PRAISE FOR *CLOSE THE WORKSHOP*

"The essence of the Church is tradition, which manifests itself in keeping diligently the faith of all ages and at the same time the liturgy of all ages. The unprecedented liturgical revolution after the Second Vatican Council therefore contradicts the essence of the Church. We are grateful to Dr. Peter Kwasniewski for showing to the readers of our day, in a competent and understandable manner, the inestimable treasure of the Catholic liturgical tradition, which, in its prayers and rites, most perfectly reflects the integrity and the ineffable mystery of the Faith, and at the same time for exposing patiently and no less thoroughly the severe flaws of its attempted replacement. *Close the Workshop* is an invaluable help for all who want to know, love, and celebrate the liturgy for the glory of God and for the true benefit of the people."

— MOST REV. ATHANASIUS SCHNEIDER, Auxiliary Bishop of Astana, author of *The Catholic Mass*

"In *Close the Workshop*, Peter Kwasniewski brings to a close his hard-hitting trilogy on the Roman rite (after *The Once and Future Roman Rite* and *Bound by Truth*). Most of Kwasniewski's conclusions in this volume are diametrically opposed to those of the Vatican, which is all the more reason they should be read—not as a proud act of dissent but in order to gain a different perspective, one that raises serious questions about a matter vital to the Church. *Close the Workshop* contains a defense of the preexisting soundness of the old rite and an argument for insoluble flaws in the new rite that both friend and foe will value for their clarity."

— MICHAEL P. FOLEY, author of *Lost in Translation: Meditating on the Orations of the Traditional Roman Rite*

"Dr. Kwasniewski's latest book will present challenges both to those who agree with him and to those who disagree with him. For those who agree with him, his evidence and arguments ask, 'Can you see your way to embrace all of the implications of this book?' For those who disagree, his evidence and arguments ask, 'State for the record your superior evidence and the arguments that justify your disagreement.' Dr. Kwasniewski has produced a volume that demands a verdict. Agree or disagree with this work as you see fit—but it cannot with integrity be dismissed or ignored."

— FR. ROBERT MCTEIGUE, S.J., host of *The Catholic Current* via the Station of the Cross Catholic Media Network; author of *Real Philosophy for Real People* and *Christendom Lost and Found*

"David slaying Goliath is the only apt metaphor for Dr. Kwasniewski. At the Goliath of systematic lies perpetuated about the traditional Mass, Kwasniewski has aimed the five shiny stones of his prodigious scholarship. He has mortally wounded the giant of liturgical mendacity; it is hard to see how any thinking Catholic could ever grant it credibility again. He has earned a secure place alongside Joseph Ratzinger and Klaus Gamber, Dietrich von Hildebrand and Martin Mosebach. In his latest volume, *Close the Workshop* (which book is this? we have lost count!), he seals his scholarly

triumph. With the knife of his compelling theological scholarship and comprehensive historical reach, he cuts through the sundry disingenuous assumptions regarding liturgy that have brought us to this pass. A return to liturgical sanity will take some time, but we have reason for consolation: the men who are our future bishops are carefully reading Kwasniewski's oeuvre with relish, waiting for their turn to chant *requiescat in pace* over one of the Church's most tragic missteps."
—FR. JOHN A. PERRICONE, Iona University, New Rochelle, New York

"*Close the Workshop* is an impassioned, uncompromising defense of the traditional Latin Mass. It's a summons to Catholics to stand fast in the face of persecution and adversity. But going beyond that, *Close the Workshop* is an encyclopedic review of the current issues in the Catholic traditionalist movement—both clarifying fundamental theological principles and offering practical advice on celebrating the TLM today. Throughout, Dr. Kwasniewski draws on his own vast experience as a scholar, musician, and participant in the traditionalist cause."
—STUART CHESSMAN, author of *Faith of Our Fathers: A Brief History of Catholic Traditionalism in the United States*

"The image of a workshop is pertinent within the context of recent liturgical history. In one sense, it represents the idea of a 'reform of the reform' which, like a mechanic, aims to repair the liturgical engine, bringing it back into line with what it understands to be the manufacturer's specifications. The second sense pertains to the reformers themselves who, like inventors in their workshops, seem to have had an insatiable desire to tinker with and modify the liturgy, to 'improve it' and make it more 'relevant.' The contention of Dr. Kwasniewski's work is that either approach falls short in both theory and practice, and that what is truly needed is a great liturgical *reset*. Certainly the reformers' innovations have not brought about the promised 'new springtime' for the Church, while the reform of the reform, however well-intentioned, cannot overcome the significant deformation to the Roman liturgy and Catholic liturgical life that resulted from too much pruning and too many modifications. Indeed, the argument can be made that the liturgical books in use in most parishes today are not only *not* what the Council Fathers envisioned or authorized, but are no longer even the Roman rite at all. That a claim like this is even tenable should be a source of great consternation for anyone with a genuine love of the Church and her venerable patrimony. Whether or not you concur with each particular conclusion proffered by Dr. Kwasniewski, he makes an important contribution to a question that has become only more urgent over time: Did we certainly and genuinely need a substantial reconfiguration of liturgical rites that exchanged a venerable patrimony for a manufactured product that was (or was at least intended to be) adapted to ourselves and to the zeitgeist—or do we actually need to reform ourselves and our culture, adopting as our own a tradition passed down from time immemorial?"
—SHAWN TRIBE, Editor, *Liturgical Arts Journal*

CLOSE THE WORKSHOP

RELATED WORKS FROM THE SAME AUTHOR

Resurgent in the Midst of Crisis
Noble Beauty, Transcendent Holiness
Tradition and Sanity
John Henry Newman on Worship, Reverence, and Ritual
And Rightly So: Selected Letters & Articles of Neil McCaffrey
Reclaiming Our Roman Catholic Birthright
The Holy Bread of Eternal Life
Ministers of Christ
True Obedience in the Church
From Benedict's Peace to Francis's War
The Once and Future Roman Rite
Good Music, Sacred Music, and Silence
Illusions of Reform
Bound by Truth
Ultramontanism and Tradition
Unresolved Tensions in Papal-Episcopal Relations
Turned Around

Close the Workshop

WHY THE OLD MASS
ISN'T BROKEN AND THE
NEW MASS CAN'T BE FIXED

PETER A. KWASNIEWSKI
Foreword by Rev. Thomas M. Kocik

First published in the USA
by Angelico Press 2025

© Angelico Press 2025

All rights reserved:
No part of this book may be reproduced
or transmitted, in any form or by any
means, without permission.

For information, address:
Angelico Press, Ltd.
169 Monitor St.
Brooklyn, NY 11222
www.angelicopress.com

ppr 979-8-89280-077-8
cloth 979-8-89280-078-5
ebook 979-8-89280-079-2

Book and cover design
by Michael Schrauzer

Dedicated to all priests whose love for truth and tradition
has led to their marginalization, cancellation, or penalization,
yet who continue to minister the word of truth and the rites of tradition
to the faithful members of the Mystical Body of Christ,
confident that one day there will be vindication and restoration

If you have taken a wrong turning, then to go forward does not get you any nearer. If you are on the wrong road, progress means doing an about-turn and walking back to the right road.... Going back is the quickest way on.

C. S. Lewis

CONTENTS

ABBREVIATIONS x
FOREWORD xi
PREFACE xvii

PART I: Detours to a Dead End 1
1. *Sacrosanctum Concilium*: The Ultimate Trojan Horse 3
2. The Irreparable Failure of the Liturgical Reform 27
3. Escaping the Infernal Workshop 47
4. Indeterminacy and Optionitis 69
5. The Outrageous Propaganda of Cardinal Roche & Co. 85
6. The Hunt for the Elusive Unicorn 108
7. Why the Reform of the Reform Is Doomed 123
8. The "Latin Novus Ordo" Is Not the Solution 145
9. Sacrifice and Desacrificialization 158
10. Time for the Soul to Absorb the Mysteries 175
11. Discovering Tradition: The Priest's Crisis of Conscience 192

PART II: Did—Does—the Old Mass Need to Be "Reformed"? 207
12. The Liturgical Rollercoaster and the Temptation of Tinkeritis 209
13. Just Say No to '65—and '62 231
14. Too Many Saints—Too Many Intercessors? 239
15. Allegory as a Key to Understanding Traditional Liturgy 248
16. The Importance of Understanding and Abiding by the Rubrics 270
17. In Defense of Readings in Latin 288
18. The Truthfulness of the Pre-1955 Good Friday Prayer for the Jews 300
19. The Grace of Stability: How Liturgy Forms the Christian Soul 306
20. The Minor Options of the Old Rite and How They Avoid Optionitis 329
21. Progressive Solemnity: Traditional Interpretations and Methods 341
22. Modest Proposals for Improving Low Mass 350
23. Should the Postures of the Laity Be Regulated, Legislated, or Revised? 362
24. The Liturgy as a Temple 368

EPILOGUE 373
APPENDIX 1: Are We Justified in Calling Paul VI's Rite the "Novus Ordo"? 383
APPENDIX 2: Discovering the Latin Mass Brings Lots of Questions 386
WORKS CITED 401
INDEX 423

ABBREVIATIONS

CDF	Congregation for the Doctrine of the Faith
EF	Extraordinary Form
EMHC	Extraordinary Minister of Holy Communion
FSSP	Priestly Fraternity of St. Peter
ICKSP	Institute of Christ the King Sovereign Priest
LAJ	*Liturgical Arts Journal*
LCD	lowest common denominator
NLM	*New Liturgical Movement*
NO	Novus Ordo
NOM	*Novus Ordo Missæ*
OF	Ordinary Form
ROTR	reform of the reform
SC	*Sacrosanctum Concilium*
SSPX	Society of St. Pius X
TC	*Traditionis Custodes*
TLM	traditional Latin Mass

Since the terminology of "OF" and "EF" was always problematic and has, in any case, been rejected by Pope Francis, it is used in this book only in quotations from other sources.

A NOTE

In these pages frequent reference is made to the Consilium, which was divided into many study groups, called *cœtūs* (singular, *cœtus*). The exact number of *cœtūs* is a matter of interpretation. Annibale Bugnini lists 45 in his *Reform of the Liturgy* (63–65). In *Notitiæ* vol. 18 (1982), Bugnini's collaborator Piero Marini lists 46 (adding XXVI*bis*). It is an open question as to whether *Cœtus* XXVIII–XXXVIII—twelve of them, including XXXII*bis*—ought to be counted as "groups" at all, since Marini says they consisted of a single *relator*. *Cœtus* XIX, moreover, seems to have produced no schemata. To complicate matters further, there were also numerous "*cœtūs peculiares*" established for specific questions, even early on in the Consilium's work. Were one to count *these*, who knows how many groups there ended up being! With those caveats, we will adopt Marini's number of 46.

FOREWORD

WHEN I LEARNED THAT THIS BOOK WAS IN THE works, my first thought was: Yet another *apologia* for "the Mass of the Ages" by the prolific (and, I would think, insomniac) Dr. Kwasniewski? But *Close the Workshop* is more than that, precisely because of *how* it fulfills that function so well. These pages expose the inadequacy, indeed the *futility*, of attempting a "reform of the liturgical reform" carried out after the Second Vatican Council (1962–65). Kwasniewski explains all the reasons why efforts to get back to "what the Council actually intended" are doomed from the start, thus showing the only viable way forward if Latin-rite Catholics are to recover their rich liturgical, spiritual, and theological heritage in full: a universal restoration of the authentic Roman rite and the divinely revealed Faith it expresses—undiluted and unabridged.

Not very long ago, I could not have imagined writing the preceding sentence. While by no means opposed to the traditional Latin Mass (in fact, I was saying the old Mass in private even before Pope Benedict XVI's Motu Proprio *Summorum Pontificum* of 2007 freed up its public celebration), I believed that the best plan of action for the Church was a faithful implementation of what the Vatican II Fathers *really* called for when they approved the 1963 Constitution on the Sacred Liturgy, *Sacrosanctum Concilium*. While that document contains no dogmatic definitions, it does articulate fundamental principles drawn from liturgical theology authoritatively taught—principles emerging from the Liturgical Movement that sprang up in the nineteenth century and was given further impetus in the twentieth century under Pope Pius X and his successors. One of those principles holds that the liturgy, by its very nature, demands the "fully conscious and active participation" by all of Christ's faithful in the Church's liturgical worship of Almighty God (no. 14). This principle necessitated liturgical adaptation and change (or so I believed), even if it did not necessitate specifically the New Order of Mass (*Novus Ordo Missæ*) promulgated by Pope Paul VI in 1969 and published in the Roman Missal of 1970. To return to the "Tridentine" Missal of 1962 (or earlier) and stop there would mean rejecting the reforming mandate of an ecumenical council of the Catholic Church—something unthinkable, no?

In 2003, Ignatius Press published a book of mine that may be familiar to Dr. Kwasniewski's readers: *The Reform of the Reform? A Liturgical Debate: Reform or Return*. Part of that work presents a dialogue between two imaginary critics of the post-Vatican II liturgical reform.

One is a "traditionalist" who argues for a return to the liturgy preceding the Council. The other is a "reformist" who wants the postconciliar liturgy brought into line with the moderate reform of the Roman rite outlined by *Sacrosanctum Concilium*, thus leaving the new Mass looking and sounding very much like the old. The book earned me some renown among Catholics who are interested in "the question of the liturgy." In the ensuing years, I thought and wrote a great deal about the "reform of the reform," thus establishing a reputation in some quarters as the doyen of that movement (if it can be called a movement). Then, a decade ago, I announced that I was "throwing in the towel," as they say in the boxing world.[1] That is the reason I was invited to contribute this foreword. People like a good conversion story, although mine involves no obvious Damascus moment.

So, what happened? I had come to realize that the "reform of the reform" is basically a dead end, whether that agenda is understood in terms of doing what is already possible (by making use of existing legitimate options), or in terms of an authoritative "correction" of the reformed liturgy as it was implemented. Let me start with what is presently doable. I knew in theory and from experience that the Mass of Paul VI can be celebrated reverently and beautifully, and with as much deference to the previous tradition as that rite makes possible. It is permissible to celebrate the Novus Ordo Mass wholly or partly in Latin, facing the liturgical east, using the (truncated) Confiteor and Kyrie, the Roman Canon and chants from the Proper, with incense, male-only service of the sanctuary, and Holy Communion received kneeling and on the tongue. But that is most often *not* how the new Mass is celebrated in the great majority of places. Both by design and by its own official development since the early 1970s,[2] the Novus Ordo is a cornucopia of options and variations. The very fact that it renders all too many traditional practices optional at the mere preference of the celebrant means that there are relatively few places where

---

[1] "Reforming the Irreformable?," *New Liturgical Movement* [*NLM*], February 9, 2014. A few years ago, another erstwhile "reform of the reform" proponent, the French theologian and Gregorian chant specialist Denis Crouan, likewise came to his senses; see Gregory DiPippo, "A Reform-of-the-Reform Paladin Throws in the Towel," *NLM*, January 29, 2022.

[2] Each successive change involves a break with longstanding tradition or discipline, beginning with the abolition of the subdiaconate and minor orders and their replacement by the "instituted ministries" of lector and acolyte, open to laymen (1972). Then followed the permissions given for lay men and women to function as extraordinary ministers of Holy Communion (1973), Communion in the hand (1977 for the USA, by virtue of an indult), altar girls (1994), the presence of cremated remains of a body at the funeral liturgy (1997 for the USA, by virtue of an indult), the washing of women's feet at the Holy Thursday Mass of the Lord's Supper (2016), and female instituted lectors and acolytes (2021).

reform-of-the-reform-style liturgy can be had on a consistent basis over a long period of time, and this, obviously, has grave implications especially for families. Clearly, much more is required for a robust liturgical life than the freedom to choose between sets of licit options.

But I have only scratched the surface. It further dawned on me that I was focusing too narrowly on external forms, failing to take adequate account of the liturgy's *contents* (the readings, chants, prayers).[3] Even when the Novus Ordo is celebrated as "traditionally" as its rules permit, when all is said and done it is not the Roman rite of Mass except in the juridical sense.[4] It is an artificial concoction, antiquarian and rationalist in conception.[5]

This is not the place to rehash the considerable differences between the missals of 1962 and 1970; nor will I elaborate on the theological and ideological motivations behind the creation of the new rite. That patient and painstaking labor has already been done by our author in *The Once and Future Roman Rite* (TAN Books, 2022) and by others before him whose works are cited in *Close the Workshop*, including Michael Davies, Msgr. Klaus Gamber, Fr. Anthony Cekada, Dr. Lauren Pristas, and Matthew Hazell. May it suffice to reiterate here what I have said elsewhere: the Novus Ordo constitutes a rupture with liturgical tradition which cannot be mended by rescuing Gregorian chant from oblivion, expanding the use of Latin and improving vernacular translations of normative Latin texts, praying the Roman Canon exclusively, reorienting the altar, and rescinding certain permissions. None of these measures can, in the words of Fr. Aidan Nichols, "restore an adequate continuity with the textuality of the Roman rite in its earlier incarnation or with its ritual integrity as a unity of word and action."[6] Any attempt at reforming the reform from within the framework of the Novus Ordo

---

[3] I use the qualifier "adequate" because it is not true that the "reform of the reform" is all about aesthetics. The traditionally minded priest who thoughtfully chooses the Confiteor and Kyrie (the first of three options for the Penitential Act) and the Roman Canon is obviously concerned with the *content* of the rite.
[4] By "juridical" is meant that the new rite was believed to have been promulgated by the same authority that promulgated the old. For someone who believes the pope has the authority to do such a thing, the Mass of Paul VI is to be considered the "Roman rite" because it was imposed by the Bishop of Rome and is the rite used by Catholics belonging to the Western patriarchate. Nevertheless, Dr. Kwasniewski has called this conclusion into question with rigorous argumentation: see his books *The Once and Future Roman Rite* and *Bound by Truth*.
[5] The non-identity of the Pauline missal with the Roman rite was affirmed by no less an authority on the subject than Joseph Gélineau, SJ, who was involved in its production. He bluntly states in *Demain la liturgie: Essai sur l'évolution des assemblées chrétiennes* (Cerf, 1976), 10: "the Roman rite as we knew it no longer exists; it has been destroyed [*Il est détruit*]."
[6] Aidan Nichols, OP, *Looking at the Liturgy: A Critical View of Its Contemporary Form* (Ignatius Press, 1996), 119. Although this passage is highlighted in my copy of the book (which I obtained and first read in early 1997), it evidently took a long time to sink in.

would be like trying to put Humpty Dumpty back together again. Once I had realized this, it became clear that the only logical starting-point for revived "organic" development is the liturgy as it was celebrated in 1963 when *Sacrosanctum Concilium* was promulgated, or possibly around 1965 when the Constitution's prescriptions had begun to be adopted but before the wrecking ball struck. But now we are no longer speaking of a "reform *of the reform*," are we? Indeed, the plot thickens: deeper research into twentieth-century developments and a more extensive (post-*Summorum*) pastoral experience of older forms such as the pre-1955 Holy Week ceremonies have led many tradition-loving Catholics to call into question the initial wave of changes made to the Roman rite in the 1950s under Pius XII, so that the "reset" moment might better be argued to be the "typical edition" of the Roman Missal promulgated by Benedict XV in 1920. Without getting into the weeds on this subject, I will simply declare my mixed feelings about the Pian liturgical reforms in general and cite Dom Alcuin Reid's opinion that "these ancient rites have much to offer the Church of the twenty-first century, not as an archaeological curiosity, nor as a rallying point for divisive ecclesiastical luddites, but as profound and worthy celebrations of the mysteries of our redemption."[7]

Although I had been disabused of the fantasy of bringing the Novus Ordo back to the point of wrong turning, I was not quite in the traditionalist camp. After all, *Sacrosanctum Concilium* prescribed specific modifications to the existing (1962) Roman rite: a fuller cycle of scriptural readings, some ritual simplifications, a wider allowance of the vernacular, priestly concelebration in some cases, and so on. Now, one can surely object that some of the liturgical reforms enacted in the name of the Council went beyond the provisions of the Council itself. Yet the fact remains that the Council Fathers *cum et sub Petro* decreed a reform of the Roman rite in a manner that would preserve its substantial unity. That fact, together with a healthy dose of realism, ruled out in my mind a permanent restoration of the "unreformed" liturgy. It was clear to me that the solution to Western Catholicism's great liturgical crisis would be a *proper* implementation (at last) of *Sacrosanctum Concilium*.

Case closed, then? Again: so I thought. While Catholic sensibility compels such deference to the Church's Magisterium (and the Liturgy Constitution *is* an act of the Magisterium), I have come to appreciate that the argument from authority cannot stand alone. The dilemmas

---

[7] Adrian Fortescue, J. B. O'Connell, and Alcuin Reid, *The Ceremonies of Holy Week & the Vigil of Pentecost Described According to the Missale Romanum editio XXIX post typicam 1953* (Éditions Pax inter Spinas, 2022), 19.

created by the reform are in large part due to the fact that *Sacrosanctum Concilium*, like the other Vatican II documents, can with justification (nay, by authorial design) be understood in contrary ways, conservatively or liberally; hence, while "there must be no innovations unless the good of the Church genuinely and certainly requires them" (no. 23), "the hour of Prime is to be suppressed" (no. 89d)!

Benedict XVI, like John Paul II before him, applied to the teachings of Vatican II a "hermeneutic of reform" in continuity with Tradition, in contrast to a "hermeneutic of discontinuity and rupture." *Summorum Pontificum* was a practical consequence of the application of the hermeneutic of continuity to the liturgy. However, as the ecclesial experience of the past decade has made painfully evident (think synods, among other things), that once-prevalent, authoritative method of reading and implementing the Council is no longer secure, if ever it was. Like America's "living constitutionalists," there will always be those who claim that *Sacrosanctum Concilium*, like the other conciliar documents, bears meaning which its drafters did not envisage—or may simply be pressed by the powerful into service of still further modernizing or inculturating agendas.

Besides, it is now six decades since the close of Vatican II, and circumstances in the Church and in the world have radically changed. If "obedience to the Council" means that we are forever bound to *Sacrosanctum Concilium*, then let us ask, with Dom Alcuin Reid, whether all of the Constitution's *subsidiary* principles and *contingent* policies, as distinct from the greater realities preceding them (i.e., the fundamental theological principles), are as vital and helpful to the Church today as they were thought to be in 1963.[8] The important distinctions made by Dom Alcuin's question drove me to reconsider whether a return to the old Roman rite *intrinsically* involves a rejection of Vatican II, at least with regard to its vision of the liturgy. In contemporary celebrations of the traditional Mass, one finds people fully involved in both interior and exterior participation, thus discrediting the claim that the renewal so fervently desired by the Council *required* a restructuring of the liturgy and could not otherwise be achieved. In fact, it is no secret, though it may be an embarrassment for some, that many of the desiderata spelled out in the Council are achieved *better*, with greater consistency, in communities that exclusively use the traditional Roman rite today.

With this brief foreword, I have traced my intellectual journey from the initially appealing but illusory "reform of the reform" to a qualified restorationism—qualified, because I do not wish to replace

---

[8] See "Editor's Preface," in *Sacred Liturgy: The Source and Summit of the Life and Mission of the Church*, ed. Alcuin Reid (Ignatius Press, 2014), 8–9.

one chimera with another. It is unrealistic to exclude the possibility of further change to the classical Roman rite, if by "change" is meant not *permutatio* (a change away from its original identity) but *profectus* (growth by augmentation), to appropriate St. Vincent of Lérins's distinction in respect of doctrinal development.[9] Nor do I think that anyone can reasonably expect a total displacement, certainly not an immediate one, of the reformed liturgy, which for the vast majority of still-practicing Catholics is, at this time, the source and summit of their Christian life. But by all means, let us pray and work for the restoration of that glorious patrimony of which three generations of Catholics have been unjustly deprived, not once but twice now. The detailed arguments in Dr. Kwasniewski's *Close the Workshop* furnish invaluable tools for this ongoing project, helping us to be conscious of, and thus to avoid, certain pitfalls of the past—and of the present.

Fr. Thomas M. Kocik
November 21, 2024
Presentation of the B.V.M.

---

[9] See St. Vincent of Lérins, *Commonitorium* 23:1–3. This sort of change has already occurred with the Holy See's allowance, since 2020, for the optional use of several new prefaces and for the optional celebration of the feasts of certain saints canonized since 1962. Arguably, it may be happening likewise by the recovery of older parts of the Roman tradition that were hastily abandoned and replaced in the postwar period.

PREFACE

IT COULD BE SAID, WITHOUT EXAGGERATION, that the book you are holding in your hands has been under development for decades—basically, for the whole adult lifetime of its author.

Born in 1971, growing up I had only ever experienced the modern rite of Paul VI and, like most Roman Catholics at the time, did not even know of the existence of any other form of worship, whether traditional Latin or Eastern Christian. Such things were never mentioned at all in the local parish or the Catholic schools I attended. Looking back, it seems to me that the ecclesiastical hierarchy desired to project a message that the Church was the same as it had ever been—a message that probably could not persuade most older people, but was ideally suited for impressionable children. Those who despised the preconciliar past and those who loved and missed it would naturally have contrary reasons for passing over it silently, yet pass over it they did: no need to call that chaotic and traumatic time to mind. A veil of secrecy descended; no one was supposed to know.

In my early twenties, I first encountered the Roman rite, that is, the rite used by the Roman Catholic Church prior to the imposition of Paul VI's modern rite. I was fascinated, puzzled, provoked, disturbed, elated. My heart was startled and my mind was bursting with questions. What *was* this? Why had it gone away—why had it been discarded? What had possessed the Church to move away from an intensely contemplative theocentric act of divine worship to the busy, talkative, anthropocentric, secular-flavored community event I grew up with, which, as I reflected on it further, never seemed to have much to do with *divine worship*? Thus began for me a journey on which countless other souls have embarked, a journey that could justly be described by the phrase "further up and further in." For indeed it seemed, as I got to know the traditional rites of the Church, both Western and Eastern, that there was a heavenly country to explore, high up in the mountains of tradition, far back into the depths of the ages, and that the way to this country had been blocked, barred, almost blacked out, by a strange, suicidal humanism of the twentieth century, when modernism morphed into revolutionary change.

Then the trouble started: the trouble of living in a broken Church, divided from itself, violently cut off from its past yet still home to believers ardently seeking continuity; a Church that seemed more like floating clusters of autonomous initiatives than a unified body of faith, worship, and life. As a lifelong church musician who only ever worked at "conservative" institutions, I was continually called upon to provide the best sacred music possible for the Novus Ordo,[1] while I never stopped participating in the traditional Mass and the Byzantine Divine Liturgy. It was like having three personalities! At the Novus Ordo, I would struggle mightily to shoehorn the tradition back into it, taking advantage of every option-point and loophole and permission, pleading or arguing with priests and even bishops to "do the Novus Ordo well," that is, with reverence, dignity, and beauty. At the Byzantine liturgy, I would, with congregational gusto, sing in English, Slavonic, Ukrainian, Romanian, or whatever other language happened to have the upper hand that day in the chapel,[2] letting myself be carried away by an utterly different but magnificent way of worshiping the Lord. At the traditional Latin Mass, I would yield myself, with a sigh of relief, to the orderly motions, sober prayers, mellifluous chants, and silent oases that it offered for the nourishment of my soul.

This triple liturgical life continued, in varying proportions, for twenty years. More often than not, I was serving as cantor or choir director. This experience was like learning languages by immersion: I came to understand deeply, experientially, how these liturgies are structured, how they operate, how their texts and music and ritual actions compare and contrast.[3] It was during this time that my traditionalist views matured. I'm not a hot-headed person who quickly jumps to conclusions or makes rash decisions; when I reach a conclusion, it is because the evidence has buried me alive and I can't escape it, and when I make a decision, it is the fruit of a long meditation (sometimes overlong). Thus, it took me a while, longer than it has taken many others, to reach a double conclusion: there was no need for the massive liturgical reform in the first place, and the new rite cannot be reformed or "done well"; rather, it must simply be retired and the traditional rite must be restored to its rightful place of honor. Similarly, it took me a while, longer than it has taken many others, to make the firm decision to attend the traditional rite[4] exclusively and, as a matter of principle, to avoid the modern rite altogether. This book is about that double conclusion and that double decision.

---

[1] Some people object to the phrase "Novus Ordo," considering it to be inaccurate or demeaning. I use it because Paul VI himself used it, as explained in Appendix I.

[2] This was at the International Theological Institute, then in Gaming, where Greek Catholics of many nationalities shared a Byzantine chapel and took turns offering the daily liturgy. Later, in Lander, Wyoming, we always conducted the Divine Liturgy in English.

[3] To read a summary of what I learned, see "Byzantine, Tridentine, Montinian: Two Brothers and a Stranger," in Peter Kwasniewski, *The Once and Future Roman Rite: Returning to the Traditional Latin Liturgy after Seventy Years of Exile* (TAN Books, 2022), 279–311.

[4] Perhaps it would be more accurate to say "*a* traditional rite": where the Tridentine rite is not available, I attend an Eastern Catholic rite.

Preface

The following passage in Msgr. Robert Hugh Benson's *Confessions of a Convert* perfectly captures the feelings of those who, having devoted many years of their lives, perhaps decades, to the laborious and often stressful business of trying to make the Novus Ordo traditional and reverent, then find blessed peace in full and exclusive adherence to a truly traditional liturgy, one to which they can trustingly surrender themselves and from which they can joyfully live. One might think of the transition from "reform of the reform" to Tridentine Restoration in reading these moving words:

> Cardinal Newman compares, somewhere, the sensations of a convert from Anglicanism to those of a man in a fairy story, who, after wandering all night in a city of enchantment, turns after sunrise to look back upon it, and finds to his astonishment that the buildings are no longer there; they have gone up like wraiths and mists under the light of the risen day. So the present writer has found. He no longer, as in the first months of his conversion, is capable of comparing the two systems of belief together, since that which he has left appears to him no longer a coherent item at all.
>
> There are, of course, associations, memories, and emotions still left in his mind—some of them very sacred and dear to his heart; he still is happy in numbering among his friends many persons who still find amongst those associations and memories a system which they believe to be the religion instituted by Jesus Christ; yet he himself can no longer see in them anything more than hints and fragments and aspirations detached from their centre and reconstructed into a purely human edifice without foundation or solidity.
>
> Yet he is conscious of no bitterness at all—at the worst experiences sometimes a touch of impatience merely at the thought of having been delayed so long by shadows from the possession of divine substance. He cannot, however, with justice, compare the two systems at all; one cannot, adequately, compare a dream with a reality.[5]

I set myself the task of writing this book over six years ago, as the fiftieth anniversary of Pope Paul VI's apostolic constitution *Missale Romanum* approached in April of 2019. Soon enough it became apparent that the project was on a vaster scale than I had initially supposed. Like triplets in the womb, three books were conceived and born. *The Once and Future Roman Rite: Returning to the Traditional Latin Liturgy after Seventy Years of Exile* (TAN Books, 2022) makes the argument that the modern rite is not and cannot be called the Roman rite, nor indeed can it be grouped with any historic apostolic rite. *Bound by Truth: Authority, Obedience, Tradition, and the Common Good* (Angelico Press, 2023) lays the theological and canonical foundations

---

[5] Robert Hugh Benson, *Confessions of a Convert* (The Cenacle Press, 2022), ix–x.

for the primacy of tradition, the duties and limits of ecclesiastical governance, and the right to offer resistance to papal acts that threaten fundamental ecclesial and spiritual goods. The present volume, finally, looks at the two issues mentioned above: why the new Mass is so flawed that it cannot be repaired and should be abandoned; and why the old Mass did not (and does not) need to be "reformed." The latter consideration is anything but speculative: proposals are always afoot for "updating" the troglodytic TLM on the false assumption that, more than sixty years after publication, *Sacrosanctum Concilium* must *still* be carried out, no matter what. (Thus, in chapter 12, I talk about what such proposals look like, and then cite recent Vatican interventions that amount to: "If we can't get rid of the traditionalists altogether, the next best thing is to insist they start reforming their old-fashioned ways. Better late than never when it comes to implementing the Council.")

As the subtitle of this book indicates, we are concerned here with two major issues: the soundness of the inherited Roman rite of the Mass, and the unsoundness of the new rite of Paul VI. Going, in a sense, from the more known (the fiasco of the new rite) to what is less known (the perfection of the old), the first part of this book will address the new Mass and the second part, the traditional Mass. Part I will explain why a "reform of the reform" is not possible without altogether deconstructing the modern rite and, in a sense, trying to re-engineer the goods of the old rite out of materials poorly suited to or incapable of such a transformation; that smells and bells can only cover up, not correct, the enormous problems embedded in the new rite, since these problems are genetic and not cosmetic in nature; and that even the quest for a "reverent celebration"—assuming it is not obstructed by hostile forces—involves serious spiritual dangers for both clergy and faithful. As for Part II, it is not this book's purpose to demonstrate in detail all the glories and perfections of the traditional rite and to respond to the arguments people never cease to hurl against it; this I have done in several other works, notably *Turned Around: Replying to Common Objections Against the Traditional Latin Mass* (TAN Books, 2024). Here, I will concentrate on how proposals to reform the old rite as well as pastoral experiments undertaken in our times to "improve" it or to "make it more relevant to the people" are contrary to the genius of the rite and disruptive to the communities that celebrate it, and, moreover, that the old rite has sufficient built-in "flexibility" to make itself at home in a great diversity of situations. The key aspect over which there *is* control is the *ars celebrandi*, that is, the manner in which the old rite is offered; and in that regard, I will indeed argue that we must take pains to celebrate it *well*, correcting certain bad habits that have a way of cropping up from time to time.

In short, I maintain, on the one hand, that there is no good way to use the new rite and it must eventually cease to be used, and, on the other hand, that there is nothing wrong with the old rite and it must be restored, or at least reclaimed by individual clerics and communities as we wait for better leadership in Rome and across the hierarchy.

In the course of this work, I shall frequently point out the vast implications of what has happened in the domain of liturgy and of what is still happening there, for good and for ill. These implications extend far beyond particulars of religious ceremonial. Though subject to ecclesiastical supervision, the Church's liturgy has always been revered by believers as a sacrosanct reality, a touchstone of orthodoxy, an embodiment of living tradition that must not be violated. It is not our possession to manhandle as we please; it is a gift entrusted to us to love, honor, and transmit to future generations. When the old liturgy of centuries, indeed millennia, was suddenly dismantled and reconfigured in modern guise as a sleek vehicle for the emerging Space Age, the defining "taboo" of the Catholic Church was shattered. Predictably, millions of the faithful deserted the Church.[6] If this, they wondered, is how the holiest of our religious rituals is treated, the quintessential symbol and radiant center of Catholicism, can there be any abiding truth in what the Church says about anything else? If the Holy Mass itself is subject to human manipulation, why not the rest of her beliefs and practices, which are obviously less sacred? Why not admit that our morality, and our doctrine too, are antiquated and need updating in light of modern thought and the experience of the men and women of today?[7] Perhaps, come to think of it, the whole religion is a fraud. To that despairing conclusion many were driven by the ceaseless barrage of changes unleashed by the Council; and to it some Catholics may yet be driven in our own day by the slouching towards Gomorrah of

---

6 The Catholics who fell away from the faith or drifted into schism due to the scandal of the liturgical reform are the "unremembered dead"—the nameless casualties of a triumphal march of progress that did not care about its victims or deemed them necessary sacrifices to the Moloch of the Future (to borrow a phrase from Benedict XVI in a different context). These people deserve our sympathetic remembrance and prayers, and our hard work to reverse something of the damage that traumatized and alienated them.
7 This is exactly the line that has been taken in the pontificate of Francis. See, out of countless examples, Jonathan Liedl, "Personal Experience, Not Moral Absolutes, to Steer Synod Study Group's Discernment on Sexuality Questions," *National Catholic Register*, October 3, 2024; Grégory Solari, "Traditionalism creates a distance between the heritage of past generations and the contemporary ecclesial community," *La Croix International*, October 4, 2024. Solari says outright: "The key difference between these two understandings of formalizations [viz., living transmission vs. dead tradition] lies in whether or not the life (*lex vivendi*) of the community is prioritized in shaping formalized prayer (*lex orandi*) and defined doctrine (*lex credendi*)." For him, prayer and doctrine should take a back seat to the ever-changing "life of the ecclesial community."

one progressive synod after another and by the assault on communities that celebrate the old Roman rite. The arguments of the enemies of tradition are the same as they were right after the Council, and they have not improved with age; the faithful's sufferings are the same, too, and they remain meritorious for those who persevere. "He that shall persevere to the end, he shall be saved" (Mt 24:13).

The expulsion of tradition from our churches after Vatican II made laymen strangers in their own ecclesial home, alienated from their ancestors and deprived of their inheritance. In a manner that left them permanently scarred, clergy and religious who had loved Catholic tradition were forced to abandon it as if it were so much useless baggage, or to repudiate it as harmful to the Church's contemporary mission.[8] The hemorrhaging of priests and religious continued throughout the 1970s and beyond, and even today we face a demographic sinkhole as retirements and deaths claim their own. Many abandoned integral Catholic social teaching in favor of humanistic and socialistic protestations of solidarity.[9] Philosophy and theology collapsed into war zones of competing ideologies. One author describes the fallout thus:

> The Sacred Heart beating at the center of the Church has not abandoned Her and never will. But how often that Sacred Heart is obscured! Many a modern Mass is replete with banal—or even bizarrely inappropriate—liturgy, yet His Sacred Heart remains beating there. It is as though this Heart is wrapped in banks of fog. Such irreverent celebrations of the Holy Mass are not sufficient to destroy Christ's presence; they only blind people to it. The results are as manifold as they are grievous. But perhaps few are as saddening as this: Catholics, even when they continue to practice, are lost. They are no longer really sure of their Faith or why it matters. The Church is torn apart by warfare between liberals and conservatives. And a house divided against itself cannot stand.[10]

---

[8] The bitterness, resentment, and anger of elderly clergy and religious towards the revival of traditional Catholicism in our day is at least partially connected with the psychological abuse visited upon them in the sixties, when they were coerced into conformity with a new paradigm that was presented as an unrepealable replacement of the Tridentine inheritance. When they see young people now happily taking hold of these things again as if the trauma of the conciliar and postconciliar period had never happened (and as if their own sufferings were in vain), it must be like salt and vinegar in the wounds. One should not overlook, as well, the Stockholm syndrome. See Peter Kwasniewski, *Reclaiming Our Roman Catholic Birthright: The Genius and Timeliness of the Traditional Latin Mass* (Angelico Press, 2020), 205–12.

[9] Abandonment is not too strong a word. When is the last time you heard mention of the kingship of Jesus Christ over nations, cultures, laws, governments?—and yet it is no less true today than it was in 1925 when Pius XI issued his encyclical *Quas Primas*. See Joseph Husslein, SJ, *The Reign of Christ, the Immortal King of Ages* (Arouca Press, 2024; originally published in 1928).

[10] Roger Buck, *Cor Jesu Sacratissimum: From Secularism and the New Age to Christendom Renewed* (Angelico Press, 2016), 10–11.

The liturgy is the glue that holds all of Catholicism together, the keystone that keeps all the stones of the arch in place. When it fell, everything else tottered or collapsed. Where it returns, the fullness of Catholicism is not far behind: the renewal of family life, the reawakening of religious life, the intensification of the intellectual life, the splendor of cultural life, the rudiments of Catholic political life. I have seen this dynamic play out many times in my lifetime, and in both directions: from disorder to order, and from order to disorder. This is why I am hopeful about the future, wherever the movement for restoring tradition has taken root and prospered; and I am equally despairing of any future for the mainstream Church, which, deformed by the spirit of Vatican II, is like the seed in the parable that falls on the path and is gobbled up by the birds, or the seed strewn on rocky ground that sprouts up, is scorched, and withers away. Tradition is a seed planted deep in the rich soil of souls that still long for absolute truth, for heroic goodness, for noble beauty. In such souls the growth and the harvest will be great—thirtyfold, sixtyfold, a hundredfold.

Catholics who practice their faith seriously and take pains to educate themselves can see right through the propaganda of the liturgical revolution and its rather tired-sounding propagandists of today. They can see right through the "Eucharistic Revival" and the "reverent Novus Ordo," concepts that flourish on the internet but, in the suffocating mediocrity of real life, die a quick death, crushed between bland chanceries and bad customs. To put it positively, such Catholics see that everything we need, everything we are trying to accomplish, is *already contained in our patrimony*, waiting to be rediscovered, recovered, lived anew. That is by no means an easy task at this strange juncture in history, but the tools for doing it are present in abundance. There have always been clergy and religious who live according to the traditional rites, so personal apprenticeship has always been and will continue to be available. Libraries of books and videos exist from which any ceremony can be learned. Priests are quietly receiving instruction in the tradition and are putting what they know into practice or biding their time for a better season. The revolution has no gas left in its tank, only fumes; and fumes can last only so long. In the Church today, the sole argument backing up the reform is the papal diktat, "Because *I* said so!" Such desperate blustering is only a few steps away from total collapse, as any standard history of dictatorship shows. Without enthusiastic buy-in, nothing can endure.

When will the institutional Church stop seeing the traditional Roman rite as a threat to its entire existence, and come to see it rather as a heaven-sent remedy for decades of anomy, anemia, and amnesia? The spokesmen of synodality, who talk endlessly about "listening to the Holy Spirit," seem to be the ones most in need of a supernatural hearing-aid.

As can be seen on many levels, from the experiential to the academic, the modern rite of Paul VI is not a legitimate development of the Roman rite or really any expression of the Roman rite—let alone its "ordinary" or "unique" expression.[11] The proposal of a "reform of the reform" is and has always been, practically speaking, a non-starter; philosophically, it is a seductive chimera that must be given up for the sake of mental and spiritual health. Unlike a sick body that can heal itself, the modern rite cannot be rescued from within. If the Catholic Church is ever to recover her internal soundness and external influence, her shepherds and her flocks must let the ill-advised Council of the 1960s and the Bauhaus liturgy fabricated in its name lapse into a well-deserved obsolescence, so that the perennially fresh theology of the Council of Trent and the immortally beautiful liturgy of the Roman Church may once again flourish unfettered.[12] A council's prudential or disciplinary recommendations—and that is primarily what *Sacrosanctum Concilium* concerned itself with—are *not* set in stone; they are *not* guaranteed to be prudent or helpful or long-lasting; they are *not* assured to be fruitful when implemented; indeed, they can be revisited, modified, or overturned as time goes on, if the common good of the Church calls for something else. In our times, that something else is a return to the tradition so foolishly discarded in a whirl of intoxicated optimism and myopic deference to "Modern Man." As H. L. Mencken once quipped: "For every complex problem, there is an answer that is clear, simple, and wrong." It was Paul VI's misfortune (and thus it became everyone else's misfortune) to have given this witticism its supreme illustration. Thanks to waves of change in the last century, each more destructive than the one before, the problem of the Church's liturgy has become more complex than ever—so complex that further tinkering will only exacerbate it. Tradition offers an answer that is theologically clear, nobly simple, and eminently right.

---

[11] I refer here to the language, respectively, of Benedict XVI's *Summorum Pontificum* and of Francis's *Traditionis Custodes*: in the former, "the Roman Missal promulgated by Paul VI is the ordinary expression of the *lex orandi* (law of prayer) of the Catholic Church of the Latin rite" (art. 1); in the latter, "the liturgical books promulgated by St. Paul VI and St. John Paul II, in conformity with the decrees of Vatican Council II, are the unique expression of the *lex orandi* of the Roman Rite" (art. 1). That both of these claims are unsustainable has been demonstrated in my book *The Once and Future Roman Rite*, but the present book will also have much to offer in refuting them.
[12] This flourishing also requires undoing the major liturgical changes from 1948 to 1962, all of which tended in the direction of the deformation of the Roman rite. See Kwasniewski, *Once and Future Roman Rite*, 333–75.

Preface

A few particulars. When citing an online article, I have preferred not to burden the footnote with a long and ungainly hyperlink but have simply provided author, article title, website name, and date—more than enough for locating it in a fraction of a second. (I made exceptions for online sources that might be hard to find without a link.) Many chapters herein saw their original publication at a number of sites to which I have regularly contributed over the years: *New Liturgical Movement*, *OnePeterFive*, *Rorate Caeli*, *Crisis Magazine*, *LifeSiteNews*, *The Remnant*, *Catholic Family News*, and *Views from the Choir Loft*. Certain chapters first appeared in *The Latin Mass* magazine as well as on my Substack *Tradition and Sanity*. All of the content has been revised, sometimes extensively, for its new home. I decided to let stand some conceptual repetitions now and again to make this or that chapter's argument more complete on its own terms—especially for those who, instead of reading the book from cover to cover, prefer to skip around to topics that interest them the most.

Enormous debts of gratitude have been amassed in the course of finishing this project. Anthony Jones acted as a superb copy-editor and a friendly critic; his work has significantly improved the clarity and rigor of my arguments. Fr. Thomas Kocik, whom I thank for his lucid and stylish Foreword, offered corrections on this or that point in the manuscript. Another traditional priest, supremely versed in rubrics and history, likewise invested considerable time to comment on my manuscript; his name cannot be mentioned due to Church politics, but God knows who he is and will reward his outstanding work. John Pepino, Matthew Hazell, Gregory DiPippo, and Dom Alcuin Reid generously responded to my calls for help. During our frequent conversations, Jeremy Holmes articulated some of the best insights to find their way into these pages, and with characteristic generosity always told me just to take his idea and run with it—which I've gladly done. For over ten years, John Riess and I have collaborated fruitfully on many publishing projects; it delights me to give Angelico Press another manuscript, just about a decade after the first book I published with John, *Resurgent in the Midst of Crisis*. He is very patient with my unrelenting perfectionism. So is my wife, after twenty-six years of marriage with a high-strung writer. Her power to encourage, moderate, and empathize is legendary to those fortunate to know her (myself most fortunate of all!). Finally, a vast number of readers have contacted me over the years with questions, objections, or insights; it was often their words that supplied missing pieces of the puzzle, pushed me to refine or replace my arguments, challenged me to dig deeper into the sources, tempered my excesses or, conversely, called out compromises. I cannot express my sense of awe and joy when I think of how much collaboration, with so many individuals, a book like this has actually involved, and I ask the gracious Lord to send His graces down on everyone who has had a part, large or small, in the genesis or completion of any of its pages.

The version of the Bible cited most often herein is the Douay-Rheims, although I will also cite the King James Version or one of its many progeny, such as the Revised Standard Version Catholic Edition.

Peter A. Kwasniewski
December 21, 2024
Feast of St. Thomas the Apostle

PART I

Detours to a Dead End

WHY THE NEW MASS
CAN'T BE SALVAGED

⋘ I ⋙
Sacrosanctum Concilium: The Ultimate Trojan Horse

HOW DID I MOVE FROM BEING A PROPONENT of the Ratzingerian reform of the reform (ROTR), the hermeneutic of continuity, and mutual enrichment, to being a traditional Latin Mass (TLM) exclusivist who thinks the attempt at finding or making harmony between the modern rite and the Roman rite is fed by illusions and fraught with dangers? I can begin with a story.

Many years ago, I submitted a beefy manuscript to Ignatius Press, sending it directly to Fr. Fessio. It was entitled *"Resplendent for Its Dignity and Harmony": A Primer on the Reform of the Reform*. Its title conveyed my ambition: this was to be the comprehensive cookbook, as it were, by which the enterprising clerical chef could turn out the perfect sacred banquet for his Catholic clientele, in a setting dignified by candles, tasteful décor, and appropriate music. It would be the *ne plus ultra* of Ratzingerian reformism.[1]

Thanks be to God, Fr. Fessio rejected my manuscript as not aligning with the Press's vision. I think this was a polite way of saying it was both too traditional in what it recommended for improving the Novus Ordo and too critical of the Novus Ordo itself. Looking at the manuscript today, I wince with embarrassment—not because it was poorly argued or topically incomplete, but because it was a grandiose structure built entirely upon sand. At the time, I had not yet probed as deeply into the gory details of the Second Vatican Council and the liturgical reform as I was subsequently to do, and this meant I was still operating on the basis of conventional truths that had to be exploded before it would be possible to locate a foundation of rock upon which to build a permanent structure of argument and advice. That foundation was nothing other than the Roman tradition in its high medieval flourishing, comprising the "received and approved" rites that St. Pius V canonized as the Church of Rome's liturgical *regula fidei*, inherited from the fathers and destined to accompany Latin Christians in divine worship until the end of time.[2]

---

[1] For a taste of what the content was like, see my article "What the Ordinary Form Could Be: The Vienna Oratory," *Views from the Choir Loft*, June 5, 2014, www.ccwatershed.org/2014/06/05/what-ordinary-form-could-be-vienna-oratory.
[2] On *Quo Primum* as dogmatic and not merely disciplinary, see Peter Kwasniewski, *True Obedience in the Church: A Guide to Discernment in Challenging Times* (Sophia Institute Press, 2021).

Further study convinced me that the Council was guilty of vanity and naïveté in its announced intention, of looseness in its methodology, and of prolixity and studied ambiguity in its documents. The Council played out under the predominant influence of the progressive faction and gave birth to an activistic, antinomian, anti-traditional, anti-liturgical "spirit" that may have been officially frowned upon but was unofficially tolerated or even nudged along at all levels.[3] I used to think that the Council, orthodox in itself, had suffered the sad fate of journalistic distortion and ecclesial misapplication, but today it seems to me to be impossible to sustain this viewpoint if one wishes to be strictly bound to the full scope of evidence.[4]

The Constitution on the Sacred Liturgy *Sacrosanctum Concilium* (*SC*), which once appeared to me as a predominantly conservative document, discloses a "subtext" or, *horribile dictu*, "spirit," that is revolutionary in nature. Even if most of what the text says might be reconciled with traditional Catholic thought and practice, there is a subtle bias in favor of change — the mastery of liturgy by expertise that parallels the Baconian/Cartesian mastery of nature by technology, and the construction of meaning by executive fiat that parallels the subjectivist epistemologies of Descartes, Kant, and other modern philosophers. For anyone with a *sensus catholicus*, it is sickening to read lines like the following: "In this restoration, both texts and rites should be drawn up [*oportet ordinari*] so that they express more clearly the holy things which they signify" (*SC* 21); "a new rite for concelebration is to be drawn up [*conficiatur*] and inserted into the Pontifical and into the Roman Missal" (*SC* 58); "a new rite is to be drawn up for converts who have already been validly baptized" (*SC* 69); "a rite of religious profession and renewal of vows shall be drawn up in order to achieve greater unity, sobriety, and dignity" (*SC* 80); and on and on, as the document conjures up visions of academics grinding away at their desks, arrogantly drawing up new rites to suit the new age of mankind of which they believe themselves to be the anointed interpreters.

As one who has sung the traditional Latin office of Compline, the night prayer of the Church, for many years of my life — indeed, often

---

3 In addition to older classics by Ralph Wiltgen, Michael Davies, Dietrich von Hildebrand, Romano Amerio, and others, several recent books enhance the critique of the Council: Roberto de Mattei, *The Second Vatican Council: An Unwritten Story*, trans. Patrick T. Brannan et al. (Loreto Publications, 2012); H. J. A. Sire, *Phoenix from the Ashes: The Making, Unmaking, and Restoration of Catholic Tradition* (Angelico Press, 2015); Yves Chiron, *Between Rome and Rebellion: A History of Catholic Traditionalism with Special Attention to France*, trans. John Pepino (Angelico Press, 2024).
4 I make the case for this interpretation in my essays "Vatican II: *Requiescat in Pace*," in Peter A. Kwasniewski, ed., *Sixty Years After: Catholic Writers Assess the Legacy of Vatican II* (Angelico Press, 2022), 93–122, and "Vatican II as Cause of Cultural Revolution: Questioning the Victim Narrative," *Tradition and Sanity* Substack, February 19, 2024.

with my wife and children singing along—and who has found great beauty, consolation, and nourishment in its chants and prayers, I cannot but cringe to read this statement: "Compline is to be *drawn up* [*instruatur*] so that it will be a *suitable prayer* for the end of the day."[5] As if the age-old form of Compline were not already the most suitable prayer imaginable for the end of the day! As if such luminous liturgical forms, the fruit of an entire civilization of piety, can simply be "drawn up" at will![6] While we're at it, why not "draw up" another Chartres Cathedral and Scrovegni Chapel, another corpus of plainchant, another *Summa theologiæ* and *Divina Commedia*, if the production of masterpieces is as easy as signing a conciliar document and handing the keys to a team of experts? The prophet Jeremiah might as well have been speaking of the results of this absurd pretentiousness: "The great ones sent their inferiors to the water: they came to draw, they found no water, they carried back their vessels empty: they were confounded and afflicted" (Jer 14:3).

On the whole, *Sacrosanctum Concilium* is marred by two errors: the rationalist assumption that things must always be easily understood by us, and the neo-Pelagian implication that we—or rather, the pope and his favored commission—are the primary architects of our worship, the ones who can build a better liturgy by our own efforts, even as post-World War II statesmen flattered themselves into thinking they could build a better world under the benevolent guidance of the United Nations. Although particular passages of *Sacrosanctum Concilium* could have been implemented in a way respectful of tradition, the entire trend and tone of the document is decisively modern, disrespectful towards the inherited liturgical wealth of the ages. The absolute nadir is reached in the following statement: "The hour of Prime is to be suppressed (*supprimatur*)" (SC 89d). As if stating a self-evident truth, St. John Henry Newman observes that the Catholic Church does not abolish liturgical rites honored by long use.[7] His observation rang

---

[5] SC 89, emphasis added.
[6] See John Lamont on the vast civilizational resources needed for the development of an orthodox prayer form suited to the Christian religion: "Dominican Theologian Attacks Catholic Tradition (Part 4): What Is At Stake in the Attempted Suppression of the TLM?," *Rorate Caeli*, September 20, 2023.
[7] See the tract "Rites and Customs of the Church" and the sermon "Ceremonies of the Church" in *John Henry Newman on Worship, Reverence, and Ritual: A Selection of Texts*, ed. Peter A. Kwasniewski (Os Justi Press, 2019), 69–80, esp. 78–79. See also Wolfram Schrems, "The Council's Constitution on the Liturgy: Reform or Revolution?," *Rorate Caeli*, May 3, 2018. As Joseph Ratzinger wrote to Wolfgang Waldstein in 1976: "The problem of the new Missal lies, on the contrary, in its abandonment of a historical process that had always gone on, before and after St. Pius V, and in the creation of an entirely new book, albeit from ancient material, and whose publication was accompanied by a kind of ban on what had existed before, a ban, moreover, never seen in juridical and liturgical history." On this statement and its implications,

true until the hubris of the 1960s, an era in which churchmen let go of piety in favor of slogans.[8] Such an all-embracing reform could have been conceived and executed only by men inflated with the pride of modernity, men who, having lost confidence in the sacred heritage of the Church, had already set out on the road to the apostasy we now see across the Western world. The result was as might have been predicted: *Facti sunt hostes eius in capite... et egressus est a filia Sion omnis decor eius.* "Her adversaries are become her lords... and from the daughter of Sion, all her beauty is departed" (Lam 1:5–6). *Posuerunt terram desiderabilem in desertum.* "They changed the delightful land into a wilderness" (Zech 7:14).

In this way, the Constitution is not in continuity with the original Liturgical Movement, which cherished a deep love for the liturgy *as given*, as an object of devotion—not the liturgy *as project*, as a subject of change.[9] That movement was characterized, at its best, by a filial attachment to the objectivity of tradition; the radical wing that took charge in the fifties and sixties was characterized by a critical detachment from anything inherited unless it could pass through the double filter of archaeology and *aggiornamento*. No wonder few things survived: this filter was designed to catch everything but the pride of its users. The lament of Dom Prosper Guéranger and others like him was that the beauty and spiritual riches of the ancient liturgy were not sufficiently known and needed to be made known through hand missals and devotional commentaries, retreats and conferences. The lament of Archbishop Annibale Bugnini and his generation was that the liturgy as handed down to us was defective and needed to be thrown into the scrap heap so that a better liturgy, one truly contemporary, could be constructed from pieces of imagined "authenticity."[10] The classical

---

see Réginald-Marie Rivoire, FSVF, *Does "Traditionis Custodes" Pass the Juridical Rationality Test? A Canonical-Theological Study*, trans. William Barker, FSSP (Os Justi Press, 2022), 40.

[8] It is a form of poetic justice that Prime, in spite of this attempted suppression, has remained alive and well among clergy, religious, and laity who adhere to the traditional liturgy.

[9] For an extended discussion of the difference between the original Liturgical Movement and its cancer phase, see Peter Kwasniewski, *Noble Beauty, Transcendent Holiness: Why the Modern Age Needs the Mass of Ages* (Angelico Press, 2017), 89–112; cf. Kwasniewski, *Reclaiming Our Roman Catholic Birthright*, 48–53.

[10] The contradiction in approaches is signaled in the names Divine Providence permitted these men to bear. The word "prosper" suggests a flourishing from presently available resources, such as those of the historic liturgy, while as a proper name it reminds us of Prosper of Aquitaine, who is credited with the original formulation of what would become the pithy maxim *lex orandi, lex credendi*—a principle Pope Pius XII would later attempt to subvert in the encyclical *Mediator Dei*, even as he earned the disgrace of being the first to appoint Bugnini to a position at the Vatican. The name Annibale, on the other hand, harks back to the military general Hannibal, a brilliant strategist who fought against Rome, even as his namesake battled for

Liturgical Movement saw the liturgy as the fruit of slow, organic growth under the guidance of Divine Providence; as a result, this liturgy constituted a timeless expression of the Catholic faith that was guaranteed to be permanently relevant to each generation—provided only that it be known and loved. The radicalized Liturgical Movement saw the liturgy as a work of human hands that had suffered waves of deformation and deviation ever since antiquity, particularly in the medieval and Baroque periods; it was, therefore, a thing that had become *inherently* irrelevant—a thing corrupted and alienating that no longer gave expression to the Catholic faith as *now* understood by (or understandable to) modern Europeans. The commission to which Paul VI entrusted the reform of the liturgy—the *Consilium ad exsequendam Constitutionem de Sacra Liturgia*, or Consilium for short—echoed the rationalist ambitions of the Synod of Pistoia (1786), an Enlightenment excrescence condemned by Pope Pius VI; it produced modernism's most enduring monument, made in Pistoia's image and likeness.[11] Jesuit liturgist John F. Baldovin admits with refreshing frankness:

> These historical studies [by Martène, Mabillon, Muratori, et al.], as well as the philosophical concerns of the Enlightenment, led to the decrees of the Synod of Pistoia (Tuscany) in 1786 under Bishop Scipione de' Ricci. In liturgical terms, this synod decreed a major streamlining and modernization of the liturgy, for example, by decreeing that there be only one altar in a church as well as limiting statues and processions. Although its decrees were swiftly suppressed by Pope Pius VI (1794), much of Pistoia's agenda survived in the liturgy constitution [viz., *Sacrosanctum Concilium*]. As a matter of fact, some of the post-Vatican II criticism of the constitution, and of the liturgical reform in general, focused on the fact that some of what was condemned by Pope Pius VI was now approved.[12]

Elsewhere, I've discussed how Pius VI's *Auctorem Fidei*—the document that condemns in detail the proposals of the Synod of Pistoia—serves as a sort of anticipatory condemnation of the Consilium's large-scale liturgical reconstructions under Bugnini's direction.[13]

---

modernity against Roman tradition.
11 On the Synod of Pistoia, see Kwasniewski, *Reclaiming Our Roman Catholic Birthright*, 149–60; John Parsons, "A Reform of the Reform?," in Thomas M. Kocik, *The Reform of the Reform? A Liturgical Debate: Reform or Return* (Ignatius Press, 2003), 211–56; Geoffrey Hull, *The Banished Heart: Origins of Heteropraxis in the Catholic Church* (T&T Clark, 2010), 53–67. In his *The Synod of Pistoia and Vatican II: Jansenism and the Struggle for Catholic Reform* (Oxford University Press, 2020), Shaun Blanchard praises Vatican II for fulfilling Pistoia's program.
12 John F. Baldovin, SJ, "Vatican II's liturgy constitution turns 60—preparing the constitution," *The Pilot*, November 3, 2023.
13 See "Does Pius VI's *Auctorem Fidei* Support Paul VI's Novus Ordo?," in Peter Kwasniewski, *The Road from Hyperpapalism to Catholicism*, vol. 1: *Theological Reflections on the Rock of the Church* (Arouca Press, 2022), 84–90.

We see here a fundamental difference in attitude and mentality. The Catholics of old respected and venerated what they received from their ancestors — to such an extent that they readily attributed later writings to famous saints, as when they attributed chant to St. Gregory the Great, or the Divine Liturgy to St. John Chrysostom, even though it is clear enough that these things existed prior to those saints and continued to develop after them. The conciliar/postconciliar mentality, in contrast, is to distrust tradition, to set oneself up in judgment over it, to pick and choose from it as it suits one's fancy, to emphasize *our* scholarship, *our* theories, *our* publications, *our* progress, improvements, insights, and, in general, superior status vis-à-vis our predecessors. Thus we debunk and deconstruct everything and remake it in our image, instead of humbly allowing ourselves to be reshaped in the image passed on to us, as the veil of Veronica received the impression of Our Lord's Face. This attitude of presumed superiority poisons our relationship to tradition and, ultimately, to divine revelation and the Christian Faith as such.

Consider that the Church's traditional worship has been likened to a great sprawling ancient estate. We inherit not a bunch of boxes of junk to sort through but a huge piece of land — a kind of *holy land* — with a grand mansion built on it: the liturgy. This mansion has been lived in and added to by countless saints. It was built by them under the hand of Divine Providence. The entire structure has become an indistinguishable conglomeration of first-, second-, and third-class relics. This doesn't mean we have to live in every room of it or that we can't paint some of the walls a different color or add new rooms or furnishings (as long as they are in good taste, matching with what is already there). What it *does* mean is that we have no business tearing down the structure and starting over from the ground up, or getting rid of the land we inherited to buy a convenient field in Babylon. Writing in 1976, the influential Jesuit liturgist and Consilium member Joseph Gélineau — whom Bugnini numbered among the "great masters of the international liturgical world"[14] — candidly stated what he believed the Consilium had achieved:

> Let those who like myself have known and sung a Latin-Gregorian High Mass remember it if they can. Let them compare it with the Mass that we now have. Not only the words, the melodies, and some of the gestures are different. To tell the truth, it is a different liturgy of the Mass [*c'est une autre liturgie de la messe*]. This needs to be said without ambiguity: the Roman rite as we knew it no longer exists [*le rite romain tel que nous l'avons connu n'existe plus*]. It has

---

14 See Annibale Bugnini, *The Reform of the Liturgy 1948–1975*, trans. Matthew J. O'Connell (The Liturgical Press, 1990), 221.

been destroyed. [*Il est détruit.*] Some walls of the former edifice have fallen while others have changed their appearance, to the extent that it appears today either as a ruin or the partial substructure of a different building.[15]

If one were to counter by saying the liturgical reform didn't tear *everything* down, the truth is that they seriously *considered* tearing everything down and believed they had the right and the authority to decide on the fate of every part except for the so-called "sacramental forms."[16] In other words, they were like doctors who "allow" the unborn to live, but who believe they would be perfectly within their rights to "terminate a pregnancy." So far from being praised for saving lives, such doctors deserve to have their licenses revoked and their practices shut down. What remained of tradition in the Novus Ordo remained because Bugnini's Consilium *willed* that it remain; it had successfully passed through their ideological filtration system. Their *individual will*—not reverence for the tradition—was the ultimate principle of everything. And this is profoundly uncatholic, I would even say anti-Catholic; it vitiates their entire project.[17]

It seems irrelevant, therefore, to object that some of the most obvious and violent changes—Mass *versus populum*, the *de facto* exclusion of Latin and Gregorian chant, women serving in ministerial roles in the sanctuary, Communion in the hand while standing—were not mandated by the Second Vatican Council and are not required by the Novus Ordo, which to some extent *permits* an *ars celebrandi* in continuity with tradition. The simple fact is that, from 1964 onwards, the highest levels of authority introduced a self-consciously modern way of celebrating the liturgy and, for all intents and purposes, imposed it on the body of the faithful. In his general audience of November 26, 1969, which is easily in the running for most repellent papal speech ever given,[18] Pope Paul VI stated that the Church must now sacrifice

---

[15] Gélineau, *Demain la liturgie*, 9–10; translation mine.
[16] Indeed, even these were modified, except not in such a way as to invalidate them.
[17] For the implications of this filtration, see my article series "The Reign of Novelty and the Sins of the Times: Why the Novus Ordo Is Solely Modern in Content," *Tradition and Sanity* Substack, August 5, 8, 12, and 15, 2024.
[18] In this speech Paul VI refers to "the liturgical innovation of the new rite of the Mass," and uses the expression "new rite" seven times; he calls the changes a "novelty" more than once, e.g., "this novelty is no small thing," and repeats the word "innovation." In Paul VI's mind, this was a new rite, a novelty, an innovation—that is why it is called the *Novus* Ordo. We should not smudge the clarity with which he speaks his intentions. A week earlier, in his audience of November 19, he uses the same vocabulary and dares to say: "It is an act of coherence of the Church with herself. It is a step forward for her authentic tradition. It is a demonstration of fidelity and vitality, to which we all must give assent.... It is a law. It has been thought out by authoritative experts of sacred Liturgy; it has been discussed and meditated upon for a long time. We shall do well to accept it with joyful interest and put it into practice

the "divine" Latin and the "incomparable" Gregorian chant for the sake of reaching Modern Man in a this-worldly vernacular, with the consequence that "pious persons are [going to be] disturbed most." This address is vintage Montini: pretending to be an upholder of the deeper values of Catholicism—a sort of neo-Platonic distillate without historical embodiment—he systematically dismantled its actual traditions and thereby paved the highway of identity-free Catholicism on which the modernizing Church, led by uncassocked priests and unhabited nuns, had already gleefully embarked after the Council. To such an incumbent of the papal throne might well be applied the words of Holy Writ: *Cogitasti confusionem domui tuæ, concidisti populos multos, et peccavit anima tua.* "Thou hast devised confusion to thy house, thou hast cut off many people, and thy soul hath sinned" (Hab 2:10). Telling are the words of John Henry Newman: "The contempt of mystery, of reverence, of devoutness, of sanctity, are notes of the heretical spirit."[19]

Bugnini, on the other hand, offered no sympathetic farewell to the liturgical patrimony of the Roman rite as he discarded it. During the same year that Paul VI gave the aforementioned address, Bugnini dispatched a flurry of demeaning rhetoric toward the Roman rite, which, if taken seriously, suggests that the Church had been unable to engage in true worship for over a millennium. In an article published in *L'Osservatore Romano* in 1969, replying to historian Hubert Jedin's regret at the loss of Latin, he wrote:

> As a good historian who knows how to weigh both sides and reach a balanced judgment, why did you not mention the millions and hundreds of millions of the faithful who have *at last achieved worship in spirit and in truth*? Who can at last pray to God in their own languages and not in meaningless sounds, and are happy that henceforth they know what they are saying? Are they not "the Church"? As for the "bond of unity": Do you believe the Church has no other ways of securing unity? Do you believe there is a deep and heartfelt unity amid lack of understanding, ignorance, and the "dark night" of a worship that lacks a face and light, at least for those out in the nave?[20]

As a result of these direct and indirect attacks upon reverence and tradition, between 1970 and circa 2005 one could count on both hands

---

punctually, unanimously, and carefully." One does not know whether to be more astonished at the brazen abuse of language or at the ominous tone with which he lowers the boom. These speeches might as well have been inspired by the propaganda depicted in George Orwell's *1984*. For more on the nomenclature associated with the modern rite, see Appendix 1. For analysis of this speech of Paul VI's, see Kwasniewski, *Once and Future Roman Rite*, 128–38.

[19] John Henry Newman, *An Essay on the Development of Christian Doctrine* (Longmans, Green, and Co., 1909), pt. 2, ch. 7, p. 354, www.newmanreader.org/works/development/chapter7.html.

[20] Cited in Parsons, "A Reform of the Reform?," in Kocik, *Reform of the Reform?*, 223.

the number of places that made serious attempts to practice what Pope Benedict XVI dubbed "the hermeneutic of continuity,"[21] that is, a Novus Ordo Mass offered *ad orientem*, in Latin, with Gregorian chant, having only properly vested male ministers in the sanctuary, Communion given on the tongue to faithful kneeling along the altar rail, and so forth. It is understandable that defenders of the modern Roman rite wish to compare the Novus Ordo "as it might be" with the traditional Latin Mass "as it actually is," but such a comparison is unreal, even fantastical. As thoroughly as the old rite is designed to be inflexibly regulated, the new rite is designed to be open-ended, malleable and mutable, "inculturated," so that it bears the seeds of its own destruction within itself; the Novus Ordo doesn't *bind* or *direct* priests in a way that is totally determinative. That is why "Father Over-here's Mass" can be so different from "Father Over-there's Mass," even when both are within bounds of the rubrics (such as they are). What happens when, so to speak, Fr. Longenecker retires and Fr. Shortnecker takes over? With Cardinal Ratzinger,

> today we might ask: *Is* there a Latin Rite at all any more? Certainly there is no awareness of it.... There was a loss of the awareness of "rite," that is, that there is a prescribed liturgical form and that liturgy can only be liturgy to the extent that it is beyond the manipulation of those who celebrate it.[22]

Yet, in another sense, the Novus Ordo on the ground is characterized by a relative *lack* of diversity, due to the adamantine grip of a one-sided body of customs built up over decades of impoverished and abusive celebration.[23] And even assuming the best-case scenario, the differences between the missals are so profound, to the disadvantage of the new, that no *ars celebrandi* can ever adequately surmount the rupture. The problem is not so much cosmetic as genetic.

As Joseph Ratzinger famously observed, the general crisis of the postcouncil is linked to the specific crisis of the liturgy.[24] In the words of French novelist and lay activist Cyril Farret d'Astiès:

---

21 Post-Synodal Apostolic Exhortation *Sacramentum Caritatis* (February 22, 2007), note 6.
22 "Change and Permanence in Liturgy: Questions to Joseph Ratzinger," in *Collected Works*, vol. 11: *Theology of the Liturgy*, ed. Michael J. Miller (Ignatius Press, 2014), 523.
23 The new-rite "solemn Mass" done by the Oratories in such cities as London, Oxford, Toronto, and Vienna are clearly not what any of the popes from Paul VI to the present has seen fit to offer the Church as a model, much less as a requirement. Msgr. Richard Schuler (1920–2007), longtime pastor of St. Agnes in St. Paul, Minnesota, is often brought up as an example of the hermeneutic of continuity (see his collected writings: *Sacred Music and Liturgy After Vatican II*, ed. Virginia A. Schubert [Arouca Press, 2024]), but the simple fact that one can name so few like him points up not only his own heroic fidelity in swimming against the tide but also the inherent improbability of the chosen approach.
24 Joseph Ratzinger, *Milestones: Memoirs 1927–1977*, trans. Erasmo Leiva-Merikakis (Ignatius Press, 1998), 148.

Certainly it was not the promulgation of the new missal that gave birth to modernism, the "collector of all heresies" that so worried St. Pius X. However, it is undeniable that all the modern thought of the twentieth century paved the way for liturgical reform; the reformers were in love with new ideas and had experimented, more or less clandestinely, with their pastoral whims, which found concrete and definitive application in the new missal—suppression of the Offertory, horizontal participation, abandonment of eastward orientation, systematic use of the vernacular, methodical simplification of all the rites...

Once these radical transformations of the entire liturgical edifice had been imposed, the faithful and the clergy who had to make use of them ended up integrating their suspect theological underpinnings, and in 2020 we have come to see bishops receiving Communion from the hands of a young girl, worship of the goddess Pachamama in the heart of the Vatican, bishops knowingly giving the Eucharist to both Protestants and civilly remarried divorced persons...

Even if worship is not a catechism, its expression is necessarily a reflection of belief. Liturgy expresses faith. And faith is expressed and spread through worship. As Fr. de Blignières so aptly put it during the pilgrimage for the tenth anniversary of *Summorum Pontificum*, ritual is what makes the truth tangible. The liturgical crisis is therefore naturally linked to the crisis of faith.[25]

The liturgical reform was the "Trojan Horse" by which modernism, liberalism, relativism, feminism, and a host of other evils invaded the Church and took possession of the city. Although in certain countries the practice of the Faith was already weakening in the 1950s and early 1960s, in most places and in most respects the Church was holding its own, and, allowing for crests and troughs that may be expected in a world of fallen human beings, such resilience could have continued for decades to come—if the Second Vatican Council had not been taken as a proclamation that all-encompassing change was overdue and that the Church *must* change to accommodate and assimilate the modern world from which it had so long been estranged.[26] The liturgical reform is exactly where these notions found their most complete acceptance, their most stunning realization, their most devastating consequences.

---

[25] "Les laïcs et la defense de la messe traditionnelle: Entretien avec Cyril Farret d'Astiès à propos de son ouvrage les cinquante ans du missel de Paul VI," *Paix Liturgique* Letter 776, December 18, 2020, www.paixliturgique.com/aff_lettre.asp?LET_N_ID=3064; translation mine. For an alternative translation of the entire interview, see my article "Why Are Laity So Involved in the Liturgical Debate? And Why Is the Continued Struggle Necessary?," *NLM*, July 10, 2023.

[26] Such, at any rate, was the claim; and yet there is much evidence that modern artists and intellectuals were fascinated with and strongly attracted to the Catholic Church's depth of tradition, culture, and thought. See Joseph Shaw, ed., *The Latin Mass and the Intellectuals: Petitions to Save the Ancient Mass from 1966 to 2007* (Arouca Press, 2023).

Those who think that *Sacrosanctum Concilium* is "just fine" if taken at face value, that the problem was people ignoring it or implementing it in a one-sided or distorted manner, and that a "reform of the reform" could take its bearings from a strict application of that document, may find themselves jarred awake from pleasant daydreams by the following two considerations.

First, one should consider how cleverly the reformatory impresario Annibale Bugnini steered the drafting committee of *Sacrosanctum Concilium* prior to the Council. Employing "the Bugnini Method" (as the acclaimed French historian Yves Chiron, who has written the best biography of Bugnini, calls it),[27] the Monsignor ensured that the text would never ask for too much, too fast, but would leave things vague enough to allow the extensive work of demolition and reconstruction he and his well-connected network of allies *already had in mind*. As he said to members of that committee on November 11, 1961 (thus, prior to the opening of the Council in October 1962):

> It would be most inconvenient for the articles of our Constitution to be rejected by the Central Commission or by the Council itself. That is why we must tread carefully and discreetly. Carefully, so that proposals be made in an acceptable manner (*modo acceptabile*), or, in my opinion, formulated in such a way that much is said without seeming to say anything: let many things be said in embryo (*in nuce*) and in this way let the door remain open to legitimate and possible postconciliar deductions and applications: let nothing be said that suggests excessive novelty and might invalidate all the rest, even what is straightforward and harmless (*ingenua et innocentia*). We must proceed discreetly. Not everything is to be asked or demanded from the Council—but the essentials, the fundamental principles [are].[28]

At the opening of the first session of the Council, when a cabal of prelates and *periti*[29] orchestrated a dramatic overturning of three years' worth of preparatory work and draft documents, *Sacrosanctum Concilium* was the only document allowed to stand. The October revolutionaries, so to speak, saw that the draft already met their expectations and future plans; it could be allowed to remain on the table while all the other drafts were shredded. This, and not a pious wish to treat the liturgy first, is the reason why *Sacrosanctum Concilium* was the first document to be discussed, then approved and promulgated.

---

27 Yves Chiron, *Annibale Bugnini: Reformer of the Liturgy*, trans. John Pepino (Angelico Press, 2018), 81–82.
28 Chiron, *Bugnini*, 82.
29 Maike Hickson, "New biography describes great influence of Fr. Joseph Ratzinger in Vatican II," *Rorate Caeli*, December 11, 2020. See Paolo Pasqualucci, *The Parallel Council: The Anomalous Beginning of the Second Vatican Council* (Gondolin Press, 2018).

Second, one must re-read *Sacrosanctum Concilium* more closely with the Bugnini Method in mind. A key tool for doing so is Christopher Ferrara's "*Sacrosanctum Concilium*: A Lawyer Examines the Loopholes."[30] I'd read this years ago, but only after reading Chiron was it able to hit me with full force. Ferrara's analysis shows, in detail, how a postconciliar liturgical reform that seems to depart so egregiously from certain stipulations of *Sacrosanctum Concilium* was, nevertheless, a consistent application of it, taking advantage of its loose language and the many openings it created for postconciliar extrapolations and adaptations.

The conclusion: *Sacrosanctum Concilium* is not only *not* a safe document, it was the greatest Trojan Horse ever introduced into the Church. It may be painful for many good Catholics to admit that a document so lauded by the establishment is, in truth, so flawed and so corrosive, but we must judge the tree by its fruits. In a debate broadcast by Radio-Courtoisie on December 19, 1993, Jean Guitton (1901–1999), philosopher and theologian, and a close personal friend of Paul VI, said the following:

> The intention of Paul VI with regard to the liturgy, with regard to what is commonly called the Mass, was to reform the Catholic liturgy in such a way that it should almost coincide with the Protestant liturgy... What is curious is that Paul VI did that to get as close as possible to the Protestant Lord's Supper... But I repeat that Paul VI did everything in his power to get the Catholic Mass, beyond the Council of Trent, closer to the Protestant Lord's Supper...
>
> I do not think I am wrong to say that the intention of Paul VI, and of the new liturgy that bears his name, was to require of the faithful a greater participation at Mass, to make more room for Scripture, and less room for all that some would call "magic," [and] others [would call] substantial, transubstantial consecration, and for what is of Catholic Faith; in other words, there was with Paul VI an ecumenical intention to remove, or at least to correct, or at least to relax what was too Catholic, in the traditional sense, in the Mass, and, I repeat, to get the Catholic Mass closer to the Calvinist mass.[31]

Just how close a friend Paul VI considered Guitton, and how openly he shared his mind with him, may be inferred from several facts: the

---

[30] Text available online at https://salbert.tripod.com/SClel.htm.
[31] The comments were first printed in the *Abbey Newsletter* by the Very Rev. Dom Gerard, OSB, Abbaye Sainte-Madeleine, Le Barroux, with a translation likely by Paul Crane, SJ in *Christian Order*, vol. 35, no. 10 (1994): 454. The interview in which Guitton made the remarks was subsequently transcribed and published in full: Yves Chiron, with François-Georges Dreyfus and Jean Guitton, "Entretien sur Paul VI" (Éditions Nivoit, 2011); see pp. 27–28, posted online by Sharon Kabel in "Catholic fact check: Jean Guitton, Pope Paul VI, and the liturgical reforms" (https://sharonkabel.com/post/guitton/); translation mine. For a different translation of part of the second paragraph, see chapter 5.

former asked the latter to suggest ideas for his inaugural encyclical; a couple of years later, the same pope asked him, along with Jacques Maritain, to draft the various "messages" that he would deliver at the end of the Second Vatican Council; and, most tellingly, Paul VI hosted him annually at the Vatican on September 8, the date they first met in 1950—a remarkable favor for anyone as busy as a pope to grant to anyone.[32] A photo exists of Guitton and Paul VI at the Vatican, working on a book together.[33] Guitton is a man who knows what he's talking about. For his part, Bugnini would surely have agreed with the aims attributed to Paul VI, for—concerning severe edits made to the traditional Good Friday orations in 1955—Bugnini wrote in the March 19, 1965, edition of *L'Osservatore Romano*: "It is the love of souls and the desire to help in any way the road to union of the separated brethren [i.e., Protestants], by removing every stone that could even remotely constitute an obstacle or difficulty, that has driven the Church to make even these painful sacrifices [in the liturgy]."

Conservative Catholics, although a quickly-vanishing breed in the face of burgeoning traditionalism, continue to repeat the bromides they have been taught, probably because they could not face what they think are the catastrophic consequences of renouncing them. Conor Dugan, in an irenic essay-review, says the following about Robert Royal's *A Deeper Vision: The Catholic Intellectual Tradition in the Twentieth Century*:

> In Royal's reading, "there is nothing whatever in any document approved by the Council Fathers that countenance[d] [the] radical departures" that followed the Council. Royal backs up his claims by a survey of the key documents. And, like Fr. Nichols' recent study, *Conciliar Octet* ... he concludes that the Council was not the Copernican Revolution of the Church, but reform in continuity.[34]

I wish I could believe this (indeed, I once *did* believe it). But having come to see that the first document approved by the Council—the *only* one where the preconciliar draft was retained because it was considered the least controversial!—is already chock-full of problematic statements and loopholes big enough to drive a fleet of Mack trucks through, it is impossible to live in the fantasy world of Catholic conservativism any longer. D. Q. McInerny well describes this problem:

---

[32] See Yves Chiron, *Paul VI: The Divided Pope*, trans. James Walther (Angelico Press, 2022), 117, 188, 215.
[33] *The Pope Speaks: Dialogues of Paul VI with Jean Guitton* (Meredith Press, 1968).
[34] Conor Dugan, "A Deeper Context: Overlooked book provides insight into Vatican II debates," *Catholic World Report*, September 2, 2020.

A characteristic of *Sacrosanctum Concilium*, and the other Council documents as well, is their adoption of a peculiar "yes... but," "certainly... maybe" mode of literary expression. A specific mandate is laid down, or a particular directive stated, and then almost immediately thereafter, in more cases than not, there follows a number of qualifying adjustments, relating to what has just been said, which have the effect of rendering a mandate not really mandatory after all, and making a directive sound as if it were little more than a suggestion, representing one possibility among others. This is what happens in *Sacrosanctum Concilium*. The effect of such an approach is to create an aura of ambiguity regarding a particular issue which allows for, or even invites, a variety of divergent interpretations, some so divergent that they are mutually contradictory. This is something which has been amply demonstrated over the last several decades.

No sooner is it specified, in *Sacrosanctum Concilium*, that Latin is to be preserved in the Latin rite than permission is granted for the vernacular to be used in the Mass and in the administration of the sacraments, and, tellingly, "the limits of its employment may be extended."... Given the vacillating manner in which the subject of Latin is handled in *Sacrosanctum Concilium*, I think it a fair judgment to say that the anti-Latin party can legitimately find greater backing in the document for their position than can those who wish to uphold tradition. What happened to Latin was the result of careful calculation.[35]

The reason we got the Novus Ordo in all of its reformation glory is that its future architects rigged the conciliar document to open the way to it, and admitted that they did so, as we have seen. If *Sacrosanctum Concilium* is the green wood of the Council, what about the dry?

Bugnini knew that he could succeed only by patient incremental efforts, so he ensured the drafting of a base text that was legalistic and "moderate" in tone, reasonable and serene in its provisions. Yet examined closely, the document finally approved contains more than a few hints of revolution to come, with scant regard for the *sensus fidelium* and *sensus catholicus*. As mentioned before, a line such as "Compline is to be drawn up so that it will be a suitable prayer for the end of the day"—as if Compline's traditional form were not already a highly suitable prayer for the day's end, and as if a worthy substitute for tradition can be summoned into existence at the snap of one's fingers—indicates the radical modernism at work in *SC*. Its spirit is rationalistic through and through, and could only have been the work of someone scornful of Catholic tradition and desirous of overthrowing it. The whole document is chipping, chipping, chipping away at

---

35 D. Q. McInerny, "Reflections on the Loss of Latin, Part I," *Latin Mass Magazine*, vol. 28, no. 4 (Christmas 2019): 33–34.

traditional piety, so that the subliminal message is: "The faith of your fathers was ill-informed, superstitious, excessive, misguided, while *your* faith will be modern, up to date, correct, truthful." It starts an avalanche of questioning, doubting, changing, changing some more, experimenting, rejecting, perverting, departing.

The foundational assumption of the liturgical reform was that the old rite was in dire need of repristination. To this end, the Council Fathers agreed to an *instauratio* (restoration), but by no means to a wholesale reconstruction[36]—at least, the vast majority of them would have said that this is not what they had agreed to. The clique of liturgical revolutionaries who worked closely to secure what they sought (as we shall see) were far more clever than the bumbling bishops whose goodwill had been abused. Ignoring their vote, Paul VI empowered the Consilium to "divide and conquer" the entire terrain of the liturgy.[37] Under Bugnini's indefatigable leadership, its members allowed themselves the widest latitude when creating new rituals out of bits and pieces of tradition fused with modern inventions.

It is worth noting that some of the most qualified participants became, over time, the ones most disturbed by the manner in which the business was conducted. Future cardinal Ferdinando Antonelli wrote in his diary in 1964 that the Consilium

> is merely an assembly of people, many of them incompetent, and others of them well advanced on the road to novelty. The discussions are extremely hurried. Discussions are based on impressions and the voting is chaotic. What is most displeasing is that the expositive Promemorias and the relative questions are drawn up in advanced terms and often in a very suggestive form. The direction is weak.[38]

---

[36] Thus, *SC* 21 authorized a "generalem instaurationem" of the liturgy, where *instaurationem* means restoration, while *generalem* means of a wide scope (in the sense that it includes the Mass, the Divine Office, etc.)—not something *integer*, "integral," concerning the totality, to its root level. Similarly, *SC* 31 says "in libris liturgicis recognoscendis," where *recognitio* means revision, not reform. Neither *instauratio* nor *recognitio* means "reform"; the Latin word *reformatio* is nowhere to be found in the Constitution. However, the Consilium interpreted its task as one of "*integer instauratio*" in the Instruction *Inter Œcumenici* 48: "Donec *integer* Ordo Missæ instauratus fuerit." One can see how boldly the Instruction takes a giant step forward. Progressivists will assert that *SC* called for "radical reform," but there is no basis for it in the Latin text. My point is that the Bugnini Method was followed rigorously: *SC* did not ask for everything the liturgists wanted—but after its promulgation they helped themselves to what they wanted nonetheless.

[37] An excellent introduction to the *Consilium* may be found in "The 'Consilium ad Exsequendam' at 50—An Interview with Dom Alcuin Reid," published in two parts at *NLM*, February 7 and February 12, 2014. For much more detail, see Christiaan W. Kappes, "Consilium and Vatican 2: Everything You Wanted to Know About Its Make-Up, Function, etc. (Replete with Graphs)," https://www.academia.edu/8837932.

[38] Nicola Giampietro, *The Development of the Liturgical Reform as Seen by Cardinal Ferdinando Antonelli from 1948 to 1970* (Roman Catholic Books, 2010), 166–67. Merriam-Webster defines promemoria as "a formal note embodying the written record of a diplomatic discussion."

The same participant observed in 1968:

> That which is sad... however, is a fundamental datum, a mutual attitude, a pre-established position, namely, many of those who have influenced the reform... and others, have no love, and no veneration of that which has been handed down to us. They begin by despising everything that is actually there. This negative mentality is unjust and pernicious, and unfortunately, Paul VI tends a little to this side. They have all the best intentions, but with this mentality they have only been able to demolish and not to restore.[39]

One of the most eminent participants, Fr. Louis Bouyer, had little praise to offer for the Consilium's fruits: "There was no hope of producing anything of greater value than what would actually come out of it, what with this claim of recasting from top to bottom and in a few months an entire liturgy it had taken twenty centuries to develop."[40] Recalling Lauren Pristas's research-based conclusion that "the post-Vatican II revisers did not adopt an antecedent tradition of usage. They produced something unique,"[41] Matthew Hazell accurately summarizes their mentality:

> For the [particular] Sunday we have looked at, the Consilium took orations from some of the well-attested Easter, Time after Pentecost, and Advent prayers, and created a new, unique Mass formulary. This process of reform could almost be seen as a kind of liturgical "greatest hits" album, with the reformers having taken what they considered to be the best orations from across the entire liturgical tradition, and collected them into one corpus of prayers. Of course, this is not a completely accurate metaphor, as, at best, the reformed Missal could only be partly considered a "greatest hits" album. Within it, there are also a sizeable number of "re-recordings" (edited orations) and "remixes" (centonisations), as well as completely new compositions—not things that people tend to buy "greatest hits" albums for!
>
> This rather cavalier approach to liturgical reform is not without its serious problems. Ultimately, it treats the liturgical tradition as a vast body of texts that can be freely deconstructed and reconstructed, like a giant piece of plasticine able to be remade in a completely different shape at the whim of the one moulding it, without any necessary reference to what it was before. No previous liturgical reform had been carried out like this; the 1570 *Missale Romanum* largely took up a corpus of prayers that, at

---

39 Giampietro, 192.
40 Louis Bouyer, *The Memoirs of Louis Bouyer: From Youth and Conversion to Vatican II, the Liturgical Reform, and After*, trans. John Pepino (Angelico Press, 2015), 219.
41 Lauren Pristas, *The Collects of the Roman Missals: A Comparative Study of the Sundays in Proper Seasons Before and After the Second Vatican Council* (Bloomsbury T&T Clark, 2013), 208.

the time, had been in use for some 800 years, making only very minor changes to it.[42]

What Hazell discovers by drilling into a particular "Sunday of Ordinary Time" has its parallel on every single page of the new liturgical books. They are not a *restoration* of anything; they are the brainchild of liturgical "experts" whom Archbishop Robert J. Dwyer, present at all four sessions of the Council, memorably called "either unscrupulous or incompetent," members of a "so-called Liturgical Establishment, a Sacred Cow which acts more like a white elephant as it tramples the shards of a shattered liturgy with ponderous abandon."[43] The idea of a liturgical rite as a *given* that deserves our deepest respect, so much stressed by Ratzinger,[44] was appallingly absent.

Let's take another example. The Ember Days are among the most ancient liturgical observances we possess. Already spoken of by Pope St. Leo the Great *in the fifth century* as a firm and fixed tradition, they predate even the Sundays of Advent (!), as beloved as those are. Michael Foley notes:

> The Ember days, which fall on a Wednesday, Friday, and Saturday of the same week, occur in conjunction with the four natural seasons of the year. Autumn brings the September Embertide, also called the Michaelmas Embertide because of their proximity to the Feast of St. Michael on September 29. Winter, on the other hand, brings the December Embertide during the third week of Advent, and spring brings the Lenten Embertide after the first Sunday of Lent. Finally, summer heralds the Whitsun Embertide, which takes place within the Octave of Pentecost. In the 1962 Missal the Ember days are ranked as ferias of the second class, weekdays of special importance that even supersede certain saints' feasts. Each day has its own proper Mass, all of which are quite old. One proof of their antiquity is that they are one of the few days in the Gregorian rite...which has as many as five lessons from the Old Testament in addition to the Epistle reading, an ancient arrangement indeed. Fasting and partial abstinence during the Ember days were also enjoined on the faithful from time immemorial until the 1960s.[45]

Early on, the Ember Saturdays were chosen as days of ordinations. As Peter Day-Milne recounts, "in the year 494, Pope Gelasius

---

42 Matthew Hazell, "The Scattering of the Propers: A Case Study in the Mass Formularies of the Ordinary Form," *NLM*, July 15, 2020.
43 See my article "'The Liturgy Has Been Dismantled': Portland Archbishop Robert Dwyer's Assessment in 1971," *NLM*, September 16, 2024.
44 See, *inter alia*, Ratzinger, *The Spirit of the Liturgy*, IV, 1, in *Theology of the Liturgy*, 98–105.
45 Michael P. Foley, "The Glow of the Ember Days," *Rorate Caeli*, September 23, 2015.

prescribed that the orders of priest and deacon be conferred on those days... around evening-time."[46] As a result, notes Fr. Arnaud Devillers, "the prayer and fasting of Ember week acquired added importance, for apostolic tradition demanded that ordinations be preceded by fast and prayer (Acts 13:3)."[47] The traditional Epistle for the Fourth Sunday of Advent (1 Cor 4:1–5), which always follows the Advent Ember Days, reflects this ancient connection with ordinations when it speaks of how the "dispensers of the mysteries of God" should be found faithful.

This ancient tradition, like so many others, was abandoned in the 1960s as part of the "extreme makeover" of the Church's worship by committees that invented what *they* thought the world *now* needed, and suppressed what they thought it had outgrown. That is completely contrary to the way the liturgy has always been treated: as an inheritance to be proudly maintained and jealously protected.[48] How could such a thing have happened?

A purge and fabrication of this magnitude arose from the belief that Modern Man is *essentially different* from his predecessors, to such an extent that what past generations possessed and made use of can no longer be assumed profitable to modern people.[49] This belief, as false as the day is long, dovetailed with the mania for system and method characteristic of modern times: with enough taxpayer dollars and enough government committees, we can build a better world—or, in this case, with enough "experts" backed by conciliar and papal muscle, we can build a better worship.

There are multiple reasons for the mania, but they converge on one thing: the triumph of rational method and its (attempted) application to every domain of human life. By "rational method" I mean the sort of thing one finds in rationalist thinkers such as Descartes, Bacon, Spinoza, Kant, or Comte: the attempt to dominate reality by a self-contained logical system of axioms, theorems, and corollaries. In civil society, this becomes the attempt to create a rational "science of politics" and a system of human rights so that man's happiness can be procured on Earth and the evils to which the flesh is heir can be

---

[46] Peter Day-Milne, "Remember the Ember Days? (Part I)," *Adoremus*, November 22, 2021.
[47] Arnaud Devillers, FSSP, "Ember Days of Lent," *The Missive*, March 13, 2019.
[48] In fact, the Ember Days were taken off the general calendar and delegated to the episcopal conferences for local adaptation. Amidst all the chaos, not a single conference got around to reestablishing them. The fact that their loss seems to have been the result of combined clumsiness and indifference underlines how badly the "reform" was managed; no secular art museum would treat even its least valuable items as carelessly. See Matthew Hazell, "Ember Days in the Post-Vatican II Liturgical Reforms: An Accidental Elimination?," *Rorate Caeli*, March 10, 2022.
[49] See my article "Is Modern Man 'Incapable of the Liturgical Act'?," *NLM*, October 12, 2020.

banished. Romanticism was a failed response to the rationalist mania, and its failure was all the heavier because it bought into the premise of the mania—namely, that system and method are the only ways to be rational. In reacting against rational method, romanticism thought it had to react against rationality itself.[50]

Bronwen McShea's groundbreaking essay "Bishops Unbound"[51] traces out how this mania invaded the Church long ago. To respond to the rise of rationally organized states, the Church adopted the same type of rational organization herself, overriding centuries of local, organic traditions. To be fair, Protestantism had played those traditions to its advantage: get all the local canons to be heretics, and they'll elect a heretical bishop. Some response, then, was needed. But in adopting the tactics of modernity, the Church began to drink in the view that system and method are the answer to every problem. We see that mentality seeping into governing structures, seminaries, advice for confession, spiritual manuals, mass-produced artworks, you name it. The Church imitated the secular state in its absolutism, its legal codes, its proceduralism, and its regimentation. John Lamont's analysis of the corruption of the concept of obedience fits into this picture as well.[52]

So when the Church faced a crisis of humanity in the twentieth century—and there can be no doubt that some such crisis had been brewing ever since the First World War and was only intensified by the Second—the natural solution seemed to be this: call a huge meeting of all the executives, draw up a new set of documents and plans, and set things to rights from the top down. What is usually billed as the moment of the Spirit, the moment of throwing off the shackles of neoscholasticism, was in its very conception one huge exercise in the mania for system and method. The ensuing liturgical construction, rationalization, and standardization at the hands of a memorandum-driven super-committee for top-down "reform" was of a piece with that.[53]

Catholics who are steeped in the modern conception of rationality can imagine no other alternative but a nostalgic romanticism. Some people think their way along, while others feel their way along. We can see this false alternative at work whenever traditionalists are accused of "nostalgia," which is regarded as a sort of weakness of the brain:

---

[50] For a full examination of this theme, see Gerard G. Steckler, SJ, *The Triumph of Romanticism* (Os Justi Press, 2023).
[51] Bronwen McShea, "Bishops Unbound," *First Things*, January 2019, www.firstthings.com/article/2019/01/bishops-unbound.
[52] John Lamont, "The Catholic Church and the Rule of Law," in Peter A. Kwasniewski, ed., *Ultramontanism and Tradition: The Role of Papal Authority in the Catholic Faith* (Os Justi Press, 2024), 78–106.
[53] See chapter 19; cf. my article "In Praise of Irregularity," *NLM*, April 4, 2016.

since system and method are the only version of rationality—there's simply no other way of being rational—it follows that being attached to place, to local tradition, to the heritage of the past, is to be irrational.

Two giants of early modern philosophy, Bacon and Descartes, reject the formal cause, the principle that accounts for *what* something is, and the final cause, the principle that accounts for why it does what it does. Scientifically-minded people are to look instead to the material cause, that is, the stuff something is made out of, and the efficient cause, what put it together or pushes it. In a similar way, the formal cause of liturgy (tradition) and the final cause (worship of the thrice-holy God) were neglected, and the "stuff" of the liturgy was subjected to manipulation by scholarly architects and engineers, for whom it was seen as raw material ready to be endowed with a new purpose: the betterment of the human condition. In other words, the same mechanistic and humanistic worldview was operative in the liturgical reform as in the Baconian and Cartesian scientific revolution.

In my experience, relatively few Catholics today are aware of just how the liturgy was "reformed."[54] The entire landscape of the liturgy—the Mass, all the sacramental rites, the Divine Office, blessings, papal ceremonies—was partitioned into 46 segments entrusted to as many subcommittees (each called a *Cœtus*, "group" in Latin), all under the expert management of Annibale Bugnini, who reported directly to Paul VI and served as the information conduit between the subcommittees that "drew up" rites and reports and the pope who had to approve their work. Within this bureaucratic juggernaut there were, for instance, nine groups for the Divine Office and eight for the *Ordo Missæ*.

The various groups disassembled the existing rites into their atomic parts and then produced new building plans out of traditional, archaic, imaginary, and novel ingredients. These were reassembled at plenary meetings, as a car factory has an assembly area for the parts fashioned in separate departments. This was Bugnini's plan from the first moment: "divide and conquer." All he had to do was to make sure that the "right" people were assigned to each subcommittee, and then sit back and orchestrate the agendas and communications. The tunnel vision of so many simultaneous tracks would ensure that the most avant-garde ideas could be pursued and given a favorable hearing, while no one but Bugnini and a few others had in mind the overall goal they were seeking. He knew that the monumental changes he and the other radical reformers had in mind would never be approved all at once in a full-frontal view; rather, Henry Ford's car-factory process would ensure success.

---

54 Of this multi-decade process, there is no better overview than Chiron's *Bugnini*.

It should be clearer now why I have said that approaching liturgy in this mechanistic, industrialized, compartmentalized way betrays a Baconian-Cartesian conception of reality. Bacon's *Novum Organum* was the methodological template of the *Novus Ordo*. The Consilium's workshop was like the laboratory of a chemist or a physicist, rather than the outdoor world of real organic beings studied by the botanist or zoologist. The liturgy was regarded and treated not as a mystery that grows with its own inner life-principle, like a child in the womb of Holy Mother Church, but rather as a series of lifeless parts that have to be rigged up a certain way to get them to "function properly." The holistic metaphysical vision of Plato and Aristotle, of Augustine and Aquinas, is absent from this atomistic reductionism and technological utilitarianism. The liturgy was treated like a deluxe set of LEGO bricks or a DIY project instead of a wondrous seed imparted by the Lord, planted by the apostles, tended by the Church Fathers, and maintained by centuries of gardeners. Although the liturgy was affected by the soil, water, and climate in which it lived, those who received it and cared for it had always respected its *givenness*, its "otherness" from us and from any age through which it passed. Such must still be our attitude today toward the great tradition. By a kind of miracle, this tradition survived alongside its attempted modern replacement, and as the years go on, we can see it thriving anew, refuting the claim that old rituals cannot speak to modern believers.

Once one understands what actually transpired at the Council by reading such works as Roberto de Mattei's *The Second Vatican Council—An Unwritten Story* and Henry Sire's *Phoenix from the Ashes*, it is no longer possible to credit the optimistic "Royal reading" of Vatican II; nor can the blossoming of Catholic intellectual life before Vatican II cancel out the machinations of the progressives and soft modernists who steered the internal discussions and drafts more or less as they wished. They saw their chance, and they took it boldly. Indeed, Bugnini himself, in his account of the years 1948–1975, self-congratulatorily invokes the saying "Fortune favors the brave" to explain how he and the other reformists shaped and guided the entire reformatory process from start to finish.[55]

---

[55] In 1948 Bugnini had a questionnaire sent to "almost a hundred liturgical experts in all parts of the world" on behalf of the Roman periodical *Ephemerides Liturgicæ*, concerning a prospective "reform of the Missal, Breviary, calendar, Martyrology, and other liturgical books." Bugnini writes: "This questionnaire, sent as it was by the editorial staff of a periodical regarded as the semi-official voice of Roman liturgical circles, was the first alarm signal that something was stirring. In those days it was unheard of for anyone to challenge even a rubric or to use the word 'reform.' The questionnaire was therefore a bold move. In this case the proverb was proved true: 'Fortune favors the brave.'" Bugnini, *Reform of the Liturgy*, 11. For commentary, see Kwasniewski, *Noble Beauty*, 281–85.

Why, then, did nearly every prelate at the Council, including Archbishop Marcel Lefebvre, vote in favor of *Sacrosanctum Concilium*—a whopping 2,147 against 4? Fr. Hunwicke suggests that they were naïve about the ultimate goals of the radical Liturgical Movement and thought they were opting for a gentle modernization of the traditional worship;[56] that they were lied to about what the plan would actually be, since the debates at the Council suggested moderate reform;[57] and, not least, that they acted by a herd instinct, which, in the midst of such an inefficient and laborious meeting as the Council was (we have many private records complaining of dreadful tedium), allowed the key players to fuel documentary finalization with the gasoline of impatience.

And why, then, did they obediently implement all the changes afterward? Ah, therein lies a different tale. Even the bishops who had serious doubts about the reforms (and there were more than a few) felt they had no choice but to obey whatever the pope decreed. A pope's word is God's word, isn't it? Cardinal John Heenan of Westminster, who felt bewildered and betrayed by the constant liturgical changes of the latter half of the 1960s, wrote to a correspondent in 1963, "When the voice of the whole Church speaks, we have to stifle our personal preferences and accept the fact that the Holy Ghost is guiding the Church.... Reserve judgement for a few years and you will see why God has led the Church to a new liturgy." To another, he wrote in 1965: "If the Pope and the bishops of the whole world have agreed on these changes the Holy Spirit must be guiding His Church." In 1967: "When the Holy See gives directions we have to obey them" (no qualifications!). In 1969: "If the Holy Father has decided to reform the liturgy, we must accept."[58] A long-ingrained sheepish hyperpapalism masquerading as piety prevented even the shepherds from protecting their flocks against revolutionary harm.[59] Sixty years of deformed

---

[56] John Hunwicke, "Liturgy and Vatican II: what did they think they were voting for?," *Fr Hunwicke's Mutual Enrichment*, March 23, 2019.
[57] See John Hunwicke, "Some priest called Ruff... and: Did Archbishop Marcel Lefebvre make a big mistake? (1)," *Fr Hunwicke's Mutual Enrichment*, March 3, 2017, and this trio of articles: Peter Kwasniewski, "The Council Fathers in Support of Latin: Correcting a Narrative Bias," *NLM*, September 13, 2017; "What They Requested, What They Expected, and What Happened: Council Fathers on the Latin Roman Canon," *NLM*, August 8, 2022; "The Lie That Was Told to Over 2,000 Council Fathers at Vatican II," *NLM*, May 27, 2024.
[58] Quoted in Alcuin Reid, ed., *A Bitter Trial: Evelyn Waugh and John Carmel Cardinal Heenan on the Liturgical Changes*, expanded edition (Ignatius Press, 2011), 23–24. For a refutation of this simplistic reasoning, see Peter Kwasniewski, "Games People Play with the Holy Spirit," in idem, ed., *Illusions of Reform: Responses to Cavadini, Healy, and Weinandy in Defense of the Traditional Mass and the Faithful Who Attend It* (Os Justi Press, 2023), 134–50.
[59] See "My Journey from Ultramontanism to Catholicism" in Kwasniewski, *The Road from Hyperpapalism to Catholicism*, 1:1–27.

parochial worship, a global network of clerical immorality, and a pope who treats the Church's faith as malleable clay are the three strikes by which hyperpapalism has at last exited the batter's box—although some are still catching up on the news.

Does the foregoing critique of *Sacrosanctum Concilium* or of the Consilium set up by Paul VI to implement it count as "dissent from the Magisterium"? No. The Constitution itself has two ingredients: a speculative account of liturgy, which is patient of an orthodox interpretation, and a long list of practical decisions about how the liturgy should be "restored," a task undertaken by the super-committee. The traditionalist critique aims at the latter ingredient, which, of its nature, concerns prudential judgments made about particulars. Such judgments about what is best to do here and now are not infallible in themselves and remain subject to reevaluation, modification, and even rejection. The same process happened with disciplinary measures of earlier ecumenical councils, some of which were never implemented or fairly quickly became moot.[60] Put simply: the plan of action to which the Council Fathers agreed, together with the way it was interpreted and applied, can and must be judged by its fruits and against the backdrop of changing circumstances; it is not an object of religious assent. Even according to the most robust valuation of an ecumenical council's status, it is well within its powers to enact a mistaken plan of action, and, *a fortiori*, well within the powers of its implementary bodies such as working groups and episcopal conferences.

The disaster of the liturgical reform ensued because a coterie of arrogant academics had convinced themselves that everything needed to be changed to catch up with, or speak effectively to, Modern Man. It did not; they were wrong. Worst of all, Modern Man did not come rushing into the doors of the Novus Ordo; rather, millions of faithful left, never to return. Contrary to the itching hands of reformers from the era of Protestantism through the Synod of Pistoia down to the cancer-phrase of the Liturgical Movement, the Roman rite of Mass, definitively codified in 1570 by St. Pius V, *did not need to be reformed*. To those humble enough to take its yoke upon them and acquire its wisdom, this rite made and still makes perfect sense in the form in which it has been handed down for so many centuries.

---

60 For example, the Fourth Lateran Ecumenical Council (1215) forbade clergy to watch mimes, entertainers, and actors, visit taverns, and play games of chance or even be present at such, and enjoined them to have a crown and tonsure, while bishops were ordered to wear linen; moreover, it was ordered that Jews and Saracens living in Christian lands had to wear a distinctive mark of dress, and could not leave their houses during the Triduum. There are many analogous examples if one reads the annals of the ecumenical councils.

It was not—*is* not—defective. Objections against it fall away when scrutinized.[61]

As St. Thomas Aquinas argues, following St. Augustine and other Church Fathers, God would not permit an evil unless He wills to bring forth from it a greater good. While none of us can see in full the good He will bring from the evils attendant on the Council and its subsequent liturgical reform, I think it is past dispute that we have learned hard lessons that have helped us over the decades and will continue to help us in the future. We can have—and an ever-growing number do have—a better understanding of why the traditional (pre-1955) Roman rite *is just the way it is,* why it functions well as it stands, and why it should not be changed in any significant way. Its perfection in texts, chants, and ceremonies has never been as evident as now, standing out against a backdrop of liturgical manglement, mediocrity, and malaise. Those who care about the liturgy care *more* about it; those who love tradition, as all Catholics should, love it all the more. These are the necessary preconditions for a flourishing of divine worship in the Church: the font and apex of the Christian life and the heart and soul of Christian culture.

More than sixty years after *Sacrosanctum Concilium,* the spirit of reform has largely lost its hold on anyone except the ever-dwindling generation that was young at the time of Vatican II, supported by a small number of ideologues who still parrot the views of Bugnini and associates. The youthful momentum and intellectual weight are on the side of tradition. We must be patient and never lose heart, for major changes—this time, good ones—are in the offing.

---

[61] I have done a good deal of this scrutinizing in my book *Turned Around*; see also Part II below.

❧ 2 ❧
The Irreparable Failure of the Liturgical Reform

THOSE WHO HAVE BEEN IN THE TRADITIONalist movement for decades can remember times when critiques of the postconciliar liturgical reform appeared in obscure corners of the Catholic world at intervals of months (for papers and magazines) or years (for books). In our day, things are far different: every week brings with it the tidings of worthwhile articles and books defending tradition and critiquing novelty, sometimes even in popular venues. In this regard, the difference between, say, 1974 and 2024 is astonishing: surely a sign of the vitality of the movement of restoration. Thanks in no small part to Pope Benedict XVI's profound liturgical theology and no-nonsense criticisms of the hack-job of the 1960s, a growing awareness that something went seriously amiss has pervaded those who are still practicing the Faith in the younger generations. Best of all, the number of clergy who are familiar with the glories of the unreformed Roman rite and celebrate it regularly is growing apace, guaranteeing its vitality long past the time when the products of the Consilium will have been relegated to a museum of twentieth-century curiosities.

THE NOVUS ORDO'S DEFECTIVE CALENDAR

Consider, to begin with, a number of authors thoughtfully tackling the question of the botched reform of the Roman calendar, which is agreed to be one of the worst casualties of the postconciliar era, and which Fr. Louis Bouyer called the work of "a trio of maniacs."[1] The "unfreezing" of the traditional calendar to such an extent that it seems to have melted into a puddle encouraged episcopal conferences to play fast and loose with holy days of obligation. Joseph Shaw, Chairman of the Latin Mass Society of England and Wales, observes:

---

[1] His critical evaluation is quoted at greater length below on p. 243. It is a little hard to know *which* three maniacs Bouyer is referring to, as there were so many involved in the project. The *Consilium*'s *Cœtus* for the calendar comprised Bugnini, A. Dirks, R. van Doren, J. Wagner, A.-G. Martimort, P. Jounel, A. Amore, and H. Schmidt, though we know that Jounel was the leading spirit. For further reading, see Michael P. Foley, "The Reform of the Calendar and the Reduction of Liturgical Recapitulation," in Alcuin Reid, ed., *Liturgy in the Twenty-First Century: Contemporary Issues and Perspectives* (Bloomsbury T&T Clark, 2016), 321–41.

The dates of the Church's major feast days are in no way random. They have deep historical and cultural roots, and immense theological significance. The Church uses the calendar to teach us things, and the means she employs include the *intervals between feast days*. Thus, most obviously, the *Ascension* is forty days after Easter. Forty is the time of waiting we find in the Old and New Testament. Moving the feast of the Ascension not only obscures this, but mucks up the interval between the Ascension and Pentecost: nine days, a novena of preparation for the Holy Spirit to descend. *Corpus Christi* is on a Thursday after Easter because it recalls the mystery of Maundy Thursday. The symbolism is destroyed if it is moved to Sunday. *Epiphany* is the Twelfth Day of Christmas: it can't be moved without damage to all the cultural associations this has. It is the primary feast of Christmas for many Oriental Churches. It was celebrated on 6th of January by the Emperor Julian in the year 360. This is pretty well as far as detailed records go back for many aspects of the liturgy. To move it is surely an act of barbarism.[2]

Fr. Richard Cipolla focuses on the deformation of the entire structure of sacred time:

> One of the saddest and most deleterious effects of the changes in the structure and content of the liturgical calendar in the post-conciliar reform is the lack of understanding of the sanctification of time by the feasts and fasts of the Church. The introduction, at least in English, of the term "ordinary time" contradicts the fact that after the Incarnation there is no "ordinary" time. There is only the extraordinary time that has been brought into being by the insertion of the dagger of the Incarnation into ordinary time. Now we know that the term "ordinary time" is a poor translation of the Latin term for "in the course of the year" [*per annum*]. But even this does not take away from the fact of the impoverishment of the liturgical calendar that has been effected by taking away the Sundays after the Epiphany and the Sundays after Pentecost. The traditional way of naming these Sundays understood that these two feasts, Epiphany and Pentecost, are the climaxes of the Christmas and Easter seasons, the seasons that celebrate the event and meaning of, respectively, the Birth, and the Death and Resurrection of Christ, and therefore these feasts become the touchstone, the source of reality of the Sundays of the Church Year....
>
> Surely we can now see the foolishness of the possibility of celebrating the Epiphany as early as on January 2, four full days before the actual feast that is celebrated in parts of the Western Church still on January 6 and celebrated on that day by our Orthodox brethren

---

[2] Joseph Shaw, "Transferred Holy Days, 2: The Dates," *LMS Chairman*, January 10, 2014; cf. idem, "Must I Go to Mass on Monday?," *Catholic Answers*, November 19, 2024, where he says of the above feasts and several more: "These are not just convenient dates; they establish a web of symbolic connections across the liturgical year."

throughout the world with the solemnity it deserves. It is foolish as well to celebrate this feast after January 6, as if it is irrelevant to the sanctification of time when any feast is celebrated, for the guiding principle in this reform is the convenience of the people: it is more convenient for the people to celebrate the Epiphany on Sunday rather than the interruption of having to go to Mass on a weekday. But it is precisely the interruption that is the point. The ir-ruption of the Incarnation demands such an inter-ruption, demands such an "inconvenience," for it is a reminder of the sanctification of time itself to those of us who forget that time and space and the world and our lives and our future have been radically changed by the Incarnation of God in Jesus Christ.[3]

Kate Edwards, an expert on the Benedictine Monastic Office, also draws attention to the abolition of Epiphanytide:

> The removal of most of the octaves from the liturgical calendar was perhaps an understandable decision. But it was, I think, one of those reforms that went more than a few steps too far, most obviously in the abolition of the octave of Pentecost in the Ordinary Form calendar. Another case in point, in my opinion, is the abolition of the octave of the Epiphany, which is, I think, one of those decisions which it would be nice to reverse as a means of giving some genuine impetus to the "New Evangelization." The calendar reforms of the twentieth century saw a progressive reduction in the importance of Epiphany, starting with the abolition of the octave of the feast, and culminating in the outright abolition, in the Novus Ordo calendar, of the traditional season of time after Epiphany. Yet Epiphany is, above all, the great feast of the revelation of God to the gentiles, represented by the three wise men. So how could reducing the importance of this feast possibly be thought consistent with the objective of making the Church more missionary oriented?[4]

In a talk given at the Brompton Oratory, Fr. Cassian Folsom summarizes the problem in a memorable image:

> The *Ordo Missæ* of the 1970 Missal was radically changed: in fact, we call it the *Novus Ordo*. Concerning the calendar, and especially the superabundant growth of the sanctoral cycle, there has always been need of periodic pruning. But in the 1970 Missal, the pruning was so radical that the original plant is sometimes unrecognizable. The

---

[3] Richard Cipolla, "Epiphany and the Unordinariness of Liturgical Time," *Rorate Caeli*, January 10, 2014. It is true, as Michael Foley has explained ("The Origins and Meaning of Ordinary Time," *Antiphon*, vol. 23, no. 1 [2019]: 43–77), that Msgr. Pierre Jounel, who proposed *Tempus per annum*, did not intend the pejorative sense of "mundane" as opposed to "special." Nevertheless, the theory behind his proposal was so arcane and implausible that it never caught on popularly; we are abandoned to the usual associations.
[4] Kate Edwards, "Not the Octave of the Epiphany!," *Saints Will Arise*, January 7, 2014, https://saintsshallarise.blogspot.com/2014/01/not-octave-of-epiphany.html.

protective fence of the rubrics, carefully developed over centuries in order to guard the Holy of Holies, was taken down, leading to unauthorized "creativity" and liturgical abuse.[5]

To the instances of calendrical iconoclasm already cited, one could add the suppression of the ancient season of Septuagesima, which, following on the heels of the joyous season of Epiphany, allots three weeks of time before Lent for the faithful to prepare themselves gradually for the rigors of fasting, abstinence, and almsgiving.[6] Such a season, while invested with symbolic meanings by commentators on the liturgy, is obviously also premised on a sound grasp of human psychology and the need for transition, so as to avoid the feeling of having been, in the words of one author, "parachuted into Lent."[7]

Over the years, many commentators have pointed out how ridiculous it is to celebrate "Ascension Sunday" or "Epiphany Sunday," and yet these things remain fixed in place, like prehistoric flies trapped in amber. There can be no change for the better, that is, no restoration of Catholic tradition, until there is a massive change of mentality, a dying off of the old guard and a genuine renewal from the grassroots. For this transition to take place—for it to have even a chance of taking place—discussion and promotion of the TLM must continue, must rise and grow into a mighty wave of unanimous and irresistible testimony: "Give us back our tradition, give us back the fullness of the Catholic faith!" This will be a second great instance in history when the *sensus fidelium* will have carried the truth of the Gospel in a time when even hierarchs compromised, denied, or disappeared.[8]

---

[5] Cassian Folsom, OSB, "*Summorum Pontificum* and Liturgical Law," a talk given at the London Oratory, December 13, 2013. Over 300 saints were removed from the Novus Ordo's calendar: see my article "The Sanctoral Killing Fields: On the Removal of Saints from the General Roman Calendar," *NLM*, November 16, 2020, and chapter 14 below.

[6] At least, when there *were* rigors of fasting and abstinence. In the old calendar, all Lenten weekdays, Ember Days, and vigils were days of fast, on which only one regular meal could be taken. Paul VI enjoys the dubious distinction of having reduced the fasting days to only two: Ash Wednesday and Good Friday. This represents a departure from the unanimous practice of East and West stretching from the earliest Christian records to the mid-1960s, or an almost 2,000-year practice. So much for looking to the ancient Church as a model.

[7] The phrase is from André Rose, who was a member of *Cœtus* 18bis but later expressed sharp criticisms of its work. See the melancholy analysis by Pristas, *Collects of the Roman Missals*, "Septuagesima," 95–111.

[8] The first, of course, was the Arian crisis. See John Henry Newman, *The Arians of the Fourth Century* (University of Notre Dame Press/Leominster: Gracewing, 2001), note 5: "It was mainly by the faithful people that Paganism was overthrown; it was by the faithful people, under the lead of Athanasius and the Egyptian bishops, and in some places supported by their Bishops or priests, that the worst of heresies was withstood and stamped out of the sacred territory" (446); "I mean still, that in that time of immense confusion the divine dogma of our Lord's divinity was proclaimed, enforced, maintained, and (humanly speaking) preserved, far more by the 'Ecclesia docta' [the Church taught, i.e., the non-hierarchy] than by the 'Ecclesia docens' [the

The issues we have touched on with the drastically altered calendar are only part of a vast field of problems. The rupture between the liturgical tradition as it stood on the eve of the Second Vatican Council and the modern rite is so comprehensive and easily demonstrated that one could choose any point of entry and mount a substantial critique of the reform on its basis: the *Ordo Missæ*, the Propers, the sanctoral cycle, the lectionary, the modifications in text and rubric that amounted to an abandonment of our musical patrimony, and so on.

THE DEATH OF THE REFORM OF THE REFORM

It seems, then, that we have entered a phase of great honesty and frankness not only in assessing the false principles behind the Pauline liturgical reform and the worldwide damage it has wrought (an assessment that has certainly not been lacking at any point over the past sixty years[9]) but also in evaluating the implausibility of an institutional correction that would remove rampant abuses and re-integrate foolishly discarded elements.

This new and more realistic phase is epitomized in an article that attracted an enormous amount of attention when it first appeared just over a decade ago, in February 2014: Fr. Thomas Kocik's "Reforming the Irreformable?"[10] It would be no exaggeration to call this article a turning point in the English-speaking world. Here we had one of the greatest experts on the subject[11] concluding that the "reform of the reform" was, in fact, not possible. The modern rite is so radical a deconstruction and reconstruction of the liturgy that it does not exist in the same line of organic development as the Roman rite. Pope Paul's

---

teaching Church, i.e., the hierarchy]; that the body of the Episcopate was unfaithful to its commission, while the body of the laity was faithful to its baptism; that at one time the pope, at other times a patriarchal, metropolitan, or other great see, at other times general councils, said what they should not have said, or did what obscured and compromised revealed truth" (465–66). See also Roberto de Mattei, "Resistance and Fidelity to the Church in Times of Crisis," in idem, *Love for the Papacy and Filial Resistance to the Pope in the History of the Church* (Angelico Press, 2019), 105–30.

9 The conversation has indeed been taking place for some decades, and we must be careful not to overlook or forget earlier contributions of the traditionalist movement, such as the work of Klaus Gamber, Michael Davies, Dietrich von Hildebrand, Jean Madiran, and Roger-Thomas Calmel. A fine example on our current topic would be John Parsons's "Reform of the Reform?," originally published in *Christian Order*, November–December 2001, and republished as Appendix 6 of Kocik's *Reform of the Reform?* Apart from its magnificent clarity and depth of thought, this article demonstrates that the skepticism about ROTR recently expressed by Fr. Kocik and others has been around for quite some time in the circles of those who know their liturgical history and theology.

10 See, too, the same author's "Reforming the Irreformable? A Postscript," *NLM*, March 1, 2014.

11 The most important publications of Kocik in this connection are the book already mentioned (*The Reform of the Reform?*); "A Reform of the Reform?," in Alcuin Reid, ed., *T&T Clark Companion to Liturgy* (Bloomsbury T&T Clark, 2016), 317–38; and "The Reform of the Reform," in Reid, *Liturgy in the Twenty-First Century*, 19–50.

liturgy is a new departure, a new thing, not a revision of the old thing that had been handed down over the centuries. As an artificial entity constructed out of bowdlerized and decontextualized pieces of the Roman heritage combined with modern inventions, any future reform of it would be no more than a mere variation on the novel theme. The only way forward is not to tinker any more with this "fabrication, a banal on-the-spot product,"[12] but to return steadfastly and stalwartly to the Catholic and Roman liturgical tradition embodied in the preconciliar (and indeed pre-Pacellian) liturgical books.

Fr. Kocik's bracing honesty was the long-awaited and necessary announcement that "the Emperor has no clothes." Even if others had said similar things over the years, people perk up when an educated priest who specialized in the study of the Roman liturgy and who for a long time defended and promoted the reform of the reform finally cashes in the chips and says: "The only viable solution is to restore the *usus antiquior* everywhere, with full, actual, and conscious participation." Honesty has a way of clearing the air, letting us breathe freely.

Taking their cue from Fr. Kocik, several authors expressed similar judgments at the time. Dom Mark Kirby bore eloquent witness to the experiences and feelings of many:

> I was, at one time, as deeply committed to the reform of the reform as was Father Kocik, having contributed to the *Beyond the Prosaic* conference at Oxford in 1996 and to the book that followed it. Like Father Kocik, although several years earlier, I came to see the futility of trying to repair something that, at bottom, is structurally unsound. Nowhere is the old adage, "Haste makes waste," truer than when applied to the precipitous reform of liturgical rites and the books that contain them. In most places the liturgical landscape has become a dreary wasteland. The liturgical rites and books prepared so feverishly in the wake of the Second Vatican Council have been tried and found wanting.
>
> There are, it is true, liturgical oases here and there, where the reformed rites are carried out intelligently, with dignity, reverence, and devotion—I am thinking of certain communities, monasteries, and parishes, the Communauté Saint-Martin, for example—but these subjective qualities cannot make up for the objective flaws and structural weaknesses inherent in the same rites....

---

[12] As Joseph Ratzinger famously called it in 1992. "What happened after the Council was something else entirely: in the place of liturgy as the fruit of development came fabricated liturgy. We abandoned the organic, living process of growth and development over centuries, and replaced it—as in a manufacturing process—with a fabrication, a banal on-the-spot product." From Ratzinger's preface to the French edition of Gamber's *The Reform of the Roman Liturgy: La Réforme Liturgique en Question* (Éditions Saint-Madeleine, 1992), 8, translated on the back cover of the English edition of the book. For the full text, see my article "Translation of Ratzinger's Preface to the French Edition of Klaus Gamber," *NLM*, February 8, 2023. An alternative and somewhat softened translation may be found in Ratzinger, *Theology of the Liturgy*, 537–38.

The passing of the years has demonstrated the intrinsic inadequacies of the reformed liturgical books of the post-conciliar era. The cracks in the post–conciliar liturgical edifice became evident almost as soon as the new rites began to be "lived in." Today, the same edifice appears like so many shabby buildings put up hastily during an economic boom, now revealing their structural flaws, and threatening imminent collapse.[13]

Another Benedictine, Dom Hugh Somerville Knapman, penned a soul-searching article in the course of which he laments:

If liturgy was a live issue before the Council of 1962–65, it has become in the wake of that Council an explosive issue. Liturgy seems never to be at rest. For some, the Council gave a licence to change comprehensively the performance of the Church's liturgy, and the change has been unrelenting. For others the changes were unjustifiable, unconscionable even, and they reject them outright. For others still, liturgy has been something to be coped with, an unavoidable battlefield on which they try to find shelter in some compromise that acknowledges the reality of change and seeks somehow to keep it organically connected to the Tradition of the Church. Few have been satisfied.

We might ask ourselves: where is my foxhole, my bunker, my bastion, on this battlefield? So much of my reading the past year or more has shown my foxhole [i.e., the reform of the reform] to be filling with mud, slowly but ever more surely. It is not a tenable position in the long-term....

It is hard not to conclude that the structure and the rubrics of the new Mass lend themselves to such a [cavalier, creative] practice and attitude. If you remove so many of the sacralizing elements of a ritual, of course it is going to end up secularized. Rather arbitrarily included after the Council among the "useless repetitions" the same Council had deprecated, nearly all the signs of the cross and genuflections and kissings of the altar were removed from the Mass. To one not formed under the old Mass, these gestures can appear to be fussy and pedantic and almost obsessive. They seem to cry out for some rationalization. But is such a principle appropriate to the symbolic and sacred ritual of the Mass? Are time-and-motion principles suited to something that should take us out of time and out of ourselves?...

In other words, there is a disjunction between what we are taught happens at Mass and what seems so often to be happening. There is an incongruence between the words and the actions. It is possible to do the new Mass properly; but the new Mass seems to have the inherent flaw that it is so easy to do improperly.[14]

---

[13] Mark Kirby, "Let nothing be preferred to the Work of God," *Vultus Christi*, February 20, 2014, https://archive.ph/lTOsz.
[14] Hugh Somerville Knapman, "The Lament of a Liturgical Loner," *Dominus Mihi Adjutor*, February 18, 2014.

In addition, we may note the problem that it is ultimately impossible to know what "doing the Novus Ordo properly" *actually means*, given that there is no rubrically-determined authoritative model, and given that successive papacies have continuously liberalized liturgical customs while simultaneously asking for a never-enforced removal of abuses.[15] There is anarchy in the place where there should be maximum order. This led Monika Rheinschmitt to formulate a sardonic judgment:

> If there is anything we can learn from considering (a) the diversity already allowed by the Novus Ordo's own rubrics, (b) the diversity added on top of this by official or unofficial attempts at "inculturation," and (c) the further diversity created by rampant abuse and bad custom, about which the Vatican pretends to care but never takes concrete action, we are justified in reaching the following conclusion: The unity of the Novus Ordo consists exclusively in not being the traditional liturgy.[16]

Fr. Richard Cipolla compared Fr. Kocik's article to the famous *Tract 90*, the final installation of the Oxford Movement's *Tracts for the Times* (1833–1841) and a symbol of the crisis and parting of the ways within the Anglo-Catholic effort to re-inject Catholicism into the English Church.

> This is indeed "Tract 90" for the "reform of the reform" and sounds the death knell of any serious attempt to hold onto the fiction of continuity between the 1970 Missal and the Traditional Roman rite. Just as Tract 90 marked the end of Newman's attempt to find a Catholic continuity and a *Via Media* in Anglicanism, so does Fr. Kocik's public articulation of the abandonment of his attempt to find a liturgical and theological continuity between the Novus Ordo and the Traditional Roman rite mark the end of the Reform of the Reform movement. What must be done now—and this will require much *laborandum et orandum*—is to make the Extraordinary ordinary [i.e., to make the classical Roman rite normative].[17]

The missal of Paul VI, the modern (and not the Roman) rite, is irreparably broken. Due to the false principles, exploded assumptions, and rationalistic method behind its composition, it was wrong from the first day, and it remains wrong, no matter how "well" it is celebrated. Its prayers and rubrics embody a hermeneutic of discontinuity that

---

[15] For example, Paul VI allowed male laity to do readings at Mass; John Paul II allowed female laity to read and serve at Mass; Francis decreed that female laity may be "installed" as "lectors and acolytes." A similar pattern may be discerned in the loosening-up of communion customs over time. As for the never-enforced call for removing abuses, see chapter 6.
[16] Monika Rheinschmitt, "Further thoughts on 'inculturation': Why ignore the liturgy that sustained the evangelization of the entire globe?," *Rorate Caeli*, July 5, 2022.
[17] Richard Cipolla, "The End of the 'Reform of the Reform': Father Kocik's 'Tract 90,'" *Rorate Caeli*, February 12, 2014.

could not be cured without a complete overhaul. In the language of the philosophers, it would require not an accidental but a substantial change.¹⁸ As far as incremental reform goes (for example, if we look to how some Oratorians celebrate the new rite), nearly every successful step has involved adding or substituting something from the old rite—for example, artificially crafting roles for a "subdeacon" and deacon at Solemn Mass, re-introducing the Offertory prayers *sotto voce*, observing silence during the Canon, and giving Communion on the tongue to faithful kneeling along an altar rail—or removing something painfully problematic, such as the singing of ditties unworthy of a third-rate Broadway musical, or the sauntering up of unvested laity into the sanctuary to read readings or distribute Communion. Using the (by now) old-fashioned terminology of Benedict XVI, one might say the Ordinary Form becomes better by becoming the Extraordinary Form. As such, the Novus Ordo needs to be *retired*, not reformed, so that the fully developed Roman rite may once again occupy its proper place in the life of the Catholic Church as it had done for centuries before.¹⁹ Granted, such a retirement will not happen overnight (nor should it), but the end goal is clear.

We have come a long way since the optimism of the 1990s, when it seemed as if one might somehow restart the process of organic development from within the Novus Ordo. As most have come to see, this is a fool's errand. Even if we may agree that the Holy Sacrifice of the Mass should always be celebrated as beautifully, reverently, and solemnly as possible—in whatever rite one is using—it is no longer necessary to pretend that, with a certain yet-to-be-found alchemy, lead can be transmuted into gold. The gold remains golden, and the lead, leaden.

---

18 I invoke this Aristotelian distinction in an analogous sense: the accidents of a rite would be the particular cut of a vestment, the variety of incense, the use of this or that type of supplementary music, and so forth; whereas its substance would be the order of ceremonies, the content of prescribed texts and chants, the rubrics that govern actions, and so forth. My claim (expatiated in my book *The Once and Future Roman Rite*) is that the Novus Ordo differs from the Roman rite in regard to the substance of the liturgical rite, not (only) its variable accidents.

19 There is nothing "irreversible" about liturgical reform, since it concerns contingent prudential decisions. Hence, Pope Francis is guilty of absurdity when he writes: "We cannot go back to that ritual form which the Council fathers, *cum Petro et sub Petro*, felt the need to reform" (Apostolic Letter *Desiderio Desideravi*, no. 61). But *of course* we can; today's pope and today's bishops are not bound to agree necessarily with the reformatory program of their predecessors in the 1960s. If their predecessors had the right to launch a reform, then their successors have no less right to direct, redirect, or undo that reform. Indeed, a rigid adherence to the 1960s would, according to their own logic, convict them of a spirit of nostalgia and backwardism that refuses to "read the signs of the times" or to remain open to the Holy Spirit. (A refutation like this has its limits, especially as I would not concede a "right" to reverse liturgical tradition on the scale on which that reversal was done. I am merely pointing out that "what is sauce for the goose is sauce for the gander.")

Careful study and long experience of the liturgy has led many Catholics who deeply love the Church to the conclusion that the reform carried out by the Consilium and promulgated by Paul VI is not just the unfortunate victim of a wave of abuses but a thing deeply and inherently flawed in structure and content.[20] For instance, consider the sobering and relatable reflections of Phillip Campbell as he reflects on his conversion and the nasty surprise that awaited him:

> When I was able to compare the prayers of the TLM to the Novus Ordo, the difference was night and day. "Why *wouldn't* anyone want to pray like this?," I thought to myself in astonishment at the obvious superiority of the old prayers.... I had the following realizations: (1) The Church I had fallen in love with through study [before converting] was the *traditional* Church, which for all intents and purposes no longer existed. (2) Whatever it was that had replaced the traditional Church was not only different, but also *inferior* to it in every way. Those things I liked about the contemporary Church were precisely those facets of traditional Catholicism that had survived *despite* the rupture of the Conciliar era. (3) Finally, this displacement of tradition was not some accident of history, but was a very deliberate act of erasure—of intentional cultural warfare waged against the Church by one of her own factions. The Church I had read my way into simply did not exist. It's hard to explain the degree of frustration I felt. Not just frustration, but a sense of having been robbed. Yes, robbed; for to intentionally cut off the great stream of tradition is to commit the sin of theft against future generations, who are thereby deprived unjustly of a heritage they ought to have inherited. Destroying tradition is to commit theft against future Catholics.[21]

In sum, Campbell, like so many others, came to realize that the Novus Ordo is not in continuity with the Roman liturgical tradition as it unfolded over the centuries of faith. As a result, it cannot serve as a suitable platform for the long-term future of the Roman rite.

The "irreparable failure" mentioned in this chapter's title comprises four aspects of the liturgical rites of Paul VI:

---

[20] One need only study Pristas's *Collects of the Roman Missal* to see what was done to the Collects and why. And this is just the tip of the iceberg; the same thing can be seen with prayers used for all of the sacraments, the Divine Office, the blessings of persons and objects, exorcisms, and so forth. There is precious little that has not been corrupted, save the bare sacramental forms necessary for validity. To say that "a rite is valid" or "a prayer is Christian" is rather like saying of a person, "he is conscious" or "he is alive." It gets you something important, to be sure, but only the first of many levels that are meant, by God's providential design, to work together.
[21] From Phillip Campbell, "The Novus Ordo and Conversion," *Unam Sanctam Catholicam*, September 20, 2020; see the same author's articles at the same place, "The Problem of the 'Reverent Novus Ordo,'" September 10, 2020; "Reform of the Reform: Liturgical Russian Roulette," December 5, 2022; "The Unsalvageable Novus Ordo," December 25, 2019.

1. their failure to uphold the inherent *auctoritas*, the morally binding authority, of the liturgical tradition as such;[22]
2. their failure to reflect the duties and limits of papal authority vis-à-vis the liturgical tradition;[23]
3. their failure to adhere to principles and desiderata of *Sacrosanctum Concilium*,[24] not to mention a host of earlier documents, especially Pius XII's *Mediator Dei*;[25]
4. their failure to respect basic laws of psychology and sociology concerning healthy behavior toward a cultural patrimony and the requirements of ritual stability for group identity and harmony.[26]

The scope of any "reform of the reform" project and its likely success are therefore intrinsically and inescapably limited. Even if we indulged the fantasy of a day when every Novus Ordo celebration across the globe would be reverent, solemn, and beautiful, in full accord with (a

---

[22] Although many have written on this topic, Fr. Hunwicke offers helpful and fascinating discussions on the *auctoritas* of Latin in the liturgy and the *auctoritas* of having but one anaphora in the Roman rite (search his weblog for "auctoritas"). For extensive discussion of the authority of tradition in general and of the traditional liturgy in particular, see Peter Kwasniewski, *Bound by Truth: Authority, Obedience, Tradition, and the Common Good* (Angelico Press, 2023).

[23] Here is how Ratzinger puts it: "After the Second Vatican Council, the impression arose that the pope really could do anything in liturgical matters, especially if he were acting on the mandate of an ecumenical council. Eventually, the idea of the givenness of the liturgy, the fact that one cannot do with it what one will, faded from the public consciousness of the West. In fact, the First Vatican Council had in no way defined the pope as an absolute monarch. On the contrary, it presented him as the guarantor of obedience to the revealed Word. The pope's authority is bound to the tradition of faith, and that also applies to the liturgy. It is not 'manufactured' by the authorities. Even the pope can only be a humble servant of its lawful development and abiding integrity and identity.... The authority of the pope is not unlimited; it is at the service of sacred tradition.... The greatness of the liturgy depends—we shall have to repeat this frequently—on its unspontaneity." *The Spirit of the Liturgy*, IV.1, in *Theology of the Liturgy*, 102–3.

[24] *Inter alia*: SC 23, 28, 36, 54, 112–116.

[25] The ignoring of the preceding Magisterium was made far easier by a last-minute decision on the part of the conciliar liturgical commission to *remove* 73 out of 115 footnotes from the final draft of *Sacrosanctum Concilium*—namely, precisely the references to such documents as *Mediator Dei* that might have "controlled" the interpretation and implementation of the constitution. Curiously, the person who explained in 1964 (after the fact) why the notes were pulled *without* explanation to the council fathers, making the lightweight version a *fait accompli*, was none other than Pierre-Marie Gy, OP, who years later would condemn Joseph Ratzinger's *Spirit of the Liturgy* as unfaithful to the Second Vatican Council. See Susan Benofy, "Footnotes for a Hermeneutic of Continuity: *Sacrosanctum Concilium*'s Vanishing Citations," *Adoremus Bulletin*, vol. 21, no. 1 (Spring 2015): 8–34, https://web.archive.org/web/20160817074120/http://adoremus.org/AdoremusSpring2015.pdf. The first two pages, summarizing her findings, can be found at https://archive.ccwatershed.org/media/pdfs/15/06/03/13-43-26_0.pdf. When Adoremus republished those two pages online on September 23, 2024, they modified the text to downplay the sleight-of-hand—an action that reflects the original sleight-of-hand.

[26] One thinks, for instance, of the work on cultural anthropology of Mary Douglas or Anthony Archer. For a discussion of the latter, see Joseph Shaw, "The Old Mass and the Workers," *LMS Chairman*, July 3, 2013.

conservative reading of) Vatican II and the postconciliar Magisterium, there would *still* be profound discontinuity between what came before the Council and what came after, in the very bones and marrow of the rites themselves—in their texts, gestures, rubrics, rationale, spirituality, and theology.

What is more, Joseph Shaw argues that a Novus Ordo Mass "dressed up" in Latin and chant often ends up awkwardly "falling between two stools" because it respects neither the genius of the Vetus Ordo nor the specific populist motivations behind the Novus Ordo.[27] Many who are involved in liturgical ministries have experienced the uphill battles Shaw describes, which make the task of any kind of reform of the reform extremely tiring, a constant struggle with the rite's plethora of options,[28] the rationalistic assumptions undergirding it, and the longstanding habits of minimalism, antinomianism, and horizontalism with which it is surrounded like a stag at bay. Shaw concludes that it is easier and better simply to begin celebrating the age-old liturgy of the Church. It *starts* at a healthy place; it is a coherent whole, serenely and admirably just what it is; and there is no nonsense about it. Whether it might need minor doctoring or not is vastly secondary to the consoling truth that it is not a bloody mess on the operating table of wartime medics.

If the analysis by Fr. Thomas Kocik, Dom Hugh Somerville Knapman, Fr. Richard Cipolla, Joseph Shaw, and others is correct—and, by this time, one could compile many volumes of such analysis, from authors writing in many languages—there are systemic, "hard-wired" problems that no reform of the reform can overcome. We should not ignore or dance gingerly around them but admit them truthfully and courageously, before directing our efforts *most of all* towards a restoration that will bear those fruits of renewal denied to the Consilium's brainchild. Lost continuity cannot be recovered by stubbornly insisting upon it; the only way it will happen is to resume the Vetus Ordo, which embodies the received Roman liturgical tradition. The Novus Ordo cannot be an evolutionary step toward a future Roman rite; it is a detour, an evolutionary dead-end, a dodo bird. It is like those modernist churches that do not suffer gently the passage of time, trapped in their own era and mentality, unable to rise above it, and worthy of nothing so much as nonexistence. The way forward in this case is not to maintain the modernist mistake but to abandon it and re-embrace

---

[27] Vetus Ordo, old order (of worship), is said by way of contrast to Novus Ordo, new order (of worship). See chapter 8 for a full treatment of the nonviability of the chanted Latin Novus Ordo, a *contradictio in terminis*.
[28] I will address this problem of "optionitis" a number of times in this book, as it is a far bigger problem than most realize, not only for strictly liturgical reasons, but also for spiritual and psychological ones.

our noble artistic tradition, which retains inexhaustible power to speak to us of realities that are timeless and transcendent. Sometimes what an ugly building or sculpture needs is not an interior decorator or a powerwash but a wrecking ball and a dump truck.

In a poignant reflection entitled "Home from the Liturgical Thirty Years' War," Dom Mark admits that, after spending decades of labor on the revised rites, working to elevate them as much as he could, he came to realize how much richer and more fruitful the traditional liturgy is—and that his time all along would have been better spent within this welcoming and lovely house.[29] Moving from the cramped urban apartment bloc into the spacious old country home ("the family seat," one might call it) may not yet be an option for some Catholics, but we must pray, hope, and work for the day when every member of the Latin Church will find his way back to that venerable house of prayer.

DIVERGENT POLITICAL MODELS

If the Novus Ordo is as defective as traditionalists say it is, how can we explain the fact that there are flourishing religious congregations exclusively reliant on it? The Missionaries of Charity and the Nashville Dominicans, for example, are full of fervent disciples of the Lord who take their nourishment from the liturgy of Paul VI, so it cannot be the case that this liturgy is "all bad."

Apart from the fact that I have never argued and never would argue that the Novus Ordo is "all bad" (something that would be metaphysically impossible), I welcome the opportunity to analyze this phenomenon. In my opinion, such religious communities are bringing to the liturgy a spiritual disposition that enables them to benefit from the Real Presence of Our Lord in the Eucharist—a disposition they are not necessarily developing *from* the liturgy as such. The Novus Ordo can be fruitful for those who already *have* a fervent and well-ordered interior life, built up by other means; but for those who do not, it will offer few pegs on which to climb up. In this respect it is unlike the traditional liturgy, which has within itself enormous resources for enkindling and expanding the interior life.

One might make a political comparison to elucidate this point. The basic philosophical problem with the American regime is not that a good use cannot be made of its political institutions, but that they *presuppose* a virtuous citizenry in order to work at all. Time and time again, the American Founding Fathers say things like: "Our Constitution was made only for a moral and religious people. It is wholly

---

29 Mark Kirby, "Home from the Liturgical Thirty Years War," *Vultus Christi*, February 23, 2014, https://archive.ph/Lw8RV.

inadequate to the government of any other."³⁰ But the aims of this government do not include *producing* a virtuous citizenry; this is seen as above and beyond the government's limited scope. Government is supposed to act like a police officer who regulates the flow of traffic; it is assumed that people know how to drive and basically drive well.

The traditional view, which we find (for instance) in Pope Leo XIII's social encyclicals, is that government has a God-given responsibility for the moral and spiritual welfare of the people. It must lead them to the observance of the natural law and dispose them as well as possible to the observance of the divine law. In this model, the government is more like a parent, teacher, and counselor who knows what the human good is and actively fosters its attainment by as many citizens as possible. This is why, for Leo XIII, a good government will necessarily involve the Catholic Church in educating the citizens of the regime, so that they may have the best possibility of developing virtue, both natural and supernatural. Virtue does not develop spontaneously or accidentally.

The liturgical parallel is not hard to see. The Novus Ordo is like the American government. It is a structure or framework within which free activity can take place, but it does not rigorously specify or dictate how that activity ought to be pursued, nor does it provide ample means for accomplishing the task. It is like the benign and neutral policeman — a certain precondition for peace, but not the representative and spokesman of peace. The minimal rubrics function like boundaries on a sports field. The people who attend are assumed to know how to pray, how to "participate actively" (as if this is at all evident!), and how to be holy. They come to display and demonstrate what is already within them.

The traditional liturgy, in contrast, forthrightly adopts the attitude of parent, teacher, and counselor. It assumes that you are in a dependent position and must be shaped in your spirituality, molded in your thoughts, educated in your piety. Its rubrics are numerous and detailed. The liturgy knows exactly what you need in terms of silence, chant, prayers, antiphons, and it delivers them authoritatively, in a way that emphasizes the liturgy's own perfection and your receptivity. The traditional liturgy establishes a standard of virtue and expects the worshiper to conform to *it*. It does not presuppose that you are virtuous.

This helps to explain the intentionally Protean adaptability of the modern liturgical rites, in their optionitis and spectrum of *artes celebrandi*. Moderns don't really think there *can* be a fixed and virtuous

---

30 John Adams, October 11, 1798, "Letter to the Officers of the First Brigade of the Third Division of the Militia of Massachusetts," in Charles Francis Adams, ed., *The Works of John Adams, Second President of the United States* (Little, Brown, and Co., 1854), 9:229.

liturgy that should form them into its image. As heirs of the Enlightenment, which enthroned human reason as king and assumed a supposedly rational control over all aspects of society, moderns feel they need to be in some way *in charge of* the liturgy. It has to have options to accommodate our pluralism.[31]

In this way the Novus Ordo betrays its provenance in a democratic and relativistic age, in stark contrast with the traditional liturgy that was born and developed entirely in monarchical and aristocratic eras (and this, of course, by Divine Providence, since God knew best what human beings needed, and ensured that the rites would embody it). Even if one wished to say, for the sake of argument, that secular society is better off democratized—a claim that would seem counterintuitive, to say the least, especially if one could canvas the opinions of the countless millions of victims of abortion murdered under the democratic regimes of the Western world—one must nevertheless maintain as a matter of principle that the divine liturgy, being from and for the King of kings and Lord of lords, cannot be democratized without ceasing to exist. It must remain monarchical and aristocratic in order to remain *divine* liturgy, as opposed to a self-derived human patriotism.[32]

If you are that fortunate person who has a robustly developed life of faith, whether from a Protestant upbringing prior to your conversion, or frequent attendance at adoration of the Blessed Sacrament, or a constant and childlike Marian devotion, you bring all of this fullness with you when you attend the Novus Ordo, and you fill the relative emptiness of the liturgical form with that fullness. In this case, your fullness (so to speak) meets Christ's fullness in the Eucharist, and there is a meeting of minds and a marriage of souls. This, it seems to me, is what is happening with those aforementioned religious communities that are flourishing in spite of the Novus Ordo's defects as a *lex orandi*, in its anthropological assumptions, theological content, and aesthetic form.

---

[31] An objection might be raised: Are there not aspects of the old liturgy that are also up to the celebrant's discretion? And should you not argue against them, as well? The truth is that the realm of choice in the old liturgy is extremely narrow, and is always a choice between fully articulated elements. In some Commons, there is a choice of Epistles or Gospels. On a solemn day, a priest may choose to wear gold instead of a different liturgical color. He may choose to sing the most solemn Preface tone rather than the more solemn tone. If his missal has the Gallican prefaces, the rubrics allow him to use them on specified days. But notice how small a range of choice is allowed, and how its components are already fully spelled out—the priest invents nothing. There is no putative right to extemporize; and the most essential elements, such as the Canon, can *never* be altered. The holiest thing is beyond the realm of choice; it is a given. The Byzantine liturgy is the same: which of the anaphoras is to be used is dictated to the priest by the calendar, not left up to his pastoral discretion. We will come back to these points in chapter 20.
[32] See "Why the Traditional Mass Is Kingly and Courtly" in Kwasniewski, *Turned Around*, 56–78.

With the traditional Mass, it is different. It awakens an awareness of the interior life that is the first step to a more profound interior conversion. It contains ample Eucharistic adoration within it, and so, it feeds this hunger of the soul and intensifies it to the point that it overflows beyond the confines of the liturgy. Its spirituality is Marian through and through, so it tends to lead souls to Our Lady, who is waiting for them there.[33] In every way, this Mass is actively calling into being a mind for worship and a heart for prayer; it carves out a space in the soul to fill it full of Christ.[34] It does not presuppose that you are at that point, but pulls and draws you there, due to its confident possession of the truth about God and man. It is not leaning on you to supply it with force or relevance; it is not waiting for you to be the active party. It is inherently full and ready to act upon *you*, to supply you with *your* meaning. And paradoxically, it does all this through *not* being focused on you, your problems, your potentialities. It works because it is so resolutely focused *on the Lord.*

There is an irony here, inasmuch as, at first glance, the didacticism of the Novus Ordo seems to be aimed at explaining and eliciting certain acts of religion, while the *usus antiquior* seems to take for granted that one knows what to do. But in reality, the new rite's didacticism interferes with the free exercise of these acts of religion, and the *usus antiquior*'s "indifference" to the attendees more subtly challenges them to build new interior habits proportioned to the earnestness and intensity of the liturgical action. By attempting to provide for the worshiper everything he "needs," the modern rite fails to provide the one thing needful: an unmistakable sense of encounter with the ineffable mystery of God, whom no words of ours can encompass, whom no actions of ours can domesticate. The *usus antiquior* knows better, and therefore strives to do both less and more—*less*, by not leading children by the apron strings of a school teacher; *more*, in terms of calling into being new ascetical-mystical capacities that depend radically on a fixed and dense "regimen" of prayer, chant, and bodily gestures.[35] "I have run the way of thy commandments, when thou didst enlarge my heart" (Ps 118:32). In this domain, the old rite shows us that space is greater than time. Having a capacious and symbolically dense space within which to "play" is of greater benefit, in the long run, than spending an hour doing verbal exercises in the confines of a modern classroom.

This is the difference between the worship inherited from the ages and the set of exercises devised by twentieth-century liturgists. The one

---

33 See "The Spirit of the Liturgy in the Words and Actions of Our Lady" in Kwasniewski, *Noble Beauty*, 53–87.
34 In chapter 10, I explain just how the TLM does this.
35 A point to which I will return in chapter 19.

is humble enough to go without the name of an author or a committee and confident enough to insist that it knows best what we need. The other contends that scholars always know best and the people must eat out of their hand, even if this dependency will always be in tension with the perpetual drive toward localization, popularization, and inculturation.[36]

THANKSGIVING FOR LITURGICAL PROVIDENCE

Progressive liturgists—that is to say, the entire establishment during and after Vatican II, with a few exceptions—make an elementary mistake in their thinking, akin to the mistakes made by historical-critical biblical scholars.

When liturgists dig into the history of rites, they discover lots of change, development, variety, and seemingly chance events ("after all, don't you know, it was because of Charlemagne that the Roman liturgy replaced the Gallican while assimilating many of its elements"). So far, so good. But then they make an unwarranted inference: beyond the postulate of a "golden age" of apostolic worship, we owe no reverence to liturgical rites at any later stage of their development. For example, since medieval and Baroque features of the Roman liturgy resulted from "historical accidents," they are viewed as ripe for purging at the hands of the *cognoscenti*—defined as those who, by their own admission (and surely they would know), know better what our current historical milieu requires.

Such reasoning betrays the lack of a metaphysical and theological framework for seeing how Divine Providence works by governing all things in general *and* in detail. To us here below, with our faint and finite grasp of causality, there appears to be chance; in the eyes of God there is no such thing as chance. He sees all, He causes all. Without an adequate conception of and trust in Providence, we will (or will be tempted to) commit sins of judging and rejecting the fruits of organic liturgical development, as if we moderns are superior to our forefathers. Nor can it be said that the twentieth-century reformers were themselves merely acting as instruments of Providence for bringing about the latest phase of rightful historical development, for their work was premised on a rejection of vast swaths of tradition, deemed the result of chance or corruption, to be replaced with a highly selective return to antiquity filtered through the assumptions of modern philosophy—an inorganic methodology incompatible with faith in the continuous rulership of God. The Christian's default assumption is that our forefathers, historically and collectively, have more wisdom

---

[36] See chapter 5.

than we do, for we are, as it were, latecomers on the scene. Our job is to receive and assimilate their wisdom, striving to live up to it if we possibly can.[37] As Newman puts it:

> It is a fault of these times (for we have nothing to do with the faults of other times) to despise the past in comparison of the present. We can scarce open any of the lighter or popular publications of the day without falling upon some panegyric on ourselves, on the illumination and humanity of the age, or upon some disparaging remarks on the wisdom and virtues of former times. Now it is a most salutary thing under this temptation to self-conceit to be reminded, that in all the highest qualifications of human excellence, we have been far outdone by men who lived centuries ago; that a standard of truth and holiness was then set up which we are not likely to reach, and that, as for thinking to become wiser and better, or more acceptable to God than they were, it is a mere dream.[38]

Thus, the liturgists' inference fails to appreciate the *spiritual* attitude that we are supposed to have towards our inheritance—towards that which "falls to our lot." The Psalmist captures this attitude perfectly: *Funes ceciderunt mihi in præclaris; etenim hæreditas mea præclara est mihi* (Ps 15:6), which the Douay-Rheims renders: "The lines are fallen unto me in goodly places: for my inheritance is goodly to me." The sense of the verse is that the boundaries God has measured out for His people in the course of His fatherly guidance of them are the

---

[37] As Jeremy Holmes explains: "'Ancestor' comes from *antecessor*, which means foregoer, forerunner, the one who goes before; 'tradition' comes from *traditio*, a delivering, derived from the verb *trado*, to give, to give over, to deliver. In this mode of experiencing time, the ancestors have gone before; they have run the path on which we are now running; they are ahead of us on that path; they have given to us or delivered to us something, perhaps trail markers, instructions on how to walk, how to run, how to climb, what to avoid, where the dangers lie, equipment for the journey, instruction on what lies at the end of the path, and so forth. We are coming behind. We receive what they have given us, and in turn we deliver it to those coming behind us.... By following them we enter into our inheritance and make it our own with them." Moreover, "because human reason is by nature tradition-dependent, a literate society naturally creates a canon, namely, a set of writings that embody and transmit a tradition. Because a canon is the means of passing on a society's innermost life, the life of the mind, it also serves as a medium for that life as members of society think via the canon, speak via the canon, and interpret the world via the canon." *Cur Deus Verba: Why the Word Became Words* (Ignatius Press, 2021), 59, 64, 66. These insights can be easily applied to the traditional liturgy as the canon formed by our Catholic *antecessores* at prayer.

A failure to receive this canon of tradition and to pass it on is a hidden but potent form of selfishness, as Roger Scruton intimates: "The dead and the unborn are as much members of society as the living. To dishonor the dead is to reject the relation on which society is built—the relation of obligation between generations. Those who have lost respect for their dead have ceased to be trustees of their inheritance. Inevitably, therefore, they lose the sense of obligation to future generations. The web of obligations shrinks to the present tense." "Rousseau and the Origins of Liberalism," *The New Criterion*, October 1998, https://newcriterion.com/article/rousseau-the-origins-of-liberalism/.

[38] John Henry Newman, "Use of Saints' Days," *Parochial and Plain Sermons* II, Sermon 32, in Kwasniewski, ed., *Newman on Worship*, 95–96.

right ones: they shine with His wisdom. The lot we have received is goodly and not to be scorned or second-guessed—"as if to say," in the words of St. Thomas, "my inheritance is not only goodly in itself, but it is goodly to me, so that I would not change it at all."[39]

Note the word used twice in the Vulgate verse just cited: *præclarus*. This word has many meanings: splendid, bright, excellent, famous, illustrious, noble, distinguished. This dictionary definition reads like a listing of all the qualities that traditional liturgical rites of Eastern and Western Christianity possess—and exactly the qualities that are wanting in the fabricated rites of the 1960s and 1970s. For however much we might dress them up, they are still like the social *parvenu*, the *nouveau riche*. The psalmist, however, exclaims that his received inheritance is *præclarus*. He says it twice, in Hebrew poetic fashion, to give it appropriate emphasis.

Where else do we see this Latin word *præclarus*? We see it twice in the principal defining feature of the Roman Mass, namely, the Roman Canon, the optionalizing and marginalization of which effectively prove the discontinuity between the old and new rites. First, we hear it in the consecration of the chalice: "taking also into His holy and venerable hands this excellent chalice, *hunc præclarum calicem*." Then we hear it immediately after the consecrations: "Wherefore, O Lord, we Thy servants as also Thy holy people ... offer to Thy supreme majesty [*præclaræ majestati tuæ*] a pure Victim, a holy Victim, an unblemished Victim, the holy bread of eternal life, and the chalice of everlasting salvation."

It is not by chance that the same psalm we cited above, Psalm 15, uses the cup or chalice as a symbol of God's generous provision to His people: *Dominus pars hæreditatis meæ, et calicis mei: tu es qui restitues hæreditatem meam mihi*, "The Lord is the portion of my inheritance and of my cup: it is thou that wilt restore my inheritance to me" (Ps 15:5). By surrounding the word *calix* with a double use of *præclarus*, the Roman Canon not only echoes but enacts Psalm 15, a favorite prayer of early Christians as we see in the Acts of the Apostles, and so reminds us of the nature of our liturgical inheritance. It is not a dead or static set of books, the fallout of meandering chance and merely human intentions, but a living tradition that begins in the *Logos* of God and culminates in the *Logos* made flesh, our eternal High Priest who guides His Church into the fullness of truth by the gift of His Spirit. Our goodly inheritance is the rich content of a cup poured out in ever greater measure on Adam, Abel, Abraham, Melchisedek, David, the temple worship,

---

39 Thomas Aquinas, *Commentary on Psalms*, trans. Albert Marie Surmanski and Maria Veritas Marks (Emmaus Academic, 2021), on Psalm 15:5, no. 112: "quasi dicat: non solum hereditas mea in se præclara est; sed est ita præclara mihi, quod nullo modo mutarem eam."

the early Christian *dies Domini*, and the Catholic centuries of faith, when the liturgy grew from a mustard seed into a great tree in whose branches the birds of the air, that is, the holy angels, lodge (cf. Lk 13:19).

As Benedict XVI said, "we are not some casual and meaningless product of evolution. Each of us is the result of a thought of God. Each of us is willed, each of us is loved, each of us is necessary."[40] We are not the accidental products of chance but the deliberate offspring of a divine intention; the universe is shot through with the *Logos* reigning above matter and chaos. Something analogous is true of the liturgy as well. It, too, is not the accidental product of chance but the deliberate offspring of a divine intention that directs the contributions of secondary causes; its path, which emerges from Israel and crisscrosses the Greco-Roman and later barbarian world, is from the *Logos*, reigning above the tumult of human affairs. This, ultimately, is the reason traditionalists reject the liturgical reform, or rather, revolution: it is a rejection of the Catholic understanding of how liturgy grows within the home of Holy Mother Church, to be transmitted and received by all members of the family. The overthrow of the traditional liturgy is, fundamentally, a rejection of the *Logos*.[41]

Similarly, St. John says the Antichrist is he who denies that Jesus Christ has come *in the flesh* (cf. 1 Jn 4:3). After the Ascension, the "flesh" of Christ, His body, is the Church (cf. Eph 5); and of this Church, the liturgy is the primary expressive sign, as the body is of the soul.[42] Thus, those who despise the inherited liturgy despise the flesh of Christ; their action has the aspect of gnostic apostasy, a negation of incarnation. The liturgical reform was in this sense antichristic, for it rejected, as corrupt or defective, elements and practices that had been in place for centuries, often for well over a millennium. "Because they do not regard the works of the Lord, nor the operation of His hands, He will break them down and not build them up" (Ps 28:5, KJV). Let us not join the number of those who care not for the Lord's works and operation; let us rather extend, here on earth, the joy of His saints in heaven.

---

[40] Benedict XVI, Homily at the Inaugural Mass for the Beginning of the Petrine Ministry, April 24, 2005.
[41] It is also, by extension, a rejection of the providential guidance of the Holy Spirit. See chapter 19; cf. "Sinning against the Holy Spirit" in Kwasniewski, *The Once and Future Roman Rite*, 67–72.
[42] St. Thomas Aquinas: "To one asking why there are so many members in a natural body — hands, feet, mouth, and the like — it could be replied that they are to serve the soul's variety of activities.... The natural body is a certain fullness of the soul; unless the members exist with an integral body, the soul cannot exercise fully its activities" (*Commentary on Ephesians* [1:23], chap. 1, lect. 8, no. 71). Thus, the body expresses what is in the soul; it is the outward face, the signature, the language, of the soul. Similarly, the liturgy expresses what is in the Church's soul; it is her face, signature, and language.

❧ 3 ❦
Escaping the Infernal Workshop

THE ARCHITECT OF THE REFORM
In G. K. Chesterton's story "The Queer Feet," Father Brown says:

> A crime is like any other work of art. Don't look surprised; crimes are by no means the only works of art that come from an infernal workshop. But every work of art, divine or diabolic, has one indispensable mark—I mean, that the centre of it is simple, however much the fulfilment may be complicated. Thus, in *Hamlet*, let us say, the grotesqueness of the grave-digger, the flowers of the mad girl, the fantastic finery of Osric, the pallor of the ghost and the grin of the skull are all oddities in a sort of tangled wreath round one plain tragic figure of a man in black.[1]

These words well describe what I was thinking as I made my way through Yves Chiron's biography of Annibale Bugnini (1912–1982). The liturgical revolution that took place in the Catholic Church predominantly between the years 1950 and 1975 was indeed, like *Hamlet*, a complicated business, involving hundreds of bishops and experts, several popes, an ecumenical council, and countless publications, but at the center of it stood "one plain tragic figure of a man in black"—or perhaps we might say black with red piping: Msgr. (later Archbishop) Annibale Bugnini, a Vincentian priest who was one of the few men who had a hand in this quarter-century drama from its beginning nearly to its end.

Those who have heard of Bugnini tend to think of him, depending on their positive or negative views of his legacy, either as an evil genius bent on the destruction of the Catholic faith or as a talented project manager who smoothly guided a gargantuan liturgical reform to its happy conclusion. Chiron's book, well-researched yet mercifully compact for a modern biography, portrays a busy bureaucrat. That he was totally convinced of and consistently acted upon various rationalist and pastoral theories about how liturgy "ought to be" is indisputable, and this book provides copious documentation of it; but not all of his ideas were welcomed by those in authority, and he did eventually run afoul of the pope to whose itching ear and promulgating pen he had enjoyed such uninhibited access.

Through Chiron's book we become acquainted with the life of a man who was singularly influential in marshaling the forces necessary for an unprecedented revision of Roman Catholic worship. One sees how it

---
[1] G. K. Chesterton, "The Queer Feet," in *The Complete Father Brown* (Penguin, 1981), 51.

came about, step by step, pope by pope, committee by committee, book by book. It is truly one of the most astonishing stories in the history of Catholicism, and one about which Henry Sire rightly quips: "The story of how the liturgical revolution was put through is one that hampers the historian by its very enormity; he would wish, for his own sake, to have a less unbelievable tale to tell."[2] With Chiron patiently taking the reader through the phases of Bugnini's life and activity, the tale becomes a little less unbelievable, albeit no less an enormity, as each daring maneuver leads to a new opening, a new opportunity, and new changes.[3]

Was Bugnini a mastermind, one of those rare Faustian individuals who singlehandedly changes the course of history, or was he a small-minded ideologue and opportunist? The evidence presented in this biography tends to support the latter view. Additional evidence not discussed by Chiron lends support to the same interpretation. In a memorable address in Montreal in 1982, Archbishop Lefebvre shared the story of a meeting he attended with other superiors general in Rome in the mid-1960s:

> I had the occasion to see for myself what influence Fr. Bugnini had. One wonders how such a thing as this could have happened at Rome. At that time immediately after the Council, I was Superior General of the Congregation of the Fathers of the Holy Ghost and we had a meeting of the Superiors General at Rome. We had asked Fr. Bugnini to explain to us what his New Mass was, for this was not at all a small event. Immediately after the Council talk was heard of the "Normative Mass," the "New Mass," the "Novus Ordo." What did all this mean?...
>
> Fr. Bugnini, with much confidence, explained what the Normative Mass would be; this will be changed, that will be changed and we will put in place another Offertory. We will be able to reduce the Communion prayers. We will be able to have several different formats for the beginning of Mass. We will be able to say the Mass in the vernacular tongue....
>
> Personally I was myself so stunned that I remained mute, although I generally speak freely when it is a question of opposing those with whom I am not in agreement. I could not utter a word. How could it be possible for this man before me to be entrusted with

---

[2] Sire, *Phoenix from the Ashes*, 251. The chapter "The Destruction of the Mass" in this book (pp. 226–86) is among the best concise accounts of what was done to the Mass in the liturgical reform, why, and how.

[3] In order to understand how it was possible for Bugnini to achieve all that he did, one must understand the self-doubting, conflicted, dialectical, and mercurial Paul VI, his prevailing fear of not keeping up with modernity and not enjoying the respect of the modern world. A careful and not unsympathetic portrait may be found in Chiron's *Paul VI*; cf. my "Animadversions on the Canonization of Paul VI," in Peter Kwasniewski, ed., *Are Canonizations Infallible?: Revisiting a Disputed Question* (Arouca Press, 2021), 219–41.

the entire reform of the Catholic Liturgy, the entire reform of the Holy Sacrifice of the Mass, of the sacraments, of the Breviary, and of all our prayers? Where are we going? Where is the Church going?

Two Superiors General had the courage to speak out. One of them asked Fr. Bugnini: "Is this an active participation, that is a bodily participation, that is to say with vocal prayers, or is it a spiritual participation? In any case you have spoken so much of the participation of the faithful that it seems you can no longer justify Mass celebrated without the faithful. Your entire Mass has been fabricated around the participation of the faithful. We Benedictines celebrate our Masses without the assistance of the faithful. Does this mean that we must discontinue our private Masses, since we do not have faithful to participate in them?"

I repeat to you exactly that which Fr. Bugnini said. I have it still in my ears, so much did it strike me: "To speak truthfully, we didn't think of that," he said!

Afterwards another arose and said: "Reverend Father, you have said that we will suppress this and we will suppress that, that we will replace this thing by that and always by shorter prayers. I have the impression that your new Mass could be said in ten or twelve minutes or at the most a quarter of an hour. This is not reasonable. This is not respectful towards such an act of the Church." Well, this is what he replied: "We can always add something." Is this for real? I heard it myself. If somebody had told me the story I would perhaps have doubted it, but I heard it myself.[4]

When we read an account like this, we are tempted to think it an exaggeration. Chiron's careful, almost surgical examination of original documents proves that it is nothing of the kind. While studiously avoiding polemics, Chiron paints a portrait of his protagonist that harmonizes with such accounts as Lefebvre's, or Bouyer's in his *Memoirs*. Bugnini was indeed an adroit manager, manipulator, massager, and messenger. He knew how to gather an "all-star" team that would work in the direction he thought best. He knew how to win the pope over to his ideas. He knew when to speak up and when to keep silent. As we saw in chapter 1, he urged the preparatory commission on liturgy for the Second Vatican Council not to spell out *too* many radical ideas lest their entire project of reform be shot down; it was enough, Bugnini said, to offer general innocuous-sounding indications and to fill out the details later in committee work. In other words, he knew what he wanted *prior* to the Council, and that's what he ended up getting, thanks to Paul VI's papal support.

---

4 From a conference given by Archbishop Lefebvre in 1982. The full text was printed in the *Angelus* magazine, vol. 15, no. 3, and may be found online at www.sspxasia.com/Documents/Archbishop-Lefebvre/The-Infiltration-of-Modernism-in-the-Church.htm.

The term "Machiavellian" might have to be excluded only because there is no smoking-gun evidence of malice. Rather, Bugnini is that oddest of odd figures: the seemingly well-intentioned double-crosser who stifles his opponents because they are obviously wrong and he is obviously right. "The end justifies the means," an error as old as the Roman hills and practiced every day by millions, requires no colossal wickedness.

In his swift-moving biography, rich with details but never bogged down in minutiae, Chiron shows us what made Bugnini "tick": a one-track obsession with "active participation," understood as the rational comprehension and production of verbal data, and, as a corollary, the need for a radical simplification of liturgical forms to meet the straightforward, efficient modern Western man. To this goal, everything else was to be subordinated: all ecclesiastical traditions were so much flotsam and jetsam compared to the pastoral urgency of immediate conveyance of Vatican II-flavored content. This explains why Latin had to give way to the vernacular, why intricate language had to be broken down into bite-sized chunks, why elaborate prayers and ceremonies had to be abbreviated or abolished, why the priest should interact familiarly with the people rather than fulfilling a distinct hieratic role, why Gregorian chant had to be sidelined in favor of popular songs, and so forth. On January 4, 1967, Bugnini read the following statement at a press conference:

> A reform of Catholic worship cannot be accomplished in a day or a month, nor even in a year. The issue is not simply one of touching up, so to speak, a priceless work of art; in some areas, entire rites have to be restructured *ex novo*. Certainly this involves restoring, but ultimately I would almost call it a remaking and at certain points a creating anew. Why a work that is so radical? Because the vision of the liturgy the Council has given us is completely different from what we had before.... We are not working on a museum piece, but aiming at a living liturgy for the living people of our own times.[5]

Modernization "makes sense" to one who regards patrimonial goods as so much debris swept along by the tide of history, just as Cartesianism "makes sense" to one who rejects the possibility of knowing any reality other than the mind, Freudianism "makes sense" to one who is already disposed to reduce interpersonal relations to sexual interests, and deconstructionism "makes sense" to one who dismisses the possibility of meaning.

How very different, indeed *contrary*, to the postconciliar project of building the first liturgy *of* moderns, *by* moderns, and *for* moderns is

---

[5] International Commission on English in the Liturgy, *Documents on the Liturgy 1963–1979: Conciliar, Papal, and Curial Texts*, trans. Thomas C. O'Brien (The Liturgical Press, 1982), no. 37.

the attitude we meet in the memoirs of Cardinal Ratzinger, speaking of his youthful discovery of the riches of the liturgy:

> It was a riveting adventure to move by degrees into the mysterious world of the liturgy, which was being enacted before us and for us there on the altar. It was becoming more and more clear to me that here I was encountering a reality that no one had simply thought up, a reality that no official authority or great individual had created. This mysterious fabric of texts and actions had grown from the faith of the Church over the centuries. It bore the whole weight of history within itself, and yet, at the same time, it was much more than the product of human history. Every century had left its mark upon it.... Not everything was logical. Things sometimes got complicated, and it was not always easy to find one's way. But precisely this is what made the whole edifice wonderful, like one's own home.[6]

UNSAVORY ASSOCIATIONS

That he was a Freemason who utilized the liturgical reform to undermine the Church from within is the conspiracy theory that will forever cling to Bugnini's name. With a professional historian's sobriety, Chiron looks at documentary evidence and concludes that it is impossible to say with certainty that he did or did not belong to the Lodge.

Since the appearance of Chiron's biography, however, new testimonies have been published by Fr. Brian Harrison and by Fr. Charles Murr.[7] Thanks to Fr. Harrison we have good reason to believe that the high-ranking official who saw the evidence and reported it to Paul VI was Cardinal Dino Staffa, whose intervention triggered Bugnini's precipitous fall from grace and exile to Tehran; and thanks to Fr. Murr's time in Rome in the 1970s as secretary to Cardinal Gagnon during the latter's investigation of Freemasonry in the Roman curia, we have access to behind-the-scenes conversations and decisions. Bugnini's indignant protestations that he had never had, nor dreamt of having, anything to do with a secret society sound much less convincing after the Fr. Harrison and Fr. Murr revelations, which replace vague and unsubstantiated rumors with names and dates. Nevertheless, we are still working with second-hand reports that do not permit a historian

---

[6] Ratzinger, *Milestones*, 19–20.
[7] See my articles "New Interview with Fr. Charles Murr on Mother Pascalina, Bugnini, Paul VI, and Other Major Figures," *Rorate Caeli*, October 10, 2020; "Rooms broken into, dossiers stolen, death threats, armed guards, assassinations... Fr. Charles Murr on Vatican intrigues surrounding Cardinals Baggio, Benelli, Villot, and Gagnon," *Rorate Caeli*, December 18, 2020; "New historical evidence emerges in support of Bugnini's association with Freemasonry—Names are named," *Rorate Caeli*, May 6, 2020; "Was the chief architect behind the New Mass a Freemason? New evidence emerges," *LifeSiteNews*, October 12, 2020. Murr's books are worth reading for the insights they provide: *The Godmother: Madre Pascalina, A Feminine Tour de Force* and *Murder in the 33rd Degree: The Gagnon Investigation into Vatican Freemasonry*.

to reach a definitive conclusion. Chiron notes that some of Bugnini's private journals and personal papers are still jealously guarded by his literary executors. One wonders if such texts will ever come to light. There are, in any case, two things to be said about this matter.

First, in the intriguing foreword to the biography, we learn of a 1996 interview in which Dom Alcuin Reid asked Cardinal Stickler if he believed that Bugnini was a Freemason and if this was the reason Paul VI dismissed him. "No," the cardinal replied, "it was something far worse." But His Eminence declined to reveal what the "far worse" was—and, frankly, the concept of something "far worse" than a Freemason opens frightening vistas of imagination.

Second, let us assume for the sake of argument that Bugnini was just who he believed himself to be: a "lover and cultivator of the liturgy," as the epitaph on his tombstone reads. In some ways, this is the most depressing of all scenarios. One might almost have more respect for Bugnini if he had operated by some grand plan to demolish the liturgy of the ages and replace it with a mechanism brilliantly contrived to undermine Catholicism, if he had been an apostate infiltrator whose only goal was wreaking havoc on the central nervous system of the Church. We tend to look for a Professor Moriarty who orchestrates the underworld. But if it turns out that he was an earnest, hardworking, small-minded man, won over by the rhetoric of the Liturgical Movement avant-garde, incapable of self-doubt in the wee hours of the night, utterly blind to the world-shifting implications of what he was doing, a diligent functionary with half-baked ideas and the stubbornness to push them along at every opportunity, then we enter into the soulless gray world of Hannah Arendt's "banality of evil."[8] We are looking at the analogue of the SS officer who killed Jews in concentration camps because it seemed like the conscientious fulfillment of his duty to the State, under lawful commands from above.

Perhaps, in the end, the irrepressible urge to make Bugnini a Freemason ("surely he *must* have been...") is a defense mechanism against having to face up to the possibility that he was, in his own mind, sincerely service-oriented as he went about dismantling twenty centuries of organically developed liturgy. That is not to say he always used worthy means; he was adroit and clever at getting his way and more than a little

---

[8] Arendt says this about Adolf Eichmann, the Nazi administrator of concentration camps during World War II: "Despite all the efforts of the prosecution, everybody could see that this man was not a 'monster,' but it was difficult indeed not to suspect that he was a clown. And since this suspicion would have been fatal to the entire enterprise [of his trial], and was also rather hard to sustain in view of the sufferings he and his like had caused to millions of people, his worst clowneries were hardly noticed and almost never reported." *Eichmann in Jerusalem: A Report on the Banality of Evil* (Penguin Classics, 2006), 54.

willing to bend the truth. But he always felt he was in the right, that such a great and difficult end justified whatever means it took to reach it, and that someday everyone would come around to his point of view.

Few managers in the history of bureaucracies have ever been so mistaken. Baptized Catholics today fall into many groups, but the majority are fallen away and attend no liturgy, or lightly skip a Mass to attend sonny's soccer game; meanwhile, practicing Catholics, aware of no alternative, or under the sway of the establishment narrative, dutifully attend the Bugnini Mass, taking the scraps that fall from the table of plenty; finally, a sizeable minority, despite differences among themselves, adhere energetically to the traditional Roman Catholic liturgy. This is not the future Bugnini dreamt of—if, in the midst of journals, conferences, meetings, audiences, and correspondence, he permitted himself the luxury of dreaming.

A clever poet has written:

> In Rome they should have known him by his name:
> the enemy descending with his brutes.
> But to our guardians' eternal shame,
> the harried faithful know him by his fruits.[9]

When I finished Chiron's *Bugnini*, I leaned back in my chair and thought wistfully about the momentous period its pages brought before my eyes—how outdated, how stale, how empty it all seems today, when it lives on in a legacy that stimulates about the same level of enthusiasm as Victorian sentimental kitsch. Bugnini's life had been spent in a sleepless effort to bring the Church "up to date," to make her an equal partner with modernity, in a bid to conquer the culture—and now look at the smoking remains, the boarded-up churches, the indifferent and ignorant laity, the infant-slaying Cuomos, Pelosis, and Bidens, the pope afflicted with heretical logorrhea, and, above all, the liturgy that bores to tears. It is not the Church that engaged modernity, but modernity that colonized the Church, reducing her to a state of vassalage. Without explicitly intending to do so, Chiron helps us to see why traditional Catholicism is the *only* way out of this pit of despair.

What the modern liturgists and churchmen who fawn on Bugnini's handiwork don't get—and really need to have spelled out for them like children slow to learn—is this: we do not welcome the postconciliar liturgical reforms, and we will never sing their praises. You cannot force us to like them; you cannot even force us to celebrate them. We think they were the product of an insane arrogance acting on faulty principles and yielding shameful results. We distrust the people who ran the

---

[9] Mark Amorose, *City under Siege: Sonnets and Other Verse* (Angelico Press, 2017), 34.

Consilium, especially Bugnini, and no matter how many purple-faced prelates stand up and haughtily proclaim: "It was the will of the Holy Spirit" or "It was the dictate of the Second Vatican Council" or "It was promulgated by Paul VI," we will always hold to the great liturgical tradition that developed organically from St. Peter, St. Damasus, and St. Gregory the Great to the twentieth century, and our numbers will continue to grow, even as dioceses consolidate parishes, sell off churches, and bleed out legal damages.[10] By the repressive policies of *Traditionis Custodes*, you are attempting to cajole and coerce us—clergy and laity across the world—into abandoning a tradition we have rediscovered with joy and zeal, as if you wish to repeat the tragedy of the '60s and '70s. We are told we must embrace the "sole expression of the *lex orandi* of the Roman rite"—a gigantic untruth if ever there was one, since it is neither the Roman rite[11] nor obligatory,[12] and the Catholic Church can never outlaw her own tradition or justly deprive her ministers and people of it.[13] We know where we stand, and you will never succeed in eliminating us, however much harm you cause as you try to exterminate the tradition we love—a harm for which you will be answerable before the fearsome judgment seat of Christ.

Allow us to paraphrase the words of David: Let the Lord be judge, and judge between us and you, and deliver us out of your hand (cf. 1 Sam 24:16). We will bide our time. The enthusiastic liturgists of the '60s and '70s are the aging nostalgics of today, as the Church increasingly splits into those who, as Catholics, take established dogma, tradition, and liturgy seriously and those who, as moderns first and foremost, would modernize or relativize them to the point of dissipation.

ON SECOND THOUGHT...

But let us not walk away so nonchalantly from the question raised in the preceding pages. How much would it actually *matter* if Bugnini was a you-know-what?

In the twilight of Francis's pontificate, we have seen an ever-shrinking brigade of "conservative Catholics" who sound jittery, short-tempered, dismissive, and intolerant towards their tradition-loving coreligionists who refuse to embrace the papally-bestowed role of scapegoat for the abrogation of *Summorum Pontificum*. One such person—no need for a name, since my point is not about a name but a phenomenon—heatedly

---

[10] See "Games People Play with the Holy Spirit," in Kwasniewski, ed., *Illusions of Reform*.
[11] As demonstrated in Kwasniewski, *Once and Future Roman Rite*.
[12] As shown by John Salza and Robert Siscoe, *True or False Pope? Refuting Sedevacantism and Other Modern Errors* (STAS Editions, 2015), 493–524.
[13] See Kwasniewski, *True Obedience* and *Bound by Truth*.

made fun of anyone who mentioned that Bugnini probably or certainly was a Freemason, mockingly referring to "Viganò's flying monkeys" and other such sarcastic turns of phrase. In fact, he betrayed nothing but insouciance about Freemasonry, as if it is a topic unworthy of a moment's serious consideration, to be put on the shelf next to self-published apocalyptic ravings or unauthorized private revelations.

A few summers ago in Mexico, I visited the sites of one martyr after another who was killed by real, live, card-carrying Freemasons. The Catholic parts of Europe and South America bear plentiful scars from the persecution and secularization driven by this sect.[14] And when Paul VI, sensing something desperately wrong at the Vatican, hand-picked Cardinal Gagnon to investigate the curia for its possible entanglements, Gagnon discovered a buzzing hive of subversive activity. As we have seen, when Chiron published his biography in 2016 (the English in 2018), he had concluded that there was no definitive evidence of Bugnini's membership in this philosophical sect. Since then, new information has shed further light on Bugnini's probable connection with Freemasonry.[15]

It is astonishing to me that some of my fellow Catholics seem not to care that the main person in charge of an all-encompassing reinvention of the Church's liturgy was likely a member of one of the world's most destructive anti-Catholic organizations. I mean, if that's not a problem, then it wouldn't be a problem for the USCCB's pro-life point person to be a board member of Planned Parenthood. On the other hand, I suppose this would be business as usual for an organization whose general secretary, a key figure in responding to sex-abuse scandals, turned out to have been an active homosexual regularly using a gay dating app.[16]

The annals of European history are full of incidents in which Freemasons were involved, often enough boasting of their accomplishments: one need only think of the many political revolutions in Catholic countries that led to anti-Catholic, anti-clerical, anti-monastic, and anti-patrimonial legislation. They boasted of destroying the Church; arguably their most triumphant moment was the Law of Separation in France, which Pope St. Pius X condemned in his 1906 encyclical *Vehementer Nos*. If much can be soberly written about the acknowledged role of this well-organized

---

[14] Saints have had run-ins: the visionaries of Fatima, for example, were persecuted by local Freemasonry; and when, in February 1917, St. Maximilian Kolbe witnessed a march of Freemasons in Rome, carrying images of St. Michael being crushed by Lucifer, he responded by creating the Knights of the Immaculate.
[15] See the sources mentioned eight notes above.
[16] See "Pillar Investigates: USCCB gen sec Burrill resigns after sexual misconduct allegations," *The Pillar*, July 20, 2021.

network of lodges, how much greater must their actual role be, given their obvious penchant for working behind the scenes? As Roberto de Mattei notes, the existence and operation of conspiracies are a plain fact of history, seen again and again from ancient times to the present.[17] To be sure, amateur historians will make mistakes in recognizing and analyzing conspiracies, but only fools will deny their reality.

Unlike some modern-day conservative commentators, the popes of old were no fools. As I describe in my overview of the subject,[18] Freemasonry was condemned and made subject to *latæ sententiæ* excommunication by no fewer than eight popes after the founding of the first lodge in London in 1717: Clement XII (1738), Benedict XIV (1751), Pius VII (1821), Leo XII (1825), Pius VIII (1829), Gregory XVI (1832), Pius IX (many documents from 1846 to 1873), and Leo XIII (1882, 1884, 1890, 1894, and 1902). Either all of these popes were reactionary "flying monkey" nutcases, as our "I'm-too-cool-for-conspiracy" conservatives would have us believe, or they actually knew a thing or two about modern revolutions and the sects that spawned them. Cardinal Ratzinger, who as head of the Congregation for the Doctrine of the Faith reiterated that membership in Freemasonry is prohibited and excommunicable, did not hesitate to say that they remain a malign influence.[19]

Moreover, it just might give one pause to learn that the Freemasons themselves celebrate the Second Vatican Council as an historic "thaw" in the Church's stance toward Modernity—which, however else we define it, is at least partially a product of revolutions against the Church and State—and that they have bestowed glowing accolades on Pope Francis for various acts of his that they recognize as characteristic of their own philosophy.[20]

Surely there are many other forces at work in the drama of dechristianization, and no organized body need be posited to explain every evil or every rejection of the Faith. The century-long influence of modernism as well as the proponents of radical change within the Liturgical Movement would be enough to account for many of the mistakes made in the reforms sparked by the Second Vatican Council. But to ignore

---

[17] See Roberto de Mattei, "True and False Conspiracies in History. In memory of Father Augustin Barruel (1741–1820)," *Rorate Caeli*, January 13, 2021; or, more extensively, idem, *The Paths of Evil: Conspiracies, Plots, and Secret Societies*, trans. Nicholas Reitzug (Sophia Institute Press, 2023).
[18] Peter Kwasniewski, "Freemasonry and Catholicism: Implacable Enemies," *The Remnant* online, July 22, 2020.
[19] See Robert Moynihan, "Letter #8: The Long Hand," at *Inside the Vatican*, April 23, 2020. Even Pope Francis and Cardinal Victor Fernández reiterated this point: see Courtney Mares, "Vatican doctrine office reaffirms that Catholics cannot be Freemasons," *Catholic News Agency*, November 15, 2023.
[20] See "Freemasons Celebrate Vatican II...," *Catholic Truth*, June 23, 2014; Timothy Flanders, "Why do the Freemasons Love Pope Francis?," *OnePeterFive*, April 7, 2017.

or glibly dismiss the masonic influence on modern European history and specifically on the Catholic Church is not only a blameworthy naiveté, it is a form of intellectual dishonesty—a sort of plugging of the ears and whistling so that one doesn't have to hear something one doesn't like.

Returning now to Annibale Bugnini, even if we say for the sake of argument that he was nothing other than an ecclesiastical functionary tirelessly dedicated to the conciliar project of reform, it nonetheless remains true that, according to rigorous historical research, Bugnini was a two-faced manipulator who lied to the Consilium and to Paul VI in order to drive through the radical reforms he had envisioned even prior to the Council.[21] He hand-picked the moderates and progressives he needed for the various subcommittees. He orchestrated the whole complex process from start to finish. He was the impresario. If one can read the life of Bugnini without a feeling of profound revulsion and a desire to distance oneself from anything he put his hands on, I'm not sure what kind of conscience one has left.

Conservative apologists will rise up in protest: "But it doesn't really matter what Bugnini thought or did or said, or how compromised were the human mechanisms, or how problematic their guiding principles—all that matters is that a pope approved the work in the end. After all, God writes straight with crooked lines!" This is where we see most dramatically the uncatholic irrationality to which the hyperpapalist position reduces itself,[22] making the pope a magician who can transform something bad into something good simply by adding his signature. About fifteen years ago, I wrote down the following observation, which acquires new pertinence in light of recent events:

> What happens if you take a lot of garbage, give it to the Pope, and he signs off on it? Does it cease to be garbage—or does it just become papally approved and enforced garbage? This is the key question about the liturgical reform. Past all doubt, it was the work of a cabal of poor theologians, ill-equipped for their work, in the grip of humanist, rationalist, and modernist assumptions and now-exploded theories, acting irresponsibly and illegally. Some of them are known to have been Freemasons, others are suspected of it. Their work was an atrocious dismantling of the most venerable possession of the Catholic Church. And when they were done with their "work," they handed the mess over to Paul VI, who approved it (under at least partially false pretenses). When all is said

---

[21] Bouyer, *Memoirs*, 225.
[22] See Peter Kwasniewski, "The Pope's Boundedness to Tradition as a Legislative Limit," in idem, ed., *From Benedict's Peace to Francis's War: Catholics Respond to the Motu Proprio Traditionis Custodes on the Latin Mass* (Angelico Press, 2021), 222–47.

and done, did his papal signature make their poverty of theology, their inadequacy to the task, their erroneous presuppositions and goals, and their irregularities vanish into thin air, like a magic wand transforming a frog into a prince?

There is no escaping it: if he signed on the dotted line, Paul VI bears full responsibility for whatever is wrong with the Novus Ordo—even when he didn't bother to read the documents submitted to him for examination,[23] and even when he was surprised and dismayed at the liturgical books he himself had approved.[24]

We return to the question of affiliations. If Bugnini truly was a Freemason, it would help explain—or, in any case, it would be fully consistent with—the anthropocentric, rationalistic, desacralizing tendencies of the liturgical reform, tendencies Paul VI sympathized with due to his own alliance with humanistic modern thought and pan-Christian ecumenism, the prelude to Assisi, Abu Dhabi, and Singapore. If, on the other hand, Bugnini was *not* a Freemason—as we have seen, Cardinal Stickler once said: "No, it was something far worse"[25]—it would be difficult to imagine how an *actual* Freemason could have accomplished something much worse. Cardinal Stickler's comment gives one pause. What, after all, would be worse than a secret society that denies divine revelation, the Holy Trinity, the redemptive Incarnation, original sin, the need for supernatural grace and the sacramental life, and seeks to replace it with a man-created, man-centered panreligious philosophy? The only thing that comes to mind is Satanism.

Whether or not this is what Cardinal Stickler had in mind, one would find it difficult to dispute the conclusion reached by Dietrich von Hildebrand in his book *The Devastated Vineyard*: "Truly if one of the devils in C. S. Lewis's *Screwtape Letters* had been entrusted with the ruin of the liturgy, he could not have done it better."[26]

LITURGICAL ECSTASY AND MECHANICAL HYPERACTIVITY

How might we contrast the products of the infernal academic workshop with heavenly worship's earthly form, transmitted by living tradition?

Ritual action is inherently non-spontaneous, non-original, and non-extemporaneous. The more perfectly one is enacting ritual, the less of

---

[23] See my article "Who Was Captain of the Ship in the Liturgical Reform? The 50th Anniversary of an Embarrassing Letter," *NLM*, June 24, 2019.
[24] See Gregory DiPippo, "Paul VI's Dislike of the Liturgical Reform," *NLM*, April 19, 2018; John Zuhlsdorf, "A Pentecost Monday lesson: 'And Paul VI wept,'" *Fr. Z's Blog*, May 21, 2018.
[25] Chiron, *Bugnini*, 7.
[26] Dietrich von Hildebrand, *The Devastated Vineyard* (Franciscan Herald Press, 1973), 71.

one's creative self is present in it, and the more one is absorbed into a vastly larger mystery. Even the pagans understood this in their mystery rites, through which the individual was meant to be drawn into the realm of the gods and to participate in their actions. The worshiper took on the identity of another, and for a moment lost sight of himself. This is the "ecstasy" about which we read in ancient authors: a "standing outside oneself" (*ek-stasis*), a going out of one's everyday world and mind, to be drawn into something primordial, archetypal, divine.

I have noticed the following about the modern rite of Paul VI, when studying the ponderous tomes of its architects and admirers: it may sometimes look good *on paper*, it may have a rationale about which one can wax eloquent, but somehow it never works *in practice*. There, it tends to look clumsy, casual, limited in expressive range and impressive power; due to its linear modular construction, it suggests a series of tasks on an agenda, and most attendees may be forgiven their desire to see the agenda completed as expeditiously as possible.

The traditional Roman liturgy, in contrast, often looks obscure, elaborate, or strangely ordered on paper, but it always works in practice. It *flows*, sweeping all along before it. The motions of the individuals in the sanctuary are scripted and coordinated; there is an organic wholeness to it, and a smoothness like that of rocks caressed by water for a thousand years. Those involved are so intent on "the Father's business" that it is easy for our attention to be absorbed in whatever they are doing, even when we don't understand it. So strongly does the rite convey a sense of something extremely important and weighty happening that it has the power to make us *want* to understand it better.

I am reminded here of the difference between stage drama and "closet drama." The one is a story meant to be acted out before an audience, the other is a musing to be read in the solitary comfort of one's study. A play by Shakespeare, while far more complex than Goethe's *Faust* in number of characters and subplots, works brilliantly on stage, while Goethe's, with a relatively straightforward plot, is not nearly as dramatically effective. The one is artistically perfect, the other an intellectual construct. It is like comparing a folk dance with a mathematical theorem.

Even though it is "easier" or "more accessible"—indeed, precisely *because* it is so—one grows weary of the new Mass over time; it has few secrets and yields them readily. It is the opposite with the old: the longer one attends, the more one discovers in it to appreciate, and one never reaches the bottom of its secrets. The many commentaries on the cherished rites of the Roman Church (Guéranger, Schuster, Parsch, Gihr, Zundel, Vandeur...) contain an inexhaustible wealth of insights, illuminating details one hadn't noticed before, pointing out reasons for some text or ritual or chant that one had not previously grasped. I like to think of the Queen of Sheba as a metaphor:

> When the queen of Sheba saw all the wisdom of Solomon, and the house which he had built, and the meat of his table, and the apartments of his servants, and the order of his ministers, and their apparel, and the cupbearers, and the holocausts, which he offered in the house of the Lord: she had no longer any spirit in her, and she said to the king: The report is true, which I heard in my own country, concerning thy words, and concerning thy wisdom. And I did not believe them that told me, till I came myself, and saw with my own eyes, and have found that the half hath not been told me: thy wisdom and thy works exceed the fame which I heard. Blessed are thy men, and blessed are thy servants, who stand before thee always, and hear thy wisdom. (1 Kg 10:1–8)

What happened to the queen in the king's court, when she cries out "The half of it wasn't told to me!," is the opposite of the experience of a person who hears or reads what Catholics believe the Mass and the Holy Eucharist to be—the supreme sacrifice that redeems mankind, our earthly participation in the heavenly liturgy, and so forth—and then goes to check out what it's like at the local parish: "Behold, this isn't even half as good as what I read about or imagined." But if that same person happened upon a Solemn High Mass in the classical Roman rite, how exactly like the Queen of Sheba's reaction would his be: "Just based on what I'd heard or read about, I couldn't have imagined such solemn splendor as this!"

The reason for these opposite reactions is simply this: the old rite is so much *more* than the words of which it is composed—it is thick with ceremonies, gestures, postures, vestments, incense, music—while the new liturgy is centered on and preoccupied with *words* and *communal action*, even when it has some of these "traditional elements" added on to it. Hence it cannot fill us with wonder or amazement because in modern times we are already saturated with words ("talk is cheap"), and the mode of their delivery at the new Mass—almost always spoken, and almost always towards us—is the most ordinary, humdrum, secular mode of communication.[27] In such circumstances, there will be no ecstasy like that of the Queen of Sheba.

When everything is visible, nothing is seen. When everything is audible, nothing is heard.

The old rite always exceeds its paper description. No individual pope, not even St. Pius V, can be identified as its author. Here, the

---

[27] See "The Peace of Low Mass and the Glory of High Mass" in Kwasniewski, *Noble Beauty*, 235–55.

whole is greater than the sum of its parts; the impact exceeds the force of its components; the experience transcends reason and imagination. There is always something that "escapes" our notice, our understanding, our human capacity.[28] We do not measure the rite, because our age did not produce it (indeed, no single age produced it, and no single milieu); we are measured by it, and we always fall short. The new rite, on the other hand, always falls short of its paper description. It bears the names of its authors and the date of its manufacture. For the rite of Paul VI, the trailer is better than the film, the advertisement better than the product.

Like all modernist projects, the reformed liturgy always sounds better when described by its proponents than it ever comes out when executed by its laborers. One sees this with modern architecture: the plans can look spiffy, but the built results always disappoint. It's the opposite with Gothic architecture: the plans of medieval architects look like quaint doodles compared with their magnificent structures of carved stone and stained glass. The same critique can be leveled at modernist poetry, which is never as satisfying as the thick philosophical commentaries written on it—a curious fact that shows the failure of art, if not the failure of thought. In the words of Henry Sire,

> The literalism that saw the Mass as merely a text to be revised found its expression [in] a one-dimensional, human liturgy. The pedantry of the liturgists in their new science showed an arrogance towards the past characteristic of twentieth-century culture. We find a parallel among the architectural purists who came to prominence after the Second World War. Le Corbusier and his disciples were so revolted by the untidiness of traditional town planning that they wanted to tear out the centres of historic cities and rebuild them in their shiny new style. In the same spirit, Bugnini and his technicians tore out the old Mass and replaced it with their own creation. Yet the defect of both conceptions is a sterility of spirit, a remoteness from human feeling, that unfits them for their proposed task. The last thing that the ordinary person wants to do with Le Corbusier's *machine à habiter* is live in it, and the last thing that Paul VI's machine for praying is good for is praying. What we find in the modern liturgy is a counterpart of the tower blocks that in the 1960s were hailed as the beacons of the new age: soulless, jerry-built, and inspired by a totalitarianism all the more odious for its democratic pretensions. It is only a matter of time before the liturgy goes the same way as the tower blocks, which now come down amid large clouds of dust and even larger public satisfaction.[29]

---

28 See "Why It Is Better Not to Understand Everything Immediately" in Kwasniewski, *Turned Around*, 191–212.
29 Sire, *Phoenix from the Ashes*, 374–75.

The Novus Ordo was built by a "dream team" of highly credentialed specialists, loquacious about their ideals, but the finished product is what one would expect from a period known for neither theological sublimity nor aesthetic brilliance. Poking fun at academics for their excessive self-regard, Pope Benedict XVI warned priests against following "experts" instead of the witness of the saints:

> I have been following theology since 1946. I began to study theology in January '46 and, therefore, I have seen about three generations of theologians, and I can say that the hypotheses that in that time, and then in the 1960s and 1980s, were the newest, absolutely scientific, absolutely *almost* dogmatic, have since aged and are no longer valid! Many of them seem almost ridiculous. So, have the courage to resist the apparently scientific approach, do not submit to all the hypotheses of the moment, but really start thinking from the great faith of the Church, which is present in all times and opens for us access to the truth.... We must have the humility not to submit to all the hypotheses of the moment and [the humility] to live by the great faith of the Church of all times. There is no majority against the majority of the Saints. Saints are the true majority in the Church and we must orient ourselves by the Saints![30]

As pope emeritus, Ratzinger returned to this point in a letter addressed to Cardinal Müller:

> In the confused times in which we are living, the whole scientific theological competence and wisdom of him who must make the final decisions seem to me of vital importance. For example, I think that things might have gone differently in the Liturgical Reform if the words of the experts had not been the last ones, but if, apart from them, a wisdom capable of recognizing the limits of a "simple" scholar's approach had passed judgment.[31]

Indeed, it shows a singular lack of self-awareness, to say nothing of wisdom, when modern Westerners believe they can surpass or even equal the patrimony of the ages. "We live in a world without poetry," said Dietrich von Hildebrand, "and this means that one should approach the treasures handed on from more fortunate times with twice as much reverence, and not with the illusion that we can do it better ourselves."[32]

Returning to David's royal son, King Solomon left a noteworthy example both of what to do and of what *not* to do. At the start of his reign, he approached the treasure of the Law with twice as much reverence as any other king had manifested; by its close, he had succumbed

---

[30] Vigil on the Occasion of the International Meeting of Priests: Dialogue of the Holy Father Benedict XVI with Priests, St. Peter's Square, June 10, 2010.
[31] "For the Record: Full translation of Benedict XVI letter of support to Müller after dismissal by Francis," trans. Francesca Romana, *Rorate Caeli*, January 2, 2018.
[32] von Hildebrand, *The Devastated Vineyard*, 70.

to the syncretistic illusion that more gods must be better than just one God, even as today some believe that God wills "the pluralism and diversity of religions" and that "all religions are a path to arrive at God."[33] Keith Lemna observes: "The wise man in Israel, such as King Solomon at the beginning of his reign—though not its end!—was characterized by humility, pious prayer, and contrition, characteristics necessary to heed the call of the divine Word."[34] The humble man is the one who knows when to lower his eyes and open his hands to receive a gift rather than keeping his hands tightly shut and his arms crossed in the pose of a "self-made man." Piety demands respect for those on whom we depend, most of all God and our predecessors. Contrition comes readily to the one who realizes how much he has failed to live up to the many graces he has been given. The traditional Latin Mass is like the youthful Solomon, a wise man seeking the Lord alone in the true religion. The Novus Ordo is rather like the old Solomon, burdened with concubines and a blend of religions.

Echoing the original Liturgical Movement, one finds Pius X, Pius XI, and Pius XII exhorting the faithful to take rightful possession of the liturgy as members of the Mystical Body of Christ: following the prayers with understanding, chanting the responses and the Ordinary of the Mass, joining in public Vespers, and so forth. This entire program was, however, premised on a fundamental truth: the liturgy is a gift to us from God through the generations that have preceded us, one that we must gratefully receive and enter into more and more fully. Participation thus meant entering into something already present in our midst, prior to our cogitation and volition: a transmitted body of symbols, cross-textured with words, melodies, gestures, actions, endowed with supernatural vitality and inexhaustible richness. It could *not* mean that we fashion something ourselves which, being in some way the image of our own mentality and our own age, we then "participate in," as we create athletic games or board games into which we then throw ourselves. The crass manner in which "hyperactive participation" (as William F. Buckley Jr. lampooned it[35]) was enforced in the mid-1960s undermined any recognizably Catholic realization of *participatio actuosa* and rendered it a "a thing of horror, a byword and an object of ridicule" (Dt 28:37) for those in search of the sacred.

---

33 The first phrase is from the "Document on Human Fraternity for World Peace and Living Together" signed by Pope Francis and Grand Imam Ahmad el-Tayeb in Abu Dhabi on February 4, 2019; the second phrase is from Pope Francis's comments during a meeting with youths in Singapore on September 13, 2024.
34 Keith Lemna, *The Apocalypse of Wisdom: Louis Bouyer's Theological Recovery of the Cosmos* (Angelico Press, 2019), 106.
35 William F. Buckley Jr., *Nearer, My God: An Autobiography of Faith* (Doubleday, 1997), 97.

As Martin Mosebach says, we do not know the names of most of the holy men who "wrote" the old liturgy.[36] But we know exactly who put together the new one—list after list of experts, carefully recorded by Bugnini in his giant book *The Reform of the Liturgy 1948–1975* (see pp. 937–55). This contrast makes all the difference. The old rite is a monumental anonymous gift that we receive from as many centuries as the Church has offered up her corporate worship to God; the new rite is the ephemeral work of a jetsetting super-committee, imposed on us from above by the stroke of a pen. The one is a collective masterpiece, the other a period piece trapped in the assumptions of a frenzied and dated movement.

Man was created for ecstasy—not sexual, athletic, aesthetic, or drug-induced, but the ecstasy of faith, of love, of beatitude in union with God for ever. Truly the traditional liturgy of the Church, celebrated with all the resources Divine Providence has bestowed on us, feeds that faith, inflames that charity, and grants us a foretaste of that heavenly consummation.

WHY I COULDN'T GO BACK... TO THE NOVUS ORDO

On March 8, 2012, the Jesuit magazine *America* published an article by Fr. Peter Schineller entitled "The Tridentine Mass: Why I Couldn't Go Back." For years, I've noticed that *America* actually pays to promote this article in online searches so that it will influence public opinion (they are evidently worried about the direction the youth are going in). That planted in me the seed of a contrasting reflection, which is intended as the other's antithesis.

For the first eighteen years of my life, I exclusively attended the new Mass. I grew up in a typical suburban parish on the East coast that celebrated the Boomer Rite. The sanctuary was covered in carpet and Extraordinary Ministers. I remember the priests; they were all more or less nice guys and more or less heretical. One of them started an Ash Wednesday homily by wiping off the ashes from his head and saying that Christ came to do away with "this kind of stuff." Another one left the priesthood to get married and work as a professional psychiatrist. Wanting to be more involved, I became, in succession, an altar boy, a lector, and an extraordinary minister.[37] My faith was active but

---

[36] That we can name the exact author of the texts for the feast of Corpus Christi—St. Thomas Aquinas, by the invitation of the pope—stands out for its rarity. We have, in addition, scattered indications: Pope St. Sergius is said to have added the Agnus Dei to the Mass, and the feast of Candlemas; Pope St. Gregory the Great moved the Our Father to a different place; Sedulius Scottus is author of the Introit text "Salve, Sancta Parens"; and so forth. But for the vast majority of what is said and done in the liturgy, the roots are deep, the authors unknown.

[37] See "Lay Ministries Obscure Both the Laity's Calling and the Clergy's" in Peter Kwasniewski, *Ministers of Christ: Recovering the Roles of Clergy and Laity in an Age of Confusion* (Crisis Publications, 2021), 83–102.

confused—just *how* confused will have to be left to my memoirs (if I ever write them), but it was bad.

Later in high school, I joined a charismatic prayer group that introduced me to committed, conservative lay Catholics who had the courage to uphold *Humanæ Vitæ*. Music played a big role in this reversion. I wrote my one and only guitar song. But quite by chance, as it seemed, I also discovered Gregorian chant, which began to exercise a fascination on me. I began to learn about St. Augustine, St. Thomas Aquinas, and Padre Pio. A friend laden with medals introduced me to St. Louis de Montfort and *The Secret of the Rosary*. After a rocky year at Georgetown University, I started over again at Thomas Aquinas College, where for all four years students could enjoy (and still do enjoy) the company of the legendary unicorn: the reverent Novus Ordo in Latin, with chant and polyphony.

It was at TAC that I discovered the TLM—somewhat in secret, like Elizabethan recusants. In the early nineties, this Mass was "permitted" by Cardinal Mahony only one Sunday a month. We had a chaplain who privately offered the old Mass whenever he could get away with it. Trustworthy students confided assignations in whispers. First I attended the Low Mass; not long after, a High Mass. My friends and I were haunted with questions: "Why was this abolished?" "Who took it away from us?" In grad school came my first experience of a Solemn Mass; years later, my first Pontifical Mass. Each was a more splendid revelation of the glory of Roman Catholic worship. The ascetical-mystical elements of the Faith suddenly made sense, reunited with their origins, finding their harbor.

In my first job out of graduate school, as an assistant professor in Austria, we had the old Mass daily for a while, at the simultaneously cruel and contemplative hour of 6:00 a.m. When this happy spell ended, my family and I made a point of driving a good distance on Sundays, either to Vienna or Linz, to get to a Latin Mass. When we moved out to Wyoming, availability was as spotty as the cell phone reception, and this time, we were five minutes away from the college chaplaincy Mass but four hours' drive from the nearest parish with a TLM. When school was in session, we enjoyed the blessing of three traditional Masses a week, but when school was out and the chaplain gone, we'd have few to none.

Throughout all the periods narrated, for a good 25+ years I "stuck it out" with the Novus Ordo as a cantor and choir director (although always in situations with access to the TLM as well—I could not do without it). With the intimate knowledge a music director acquires, I gradually came to see how profound a rupture is the reformed liturgy *at every level* save that of bare sacramental efficacy. The evil of that rupture grated on my mind more and more. The new rite is an artificial liturgy, as Esperanto is an artificial language or aspartame an artificial sweetener.

One of the reasons I decided to leave Wyoming in 2018, as much as I loved it there for all kinds of *other* reasons, was an urgent longing for a fully traditional parish with a daily Tridentine Mass. The time had come to make a decisive break. Now that I've been living for over six years in that haven, I could honestly never go back to anything else.

During these years I have attended a Novus Ordo Mass only once, as a favor for someone. Having been away from it for so long, the experience was far more jarring than I could have imagined possible. It felt as if my eyes were fully opened to the magnitude of the *contradiction*, not just difference, between the two rites.[38] Mind you, I am not talking about "abuses." Legally speaking, there had been no abuses in this particular instantiation of Paul VI's polymorphous prayer service. It "did the red and said the black," *sans* altar girls, extraordinary ministers, or strumming guitars. The faithful knelt for Communion and the priest even wore a fiddleback chasuble. No, it was about the *spirit* of the thing, its *Gestalt* or total form. I was put off not by any particular thing, but simply by the thing itself. *What was wrong was the Novus Ordo.*

Static and arid because of the constant flow of words—from the priest, the lector, the congregation—the liturgy skipped along the surface of the sacred like a flat stone thrown skillfully across a lake. The sense of mystery utterly evaporated, or rather, never condensed to begin with. Only the occasional chant gave it a touch of sacrality, but this was more like "atmosphere" provided by mood music than an integral part of the action. The chant seemed like a foreign import to the rite rather than an organic part of a single flowing motion. Above all, the Mass was lacking in unity: it did not unfold, but rather plodded from one discrete task to the next, like a sequence of setting-up exercises. The modular sequence of generically pious texts starved my prayer of oxygen, as if the liturgy were grudging me both ordinary and extraordinary means of life support. There was no time to breathe, to reflect, to savor, to be carried beyond this earthly realm to the edge of the heavenly fatherland.

Afterwards, I thought to myself: no wonder the Church is sickening

---

[38] And they *are* two rites, even if the convenient legal fiction of two "forms" was felt to be necessary to medicate a schizophrenic situation. This nomenclature lasted from 2007 to 2021. Pope Francis correctly set it aside in *Traditionis Custodes*—but mistakenly equated the Novus Ordo with the Roman rite. See "Two 'Forms': Liturgical Fact or Canonical Fiat?" in Kwasniewski, *Once and Future Roman Rite*, 145–77.

and dying. It is just as St. Paul says in 1 Corinthians 11:30, about those who assist at the Holy Sacrifice without discerning what they are doing, *whom* they are receiving into their midst: "Therefore are there many infirm and weak among you, and many sleep." Somehow this one Mass, out of thousands I've attended, crystallized it for me—clarified all the reasons I have shaken the dust from my feet.

I would never be able to give up the blessed silence of the contemplative Low Mass or the stirring integral chants of the flowing High Mass, in exchange for the bumpy vernacular verbosity of the new Mass. The communion of prayer, the fellowship with the Church on Earth, the Church in Heaven, the Church in Purgatory—I don't want it to be shattered by the next barrage of verbiage.

I don't care to have the priest always trying to "connect" with the people in the pews; he is there for one reason, to connect us with God, and to connect himself with God. When he stands there facing us, at that moment prayer dies and God departs. I don't want his eye contact, his practiced smiles, his best rendition of a pastoral Mister Rogers, or (in worst-case scenarios) the congratulations meted out to various and sundry, with the eruption of applause.

I don't want to see Father give in to temptations of spontaneity and creativity, like a well-intentioned alcoholic defeated by a well-stocked liquor cabinet—or even to be put in a position where he has no choice but to *choose* how the liturgy is going to be done.[39]

I don't want the nearly fatal shock of discovering that this weekend the young priest who "does a reverent Novus Ordo" is sick or out of town or on vacation, and Mass will be said by a visiting priest from an ashram in India, a Jesuit rainbow retreat center, or a home for retired iconoclasts.

I'm forever done with seeing unvested lay readers walking up from their pews into the sanctuary, as if reading the Word of God were nothing more special than reading a story from the newspaper, as if—contrary to the unanimous testimony of ancient Israel and its continuation and fulfillment in the Catholic Church—no special office or consecration, no special holy garment, were required on the part of the one who dares to touch the book and take its awful divine words upon his lips.

I'm through with seeing the army of old ladies march up to take charge of the distribution of Communion, for all the world as if they owned the place and had a right to handle the Body and Blood of God. It always made me sick to see this pseudo-priestly caste, in its

---

39 On the evils of indeterminacy, optionitis, and liturgy as personal accomplishment, see chapters 4 and 7.

clueless way, take up like bingo cards that which would have induced fear and trembling in any Christian during the centuries when men had faith in the All-Holy.

I want to have nothing to do with the Hobbesian Peace of All against All. (That was one silver lining of Covidtide: the handshake of bonhomie vanished.)

I would not give up the freedom to pray, to meditate, to let myself be drawn into Christ my Lord, for a jamboree of communal self-celebration, with its straightjacketed way of "actively participating." I never knew what participation could be until I discovered the traditional Mass. This taught me, at a level deeper than catechesis, what the Mass really is and how I can enter into it through adoration, contrition, supplication, and giving thanks.

Now that I have enjoyed a foretaste of heaven and caught a glimpse of angels' worship, now that I have reconnected with centuries of my predecessors, on their knees gazing up to the high altar, wrapped in a mantle of a thousand years of ritual, I could never, ever go back to the 1970s. May the Lord in His mercy send us someday a Holy Father who will lead the Church at once truly forward and much further back, to the timeless treasury of immemorial tradition.

Having escaped Bugnini's infernal workshop, I will never go back — nor should any Catholic who has seen the glory as of the Only-begotten, full of grace and truth.

❦ 4 ❧
Indeterminacy and Optionitis

IN CRITIQUES OF THE RITE OF PAUL VI, ONE finds a special intensity of complaint about its indeterminacy or, to give this problem a more precise name, *optionitis*. The rite is pluriform by design, different in different places; to paraphrase Heraclitus, you cannot step into the same Mass twice. My experience of the Novus Ordo may be radically different from your experience, and both yours and mine from that of another person. As linguistically convenient as it is to speak of "the Novus Ordo," it is by no means guaranteed that we will have in mind the same thing *in practice*. How did this situation come about?

There are at least three levels at which the modern rite can be evaluated, each one bringing with it a new level of instability and indeterminacy.

1. The modern rite can be viewed against the backdrop of what the Fathers of the Second Vatican Council called for in the Constitution *Sacrosanctum Concilium* when supporting the restoration of the liturgy—namely, generally modest changes to the inherited Latin liturgical tradition, which was presented there as an obvious good to be preserved. It is easy to trace the many ways in which the Consilium's subsequent work trespassed the plan agreed to by the Council Fathers (including Archbishop Lefebvre).[1] Even so, as Michael Davies, Christopher Ferrara, and others have pointed out, the Constitution has enough loopholes to drive several moderately-sized Italian lorries through.[2] We know that Bugnini urged the preparatory commission to write a vague and open-ended text, without committing all their plans to paper, so that the document's passage would be ensured and the signatories would not know what they were agreeing to.[3]

---

[1] See, for starters, Alfons Cardinal Stickler, "Recollections of a Vatican II Peritus," *NLM*, June 29, 2022; Alcuin Reid, "*Sacrosanctum concilium* and the Reform of the Ordo Missae," *Antiphon* 10.3 (2006): 277–95; idem, "The Liturgy, Fifty Years after *Sacrosanctum Concilium*," *Catholic World Report*, December 4, 2013; idem, "Does *Traditionis Custodes* Pass Liturgical History 101?," in Kwasniewski, ed., *From Benedict's Peace to Francis's War*, 252–59; Joseph Shaw, "Vatican II on Liturgical Preservation," *LMS Chairman*, January 17, 2017; idem, "What Sort of Mass Did 'Vatican II' Want?," *LMS Chairman*, May 24, 2016; Anonymous, "The Old Liturgy and the New Despisers of the Council," *Rorate Caeli*, July 5, 2022; Robert W. Shaffern, "The Mass According to Vatican II," *The Catholic Thing*, July 10, 2022. See also note 56 on p. 24.

[2] On Ferrara, see p. 14.

[3] See chapter 1.

2. Then there is what the official text of the *Novus Ordo Missæ* calls for, in tandem with the *General Instruction of the Roman Missal* (one might call this "the letter" of the Novus Ordo). Here we are already in difficulties, since even if the celebrant stays within the rubrics, there is plenty of room for him to make himself the master of each liturgical celebration, such that no two Masses need be alike. If one takes into account the options for each step of the liturgy and all of their possible combinations, one would arrive at trillions of permutations.[4] In contrast, in the traditional Mass the priest is plainly the servant of the stipulated text and its prescribed ritual.

3. Lastly, there is the reality at the parish level. This, as we know too well, often goes far beyond (or falls far beneath) what is permitted or required either by the missal or by anything that could be described as Catholicism, as when a priest suggested putting a six-pack of beer on an altar during a pre-Lenten pitch to urge the faithful to put their beer money towards alms instead. Here we are dealing with what might be called "the spirit" of the Novus Ordo, which for over half a century has sheltered experimentation, anarchy, idiosyncrasy, laxity, minimalism, and sentimentalism.

In ages past, there was an instinctive, if waning, tendency to adhere to the larger tradition — "the way things had always been done" — and to follow the law because it was the law. This mindset was already endangered well before Vatican II was convened. Modern liberalism, which exalts freedom and individual expression at the expense of community tradition and law-abidingness, infected the mentality of many clergy. The Council itself offered the Catholic world a pretext for throwing everything overboard in a huge adolescent fit of raw emotional energy. By the time the young Turks announced the triumph of the Liturgical Movement, the good spirit that animated its origins was dead and gone. Not only was there no Liturgical Movement anymore; there was all movement and no liturgy.

What the Council taught means nothing today for most Catholics, whether laity or clergy. It was a sad spectacle to watch John Paul II or Benedict XVI attempting to refute erring progressives, year in and year

---

[4] This is no exaggeration. A German mathematician calculated that, given all the moving pieces in the introductory rites, the readings, the Eucharistic Prayers, the selection of music, the use (or not) of lay ministers, the language employed, what is spoken or sung, etc., the total number of possible configurations of the Novus Ordo would be $5{,}000 \times 500{,}000{,}000 = 5 \times 10^3 \times 5 \times 10^8 = 25 \times 10^{11} = 2.5 \times 10^{12}$, or more than two trillion possibilities. A similarly staggering calculation can be made in regard to the new rite of baptism: "Not counting the possible variety in the use of 'similar words,' the total number of possible combinations for the Novus Ordo Baptism is $3 \times 96 \times 2 \times 2 \times 4 \times 2 \times 3 \times 2 \times 2 \times 2 \times 3 \times 2 = 1{,}327{,}104$." Daniel Graham, *Lex Orandi: A Comparison of the Traditional and Novus Ordo Rites of the Seven Sacraments* (Loreto Publications, 2017), 13.

out, by quoting at them *Lumen Gentium, Dei Verbum*, and other conciliar documents, when these individuals couldn't care less about such documents. *They* never saw Vatican II as a body of authoritative teachings to be carried out; for them, it was (as they often explicitly say) an "event" with a "spirit," a certain program or inspiration or ideology that was meant to be creatively evolved until a new Church came into being. Pope Francis has endeavored to institutionalize this progressive approach.

In the area of liturgy, too, the new missal was, from the beginning, not so much a concrete path to be diligently followed as a new attitude, a sounding board, a suggested point of departure for personal and communal self-expression. Hence there must be a Zaire use, a Mayan use, an Amazonian use, and so forth, to join the multiplicity of urban and suburban uses already in play. It is hard to talk about "the Novus Ordo" with any definiteness because it allows so much creativity and spontaneity. Ratzinger argues that three qualities characterize the modern conception of liturgy as group self-expression: arbitrariness, unrepeatability, and artificiality.[5]

Optionitis is a disease of which the world needs to be rid to make it safe for liturgy. Even when men are well disposed and properly taught, it is expecting too much of human nature to think that they will freely choose the best or the better when given a number of options along the spectrum. Many will succumb to the shortest or easiest path out of laziness or a false notion of efficiency. Those who are holy and learned can elaborate strange practices that disturb the rhythm and shape of the liturgy. As we know, priests often avoid the Roman Canon because it is "too long," yet always seem to find time for rambling homilies and general intercessions.[6]

The problem we are considering goes well beyond deficiencies in the content of any given option; the chief problem is a liturgy that allows so many options to be chosen. Advocates of the "reverent Novus Ordo" simply do not wish to acknowledge the fact that a rite capable of being

---

[5] Joseph Ratzinger, "The Image of the World and of Man in the Liturgy and Its Expression in Church Music," in *Theology of the Liturgy*, 451.
[6] The innovation of the General Intercessions (or Prayer of the Faithful) is particularly gratuitous, since the kind of intercessions found on Good Friday were never in daily or weekly use in the Roman tradition, and the Roman Canon already intercedes for the Church's leaders, all those gathered at Mass and those dear to them, and the entire Church on earth and in Purgatory. Moreover, prior to 1955, a second and third oration were always added to the primary orations of the day, with petitions for seasonal or specific needs. Bidding prayers did exist in other contexts in the West, e.g., before the Sermon and notices at Sunday Mass in the Sarum use, and the litany added to Lauds and Vespers in penitential seasons. They are omnipresent in the East. The Roman Rite is just not that concerned with specific intentions being stated at every Mass—though naturally every layman was encouraged to bring his own petitions to the Mass and offer them in the many silent spaces that accommodated personal prayer in symbiosis with liturgical offering.

celebrated in almost total discontinuity with the received Roman rite is *itself*, as such, a discontinuity—indeed the primordial and singular rupture. *This* is what must be rejected, not merely abuses or bad taste or poor judgment. Andrew Shivone astutely observes that there is a ruthless logic built into the new rite that militates against traditional forms:

> The Ordinary Form ... perpetually communicates the disunity of spiritual intent and external gesture. The plethora of options for both laity and priests in the liturgy contributes to the sense that physical gestures and symbols are merely sentimental adornments to real internal worship. While one could celebrate it quite reverently with the Proper chants, reciting the Roman Canon, and in Latin, the very fact that all these forms are optional suggests that they are unnecessary aesthetic accoutrements for elitist retrogrades rather than integral parts of a whole.[7]

The Novus Ordo cannot be done "just as well" as the Tridentine rite, because it was not *built* to be traditional, that is, to privilege adoration, beauty, and contemplative prayer; it was built to be efficient, congregation-oriented, and ever-adaptable. These it surely is, but to the detriment of the liturgy's deepest essence.

The long-term solution to our present malaise, then, will necessarily involve the abolition of options and the re-establishment of clear and detailed rubrics that foster a most profound reverence for the Blessed Sacrament and a leisurely embrace of all the ritual involved in enacting the sacraments and honoring the Word of God. In other words, the solution is the restoration of the classical Roman rite. The great founders of religious orders wrote detailed rules instead of just saying, "Form holy brothers and sisters, and they will instinctively know what to do." Everyone has his own opinions and private preferences about things. No matter how well one trains a priest, and no matter how holy he might be, if the missal allows him to translate his personal opinions and preferences into the arena of public worship, he will inevitably come to see himself as the master of the liturgy instead of its servant.

THE DANGER OF ARBITRARINESS

Because the Novus Ordo features so many options, allows so many ways of doing things, consists of so many modules that can be fitted together this way or that, it is exceedingly difficult to achieve coherence—especially in what may be called "compromise Masses," where different "sensibilities" must all be included in the liturgical planning and are therefore discernible in the resulting concoction.

---

7 Andrew Shivone, "The Glorious Form of the Liturgy," *Humanum Review*, Language: Issue Two, https://humanumreview.com/articles/the-glorious-form-of-the-liturgy.

But why take one traditional feature and reject another? Why take one modern feature and reject another? Have we lost our instinct for consistency? Do we even know what consistency looks like when we see it? Who says that we are qualified to judge? "Asses prefer straw to gold," to quote Heraclitus again. The traditional practices form a coherent whole; they developed organically together, like a plant or animal maturing over time, its parts in proportion, becoming more and more wholly itself. The reform, whether you consider it well-motivated or ill-motivated, was, in any case, inorganic; in the same way modern science views nature as a machine or mechanism, modern liturgists viewed public worship as a human construct with interchangeable pieces. It is not a whole that is greater than its parts but a mere sum of parts. And once you begin to change this or that part, you might as well change all of them. If the *whole* does not command a fundamental reverence, why would one stop messing with it here or there? While still an Anglican, John Henry Newman argued passionately against satisfying the itch for "making improvements" to liturgical rites, in words that have a melancholy ring for Catholics as we look back over the past sixty years and more:

> Attempts are making to get the Liturgy altered. My dear Brethren, I beseech you, consider with me, whether you ought not to resist the alteration of even one jot or tittle of it. Though you would in your own private judgments wish to have this or that phrase or arrangement amended, is this a time to concede one tittle?
>
> Why do I say this? because, though most of you would wish some immaterial points altered, yet not many of you agree in those points, and not many of you agree what is and what is not immaterial. If all your respective emendations are taken, the alterations in the Services will be extensive; and though each will gain something he wishes, he will lose more from those alterations which he did not wish. Tell me, are the present imperfections (as they seem to each) of such a nature, and so many, that their removal will compensate for the recasting of much which each thinks to be no imperfection, or rather an excellence?
>
> There are persons who wish the Marriage Service emended; there are others who would be indignant at the changes proposed.... There are some who wish the imprecatory Psalms omitted; there are others who would lament this omission as savouring of the shallow and detestable liberalism of the day. There are some who wish the Services shortened; there are others who think we should have far more Services, and more frequent attendance at public worship than we have. How few would be pleased by *any given* alterations; and how many pained!
>
> But once begin altering, and there will be no reason or justice in stopping, till the criticisms of all parties are satisfied. Thus, will not the Liturgy be in the evil case described in the well-known

story, of the picture subjected by the artist to the observations of passers-by? And, even to speak at present of comparatively immaterial alterations, I mean such as do not infringe upon the doctrines of the Prayer Book, will not it even with these be a changed book, and will not that new book be for certain an inconsistent one, the alterations being made, not on principle, but upon chance objections urged from various quarters?

But this is not all. A taste for criticism grows upon the mind. When we begin to examine and take to pieces, our judgment becomes perplexed, and our feelings unsettled.... Now I think this unsettling of the mind a frightful thing; both to ourselves, and more so to our flocks.... [W]ill not the unstable learn from us a habit of criticising what they should never think of but as a divine voice supplied by the Church for their need? But as regards ourselves, the Clergy, what will be the effect of this temper of innovation in us? We have the power to bring about changes in the Liturgy; shall we not exert it? have we any security, if we once begin, that we shall ever end? Shall not we pass from non-essentials to essentials? And then, on looking back after the mischief is done, what excuse shall we be able to make for ourselves for having encouraged such proceedings at first?[8]

The *tendency* of the postconciliar liturgy has been towards jettisoning one traditional feature or element after another. Brass candlesticks are locked away, to be replaced by stumps on square pillars; grand high altars or altars with antependia are replaced by tables; beautiful vestments are thrown away or locked away, and polyester drapery takes their place; noble music from the ages of faith is forgotten in the strumming of guitars or the plinking of pianos. If it *can* change, it *will* change.

A Church limping along in a state of discontinuity and rupture must make heroic efforts to find her way back to a vital connection with her history and heritage. Pope Benedict XVI knew that the sacred liturgy is the heart of the Church's life, the most exact and expressive symbol of her faith, and the vehicle through which the faithful are always being catechized by word and sign. Hence this pope began, modestly it is true, to demonstrate what continuity looks like by the way he himself celebrated the liturgy, and by continually pointing us to the Church's past inheritance as well as her present rules and norms. He restored the traditional arrangement of candles and crucifix across the altar; he brought back the beautiful vestments long locked away; he restored grand processions with cope and cross; he ensured that the music was

---

[8] John Henry Newman, "Thoughts Respectfully Addressed to the Clergy On Alterations in the Liturgy," in Kwasniewski, ed., *Newman on Worship*, 1–2. Note that Newman's example of a change motivated by a "shallow and detestable liberalism"—the removal of the imprecatory psalms—was enacted by Paul VI in the new Liturgy of the Hours. See my article "The Omission of 'Difficult' Psalms and the Spreading-Thin of the Psalter," *Rorate Caeli*, November 15, 2016.

reverent and sacred, suggestive of divine majesty and the loftiness of the immortal soul. In such ways he transmitted the message that the Church's ecclesiastical traditions, and above all, her solemn rituals and artistic accomplishments, are not something to be ashamed of or embarrassed about; on the contrary, they are witnesses to glory, "the light of the knowledge of the glory of God, in the face of Christ Jesus" (2 Cor 4:6). Pope Benedict was a voice crying out in the wilderness, proclaiming that we *need* to restore and rediscover these epiphanies of beauty, since our identity, our mission in this world, even our survival, depend on it. The faithful have a right to the truth—what is more, they have a right to tradition.

The modern liturgy might make a bid for non-arbitrariness only were it celebrated with *both* total fidelity to its rubrics, such as they are, *and* in the maximum possible continuity with the Roman liturgical heritage that preceded it for two millennia. To do anything less would be personally to endorse the ideology of rupture that has lacerated the Church for over half a century. Yet such an endorsement already seems to be inherent in every celebration of the Novus Ordo, even the most reverent, since the spirit of maximal continuity is impossible to achieve within its bounds, not least because of the inadequacy of the rubrics and the jarring absence of the traditional *lex orandi*, overshadowed by the fundamental *option* that must be made to side with traditional as opposed to novel praxis (the new rite itself being deliberately open to either—indeed, to an indeterminate number of "adaptations" to local cultures and ill-defined "pastoral needs"). As soon as we see that certain changes were unnecessary and unmandated—that they occurred because of academic theories fused with lust for novelty—the only consistent and principled thing to do is to reject these changes *tout court* and return to the tradition of the Fathers, with the humble repentance of prodigal sons. Speaking from his long experience as a priest, a liturgist, and a mystagogue, Dom Mark gently signifies his departure from the effort to reform the irreformable:

> I laud and support the brilliant achievements of individual parish priests and of groups that use the so-called Ordinary Form or *Novus Ordo Missæ* with dignity, beauty, and reverence. I am thinking, in particular, of the stellar Communauté de Saint-Martin, and of various abbeys and Oratories. For myself, I can no longer spend my energies in that particular exercise.... I seem to hear Our Lord chiding me, saying: "How many cares and troubles thou hast! But only one thing is necessary; and Mary hath chosen for herself the best part of all, that which shall never be taken away from her" (Lk 10:41–41).
>
> I maintain that the real difficulty with the current reformed Missal is that its flawed infrastructure cannot bear the weight of

continual wear and tear. It is a modular liturgy which, because of the multiplicity of options inherent in it, makes unrealistic demands on both priest and people. One finds oneself occupied and preoccupied with assembling and disassembling the various modular elements that make it up. The liturgy [as it was and should be] is not something that men fashion for various occasions and venues; it is the mystery, ancient and ever new, wherein the Church is fashioned and re-fashioned by the gentle and mighty action of the Holy Spirit.[9]

Eripies me de contradictionibus populi: "Thou wilt deliver me from the contradictions of the people" (Ps 17:44). The psalmist expresses to perfection the feeling of one who has been liberated from the world of optionitis. For many years, I struggled to square the circle of the Novus Ordo. I urged, with all the knowledge and eloquence at my command, the use of Latin, chant, and polyphony. I led choirs and scholas. I patiently counseled priests on their *ars celebrandi*. I read *Sacrosanctum Concilium* with continuity-colored glasses. In the end, there was no victory; there could be no victory. The reason is simple: however much you improve one iteration of the Mass, or one month's or year's worth, the success of your campaign (for it always has something of the feel of a political campaign) is tentative and tenuous, dependent on good will, the right circumstances, and a lack of murmurers. There are no long-term gains; it is like writing in the sand at the beach. The waves roll in — a new pastor, a new bishop, a new pope — and wash everything away. The gentle encouragement of good ideas and initiatives that characterized the pontificate of the scholarly Benedict XVI has given way to the nightmare of the Bergoglian police state, in which thriving communities of priests and religious are crushed at whim, while abusers of sex and liturgy roam free or gain promotion.[10]

The Novus Ordo is not one thing but many; it is not a liturgy but a framework for liturgy, a schema for "making liturgy happen." Thus,

---

[9] From an article no longer online, the text of which was copied in 2014. This analysis of the "modularity" of the Novus Ordo explains why some less kind but no less correct commentators have called it the "Frankenmass": as previously mentioned, the content of the liturgy was divided among 46 groups or *coetūs* of experts who trotted off to separate little arenas wearing their scholarly blinders. The results of the groups were sewn together by a central committee, under the directorship of Bugnini, then artificially animated by papal decree. The result may be something that clumsily steps around like a living thing, but all the sutures are clearly visible, and the light of integrity is absent in the eyes.

[10] After *Traditionis Custodes*, we have seen the same dynamic playing out among traditional clergy and with traditional communities: the "new policy" is to cancel them, washing away years of spiritual and physical growth. It is absolutely wrong to allow the work of God to be canceled by ecclesiastical dictators; the clergy and communities dedicated to the TLM must stand up in defense of what they know to be true, good, right, and holy, persevering with a clear conscience, regardless of the consequences. Canon law wielded as a weapon of wickedness has no more efficacy than the fantasies of a madman.

devoting effort to its improvement can feel like pouring money into repairing a poorly-built house held up by rotting timbers and perched on the edge of a cliff. Either the house will totter or the cliff will collapse, but in either case, one's investment would have been more wisely spent restoring a beautiful old building many miles away from the edge.

OPTIONED OUT OF EXISTENCE

I was once talking with a priest about the strange phenomenon of options in the new rite of Mass and the other sacraments. He made the observation that whenever there are multiple options, one of which is traditional and the others more recent inventions, there seems to be a subtle pressure to choose the more recent inventions, with the consequence that, as he put it, the traditional practice is "optioned out of existence."[11]

We know this happens a great deal when it comes to anything that's longer or more complex, or requires a special effort. For example, if the lectionary provides optional readings for a particular saint or category of saint, chances are they'll be skipped, just because it's so much easier to march through the daily cycle page by page rather than being bothered to look up the optional reading. An example of length would be the Confiteor: it takes a little longer to pray the Confiteor and the Kyrie than it does to use the pseudo-troped Kyrie. And so the Confiteor often falls by the wayside.

A dangerous tendency is at work here. Although many options are theoretically put at the celebrant's disposal, in reality there is a certain pressure against choosing the traditional option precisely because it is traditional and a certain pressure in favor of choosing the modern option because it's modern, because it can be done, perhaps because it's more politically correct or more feminist-friendly. One is reminded here of the hubristic vanity of modern applied science, which seems to function by the technobarbaric principle "if we *can* do it, we *should* do it." No matter the larger questions of right or wrong, the nuclear bombs must be built, the organs must be harvested, the test tube babies produced, the embryos frozen, the animals cloned, or whatever it might be.

An excellent example is how the new missal gives the priest the option to say "Pray, brethren." Nobody *ever* says "Pray, brethren"; they always say "Pray, brothers and sisters" (or sometimes "Pray, sisters and brothers," although that's not an option given in the missal).

The same problem pops up everywhere. Take, for example, the ceremony of the washing of the feet on Holy Thursday. For decades, clergy

---

[11] For further thoughts along these lines, see my article "'The Rupturist Rubric': The Attempt to Cut Off the Liturgy from Tradition," *NLM*, July 14, 2022; and Cyril Farret d'Astiès, "The Mass of Paul VI 'Well Celebrated'—a Myth!," *Rorate Caeli*, November 17, 2021.

throughout the world were simply violating the rubrics that said if feet were to be washed, they had to be those of *viri* or men. Although a number was not specified, often twelve men were chosen to represent the twelve Apostles. This simultaneously symbolized two things: the universal commandment of charity, and—more specifically tied to Holy Thursday and the commemoration of the Last Supper—the institution of the priesthood in the first Apostles and the institution of the Most Holy Eucharist, which only priests can confect. So if you have *twelve men*, you successfully capture both sides of the symbolism. The twelve Apostles, as the foundation stones of the Church, represent all of us, so the universal commandment of charity is there as well. On the other hand, if you have a mixed group of men and women, it cancels out the symbolism of the institution of the priesthood and of the Eucharist, and emphasizes only the commandment of charity. Therefore, these two different approaches are *not* equivalent to each other. One of them is more comprehensive while the other is more narrow, and (arguably) politically motivated.

Even after Pope Francis's 2016 change to the rubrics so that women are permitted, it is of course still allowable to wash the feet of twelve men, or some number of men. The exclusive use of *viri* has not been forbidden. But there's an attitude among many clergy that this option is a theoretical option only. We *have* to include women, now that Pope Francis does it, now that so many places do it: "If we *can* have women, we *should* have women." If we don't include women, we must be prejudiced against them, discriminatory, chauvinistic. In this way, an option that really remains—having only men's feet washed—is optioned out of existence.

The foot-washing debacle illustrates a more general principle of action I've encountered in certain priests, namely, that traditional options are *nowhere* to be chosen: they are *never* appropriately chosen anywhere. This, after all, is the modern Church; we're in the contemporary world and we need to do what's relevant, up to date, in fashion. Consequently, the traditional options, though they exist on paper, have to stay on paper.

To take another example, we know that it's possible to sing the entire Mass in Gregorian chant, and this even appears to be favored by the Second Vatican Council; but a chanted Mass was one of the first casualties of allowing many options for music.[12] Most places don't use the Entrance, Offertory, or Communion antiphons. The music

---

[12] On the loss of chant as a result of the way the Council embraced musical pluralism, see Garrett Meyer, "'Other Things Being... Equal'? A Critique of *Sacrosanctum Concilium* 116," *NLM*, October 14, 2024.

ministers simply substitute other, more or less appropriate (usually less appropriate) hymns for those Propers, which are actually part of the structure of the Mass in a way that hymns never have been and never will be. Miscellaneous vernacular hymns are not printed in the official liturgical books; they're not printed in the missal; they're not part of the liturgy; they're just optional add-ons. But the optional add-ons have become the norm, almost as if they're required, and the traditional options, which are a part of the structure of the liturgy and its history, are practically optioned out of existence.

Similarly, we all know that *ad orientem* is a legitimate option for the celebration of the Novus Ordo.[13] But once again, the huge pressure of *versus populum* celebration—the psychological insecurity of clergy who have to be validated by their relationship with the congregation, and also the egocentricity of the congregation expecting to be coddled and catered to—these forces make a return to *ad orientem* extremely difficult, even though we know that it's a perfectly legitimate option on paper.

Such examples could be multiplied. What we see in the world of the reformed liturgy, in short, is a continual drift towards a more and more meaningless, vestigial, paper-thin permission for traditional practices. These practices are like a rare species of delicate flower that's being driven out of its ecosystem by an aggressive, invasive species of noxious weeds.

As a name for this phenomenon, I suggest "the imperialism of novelty," a kind of undiscerning, indiscriminate favoritism toward or advancement of all that is new and recent and shiny, the latest model rolling off the production line. Tradition has no voice with which to defend itself; it has no armies, no force. It compels solely by its inner rationale, its beauty, its value as something passed down to us. But because modern people don't care about what has been passed down to us, tradition's voice is muted; the moral force that it should have is tempered, if not suppressed altogether. Modernity is fundamentally anti-traditional: recall Thomas Jefferson talking about how the enlightened governments of his day will at last throw off medieval priestcraft, monkery, and superstition as they embark on a new Age of Reason, *Novus Ordo Seclorum*. The only positions that have any clout are those that are espoused by people today—not surprisingly, because the people today who espouse them are alive, with muscles and vocal chords, and they will do what they want to do because they're in charge right now.

This having been the case and still being the case in so many places, I am struck by how often I encounter in younger generations

---

[13] Indeed, it is the default assumption. See my article "The Normativity of *Ad Orientem* Worship According to the Ordinary Form's Rubrics," *NLM*, November 23, 2015.

a re-thinking of all this. Not weighted down by the baggage of the Second Vatican Council, these generations can look at the imperialism of novelty and see it for the empty do-it-yourself religion that it is. They can see that it's a form of chronological snobbery, an egocentricity of the age. They can see that modern Christian people and leaders are, in essence, slapping each other on the back and saying: "Isn't it great to be modern, isn't it great to be up-to-date, isn't it great to be politically correct and democratic and sensitive?," and so on. It all rings hollow; to paraphrase Ratzinger, when the community celebrates itself, the liturgy becomes an exercise in boredom and futility.

Young people, if they still have faith and still wish to use their reason, are becoming more and more aware of the inherent value, one might say the silent but immensely powerful value, of tradition. They are becoming its spokesmen; they are taking up the cause, giving it voice and muscle. They are asking, in some cases demanding, that traditional options be exercised — that traditional practices be rescued from oblivion and be allowed a genuine foothold in the Catholic world, in the Catholic consciousness. The very least we can ask is that the traditional options not be optioned out of existence. May all Catholics come to see, sooner or later, that the very best option is to return to a liturgy not at the mercy of options, a liturgy not of modular components associable in countless permutations but a single sacred tunic woven from top to bottom by our Holy Mother, ready to give us warmth and beauty if we will but take it up again and wear it.

RESISTING THE LOWEST COMMON DENOMINATOR

A priest shared with me some insights from a meeting he attended of diocesan priests with their bishop. In what follows, I will be drawing upon what he told me.

In the meeting, the bishop said that the clergy should work against the temptation to settle for the "LCD," the lowest common denominator. For, if we allow every member of the clergy to "roam free," as it were, and aspire to no diocesan-wide standards of excellence, the principle of entropy — or we could just say man's fallen nature — tells us that things will tend to roll downhill and decay over time, and eventually, at some point not too far down the road, every parish will face immense pressure to conform to this LCD: whatever options are least confrontational, most politically correct, and most socially acceptable will eventually win the day. It takes real vision to see this inevitable outcome and to combat it from the start. Free choice can be attractive, but ultimately results in division and degradation.

The priest then reflected: this is exactly what I and many brother priests have seen happening with the liturgy. Because of the equivocal nature of the missal of Paul VI, which leaves so much at the disposal of the celebrant, we have quickly slid to the LCD in every area where there is legitimate free choice. In other words, there is no free choice within the system.

Let's look at some examples.

A priest (as I mentioned above) is free to celebrate *ad orientem* or *versus populum*—in fact, the missal presumes celebrating *ad orientem*, which would put us in harmony with the rest of Tradition. But because of the LCD factor, only *versus populum* is acceptable. Any priest who chooses to celebrate *ad orientem* is seen as divisive and is eventually pressured into conforming, unless he wants to be ostracized not only from the faithful but even from his bishop and brother priests. But is it the priest who is the source of division? Or is it the freedom to choose either option that creates the division? It is the inevitable result of the LCD factor. Priests are accused of fighting what are called "the liturgy wars," but are they to be blamed, or does the blame not rest squarely on the shoulders of Paul VI and his ambivalent missal?

A priest is free to incorporate as much Latin as he would like. But because of the LCD, de facto *only* the vernacular is possible—despite the anathema from the Council of Trent: "If anyone says...that the Mass ought to be celebrated in the vernacular tongue *only*...let him be anathema."[14]

A priest is—or was, prior to *Traditionis Custodes*—free to incorporate the traditional Mass into his parish or his ministry, but again because of the LCD factor, this is seen as extreme and rigid, and is frowned upon to the point where it is de facto nearly impossible.

A priest is under no obligation to concelebrate and is perfectly free to choose to assist in choir so as to be able to celebrate his own Mass at a separate time in the day, a custom hallowed by many centuries of tradition in the Roman rite and clearly upheld by the 1983 Code of Canon Law.[15] But de facto, there is immense pressure upon him to concelebrate because of the LCD factor; to resist conformity will result in his receiving the label of being "not community-minded." At some large gatherings for retreats, conventions, or meetings, there is literally no possibility of a private Mass unless you bring your own portable altar or use a dresser in your room, since such a thing is no longer even contemplated by the organizers, let alone provided for.

A priest is supposed to use a Communion paten and *not* to use extraordinary ministers of Holy Communion (EMHCs) except in

---

[14] Session XXII, Chapter 9, canon 9; www.ewtn.com/catholicism/library/twentysecond-session-of-the-council-of-trent-1489.
[15] See my article "The Mounting Threat of Coercive Concelebration," *NLM*, July 22, 2019.

circumstances *outside* the ordinary, as the very name indicates;[16] but because of systemic habitual abuse in the American Church and the LCD factor, doing either of these things would be seen as suspiciously extreme. The pragmatic norm, on the contrary, is to *not* have a Communion paten but to employ a roster's worth of EMHCs.

The faithful are encouraged to receive Holy Communion on the tongue, which is the traditional custom and still the universal norm as per the Vatican; meanwhile, they are permitted to receive in the hand as long as certain serious conditions are met. But because of the LCD factor, probably 95% of the faithful receive in the hand. And children preparing for First Communion are seldom even *taught* the traditional practice, in spite of its still being "on the books."

The same can be said of sacred music, church architecture, sacred vessels, vestments, preaching, etc., etc., etc. We are all now forced by social pressure to conform to the LCD. And what happens when a priest doesn't want to conform to the LCD but wants to raise the bar? Well, typically the choice is either: *conform to the LCD, or hit the highway*. The dynamic subtly eats away at the bishop's own integrity, because when he is confronted with complaints about a "difficult" or "demanding" priest—as identified promptly by Susan from the Parish Council—he must either stick his neck out and risk his reputation to defend the priest, or take the quieter path of pressuring the priest to conform to the LCD (or face exile to the boondocks, removal from ministry, or some other form of cancellation).

It is as if everyone is laboring under the spell of the LCD. Such is the division that has been sown into the heart of the Church, and especially into the heart of the priesthood and religious life, by the missal of Paul VI.

The laity need to understand this phenomenon if they wish to grasp why so many good priests who want to celebrate in harmony with tradition and want the faithful to experience the fullness of this rich treasure that we have as Catholics are afraid to do so, or perhaps suffer a crisis when the tension between their ideals and the LCD reality becomes too intense. Some think there is a huge conspiracy that carefully planned the situation I've described, and certainly this may be true, since no doubt the cunning of the devil is involved. But it can also be explained as the result of *societal entropy*.[17] Because of original sin, everything tends towards decay, as we see in the movies, music, and media of our culture. The Church is immune from this decay only in

---

[16] See Peter Kwasniewski, *The Holy Bread of Eternal Life: Restoring Eucharistic Reverence in an Age of Impiety* (Sophia Institute Press, 2020), 93 n94, 147–50.
[17] See Kwasniewski, *Noble Beauty*, 181–86.

her divine element; she is by no means immune to it in her human element, unless her members fight consciously and vigorously against it. The traditional liturgy had long been a barrier against this natural process, but the new Mass has opened the floodgates to it.

This "Trojan horse in the City of God"[18]—the new Mass in the sanctuary—did not spring up out of nowhere. Its principles had been brewing among modernist theologians and their heirs, the theologians of the *nouvelle théologie*, expressed in the false distinction made by Fr. Yves Congar between the "unalterable structures" of the Church and the "accessory, changeable superstructures," allowing the latter to be discarded and reinvented *ad libitum*. But this mentality is nothing less than a betrayal of a mystical person, as one lover of tradition poetically expressed it:

> I do not love a skeleton nor vital organs, I love her face, her sparkling clothes and even her sandals, her entire being. With the spiritual canticle I will sing of the hair on her neck that charmed us as well, her children, as it ravished the heart of her Spouse. Oh, may those who love the Church understand! In her features and her slightest gestures, something indescribably exquisite enraptures us to the summit of her essential Mystery. The liturgical movements, the hymns, the ornamentation of churches, the words of the catechism and the sermon, this flesh, this manner of walking, the sound of the voice, the color of the eyes, revealed the very soul, immediately, and we were struck, intoxicated by it, for her ancient and universal soul, her intimate life that came to comfort us, was the Holy Spirit in Person![19]

This is the reverence that a Catholic should have towards the received rites that come down to us from tradition, and all of their ornamentation. But the new Mass incarnates the false principle of Fr. Congar by deliberately tossing all this out the window in a massive overhaul, giving the impression to faithful Catholics and to the world that the Catholic faith can change its entire appearance. Ever since the so-called "accessory, changeable superstructures" were overthrown, we have become painfully aware that they were instead a constitutive part of the solid rock that formed our sure foundation, or, to use the above imagery, the beautiful wedding garments of Holy Mother Church, visibly radiant in her sacred rites. And now we find ourselves upon a foundation of sand, always shifting, and—if we are willing to be honest

---

18 To use an expression of Dietrich von Hildebrand's.
19 From the Abbé Georges de Nantes's "Letter to My Friends," no. 178, August 6, 1964. Like Padre Pio, de Nantes was reacting to the devastation already being visited on the Tridentine Mass in the mid-sixties, prior to the *coup de grâce* of 1969. For the quotation as well as the mention of Congar, see https://crc-internet.org/our-doctrine/catholic-counter-reformation/critical-study-second-vatican-council/de-ecclesia-lumen-gentium.html.

with ourselves — a foundation always eroding down to the LCD, again and again. Like a bird with a broken wing that can only manage to throw itself a few inches, or an airplane with faulty engines that rises up from the runway only to crash just beyond it, so is our lot, so it has been and so it will remain, until the Church is no longer deprived of the liturgy that belongs to her.

The priest with whom I was corresponding concluded with this *cri de cœur*:

> If other priests want to accept the status quo, the tyranny of the LCD, that is their decision, between them and God. Perhaps not everyone needs to fight on the front lines and resist *usque ad sanguinem*. But for us whose hearts belong to the Church of all times, and to her traditional rites, we seek nothing more than to access them in freedom, nothing else than to live and die with them, nothing other than to nourish the faithful with this potent food and drink.

May God raise up more and more priests with such a heart.

❧ 5 ❧
The Outrageous Propaganda of Cardinal Roche & Co.

AT ONE POINT IN HIS AUTOBIOGRAPHY *Unwanted Priest* (p. 158), Fr. Bryan Houghton talks about anti-religious posters he came by on a trip to Russia:

> I had picked up the first group [of posters] in 1931 from an upper school in Moscow. They are forcefully designed but the content is rather naive. They are anti-clerical rather than anti-religious. A typical example is one for use in a history class... It represents the square in front of Notre-Dame de Paris with the cathedral in the background. To the right is a leering capitalist, identifiable by his top hat, in front of whom are Cardinal Verdier (Archbishop of Paris in 1931) and Marshal Foch, who are encouraging some troops on the left side of the poster to massacre a crowd of defenceless workers. Underneath is a quotation from Karl Marx referring to the Paris Commune of 1870/71.
>
> Now it is obvious that the religion might still be true even if cardinals were in the habit of mowing down the populace. As anti-religious propaganda it is naive. What is wicked and typically communist about the poster is its falsification of history. It so happens that in May 1871 it was the then Archbishop of Paris, Georges Darboy, who while in prison was murdered in cold blood by the communists.... You do not just tell a lie but the exact opposite of the truth; it leaves your opponent speechless. It is the technique used so successfully by progressives when they accuse traditionalists of being divisive.

I had this passage in mind as I read an interview with then-Archbishop Roche, in which he does not merely tell lies, but says the exact opposite of the truth.[1] However, unlike the audience of communist propaganda, Roche's opponents will not be found speechless; no, they will have plenty to say, for they have been assiduously following these matters for a much longer time, and far more carefully, than the prefect of the Dicastery for Divine Worship has done. We take pains with Roche not because he will sit forever in the office he occupies but because he epitomizes an ideology and an attitude that we have had to suffer under for a long time and may still have to endure for many years to come.

---

[1] Cindy Wooden, "Archbishop says most bishops see importance of 'Traditionis Custodes,'" *National Catholic Reporter*, January 21, 2022. The quotations of Roche through p. 91 are taken from this interview.

One can hardly read a paragraph without cringing at the interviewee's befuddlement.

"I think one of the problems that we are facing today is that we are living in a very individualistic world, a very relativistic world, and where the individual preference promotes itself above the common good and the common expression," he said. "I think that that is a very dangerous thing, and it is something that as Christians, we really need to take very careful note of."

So: how exactly does a liturgy notorious for its "optionitis," which makes of it the personal project of whoever is celebrating it, escape from "individual preference"? The priest gets to make choices about the penitential rite; whether or not to improvise mini-commentaries on the readings; whether or not to have an Alleluia; whether or not to say the Offertory out loud; sometimes which Preface to say; which Eucharistic Prayer to say (!); whether to use some Latin or not; *ad orientem* or *versus populum*; and so on and so forth. Add to this the completely open-ended possibilities for the music, what kinds of music, which texts, when to sing and when not to sing, possibilities of readings, optional memorials, periods of silence, etc.... As any amateur mathematician may see, there are trillions of possible configurations of the Novus Ordo,[2] all of them summoned into being by "individual preference," which, of course, rules out altogether a liturgical "common expression" of the Faith! That's a "very dangerous thing" that "we really need to take very careful note of"!

"This is not the pope's Mass, it's not my Mass, it's not your Mass. This is the Mass of the church," the archbishop said. "This is what the church has decided how we express ourselves as a community in worship, and how we imbibe from the books of the liturgy the doctrine of the church."

Apart from His Excellency's tipsy grammar, we may note the profound irony of saying, about a Mass created for and issued by Paul VI in an absolutely unprecedented flexing of papal creativity, that "this is not the pope's Mass." But *of course* it is: it is *Paul VI's* Mass, in a way that the Tridentine rite was *never* "the Mass of" St. Pius V or Benedict XV or John XXIII, for it was the Roman rite handed down from century to century by all who used this missal.[3] Only of the TLM and of other traditional Eucharistic liturgies could it be truthfully said: "This is not the pope's Mass; it's not my Mass; it's not your Mass. This is the Mass of the Church."

---

[2] See note 4 on p. 70.
[3] See Shaw, "Pope Pius V and Liturgical Reform," in idem, ed., *The Latin Mass and the Intellectuals*, 3–17.

Here is where Roche makes a fatal move:

> The differences between the pre-Vatican II and post-Vatican II Masses, he said, are not simply the use of Latin, chant, silence and the direction the priest faces. The promotion of the pre-Vatican II liturgy as somehow more holy or prayerful than the current liturgy "is not basically a liturgical problem, it is an ecclesial problem," the archbishop said.

By admitting that the differences between the missals are not just "skin-deep" (they go beyond the "smells and bells") and by stating that the promotion of the preconciliar rite is "not basically a liturgical problem, it is an *ecclesial problem*" (that is, one that concerns fundamental theology, the *lex credendi* expressed by the *lex orandi*), the Archbishop once again asserts the rupture thesis[4] that condemns *Traditionis Custodes* to the dustbin: if the new rite is antithetical to the old rite, yet the old rite expressed the faith of the Church for well over a millennium, which of the two is the loser? Surely the new rite, unless we want to say the Church had a faulty and damaging notion of itself and of its faith for most of its history—which sounds oddly like the view many Protestants hold.

Now we come to the most monumental of the errors:

> The current Mass, with a richer selection of prayers and Scripture readings, reflects and reinforces the church's understanding of itself as the people of God.

Roche tells us every chance he gets that the "current Mass" boasts a "richer selection of prayers and Scripture readings." True, the missal of Paul VI draws its euchology or prayer texts from a wider variety of sources in ancient manuscripts. However, what people like Roche do not want to tell you is that Bugnini's Consilium heavily redacted most of the texts it borrowed, altering their message, removing material deemed "difficult" or "irrelevant" for Modern Man. What you end up with in the missal is not a plethora of ancient sources but a carefully filtered and rewritten 1960s "take" on them.[5] This chronological snobbery is perfectly conveyed in a memorandum from the Consilium in charge of the liturgical reform, dated September 9, 1968:

> It is often impossible to preserve either orations that are found in the [1962] Roman Missal or to borrow suitable orations from the treasury of ancient euchology. Indeed, prayer ought to express the mind of our current age, especially with regard to temporal

---

[4] See Michael Charlier, "'He is damaging the entire series of his predecessors... and thus himself and the papacy': The insoluble contradiction between Francis and Paul VI," *Rorate Caeli*, January 21, 2022.
[5] On this problem, see my article series "The Reign of Novelty and the Sins of the Times."

necessities like the unity of Christians, peace, and famine… In addition, it seems to us that it is not always possible for the Church on every occasion to make use of ancient orations, which do not correspond with the doctrinal progress visible in recent encyclicals such as *Pacem in terris* and *Populorum progressio*, and in conciliar documents such as *Gaudium et spes*.[6]

In keeping with this policy, only 13% of the orations of the old missal, once the backbone of Roman Catholic worship, found their way into the new missal unchanged.[7] The scholars with their scissors and paste were busy rejecting or rewriting most of what they came upon. The editing process was ruthless, removing most of the references to

> detachment from the temporal and desire for the eternal; the Kingship of Christ over the world and society; the battle against heresy and schism, the conversion of non-believers, the necessity of the return to the Catholic Church and genuine truth; merits, miracles, and apparitions of the saints; God's wrath for sin and the possibility of eternal damnation.[8]

Gone are most references to the struggle against our sinful fallen nature, offenses against the Divine Majesty, wounds of the soul, worthy repentance, remorse, and reparation; the need for grace to do any good acts; the mystery of predestination; the relics of saints; the subordination of the secular sphere to the sacred; the snares of the enemy; victory over hostile forces, including the pagans; orations specifically addressed to Jesus Christ as God.[9]

How, exactly, can a missal missing all these old riches be said to represent "a richer selection of prayers"? On the contrary, the selection — precisely because it *is* a selection by 1960s "experts" — is theologically narrower, culturally thinner, and spiritually poorer.[10] The old

---

[6] Translated by Matthew Hazell in "The Eastertide Collects in the Post-Vatican II Missal: A Problematic Reform," *Rorate Caeli*, May 17, 2021.
[7] Matthew Hazell, "'All the Elements of the Roman Rite'? Mythbusting, Part II," *NLM*, October 1, 2021.
[8] Michael Fiedrowicz, *The Traditional Mass: History, Form, and Theology of the Classical Roman Rite*, trans. Rose Pfeifer (Angelico Press, 2020), 239, with ample notes there.
[9] Illustrations of these points can be seen by looking, for example, at the old orations for February 8, 10, 22, and 27, March 24, April 28, May 3, June 22, September 15 and 17, October 3, 10, 16, and 17, November 6, 15, and 25, the Sacred Heart, the Holy Family, the Holy Name of Jesus, the Seventeenth Sunday after Pentecost. A comparison with the new rite at almost any point will disclose how much of the traditional *lex orandi* has been erased.
[10] For examples that are by no means atypical, see my articles "Adventures in the *Lex Orandi*: Comparing Traditional and Modern Orations for St. Augustine of Canterbury," *Rorate Caeli*, May 28, 2020; "Adventures in the *Lex Orandi* #2: Old and New Versions of St. Ephrem the Syrian," *Rorate Caeli*, June 18, 2020; "Adventures in the *Lex Orandi* #3: Comparing the Old and New Orations for Our Lady of Sorrows," *Rorate Caeli*, September 15, 2021.

missal's prayers express much more of the full height and depth of the divine mysteries and the variegated human response to them. For those who are not persuaded, I recommend, in addition to Fiedrowicz, the unanswerable research of Lauren Pristas in her *Collects of the Roman Missals: A Comparative Study of the Sundays in Proper Seasons before and after the Second Vatican Council*. (Don't these Sant'Anselmians ever study any books? They seem to have read nothing after circa 1975.)

The same thing can be said of the "richer selection of Scripture readings." Yes, there are more readings, numerically speaking. However, some of the highly appropriate and crucial readings found in the old missal were excluded from the new lectionary, and the new one, for its part, skips verses deemed (you guessed it) "difficult" for Modern Man.[11] The old readings, like the old orations, express a wider range of certain themes than the new lectionary, in spite of its vastly greater size. As a matter of fact, the old lectionary boasts numerous advantages over the new one, as traditionalists have long maintained.[12]

Returning now to Roche:

"That which was given to us by the council, which classified, concretized the teaching of the church about itself and its understanding of the role of the baptized and the importance of the Eucharist and the sacramental life of the church, is not without significance for the future of the church," he said.

Please repeat three times: "The Novus Ordo was not given to us by the council." As we saw in chapter 1, the premises of *Sacrosanctum Concilium* could have been fulfilled in many different ways. Their actual application in the form of the new liturgical books of Paul VI has led to unceasing controversy and complaints at all levels and from all sides, because it will never be traditional enough for those who love immemorial tradition and never progressive enough for those who favor constant "inculturation" or "adaptation." Nevertheless, it would be impossible to find a single statement in Vatican II that would *necessarily yield* the Novus Ordo as it now exists. Nor can it ever be said that the preconciliar period lacked a profound awareness of "the role of the baptized and the importance of the Eucharist and the sacramental life of the church"; on the contrary, this awareness was far stronger, as the vastly greater participation of Catholics before the Council in Sunday Mass, their frequent use of Confession, their

---

[11] See my foreword, "Not Just More Scripture, But Different Scripture," in Matthew P. Hazell, *Index Lectionum: A Comparative Table of Readings for the Ordinary and Extraordinary Forms of the Roman Rite* (Lectionary Study Press, 2016).

[12] See Kwasniewski, "Why We Use a One-Year Lectionary of Readings," in *Turned Around*, 133–66.

choice of matrimony in the Church and the consequent baptism of more numerous offspring, and the higher numbers of priestly and religious vocations, would evidently suggest to anyone but an ideologue.

> And the bishops gathered for the Second Vatican Council, under the inspiration of the Holy Spirit, said, "this is the direction in which we are going," Archbishop Roche said.

No reputable theologian has ever claimed that bishops at an ecumenical council act "under the inspiration of the Holy Spirit" simply speaking; nor was "this direction" pointing as clearly to the Novus Ordo as Roche must assume in order to support his dogmatism.[13]

> Through regular contacts with bishops and bishops' conferences, he said, he knows most bishops have "greeted the pope's call back to the council and also to the unity of the church with open arms and are very much behind what the Holy Father is saying."

This sounds like the mandatory optimism of the Communist Party, according to which everything is always getting better, and everyone is marching side-by-side, arm-in-arm, into a glorious future! If Roche is correct, why is it that so many bishops either have done nothing about *Traditiones Custodes* and the *Responsa* of the (then) Congregation for Divine Worship, or have sought ways to work around their onerous and episcopally insulting provisions? The available statistics and statements suggest—as Diane Montagna already reported[14]—that most bishops had either positive or neutral things to say about *Summorum Pontificum*, or indeed, had nothing to say at all, since only 30% responded to the pope's survey. This doesn't sound like "most bishops...are very much behind what the Holy Father is saying."

But His Excellency saves the most delicious absurdity for last:

> Obviously, people have preferences, the archbishop said. But Catholics need to look more deeply at what they are saying when they express those preferences. "When people say, 'Well, I'm going to Father So-and-So's Mass,' well Father So-and-So is only the agent. It is Christ who is active in the Mass, it is the priest who acts in 'persona Christi'—the person of Christ, the head of the church," he said.

Are traditionalists really individualists who exalt their personal preferences above the Church's shared liturgy? Or is it rather the Novus Ordo that has privileged clerical choices and community preferences

---

[13] See "Games People Play with the Holy Spirit," in Kwasniewski, ed., *Illusions of Reform*, 134–50.
[14] Diane Montagna, "*Traditionis Custodes*: Separating Fact from Fiction," *The Remnant*, October 7, 2021; "*Traditionis Custodes*: More Facts Emerge (What the Bishops of the World Actually Told Francis)," *The Remnant*, October 28, 2021; "*Traditionis Custodes*: A Weapon of Mass Destruction," *The Remnant*, November 29, 2021.

for five and a half decades, as we saw in chapter 4? The old liturgy consistently bears witness to a common faith and worship across the ages and around the world; it possesses a durable diachronic unity and a sensible synchronic unity. The phenomenon of "Fr. So-and-so's Mass" generally happens only in the realm of the Novus Ordo due to all the options and interpretations and loose rubrics, which can make two Masses radically different from each other *even at the same parish on the same morning.* No wonder Catholics choose between "Fr. Pius Fiddleback" and "Fr. Lookatme Adlibber": they are compelled to make a choice between those who make choices. The loser here is the *persona Christi*, the One who should shine through and dominate.

> "When we go to Mass, even when the music perhaps isn't something that we would personally choose—and again, this is individualism coming in—then we've got to realize that we are standing at the side of Christ on his cross, who gives everything back to the Father through this Eucharist," Archbishop Roche said.

Here Roche implies that those who attend the old rite do so out of a personal desire for a certain variety of sacred music, as if chasing after their own Spotify playlist. Once again, the opposite is the truth: at the traditional Latin Mass, the music you will hear is (most often) either age-old chant *dictated by the liturgy itself* or polyphony based off of that chant—in short, the music long praised by the Magisterium and well suited for universal use, not "what we would personally choose" (although we may prefer it for aesthetic reasons, too, since it is in fact superior).[15] This is—*surprise!*—what Vatican II called for: "The Church acknowledges Gregorian chant as specially suited to the Roman liturgy: therefore, *ceteris paribus* [all things being equal], it should be given chief place in liturgical services" (*SC* 116). Dear Prefect, be careful how you wave about that Constitution on the Liturgy! Whereas in the Novus Ordo, contrary to this conciliar directive, somebody else—the pastor, the guitarist, the parish council, GIA, etc.—gets to impose his or its personal choice of music on the hapless people in the pews, dismissing the unitive power of the Church's tradition. As with liberal political propaganda, so too with ecclesiastical: in nearly every case, the vices of which one is accused are the vices of the accuser. Fr. Houghton's Soviet posters would be right at home on the walls of Roche's office.

A breathtaking example of self-indictment came in an interview conducted by Christopher Lamb, where Cardinal Roche manages to utter what may well be the most ironic statement since Vatican II:

---

15 See "Gregorian Chant: Perfect Music for Christian Worship" in Peter Kwasniewski, *Good Music, Sacred Music, and Silence: Three Gifts of God for Liturgy and for Life* (TAN Books, 2023), 88–115.

That reform [of Catholic worship since the Council] is taking place, but it's a slow process because there are those who are dragging their feet with regard to this and not only dragging their feet but stubbornly opposing what the Church has actually decreed. That's a very serious matter. In the end, people have to ask themselves: am I really a Catholic, or am I more of a Protestant?[16]

Let's think about this for a moment. As Michael Davies demonstrated in his masterpiece *Cranmer's Godly Order: The Destruction of Catholicism through Liturgical Change*, the liturgical reform after Vatican II emulated, in dozens of ways, the liturgical "reforms" fashioned by Cranmer and imposed on England by its rulers. *The Book of Common Prayer* was a revolution in the *lex orandi*, made to reflect and promote a Protestant *lex credendi*. The website *Whispers of Restoration* has prepared a handy chart that shows these parallels.[17]

For example, the Novus Ordo, like Cranmer's missal, repudiates an oblative Offertory, replacing it with a supper-oriented "presentation of gifts" based on the Jewish *berakah*, which does not unambiguously signify that the Mass is a true and proper sacrifice in propitiation for sins and for the good estate of the living and of the dead, offered to the Most Holy Trinity by the Son of God according to His human nature. As F. A. Gasquet and E. Bishop write:

> The ancient ritual oblation, with the whole of which the idea of sacrifice was so intimately associated, was swept away. This was certainly in accord with Cranmer's known opinions.... To understand the full import of the novelty it must be borne in mind that this ritual oblation had a place in all liturgies [of Christendom].[18]

It is worthy of note that Luther, when designing his own Order of Mass for his followers, omitted the Roman Offertory, which he called "that complete abomination into the service of which all that precedes in the Mass has been forced, whence it is called Offertorium, and on account of which nearly everything sounds and reeks of oblation."[19]

---

[16] Christopher Lamb, "Stubborn opposition to Vatican II 'not Catholic' says cardinal," *The Tablet*, August 28, 2022.
[17] See https://whispersofrestoration.blog/2018/02/28/resource-liturgy-comparison-chart/. In chapter 1 of *Lex Orandi*, Daniel Graham offers a similarly harrowing and undeniable account of eleven parallels between the Novus Ordo rite of baptism and pre-existing Protestant versions of the rite.
[18] F. A. Gasquet and E. Bishop, *Edward VI and the Book of Common Prayer* (John Hodges, 1891), 196. Already long before the Council of Trent, Western liturgical rites and uses featured just such a proleptic oblative Offertory: see Gregory DiPippo, "The Theology of the Offertory—Series to Resume," *NLM*, February 27, 2015.
[19] See Martin Luther, *Formula missæ et communionis pro ecclesia Wittembergensis* (1523), in *Works of Martin Luther*, vol. 6 (Muhlenberg Press, 1932), 88. A description of Luther's plan for Mass and his reasoning about what to keep and what to reject is found in Gasquet and Bishop, *Edward VI*, 220–24.

Not only Cranmer's actions, then, but Luther's theology also influenced the architects of the Novus Ordo. As Joseph Ratzinger observed in his lecture "Theology of the Liturgy" given at Fontgombault in July 2001:

> Who still talks today about "the divine Sacrifice of the Eucharist"?... Stefan Orth, in the vast panorama of a bibliography of recent works devoted to the theme of sacrifice, believed he could make the following statement as a summary of his research: "In fact, many Catholics themselves today ratify the verdict and the conclusions of Martin Luther, who says that to speak of sacrifice is 'the greatest and most appalling horror' and a 'damnable idolatry'; this is why we want to refrain from all that smacks of sacrifice, including the whole Canon, and retain only that which is pure and holy." Then Orth adds: "This maxim was also followed in the Catholic Church after Vatican II, or at least tended to be, and led people to think of divine worship chiefly in terms of the feast of the Passover related in the accounts of the Last Supper."...
>
> A sizable party of Catholic liturgists seems to have practically arrived at the conclusion that Luther, rather than Trent, was substantially right in the sixteenth-century debate; one can detect much the same position in the postconciliar discussions on the Priesthood. The great historian of the Council of Trent, Hubert Jedin, pointed this out in 1975, in the preface to the last volume of his history of the Council of Trent: "The attentive reader ... in reading this will not be less dismayed than the author, when he realizes that many of the things—in fact, almost everything—that disturbed the men of the past is being put forward anew today." Only against this background of the effective denial of the authority of Trent can one understand the bitterness of the struggle against allowing the celebration of Mass according to the 1962 Missal after the liturgical reform. The possibility of so celebrating constitutes the strongest and thus (for them) the most intolerable contradiction of the opinion of those who believe that the faith in the Eucharist formulated by Trent has lost its validity.... Meßner, who says a great deal that is worth pondering, nonetheless arrives at the conclusion that Luther understood the early Church better than the Council of Trent did.[20]

The view that the early Christian Mass was more "authentic," more in keeping with what Jesus intended—free from all the medieval clutter, repetition, bowing and scraping, pious mumbo-jumbo, devotionalism, and even superstition that grew up around it later—is precisely the view that unites the original Protestants with their latter-day descendants

---

[20] From "The Theology of the Liturgy" in Ratzinger, *Theology of the Liturgy*, 542–45; cf. 207–17. See also Michael Davies, *Pope Paul's New Mass* (Angelus Press, 2009), 329–47. In connection with the theme of sacrifice, see José Ureta's illuminating essay: "A Brief Study of Certain Theological Deviations in *Desiderio Desideravi*," https://onepeterfive.com/wp-content/uploads/2022/08/Ureta-Complete.pdf.

in the radical wing of the Liturgical Movement that produced the Novus Ordo. I discuss this point at length elsewhere.[21] Let it suffice, for the nonce, to provide a picture-perfect example of such antiquarian reformism:

> The liturgy we experience today is quite different from that of fifty or sixty years ago. Over the ages, what began as a gathering of friends and followers of Jesus sharing a meal and remembering his teachings became an increasingly elaborate ceremony of sacrifice. The celebrations of the Lord's Supper, held in secret in people's homes during the times of persecution, gave way to highly ritualized ceremonies held in beautiful churches. By the Middle Ages, the priest was saying Mass while the people watched in silence. The focus was primarily on Jesus' sacrifice, which diminished the symbol of a shared meal. Those attending were not participants as much as watchers. In the 1960s the bishops from around the world gathered at the Second Vatican Council. They called for important reforms to renew the liturgy. The language of the liturgy changed from Latin to the vernacular, so that for the first time in hundreds of years, the people could hear and understand the prayers being said. People were also encouraged to receive Communion, in the hand, and from the cup. The idea of a shared meal around a table was reclaimed from the early years of Christianity.

This passage is taken from a middle-school Religious Ed textbook: *Catholic Faith Handbook for Youth*, published by Saint Mary's Press in 2008. It even has the *nihil obstat* and *imprimatur* (the devaluation of Catholic currency on full display). It is precisely this "quite different experience" of liturgy that not only prompted a mass exodus of Catholics after the Council[22] but also, and more damningly still, led to the well-documented erosion of faith in the Real Presence, of awareness of moral conditions for receiving the Eucharist (including recourse to Confession), of fidelity to the Sunday obligation, and so forth. The past sixty years have offered an unanswerable demonstration — if anyone needed convincing — of the ironclad axiom *lex orandi, lex credendi*.

Nor should we be surprised by these Protestant/Novus Ordo parallels. An explicit motivation of the modern Catholic liturgical reform was an ecumenism designed to bring Catholics and Protestants together. As Annibale Bugnini famously wrote in the March 19, 1965 edition of *L'Osservatore Romano* concerning the softening of the prayer for the conversion of heretics and schismatics on Good Friday:

---

[21] See Kwasniewski, "False Antiquarianism and Liturgical Reform," NLM, September 2, 2024; *Once and Future Roman Rite*, 197–215; *Reclaiming Our Roman Catholic Birthright*, 149–57.
[22] See Stephen Bullivant, *Mass Exodus: Catholic Disaffiliation in Britain and America since Vatican II*, second edition (Oxford University Press, 2019).

Let's say that often the work [of the Consilium's ongoing editing of prayers] proceeded "with fear and trembling" by sacrificing terms and concepts so dear, and now part of the long family tradition. How not to regret that "Mother Church—Holy, Catholic and Apostolic—deigned to revoke" the seventh prayer? And yet the love of souls and the desire to help in any way the road to union for the separated brethren, by removing every stone that could even remotely constitute an obstacle or source of difficulty, have driven the Church to make even these painful sacrifices.[23]

This interpretation is confirmed not only by the oft-mentioned participation of six Protestants in the Consilium that worked on the new liturgy[24] (their role was mainly confined to the new lectionary) but even more by the testimony of Paul VI's close personal friend, the philosopher Jean Guitton. I quoted this paragraph earlier, but it deserves to be repeated:

> First of all, Paul VI's Mass is presented as a banquet, and emphasizes much more the participatory aspect of a banquet and much less the notion of sacrifice, of a ritual sacrifice before God with the priest showing only his back. So, I don't think I'm mistaken in saying that the intention of Paul VI and the new liturgy that bears his name is to ask of the faithful a greater participation at Mass; it is to make more room for Scripture, and less room for all that is, some would say magical, others, transubstantial consecration, which is the Catholic faith. In other words, there was with Paul VI an ecumenical intention to remove, or at least to correct or to relax what was too Catholic, in the traditional sense, in the Mass, and, I repeat, to bring the Catholic Mass closer to the Calvinist Mass.[25]

---

[23] This quotation came under renewed discussion because the second episode of the *Mass of the Ages* film trilogy misquoted it as if it referred to the entire Mass rather than to the prayer of Good Friday. The *Mass of the Ages* issued an official apology and correction. Yet as Gregory DiPippo pointed out: "The statement is nevertheless a fair summary of the ethos of the reform as a whole. The reformers unquestionably saw their mission not as the restoration of the liturgy which the Council had asked for, but the remaking of it in their own image and likeness. Ferdinando Cardinal Antonelli, who was a member of the Consilium, and in principle very much in favor of reform, stated this outright in his memoirs. And furthermore, this remaking did unquestionably consist in the reformers identifying, each according to his own personal ideas, what in the liturgy constituted an 'obstacle,' whether it be to the comprehension of the faithful, ecumenical progress, or some other hazily identified but unquestionably desirable goal, and taking it out. And this is why they took advantage of the highly imprudent ambiguity of *Sacrosanctum Concilium*'s statement that 'elements which... were added (to the liturgy) with but little advantage are now to be discarded,' and discarded any number of elements that are attested in every single pertinent liturgical book of the Roman Rite as far back as we have them." DiPippo, "Muphry's Law Comes After Mass of the Ages (Part 1)," *NLM*, July 23, 2022.
[24] See "The Participation of the Protestant Observers in the Compilation of the New Catholic Liturgical Texts" in Davies, *Pope Paul's New Mass*, 625–29.
[25] Chiron, with Dreyfus and Guitton, "Entretien sur Paul VI," 27–28.

Bishop Athanasius Schneider points out another way in which Calvinism influenced the liturgical reform:

Today the faithful take and touch the Host directly with their fingers and then put the Host in the mouth: this gesture has never been known in the entire history of the Catholic Church but was invented by Calvin—not even by Martin Luther. The Lutherans have typically received the Eucharist kneeling and on the tongue, although of course they do not have the Real Presence because they do not have a valid priesthood. The Calvinists and other Protestant free churches, who do not believe at all in the Real Presence of Christ in the Eucharist, invented a rite which is void of almost all gestures of sacredness and of exterior adoration, i.e., receiving "Communion" standing upright, and touching the bread "host" with their fingers and putting it in their mouth in the way people treat ordinary bread....

For them, this was just a symbol, so their exterior behavior towards Communion was similar to behavior towards a symbol. During the Second Vatican Council, Catholic Modernists—especially in the Netherlands—took this Calvinist Communion rite and wrongly attributed it to the Early Church, in order to spread it more easily throughout the Church. We have to dismantle this myth and these insidious tactics, which started in the Catholic Church more than fifty years ago, and which like an avalanche have now rolled through, crushing almost all Catholic churches in the entire world, with the exception of some Catholic countries in Eastern Europe and a few places in Asia and Africa.[26]

Cranmer... Luther... Calvin... "That's a very serious matter. In the end, people have to ask themselves: am I really a Catholic, or am I more of a Protestant?"

I have a piece of advice for Cardinal Roche's friends and associates. They should tell him to stop speaking and especially to stop giving interviews. Every time he opens his mouth, he inadvertently advances the cause of Tradition. In this respect, he imitates to perfection the one who created him cardinal.

RELEASING ENERGIES

The term "inculturation" is certainly one of the favorite buzzwords of progressives. We have heard it flung about for decades. It was the original rationale for updating or modernizing the liturgy: the old liturgical rites (so it was said) are excessively beholden to and redolent

---

[26] Athanasius Schneider, in conversation with Diane Montagna, *Christus Vincit: Christ's Triumph over the Darkness of the Age* (Angelico Press, 2019), 223–24. Right before this, Bishop Schneider explains how the Calvinist communion method differs from the one described by St. Cyril of Jerusalem in the fourth century.

of a past age of European Christendom, and modern Christians need a recognizably modern set of rites, sleek, direct, patent, simple, comprehensible, action-oriented. The fact that Catholics did not *ask* for such rites is only a sign of their habitual modesty and passivity; nevertheless, scholars were capable of divining hidden intentions that a grateful laity subsequently recognized and welcomed as if these had proceeded forth from their own breasts. It was also claimed, although the impression of hocus-pocus was a little too strong to ignore, that these modern qualities were, remarkably, the very same as those prized by early Christians in *their* rites, about which we have almost no extant records but of which German scholarly reconstructions could achieve the highest verisimilitude.

For a time, such futuristic fantasies took a back seat as the Church under Benedict XVI hunkered down to restore a modicum of dignity to the new rites and began to restore the old ones. At first, one saw the effects of the Ratzingerian approach only in this or that city, but over time they could be detected in many dioceses around the world. The pulsing drumbeat of inculturation died down for a time; one might have thought it had gone extinct. Yet like a rare species of poisonous frog sighted in the remotest part of a rainforest, it has returned in the form of Cardinal Arthur Roche, a most unlikely proponent of flexibility and exoticism. In an interview with the Spanish Catholic magazine *Omnes*, he said the following:

> On this subject, I have often said to the bishops that we have spent the last fifty years preparing the translation of the liturgical texts; and now we must move on to the second phase, which is already foreseen by *Sacrosanctum Concilium*, and that is the inculturation or adaptation of the Liturgy to the other different cultures, while maintaining unity. I think that we should start this work now. But I would like to point out that today there is only one [other Novus Ordo] liturgical "use," not a "rite," and that is in Zaire, in Africa.
>
> It is important to understand what it means that Jesus has shared our nature, and in a historical moment. We have to consider the importance of the Incarnation and, if we can say so, of the action of grace being incarnated in other cultures, with various expressions that are *completely different* from what we have seen and appreciated in Europe for so many years.[27]

The self-appointed spokesman of liturgical reformism, Andrea Grillo, espouses the same program. In a reflection he posted for the one-year anniversary of *Traditionis Custodes*, Grillo writes:

---

[27] "Archbishop Roche: Vatican is Preparing New Document on Liturgical Formation," *Gaudium Press*, English edition, May 16, 2022, www.gaudiumpress.ca/archbishop-roche-vatican-is-preparing-new-document-on-liturgical-formation/; emphasis added.

It is about releasing the true energies of ritual language (verbal and non-verbal) as the *culmen et fons* [summit and source] of all the action of the Church. Today this happens no longer primarily in Latin and in a rite of priests and not of the assembly, but in many languages whose cultures have entered, for sixty years, into the common patrimony of the great ecclesial tradition. A Church that wants to "guard the tradition" must not be afraid of the different cultures with which we can experience faith and express our creed today. This "communal table" will be able to make it possible to assess the limits of what has been done so far and boldly take the way forward on the level of verbal and non-verbal languages. A great construction site can open up: for the tradition of guarding by walking forward, not backward.[28]

When I read such things, my mind wanders back to an intriguing conversation I once held with an older priest who had done his liturgical studies in the 1970s at the Pontifical Athenaeum Sant'Anselmo, an international Benedictine university in Rome that has been known, for quite some time, as a breeding-ground of progressive liturgists (even if, to give the angels their due, there have also been good students and faculty as well).[29] This priest had had the rare good luck to find himself going out to lunch one day with Annibale Bugnini, shortly before the latter's fall from grace. In their tabletalk, Bugnini, a regular *raconteur*, finally came around to the topic of the liturgical reform. The mastermind of the Consilium said to him essentially this:

> What you need to see is that the new liturgy involves *three* stages. First, we had to eliminate the old way of doing things. This was mainly the work of the 1960s, and in thirty years' time, everyone will have forgotten what came before. Second, we had to create something new for the time being: this is what people are calling the "Novus Ordo." But even *this* must disappear, giving way to *complete inculturation*: every liturgy should be made by the community, for its own immediate needs. No liturgical books, just like it was in the ancient church! Even *my* Mass will disappear, by the year 2000.

Lest it be thought that we are putting words into Bugnini's mouth, words he never would have said, consider the following paragraph from a press conference in 1967, in which he goes into considerable detail about the novelty of the Consilium's project:

---

[28] "Il papa bambino e il primo compleanno di *Traditionis custodes*," *Munera: Rivista Europea di Cultura*, July 15, 2022, quoted by Luke Coppen, "*Traditionis custodes*—1 year on," *The Pillar*, July 15, 2022.

[29] See Andrea Gagliarducci, "The increasing influence of the liturgical school Sant'Anselmo in the Vatican," *Catholic News Agency*, July 22, 2021; Luisella Scrosati, "The clique of Saint Anselm conducts the war against ancient Mass," *Rorate Caeli*, February 27, 2023.

The liturgy is in the midst of a period of transition.... It is not only a question of touching up a work of art of great value, but sometimes it is necessary to give new structures to entire rites. It is indeed a question of a fundamental restoration, I would almost say of a recasting and, for certain points, of an actual new creation. Why this fundamental work? Because the image of the liturgy given by the Council is completely different from what it was before, that is, above all rubricist, formalist, centralizing. Now the liturgy expresses itself vigorously in its dogmatic, biblical, and pastoral aspects; it seeks to make itself intelligible in the word, in symbols, in gestures, in signs; it strives to adapt itself to the mentality, to the genius, to the aspirations, and to the demands of each people, in order to penetrate it intimately and to bring Christ there. From a juridical point of view, its fate is largely in the hands of the episcopal conferences, sometimes of the bishops, if not even of the celebrating priests. If the restored liturgy—which some disparagingly call the "new" liturgy—did not achieve this goal, the work of restoration would fail.[30]

Readers familiar with the immediate postconciliar literature will recognize, in this vision, the viewpoint given eloquent expression by the Jesuit songster Joseph Gélineau: that the liturgy is a "permanent workshop" (Grillo's "great construction site").[31] It can be easily shown that the mentality is widespread. Three examples will suffice. First, to resume with master architect Bugnini himself:

The liturgical reform will continue without limits of time and space, initiative and person, modality and rite, so that the liturgy may remain alive for people of all times and every generation.[32]

Echoing him is Dom Anscar J. Chupungco (1939–2013), an influential teacher of generations of students at Sant'Anselmo in Rome:

---

[30] Annibale Bugnini, C. M., Press Conference, January 4, 1967, in *Documentation Catholique* 1967, col. 829, cited in Rivoire, *Does "TC" Pass the Juridical Rationality Test?*, 30–31. For a different translation of the first part of this quotation, see p. 50 above. Cf. Bugnini, *Reform of the Liturgy*, 267–68: "The ideas of experiment and adaptation are closely linked. Adaptation is a necessity if the liturgy is to be the action of all God's people and, while maintaining its essentials everywhere the same, to be integrated with the reality of each people and each nation.... A decisive approach to them [viz., adaptations] will be the task of the third phase of the reform, once the general revision of the liturgical books has been completed, since the latter provide the basic structure...." The entire chapter (267–76), indeed the whole of Bugnini's tome, makes it clear past all gainsaying that such figures as Bergoglio, Roche, Viola, and Grillo adhere with religious submission of will and intellect to Bugnini's vision.
[31] "It would not be right to identify this liturgical renewal with the reform of rites decided on by Vatican II. This reform goes back much further and forward beyond the conciliar prescriptions. The liturgy is a permanent workshop." Joseph Gélineau, SJ, *The Liturgy: Today and Tomorrow*, trans. Dinah Livingstone (Paulist Press, 1978), 11. As we saw earlier, Bugnini (*Reform of the Liturgy*, 221) describes Gélineau as "one of the great masters of the international liturgical world."
[32] Annibale Bugnini, "Rinnovamento nell'ordine," *Notitiæ* 61 (February 1971): 52.

The work of liturgical reform is not finished and, in the spirit of the Council, must never end. The liturgy, like the Church in its human aspect, is inevitably subject to continuous reform, so that it may truly and in every time, and for every culture and historical moment, be the wellspring of ecclesial life.[33]

In 1966, Fr. Clement McNaspy, SJ, perceptively identifies liturgical change as the tip of the iceberg for (unspecified) change in the Church:

> Since we learn by doing, it was plain that by experiencing change in our everyday life of worship we might all become better prepared to accept the further changes called for in other conciliar decisions.... Liturgical change was to be only the beginning; but it did establish the principle.[34]

In laying out his timeline for utopia, Bugnini proved to be no prophet. By the year 2000, the Novus Ordo was still plodding along in its thousand vernaculars, subject to widespread abuse and feeble attempts at community customization that never amounted to much more than a presider's or a committee's vague and often silly ideas about what a celebration "for us" should look like. One might call it creative mediocrity or mediocre creativity, but it was a far cry from the lunchtime prognostication.

Not deceived by the siren song of inculturation or perpetual adaptation, Dom Hugh Somerville Knapman puts his finger on the inevitable result:

> The progressive element among the reforming liturgists saw the 1969 missal as but a stage — a significant one, mind you — in the new project of reconstituting the liturgy as something that continually adapts to the age in which it is celebrated. As we have seen, the result is that the liturgy generally degenerates into reflecting the age rather than speaking to it and sanctifying it. Or more to the point, radical deformations of the liturgy reflect not the face of Christ but the face of the dominant person or clique that imposes them, and so become vehicles not of worship but of narcissism, the cult of self which is the de facto creed of postmodern western society.... We are rootless and thus heartless, replacing self-sacrifice with self-service, with self as the only moral absolute, its inescapable subjectivity and impermanence denying the absolutism it demands for itself. Its secondary absolute, novelty, suffers the same inherent flaw.[35]

---

33 Anscar J. Chupungco, "Costituzione conciliare sulla sacra liturgia. 15° anniversario," *Notitiæ* 149 (December 1978): 580.
34 Clement McNaspy, SJ, *Our Changing Liturgy* (Hawthorn Books, 1966), 32–33. McNaspy was a member of the Board of Directors of the Liturgical Conference and then editor of the magazine *America*.
35 Hugh Somerville Knapman, "Pursuing a Point," *One Foot in the Cloister*, April 13, 2019.

In Roger Buck's entertaining romp *The Gentle Traditionalist Returns*, there is a point in the imaginary conversation where a thoroughly modern person objects that GT (i.e., the Gentle Traditionalist) is nothing other than a medievalist, an escapist, a nostalgic. In reply, GT explains why he loves *tradition in its totality*—from every stage, every place, every period, every culture through which the Catholic religion has passed, not limiting himself to the Middle Ages but not willing to limit himself to modernity either, particularly because the latter seems to operate under an oddly reactionary mentality that traps it in a little box marked "Now":

> Well, the medieval era is an important stage in Catholic tradition. But it's *just one stage*. Catholic tradition covers 3,000 years—not just modern media culture! It begins with the Old Testament, becomes infinitely enriched by the Gospel, takes in Greek thinking with the Patristic era, develops through the so-called "Dark Ages." *Then* comes the medieval era. Finally, the tradition significantly develops in modern times, as well. That, my dear fellow, is the whole point to Tradition—respecting three thousand years of Divine Revelation and dedicated human effort to engage that Revelation. Three thousand years of prayer, thought, study, sacrifice—indeed blood, sweat and tears. But all that, I know, is just three thousand years of encrusted patriarchal baggage to you....
>
> You see why the destruction of tradition troubles me. One so easily gets enslaved to the present moment. All this "Power of Now" stuff is dangerous, if you ask me. It's also arrogant. Thousands of years of human insight, human enquiry, human intellectual and spiritual endeavour—not to mention Divine Revelation—thrown to the winds. And why? Because it didn't jive with the Baby Boomers after the "Summer of Love"?[36]

The liturgy so prized by Roche & Co. is, contrary to their mindlessly-repeated claims about breadth of inclusivity and depth of sources, staggeringly provincial in time and space; it reflects the preoccupations of mid-twentieth-century liturgists of postwar "enlightened" Europe, through whose filtration devices every item of ritual and rubric had to pass.

To the cardinal now in charge of liturgy, we express our modest and humble opinion: we do not want this Bugninian futuristic indigenous/cosmopolitan self-inculturated workshop. Its first iteration failed, and the current geriatric fad for attempting to revive the mimeographed agenda of the reformers not only fails to enthuse, it positively nauseates most of us who still frequent the pews, study in seminaries, or go in unto the altar of God—unto God who giveth joy to our youth.

---

36 Roger Buck, *The Gentle Traditionalist Returns: A Catholic Knight's Tale from Ireland* (Angelico Press, 2019), 126, 129–30.

A LOST CAUSE

Today—and it has already been thus for some years—the intellectual firepower, not to mention the virtue of basic honesty when it comes to Church history and dogmatic theology, is all on the side of traditional Catholic writers. If one wishes to laugh or groan, one need only visit the blogs *Pray, Tell* or *Where Peter Is* to see on display the mettle (such as it is) of the opposing side's views.

In fact, so desperate are the apologists of the new order that they have even tried to make selling points out of defects, as if a used car salesman were to advertise the defects of the lemons in his lot. "This automobile here has bald tires, an iffy alternator, and a transmission on its last legs, but the bright side is that you get to invest your own effort in making it better! That's what we call full, conscious, active ownership, which is your right and duty as a member of a market society!" Here's what one writer found it possible to say on behalf of Paul VI's great project for renewal:

> The liturgy of Paul VI is rather plain.... In fact, the plainness of the Vatican II liturgy is an intentional strategy for the renewal of the Church.... [It can be] compared to a painting class, in which each of the students, guided by an instructor, paints a depiction of the same religious scene.... We need to do the hard work of embracing voluntary poverty and true community. If we do so, the "emptiness" of the Vatican II liturgy will prove to be the fertile emptiness of a tilled field, expectantly waiting for the growth of a new, enculturated, liturgical form.[37]

So, the liturgy, to be better, has to become less liturgical; divine worship, to meet our needs, has to become less divine; what was full of beauty and symbolism and dogma has to be evacuated to make room for our creativity. It's a mighty wonder that none of this was ever on the minds of any Catholics at any time in the history of the Church. Well, okay, there's the Synod of Pistoia, which was condemned by Pope Pius VI.[38] I wonder what Eastern Christians (both Catholic and Orthodox) would have to say to the suggestion that their Divine Liturgy needs a major overhaul because it's far too grandiose.

The same author criticizes the Tridentine Mass for being always the same, which he compares to "a mass-produced image of a religious scene, likely at least a little dated-looking, probably showing Christ as looking strangely European, and laminated in plastic to avoid any tampering." Its sameness prevents, he thinks, its reception and inculturation.

---

[37] Malcolm Schluenderfritz, "Prayer Cards, Painting Class, and Liturgy Wars," *Where Peter Is*, December 9, 2021.
[38] See note 11 on p. 7.

Strange, isn't it, that this was the liturgy with which the entire world was evangelized, leading to flourishing local churches planted everywhere—churches that were rich in vocations when the liturgy was still in Latin, but have so often suffered an inexorable decline after Vatican II and the prioritization of the local and regional (which reached its absurd climax with the Amazon Synod)?[39] Strange, too, that we can find magnificent examples of legitimate inculturation well before the Second Vatican Council...[40]

Again, one has to wonder if Schluenderfritz would dare to make such a critique of Eastern liturgical rites, which have (on the whole) changed even less than the Western ones. Ultimately, only someone absolutely ignorant of ritual and rituality would be able to say that a rite's stability, its givenness, its "unspontaneity" (to use Ratzinger's favored expression), is a defect, rather than a pre-eminent virtue.[41] One is reminded of the bracing remark of C. S. Lewis: "The modern habit of doing ceremonial things unceremoniously is no proof of humility; rather it proves the offender's inability to forget himself in the rite, and his readiness to spoil for everyone else the proper pleasure of ritual."[42]

A rather different Lewis, one Mike Lewis—the most brazen representative of a breakaway movement that could be called "Peterism"—rushed to the defense of his fellow disciple by reminding everyone, in case we might have forgotten, that the Tridentine rite as promulgated by St. Pius V has "unnecessary elements."[43] When challenged about this claim online, Lewis doubled down: "They have plenty of arguments for why even the stupidest parts are absolutely necessary."[44] Silly me, I had been predisposed to think well of the old Mass in its broad lines and tiny details due to the testimony of the Catechism of the Council of Trent, which says there is "nothing superfluous" in the rite of Holy

---

[39] This is manifestly true of South America. Africa is a more complex question, but the growth of the Church there is no victory tale for Vatican II, as it has markedly slowed in the decades since the Council. See *Is African Catholicism a "Vatican II Success Story"? Questioning the Conventional Narrative*, ed. Peter Kwasniewski (Os Justi Press, 2025), 33–42.

[40] See Shawn Tribe, "Inculturation: Japanese and Chinese Madonnas," *Liturgical Arts Journal* [*LAJ*], May 15, 2018; "The Oriental Chasuble of Dom Pierre-Célestin Lou Tseng-Tsiang, OSB," *LAJ*, October 4, 2017; "Liturgical Arts Quarterly 1935: 'Christian Art in the Far East,'" *NLM*, April 20, 2010. Claudio Salvucci has done yeoman's work in the area of Catholic Native American inculturation. See, e.g., his "Forming Scholars of Native American Liturgical 'Uses,'" *LAJ*, February 27, 2018, and https://hoquessing.com/native-liturgies/ for in-depth research tools.

[41] See chapter 19.

[42] C. S. Lewis, *A Preface to Paradise Lost* (Oxford University Press, 1942), 17.

[43] Mike Lewis, "Liturgical Renewal and Traditionalist Trolls," *Where Peter Is*, December 11, 2021.

[44] Mike Lewis (@mfjlewis), "They have plenty of arguments for why even the stupidest parts are absolutely necessary," X, December 11, 2021, https://x.com/mfjlewis/status/1469847612484472837.

Mass, and was later convinced of it by the richly researched arguments in Michael Fiedrowicz's *The Traditional Mass: History, Form, and Theology of the Classical Roman Rite*. Perhaps one day Mike Lewis will attempt to explain why the Roman Catechism is mistaken and will refute Fiedrowicz in scholarship of comparable depth, ideally suffused with intimate experience of his subject matter.

I will not linger any longer over these pathetic articles, which have already been battered to a bloody pulp by the likes of Matthew Hazell and Joseph Shaw. If this is the kind of thing that proponents of the Novus Ordo are reduced to saying, theirs is a lost cause—all the more lost for their painful obliviousness. Other types of argument one will encounter include:

"*The new Mass isn't really as bad as it seems, because with a lot of effort and some luck you can make it almost as beautiful as the old liturgy.*" How often have we seen the noblest efforts of the "reform of the reform" shot down by prelates, like clay pigeons on a shooting range?[45]

"*The decline in the Church would have been even worse if we hadn't changed the liturgy.*" A patent absurdity on the face of it, given that one of the most commonly cited causes for people dropping away from the Church after the Council was the relentless and inexplicable obsession with change, or rather, that peculiar kind of suicidal change that consists of becoming ever more like the world, which, naturally, renders the Church nugatory in the minds of many.[46]

"*What was produced [by Pius V] in 1570 was entirely appropriate for the time. What is produced in this age [by Bugnini, Montini, et al.] is also entirely appropriate for the time.*" This emission of nonsense is taken straight from the lips of Cardinal Roche,[47] astonishingly the Prefect of the Dicastery for Divine Worship, who betrays a total lack of understanding of both what the 1570 missal actually is—a codification of what the Roman Church was already doing[48]—and of liturgical history, where we never see the rites changed from century to century to accommodate what a team of "experts" thinks people need at that moment.

"*The OF and EF [i.e., new rite and old rite] represent two different understandings of the Eucharist, Ecclesiology, the baptismal priesthood,*

---

[45] See, for instance, Eric Sammons, "The Politicization of *Ad Orientem*," *Crisis Magazine*, February 7, 2022.
[46] See Joseph Shaw, "Why Catholics started leaving the Church in droves after Vatican II," *LifeSiteNews*, July 18, 2019; idem, "Survey reveals why Catholics leave Church, including because of watered down teaching," *LifeSiteNews*, July 19, 2019.
[47] Hannah Brockhaus, "Vatican archbishop: Traditional Latin Mass 'experiment' not successful in reconciling SSPX," *Catholic News Agency*, November 16, 2021.
[48] See "Pope Pius V and Liturgical Reform," in Shaw, ed., *The Latin Mass and the Intellectuals*, 3–17.

and the sacrament of Orders (just to mention the most obvious theological differences)." This sentence was submitted to the CDF by a Japanese bishop, one of the nay-sayers quoted in the survey report—you know, the one which Pope Francis directly misrepresents in the letter accompanying *Traditionis Custodes*, as Diane Montagna reported.[49] If the theologies are *that* different—so different that the new rite excludes the old, leaving no place for it in the Church of today—then it's not the Mass of Catholic tradition that's in error but its new fabricated replacement; otherwise, the Catholic Church was never the true Church.[50]

"We have to accept this reform because it was demanded by the Second Vatican Council." Conveniently glossing over the fact that the Council Fathers most certainly did not demand the butchery conducted in the abattoir of the Consilium,[51] and that, in any case, there is no such thing as *the* Novus Ordo, since by its own design it can be done in *literally* a trillion different ways.[52] So what exactly are we talking about anyway?

And so it goes. There is not a single substantive argument in favor of the Novus Ordo, and about ten thousand against it. The only thing its desperate votaries can do, in the end, is to shout *"obey!"* But they forget that the "pay, pray, and obey" mentality has been relentlessly besieged by successive waves of clerical scandals—sexual abuse, financial criminality, doctrinal aberrations, and yes, liturgical offenses that cry out to heaven for vengeance; they forget that, by this point in time, committed orthodox Catholics have learned that when they are told they "must" do or believe something "for their own good" or "for the good of the Church" without further explanation, they have an intuition based on irrefutable experience that this is very likely what they must *not* do or believe. Contrary to the impotent thundering of Michael Sean Winters ("It is time, it is past time, for everybody who is interested in remaining Catholic to receive the conciliar liturgical reforms"[53]), the truth of the matter is quite the contrary: it is time, past time, for everybody who is interested in remaining Catholic to

---

49 See note 14 on p. 90.
50 In short, if *Traditionis Custodes* is right, then it is wrong; for if the new liturgy reflects a new theology not in continuity with the past, then it is not the past that is wrong, but Francis and by extension the heretical school of thought for which he serves as the mouthpiece (see Julia Meloni, *The St. Gallen Mafia Exposed* [TAN Books, 2021]; "The Crimes and Heresies of Pope Francis, Their Causes and Effects, and the Action to Be Taken," *Rorate Caeli*, May 2, 2024). For an irrefutable argument against *TC* based on the impossibility of the Church contradicting herself in the way in which the motu proprio would necessitate, see the essay by an anonymous priest, "The 'Hermeneutic of Rupture' Cancels Pope Benedict—and the Council," in Kwasniewski, ed., *From Benedict's Peace to Francis's War*, 341–56.
51 See note 1 on p. 69.
52 See note 4 on p. 70, and Farret d'Astiès, "Mass of Paul VI 'Well Celebrated'—a Myth!"
53 Michael Sean Winters, "As Francis reinforces limits on Latin Mass, it's past time to embrace Vatican II," *National Catholic Reporter*, February 27, 2023.

abandon a reform so arrogantly concocted, so grievously botched, so destructive in consequences.

Over the course of five and a half decades of artificial life-support, the Novus Ordo has been pushed by bureaucratic functionaries and career liturgists, but has managed to attract few zealous lovers. Its enforcing martinets have had to resort to increasingly dishonest and brutal methods. Unable to vindicate their cause by argument or demographics, they flex the muscle of papal authoritarianism, which is the only thing they have left. This is why, as many observers have pointed out, *Traditionis Custodes* is a monumental and embarrassing admission of defeat. Gregory DiPippo explains why:

> In the wake of this failure [of the promised "new Pentecost"], the post-Conciliar Catholic Church finds itself a post-revolutionary society, no less than France was in 1794, or Russia was in 1925. And when a revolution fails, when "freedom, equality and brotherhood" lie buried under a pyramid of severed heads, when the worker's paradise consists of millions of square miles of rust and cadavers, its paladins can go forward on one of two paths. The hard path is to recognize that the revolution has not achieved its goals, and work to rebuild their society in the light of that recognition. The easy path is to find some "reactionaries" and "counter-revolutionaries," and blame the revolution's failure on them.
>
> The surest sign that a revolution has failed, and chosen to take the easy path, is its fear of the past, its fear of the memory of what life was really like before the revolution. And this is why, in the midst of a tidal wave of crises within the Church, a hammer has been dropped where it has been dropped: not on the German Synodal Way, or the various Catholic institutions that have to all intents and purposes walked away from the Faith. The problem so grave that it must be met with the same furious scribbled-on-the-back-of-a-napkin haste that we remember from Fr. Bouyer's memoirs is not the long-standing persistence of grave liturgical abuses, the de facto absence of catechetical formation in once-Catholic nations, or widespread moral, doctrinal and financial corruption. The hammer has been dropped, rather, on the father and mother who were born at least 20 years after the last time a cleric used the word "aggiornamento" unironically, and on their children who are too young to remember the papacy of Benedict XVI.
>
> There can be no clearer sign that the post-Conciliar revolution is totally uninteresting to the rising generations, and knowing this, [it] grows deathly afraid, and resorts to doing by force what it cannot do by persuasion.... A dying revolution is not a dead revolution; it can still strike out and cause pain, and will likely do so. But in the very act of doing so, it confesses that it has failed and is dying. Do not be afraid. The revolution is over.[54]

---

[54] Gregory DiPippo, "The Revolution Is Over," *NLM*, August 1, 2021.

We who love the Church our Mother and her treasury of tradition offer our intelligent obedience to the coherent and consistent Magisterium of the ages, and—if we are Catholics of *the Latin rite*—offer to God our rational worship (*logike latreia*, Rom 12:1) through the traditional Roman liturgy or one of its close relations, and, above all, through the Mass of the Ages.[55] That is what the wearisome exile of the past several decades has taught us, with an ever-increasing clarity as time goes on. The traditionalist movement arises from and manifests the supernaturally ingrafted "sense of the faith" of faithful Catholics:

> The *sensus fidei fidelis* confers on the believer the capacity to discern whether or not a teaching or practice is coherent with the true faith by which he or she already lives.... The *sensus fidei fidelis* also enables individual believers to perceive any disharmony, incoherence, or contradiction between a teaching or practice and the authentic Christian faith by which they live. They react as a music lover does to false notes in the performance of a piece of music. In such cases, believers interiorly resist the teachings or practices concerned and do not accept them or participate in them.... Alerted by their *sensus fidei*, individual believers may deny assent even to the teaching of legitimate pastors if they do not recognise in that teaching the voice of Christ, the Good Shepherd. "The sheep follow [the Good Shepherd] because they know his voice. They will not follow a stranger, but they will run away from him because they do not know the voice of strangers" (Jn 10:4–5).... Thanks to the *sensus fidei fidelis* and sustained by the supernatural prudence that the Spirit confers, the believer is able to sense, in new historical and cultural contexts, what might be the most appropriate ways in which to give an authentic witness to the truth of Jesus Christ, and moreover to act accordingly.[56]

By this sense of the faith, we hear and recognize the Shepherd's voice and distinguish it from the voice of hirelings who serve the sheep malnourishing or toxiferous fodder.

---

[55] And yes, this phrase is totally justifiable: see Kwasniewski, *Once and Future Roman Rite*, 33–77. The *Quam oblationem* of the Roman Canon conveys this Pauline idea in Rom 12:1 to perfection: see ibid., 236–37.
[56] International Theological Commission, "*Sensus Fidei* in the Life of the Church" (2014), nos. 61–63; 65.

❦ 6 ❧
The Hunt for the Elusive Unicorn

> At the same time, I ask you [bishops] to be vigilant in ensuring that every liturgy be celebrated with decorum and fidelity to the liturgical books promulgated after Vatican Council II, without the eccentricities that can easily degenerate into abuses…

THESE ARE THE WORDS OF POPE FRANCIS, in the letter that accompanies his motu proprio *Traditionis Custodes* of July 16, 2021.

Two days later, on July 18, we were given a textbook example of eccentricity in a Sunday Mass held by pastor Rainer Maria Schießler at the Hofbräuhaus München, a famous brewery restaurant, where Mass is held once a month in the midst of mascots and Biersteins. On July 23, we were given an example of abuse (to say the least) in a Gay Mass in the Archdiocese of Berlin, featuring rainbow-colored cloths leading up to the altar and hanging from the ambo. These may be outliers—although one sees evidence of a disturbing number of such "outliers."

Yes, it's true: not *every* local church has the ambition to simulate Mass at a beerhall or drape ecclesiastical furnishings in rainbow flags. But why have such things happened *even once*? And why do sacrileges *keep happening*, again and again? For they do; the evidence is always fresh, and only ostriches of Olympic head-burying skill deny it. Yet the manner in which the new liturgy is celebrated all across the world hardly gives one reason for elation. In addition to universal banality and entrenched abuses, one need only think of the ubiquitous promotion of girls and women into liturgical roles in the sanctuary (no wonder some are agitating to become deaconesses—at the least!)[1] and the crazy Communion time, where everyone lines up as if queuing at a snack bar, where Our Lord is dishonored repeatedly, where fragments are lost and trampled under foot, and where, once again, the non-ordainable are deployed in full force, in spite of nearly twenty centuries of contrary practice in the Church of God.[2] Examples like this can, needless to say, be multiplied *ad nauseam*.[3] And what of the *everyday crimes* against

---
[1] For the theological case against female altar servers and lectors, see my book *Ministers of Christ*.
[2] On Eucharistic good practice and contrasting abuses, see my book *Holy Bread of Eternal Life*.
[3] Numerous photos illustrating the things just mentioned are compiled at the post "Crocodile Tears and Hand-Wringing: No GPS Coordinates for the Unicorn," *Tradition and Sanity* Substack, August 26, 2024. YouTube has made possible the compilation of

tradition, sound theology, piety, decorum, and care for the Body and Blood of Christ[4]—crimes that are no less offensive to God and no less harmful to the faith of the people, yet attract little notice because they are everywhere taken for granted?

Let's not forget that 99% of Novus Ordo Masses are marred by egregious abuses that are not legally-positivistically *defined* as abuses, but are still abuses in the sight of God and man, for all the bad effects they have had and will always have: *versus populum* celebration; Communion taken in the hand, standing in a bus-ticket queue; the traffic of unvested lay "ministers" between nave and sanctuary, and the feminization of ministerial roles; the relentless banality of non-sacred music; the total non-presence of the native language of the Latin rite; et cetera and so forth. No shopwork can repair this defective vehicle.

What has really happened, if we are being completely honest with ourselves, is that our bar for what counts as "reverent" is incredibly low at this point; it means something like "sprinkled with Catholic touches" or perhaps even "not intolerable." Let's face it: if a Catholic from 1950 could be suddenly transported to a church where a "reverent (according to its participants) Novus Ordo" is going on, he would quickly exit, thinking he had mistakenly entered a Protestant church or the temple of a sect. If a pope from the Middle Ages were parachuted into a "reverent Novus Ordo," he would probably summon the Holy Inquisition to prepare some pyres outside, or, at very least, dictate to his amanuensis a bull of excommunication.

That's why I don't buy this business about "only 1% of new Masses are seriously abusive." This is to miss the point entirely, for the Novus Ordo *itself* is a standing abuse in the Roman Church. It forces upon us the stark alternative between a form of liturgy handed down and received, whole and entire, as a rule of faith and law of life, and a form of liturgy willfully fabricated, violently imposed, and savagely destructive of credal, devotional, and moral ecosystems. The former is a healing and elevating presence wherever it exists; the latter remains a monument of rupture however it exists. Until the rupture is healed by the full restoration of the traditional rite and the phasing-out of

---

a vast catalog of liturgical abuse footage, from decades ago down to the present, that substantiates the claims of traditionalists. I know personally a man who, on a visit to a foreign country for a conference, just happened to step inside a church where a priest was performing a New Age-style baptism, caught it on video, and sent it to the Vatican, which subsequently, on further investigation, discovered that this priest had used an invalid formula for hundreds of people, none of whom were therefore actually baptized. If this layman had not decided to step into that church, how much longer would the travesty have continued? What we see online, so far from representing "only the worst," represents the tip of the iceberg.

4 See "No Eucharistic Revival without Restoration," *Tradition and Sanity* Substack, April 20, 2023.

the modern rite, there is no solution to the "liturgy wars" — only more or less temporary truces.

It's time we admit it. The fabled "unicorn" (code language for the reverent, traditional-looking, Ratzingerian Novus Ordo, which is supposed to satisfy the yearnings of devout Catholics) is still wandering at large and rarely sighted. The 1% statistic sometimes peddled in reference to abusive Masses is more likely to describe the unicorn Novus Ordo. After all, even where eccentricities and abuses are not abundant, banality, verbosity, anthropocentrism, and feminism still prevail.

For over fifty years, popes have been wringing their hands about various kinds of abuses and the prevailing lack of reverence and beauty in the Novus Ordo.[5] Yet nothing much has happened. Neither popes nor bishops have enforced the existing rules. Neither popes nor bishops have punished the recalcitrant or promoted outstanding models. Paul VI, who saddled the Church with this crisis to begin with, complained about ongoing liturgical abuse; nothing changed. John Paul II complained about liturgical abuse, even apologizing for it (as he apologized for lots of things). He lifted a finger or two, but only a little bit changed, and only here or there. Indeed, in Poland, where the new liturgy had been done about as conservatively as can be imagined, kneeling for Communion was eventually replaced by standing, and then, at last, Communion in the hand was introduced during Covid and has now spread like a cancer. The Novus Ordo cannot long abide tradition; it will dissolve it in due course. The tough-love Instruction *Redemptionis Sacramentum* of 2004 was supposed to be the great moment, in the wake of John Paul II's encyclical *Ecclesia de Eucharistia*, when the new Mass would *finally* be restored to rubrical rightness and resplendent reverence. What happened? Fields of crickets from one end of the earth to the other. A friend of mine called the chancery of her diocese one day and asked if she could report a violation against *Redemptionis Sacramentum* (following that document's recommended procedure). The person who had taken the call went around the office asking if anyone had heard of the document, and then told her: "No, we haven't heard of it. We're sorry." End of conversation. Benedict XVI, too, complained about liturgical abuse; his shy personality and premature resignation prevented him from carrying through the program of revitalization outlined in his writings.[6] Pope Francis has added his crocodile tears to the handwringing of his predecessors:

---

[5] See my article "Fidelity to Liturgical Law and the Rights of the Faithful," *OnePeterFive*, July 3, 2017.

[6] Unlike his predecessors (and his successor), Benedict XVI actually *did* something to initiate a counterforce: he liberalized the old Roman rite to serve as an objective standard, a stable reference point, an impetus for a "new Liturgical Movement." The

I am saddened by abuses in the celebration of the liturgy on all sides. In common with Benedict XVI, I deplore the fact that "in many places the prescriptions of the new Missal are not observed in celebration, but indeed come to be interpreted as an authorization for or even a requirement of creativity, which leads to almost unbearable distortions."[7]

Saddening abuses. *Deplorable* facts. *Unbearable* distortions. Surely, then, they must be dealt with swiftly and mercilessly, in the same manner in which the pope and his courtiers have chosen to deal with the pressing problem of the traditionalists!

Such rhetorical tropes are as shallow as the feelings of comfort they evoke. How do we know that Pope Francis won't take the well-rooted problem of bad liturgy seriously? Look at footage of a papal Mass: it is the dull and horizontal ritual of a dying *Weltanschauung*. This is the pope who violated the rules for whose feet could be washed on Holy Thursday, and then, having modified the rules, proceeded to violate the new ones; who, indeed, chronically violates the rules concerning vestments and the manner of concelebration.[8] This is the pope who does not kneel or genuflect before the Most Holy Sacrament of the Altar, but who becomes surprisingly flexible when it's time to kneel, literally, at the feet of politicians.[9] This is the pope on whose watch the Basilica of St. Peter, the premiere pilgrimage church of Christendom, has outlawed Masses at side altars, undergrounded the Mass of the Ages, and nearly banished the use of Latin — at *St. Peter's*, for crying out loud, the one shrine in the world where the Church's mother tongue has always been at home since the fourth century and would always be fitting.[10] This is the pope under whom the Vatican's publishing house decided not to reprint the Liturgy of the Hours in Latin — its *editio typica* or standard edition — since it might foster dangerous linguistic liaisons.[11] Finally, this

---

policy of *Summorum Pontificum*, welcomed by younger clergy and magnified by the internet, was beginning to have a knock-on effect in the Novus Ordo sphere — and that is the *primary* reason things were beginning to improve on that side of the liturgical divide: the "gravitational pull" of the old rite.
[7] Francis, Letter to the Bishops of the Whole World Accompanying the Apostolic Letter *Traditionis Custodes*.
[8] See Gerald Murray, "Papal Abuse of Liturgical Law," *The Catholic Thing*, March 22, 2022.
[9] See, e.g., "Why Doesn't Pope Francis Kneel Before the Blessed Sacrament?," *Torch of the Faith News*, June 2, 2016, www.torchofthefaith.com/news.php?extend.1332; Philip Pullella, "Pope kisses feet of South Sudan leaders, urging them to keep the peace," *Reuters*, April 12, 2019.
[10] So great a global protest met the initial draconian rules that some exceptions had to be made; nevertheless, the policy remains contrary to canon law, a fine exhibit of the antinomianism that reigns in the upper echelons of the Church these days. See Edward Pentin, "After Outcry, Vatican Eases Restrictions on Individual Masses in St. Peter's Basilica," *National Catholic Register*, June 22, 2021.
[11] See John Zuhlsdorf, "Can't get 'Liturgy of the Hours' in Latin," *Fr. Z's Blog*, September 6, 2017.

is the pope who, impatient of centuries of custom, further simplified the already simplified rite for a papal funeral, as if to get the nuisance over with.[12] No, this pope is no "guardian of tradition" (*traditionis custos*), nor will he lead the long-awaited crusade to bring forth "the spiritual richness and the theological depth of this [new] Missal" (to borrow a hyperbolic phrase from Benedict XVI's letter to the bishops of July 7, 2007). Nor can we expect any better from the influential churchmen of his making, who are as eager to cancel Tridentine Masses as they are to allow or even celebrate Masses for any and every subculture, especially if it calls itself by a string of capital letters.[13]

God Himself, Alpha and Omega, to whom all things bow, graces us with His presence in the Holy Mass. Because it is His gift to us of what is divine and most holy, the Mass must be rubrically inflexible, thoroughly scripted, as objective as the everlasting hills and the surging seas, carving out a space free of private personality in order to let the unchanging God of love act in our midst, Three Persons acting upon all persons. With the TLM, it makes almost no difference who the priest is, as long as he knows what he's doing. I can go (and I have been) to Latin Masses all over the world, and I know just what I'm getting. The priest does a ritual that corresponds to what is printed in my hand missal. I might barely see his face, and at a Low Mass might never hear him speak a vernacular language. He is, as St. Thomas says, an "animated instrument" of the High Priest: it is quite clear Who is in charge, Who is the primary actor. It is theocentric and Christocentric.

In contrast, the Novus Ordo is clericocentric, depending on the priest for its "reverent" realization. A lover of sights and sounds might praise Holy Loftitude Parish because *that* priest at *that* place does it *that* way: with smells and bells, *ad orientem*, a pinch of Latin for Roman Catholic effect, kneeling for Communion, and so forth. As discussed in chapter 4, all of it is optional: at the option of the priest and his "team," at the option of a willing congregation without speed-dial Susans, at the option of a willing bishop. It quickly becomes a matter of "this good and holy priest does the Mass right," instead of "the good and holy God gave us in His Providence a good and holy liturgy, on which we can always rely." Martin Mosebach leans into this contrast:

> Many people ... will ask, "Isn't it still possible to celebrate the new liturgy of Pope Paul VI worthily and reverently?" Naturally it is possible, but the very fact that *it is possible* is the weightiest

---

[12] See "Pope Francis simplifies papal funeral rites," *Aleteia*, November 21, 2024; Michael Hoffman, "Putting the Nail in the (Pope's) Coffin," *Crisis Magazine*, December 6, 2024.
[13] See, e.g., Michael J. O'Loughlin, "Mass for LGBTQ Catholics met with protesters in St. Louis," *Outreach*, April 26, 2024, https://outreach.faith/2024/04/mass-for-lgbtq-catholics-met-with-protesters-in-st-louis/.

argument against the new liturgy. It has been said that monarchy's death knell sounds once it becomes necessary for a monarch to be competent: this is because the monarch, in the old sense, is legitimated by his birth, not his talent. This observation is even truer in the case of the liturgy: liturgy's death knell is sounded once it requires a holy and good priest to perform it. The faithful must never regard the liturgy as something the priest does by his own efforts. It is not something that happens by good fortune or as the result of a personal charism or merit.[14]

The traditionalists' issue with the Novus Ordo has never fundamentally been at the level of good looks, even if we'd readily admit that a new Mass dressed like the old Mass can be a feast for sore eyes. No. It is about the traditional liturgy in its total integrity on every level, starting with its ancient and venerable *lex orandi* found in the corpus of prayers, the chants, ceremonies, rubrics, and customs. These are either utterly missing, wildly mingled, or woefully mangled in the new liturgical books.[15] The new and old rites (thankfully, Pope Francis has rid us of the clumsy "ordinary" and "extraordinary" jargon) are, in fact, nearly always different[16]—and often radically so.[17] This is why, quite apart from its rarity, the "high Novus Ordo" is not and never could be appealing to Latin Mass-goers. They might even say, in the words of the Psalmist, *Salva me ex ore leonis, et a cornibus unicornium humilitatem meam,* "Save me from the lion's mouth, and my lowness from the horns of the unicorns" (Ps 21:22).

In the years that have passed since July 16, 2021, we have been treated to a chorus of well-meaning bishops and priests who repeat some version of the refrain: "We're very sorry to have to stop the traditional Latin Mass, but we're sure you'll learn to adjust to the Novus Ordo—if only you bring the right spirit to it." Whoever can speak thus hasn't got a clue about what attracts Catholics to the old rite, how profoundly the rites are different, and how inadequate the modern rite will always seem in comparison. Nor do they understand why educated, serious, and devout Catholics have been sparring over this issue *for more than*

---

14 Martin Mosebach, *The Heresy of Formlessness: The Roman Liturgy and Its Enemy,* trans. Graham Harrison (Angelico Press, 2018), 15–16.
15 On these three kinds of problems, see the two articles by Matthew Hazell already mentioned, "'All the Elements of the Roman Rite'?" and "The Scattering of the Propers," and his "The Prayers for the Feast of St. Lawrence in the Post-Vatican II Liturgical Reforms," *Rorate Caeli,* August 10, 2021.
16 See, *inter alia,* Pristas, *Collects of the Roman Missals.*
17 Anthony Cekada, *Work of Human Hands: A Theological Critique of the Mass of Paul VI* (Philothea Press, 2010). Cekada's work is invaluable for its exhaustive analysis of the tendencies found in the Novus Ordo, but his assertion of its invalidity is unwarranted by the evidence. All the same, sacramental validity is not a panacea; for the validity of the new Mass makes its lack of respect for tradition, for the priesthood, for the faithful, and for Christ Himself, all the worse.

half a century. It's not the sort of thing about which you can shrug your shoulders and "move on." You cannot unsee what you have seen, unknow what you have come to know.[18] And that is why, in the absence of a competent pope, the troubles will continue and indeed multiply. Problems of this magnitude don't evaporate simply because a powerful person orders them to vanish. *They go away when truth and justice are recognized and accepted*. Physical healing may be more or less automatic, but moral and spiritual healing doesn't work that way.

Yes, God may be asking you to suffer, for a time, the loss of your local TLM. *But this loss is still an evil*. To begin with, it is objectively evil for a liturgical rite organically developed over more than 1,600 years to be repudiated. It is objectively evil for us to be cut off from the gift of tradition.[19] It is objectively evil to be deprived of a strong daily link with our ancestors in the Faith and of a rich source of spiritual nourishment on which we had come to rely. God does not and cannot will these evils as such (*pace* the Abu Dhabi declaration), for He does not deny Himself or repent of His gifts. Yes, He sometimes asks priests to suffer imprisonment in a concentration camp where they cannot say Mass or must say a rushed and whispered Mass with a scrap of smuggled bread and a thimbleful of wine. Needless to say (or is it?), this is not the normal, natural, social and cultural situation that is fitting for tradition-constituted rational animals. That is why God has not willed that most Christians most of the time should be incarcerated and deprived of their basic rights *or* rites. In short, the suppression of the Roman Church's traditional form of worship is an evil that God could never will, nor could He drape the mantle of his holy authority over the churchmen who inflict it; this is why they should be resisted with all our might—resisted especially by the clergy.

We've all heard of "fiat currency." Pope Francis believes in "fiat culture." As Tracey Rowland shows in *Culture and the Thomist Tradition: After Vatican II*, the Fathers of the Council neither possessed nor were able to formulate a coherent account of culture and therefore of how Catholicism was supposed to permeate and animate culture. This is why they ended up with an awkward view in which two forces—a religious subculture and a modern anti-culture—were supposed to blend and produce a new synthesis, which, however, must remain as crippled as either of its elements. Pope Francis's *Traditionis Custodes* shows that he thinks it's possible, by papal *ukase*, to tell Catholics who have embraced

---

[18] See my articles "Comparison of Old and New Prayers for Blessing of Ashes," *OnePeterFive*, February 26, 2020; "A Comparison of the Old and New Blessing of Candles on Candlemas," *NLM*, February 1, 2021.

[19] See "The Gift of Liturgical Tradition" in Kwasniewski, *Reclaiming Our Roman Catholic Birthright*, 161–79.

and internalized traditional worship—which it is perfectly *dignum et justum* for them to engage in—that they must simply "transition" over to the modern liturgy of Paul VI, sooner or later. As if we just put on or put off our deepest thoughts and feelings, our surrounding world, like a piece of clothing. That, however, is modernity's view: we *are* what we *will* ourselves to be; we are disembodied minds that choose our identity.[20] So false is this view that it cannot be refuted by argument; it is refuted by the whole of reality at every moment.

The authors and promoters of *Traditionis Custodes* are not concerned only about whether or not Catholics "accept" Vatican II or the new liturgy. Of course they want us to say we do. But their goal is not verifying our assent to some propositions and then letting us get on with our lives. Their goal is to exterminate the possibility of our living a coherently traditional Catholic life in adherence to the perennial Magisterium. It is, in that sense, precisely an anti-Catholic campaign, as Sebastian Morello and Massimo Viglione bring out so well.[21] The partisans of Bergoglianity would rather see a sparsely-attended Novus Ordo church than a full one with the traditional Mass; a tiny family that worships contemporarily than a large family that worships timelessly; fewer priestly and religious vocations, as long as they are liberal and lavender, than an abundance of vocations cut from old-fashioned cloth, be it black, brown, or gray. The specious hermeneutic of continuity has been summarily swapped out for the *hermeneutic of hatred*—a hatred of the past, of memory and identity, of history, of reality.

A priest friend wrote to me:

> I think that people need to wake up to the fact that this is about so much more than the TLM—Francis is attempting to eliminate a whole way of being Catholic, even for people who never go to the TLM. The English liturgist Clifford Howell was wont to say that the use of vernacular in the Liturgy was pointing towards a new world order that couldn't be expressed coterminously in Latin. I realize now that what he meant is that essentially the new liturgy is a social movement based on the wholesale rejection of the Catholic worldview. The Old Mass is too off-message now to be allowed to continue.

To our conservative Catholic friends we say: thanks for the reminders about how the pope's motu proprio is a cross, willed by God, that we must carry. That's true. At the same time, let's not turn our

---

20 See Jason Morgan, "Triumph of the Will: The Novus Ordo, RIP," *The Remnant* online, August 3, 2021.
21 See Sebastian Morello, "Revolution and Repudiation: Governance Gone Awry" and Massimo Viglione, "'They Will Throw You out of the Synagogues' (John 16:2): The Hermeneutic of Cain's Envy against Abel," in Kwasniewski, ed., *From Benedict's Peace to Francis's War*, 94–99 and 103–11.

religion, centered on the sacrifice of Calvary, into a version of Buddhism bedecked with a Christian symbol. We do not wave aside evils as illusions on the path to enlightenment and nirvana; we recognize them for what they are—ontological parasites—and we strive to overcome them by the grace of a personal God who reveals Himself to us. As Leo XIII says in his encyclical *Libertas Præstantissimum*, evils in a society may need to be tolerated for a time, but they may never be approved as regular fixtures, much less hailed as advantages. And if the injustice is deep enough, it must call forth our total effort at eradicating it.

Meanwhile, program your GPS to find the nearest Latin Mass. Though it may be far away, it will likely be easier to find—and will certainly be more Catholic—than the fabled unicorn.

THE PROGRESSIVE NARRATIVE CRUMBLES BEFORE REALITY

Pope Francis's various documents on the liturgy from the past eleven years—*Traditionis Custodes, Desiderio Desideravi*, his speeches at Sant'Anselmo, and the like—are remarkable displays of the extent to which the aging nostalgics of Vatican II have simply refused to let go of their utopian dream, in spite of all argument and evidence opposing it; have refused even to consider that it might be time to release their death-grip on the Novus Ordo, that unkempt love-child of liturgical freethinkers. With an obliviousness that stretches the bounds of credulity, the pope—in this respect no different from most of the curial court that surrounds him, as well as their friends in high places throughout the hierarchy—eloquently shores up an official narrative totally disconnected from the reality on the ground.[22]

The pope's narrative—identical to that which any member of the liturgical establishment would espouse—is that the Council brought about a tremendous renewal in the Church, with people eagerly worshiping, more actively than ever, having swept away the accumulated cobwebs of a dusty past to let the light of renewal stream in. The only dark cloud in an otherwise bright sky consists of the anti-ecclesial backwardists who, in their discontented nostalgia, idolize and ideologize a superseded liturgy for their own sinister purposes. Thus, addressing students and faculty at Sant'Anselmo on May 7, 2022, he said:

> I would like to underline the danger, the temptation of *liturgical formalism*: going after forms, formalities rather than reality, as we see today in those movements that try to go backwards and deny Vatican Council II itself. In this way, the celebration is recitation, it is something without life, without joy.... I emphasize again that the liturgical life, and the study of it, must lead to greater ecclesial

---

[22] See Gregory DiPippo, "What Is an Ideology?," *NLM*, May 7, 2022.

unity, not division. When liturgical life becomes something of a banner of division, there is the odour of the devil, the deceiver, in there. It is not possible to worship God and at the same time turn liturgy into a battlefield for issues that are not essential, or indeed for outdated questions and to take sides, starting from the liturgy, on ideologies that divide the Church.

The pope then compared those who lamented Pius XII's deconstruction of Holy Week to the Pharisees who rent their garments. Similarly, in the address he gave at the same Pontifical Institute on January 20, 2023 as part of a course for diocesan liturgy officials, Pope Francis sternly warned against putting "beautiful ritual" ahead of Christ. (What about those who appreciate beautiful ritual because it unites them to Christ in knowledge and love, and helps them to share His transcendent peace with their fellow Christians at worship?)

The pope's perceptions are so far removed from reality, on so many levels, that it causes one to wonder which planet he is living on, or whether he receives any accurate information whatsoever from his handlers. For a man who travels a lot, stopping in Singapore to tell Southeast Asians that all religions are paths to God and are rather like the different languages people speak, he seems entirely averse to making time on his schedule to visit communities of traditional Catholics, even though, in the order of charity, they deserve his fatherly support and benevolent assistance infinitely more than polytheists and animists do. The pope has no experience at all of the "life and energy" of the traditional movement, and seemingly no awareness of how deathly dull is the Novus Ordo in most parishes — aging, shrinking, few children, few or no vocations, representing the "active participation" of a few percent of once-Catholic populations driven away from the "Church of Vatican II" by its sheer banality, irreverence, irrelevance, and lack of anything meaningful to say to anyone hungry for encounter with the mystery of God. *That's* what's "senza vita, senza gioia."

Now let us depart from fantasy and look at the way things actually are.

For over fifty years, the architects, proponents, and enforcers of the liturgical reform have had every opportunity, resource, and advantage to promote the glories of their new rites. They have had behind them the most powerful institutional force in the world (the papacy) and all the episcopal conferences of the globe; all the university departments, institutes, seminaries, and chanceries; all the propaganda and publishing rights; and nearly endless funding. Yet their work has rarely generated notable enthusiasm among the faithful. At most, it was accepted as "what the authorities require." Some accepted it with regrets or misgivings. Some used it as an excuse to indulge in a game of "make-your-own-liturgy." A large number simply left the Church and never came back. True, there were many reasons for that exodus, but there is no doubt that many could no longer recognize in the liturgy the marks of the true Church: one, holy, catholic, and apostolic. The Church's loss of Catholics after the Council, during the period of liturgical volatility, rivals in magnitude the exodus of Catholics to the Protestant revolt in the sixteenth century. At least in Western countries, which were the cradle and laboratory of the "new and improved Mass," the most striking feature of the period of the reform—which, let's recall, was packaged and sold as the great liberator of active participation and as the key to unleashing the dormant evangelizing force of the Church in the modern world—has been a relentless downward trend in every relevant indicator of Catholic life. One need only recall the pathetic numbers of new priests and new religious in the dioceses.

Meanwhile, across all these desert decades, the traditional liturgy lived on, in spite of every imaginable disadvantage. The pope was against it. Most of the bishops were against it. The clergy usually would not bother to listen to the "malcontents." The laity often did not know how to organize themselves or how to accomplish their aims. Its greatest apologist early on was a Welsh schoolteacher, Michael Davies, whom no professional liturgist would deign even to mention. He was beneath notice, perhaps even beneath contempt—someone who, for lack of a university position among the Consilium cognoscenti, went around speaking to ragtag and bobtail audiences of ordinary Catholics who just loved the Catholic faith and its noble traditions. Events were held off-premises in those dark days, because no Catholic institution would lend a platform to such a seditious figure. (I'll never forget the one time I heard Davies speak in person, during my grad school days. In a stuffy room somewhere in Arlington, Virginia, he spoke on the uprising in the Vendée. We greeted each other afterwards, and in the months thereafter, exchanged a few letters in the mail. A seed was planted.)

Still, the movement doggedly advanced. Some bishops and cardinals began to offer the old rite in public. Traditional priestly and religious communities kept up a steady rate of growth at a time when vocations in dioceses and conventional religious orders were well beneath replacement rate (apart from the Legionaries of Christ—a bastion of manipulative mind-control run by a monstrous abuser). Then, in an ecclesiastical Perestroika, John Paul II recognized the "rightful aspirations" of lovers of tradition, and finally Benedict XVI vindicated them by confirming what many traditionalists had maintained all along: that the traditional Roman rite had never been abrogated and that it remains a heritage "sacred and great" for all of us. Benedict

XVI's admiration and acknowledgement of the permanent place of liturgical tradition is, needless to say, the only attitude consistent with confessional Catholicism. To this day, the traditional liturgy generates a joyful enthusiasm that can be seen in packed pews, copious cadres of altar servers, choirs and scholas singing great music, coffee hours and book clubs, mothers' groups and intramural kickball. And barely a touch of nostalgia, because the average age of these communities is somewhere between 15 and 25.

Consider the facts, then.

The reformed liturgy, in spite of enjoying every possible institutional advantage, has failed to bring about the dramatic re-energizing of the laity and re-Christianization of the world that was promised as its sole justification. In many Western nations the number of Massgoers has dwindled to a mere fraction of the baptized, and even the rudiments of practice — baptism, marriage, and church funerals — are increasingly abandoned. Priests in the United States are, by now, well aware that Novus Ordo congregations have lost as much as a third of their numbers due to Covidtide shutdowns and the episcopal "lifting of the requirement to attend Mass," which severed the last feeble tie that connected some Catholics to their Church. These people are not coming back and represent the next greatest exodus since that of the immediate aftermath of the Council.

Though the traditional movement has suffered under every disadvantage, it has never stopped growing since its birth in the mid-1960s. Since it is widely characterized by families generously open to life and by an abundant harvest (proportionally speaking) of priestly and religious vocations, it shows every sign of growing exponentially, as indeed the Amish have done as they quietly become the most vibrant of the USA's Protestant branches.[23] Maybe the slur on traditionalists as "Amish Catholics" should be taken as a compliment in disguise. Faithful men and women disgusted with Covid-related policies (no Mass, no Communion on the tongue, the sacramental of the mask, the rite of Purellification, etc.) migrated to TLM communities and found a new home in the only place in town with Eucharistic reverence or even a Mass to attend; and still another mighty influx occurred after the pope provided global free advertising with his motu proprio. As I like to say, if traditionalists had pooled all their bank accounts across the world, we could never have purchased as much effective advertising as *Traditionis Custodes* bought us, without our even asking for it.

We have, however, one crucial advantage that outweighs all the disadvantages: the most ancient, most resilient, most widespread rite of

---

[23] See David Larson, "Live Like the Amish?," *Crisis Magazine*, September 8, 2021.

Christendom, one that never ceases to dazzle and delight God-thirsting souls. And they, the partisans of an exhausted reform, have one crucial disadvantage that outweighs all their advantages: a banal, on-the-spot fabrication that felt dated practically the day it appeared, a committee compromise that lacks the nobility sought by conservatives as well as the "permanent workshop" sought by progressives in their fatal love affair with inculturation.[24]

In an era of declining sacramental participation or even of basic Christian belief, one would think that a pope should rejoice when Catholics love to go to Mass—even if it's in Latin, *ad orientem*, according to the missal once used everywhere, rather than Paul VI's replacement of it. But no. The ideologue cannot stand any disagreements with his ideology. Better an empty, chained-up church than a church packed with Latin Mass Catholics.

If churchmen's real concern were "active participation," they should welcome whatever most deeply and fully calls forth such participation. At traditional Masses, the faithful follow the liturgy closely; they kneel, stand, sit, make signs of the cross; they often sing the responses and Ordinary with more gusto than that with which their Novus Ordo counterparts sing the dreck published by GIA or OCP. But no. What is important to Pope Francis and his courtiers is *not* prayer, *not* embracing the "spirit of the liturgy," *not* entering into the divine worship that brought to the heights of sanctity the ten saints canonized by Francis only a week after his May 7 speech,[25] but rather, the *Novus Ordo itself*. This is the one and only end, aim, objective. The sum total of worship, at least for Latin-rite Catholics, is the Novus Ordo. This is the logic of the May 7 speech, of Archbishop Roche's interviews, of the *Responsa ad Dubia*, and of *Traditionis Custodes* itself. And this is the logic of idolatry: turning a means of sanctity into an ultimate end to which all must bow down. Who, then, makes an idol out of liturgy? Who is preoccupied with formalism? Who is the ideologue?

Curiously, the progressives are guilty of a double inversion. In the way in which the Eucharistic liturgy is truly an *end*—because it makes

---

[24] See note 31 on p. 99.
[25] All ten saints—Titus Brandsma (†1942); Devasahayam Pillai (†1752); César de Bus (†1607); Luigi Maria Palazzolo (†1886); Giustino Russolillo (†1955); Charles de Foucauld (†1916); Anne-Marie Rivier (†1838); Maria Francesca di Gesù Rubatto (†1904); Maria di Gesù Santocanale (†1923); Maria Domenica Mantovani (†1934)—knew *exclusively* the old Mass, for whom it offered a golden path to holiness; they had died in the odor of sanctity well before the Novus Ordo was even a twinkle in the young Bugnini's eye. It is very difficult to see how the times in which they lived, especially those who lived into the twentieth century, were so spectacularly different from the 1960s/70s or from today that the old rite would have been suitable for them but *not* for us. Conversely, if there is something so wrong with the old rite that it must be banished altogether, why was it so prized by these saints whom the Church has honored in the highest possible way?

really present to us Christ Himself, the Victim of Calvary, in His supreme redemptive act, through which we glorify God as the one and only end of all creation—they downplay it into a *means*, a vehicle for horizontal fellowship, social justice, applaudable entertainment, self-realization, cultural exhibitionism, or what have you. Simultaneously, in the way in which the Eucharistic liturgy is truly a *means*—one of many means given by God for the sanctification and salvation of our souls, having as its end God Himself and our enjoyment of Him in the beatific vision—they distort it into an *end*, something to be stubbornly pursued for its own sake, compulsively adhered to even when it ceases to be useful or when something else is more useful to (at least some of) the faithful. In short: where the traditional Catholic sees the liturgy as an end, the progressive sees it as a means; where the traditional Catholic sees the liturgy as a means, the progressive sees it as an end. This ought to be enough to show why we are utterly at loggerheads.

Trees are to be judged by their fruits, says Our Lord. We do not need an audience with the pope to be able to interpret the signs of the times; we do not need a liturgical institute in Rome to tell us where liturgical renewal is actually happening—and where it is failing.

In a Facebook group devoted to the clash between *Summorum Pontificum* and *Traditionis Custodes*, Shawn Tribe, editor of the *Liturgical Arts Journal*, left this incisive commentary:

> Anyone who goes to Rome will see that for all intents and purposes the local church is dead there. The great basilicas function now only as museums. When one happens to come across a liturgy taking place, it almost comes off as a curiosity and eccentricity that is out of place—not to mention very dull at that, poorly attended and attended only by an aged population. Seemingly the only thing maintaining any illusion of Catholic life is the fact so many religious orders and national churches have houses there.
>
> The fact that the post-conciliar experience has borne so little fruit now a half century later despite a half century of peddling and promotion should result in a serious examination of conscience on the part of our churchmen. The fact that despite all of those advantages the post-conciliar rite still finds itself threatened and in a defensive, reactive posture should cause more of the same.
>
> Could it be possible, just possible I say, that the notion and premise of "pastoral liturgy" so promoted after the Council, even to the exclusion of more traditional expressions of it, was based upon a faulty notion—a notion which undergirded the postconciliar reforms and which was ultimately naive and shortsighted, mistaking what was arguably merely the transitory, ephemeral spirit of one particular time for something that was more lasting and permanent? Did they misread the accidental for the substantial?

Could it be that as children of that period, they themselves were blinded by this mistake of a "*homo novus*"? Is this now why the "modern" liturgy itself seems more an ossified liturgical time piece than any traditional liturgical rite whether Eastern or Western, stuck in the ethos of a particular time and place; caught in a trend that is no longer trendy and therefore lacking in any sense of timelessness or permanence? It seems to me if simply proposing the question is deemed a threat, and results in lashing out, that in itself is rather telling. But regardless, the question must be asked.

~ 7 ~
Why the Reform of the Reform Is Doomed

AFTER MORE THAN FIFTY YEARS IN WHICH the Novus Ordo has been given ample opportunity to "prove its worth" and has singularly failed to do so—years in which a minority of strong-willed priests, attempting to turn the tide against banality and irreverence, have for their pains been sent to the boondocks, if not the shrink's couch—why are there still liturgically-minded people defending the Novus Ordo or promoting its "redemption" through Ratzingerian improvements? One can understand a pessimistic pragmatist who believes there's no other show on the road; perhaps he thinks, mistakenly, that he has no other choice in the matter. It is harder to understand the optimistic idealist who believes that this particular song-and-dance routine deserves to run another fifty years, with occasional tweaks to the casting and the pit orchestra. Perhaps we are dealing here with the final fumes of the conservative mentality, which I would characterize as follows: "Whatever Church authorities give us must be the best for us—or, at very least, adequate for us, and what we need at this time in history."

But this mentality is quite incorrect.

1. What *the Church* gives us is, and can only ever be, her *tradition*. Violence done by *churchmen* abusing their authority, working overtime to suppress or blenderize Catholic tradition, is a different story. What churchmen have given us in the liturgical reform is clearly not *the best* for us—neither in how it was produced nor in what it contains and presents, nor in how it was rolled out and implemented. There was massive rupture in *all* of these ways. There is almost no one left at this point who would defend the view, redolent of Woodstock, that, thanks to Paul VI, we have entered or will enter a liturgical Age of Aquarius.

2. Is the Novus Ordo "adequate" or "good enough"? That is never the way the Church has thought about divine worship. God deserves all that we can give, the best, the holiest, the purest, the noblest—but even more than that, He has a right to receive back from us that which He Himself has inspired among us over many centuries of liturgical prayer. The liturgy developed in depth and amplitude over many centuries under His beneficent divine causality, by His providential care for the Mystical Body. We therefore owe it to Him in justice to make use of the gifts

He has given us. To strip away much of the content of our liturgy that nourished countless Christians and then offer Him a sacramentally valid but weird combination of reinterpreted bits of antiquity combined with rootless novelties is at best a surprising way to beseech His continued blessings and, at worst, an insult to His generosity and kindness.

3. Are the reformed rites "what we need at this time in history"? Sociology, psychology, anthropology, theology, stand in formidable array to voice their negative answer.

Beyond these points, we should consider the ways in which the "reform of the reform"—to the extent that it has survived the resignation of its principal patron, Benedict XVI—is harmful to the cause of liturgical renewal at this juncture in the Church's history.

First and foremost, it harms the cause by reinforcing one of the basic errors of the Novus Ordo, which we examined in chapter 4: it requires repeated, deliberate, and somewhat arbitrary determinations on the part of the celebrant, instead of the content and manner of worship being predetermined by a tradition to which all are equally subject. A "beautiful, reverent" Novus Ordo is as much a product of the choices of its celebrant as is a bongo-drum clown Mass or a suburban talk show with a lady assistant for Communion.

The only way around this problem would be if the celebrant made a private vow "always to do the better thing"—that is, to choose always and only what is either traditional or closer to tradition—e.g., always saying "the Lord be with you" and "Kyrie eleison," always using the Roman Canon, always standing *ad orientem*, always giving Communion on the tongue, and so forth. However, this would create a world of difficulties for his conscience: what *is* the better thing in this or that case? Discernments and decisions would still have to be made, sometimes on the spur of the moment, that are foreign to the spirit of the liturgy, which implies receipt of a gift and adherence to a rule. Attempting to act upon such a vow would, sooner or later, trigger some of the parishioners, inaugurating a series of unwelcome phone calls or letters from the local chancery.

A seminarian correspondent put it as succinctly as I've ever seen it put:

> While we're out there actively trying to conform the Novus Ordo to tradition, these guys [FSSP, ICKSP, etc.] are simply letting the tradition form them. Seen that way, the NO restorationist, no matter how closely he adheres to traditional beliefs and practices, is still engaged in a self-contradictory project: to be truly traditional, one has to become smaller and smaller; to conform the Novus Ordo to tradition, one has to become bigger and bigger.[1]

---

[1] I will return to this poignant observation in the next section of this chapter.

The point is that when such a well-intending priest comes along and decides to do the Novus Ordo "in the most traditional way," it is still *his own personal accomplishment*, not the result of humbly following strict rubrics and texts in front of him. If he chooses the Roman Canon, chant, *ad orientem*, Communion at the rail, etc., all this is his own conglomerate of choices from the smorgasbord of the modern multiplex rite, and he is doing it usually with full knowledge that it's not favored by Rome, by the chancery, or even by his fellow presbyters. This is a real spiritual danger. It is "*his Mass*" in a way that the TLM is never any priest's Mass. There is an exact analogy to the missal: the Roman rite is not "Pius V's rite," but the Novus Ordo is certainly "Paul VI's rite." In the Novus Ordo, and by its very principles, the problem of a permanent lack of an objective, unarguable standard remains; it is paradoxically the only thing one can be certain of. It's every man for himself; every parish, every diocese, every country for itself.

Moreover, the ROTR prolongs the agony of the Church and of the people of God. Just as one does not give more alcohol to someone already drunk, or more of a drug to someone whose only hope of survival is quitting the drug, so one must not continue to use, even with the best of intentions, the very rite that marked a rupture with Catholic tradition and perpetuates that rupture. Even if, after many decades, something *more like* the Tridentine rite could be reassembled within the context of the Novus Ordo, it would have been simpler, safer, and better for the faithful *and* for the priest to have taken up the gold standard from the start and left aside a rite so defective. Why pursue the ROTR if each step brings us closer to—without ever finally arriving at—the authentic liturgy we already had *and still have*? I am reminded of a painfully true metaphor I saw online: "There are two pizzas in front of you: A and B. You could have Pizza A, but you choose Pizza B. Then you put all your effort into making Pizza B more like Pizza A. This is the Reform of the Reform."[2]

Thus, for example, one hears of priests celebrating the Novus Ordo who recite Psalm 42 during the procession from the sacristy, recite the *Aufer a nobis* on the way to kissing the altar, quietly mutter some of the old Offertory prayers during a silent preparation of the gifts, choose the Roman Canon and say it in a somewhat lower voice, hold thumb and forefinger together until the ablutions, and so forth. I used to be totally sympathetic to this kind of "enrichment"—until I saw that it

---

[2] Zac Mabry (@ZacMabry), "There are two pizzas in front of you: A and B. You could have Pizza A, but you choose Pizza B. Then you put all your effort into making Pizza B more like Pizza A," X, August 24, 2019, https://x.com/ZacMabry/status/1165337938210766848.

reinserts, by an act of private volition, elements that were deliberately removed by papal absolutism. It fights one abuse by another of the same sort, as if they will cancel out algebraically.[3]

Adding "smellz-n-bellz" is good and important, as far as it goes, even as toppings on a pizza make it more appetizing and more filling. But if there is something wrong with the dough, or if the sauce is missing or the cheese is low-quality, something more basic needs to be done; heaping on more pepperoni is not the solution. As Archbishop Thomas Gullickson candidly admitted:

> I think the discursive and arbitrary nature of the reformed liturgy is a big part of the problem. Liturgical abuse is rampant, yes, but I draw this conclusion about the discursive and arbitrary (I am referring to the rubrics, which read: "in these or similar words," "option A, B, or C," etc.) also from observing young priests from various parts of the world, whom you would probably label pious or at least not abusive of worship. These priests can come from most any country and most any place on the political, philosophical, or theological spectrum, that is, from the middle of the road to stock conservative. The reformed liturgy faithfully celebrated is seemingly not enough for them. They add gestures and words, sometimes deliberately and sometimes it would seem almost instinctively or unconsciously, especially during the Eucharistic prayer. They modify the Mass very simply to make it better, or so I would guess. We have a problem with the Novus Ordo that a couple of tweaks just may not solve.[4]

A sign that this is really how things are is that no one, at the end of the day, is *really* satisfied with the ROTR Novus Ordo. Those who are already well acquainted with traditional liturgy cannot help but find it inadequate compared to the "real McCoy": it is just so lacking in its texts and ceremonies. Yet the same attempt at a ROTR Mass often sorely troubles and irritates laymen who are accustomed to the reformed liturgy. The unexpected "traditional elements" cut against strong and universal expectations about the "goods" that the Novus Ordo is supposed to deliver, especially the direct and easy comprehension of words and a certain modern sensibility. Joseph Shaw has called this problem "falling between two stools": it's not traditional enough for some, and way too traditional for others.[5] The liturgy becomes, once again, a battlefield when it is supposed to be a haven of peace and

---

[3] See the section "Two 'disobediences' compared" in chapter 16.
[4] Thomas Gullickson, "Liturgy Summer Course 2019: Moving Forward—My Plea for Full Liturgical Restoration," *ad montem myrrhae*, August 2, 2019, https://admontemmyrrhae.blogspot.com/2019/08/the-best-vehicle-for-church-renewal-and.html.
[5] See Joseph Shaw, "The Death of the Reform of the Reform Part 3: Falling between two stools," *LMS Chairman*, February 25, 2014. I will develop this point further in the next chapter.

unity. The TLM cannot be blamed for being what it must be; you take all of it or none of it, inflexibly, stably, and... peacefully.

A priest I know who normatively celebrates the TLM but on rarest occasions will do the NO if requested once said to me: "Being accustomed as I am to the old Roman missal, I find it unbearable to use the Roman Canon when I say the new Mass. So much of the liturgy is so different that it seems bizarre, even irreverent, to then recite this great ancient prayer, which perhaps more than anything else shouts *Tridentine Mass*. Something like the Eucharistic Prayer III seems to slide in much better, and makes me feel like I'm just saying a different rite — which is essentially what it is." I understand perfectly why the priest feels this way. If he were to celebrate the new Mass making use of whatever elements of Roman tradition are still left in it, he would be fostering an illusion of continuity that largely does not exist when one views it euchologically, ceremonially, or phenomenologically; he would be artificially extending the lifespan of an entity that is better off dying. Yet if the same priest were to celebrate the new Mass "in *dis*continuity," letting it "be itself," he would thereby contribute to the breakdown of Catholicism's internal identity and the custodianship of its inheritance. In short: *damned if you do, damned if you don't*.

Indeed, even the idea that there is a "normative" Novus Ordo is laughable, and the idea that the Vatican wants us to celebrate with a "hermeneutic of continuity" is even more ridiculous. I am surprised that people still fall for this shell game. Have you ever noticed the consummate illogic with which the new Mass is shielded from any criticism? If someone says: "You know, it's a big problem to have sacro-pop music and altar girls and the priest facing the people and (fill-in-the-blank)," the response is: "Ah, but that's not the Novus Ordo as promulgated by Paul VI and as celebrated by its best celebrants!" But then if someone says: "You know, why don't we start having Mass here at our parish in Latin, with chant, *ad orientem*, served only by men (etc.)," the response is: "Ah, but the Novus Ordo was introduced to respond to the needs of our times, which are not those of the sixteenth century, so I'm afraid the answer is no." *Damned if you do, damned if you don't*.

One will sometimes hear a person say that the Novus Ordo is "traditional" because it has been around for over fifty years. Someone recently wrote to me: "You should stop calling it 'the new Mass' because it's not new anymore." What this objection fails to grasp is that the rationalism according to which the liturgical reform was conducted rules out a normative role for tradition as such; what is all-important is abstract truth, as the rationalist conceives it. To give an example: the United States of America will soon be 250 years old, yet its genesis in an eighteenth-century blend of social compact theory, Deism, Freemasonry, and Protestantism that abstracts from and precludes incarnational culture and tradition-based rationality means that the USA might as well be yesterday's embryo or an embalmed Pharaoh. "Venerable age" means nothing on rationalist terms. The new Mass was created for a new kind of man, Modern Man, who exists in the abstract, detached from the long and complex history of Catholic culture; it was to be a rite that appeals, with simplicity, to the man who lives by simple ideas and words. The new rite in this sense can never be traditional, a *heritage* to receive solely because it is handed down, for that would make it a foreign, static imposition on the ever-changing present into which it is supposed to be inculturated (as we saw in chapter 5).

One might also point out that fifty-five years is a minuscule 3.24% of the 1,700-year history of the Roman rite. While the handiwork of Paul VI may be old in terms of the life of a single man, it is shiny-new in comparison with the more-than-millennium-and-a-half arc of the Western liturgy's continuous development. Indeed, Catholic tradition is something *alive* in the practice of the Faith and in the continuity of *paradosis* or handing down from generation to generation; therefore, its inheritable wisdom is directly proportional to its length of days. In contrast, the Novus Ordo, because it is the result of a sort of laboratory experiment, has neither a natural birth nor a natural lifespan, just as a machine has no birthday, infancy, childhood, youth, and maturity. It simply ages the way a rock or a piece of metal ages, worn away by the winds of time and apathy.

When, later in life, John Henry Newman looked back on his youth as a highly principled and nobly minded Anglican, he had only these sobering words to say:

> I looked at her [the Catholic Church];—at her rites, her ceremonial, and her precepts; and I said, "This *is* a religion;" and then, when I looked back upon the poor Anglican Church, for which I had laboured so hard, and upon all that appertained to it, and thought of our various attempts to dress it up doctrinally and esthetically, it seemed to me to be the veriest of nonentities.[6]

How similar is the experience of so many Catholics—especially music directors, catechism teachers, and others who have a more direct involvement in typical parishes—when they shift from the NO to the TLM. "I looked at the classic Roman Mass, its rites, ceremonial, and precepts, and I said: 'This *is* worship'; and then, when I looked back on the poor Novus Ordo, for which I had labored so hard, and thought of

---

[6] John Henry Newman, *Apologia Pro Vita Sua*, ed. David J. DeLaura (W.W. Norton & Co., 1968), Note E. The Anglican Church, p. 254.

our attempts to dress it up, it seemed to me to be the veriest of nonentities." Valid, yes; but lacking in every other quality that a liturgy is supposed to have.

When Newman was a young preacher at Oxford, the Anglican establishment had existed for about 300 years (1534–1830s/40s). This is five and a half times longer than the Novus Ordo has lasted—and in spite of that duration, which is far greater than that enjoyed by Paul VI's experiment, Newman describes the Anglican Church as "poor," "the veriest of nonentities." So it is, and so it shall remain, no matter how many more centuries it may endure. The same is true of the Roman *Consilium* Rite. It is incapable of being traditional no matter how many centuries (God forbid) it may endure. If the new Mass survives another five hundred years, it will be no more traditional at the end than it is today. Just as Descartes and Kant are inescapably modern while Aristotle and Plato are timeless, the new rites are inescapably modern while the traditional rites are timeless.

History never repeats itself—but it rhymes again and again. As I was reading one of those books about books that a person reads in order to feel a little less illiterate, I came across a passage on the poet Richard Crashaw (c. 1613–1649) that startlingly reminded me of the well-intentioned but doomed spirit of the ROTR and the contemporaneous revival of the TLM:

> A significant minority in the Church of England, including William Laud, who became Archbishop of Canterbury in 1633, had become disillusioned with mainstream Protestantism and were searching for a way to restore "the beauty of holiness" to the Church without having to burn their bridges entirely by returning to Rome. After becoming a fellow of Peterhouse, Cambridge in 1635, Crashaw quickly emerged as an important figure in this High Church movement, restoring what were widely felt to be Catholic devotional objects to Little St Mary's, the church next door to Peterhouse, when he became curate there.[7]

This might be rewritten by analogy: "A significant minority in the Catholic Church had become disillusioned with the Bugnini liturgy and were searching for a way to restore 'the beauty of holiness' to the Church without having to burn their bridges entirely by returning to the traditional Roman rite." (A late beloved blogger and former Anglican might even come to mind—one who was bent on "restoring what were widely felt to be Catholic devotional objects.")[8]

But then the inevitable backlash came:

---
[7] Roy Peachey, *50 Books for Life: A Concise Guide to Catholic Literature* (Angelico Press, 2019), 58.
[8] I refer to the late and much-missed Fr. John Hunwicke. See his excellent blog, *Fr Hunwicke's Mutual Enrichment*, which his family is keeping online.

He didn't get away with his actions for long. With the start of the Civil War raising tensions, Laudian Cambridge became a target. Parliamentary commissioners ransacked Little St Mary's in 1643, tearing down crucifixes and other objects of devotion. Crashaw was forced out of Cambridge and shortly afterwards left the country, emerging in Paris three years later, by which time he had converted to Catholicism. Traveling to Italy, he became canon at the Santa Casa di Loreto, which enshrines the house where Our Lady was said to have been born and received the Annunciation. He died a few months later at the age of 36.[9]

The parliamentary commissioners who ransacked Crashaw's Little St. Mary's are reminiscent of the papal commissioners tasked with suppressing traditional and even conservative religious communities, often the only sign of vibrant Catholicism in certain dioceses or regions. Soon the Laudian curate fled to a truly Catholic country, embraced the faith of the ages, and died in communion with tradition.

It may seem that stepping from the Novus Ordo to the TLM is less momentous, less radical, than stepping from Anglicanism to Catholicism. In important ways, that is true. But those who have delved deeply into the liturgy know from intimate experience that the classic Roman rite and the modern rite of Paul VI look, sound, and feel very much like expressions of two different religions. It is no exaggeration to say a conversion is necessary—a conversion from the novelty of rupture to the integrity of tradition. As Newman called liberalism a halfway house between Catholicism and atheism, we may say the same of the reform of the reform: it is a halfway house between full tradition and liturgical relativism.

"MEN MUST BE CHANGED BY SACRED THINGS, AND NOT SACRED THINGS BY MEN"

These words were uttered by Cardinal Egidio da Viterbo in 1512 during the inaugural oration of the Fifth Lateran Council: "Homines per sacra immutari fas est, non sacra per homines." Against that backdrop, imagine the following conversation between two seminarians, both studying for their dioceses. They have discovered and fallen in love with the traditional Latin Mass and want to embrace its riches, but they disagree over how to go about doing so.

MICHAEL: It's *possible* to bring tradition into the Novus Ordo Mass. We just choose better vestments, better music, a better ceremonial guidebook, we use incense, and so forth… We learn from the Latin Mass how things ought to be done.

---

[9] Peachey, 58.

JOHN: Here's my hesitation. Isn't every attempt to make the new Mass more traditional a kind of innovation—at least compared to what bishops, other clergy, and most laity are expecting, and especially if one steps much beyond the available matrix of options? And, even in the best-case scenario, where a priest can "get away with it," what happens interiorly to a priest who's making his Mass "traditional" week after week, year after year—doesn't that habituate him into thinking that *he* is the architect of his fine liturgies? That they are *his*, to traditionalize as he will?

MICHAEL: Well, no, I think he's trying to choose what is best from the past, and therefore it's not something personally his own. He is looking to an external reference, not just an internal compass.

JOHN: But it's still a *choice* he has to make, and it's a choice he makes against the known backdrop both of a half-century of mostly contrary choices and of the generally less traditional choices of his confreres and of most other dioceses. This is very different from how worship was understood and practiced in Catholicism before the reform.

MICHAEL: What do you mean?

JOHN: While "reverse-infiltrating" diocesan clergy are laboring to crowbar the Novus Ordo back into Roman tradition, members of traditional priestly institutes take a backseat and let tradition *form them* by its own power and perfection. The reformist, no matter how enthusiastically he adheres to tradition, is caught up in a self-contradictory project. To be genuinely traditional, a disciple has to become *smaller*; to make the Novus Ordo traditional, he has to become *bigger*. The former path is an evacuation of the ego: a layman can say "oh, any priest will do, as long as he says the old Mass." The latter path is—an accomplishment! The celebrant becomes known for miles around as "the one who offers the reverent Novus Ordo." As much as the one priest vanishes in the rite, the other priest, ironically, is magnified by it.

MICHAEL: From that vantage, wouldn't it be better—more conducive to sanctity—to be a layman in a traditional parish than to be a conservative priest in the Novus Ordo world?

JOHN: It's hard to escape that conclusion. The layman is free to conform himself to an objective tradition while the Novus Ordo priest is constantly conforming the liturgy to his own (probably better) ideas of what it should be but isn't and need not be (and, for some bishops, must never be). And let's not forget that even the freedom to accomplish his well-intentioned goal can by no means be guaranteed. More likely than not, he will be forced again and again to go against his conscience, against his knowledge of what is better.

MICHAEL: It reminds me of a family I know about, where the dad became a traditional Catholic while the mom didn't, and it led to all kinds of problems. It seems as if a tradition-loving diocesan seminarian is entering a sort of mixed marriage with a typical Novus Ordo diocese, even when everyone in the picture consents with a good will; and such a marriage can rapidly break down.

JOHN: Right. If he had picked a better partner to begin with, the "marriage" would have a much higher likelihood of success.

MICHAEL: (*After a pause*) What should we do, then? What's the solution?

JOHN: I don't know if there's only *one* solution. But I know what *my* solution is—to leave the diocesan seminary and start over again in a traditional institute or community.

MICHAEL: What if the Vatican prohibits such groups from accepting new members, or even shuts down their seminaries, as rumors are saying may happen soon?

JOHN: If that occurs, the superiors should have the clarity of mind to recognize that an assault is being made against the common good of the Church—against her faith, her tradition, her past, her heritage, the consensus of all earlier popes and councils, the most sacred realities, the good of families and especially of children, and the divine gift of vocations—and should have the courage to refuse to recognize any such prohibitions or closures. The seminaries should remain open and functional, carrying on calmly as before. They should continue accepting new members, regardless of their canonical status, and carry on with priestly or religious formation, regardless of threatened or delivered penalties, all of which would be null and void, as they emanate from those acting in hatred and contempt of the Faith, contrary to divine and natural law. The lay faithful would generously support the personnel, facilities, and activities of all these groups, sustaining them until a better day dawned when the inherent legitimacy of their position is once again recognized.

MICHAEL: That's a bold set of statements you just made!

JOHN: Either we do this, or we let the modernists trample us and the traditional Faith to death. Which is what they want. Why should we let them have it? We could never have peace in our consciences if we turned our back on what the Lord has permitted us to see. *We are changed men.* And we must live as changed men. That is what God expects of us. We must not squander His graces. Besides, you know this as well as I do: a priest who has grown accustomed to the incomparable nourishment of the ancient Mass cannot, at the command of a petty dictator, simply cast it aside like an old rag.[10] That would be a kind of spiritual euthanasia. And I think the same is true for us.

MICHAEL: Yes...you are right. I can't not see what I now see. Tradition *is* a grace. I mean—to see it, to fall in love with it, to let it shape your mind and heart... What a grace to have received! *Domine, non sum dignus...*

This conversation may help crystallize a truth that remains unclear for too many people. It is indeed a contradiction in terms to say that one has to become bigger and bigger (in the sense of exercising one's own judgments and volitional force) to make the Novus Ordo "traditional" when the greatest benefit of tradition is that it allows one to become smaller and smaller, so as to let the wisdom and charity of the Church shine out through one's iconic representation of Christ.

Strictly from that point of view, to be a layman living a fully traditional liturgical life would be superior to being a priest who must celebrate the Novus Ordo either exclusively or frequently. There is no question here of attributing blame to anyone; most priests who have discovered tradition did so after their ordination, when it was too late (so to speak) to orient themselves exclusively by it. On the other hand, a priest who knew *ahead of time* that, by remaining within a diocese, he would be perpetually swimming against the current in his efforts to make the new rite something it was never intended to be—something, moreover, that the ecclesiastical hierarchy are hell-bent on preventing—would have plenty of reasons to lie awake at night, wondering what he is doing with (or to) himself.

It's not surprising, therefore, that Novus Ordo clergy who "wake up" later on to the full magnitude of the liturgical problem experience a huge crisis.[11] Some of them try to leave the diocese to join a traditional community—itself no easy step to take, with all the permissions needed on both sides, the challenge of temporary assignments during a probationary period, and no certain outcome. Others, like Fr. Bryan Houghton—author of *Judith's Marriage* and *Mitre & Crook*—realize that they must take an early retirement or find a different "line of work." As narrated in his autobiography *Unwanted Priest*, Fr. Houghton resigned his pastorship at midnight on November 30, 1969 (the day the Novus Ordo went into effect), settled in southern France, and ended up a contented chaplain of a small and rather informal group of laity who assisted at his Latin Masses. Today, laity are entirely willing to

---

10 See "When a Bishop Outlaws or Restricts Private Traditional Masses" in Kwasniewski, *Bound by Truth*, 200–13.
11 See chapter 11.

pool resources to support "canceled clergy," priests who continue to offer the TLM because they know they must.[12]

There is, of course, a very different future that could someday come into existence. Since prospective candidates for the priesthood are increasingly drawn to the Latin Mass, a forward-thinking diocese—even in the wake of *Traditionis Custodes*—could quietly create a "Latin Mass track" in which seminarians who wish to offer exclusively the traditional liturgy would be assigned eventually to shrines, basilicas, oratories, and chapels (not parishes, mind you...) that would specialize in it, for the growing number of faithful who request it, and for their growing families. Dioceses that wish to survive will have to adapt to the changing needs of the faithful and the changing aspirations of actual or potential seminarians. A few wiser dioceses in pre-*Traditionis Custodes* days were already on to this and starting to plan ahead for the inevitable, as Fr. Zuhlsdorf reported.[13]

But unless and until this happens, men who are among the "young persons [who] have discovered this liturgical form, felt its attraction, and found in it a form of encounter with the Mystery of the Most Holy Eucharist, particularly suited to them"[14] will find themselves in the position of Michael and John in my imaginary dialogue: needing to find a traditional order or community. That, too, is in God's Providence, for He is raising up luminous beacons of tradition amidst the darkness of ecclesial anarchy. And it is no less in God's providential plan that enemy forces at the Vatican are being suffered to publicly align themselves against the true guardians of tradition. The battle is on. There is great glory to be won, or the misery of desertion and surrender.

This much we know for sure: a person has an obligation to take himself out of situations in which he is continually bombarded with requirements or requests that strain or injure his conscience. Even if he could make a quick mental reservation to justify (or excuse) some act of complicity, it's like living on the edge of a sharp and unforgiving knife. It's not a healthy way to live, and the Mass is not meant to be a form of torture.[15] We are supposed to be able to yield ourselves to

---

[12] The list of priests who valiantly carried on offering the TLM in spite of illicit prohibitions is long and includes many impressive figures. In addition to Fr. Bryan Houghton, one may recall Fr. Roger-Thomas Calmel, OP; Dom Gérard Calvet, OSB; Fr. Yves Normandin; and Fr. George Kathrein, CSsR. I list the books about them or written by them in the chapter "The Rights of Immemorial Tradition and the Limits of Papal Positivism" in *Bound by Truth*, 102–20; see 114n19.
[13] John Zuhlsdorf, "A diocese smells the coffee: starts planning for decline of the Novus Ordo and growth of the TLM," *Fr. Z's Blog*, January 20, 2020.
[14] Benedict XVI, Letter to Bishops Accompanying the Apostolic Letter *Summorum Pontificum*, July 7, 2007.
[15] See my article "The Mass Should Not Be a Torture Device," *NLM*, February 7, 2022.

the liturgy as to a superior trainer who can be absolutely trusted with our spiritual good.

CAN *ANY* CASE BE MADE FOR "THE REVERENT NOVUS ORDO"?[16]

Dear Dr. Kwasniewski,

Having read your essay "Why the 'Reform of the Reform' Is Doomed," I would like, in a spirit of truth-seeking, to present some objections that might be made to it.

To start with, I do agree that the Novus Ordo is "ungraftable" onto the living tradition of the Roman liturgy, considered liturgically (as opposed to juridically, etc.). One of the great benefits of the admittedly awkward situation of "two forms"—a situation that continues to exist after *Traditionis Custodes* and shows no signs of going away in general—is that, in principle, a simple "return" to the *usus antiquior* is possible and, in some sense, already exists in many places. In a couple generations there will be, at the current rate, a strong minority of those who know and love the old Mass and have only the most remote experience, if any, of the new rite. In addition, many of the younger generations who are not die-hard devotees of the older rites are nevertheless free from the ideological bitterness against anything pre-1970 and are open to "big-picture" traditional practices, e.g., *ad orientem*, Communion while kneeling, Gregorian chant, beautiful vestments, and the like.

That being said, one might argue that there's something impractical, and something unfitting, about the tradition-minded simply abandoning the Novus Ordo.

Impracticality. The Novus Ordo is not going away any time soon, and many people, even those otherwise open to tradition, are not willing to abandon it. Thus, it seems like a more effective strategy would be to add more traditional elements to celebrations according to the new books—not just in the Order of Mass (the *Judica me*, the Offertory, etc.) but in the temporal calendar and orations. While we both agree that this is no more than an interim measure, and one that is generally unpleasing, it is nonetheless a way to get people *used* to the idea of traditional liturgical praxis in a manner that is not jolting.

I find it hard to believe that someone who comes to love a "traditionalized" Novus Ordo will not be drawn further into the sources and richness of the Roman tradition. Many people I know (myself included, and apparently you, as well) who have come to embrace an "integral" practice of traditional Catholicism first went through their

---

[16] The following is based on a real exchange of letters occasioned by the first section of this chapter.

"ROTR phase," perhaps because it is an easy way to be traditional while also remaining squarely within "the establishment." One might even point to Pope Gregory I's advice to St. Augustine of Canterbury regarding the Saxon shrines: people will be more at ease in a familiar environment while their *mores* are slowly converted, and in due time, once the dispositions are there, one can build new shrines and "go all the way." Here is what St. Gregory wrote to Abbot Mellitus, who was about to join St. Augustine:

> Tell Augustine that he should by no means destroy the temples of the gods but rather the idols within those temples. Let him, after he has purified them with holy water, place altars and relics of the saints in them. For, if those temples are well built, they should be converted from the worship of demons to the service of the true God. Thus, seeing that their places of worship are not destroyed, the people will banish error from their hearts and come to places familiar and dear to them in acknowledgement and worship of the true God.[17]

Analogously, it seems that applying one's talents to the best Novus Ordo possible, via use of the *Graduale Romanum*, Msgr. Peter J. Elliott's rubrics, and the like would actually serve the traditional Mass in the long run.

Unfittingness: Intrinsically, the Novus Ordo is pleasing to God, due to the objective confection of the Eucharist, juridical approval, and the presence of many objectively wholesome elements (and the absence of directly unwholesome ones). To my mind, the defects of the Novus Ordo lie instead in what it represents, namely, a rejection of the inherited tradition, and in what it omits, such as certain "hard teachings" of the Faith. Nothing is objectively *false* in, say, the second Eucharistic Prayer; rather, its circumstances of composition and the fact that it virtually displaced the Roman Canon are what make it truly objectionable. If the text as we have it were a received text from antiquity and preserved in some obscure autocephalous rite, I do not believe that its mere existence would pose a problem to which anyone should object (again, hypothetically speaking). As a result, it would seem unfitting, by means of a policy of abandoning the Novus Ordo "to its own devices," to relegate the vast majority of liturgical worship to virtually inevitable mediocrity.

I understand that traditionalizing the Novus Ordo would likely extend its lifespan. Still, drawing others into a positive experience of tradition, and the corresponding increase in rendering glory unto God,

---

[17] Gregory the Great, *Epistola* 76, *PL* 77:1215–16, www.fordham.edu/Halsall/source/gregi-mellitus.txt.

would seem to trump any tactical considerations when it comes to attaining the end goal which you and I share: the complete restoration of the Roman tradition.

Best regards,
Fr. Inquiring Incrementalist

Dear Father,

Thank you for your thoughts, which I welcome.

I do think it is not to the benefit of the Church that a faulty *lex orandi*, namely, that of the Novus Ordo, should be perpetuated under the guidance of a good *lex orandi*, that of the Tridentine rite. Such an approach is a bit deceptive, as it seems to depart from the clear intentions of Paul VI and of those who created the Novus Ordo, who made no attempt to hide the fact that they wanted to replace the Tridentine rite with something quite different, which they believed would be more suitable for Modern Man.™ I talk about this in detail in my book *The Once and Future Roman Rite*. And there are aspects of the new rite that manifestly cannot be done in a spirit of continuity with the old rite, so a priest attempting to follow the "hermeneutic of continuity" to its logical end either runs up against a brick wall or takes matters into his own hands. The traditional Offertory is a perfect case in point: either the Mass will be lacking it, which is a major defect against the backdrop of the mighty developments that took place in both Eastern and Western Christian rites, *or* the priest will insert the traditional Offertory *ad libitum*, which seems like a more extreme example of the vice of optionitis, since it is not a licit option within the bounds of the new liturgical rubrics.

In addition, we mustn't forget that we're not looking at the Mass alone, but at all the sacramental rites, the Divine Office, the blessings, etc., *all* of which have been deconstructed and dumbed-down past any substantive resemblance to how the Church used to offer them. "But they're valid!" or "they still have some positive content!," say the by-now tired and slightly despairing counterarguments. Yes—but should we be serving a delicious meal and the finest wine (metaphorically, the content of a sacrament) on styrofoam with plastic cutlery and in paper cups? Should we be trying to perform a symphony on kazoos, harmonicas, banjos, and washboards? No. The authenticity and fittingness of our worship hugely matter when it comes to impressing the Faith on our souls and offering to God the best He has given us and the best we can give Him. Priests who say the old Mass but pray the Liturgy of the Hours, or who say the new Mass but pray the old Roman Breviary, quickly see the stark disconnect: *it's like two different worlds*. It's even more dramatic if one compares the new rite of baptism to the old rite: there is no possible evolutionary path from old to new, and no possible reformatory path from the new back to the great tradition.

However, relatively speaking, and in particular cases, I know that a "Tridentinizing" approach to the new rite has led many Catholics back to tradition. It has acted as a bridge. It has consoled clergy who have been bullied into compliance with *TC* or who believe (whether rightly or wrongly) that they must obey the anti-TLM policy of their bishop. It has undoubtedly saved some vocations. I wouldn't be surprised if the majority of traditionalists are conflicted in mind about the ROTR *from a practical point of view*. Sure, we want Catholics exposed to good things even in the Novus Ordo... but the *environment* in which those good things occur, that is, the new rite itself, has a dismaying fakeness to it at the end of the day. It remains a construct of modern liturgists acting on the basis of false or dubious theories, and the "good use" of it is a conquest of taste, not an inheritance received whole and entire. By using the new liturgical books, we are not doing what our forefathers gave us (and gave us for good reason); we are extending the lease of Paul VI's abuse of power, and, while we're at it, validating Francis's abuse of power. Are we delaying the longed-for and long-overdue mucking out of the stables?

The new missal, after all, has its own "spirit": a spirit of simplicity, directness, and clarity. That's what it was designed to optimize. With respect to this distinct spirit, a priest is probably doing a disservice to people *in a different way* if he starts reciting a lot of the new rite in Latin and adds stuff in from the TLM that isn't there in the rubrics. He is building his own semi-Tridentine personal rite. However, on one point I can be adamant: every priest should go *ad orientem*. That is non-negotiable. After all, regardless of Paul VI's own preference for *versus populum*, the rubrics of the Novus Ordo and all other relevant documentation very obviously allow for *ad orientem* and indeed presuppose it.[18]

Is this position of mine—that it would be better to abandon the new rite in favor of the traditional rite, but at the same time, attempts should not be made to Tridentinize the new rite and put old things back into it—self-contradictory? No, because the rites have their own design, their own way of doing things (and goals that go along with it), and mixing them in either direction may not result in mutual enrichment but in mutual muddiness or mutilation. A TLM in the vernacular would be as inappropriate, given what it is and how it "works," as a

---

[18] See Kwasniewski, "The Normativity of *Ad Orientem* Worship."

Novus Ordo in whispered Latin, given what *it* is and how *it* works. I blame this mess on Paul VI: he created the unprecedented conundrum, and we are living in its chaotic aftermath.

I suppose one difference between us is that I have come to think it would be objectively wrong for the Church ever to *cease* to offer to God the orthodox prayers and rituals of reverence that He led her to embrace over many centuries of piety. This conviction did not so forcefully impress itself on me for as long as I thought that the Novus Ordo was free from objectionable material *in itself* while characterized by the privation of much good and too prone to easy abuse on account of deficient rubrics. After further study, it became clear that its architects, who held views incompatible with the Faith, designed a product that cannot but mislead the faithful, unless they are unusually well educated and zealous to make up for its deficiencies.[19] Many books converge on this conclusion, but I will mention two in particular: Lauren Pristas's *Collects of the Roman Missals: A Comparative Study of the Sundays in Proper Seasons before and after the Second Vatican Council* and Michael Fiedrowicz's *The Traditional Mass: History, Form, and Theology of the Classical Roman Rite*.

It's not possible to read this pair of books (or others like them) and not see intellectually and feel viscerally the magnitude of the crisis created by the liturgical reform—a crisis that will never be overcome until the modern rite is finally repudiated and the traditional rite is restored in its fullness. Each priest will need to decide, before God, in his own conscience, and well prepared by study and prayer, what this crisis demands of him personally. There are many paths that converge on tradition—muddling along as best one can with the occasional TLM or the souped-up NOM [*Novus Ordo Missæ*]; petitioning to join the FSSP or other such community; going into early retirement and helping discreetly on the TLM underground circuit; imitating heroes of the Faith like Fr. Yves Normandin, who brought the TLM to countless faithful across Canada in the dark days;[20] accepting the generosity of traditional laity in return for provision of the traditional sacraments;

---

[19] Some apologists for the Novus Ordo will cite canon 7 of the Council of Trent's Session XXII: "If anyone says that the ceremonies, vestments, and outward signs, which the Catholic Church uses in the celebration of Masses, are incentives to impiety rather than the services of piety: let him be anathema." Sadly for these apologists, the anathema vindicates precisely those ceremonies, vestments, and outward signs of the "received and approved rites" of tradition that were considered deficient or defective by twentieth-century reformers, who therefore believed they had the right and the duty to overhaul the rites, rejecting many elements. Consequently, so far from supporting the Novus Ordo, this canon rather undermines the entire logic behind it.

[20] Yves Normandin, *Pastor Out in the Cold: The Story of Fr. Normandin's Fight for the Latin Mass in Canada* (Angelus Press, 2021).

and so on. What is clear, in any case, is that both the reform and the reform of the reform have led to the same place, namely, a dead end. It's time to turn around.

Cordially in Christ,
Dr. Kwasniewski

WHY ART AND REVERENCE ARE *NOT* THE KEY TO RESTORING CATHOLIC LITURGY

A friend had expressed his concerns about my strong advocacy of the traditional Latin Mass and my ongoing critique of the liturgical reform. He asked me why it was not sufficient to enrich the reformed Mass with elements of Catholic tradition bit by bit, as occasion allows. He also asked about the basis of my skepticism of Church authority and whether I am not at risk of rejecting it in a Protestant fashion. Here is how I replied.

Dear Sir,

Thank you for your letter, and especially for your friendly words and concerns. I am on record saying that it's a good thing whenever Catholics are exposed to tradition—be it chant, beautiful hymnody or polyphony, male altar servers properly vested, Mass *ad orientem*, Communion on the tongue kneeling, etc. Each of these things is part of our patrimony and forms us in the true Faith.

At the same time, the relatively isolated and dissociated condition of these elements in postconciliar Catholicism makes them rather like flotsam and jetsam left from the titanic wreck of the 1960s. They are found all together—at home, in their original and harmonious configuration—in the apostolic liturgical rites of the Church, Eastern and Western. It is relatively straightforward to identify inductively the universal attributes of traditional Eucharistic rites that predate the Novus Ordo.[21] We need to get back to that traditional order of worship, fixed, stable, and dense, rather than perpetuating a modern mishmash that lacks most of those attributes or makes them "ad lib."

Not all can return immediately to the point before the serious deviations began—shortly after World War II, as the Liturgical Movement turned radical and lost its bearings—but the younger generations are quite open to the work of restoration, being free of the baggage carried by older folks who had to make do with what was given to them (or not given to them). The most effective evangelization in our times will be one that accentuates the wonder, beauty, and "strangeness" of the divine, not its domesticated familiarity and rational accessibility.

---

[21] See Kwasniewski, *Once and Future Roman Rite*, 33–77; 279–311.

It's hard for me to see how, *within* the Novus Ordo world, there could ever be the clarity of vision, determination, organization, and episcopal support to bring about what the proponents of the "reverent new Mass" envision. Outside of rare outposts, that project is more of a sinking ship than a vessel yet untested. If I had to place bets, they'd all be on the traditional Mass—not just because I love it, but because I think it has staying power. If it weathered an attempt at utter suppression by the most powerful institution in the world claiming to act in the name of God and demanding blind obedience, it can obviously weather anything else that modernity or postmodernity has thrown or could throw at it. The warning of Gamaliel applies here: "But if it be of God, you cannot overthrow it, lest perhaps you be found even to fight against God" (Acts 5:39).

You and I are both musicians strongly shaped by the pursuit of the beautiful; we have both composed music for the new liturgy. I've set as many English texts as I have Latin, and my English pieces will almost never be used at a TLM. The fact is, during the years when I directed choirs at the Novus Ordo, the art of music became my "hiding place" where I found refuge from the pain of the knowledge I had acquired by studying the history and theology of liturgy. There came a point when I had to admit that fine art, however captivating, was simply not enough to address the root problem; it was like wrapping a bandage around a severed limb and expecting it to regenerate. The bandage may staunch the blood, but it will not restore integrity to the damaged body, nor functionality where the limb is missing. This by no means detracts from the inherent value of well-made art, or its power to move, to edify, to elevate; and to that extent, I admire all that good Catholic composers, architects, and other artists are doing to improve the "tone" in parishes. But when I look at the larger picture, I see this kind of endeavor as a rickety bridge that helps wayfarers pass from a flawed reform over to a full inheritance.

Even though I consider the reformed rites to be defective and harmful, I also acknowledge that they have been and can be occasions of grace for individuals. The all-powerful Lord can bring good out of evil, as St. Augustine and St. Thomas teach, faithfully adhering to Scripture. In my view of things, it is possible both to reject the goodness of the reform *and* to accept that it has been a vehicle of grace for some individuals—although it has been an occasion of sin for many others, beginning with its architects, who sinned gravely against the virtue of piety for tradition, and its celebrants, who can abuse it or even use it well with vanity (I refer to the subtle vanity of good taste and religiosity—a temptation absent in the old rite, entirely determinate in its inflexible rubrics).

You then raise the million-dollar question: What are we to make of Church authority in all this? Has it been asleep at the wheel? Has it been undermining the very Church it is supposed to support and serve? Are we ever justified in setting ourselves against what ecclesiastical authorities have determined to be best for us in the realm of the liturgy—or does that make us renegades driven by private judgment?

One of the hardest things for me in my life as a Catholic has been coming to grips with the problem of *major* failures on the part of Catholic bishops. Minor failings have we all, and no one can escape them; but we are looking at a double systemic abuse: abuse of the liturgical inheritance and abuse of the most innocent and vulnerable of the Lord's people. These are, regrettably, related to one another.[22] Take someone like Rembert Weakland, who was both a major figure in the liturgical reform and, as we later discovered, an active homosexual; and he is far from alone.

I think it is part of a difficult but necessary renunciation to be able to admit—without denying that bishops and popes truly possess their offices, and without contumaciously or pertinaciously disobeying them in those matters over which they have legitimate authority—that our prelates have been and still are guilty of serious errors, abuses, and crimes, including catastrophic failures in prudential judgment, and that we have a duty to resist these prelates to the extent that they are responsible for or complicit in such things.[23] The Lord has raised up many laity to lead this faithful resistance (and the conservation effort that always goes with it), and there are good priests and bishops in the same movement of true reform, which means, as Martin Mosebach says, a *return to form*, that is, an intensification of sound, traditional discipline, not its relaxation or abolition:

> We must not forget what the term "reform," well anchored in the history of the Church, meant until Vatican II: a restoration of discipline, a tightening of the reins, an end to profligacy and a return to the traditional order. The "reforms" of the Second Vatican Council are the first in the entire history of the Church to deviate from this view; they no longer trusted the tradition to reach the people of the present and therefore relied on a general

---

[22] See "Liturgical Abuse, Sexual Abuse, and Clericalism" in Kwasniewski, *Holy Bread of Eternal Life*, 203–13.
[23] For example, bishops—like Cardinal Cupich in Chicago—who discourage or even try to forbid Catholics from receiving Our Lord kneeling and/or on the tongue. See "Limits to Episcopal Authority over Holy Communion" in Kwasniewski, *Holy Bread of Eternal Life*, 227–39; Amy Welborn, "Up...off your knees!," *Catholic World Report*, December 13, 2024; Anthony Esolen, "Tradition and Treachery," *Crisis Magazine*, December 27, 2024; Fr. John A. Perricone, "Chicago: Where Eucharistic Revival Goes to Die," *Crisis Magazine*, January 2, 2025.

softening of practice and doctrine, although without successfully keeping people in the Church as a result of this pastoral relativism. It is not a Church that is ossified in its rites and fossilized in its doctrines that has been losing the faithful in a steadily increasing stream since Vatican II, but rather, a Church that has softened in doctrine and become liturgically formless.[24]

In a way one could not have predicted solely on the basis of a neo-scholastic conception of how church authority works, it seems not only possible but undeniably true that major deviations have occurred through the abusive exercise of that authority. It has proved necessary and salutary for members of Christ's flock not only to refuse to follow certain directives, but also actively to oppose the softening of doctrine and the deformation of liturgy.[25] Even *Summorum Pontificum*, the pacific tone of which might make one think Benedict XVI was merely clearing up some unfortunate misunderstanding, is the result of decades of struggle in which laity and lower clergy were pitted against a hierarchy determined to crush them (and that is no exaggeration, as Leo Darroch's book shows in horrific detail).[26] Recall, just to take one example, that the reformed liturgical rites do not *in principle* exclude the use of traditional sacred music or the Latin language; yet as we saw in chapter 1, it was Paul VI himself who, in a speech delivered on November 26, 1969, diverted the Latin-rite Church from her own tradition (and, incidentally, from Vatican II) when he earnestly told the world that Latin and chant had to disappear from parochial liturgies. We are, he says, bidding them goodbye, and we *should* bid them goodbye. From 1964 onwards (that is, even before the Novus Ordo), this was the mentality of rupture that churchmen sought to enforce upon all—and there was rarely any departure from the policy.

Thus, the surprising fact emerges that it is only to the extent that Paul VI has been and is resisted by Catholics—either doing the *old* Mass against his wishes, or doing the *new* Mass against his wishes—that there has been, in the West, any historically continuous, anthropologically sound, culturally worthwhile *cultus* to offer to God and to share with the people. Everyone needs to recognize that if they are doing the right thing, they are disobeying the whims and wishes of some pope or other.

---

[24] Martin Mosebach, "The Church's reform disaster: No one wants to see the causes of the abuse scandal. Yet they can be clearly identified," *Rorate Caeli*, July 24, 2024.
[25] See my book *True Obedience* for an explanation of why such opposition cannot properly be considered disobedience but is obedience to higher obligations. See also my article, "Why Are Laity So Involved in the Liturgical Debate?"
[26] Leo Darroch, *Una Voce: The History of the Fœderatio Universalis Una Voce* (Gracewing, 2017).

The key is to do the *right* thing, even when popes are blathering on or busy contradicting their predecessors and even themselves.

It was during the Protestant Revolt that reformers first took it upon themselves to construct liturgies according to their own interpretation of early Christian worship before its "corruption" by Catholics, as they spun out their novel doctrine from threads of St. Paul and made themselves the divinely-appointed instruments of what their contemporaries "needed."[27] The Consilium in the 1960s acted in quite the same manner, *producing* rites, not *inheriting* rites as Catholics had always done before—test-tube babies rather than children conceived in natural wedlock. In a bitter irony, the ones who acted like Protestants were the liturgical reformers working for the Vatican, not the Catholics who held fast to the stable tradition that perfectly expresses the true teaching of the Bible and the dogmatic decrees of the ecumenical Councils, especially the Council of Trent. In being asked to accept such fabricated rites as authoritative and Catholic, I am not convinced that one is not being asked to act against a well-informed conscience. It seems to me something like intellectual suicide to accept that what Bugnini & Co. have given us is in harmony with the foregoing tradition. If one can believe this, one can believe anything; if one can say this, one can say anything.

We are dealing here with a *mysterium iniquitatis* that beggars belief but is nevertheless encompassed within the *kenosis* and victory of Christ as we move toward the end times. May the Lord lead us forward along the path of a tradition received in humility, cultivated in love, and enriched with the fruits of centuries of fidelity and Catholic culture.

Cordially yours in Christ,
Dr. Kwasniewski

---

[27] See Michael Davies's masterpiece *Cranmer's Godly Order: The Destruction of Catholicism through Liturgical Change*, rev. ed. (Roman Catholic Books, 1995).

8

The "Latin Novus Ordo" Is Not the Solution

IN THE WAKE OF *TRADITIONIS CUSTODES*, SOME have made the good-faith suggestion that a "solution" for a future depleted of traditional Latin Masses is "doing the Novus Ordo in Latin." This is an absolute non-starter for several reasons.

THE RITES THEMSELVES ARE PROFOUNDLY DIFFERENT

First, the missals have surprisingly little overlap. All one has to do is compare them side-by-side to see that both the Order of Mass and the Propers of the Mass are largely divergent. The classic article here is Matthew Hazell's, demonstrating that only 13% of the orations of the old missal are found intact in the new one (and not 17%, the already-low figure at which Fr. Anthony Cekada had arrived, but which turns out on closer inspection to be too generous).[1] As I demonstrate in *The Once and Future Roman Rite*, we are dealing here not with two versions of the Roman rite but with two *rites*: the Roman rite and whatever one must call the other: let us say, the "modern rite of Paul VI." If someone happens to *enjoy* the modern rite in Latin, by all means let him have it; but that's not an adequate substitute for the TLM, and no one who is even a little bit familiar with the TLM would be able to perceive it to be such. An acquaintance of mine explained to her ten-year-old son, an avid altar server, that the local bishop, when he announced the end of the TLM, offered to substitute for it a Novus Ordo in Latin, *ad orientem*, with chant. The boy replied: "Ohhhh, so they're trying to pretend!" It's insulting to be offered something that kinda-sorta looks like the TLM but isn't, as if experienced attendees of the TLM are ignorant of the fact that the TLM and the Novus Ordo are two separate rites—indeed, as if all we care about is eye-candy. A virtuous man looks for a wife who is beautiful on the inside as well as on the outside, with the former—the internal character—valued most of all. He's not interested *only* in the externals, and neither are traditional Catholics. Speaking and acting as if we were is a not-so-subtle disparagement. At the same time, we understand that the externals *ought* to match the internal reality—Mosebach says there is no shame

---

[1] Matthew Hazell, "'All the Elements of the Roman Rite'?"

in being "one of those naïve folk who look at the surface, the external appearance of things, in order to judge their inner nature, their truth, or their spuriousness"[2]—and we object to any rite that *disconnects* them, leaving their relationship to free choice, as if we we ought to be reliant on the chance intersection of local politics and subjective good taste. (I will return shortly to the question of aestheticism.)

THE NEW RITE'S ARCHITECTS WANTED ONLY VERNACULAR

Second, the new liturgy was never designed by its architects and implementers to be said in Latin. Pope Paul VI bade adieu to Latin (and Gregorian chant along with it) in his infamous general audiences of March 1965 and November 1969, as I discuss in the aforementioned book.[3] On November 19, 1969, he declared:

> The introduction of the vernacular will certainly be a great sacrifice for those who know the beauty, the power, and the expressive sacrality of Latin. We are parting with the speech of the Christian centuries; we are becoming like profane intruders in the literary preserve of sacred utterance. We will lose a great part of that stupendous and incomparable artistic and spiritual thing, the Gregorian chant. We have reason indeed for regret, reason almost for bewilderment. What can we put in the place of that language of the angels? We are giving up something of priceless worth. But why? What is more precious than these loftiest of our Church's values? The answer will seem banal, prosaic. Yet it is a good answer, because it is human, because it is apostolic. Understanding of prayer is worth more than the silken garments in which it is royally dressed. Participation by the people is worth more—particularly participation by modern people, so fond of plain language which is easily understood and converted into everyday speech.

This is the same pope who noted only five years later, in a melancholy observation that called into question the most obvious characteristic of the new rite, its vernacular verbosity: "Modern man is sated by talk; he is obviously tired of listening, and what is worse, impervious to words."[4]

---

[2] Mosebach, *Heresy of Formlessness*, 2. This author is certainly right to say that the external beauty *must* be sought for, and that the willed absence of it is evil: "The doctrine of supposedly 'inner values' hidden under a dirty and decrepit shell is something I find highly suspicious. I already believed that the soul imparts a form, a face, a surface to the body, even before I learned that it was a truth defined by the Church's teaching authority. Consider me a Mediterranean primitive, but I do not believe a language that is untrue, full of deceit, and lacking in feeling can contain ideas of any value. What applies in art must apply to a far higher degree in the public prayer of the Church; if, in ordinary life, ugliness shows us the presence of untruth, in the realm of religion it may indicate something worse" (ibid.).
[3] See "Revisiting Paul VI's *Apologia* for the New Mass" in Kwasniewski, *Once and Future Roman Rite*, 109–43.
[4] Paul VI, Apostolic Exhortation *Evangelii Nuntiandi*, no. 42.

In the giant doorstopper of a book *Documents on the Liturgy 1963– 1979*, one can find hundreds of references to Mass in the vernacular, and scarcely any reference to Mass in Latin. The Latin *editio typica* of Paul VI's *Missale Romanum* [sic] was understood by all, except perhaps Opus Dei clergy, as a launching-point for the multitudinous vernacular versions. One can tell because the new missal's very Latinity, as numerous Latinists have explained to me, is clunky and clumsy throughout; it's a committee product intended for practical extrapolations.

THE NEW RITE IS BUILT FOR EASY VERBAL COMPREHENSION

Third, and moving more deeply into the heart of the matter, the Novus Ordo is in fact built for a kind of immediate rational comprehension and active engagement that is foreign to traditional liturgy conducted in an archaic sacral language, where much that is said and done is not being said and done for or towards the congregation at all, and where being caught up in the larger liturgical action is the main point: the "creation of a presence,"[5] or, in Newman's words, "not the invocation merely, but... the evocation of the Eternal."[6]

No one has analyzed the stark differences between the rites, as far as language goes, better than Joseph Shaw. In a masterful five-part series published from February 23 to 27, 2014 at his blog *LMS Chairman*, Shaw explains why the "reform of the reform" was dead in the water even before it started (and before it was euthanized for good effect by Pope Francis).[7] Here I would like to take up a few of the major points he makes.

In Part 1, "The Death of the Reform of the Reform?," Shaw introduces his main argument:

> While I am in favour of Latin, worship *ad orientem* and pretty well everything the ROTR promotes, it is clear to me that the difficulty of imposing them on the Novus Ordo is not just a matter of parochial habits. The problem with the texts and ceremonies, in terms of bringing them closer to the Traditional Mass, is not just a matter of how many changes you would need to make. The problem is that the Novus Ordo has its own ethos, rationale and spirituality. It encapsulates its own distinct understanding of what liturgical participation is. It is to promote this kind of participation that its various texts and ceremonies have been done as they are. If you put it in Latin,

---

5 Mosebach (*Heresy of Formlessness*, 186) used this phrase to describe the traditional ceremonial for reading the Gospel, but it readily lends itself to the way the entire classical liturgy works, as Joseph Shaw explains in *Sacred and Great: A Brief Introduction to the Traditional Latin Mass* (Os Justi Press, 2023).
6 Kwasniewski, ed., *Newman on Worship*, 386.
7 See my article "Why Restricting the TLM Harms Every Parish Mass," *Crisis Magazine*, August 13, 2021; cf. chapter 7.

ad orientem, and especially if you start having things not currently allowed, like the silent Canon, then you undermine the kind of participation for which the Novus Ordo was designed. This means that there is a danger, in promoting something which amounts to a compromise between the two Missals, of falling between two stools.

In Part 2, "The Liturgical Movement," Shaw notes that the movers and shakers of the Liturgical Movement were frustrated that the people before the Council were not more "into" the liturgy (according to presumably enlightened notions of what such "into-ness" should look like). The poor folks did not *understand* its content as well as the experts themselves did, being fluent in Latin as they were and having lots of time to study and so forth. Having grown impatient with educational approaches, they tried a blunter method:

> Some liturgists made a final effort to get the wonderful texts of the ancient liturgical tradition across to the Faithful. They experimented with having Mass facing the people, so everyone could see what was going on. Then they realised that, if you want people to understand the texts, you really are a lot better off having the texts read aloud, and in the vernacular. It stands to reason! But things were moving on. Even aloud, and in English, the texts were too long, too complicated. In fact, putting them into the vernacular simply served to emphasise that these texts were unsuitable for repetitive use in the congregation's mother tongue. Furthermore, the order in which things happened was confusing and (apparently) illogical. And then there were other theological fashions which disliked the emphasis on sin, penance, and the saints. It all had to go.
>
> What we got instead was a Missal which the Faithful could follow word by word, without the need (after a while) of hand-missals. The prayers were simple, the ceremonies short and cut down to the bone, and (apparently) logical. It was in the vernacular. It faced the people. The translation used words of one syllable wherever possible. It all fitted together.

When the ROTR folks look at the result of this process, they sense, quite rightly, that there's a great lack:

> Something is missing from the Mass, the sacrality has gone. So they want to put some sacrality back. They see the things which seem most associated with it in the Traditional Mass, and they want to put them back. So they propose, and actually practice, the use of Latin, celebration *ad orientem*, Gregorian Chant and so on. These are all good things. But when the reformers said that they had to be sacrificed for the sake of comprehensibility, they weren't entirely wrong. Thinking about word-by-word understanding, verbal communication, it is perfectly true that, unless you are a superhuman Latinist, it is harder to follow the Canon in Latin than it is in English.

Unless you are lip-reader, it is harder still if it is silent. Unless you have X-Ray eyes, it is harder still if the priest has his back to you.

Pope Paul VI famously said, using a phrase of Jungmann's, that Latin was a "curtain" which obscured the liturgy, it had to be drawn back. Yes: *if* you have a very narrow understanding of participation.[8] But that is the understanding of participation upon which the entire reform was based.

In Part 3, "Falling Between Two Stools," Shaw makes explicit the assumptions of the reformers and why they are mistaken:

> I described the historical process by which we ended up with a liturgy from which drama, gesture, mystery, awe, and beauty have been systematically removed. There is still some left, but less than before; the point is that their removal was not accidental, but deliberate and systematic. There was a principle at work: *Mass should be readily comprehensible.* Drama, poetry, anything which is hidden from sight or in a foreign language: these are inevitably harder to understand. And who can argue with the principle? What the reformers took for granted was the presupposition that we are talking about verbal communication. So let's get this assumption out in the open: Mass should be readily comprehensible *at the level of verbal communication.*
>
> Suddenly it looks less obvious. Might it be possible that what is more readily comprehensible at the verbal level is actually less readily comprehensible, or, to use another term favoured by liturgists, *meaningful,* taking verbal and non-verbal forms of communication together? Listen to what Fr. Aidan Nichols OP observed (*Looking at the Liturgy,* 59): "To the sociologist, it is by no means self-evident that brief, clear rites have greater transformative potential than complex, abundant, lavish, rich, long rites, furnished with elaborate ceremonial."
>
> When you put it like that, it is clear enough. It is perfectly possible that the effort to make Mass more meaningful at a verbal level has had such a deleterious effect on its non-verbal aspect that we've ended up with something which is less meaningful, all things considered.

He then explains what happens when you try to "mix 'n' match":

> The Novus Ordo is geared towards verbal comprehension. It may be lacking in other things—certainly the Reform of the Reform people tell us so—but in terms of understanding the liturgical texts it must be said it is pretty successful. They are read nice and clearly, usually amplified, in one's mother tongue (at least for those of us who have a major language as a mother tongue, and live where it is an official language); the vocabulary (at least until the

---

8 For Shaw's extended treatment of this topic, see "Understanding Liturgical Participation" in Joseph Shaw, *The Liturgy, the Family, and the Crisis of Modernity: Essays of a Traditional Catholic* (Os Justi, 2023), 57–85.

new translation [of 2011]) is not challenging. Yes, we get the message, at the intellectual, word-by-word level. To say the Vetus Ordo operates at another level is to state the obvious. You can't even hear the most important bits—they are said silently. If you could hear them, they'd be in Latin. And yet, somehow, it has its supporters. It communicates something, not *in spite* of these barriers to verbal communication, but *by means* of the very things which are clearly barriers to verbal communication. The silence and the Latin are indeed among the most effective means the Vetus Ordo employs to communicate what it communicates: the *mysterium tremendum*, the amazing reality of God made present in the liturgy. If you take the Novus Ordo and make it verbally incomprehensible, or take the Vetus Ordo and take away the Latin and the silence, you are not creating the ideal liturgy. You are in grave danger of creating something that is neither fish nor fowl: that doesn't work at either level.

In Part 4, "Novus Ordo in Latin?," Shaw ties together his various points:

> A compromise missal, with "the best" of the Ordinary Form and of the Extraordinary Form, could turn out to be something which doesn't allow the Faithful to engage with it effectively, in either the typical traditional fashion or the typical Novus Ordo fashion. The idea that you can make the Traditional Latin Mass easier to participate in by making various changes—using the vernacular, having [formerly] silent prayers [said] aloud, having the priest face the people—is based on the idea that there is only one kind of meaningful participation, and that is an intellectual, verbal participation: a comprehension of the liturgy by a grasp of the liturgical texts word by word, as they are said. But, as I argued, this is not so....
>
> I also warned that something similar can happen from the other direction. If you take the Novus Ordo and put it into Latin, for example, you instantly take away much of the intellectual, verbal engagement for which the 1970 Missal was designed. Will you create a sense of the sacred to compensate? Perhaps. But the whole rite has been set up wrong, from that point of view, and most Catholics in the pew will not find it at all obvious how to allow themselves to engage with it in the appropriate way, in the context of the mixed signals they are getting from the ceremonies and texts....
>
> If we are going to talk about the future, of what there is some chance of really working with the bulk of ordinary Catholics, the Reform of the Reform is based on a terrible mistake. The mistake is to assume you can preserve what is attractive about one Form while combining it with what is attractive about the other. You can't, because they are incompatible.... In the EF it is *precisely those things which impede verbal communication which facilitate non-verbal communication:* Latin, silence, worship *ad orientem* and so on. An attempt to ramp up verbal communication in the

EF will destroy what makes it attractive. Similarly, an attempt to bring in more "sense of the sacred" in the OF will radically reduce its big selling point: the ease of verbal communication.

Shaw has astutely recognized that you can't have every possible good simultaneously, and that some goods exclude other goods. It is well to bear this in mind, for it also applies to defenders of the Eastern rites, who in their laudable enthusiasm for their own traditions often prove to be blind and deaf to the distinctive perfections of Western tradition.[9]

THE REPROACH OF AESTHETICISM

Fourth and finally, devotees of the TLM are often reproached for having too "aesthetic" a view of the liturgy and for thinking too much in terms of "devotion" and "reverence" (as if these attitudes could ever be a problem to worry about!).[10] But the truth is, the TLM is *inherently* aesthetic and devotional, and the Latin language is an important component in its genetic makeup. Those, on the other hand, who, knowing that the Novus Ordo was meant by Paul VI (et al.) to be in the vernacular, now seek for it to be in Latin—*they* are indeed guilty of a kind of aestheticism. For, in this scenario, the Latin becomes a decoration and a mystification, like other "smells and bells" that give the illusion of continuity in our liturgical worship and smudge the profound differences in content between old and new.[11]

It's that dragon of "optionitis" rearing its ugly head once more. The TLM basically *has* to be in Latin: the language is bone of its bone, flesh of its flesh. It is written on its birth certificate and its passport.[12] Yes, I know: the Iroquois ended up getting some of the old liturgy in their own language, and there's a Glagolitic Mass, and the high-church Anglicans did up a Cranmerized Roman Missal, etc. But 99.9% of the time, the old Roman liturgy was offered in Latin—and the same thing is true today in thousands of Mass locations across a hundred countries. In the Novus Ordo, however, even the language used is an option, like so much else. As a result, somebody has to *choose* to do the new Mass in Latin. This choice, like other choices, instantly creates polarization, in a way that something inevitable, something simply *given*, does not do.[13]

---

9 Shaw's final article in the series, "Part 5: 1965?," falls outside the current discussion. I return to the 1965 interim missal in chapter 13.
10 See Dietrich von Hildebrand, *Liturgy and Personality* (The Hildebrand Project, 2016).
11 Recall the words of Andrew Shivone on p. 72.
12 For a defense of this claim in relation to the Roman liturgy's shift from Greek to Latin, see "Was Liturgical Latin Introduced As—and Because It Was—the Vernacular?," in Kwasniewski, ed., *Illusions of Reform*, 114–22.
13 Moreover, when anything traditional but optional in the Novus Ordo is done, it thereby becomes a personal accomplishment posited by the pastoral discretion, intellectual conviction, and good taste of the celebrant, and thus reflective of his personality

In fact, there is a still deeper level to consider. The traditional Roman liturgy is based upon the pontifical liturgy in its solemn form. Every other version—Solemn High Mass, High or Sung Mass, and Low Mass—is a pragmatic reduction for pastoral exigencies. It's as if, in theory, you'd always want to have a pontifical Mass (since the bishop is Christ *par excellence*, as the Church Fathers insistently say, and the primordial Mass is the whole Church gathered around its bishop), but since that's impossible, you take the next achievable level.[14] This paradigm was rejected by the liturgical reform, which took the individual priest's liturgy as the fundamental form and made anything else a matter of *adding* things on to the parish Mass template.[15] That is a major reversal of organic liturgical development. It explains why, whenever a priest does the liturgy in keeping with our Roman traditions, he is thought to be an "aesthete," since all those additions are, in the Bugnini perspective, unnecessary additions. The reformers, at least to this extent, were trapped within the Low Mass culture and the excessive prioritization of validity, to the neglect of authenticity and fittingness.[16]

In short, the Latin Novus Ordo is not a solution for our woes. It is an awkward misfit that will confuse some, disappoint others, and inspire no one. The one and only solution, in both the short term and the long term, is a principled, inflexible adherence to the great Latin liturgical tradition, which no one on earth has the authority to outlaw, and which it would be spiritual suicide to surrender.

PRAYING IN THE SAME WORDS AS THE SAINTS

Those who sling around the charge of "aestheticism" seem to forget that, by God's design, the first level in learning how to take Catholic

---

or "*ars celebrandi.*" That is my own primary critique of the "reverent Novus Ordo" and the ROTR, as chapter 7 set forth.

[14] This, incidentally, shows that the *Missa cantata* should be privileged in traditional circles a great deal more than it tends to be. The read Mass (*Missa lecta*) or Low Mass is understandable for reasons of devotion and convenience, but its prevalence in parishes is partially the result of a subtle form of Western liturgical minimalism that sees many of the normative "externals" of the Roman rite as dispensable or even distracting/detracting from spirituality—an attitude dangerously akin to Protestant iconoclasm. In reality, the gestures, postures, vestments, music, and architecture are icons of the wedding feast of the Lamb. In the East there is a Sunday annually celebrated as the "Triumph of Orthodoxy," commemorating the victory of the iconophiles and exalting the holy icons; in the West we are still fighting for our triumph over iconoclasm.

[15] Bugnini (*Reform of the Liturgy*, 340) is explicit about this: "The point of departure for the reform should not be 'private' Mass but 'Mass with a congregation'; not Mass as read but Mass with singing. But which Mass with song—the pontifical, the solemn, or the simple sung Mass? Given the concrete situation in the churches, the answer can only be: Mass celebrated by a priest, with a reader, servers, a choir or cantor, and a congregation. All other forms, such as pontifical Mass, solemn Mass, Mass with a deacon, will be amplifications or further simplifications of this basic Mass, which is therefore called 'normative.'"

[16] See my article "The Four Qualities of Liturgy: Validity, Licitness, Fittingness, and Authenticity," *NLM*, November 9, 2020.

liturgy seriously, how to enter into it and yield to its influence, is typically none other than the "smells and bells" that capture our attention and start training us in rituality and symbolism. As rational animals who learn through our senses, we notice and appreciate beautiful vestments, furnishings, bells, incense, and music; we infer, without much difficulty, that if special things are used or done, something special must be taking place. These elements are important: not only do they subtly instruct us as to what is going on and how we should respond to it, they also inoculate us against the errors of minimalism and spiritualism. We might call this *"extrinsic* maximalism." It is sad to think that many Catholics, perhaps most, have never experienced it.

But, at times, the smells and bells can be largely absent without fatal results, as in a devout Low Mass. Ascetical in its quiet simplicity, the Low Mass helps us to apprehend the second level of liturgical soundness: the integral, substantive, expressively adequate or even superabundant prayers and ceremonies contained in the traditional missal, which the priest is *required* to use, no options about it. We might call this an *"intrinsic* maximalism" that should never be absent from the liturgy, no matter the type of celebration—whether pontifical, solemn, sung, or recited. This level bespeaks adherence to a living tradition belonging to a community stretching back 2,000 years (or even 3,000 if we take the Jewish roots into account: a truth of which the commemoration of the Holy Maccabees on August 1 reminds us), but extending also to the Church triumphant in heaven.

It is no small matter that we have the privilege of praying in the very same words as our predecessors. The *Liber specialis gratiæ* of St. Mechtild of Hackeborn (c. 1240–1298)[17] contains frequent and detailed visions springing forth from the Latin texts of the liturgy. The Church's rites came alive before her as Christ enacted the meaning of the texts. At one point, describing a liturgy she beheld ("After this our Lord sang the Mass, dressed in a red chasuble and bishop's trappings"),[18] Mechtild hears the Lord telling her: "You shall understand that when you say any psalm or prayer which any saints prayed when they were alive on earth, then all of those saints pray to me for you. Additionally, when you are in your devotions and speak with me, then all of the saints are joyful and worship and thank me."[19] Of all the prayers

---

17 *Book of Special Grace*, which was translated in medieval England as *Booke of Gostlye Grace*. Mechtild was *domina cantrix* (head cantress) at the renowned Benedictine monastery of Helfta until her death; in a vision Christ called her his "nightingale."
18 Christian Gregory Savage, "Music and the Writings of the Helfta Mystics," Thesis for the Master of Music, Florida State University, 2012, p. 47.
19 "Cum autem psalmos aut aliquam orationem tuam Sancti in terris oraverunt legis, omnes Sancti pro te orant. Cum vero meditaris, vel mecum loqueris, omnes Sancti gaudentes me benedicunt" (*Liber* 3:11, 210), cited in Savage, 53. The rejoinder

offered up by the saints, the Roman Canon is surely the foremost in age and dignity. As Dom Edouard Guillou says:

> This main prayer of the Canon has been meditated by so many saints, murmured by so many priests, that it cannot be compared to any other prayer. Keeping its original Latin form is the dazzling testimony of the necessary unity of the Roman Church in time and space. Its abandonment in practice would be an act of impiety.[20]

In like manner, the Benedictine monk Fr. Joseph Kreuter wrote in 1933:

> Is it not a prolific source of devotion, of spiritual joy and consolation, to know that you are privileged to call holy Mass your own Sacrifice, to share in it with Christ and His ordained priest? Happy those who say those ancient and divinely inspired words together with the priest, for they thus become intimately united with the generations of Christians who have preceded them. For centuries the faithful have prayed those words. What emotions, what joys, what sentiments of praise, adoration, thanksgiving and expiation have found their expression in these prayers of the Missal! What torrents of grace and blessings, temporal and spiritual, have they drawn down from on High upon the faithful worshipers![21]

Since we all know now that *only 13% of the orations* of the old missal made their way intact into the new missal—and therefore 87% of the verbatim prayer of the Roman Church prior to 1969 has been tampered with or canceled out[22]—it is worth asking what are the cosmic, heavenly, eschatological, and ecclesiological implications of such memoricide, or, to use Guillou's word, impiety.

The gradual discovery of tradition by Msgr. James Byrnes, a priest originally of the archdiocese of New York, obliged him to grapple with the "Novus Ordo question," which resulted in his ultimately deciding to celebrate the new rite no longer. He said in a talk he gave in 2014:

> It was during the Prayers at the Foot of the Altar that the thought struck me. This was the Mass offered by those priest-saints I had

---

that there are now saints in heaven who were accustomed to praying with the rites of Paul VI does not change the fact that at least 99% of the saints were familiar with traditional liturgical rites, versus at most 1% who were not. Moreover, that one could be sanctified in spite of an impoverished liturgy should be no surprise from the vantage of God's power, but it does nothing to change objectively what is wrong with a ruptured liturgy and how this rupture generally impedes the work of sanctification in the Church militant.

[20] Edouard Guillou, *Le livre de la messe: Mysterium fidei—Le texte de la messe de saint Pie V*, with a foreword by Msgr. Marcel Lefebvre (Éditions Fideliter, 1992; originally published in 1975).

[21] Joseph Kreuter, OSB, "A 1933 Sermon on the Missal: 'Having perfectly worshiped God in this life, the faithful will be prepared to take part in the heavenly praises,'" first published in the journal *Orate Fratres* of October 7, 1933; reprinted at *Rorate Caeli*, June 28, 2019.

[22] See Hazell, "'All the Elements of the Roman Rite'?"

read biographies of when I was young, particularly St. Isaac Jogues. I could and did imagine him standing before a crude altar in the wilds of northern New York State, uttering these very same words. It was this overwhelming sense of continuity that stayed with me, this sense that I had never experienced during my twenty-one years of offering the Novus Ordo, and made me realize what had been stolen from myself and others of my generation. We had been the victims of spiritual identity theft and we hadn't even realized it. That was the worst part. So much was taken from us and we didn't know it. I can say definitively that that is the reaction of most folks my age (53, almost 54) and younger who still attend the Novus Ordo but sense something isn't quite right. After experiencing the traditional Mass and beginning to fill in all the gaps of their spiritual life with tradition, all they can do is proclaim loudly, "We. Were. Robbed."[23]

We can probe more deeply into the moral dimensions of this problem by reflecting on the fourth commandment: "Honor thy father and thy mother, that thou mayest have long life in the land that the Lord thy God will show thee." The philosopher Robert Spaemann was wont to ask: When we abandon the Roman Canon and the piety of our forefathers, how are we being obedient to this commandment *in its ecclesial reality*? We have not only biological fathers and mothers, but spiritual ones as well. In the words of the prophet Isaiah: "Our holy and our beautiful house, where our fathers praised thee, is burned up with fire: and all our pleasant things are laid waste" (Is 64:11).

By rejecting centuries of Catholic liturgy and devotion, the clergy involved in the liturgical reform of the 1960s and 1970s were, in essence, trash-talking their Mother. They were outrageously violating the fourth commandment: "Honor thy father [God in His Providence] and thy mother [the Church in her order of worship and her customs]." It was a sin of, and against, the spiritual paternity of the priest, who is supposed to pass on the family inheritance, the social and cultural life of the people—a transmission far more important than that of mere biological life.[24]

What we do to, or with, our family inheritance shows what we think of our father and of our entire family. Whatever one might say about rococo churches or fiddleback chasubles, no one can deny that such things as the *Latin missal's content*, the *Gregorian chant* that cantillates it, and the *eastward orientation* are central, constitutive, and

---

[23] "A Diocesan Priest Discovers the Traditional Mass," from the 2014 Conference for Catholic Tradition: The Mass, Heart of the Church, audio at https://soundcloud.com/angeluspress/a-diocesan-priest-discovers-the-traditional-mass. Recall Phillip Campbell's similar conclusion, quoted on p. 36.

[24] On the pivotal role of tradition and literary canon in the formation of human beings and societies, see Holmes, *Cur Deus Verba*, 57–68.

characteristic treasures of our patrimony. Therefore the proponents and adherents of the liturgical reform cannot escape culpability (to varying degrees) for the grave sins of patricide, matricide, pride, ingratitude, and contempt. These are the very same sins as those of the Prodigal Son—and they can be expiated, and their bitter fruits overcome, *only* in the same way: "Father, I have sinned against heaven [Providence] and against you [the Latin tradition]; I no longer deserve to be called your son. Take me on as one of your hired hands." Take me on as a servant who will punctiliously serve the family once again and devote himself to its well-being.

Sebastian Morello synthesizes the various points I have been making:

> Only by recovering a love for its own tradition as a gift providentially bestowed down the centuries will the Church respond to the dual crisis of loss of meaning and loss of authority.... The Church is thwarted in bestowing its gift upon mankind because, in its ongoing repudiation of its own tradition, it is currently preoccupied in killing its father and mother....
>
> Latin Christians have long emphasised "assent," and hence the possession of *ideas*, over existential transformation through right worship (an emphasis that has only swelled due to the unexamined acceptance of the rationalist paradigm). It is unsurprising, then, that serious Catholicism is more likely to be found online—where ideas are offered and bought up—than in the local church. And those Catholics who have retained the organic conception of the Church as the institution that gifts to the baptised the virtues of right relationality with God—a conception of the Christian as a *liturgical creature*—have for some time now been actively persecuted by the incumbents of the Church's highest offices. Such Catholics are seen as betrayers of the modern project of Enlightened man, whom the Church's leaders have enthroned in their demotion of Christ the King. And in seeing such Catholics in this way, the Church's government is entirely correct....
>
> The cycle of revolution and repudiation, from which the West will never escape under Enlightened man, is rapidly aging the West, and it will continue to do so until the West obeys the fourth commandment and reinducts itself into its tradition.[25]

In its spirit, certainly, the commandment to honor our father and mother carries implications in how we treat the ways of tradition and the teachings of our parents—not only our parents individually but also our forefathers collectively, including the Church Fathers and the hundreds of popes[26] who handed down to their successors

---
[25] Sebastian Morello, *Mysticism, Magic, and Monasteries: Recovering the Sacred Mystery at the Heart of Reality* (Os Justi Press, 2024), 65–67.
[26] The word "pope" coming, of course, from the Greek word *páppas*, an affectionate way of saying "father."

the inheritance each had received. The reward of faithfulness to the commandment is obvious: a clear sense of identity, a community life that is coherent and creative and reasonable. In treating respectfully the traditions (and hence the teachings!) of our ancestors, we take our place in the *continuing* dialogue that God started with mankind in the persons of our first parents. Even if the central portion of it was recorded in the Sacred Scriptures, the dialogue of love within the family of faith continues past the final page of Revelation and into the history of the Church, the Body of Christ. Faithfulness to the ecclesial fourth commandment is, one might say, letting God continue to take part in the same discussion, with all of its former exchanges presupposed; whereas lack of faithfulness interrupts the discussion or starts it over from scratch—like one who would depart from the main highway in favor of rough and difficult side paths, and who, as a consequence, makes slow headway or gets lost or stuck. The evil fruits of rejecting the commandment are visible in the unraveling of a society, the waywardness, untetheredness, and confusion of the younger generations.

There is no question that this is a difficult time for Catholics who love their faith and are eager to assist at a worthy liturgy, a Eucharistic liturgy faithful to the purpose and significance of the Mass. To reap the good fruits of life in Christ, we must follow the commandments of God in their individual, social, and ecclesial dimensions. We must abandon the impiety of rupturing ourselves from the common voice of tradition; we must embrace anew the status of descendants, heirs, trustees, servants, and pupils. We must renounce antichristic "reform" and *return to form*. This we will do, to be sure—if we are Catholics of the Latin rite—by taking up once again the Latin language, in which we will study, sing, talk, and pray. Yet we will honor our providential Father in heaven and our holy Mother the Church most profoundly, most coherently, most effectively, when we take up again the Roman rite in its integrity, bringing joy to the court of heaven with the words they once formed on their lips and still love in their hearts.

9

Sacrifice and Desacrificialization

THE CLAIM IS OFTEN MADE THAT THE TRAditional Roman rite conveys more clearly than the Novus Ordo does that the Mass is a true and proper sacrifice, the unbloody re-presentation of the bloody sacrifice of Christ on the Cross. As this dogmatic truth is a point of central importance for living the Catholic faith and passing it on, we ought to look into this contrast between the two rites. Can we identify the features of the traditional Latin Mass that convey so clearly its sacrificial nature? If we can, and if it turns out that the new rite omits these things, we will have gained a valuable insight into the causes of the precipitous decline in orthodox Eucharistic faith as well as a crucial indicator of where we must look for Eucharistic revival. With a healthy fear of omissions, I suggest the following as a start. I do not list these features in any particular order of importance, as I believe *all* of them work together to produce a cumulative and overwhelming effect.

THE *AD ORIENTEM* STANCE

In every traditional liturgy, Christians face the East, the rising sun, symbol of Christ coming in glory, and of the inextinguishable light of God.[1] When the priest comes to the altar, stands facing east *with* us, and offers the holy gifts, it is obvious that he is doing something *for* us, as our mediator with God and as the image of the one Mediator between God and man, Christ Jesus. He is about the Father's business (Lk 2:49), occupied with the work of the altar, intent on offering to the Most Holy Trinity the unblemished Lamb of God who takes away our sins—there can be no illusion that Mass is all about us, in the sense of the "self-enclosed circle" Joseph Ratzinger speaks of.[2]

---

[1] There are many fine treatments of this subject, both online and in print. Uwe Michael Lang's *Turning Towards the Lord: Orientation in Liturgical Prayer* (Ignatius Press, 2009) is the place to start. A definitive scholarly account has been published by Stefan Heid, *Altar and Church: Principles of Liturgy from Early Christianity* (The Catholic University of America Press, 2024). For an overview, see "Why We Worship Facing East" in Kwasniewski, *Turned Around*, 1–28.

[2] "The turning of the priest toward the people has turned the community into a self-enclosed circle. In its outward form, it no longer opens out on what lies ahead and above, but is closed in on itself." Ratzinger, *The Spirit of the Liturgy*, II, 3, in *Theology of the Liturgy*, 49. Writes Thomas Howard: "People who are fellowshipping with each other, and sharing, are, characteristically, facing each other. People who are worshipping are, all together, facing something else, namely, the Sapphire Throne." *The Night Is Far Spent: A Treasury of Thomas Howard*, ed. Vivian W. Dudro (Ignatius Press, 2007), 255.

Now, we can always point out that *versus populum* was never mandated by Vatican II or subsequent documents and that *ad orientem* is perfectly "permissible" in the Novus Ordo, but as the years go on and we see, on the one hand, Cardinal Sarah slammed by the Vatican for endorsing *ad orientem* and, on the other, Cardinal Cupich outlawing it *ultra vires*, we can safely say there will never be a general return to the eastward posture in the Novus Ordo context.[3] If it didn't happen under Pope Benedict XVI who was deeply favorable to it, it seems unlikely to do so in the future, when a combination of institutional inertia and a renewed neo-modernist agenda will probably nip most attempts at liturgical reform in the tender bud.

In truth, the traditional orientation returns whenever and wherever the traditional liturgy returns. The "psychology" of the new Mass as it was imposed and inculturated is wrapped up with the horizontalist mentality Ratzinger critiques, and it will be much harder to budge this error than to re-introduce the *usus antiquior* as something new and different, already in possession of a consistent set of harmonizing traits.

PREPARATION AT THE FOOT OF THE ALTAR

Psalm 42, which speaks of going in unto the altar of God, of being led by His light and His truth to the holy mountain and the tabernacle of the Lord, of giving praise unto salvation (think of how the Mass is referred to in the Roman Canon as the "*sacrificium laudis*"), makes for an ideal entry into the Mass. This Psalm is shot through with the language of offering, sacrifice, suffering, the hope of redemption—all of which highlight the forthcoming mystical re-presentation of the Passion of our Lord.

The extensive penitential rite emphasizes that we are setting about a serious work, not something to take lightly. The human psyche cannot help but wonder: "What's it all about? What are we preparing to do?" The fairly substantial delay between the opening sign of the cross and the recitation of the Introit at the altar affords a much-needed opportunity to orient oneself toward the forthcoming sacrifice, to express sorrow for sins, and to beg for mercy. As Will Haun explains:

---

[3] See Gerard O'Connell, "Pope Francis: There will be no 'reform of the reform' of the liturgy," *America*, December 6, 2016; Jonathan Liedl, "The City of Big Shoulders—and Liturgical Confusion: Chicago Faithful Flummoxed by Inconsistent Liturgy Policy," *National Catholic Register*, June 27, 2022. Channeling the current Vatican line, Cardinal Roche said in an address given to newly ordained bishops gathered in Rome: "The cause of ecclesial communion will be best served if you are faithful to the principles of the reform and faithfully internalise them. We are not called to rethink, much less 'reform' the reform, rather we are called to understand it, receive it, and apply it. There is no turning back from this path." Arthur Roche, "Ecclesial Communion and the Motu Proprio *Traditionis Custodes*," in Dicastero per i Vescovi, *Il Ministero Episcopale in Una Chiesa Sinodale* (Libreria Editrice Vaticana, 2024), 146.

The priest makes the Sign of the Cross and says with the servers (this is the English translation of the Latin), "I will go into the altar of God, the God who giveth joy to my youth." Then the priest begins Psalm 42, where the first words out of his mouth are, "Judge me, O God, and distinguish my cause from the nation that is not holy; deliver me from the unjust and deceitful man." Judge me, O God. Could any phrase be, both at the same time, an intense counter to the self-oriented conception of conscience and also an entirely appropriate statement before we ascend to the throne of God Himself? God knows all that we are, and so before any one of us presume to go to the altar where he sacrifices Himself for us, we must acknowledge that frankly we don't deserve to be there. None of us do, and [it's] only by His grace and mercy that we are delivered from the unjust and deceitful man—which, if we're honest with ourselves, is *us*. It could be ourselves at any moment, and it is the God who gives joy to our youth that, despite all of our flaws, lets us have the Church that, by [our] submitting to the sacraments and the power that He gave it, allows us to access Him.[4]

Anyone who has ever served the Latin Mass and made these responses with understanding knows how piercing they are—even as Will Haun describes them. The little boys who most often parrot the words do not understand them, but they have memorized them, and the words have settled into the innermost recesses of their souls, where they may later blossom—as they have done in me, decades after I first heard them. That is how the old rite works: with immense patience, on a slow time-scale, playing the long game. Unfortunately, these prayers at the foot of the altar were entirely abolished in the Novus Ordo. Never was any edit more efficient and more stupid.

SEPARATION OF PRIEST FROM PEOPLE

There are many ways in which the old rite clearly *distinguishes* between the priest and the people—they are not lumped together, as in the modern rite, but are treated in accordance with their ontological distinction.[5] For example, the priest recites the Confiteor first, for himself, and then the servers recite the Confiteor, which serves as an occasion for the people to confess their sins in league with them. At High Mass, he and he alone intones the Gloria and the Creed, and then continues to recite them separately, while the people or the choir sing.[6] In the Offertory, the *Suscipe, Sancte Pater* strongly brings out the priest's role as mediator, as well as his personal sinfulness:

---

[4] Audio at www.youtube.com/watch?v=B5NghUaqUIY.
[5] For a thorough treatment of this contrast, see "Why the Priest Is Separated from the People" in Kwasniewski, *Turned Around*, 29–55; cf. 123–26.
[6] I defend this practice—an instance of the influence of the Low Mass on the High Mass, which most liturgists deplore—in chapter 15.

> Accept, O holy Father, almighty and eternal God, this unspotted host, *which I, Thy unworthy servant, offer unto Thee,* my living and true God, for *my* innumerable sins, offenses, and negligences, *and for all here present:* as also for all faithful Christians, both living and dead, that it may avail *both me and them* for salvation unto life everlasting. Amen.

The priest receives Holy Communion first, in order to complete the sacrifice, and only then offers it to the people. He says the *Domine, non sum dignus* three times, and only afterwards do the servers or the people say it three times.[7] The *Placeat tibi* once again brings out the special role of the priest:

> May the performance of my homage be pleasing to Thee, O holy Trinity: and grant that the Sacrifice which I, though unworthy, have offered up in the sight of Thy Majesty, may be acceptable to Thee, and through Thy mercy, be a propitiation for me, and for all those for whom I have offered it.

Such is not the prayer of a mere "presider" or "president of the assembly."[8]

How is such distinction and separation pertinent to our theme? Consider the doctrine of the Epistle to the Hebrews: "Every high priest taken from among men is ordained for men in the things that appertain to God, that he may offer up gifts and sacrifices for sins" (Heb 5:1; cf. 2:17, 8:3). This is the *definition* of a priest: the one who, as a mediator, offers gifts and sacrifices for sins. Anything that detracts from or mutes the clear expression of the priestly office also detracts from the sacrificial quality of his actions. The priest at the altar truly acts *in persona Christi*, in a way qualitatively different from the ways in which the laity or subordinate ministers participate, and the old Mass brings this out with total clarity. Surely its luminous expression of this high-priestly mediation is part of the reason why the priesthood is viewed and treated with more esteem and respect in communities centered on the traditional

---

[7] The way that the Novus Ordo conflates the priest's communion and that of the people testifies to Protestant influence. As Catholic theology teaches, while it is desirable for as many of the people as possible to receive communion (provided they are in a state of grace and properly disposed to do so), it is necessary *only* for the priest to communicate in order to have a valid celebration of the Mass. This is because the priest, in representing Christ, represents the entire Mystical Body, head and members; the sacrifice of the Cross is complete in and of itself even before its fruits are communicated to individual members of the human race.

[8] Recall Ratzinger's description of how "an unprecedented clericalization came on the scene" after the Council: "Now the priest—the 'presider,' as they now prefer to call him—becomes the real point of reference for the whole liturgy. Everything depends on him. We have to see him, to respond to him, to be involved in what he is doing. His creativity sustains the whole thing." *The Spirit of the Liturgy*, II, 3, in *Theology of the Liturgy*, 48.

Mass, and why vocations from them will always be proportionally more numerous, as it places in relief the attractive and lofty beauty of the ministerial priesthood's special conformity to Christ.

THE MANY KISSINGS OF THE ALTAR

When first introduced to traditional Catholic worship in my twenties, I remember my delight at noticing how much more often the priest kisses the altar in the old rite than in the new rite, where he does so only twice—at the start and at the finish of Mass. What a desperate relinquishment of meaning, beauty, and affection can be seen in this reduction! The many kisses in the *usus antiquior* draw our attention to the altar again and again throughout Mass, putting our focus there, at the place of the sacrifice for which the priest has been ordained, to which he continually ascends, with which he is intimately united as one of the chosen friends of Our Lord. Since the altar represents Christ, these kisses are genuine tokens of love, service, and devotion to Him. It is one more of those small but poignant ways in which the traditional Mass keeps one's mind and heart fixed on the Lord and on the immensity of His love for us—expressed above all in His Passion—and how its symbols prompt in us a desire to return love for love.[9]

THE PRAYERS THEMSELVES

The traditional Offertory prayers, the Roman Canon, and the *Placeat tibi* express to absolute perfection the doctrine of the Mass as a true, proper, expiatory, impetratory sacrifice for the living and for the dead—a doctrine given its consummate formulation by the Council of Trent and surrounded with a sturdy hedge of anathemas.

The Offertory rite is one of the Mass's medieval gems, present in a variety of forms across all of Europe in every rite and use. It was stripped away and discarded as a "medieval accretion" by the antiquarianist reformers of both the sixteenth and the twentieth centuries. The Roman Canon, which some of the more zealous Modernists of Paul VI's era wanted to expunge altogether from their avant-garde Missal, is always used in the traditional Latin Mass—no surprise, since it is *the* defining feature of the Roman rite. Lump the entire committee-created smorgasbord of alternative Eucharistic Prayers together and it will still not succeed in expressing the doctrine of the sacrifice of the Mass as lucidly and reverentially as the Roman Canon does all by itself. At their best, these other Eucharistic Prayers are novel constructs free of doctrinal errors; at their worst, they seem to dance around doctrine, for fear of excluding Lutherans from the table of plenty.

---

[9] See my article "'For I Will Not Give You a Kiss as Did Judas': On Sacred and Profane Kissing," *NLM*, April 6, 2020.

THE SILENCE OF THE CANON

The silence that falls upon the church during the Roman Canon is one of the most beautiful features of the *usus antiquior*. You can be at the most glorious Mass in the world, with organs and choirs to vie with the angels—but when it comes time for the great miracle, everyone falls silent and adores. The elevations are like visual thunder in the midst of this inaudible storm of prayer. Bells erupt into a hushed space, heightening our awareness still further, so that every sense is strained, and yet the heart is at peace. The cavernous silence makes it obvious, again, just like the *ad orientem* posture, that the priest is focused on the great work of our redemption, something obviously *from* God and *for* God; it isn't about *you*—at least, not immediately; it is about *Christ*, the Head of the Mystical Body, and therefore about you and me inasmuch as we are His members.[10]

ELEVATIONS WITHIN TWOFOLD GENUFLECTIONS

The fact that the priest is instructed in the Novus Ordo to elevate the host or the chalice immediately after consecration and only *afterwards* to genuflect before the Lord is clearly a change of which nothing good can be said, even by papal maximalists. The traditional purpose of elevating the host and chalice is to give the faithful an opportunity to adore the Blessed Sacrament *after* the priest has first adored It; the host and chalice must be raised up *because* the priest is facing eastwards and his body is blocking our view of the consecrated gifts. To the miracle of transubstantiation, there is no more natural, obvious, correct, and pious reaction than immediately to drop down on one's knee in adoration. The twofold genuflection of the *usus antiquior*—that is, both before the elevation and after it—conveys the humble awe and fitting homage of the servant before his Master, the creature before his Creator. This unmistakable emphasis on the reality of the divine Victim, like so many other details, serves to underline the Mass as a true sacrifice, not merely a symbolic one.[11]

Moreover, with the lifting of the chasuble, the repeated ringing of bells, and often clouds of incense, the elevation at a traditional Latin Mass is a far more emphatic moment, feeding multiple senses with a richer symbolism. As William Mahrt writes:

---

10 For more on the silent Canon, see Kwasniewski, *Good Music*, 283–92.
11 As I have had occasion to say many times, it does not matter that the Roman rite once lacked these genuflections and that they entered into practice at different moments of history and in different ways. What matters is the repudiation *today* of customs that developed *for good reason* and have existed for centuries of unbroken practice in our corporate worship. It is one thing to lack some perfection, and another to tear it out. No one is to blame for a man born without sight; Cornwall is rightly blamed for gouging out Gloucester's eyeballs. One imagines our liturgical Cornwalls bending to their task: "Out, vile genuflection! Where is thy groveling now?"

When the Mass is celebrated facing the altar ([the priest] facing God and not just turning his back on the people), the sacrament is consecrated in an aura of mystery and wonder, and when it is elevated for the people's adoration, they see it as something to be worshipped. When the Mass is celebrated at the altar facing the people, they see every action of the priest, after which the elevation is not as great a climax.[12]

The elevation is the *visual* high point of the Mass, a gesture that reminds us of the offering of the Son to the Father, the spotless Lamb to the eternal Trinity, for us men and for our salvation. No one who is paying the slightest attention can fail to see that something dramatic is happening at this moment. In evoking the raising up of Christ on the Cross, it rightly draws our minds to Good Friday, the redemptive Passion, and the generosity by which Our Lord makes this gift of Himself in our midst, lavishing upon us the same attentive charity that He showed on Calvary to His most holy Mother and His beloved disciple St. John. Because the Mass is a true and proper sacrifice—the very sacrifice of Calvary, a dogma of the Catholic faith as established at Trent—it ought to be offered in a way that does not look like the Passover meal of Holy Thursday, which was done in anticipation of the redemptive sacrifice yet to come.

In the Novus Ordo context, we end up with neither a straight-out sacrificial setting nor a straight-out social meal setting but an incongruous blend of the two that makes the result neither fish nor fowl. For this reason, the new liturgy will never satisfy *either* the progressives *or* the conservatives, and that is why its *ars celebrandi* has been a tug-of-war for over fifty years. The old liturgy is not a tug-of-war in this way, because it, like all apostolic rites, plainly puts the sacrificial offering front and center, and ranges everything else around that.

THE PRIEST'S COMMUNION AND ABLUTIONS

As with the preparation at the foot of the altar, the seriousness with which the priest receives Communion in the *usus antiquior*—the greater number and amplitude of the prayers, the reciting of verses from the psalms, the more deliberate handling of the chalice (making the sign of the cross with it), etc.—reinforces the solemnity of the moment, the fact that he is indeed partaking of the holy, awesome, immortal and life-giving mysteries of Christ. The ablutions, more ample in their prayers and in their thoroughness, involving the washing of forefinger, thumb, and chalice with wine and water, underline the same truth, and prevent the priest from incurring the enormous guilt of treating the Son of God

---

[12] William Mahrt, "Unintended Consequences," *Sacred Music*, vol. 142, no. 2 (Summer 2015): 4.

carelessly; his holding of thumb and forefinger together from the consecration until ablutions vividly accentuates this care. The Communion rite and the ablutions together emphasize the reality of the sacrificial Victim made present in our midst by the consecration, once again showing that what we do *around* the consecration, before and after, is by no means negligible to the overall understanding of what is happening in the Mass.

In the Novus Ordo most of these prayers and ablutions were abolished, with horrifying results witnessed by countless sacristans, servers, and attendees. The simplification of these elements of the Mass has not encouraged orthodox faith in the Holy Eucharist as the true Body and Blood of Christ or the Mass as His true and proper sacrifice.

THE LAST GOSPEL

The almost-daily recitation of the Prologue of the Gospel of Saint John after the final blessing reinforces that the drama at which we have been present is a kind of continuation of the mystery of the Incarnation itself. It is the knowledge of this awesome reality that sustains Catholics who, for whatever reason, may not receive Communion at a given Mass; they are there because the Mass is, *in and of itself*, the ultimate act of adoration, praise, thanksgiving, and supplication—not because it is a glorified Communion service.

ASSESSMENT AND PROSPECTS

As regards the "reform of the reform," one might note the sobering fact that the Novus Ordo as it now stands, even with its cornucopia of options, can emulate only a few of the features described above, and only in hothouse circumstances. Most of these elements are so far from its ethos and rubrics that the new rite would have to be significantly overhauled to accommodate them. Let's face it: the architects of the new rite *wanted* to evict what they regarded as an imbalanced medieval emphasis on the Eucharistic sacrifice, in order to reorient the celebration on the "people of God" as the "Body of Christ."[13] That is why they went through the old rite deliberately removing nearly everything listed above. And that is why the reintroduction of the *usus antiquior* appalls the progressives, unsettles them like the sound of fingernails on a chalkboard: they know it is a rejection of the doctrinal modernism and the moral laxity they stand for, of all that they have attempted to impose and permanently enshrine in their postconciliar "renewal."

---

13 This is too well documented to be denied anymore except by the Pollyannas of the world. See Ratzinger, *Theology of the Liturgy*, 541–57, and the extensive discussion of the liturgical reform in Sire, *Phoenix from the Ashes*. In one parish in Montana, when the minister of Communion said "The Body of Christ," recipients were instructed to reply, "Yes we are!" (instead of "Amen"). This innovation was then replicated elsewhere.

It is not possible to attend the traditional Latin Mass and *not*, at some level, experience it as a ritual of sacrifice, as the offering of the Son of God in His human nature to the Most Holy Trinity. The above-mentioned features, which are part and parcel of the rite and cannot be omitted, plainly teach and demonstrate this. Conversely, even a catechized Catholic will have more difficulty seeing the truth about the Mass in the new rite. Because the reformers introduced a new focus on the community and its active participation, the sacrificial prayers and ceremonies — most of them the province of the priest and the other ministers in the sanctuary — had to be reduced or eliminated. This new populist or congregational direction conflicts with a heightened awareness of the immediate and proper meaning of the mysteries being enacted.

It is true that once we have understood that the Mass is the sacrifice of Christ, the head of the Mystical Body, it *then* becomes possible for us to understand it as *our* sacrifice, the ultimate act of charity that unites us as members of the same Body.[14] But the horizontal depends utterly on the vertical, the human on the divine, the Christian community on Christ's priesthood and sacrifice.

Another way of putting this is to say that the primary realities are what the liturgy is made to embody and communicate, so that the secondary realities may flow forth in abundance. It is far more important to be brought into contact with the Body and Blood of the all-pleasing Victim than it is to be brought into fellowship with one's neighbor; the latter will be nothing but shallow pleasantry and empty goodwill until it is deeply and radically united with Jesus Christ in the mystery of His very Person. The *usus antiquior*, in all its dimensions, is focused unambiguously on the primary realities. This is where it dwells; this is where it leads us, habitually, relentlessly: it is a road to Calvary with no exits, pull-offs, culverts, or detours.

The Novus Ordo seems to offer two roads: the vertical and the horizontal, which sometimes run parallel, very occasionally merge, but most of the time run off in opposite directions, with the celebrant and/ or community choosing one or the other, but not both. At its best, it weakly imitates the transcendent verticality and pure focus on the

---

[14] St. Augustine loves to speak about the communal meaning of the Holy Eucharist, e.g., in Book 10 of the *City of God*. In his Encyclical *Ecclesia de Eucharistia* no. 40, John Paul II addresses this point: "Augustine effectively echoed this call when, in recalling the Apostle's words: 'You are the body of Christ and individually members of it' (1 Cor 12: 27), he went on to say: 'If you are his body and members of him, then you will find set on the Lord's table your own mystery. Yes, you receive your own mystery' (*Sermo* 272: *PL* 38, 1247). And from this observation he concludes: 'Christ the Lord . . . hallowed at his table the mystery of our peace and unity. Whoever receives the mystery of unity without preserving the bonds of peace receives not a mystery for his benefit but evidence against himself' (ibid., 1248)." This rich Augustinian theme has nevertheless been abused by being taken out of its metaphysical and liturgical context.

sacrifice found in the traditional Latin Mass; at its worst, it becomes a paraliturgy expressive of a religion other than the Catholic, with a valid consecration stranded forlornly in its midst, like a castaway on a desert island. With this "divided mind," as it were, hesitating and hovering between primary and secondary—a weakness augmented by its vast diversity of possible implementations—the Novus Ordo is a true reflection of the divided mind of its designers, intent as they were on rapprochement with the world, modernity, and Protestantism, as well as a contributing cause of the divided mind within the Church today, whereby Catholics seem to want to be "Catholic" and, at the same time, believe and live in ways that are antithetical to the Faith.

Once a Catholic profoundly embraces the truth that the principal purpose of the Mass is to offer up the one and only all-pleasing sacrifice to God for the life of the world and to receive its spiritual fruits, it will be difficult or impossible for that Catholic to tolerate the Novus Ordo. He will begin the search for a Mass that "looks" like what the Mass actually *is*, where the clergy and laity act, and *receive*, as if they *know* what it is; where every prayer, every gesture, the music, the expected behavior, all bear witness to what it is. Once he encounters the traditional Latin Mass, he will recognize deep within that *this* is the Catholic Mass, the liturgy that embodies the Faith of the Church. In time he will switch over to this Mass; it will be necessary to drop all pretenses and admit that he has finally found his place at the foot of the Cross, with the Blessed Virgin Mary and St. John—and there's no going back.

CONSEQUENCES OF DESACRIFICIALIZATION

The trouble does not end with a loss of focus on the mystery of the saving Passion of the Lord and the ensuing false belief or lack of belief in the constitutive essence of the Mass. There are ripple effects, the foremost of which is the removal of the tabernacle from the high altar, its being shunted aside in the majority of churches designed since the Council. There are many reasons one could give for this decentering of our Lord Jesus Christ in the miracle of His abiding Eucharistic Presence among us, including specious academic rationales refuted by better scholars. But it may be that a subtler dynamic was also at work (and, sadly, sometimes still is).

As I discussed above, the classical Roman rite enshrines and expresses in the most perfect way the reality that the Mass *is essentially* the Sacrifice of Calvary made present in our midst, the immolation of the Son of God who wrought our salvation by His death of love on the Cross and never ceases to enfold us in it down through the ages.

The expression of this sacrificial dimension is not merely muted in the Novus Ordo, it is largely *absent*. In a vernacular Mass said *versus populum* in the usual manner, with Eucharistic Prayer II as a default, how much is there in text or ceremony that strongly and unambiguously conveys the Sacrifice of the Cross? Granted, the new Offertory retained one unambiguously sacrificial phrase from the old missal: "Pray, brethren, that my sacrifice and yours may be acceptable to God, the almighty Father." In the traditional Roman rite, however, the Offertory more luminously foreshadows this very sacrifice, clearly establishing the priest's right intention; the Roman Canon is permeated with the language of oblation and sacrifice; the consecrations for which the Offertory prepares, with their twofold genuflections and glorious elevations in the midst of an ocean of silence, piercingly evoke the lifting up of the Son of Man on Golgotha (Jn 3:14; Jn 12:32). In contrast, one might say that the Novus Ordo emphasizes the *presence* of Christ in our midst, but not His *sacrifice*.[15] An omission of such an Offertory, especially against the backdrop of centuries of having it, seems to assert that the use of bread and wine is primarily for the purpose of sharing a meal. This suggestion is dangerous, as it would be contrary to Catholic doctrine.

The danger manifests itself in a difference in catechesis that follows upon the difference in phenomenology, that is, in how things appear to the viewer. When teaching children what happens at Mass, one ideally says something like the following, which comes in different packagings for different age levels:

> Jesus dying on the Cross offered His life to God, so that sins could be washed away by His precious Blood. Jesus wanted to make it possible for us to be *right there*, so that *our* sins could be washed away, too, and we could be one with Him. So, He gave us the Mass. The priest at the altar takes bread and wine, as Jesus did at the Last Supper, and, by God's power, changes these things into the Body and Blood of Jesus and raises them up on high, as Jesus was raised up high on the Cross. God rejoices in this perfect gift of His Son and, in His love for Him and for us who belong to Him, He lets us receive the Body and Blood of Jesus in Communion. This makes us as completely one with Jesus as we can be in this life; the Father is pleased with us as He is pleased with His Son; and we are prepared

---

[15] The architects of the liturgical reform were enamored of ecumenism to such an extent that they admitted they were trying to recast the Roman rite in a manner that would be acceptable to Protestants, as we saw in chapter 5. The conservative Protestants were only too happy to concede a "presence" of Christ in the Mass, but emphasis on sacrifice was anathema to them (as it were). For extensive documentation, see Davies, *Pope Paul's New Mass*, 269–380. Admittedly, the new rite retains the *Orate, fratres* (in spite of the desire of many on the Consilium to do away with it: see Bugnini, *Reform of the Liturgy*, 180n79, 358, 371n38, 379), which shows that the Protestant mentality did not conquer altogether. However, what remains in regard to sacrifice is exiguous in comparison with what the traditional rite possesses, showing a decisive shift of focus and emphasis.

for heaven, when it is our turn to permanently offer up our own life to God, with Jesus, at the moment of our death.

Granted, one might find a better way of putting it, but something along those lines will get a conversation going. Yet what really struck me years ago in working with my own children was how *little* catechesis, relatively speaking, was required in order for them to be able to perceive the meaning of the gestures of the priest at the traditional Mass—and how powerfully those gestures *remind* us of truths we have learned and continually *reinforce* them. Once you know a little about what Jesus did at the Last Supper and on Good Friday, the actions and prayers practically hit you over the head with a chain of mysteries—mediation, redemption, atonement, satisfaction, adoration. It doesn't take much training to see in the traditional Mass an awesome sacrifice joining earth to heaven, the sinner to the Savior, the altar to the cross.

Conversely, I discovered that children did not as easily see the same connections at the Novus Ordo Masses we attended. The connections were not nearly so obvious. This Mass seemed rather different in its purpose—more focused on the people, with a lot of talking, winding up with the reception of Communion. What was most of all *hidden* to the senses was that this liturgy is a *sacrifice*. It looks more like a handling of bread and wine over a table, a meal in imitation of the Last Supper. What I realized, to my chagrin, is that I had to *assert*, without much in the way of supporting evidence, that the Novus Ordo *really was* the Holy Sacrifice, even though it didn't look like it, not having the old rite's marvelous array of texts and ceremonies to underline the sacrificial nature of the action.

That bothered me then, and it still bothers me now. It's as if the new rite was designed by someone who wanted it *not* to be easy to perceive, by the combined strength of a *simple* catechism and a *complex* liturgy, that the Mass is the unbloody re-presentation of the bloody sacrifice of Our Lord on Calvary. In the sphere of the Novus Ordo we need a *complex* catechism to go with a *simple* liturgy; otherwise the truth won't be known. Because the liturgy does not embody and proclaim the truth with resounding clarity, we have to spend more time explaining, asserting, and keeping our fingers crossed that the brittle fideism will not yield to the ravages of forgetfulness, boredom, or heresy.

WHY WERE THE TABERNACLES MOVED?

After the Second Vatican Council, in countless churches across the world, the tabernacle housing the Blessed Sacrament was moved away from a central position of honor at the high altar, off to a side chapel or sometimes to a refurbished broom closet. In the church of the high school I attended, it would have been impossible to know where the tabernacle was without asking for directions, as it was hidden in a cave-like room that blended into the rest of the modernist aesthetic. While many rationalizations have been given for this exile of the Host, I have a theory about why it took place at the same time as the liturgical reform.

The overwhelming miracle of Our Lord's Real Presence in the Blessed Sacrament, reserved in the tabernacle, sets, if you will, a challenge to the Mass. To speak in halting human terms, the only way the Mass could be or do something *greater* than that miracle — the only way there could be no confusion of different "orders" of symbolism — is if the liturgy had the wherewithal to show forth *the very Sacrifice* that allows for the abiding presence of the divine Victim in the tabernacle. In other words, the Mass must be seen and felt to *outweigh* the tabernacle, so that there can be no confusion between the two orders: Sacrifice and Presence.

That this is the case with the traditional Mass vis-à-vis the Tabernacle I have no doubt; even in European churches housing enormous gilded tabernacles bedecked with extravagant decoration, the ancient Mass holds its own, drawing all eyes and hearts to itself while it is happening and remaining the total master of the building, the altar, and the furnishings. It is clearly *the reason* for everything else, and its earnest spirit of prayer, with invisible arms spread out and raised aloft, gathers all into a single offering of praise.

In contrast, a centrally-located tabernacle has the wherewithal to overwhelm the Novus Ordo, which is, in many respects, thin and fragile, barely able to hold its own in a magnificent church or at a splendid high altar. The Sacrifice is phenomenologically overshadowed by the Presence (both as it resides in the Tabernacle and as it will reside upon the table). Therefore, by a kind of instinct for compensation, "the Tabernacle has to go!": it must be removed, decentralized, hidden, so that a shy liturgy can muster some communicative force of its own. The liturgy has to be unobstructed, with no symbolic competition and no larger context, or it will vanish into the background. It has to claim as much space for itself as it can and push out all vestiges of a world of greater mass and gravity.

Doesn't this make more sense out of the postconciliar epidemic of ecclesiastical wreckovations and artistic monstrosities? Not only must the tabernacle go, but so must the high altar, and maybe the crucifix or stained-glass windows or elevated pulpit or Communion rail, etc., etc. Maybe we need to *tear it all down* and replace it with an empty gray box that has no symmetrical curves and no ornamentation. *At last,* against that sterile stage, the clean, efficient, succinct lines of the Novus Ordo will ring out with metallic clarity! And the people who still care for old-fashioned "devotions" might find the reserved Sacrament behind or over to the side somewhere, as if placed in an Ordinary Time-out.[16]

THE NEED TO REPEAT WHAT IS NOT EVIDENT

Why, ever since the liturgical reform, has there been so great a need for the Church's pastors to emphasize the truth—never disputed since the Council of Trent—that the Mass is *really and truly a sacrifice*? Why such a stream of papal and curial documents, most of them ignored? Why do the statistics get worse and worse?

If what is done at the Novus Ordo Mass looked more *like* a sacrifice, if it expressed the sacrificial reality in a sensible and intelligible way, there would be no need for endless reassertions and clarifications. The doctrine that the Mass is a true and proper sacrifice was taught *de fide* by the Council of Trent and all denials of it were anathematized. The Mass of St. Pius V embodies that Tridentine doctrine perfectly. As long as the Mass remains faithful to a general principle of sacramentality—namely, that something *signifies* what it *does* and *does* what it *signifies*—it will be known to do what it really does by a manifest and unambiguous signification. In a passage I cited earlier (p. 93), Ratzinger pinpointed this connection with Trent in the liturgy wars:

> Only against this background of the effective denial of the authority of Trent can one understand the bitterness of the struggle against allowing the celebration of Mass according to the 1962 Missal after the liturgical reform. The possibility of so celebrating constitutes the strongest and thus (for them) the most intolerable contradiction of the opinion of those who believe that the faith in the Eucharist formulated by Trent has lost its validity.[17]

We have seen the polls that prove the loss of faith among Catholics in the real, substantial presence of Our Lord in "the Most Blessed Sacrament of the Altar" (as everyone used to call it). What would be enormously interesting to see is a poll that, having first with a few deft questions identified Catholics who attend the Novus Ordo and Catholics who attend the traditional Latin Mass, proceeded to ask

---

[16] I recognize that it is customary for cathedrals, due to their size and the continual traffic of pilgrims, to have a special Blessed Sacrament chapel, nor does this seem unfitting, considering that often the chapel itself is the size of a parish church and is splendid decorated for its purpose, offering a place of quiet out of the bustle in the nave. Additionally, the traditional *Pontificale Romanum* calls for the tabernacle to be empty for certain pontifical ceremonies—presumably the better to emulate the situation expected in a cathedral—but when the ceremonies are over, the Holy Sacrament is reposed with appropriate signs of respect.

[17] Ratzinger, *Theology of the Liturgy*, 544.

each group: "Do you believe that the Mass is a real sacrifice—that of Christ on the Cross?" It is not hard to imagine the results: many in the former group would say no (as a matter of fact, more than a few might be surprised or shocked at the question itself, because it would be introducing a concept they might never have heard of), while most if not all of the latter group would say yes. Their answers would tend to mirror their experience of the liturgy.

If someone says that the difference in results can be readily explained by Latin Mass-goers being a self-selecting and highly specialized portion of the faithful who tend to be better catechized than the mainstream, that only pushes the question further back. Why are the more serious Catholics so often found at the *usus antiquior*? Why, when they have a choice, is *this* their choice? Why are the faithful who attend it more inclined to seek their own ongoing formation and to offer authentic catechetical formation to their children? One cannot appeal to more or less adequate catechesis without pointing to a real empirical *connection* between the level of catechesis and the type of liturgy attended. The causality flows in both directions. The classic axiom *lex orandi, lex credendi* tells us not only that the way we pray shapes the way we believe, but also that what we believe is going to shape the way we pray—and the choices we make about where and how we pray as Catholics. The fact that more educated and more devout Catholics frequently select the *usus antiquior* Mass affirms the very point I am arguing: if those who believe what the Church teaches and wish to worship according to it seek out the *usus antiquior*, often making great sacrifices to get to it, or if they rejoice in it when they unexpectedly discover it, doesn't that indicate a massive *lack* in the Church's mainstream worship and a contrasting *perfection* in the classical form? Nor can we take seriously the view that the problem is a failure to implement the "real intentions" of the Council or of Paul VI. For over fifty years, the vast majority of celebrations of the Novus Ordo have been conducted in a spirit of rupture and discontinuity with the Catholic past, yet almost nothing has been done to correct the status quo. This indicates a tacit acceptance of the connection between the new liturgy and the rupture with ecclesiastical tradition, which has now become an explicit and deliberate policy under *Traditionis Custodes* and Cardinal Roche's Dicastery for Divine Worship.

Chad Pecknold suggests that we should pay closer attention to the "counter-catechesis" at work in the new rite:

> Many have said that the Pew study [of August 2019] reflects a catechetical failure. I fear the opposite: it reflects a certain kind of catechetical success. It is the result of an unwritten catechesis that

American Catholics have been slowly learning. Through a deracinated, spiritualistic, and emotivistic treatment of the Eucharist, many Catholics have learned their faith from a generation of pastors who stripped the altars, razed the bastions of reverence around the Lord in the sacrament, and generally treated the Most Holy Eucharist itself as something to be passed out like a leaflet rather than received in awe, as people prostrate before the fire of divinity. Far too many have received this kind of unwritten catechesis.

It's past time that our pastors preach what St. Cyril of Alexandria taught. Namely that the Eucharist is divine fire. Mistreat it, and it will burn you. The whole "razing of the bastions" theme has played itself out to disastrous effect in the Church. The bastions turned out to be things like altar rails, and liturgical actions which conform us to the reality of the Eucharist. The Pew study proves that it's time to put the bastions back.[18]

Although its inherent purpose is the glorification of God and the sanctification of man, the liturgy has always been a powerful catechizer. With the reformed Mass, there is a dearth of symbolic and textual catechesis at the heart of Catholic life. Although repetition is always necessary for human learning, a distinction must be made between repetition that works because it functions mnemonically and repetition that indicates a failure of something's actually "sticking." Catechists, preachers, and parents locked into the Novus Ordo need to keep repeating that "the Mass IS a sacrifice" because the modern rite has so little that even remotely suggests it. Trying to convince people that they should believe something when what they see or hear conflicts with or even fails to acknowledge what they are supposed to believe is, to say the least, an uphill battle.[19]

---

[18] Chad Pecknold, "Why do so few US Catholics believe in the Real Presence? Look at the liturgy," *Catholic Herald*, August 9, 2019.

[19] What I am driving at here is given consummate expression by Fiedrowicz (*The Traditional Mass*, 214–15): "The exterior forms of veneration and adoration that belong to the classical rite of the Mass are the best way of guaranteeing the corresponding interior attitudes. Prayers of preparation, genuflections, and bows are not trifles that could be omitted without diminishing the faithful completion of the holy action. The interior encounter with the sacred must manifest itself outwardly, involving and being supported by an exterior form. The traditional liturgy insists that interior sentiments are plausible only if at the same time they appear in an outwardly appropriate manner. In the same way, the liturgy is aware of the formative power that the sensible can exercise on the spiritual condition.

"With the number of its sacred signs, the beauty of its altars, the preciousness of its chalices and vestments, and its ceaseless expressions of reverence, the classical rite guarantees this correspondence of interior belief and exterior form. This rite is, so to speak, safeguarded against a possible discord between that which one believes and that which one sees. Here is found the perfected unity and harmony between that which is to be performed and the way in which it is performed. The classical rite does not require anything to be believed that one does not — symbolically — see."

A FIRE THAT WARMS AND ILLUMINATES THE SAINTS

The difference between the *usus antiquior* and the Novus Ordo is experienced on many levels: on the aesthetic level (what we are seeing and hearing); on the emotional level (what we are feeling); on the intellectual level (what we are thinking, what we know in faith to be taking place); on the devotional level (how we are praying, how we enter into the mystery). Without doubting that the same representation of the sacrifice of Calvary is objectively present in both the classical and the modern rites of Mass, traditionalists believe that it is time — indeed, well past time — for leaders in the Church to assess the damage that has been done and is being done to the spiritual lives of the faithful by a deficient and ambiguous liturgical form, and to address the lack of due homage it pays to almighty God in proportion to its lack of clarity in expressing what it offers Him and why.

It would be one thing if, living back in the earliest centuries, at a time of transition from Hebrew rituals and of bitter Roman persecution, we had on our hands a fairly simple liturgical form that (so to speak) could do no better and was giving its all — like a healthy, shiny, promising acorn that cannot be blamed for not being already a mature and majestic oak tree. But that was not at all the situation of Roman Catholics in the 1960s. We had a venerable, orthodox, richly-developed rite of Mass beloved to countless clergy, religious, and laity, a rite that gave glory to God in its richness, fullness, and beauty. Every text, gesture, and sign that pointed to the sublime sacrifice of charity was a way for the Church to tell her Lord, her Bridegroom, that she loved Him, would never be parted from Him, would rather die than leave Him. *This* is what was rejected by the reformers and, in the maelstrom of the Council, by priests and religious in their thousands whose first love grew cold.

But those who are searching anew for ways to express the extravagance and inebriation of love know where to look. We will look to that fire which warmed and illuminated the great saints, who are the greatest lovers — the fire that burned as a bright beacon for contemplatives and, like a raging conflagration in their bones, drove restless missionaries to plant the Cross of Christ in soil and souls across the entire globe. Age after age, it will always satisfy those who hunger and thirst for a righteousness not of this world. We rejoice, again and again, to be the unworthy heirs of such a tremendous liturgical treasure as the traditional Roman rite of the Mass, which beautifully, reverently, and unambiguously expresses, confirms, and exults in the holy mysteries of the Catholic faith.

10

Time for the Soul to Absorb the Mysteries

THE LORD HAS BLESSED ME IN MY LIFE WITH three crucial experiences that have molded my understanding of the sacred liturgy. The first is the privilege of having been able to sing chant and polyphony at Sunday High Masses (and sometimes feastdays) in the *usus antiquior* for the better part of thirty years. The second is the privilege of having been able to participate frequently in the Byzantine Divine Liturgy, particularly in the period when I taught at the International Theological Institute in Austria, where we sang the liturgy on different days in Ukrainian, Romanian, and English, with bits of Church Slavonic and Greek. The third is the privilege of having been given many opportunities to lead music at a high level of beauty and artistic competence for the Novus Ordo, in (more or less) "reform of the reform" settings. The many lessons I have learned from this continual "trilingual" exposure inform every page of this book. In the present chapter, I would like to focus on just one conclusion that has become more and more clear to me as the years go on.

As the liturgy developed historically and its ritual and aesthetic elements became more fully developed, it seems that the Christian clergy and people followed an unerring instinct towards the creation of prayers, chants, and ceremonies that allow *time* for the soul to absorb the meaning of what is happening. This psychological-spiritual opening up of space and time for the soul's growth is accomplished in many ways in different rites or rituals. It is done through repetitious prayers, as in the Byzantine litanies, many of them redundant, though always eloquently worded; it is done through periods of silence between periods of proclamation; it is done through motions, processions, non-verbal actions; it is done most of all through meditative chants that do not seem to be in any hurry to be finished, and which allow the mind a certain holy leisure or rest. There are repetitions, gaps, spaces, pauses, and visual signs that do not demand of the mind the constant tackling of new ideas or concepts, but permit it to dwell or linger somewhere before moving on. A traditional liturgy is like a winding path up a steep mountain, with open ledges on which one can rest before continuing. In this way, it emulates the spiral motion, the combination of the straight and the circular, that Dionysius the Areopagite envisages as the soul's path into God. There is a forward progression, yes, *but it takes its time winding around*, in order to move up at a human pace. Attempting to go straight up or straight in would defeat us.

The classical Roman rite of Mass, particularly in the form of the High Mass or Solemn Mass, admirably displays the spiritual pedagogy of the spiral motion, the frequent ledges, the moments of prayerful repose, before continuing on with our climb up Mount Calvary, Mount Tabor, Mount Sion. In contrast, the Novus Ordo is designed in a manner contrary to this spiritual pedagogy, and thwarts the soul's ascent up the holy mountain.

THE PROCESSIONS

Traditional liturgical rites of East and West are fertile in processions. We are pilgrims and we act out our condition. A town, the grounds of a church, and the church's interior offer a symbolic geography to be covered and converted as we move from point to point. The time it takes for a leisurely procession is one of the most important "burnt offerings" we can raise up, since our time *is*, in a way, our life and energy.

The Holy Sacrifice of the Mass, in particular, should open with a stately, unrushed procession of splendidly vested ministers towards the sanctuary, accompanied by grand music (instrumental or choral or both). Those ministers represent us, and we are walking with them to the Holy of Holies. This is a solemn and wonderful moment, with its own distinctive meaning and satisfaction. Why do we completely spoil the effect by asking people to put their noses in a hymn book? The choir or schola should be lifting our minds to God and allowing us to experience this procession *as* a procession, with all our senses in act. Where the procession is well done, it becomes an occasion of journeying to a higher place, free of the baggage of the workaday world's nagging necessities.

On Sundays, we are treated to the *Asperges*, a sprinkling with holy water that puts us in mind of our baptism and remits our venial sins.[1]

THE PRAYERS AT THE FOOT OF THE ALTAR

Then we come to the marvelous preparatory prayers, in which the traditional liturgy pauses for a breath at the end of the procession and, rather than striding right up to the altar, holds back to recite Psalm 42, the Confiteor (twice), and versicles and prayers expressive of the forthcoming sacrifice. We are suspended between the entrance and the commencement, the intention and the execution, and our souls can

---

[1] See my articles "St. Thomas on the 'Asperges' (Sprinkling Rite)," *Views from the Choir Loft*, August 7, 2014, and "Things That Remit Venial Sins—The Traditional Liturgy Is Full of Them," *NLM*, February 8, 2016.

expand, adjust, collaborate, gear up to move on. It reminds me of the process whereby one's eyes adjust themselves to the indoors when one enters a dark room from a bright sunny day outside. Our spiritual sight is accustomed to the garish day, with its obvious objects and confident navigation. In divine worship we are being drawn into the interior, the innermost, the mystery that is luminously dark, caliginously blazing, and we do not know our way. We need some time to adjust. What blessed minutes, which carry us gently yet irresistibly into the sphere of the divine!

The Novus Ordo's absence of prayers at the foot of the altar has the effect of a race that starts off with a *bang!* and no time for stretching and preparing. The lack of appropriate humility in keeping an initial distance, bowing to confess, ascending with petitions, kissing the altar, and *finally* arriving at the Introit as after a pilgrimage, is among the most irritating, not to say impious, aspects of the new rite. And this is not something that can be fixed by well-intentioned priests, as it is hard-wired into it.

FROM THE INTROIT TO THE LESSON

Whether we are at a Low Mass or a High Mass, one of the greatest blessings of the TLM is that, on the one hand, we are gently drawn into prayer, as if by an invisible guide nudging us forward, and, on the other hand, *we are not immediately talked to and expected to talk back*. We are surely participating in the unfolding drama, but we are not targeted and harried; the activity does not get bogged down in a closed circle, like a boring classroom. The liturgy seems to be going on over our heads or around us or in front of us, and we can relate to it all the more deeply *because* it is outside our grasp, beyond our ken, with no possible illusions that we are the ones driving it forward. Of course we have a role to play, and this will sometimes include verbal responses; but the overall effect is one of a giant motion that we can join, if we will, that will take us somewhere our own resources could never get us. The unfailing Introit, announcing the day's mystery, throws down a sort of spiritual gauntlet: "Friend, wherefore art thou come?" (Mt 26:50).[2] The cascading Kyries, the exultant Gloria, the richly compact Collect, the apt Lesson, invite us to come deeper and deeper into worship, putting on the mind of Christ.

---

[2] St. Benedict cites this verse in chapter 60 of his *Rule* when speaking about a priest who desires admission to the monastery, who, he says, may be admitted only on condition of agreeing to abide by the *entire* rule—as if to say: the only reason for him to come here is to embrace and benefit from the monastic discipline. The liturgy, too, is something we should approach only if we are ready to embrace its discipline, which is the sole way to obtain its benefits.

THE INTERLECTIONAL CHANTS

If the preparatory prayers seal the door to the world and habituate us to the new climate of worship, and if the subsequent prayers and Epistle demand of us the exercise of our spiritual capacities, it is the interlectional chants, *sung in full*, that have the special power to plunge us into meditation and even contemplation. As at other points in the Mass, multiple things can be happening at once (the peculiar perfection called "parallel liturgy"), as when the readings and antiphons are quietly doubled;[3] but with the Gradual and Alleluia—or the Gradual and Tract in Lent, or the pair of Alleluias in Paschaltide—a restfulness descends together with the chant; time seems to stand still; the melismatic melodies draw out lovingly, syllable by syllable, the exquisitely beloved words of God, so that we cannot rush past them, or treat them in a utilitarian way, or think of them as mechanical responses made to a dreary rehearsal. The chanted psalms exist in and for themselves, living monuments of God's faithfulness and love; we are permitted to sit in their presence, take them into our ears, store them in our hearts. They are a ladder let down from above on which we are bidden to climb up. In this way, the Lesson and all that has come before has a chance to sink in, and the soil is plowed with deep furrows for the Gospel and all that will come after.

THE OFFERTORY

It hardly needs to be said that the Offertory, with its richness of content and ample length, is one of the parts of the traditional liturgy most appreciated by clergy and laity alike. One does not feel, as one does in the rite of Paul VI, rushed into the Eucharistic Prayer; there is generous time and space for blessing and setting apart the gifts for sacrifice, making the significance of their offering known, *felt*.

In the Novus Ordo, the "presentation" of the bread and wine shifts attention to the "work of human hands" and barely touches on their connection with the offering of sacrifice, dwelling rather on their status as food and drink—which is true, but misplaced, since, while a sacrifice can also be a meal, no meal, as such, is a sacrifice.[4] One strains to recognize them as proto-sacrificial offerings that will subsequently be transformed by divine power into the sacrifice that wins our redemption and, as a result, into the banquet that unites us to the Savior of all; emphasis is

---

[3] According to the older and better rubrics, the celebrant doubles (that is, quietly recites) the Epistle while it is being chanted by the subdeacon. After giving the subdeacon the blessing, he then doubles the interlectional antiphons. Once he is finished, the subdeacon transfers the missal to the Gospel corner and the deacon receives the Evangeliarium. The celebrant then doubles the Gospel while the schola continues the chants. By the time the celebrant has finished the Gospel, it is usually time to impose incense and get ready for the Gospel procession.

[4] Various experts in the liturgical reform originally proposed that there should be no prayers for the bread and wine at all but that they be simply lifted up and put back

placed rather on man's own work in preparing food and drink, which will become food and drink—a true sentiment as far as it goes, but not at all the focus of the authentic Offertories of historic apostolic rites.

The traditional Offertory is a dramatic caesura, a long drawn-out breath in which we clearly show forth what we are about to do and how it will redound to our benefit, unworthy though we are to approach the awesome mysteries of Christ. *That* Offertory makes it possible for us to participate fruitfully in the Canon of the Mass. Without it, something vital is missing. Even worse, when the modern rabbinical-sounding pseudo-Offertory is combined with the second Eucharistic Prayer, the sacrificial portion of the Mass—its very essence—can pass by so rapidly that one might be forgiven for thinking that the Mass is a lengthy liturgy of words followed by a rapid distribution of tokens of our confidence in words, which is a purely Protestant conception.

THE CANON OF THE MASS

Much can be said on behalf of the fittingness of the silent Canon.[5] Suffice it to say that many among the clergy and the faithful are sharply aware of the loss of this contemplative reservoir at the heart of the holy Sacrifice. Cardinal Ratzinger wrote in *The Spirit of the Liturgy*:

> Anyone who has experienced a church united in the silent praying of the Canon will know what a really *filled* silence is. It is at once a loud and penetrating cry to God and a Spirit-filled act of prayer. Here everyone does pray the Canon together, albeit in a bond with the special task of the priestly ministry. Here everyone is united, laid hold of by Christ, and led by the Holy Spirit into that common prayer to the Father which is the true sacrifice—the love that reconciles and unites God and the world.[6]

Having cited this passage in his magnificent book *The Power of Silence*, Cardinal Sarah observes:

> I am familiar with the regrets expressed by many young priests who would like the Canon of the Mass to be recited in complete silence. The unity of the whole assembly, communing with the words pronounced in a sacred murmur, was a splendid sign of a contemplative Church gathered around the sacrifice of her Savior.[7]

---

down, in what was called a *depositio* (see Angelo Lameri, *La «Pontificia Commissio de sacra liturgia praeparatoria Concilii Vaticani II». Documenti, Testi, Verbi* [CLV, 2013], 238, 347, 474, citing documents from 1961, 1964, and 1966). This was too much even for Paul VI, an otherwise enthusiastic proponent of Bauhaus liturgy; along with some of the other members of the Consilium, he insisted that the actions had to be accompanied by some words (see Bugnini, *Reform of the Liturgy*, 358, 375, 379). Bugnini and Co. complied, but looked to Jewish precedent rather than Catholic.

[5] See Kwasniewski, *Good Music*, 283–92; *Noble Beauty*, 71–74, 202–3, 241–47; *Once and Future Roman Rite*, 251–52.
[6] Ratzinger, *The Spirit of the Liturgy*, IV, 5, in *Theology of the Liturgy*, 136–37.
[7] Robert Sarah, with Nicolas Diat, *The Power of Silence: Against the Dictatorship of Noise*, trans. Michael J. Miller (Ignatius Press, 2017), 129.

A priest with whom I was corresponding once wrote these words to me, as if to confirm Cardinal Sarah's observation:

> If I were permitted the quasi-papal power to make just one change to the present OF [Novus Ordo], it would be to bring back the silent Canon. As one who regularly celebrates both OF and EF [TLM], that is the single difference that I find makes the most spiritual impact. And quite a few lay people I know have made similar comments. That silence, after all, is much more obviously noticeable to the congregation than, say, the omission of certain medieval Offertory prayers.

At a Novus Ordo Mass, it is all one can do to focus one's wandering attention on the mystery taking place, since there is a constant washing of words over one's ears—words that lose their force *either* from their familiarity (Eucharistic Prayer II, a.k.a. the "Roman Canonette," needs to be heard only so many times before it sounds like an eye-rolling cliché) or from their length (the historic Roman Canon said *out loud* in English, facing the people, can feel interminable—it was never meant to be recited towards a congregation) or from their grating *un*familiarity (as when a priest, in a sudden Lucretian swerve, picks out one of the Eucharistic Prayers of Reconciliation). None of this is conducive in any way to prayer, to the adoration and spiritual longing we should cultivate in the presence of our Savior as we join our hearts to His Sacred Heart in the holy offering at the altar. This is no less true, indeed it is rather more true, for the poor celebrant who gets hardly a moment of mental peace, hardly a moment to repose his head against the Lord's breast in company with St. John. The new rite keeps the faucet of loquacity nearly always turned on.

After the new Mass is over, a person might genuinely wonder: "Did I pray at all during that long harangue from the sanctuary?" And one cannot be sure that one has done so. On the contrary, sometimes one is aware of a suffocating lack of time and space to pray. But I cannot remember a single traditional Mass at which I did not experience, at least for a few fleeting moments, a vivid awareness of the prayer of Christ, a palpable sense of the mystery of God, a real *connection* with the divine. In stark contrast with its intended replacement, the old Mass—whether Low, High, Solemn, or Pontifical—seems custom-made to connect one to the divine in this way. Its whole *raison d'être* is union with God, and it pursues this with relentless determination, with a lover's preoccupation. It reminds me of Kierkegaard's statement that "purity of heart is to will a single thing." This environment of saturated theocentric prayer carves out the necessary "interior space" for a fruitful Communion on the part of priest and people, which is what comes next.

THE COMMUNION RITE

Continuing our exploration of how the ancient Roman rite has, built into it, sufficient time or leisure for the appropriation of its sacred content, consider the segment of the liturgy usually referred to as the Communion rite, which, in a well-celebrated *usus antiquior*, is a veritable oasis of tranquility. "Deep calleth on deep, at the noise of thy flood-gates. All thy heights and thy billows have passed over me" (Ps 41:8). After the long silence of the Roman Canon, the uttering or chanting of the Lord's Prayer emerges like the cry of a swimmer raising his head above the water. Soon, though, he is submerged again in the embolism,[8] followed shortly after by the Agnus Dei, a trio of prayers in preparation for Holy Communion, the threefold *Domine, non sum dignus*, and the poignant psalm verses.

I'll admit that I used to feel a little impatient right around this time. We've had our king's portion of silent worship during the Canon, and just as the sung or recited prayers are cranking up again, we find ourselves confronted once more with several sizeable pauses: the gap between the Lord's Prayer and the *per omnia sæcula sæculorum* preceding the *Pax Domini*, and then the gap between the Agnus Dei and the Confiteor/*Ecce Agnus Dei*. Why are we standing or kneeling and waiting for stuff to happen? Can't we move on already?

One could answer this question with a disquisition on the historical development of this part of the liturgy and the importance of the various prayers and gestures that the priest is busy with at that moment. But here we are considering the moral and spiritual benefit that accrues to the people from the traditional liturgy as we have it. This benefit is summed up in the famous words of Milton: "They also serve who only stand and wait." Certain virtues or spiritual dispositions are formed precisely in these gaps or pauses, these stretches of profound and expectant silence, when, like the prudent virgins in the parable, we wait and watch. We know what is coming, and yet it still has to come, in its own way and at its own time. We may not, must not, rush it in our desire to be "in charge." It is like having to wait nine months for a child to be born. How hard it is to go for so many months without seeing the child, or even, in many cases, without knowing whether it's a boy or a girl! Waiting for the priest at the altar, waiting for the liturgy to do its work at its own pace, is a model of our stance vis-à-vis life and death. Think of the Blessed Virgin Mary, who had to wait patiently for her Son to suffer his agony, die upon the cross, and be taken down. The Mass reflects this trustful stance of waiting for God to act and readying

---

[8] A prayer beginning with the words *Libera nos*. On the superiority of the traditional embolism over its Paul VI replacement, see my article "Deliver us, we beseech Thee, O Lord, from all evils past, present, and to come," *Tradition and Sanity* Substack, October 10, 2024.

oneself to meet Him, to be acted upon—that is, to suffer, and thus, to partake of His victory, when and as He wishes to share it. Thinking of it this way, I have learned not only to accept but to welcome and relish these pauses in the post-Canon portion of the Mass.

Most of the rich prayers of the liturgy at this juncture are said silently by the priest. Laity with daily missals often make these prayers their own, but just as often they may pray in their own words or thoughts or desires or emptiness as they await their invitation to the banquet of immortality. As Pius XII affirms, "The needs and inclinations of all are not the same, nor are they always constant in the same individual.... They can adopt some other method which proves easier for certain people; for instance, they can lovingly meditate on the mysteries of Jesus Christ or perform other exercises of piety or recite prayers which, though they differ from the sacred rites, are still essentially in harmony with them."[9] The priest's separate Communion brings two immense goods: first, it strongly accentuates the *de fide* teaching that the priesthood of the priest and the priesthood of the faithful are essentially different and that, as a result, only the priest's Communion is required for the completion of the holy sacrifice; secondly, it allows the faithful an ample moment of proximate preparation, in which we can take a big spiritual breath (so to speak) before we approach the altar ourselves. I was recently reminded of the importance of this moment when reading about St. Mechtild of Hackeborn's pious custom of reciting five Hail Marys before receiving Holy Communion:

> At the first Hail Mary, she reminded our Lady of the solemn hour when she conceived a Son in her virginal womb, at the word of the Angel, and drew Him to her from heaven by her profound humility. She asked her to obtain for her a pure conscience and profound humility.
>
> At the second Hail Mary, she reminded her of the happy moment when she took Jesus for the first time into her arms and first saw Him in His Sacred Humanity. She prayed Mary to obtain for her a true knowledge of herself.
>
> At the third Hail Mary, she begged our Lady to remember that she had always been prepared to receive grace and had never placed any obstacle to its operation. She begged Mary to obtain for her a heart always ready to receive divine grace.
>
> At the fourth Hail Mary, she reminded our Lady with what devotion and gratitude she received on earth the body of her well-beloved Son, knowing better than anyone the salvation to be found there by mankind. Mechtilde begged her to obtain that her heart might be filled with worthy feelings of gratitude. If men knew the blessings which flow for them from the body of Jesus Christ, they would faint with joy.

---

9 Pius XII, Encyclical *Mediator Dei*, no. 108.

At the fifth Hail Mary, she reminded our Lady of the reception given to her by her divine Son when He invited her to take her place near Him in heaven in the midst of transports of joy.[10]

Everyone who attends the *usus antiquior* can understand why St. Mechtild was able to do this as her own "pious custom." Quite simply: she had the time, the space, the silence, to recite five Hail Marys before going to Communion. Alas, such a thing is well-nigh unimaginable in the Novus Ordo, where one is scarcely allowed an opportunity to collect one's thoughts, let alone enjoy the presence of mind to pray five Hail Marys for these noble intentions! A mystic like St. Mechtild would have fared rather badly any time after about 1964, since the liturgy would no longer have been able to nourish her interior life to the extent that it had before.

A different Mechtild, Mother Mectilde de Bar (1614–1698), foundress of the Benedictines of Perpetual Adoration, describes what happens when a person receives Communion. Her description helps us to appreciate why St. Thomas Aquinas says that two things are required for a fruitful Communion: being in a state of grace, and being in a state of actual devotion.[11] A certain devout recollection is required in the communicant in order to follow Our Lord whither He goes, for He hides Himself in the depths of the soul:

> Jesus Christ, being thus in the soul, whither does He withdraw? As I said, to the *sancta sanctorum* of the soul, its most intimate depth, which serves as a sanctuary for this High Priest and as a temple where He celebrates His divine and terrible sacrifice of all that He is to His Father. This sacrifice He wants to renew in the depth of each soul as in a holy temple, which He consecrated on the day of its baptism. O inconceivable marvel! Jesus Christ descends into our heart to be immolated and to celebrate there His Solemn Mass, although in profound silence. All is quiet in that temple, the angels and saints admire and adore the way the Lord abases Himself there, and the Eternal Father is well pleased.[12]

If the saints of the past warned us against lapsing into a routine of thoughtless, unprepared Communions — and gave such warning even at a time when the liturgy itself, with earnest prayer and pools of silence, furnished every opportunity to rise above this fault! — what would they say about our situation today, when the casual, routine, indiscriminate, and undiscerning reception of the Holy Eucharist is the norm throughout the Catholic Church, rather than the exception? The rushed, abbreviated,

---

10 From *The Love of the Sacred Heart, Illustrated by St. Mechtilde* (Burns, Oates, and Washbourne, 1922), 164.
11 See, for example, *Scriptum super Sententiarum* IV, D. 9, Q. 1, art. 4, qa. 2, sol., quoted and discussed in Kwasniewski, *Once and Future Roman Rite*, 225–26.
12 Mother Mectilde, *The True Spirit of the Perpetual Adorers of the Most Holy Sacrament of the Altar*, ch. 6; unpublished translation.

breathless pace of the Novus Ordo and its lack of natural periods of silence for recollection and preparation may be more of a contributor to this plague of sacrilege than has yet been acknowledged.

I might add in passing that the new rite's theoretically optional but, in practice, long-mandatory "sign of peace"—that "simultaneous eruption of bonhomie"[13]—only contributes to the superficiality and spirit of distraction.[14] (One of the few silver linings of Covidtide was the disappearance, in some cases permanently, of this interruption.) The Novus Ordo seemingly does not want you ever to move away from the surface of things: since it is supposed to build up the community as the People of God, you must be forcibly reminded of that at every turn. This, I think, might explain why so many pastors seem content to allow the faithful to chit-chat before and after Mass rather than catechizing them about the sacred silence that befits the temple of God. This chit-chat is, in a way, the conversation one would expect at the family dinner table, which is how progressives conceive of the Mass. Guests at a meal don't close their eyes and keep silent or speak only in whispers! But we are *not* at a mere meal; we are at a sacrificial banquet, whose host is the crucified and risen Lord. Our behavior should be utterly different from that of diners. It should never remain on the surface but respond to the still, small voice that calls us to the heights and depths of Our Lord's infernal sorrow and celestial joy: "Deep calleth on deep..."

The Communion rite in the traditional Mass afford a spacious home for corporate *and* personal prayer, so that the virtue of actual devotion, which is required for fruitful communication, may thrive in clergy and in laity alike. One may say, in fact, that the traditional Mass continually supports and strongly encourages the positing of all the acts of the virtue of religion discussed by St. Thomas Aquinas in the *Summa*, such as devotion, prayer, adoration, sacrifice, and praise.[15] In this way, the Mass is not only an "oasis" of peace in which prayer may be kindled and fed, but also a training or proving ground for the heavenly Jerusalem, whose citizens heroically exercise just these virtues.

THE ABLUTIONS

Now I turn to the portion of the Mass from the ablutions to the Last Gospel, where we find, once again, that the *usus antiquior* as it has developed under the care of Divine Providence displays a subtle grasp of human psychology and divine largesse in the pacing of its conclusion.

---

[13] See Kwasniewski, *Reclaiming Our Roman Catholic Birthright*, 17 n17; 251; 294.
[14] There is, of course, a traditional form of the giving of the *Pax*, in which the image of the High Priest bestows it first on the major ministers around him, and the latter, in turn, carry it further down the hierarchy. See Joseph Shaw, *The Case for Liturgical Restoration* (Angelico Press, 2019), 75–80.
[15] See *Summa theologiæ* II-II, QQ. 81–91.

After Communion, there is a long pause for the people while the priest cleanses his fingers and the sacred vessels, and the other ministers put things aside or back to their places for the end of Mass. Here again we see the genius of the Roman rite as it developed organically: there is no unseemly haste in this matter of ablutions, and, as a providential side effect, there need be no haste in the people's time of thanksgiving. How welcome, how utterly necessary is this time of grace, when the Lord is most intimately present to us and within us! Many great saints have spoken about the privileged prayer that is possible only at this time, in the minutes following sacramental Communion with the Word made flesh; many have even composed tender prayers that can be used to enrich it. What a shame if the very form of the liturgy—or, it must be added, the particular customs of a given community, even in the sphere of the *usus antiquior*[16]—should thwart this communion of minds and hearts!

THE *PLACEAT TIBI*

Instead of racing to the finish line as does the Novus Ordo in its eagerness to "send us out on mission," the old Mass takes a moment to beseech the Lord in a prayer of burning intensity, said by the priest bowing before the altar, in between the *Ite missa est* and the final blessing: "May the performance of my homage be pleasing to Thee, O holy Trinity, and grant that the Sacrifice which I, though unworthy, have offered up in the sight of Thy Majesty, may be acceptable to Thee, and through Thy mercy, may be a propitiation for me and for all those for whom I have offered it." Behold: a magnificent summary of the very essence of the Mass, and a summons to embrace its ascetical-mystical reality! The *usus antiquior* never forgets and never allows us to forget God's majesty and our unworthiness, God's mercy and our dire need of it. Centered from start to finish on the primal mystery of the Holy Trinity, serious about the Father's business, the Mass is here simply styled "the Sacrifice." That is what it is—and that is how it should look, sound, feel, and exist for us.

THE LAST GOSPEL

Over the years, one of the things about the Novus Ordo that grated on me the most was the rapid-fire conclusion. The celebrant may well take his time with the homily (sometimes the homily seems to be viewed, by the preacher and by attendees, as the "main attraction" of the Mass), but when it comes to everything afterwards, it's typically "life

---

16 I allude here to well-meaning musicians who endeavor to fill every spare moment of a sung Mass with music, as if it would somehow be a failure in competence to allow a period of silence toward the end of the Offertory or the end of Communion time. On this problem, see Kwasniewski, *Good Music*, 276–82.

in the fast lane"—particularly when Communion is over. The vessels are hastily put away and "Let us pray" booms out like an ultimatum over the heads of people who could not have had the slightest chance *to* pray. Within seconds, the floodgates are opened and the crowds, impatient to get home to leisure pursuits that seem vastly more significant than anything that happened on Calvary, pour into the parking lot to simulate bumper cars. It is thoroughly unedifying for the few devout Catholics who, due to some unanticipated freethinking, wish to stay in the pews to make their thanksgiving after Mass.

At a traditional Mass, this travesty is unheard of.[17] Time for thanksgiving is providentially built into the ancient liturgy, from the ablutions through the *Placeat tibi*; finally comes the sweet balm of the Last Gospel, which, no matter how slowly or quickly it is read, whether aloud or *sotto voce*, always seems like a well-placed comma or ellipsis in the grammar of worship. The end is rejoined with the beginning, like the circulation of divine lifeblood: "In the beginning was the Word... In Him was life, and the life was the light of men. And the light shineth in darkness, and the darkness did not comprehend it.... And the Word was made flesh and dwelt among us, and we saw His glory.... *Deo gratias.*" The words of André Gushurst-Moore seem to fit this Prologue especially well:

> The Gospel reveals a radiance at the heart of things, a glorious shining, the uncreated light of the *logos* which is the opposite of the postmodern abyss: there is no emptiness. This is the true light that the Enlightenment threatened to banish, and in fact, for many, did cast into shadow.[18]

It is well to recall the beauty of the Last Gospel, the grand prologue to the loftiest of biblical books. For it is St. John the Evangelist who teaches us, perhaps better than anyone else, the neglected virtue of restfulness in God that the present chapter has argued is one of the chief characteristics of the ancient rite. The Beloved Disciple took his time at the Last Supper when leaning on the breast of Jesus; he did not think there were more urgent things to do, be it selling ointments to get money for the poor, strategizing against the enemies of his Lord, or even preaching the good news that he was later inspired to write down. No, at the solemn moment when the Holy Sacrifice of the Mass was instituted, John knew where he had to be: at the side of his Master, in the adoring silence of a friendship so intimate that it would later spill out in the most sublime revelations vouchsafed to

---

[17] See Kwasniewski, *Holy Bread of Eternal Life*, 78–88. I will not comment here on the Leonine Prayers recited after Low Mass, but they too fittingly keep the faithful on their knees in corporate supplication, serving as a welcome "buffer" between the conclusion of Mass and exiting into the world.
[18] André Gushurst-Moore, *Glory in All Things: Saint Benedict and Catholic Education Today* (Angelico Press, 2020), 161.

man. John heard his Gospel beating in the heart of Jesus, High Priest and Victim; there he learned the meaning of adoration, reparation, supplication, and thanksgiving—*Eucharistia*. St. John is therefore the patron not only of theologians but of all who "worship God in spirit and in truth" (Jn 4:24). He leads us back, again and again, to the authentic liturgies of the Catholic Church, whose seeds the Lord sowed into the soil of His apostles' souls in the Upper Room.

LITURGICAL SLOWNESS AS INDUCEMENT TO INTERIOR WORSHIP

Looking back over our survey of the classical rite—the processions, the prayers at the foot of the altar, the *ad orientem* stance, the interlectional chants (Gradual/Tract, Alleluia), the Offertory rite, the silent Canon, the leisurely way the Communion rite proceeds, the thorough ablutions, the *Placeat tibi*, the Last Gospel—we see that all the elements we have considered produce the effect of a certain timelessness, of a floating *in between* matters of mere practicality or business. One is not checking items off a list, but rather, ceasing to think just about getting things done; one is "setting aside all earthly cares" and letting oneself be carried along by an action vast and deep, a reality that shows its face only in response to our patience, attentiveness, and surrender. The more we talk, do stuff, make noise, and carry on, the less we see of that reality, the less we enter that cosmic and eternal action. When the liturgy is allowed to be itself and to do what is proper to it—slowly, repetitiously, carefully, and beautifully—we are pulled out of ourselves, our finite world and ticking time, and made partakers of the divine nature. This is when liturgy is a foretaste of the heavenly banquet and gives us the strength to persevere in the long pilgrimage towards it.

In fact, it would be no exaggeration to say that the Novus Ordo, in its very design and especially in its typical instantiation, stands in tension with interiority, recollection, self-awareness, and sensitivity to the divine—that keen *sensus mysteriorum* that is practically convertible with the traditional Roman rite in any of its levels (Low, High, Solemn, Pontifical). The old rite, in contrast, forces us to develop habits of prayer—self-motivated prayer, since you are thrown, to a large extent, on your own resources. As an online author put it:

> One can still hold the new rite to be integrally Catholic, and yet consider that the culture of the extraordinary form [TLM], where the people are supposedly passive, tends to teach people to pray independently, while the culture of the ordinary form [NOM] often tends to create a dynamic in which people just chat to each other in church unless they are being actively animated by a minister.[19]

---

[19] "The Sensible Bond: Why I left the SSPX milieu," *Learning My Catholic Faith*, September 28, 2013, https://web.archive.org/web/20231124125101/https://

In other words, because the liturgy has been aimed *at the people*, they are apt to think that nothing important is going on until the noise starts up and they are expected to *do* something. Traditionally, however, action begins within. As Pius XII reminds us, "the external sacrificial rite should, of its very nature, signify the internal worship of the heart."[20] The thought that the liturgy is, in a way, *already* going on, before, during, and after Mass—the glorious liturgy of the heavenly Jerusalem; the liturgy of one's interior life, consisting of our acts of adoration, contrition, thanksgiving, and supplication; the liturgy of the Church universal, from the rising of the sun to the setting of the same—would rarely occur to someone in a Novus Ordo context. The liturgy has become so closely identified with doing, saying, and hearing stuff that when these stimuli are absent, the personal prayer that is supposed to be at once the wellspring and overflow of public worship can easily be absent, too. Fr. Chad Ripperger expands on this point:

> St. Augustine said that no person can save his soul if he does not pray. Now it is a fact that mental prayer and prayer in general have collapsed among the laity (and the clergy, for that matter) in the past thirty years [he is writing in 2001—*PK*]. It is my own impression that this development actually has to do with the ritual of the Mass. Now in the new rite, everything centers around vocal prayer, and the communal aspects of the prayer are heavily emphasized. This has led people to believe that only those forms of prayer that are vocal and communal have any real value....
>
> The ancient ritual, on the other hand, actually fosters a prayer life. *The silence during the Mass actually teaches people that they must pray.* Either one will get lost in distraction during the ancient ritual or one will pray. The silence and encouragement to pray during the Mass teach people to pray on their own. While, strictly speaking, they are not praying on their own insofar as they should be joining their prayers and sacrifices to the Sacrifice and prayer of the priest, these actions are done interiorly and mentally and so naturally dispose them toward that form of prayer. This is one of the reasons that, after the Mass is said according to the ancient ritual, people are naturally quieter and tend to pray afterwards. If everything is done vocally and out loud, then once the vocal [prayer] stops, people think it is over. It is very difficult to get people who attend the new rite of Mass to make a proper thanksgiving by praying afterward because their appetites and faculties have habituated them toward talking out loud.[21]

---

learningmycatholicfaith.blogspot.com/2013/09/the-sensible-bond-why-i-left-sspx-milieu.html. It bears saying that I do not quote from this essay to endorse its overall argument.
[20] Pius XII, *Mediator Dei*, no. 93.
[21] Chad Ripperger, "The Spirituality of the Ancient Liturgy, Part 2," in *Latin Mass Magazine*, vol. 10, no. 4 (Fall 2001): 31.

Fr. Ray Blake wonders if the emphasis on the spoken word has led us so far away from the interior spirit of worship that we might not be engaging in the supreme act of adoration or *latria* at all, but only filling the air with well-meaning verbiage, as if the church were a holy lecture hall.

> True worship leads us to contemplate the God who is always beyond us, the God before whom Old Testament patriarchs and prophets fall on their faces in worship. Practically at every Mass I have celebrated over the thirty years I have been ordained I have felt the need "to break the bread of the word," to preach—except at the Traditional Mass, where all I want to do is adore the Father through the Son, in the unity of the Holy Spirit. I am beginning to believe that if the Word of God does not lead us to the act of worship, there is something wrong in its presentation, and if the Mass does not lead us to fall on our knees to be fed by God, there is something wrong here, too. Contemplating the Mystery of the Trinity should lead us to be lost in the immensity and beauty of God, realising His greatness and our nothingness, desiring only to abandon ourselves to Him, crying out with Christ: "Father, into your hands I commend my Spirit." If this realisation is not the result of worship, perhaps we are not worshipping at all![22]

Joseph Shaw contrasts the scripted, regimented style of lay participation in the new Mass[23] with the freer "open worship" characteristic of the old liturgy, which generates a peculiar sense of togetherness by the intensity of each individual worshiping the same mystery, each in his own way:

> What is quite out of the question, in this kind of liturgy [viz., the Novus Ordo], is that you should engage with it at your own pace, on your own level, in prayer. Prayerful contemplation is simply not allowed: it will be interrupted within a few minutes, and you'll get funny looks. The opposite is the case with the Traditional Mass. You are, essentially, left alone, but left alone united with the community

---

[22] Ray Blake, "Mystery of the Trinity," *Fr Ray Blake's Blog*, June 15, 2014, https://web.archive.org/web/20240523184152/http://marymagdalen.blogspot.com/2014/06/mystery-of-trinity.html.
[23] The Novus Ordo is the first liturgy in the history of the Church to specify in rubrics the postures required of the laity at each point (sitting, standing, kneeling) as well as the gestures they are to do (and not do, as per the journal *Notitiae*); it is also the first liturgy to presuppose the presence of pews. Prior to this, all postures were governed by custom alone, which remains the case in old-rite communities (and which explains why one will find a certain diversity of customs around the world). For documentation, see my article "Are Pews in Churches a Problem—and, If So, How Much of a Problem?," *NLM*, July 27, 2020. Amy Welborn ("Up...off your knees!") notes a sharp irony for the so-called "age of the laity" ushered in by the Council: "Pre-V2, the rubrics micro-managed the clergy and let the laity alone for the most part. Post-V2, the landscape is reversed. The clergy can do whatever, er, *these or similar words*, sorry, and the laity are micromanaged."

in the act of worship. You may have things given to you to help you follow the Mass, there may even be responses (especially at a sung Mass), but no one will think you odd if you just look at what is happening on the altar in prayerful silence. And for the Canon, that is what everyone is doing. You are drawn in: it may be to something unfamiliar, if contemplative prayer is unfamiliar, but it is something which you can do your own way. It is not a Procrustean bed; you can make of it what you will.[24]

We are thus confronted with a supreme irony: the Latin-rite liturgy of the Catholic Church was turned upside-down and inside-out to promote "active participation," but the faithful who attend the old Mass today evince a superior personal engagement in what they are doing.[25] Why is this the case? Dom Alcuin Reid suggests two reasons: first, people who are drawn to traditional worship must make significant sacrifices to find it and have often invested seriously in forming their own understanding. But there is a second reason having to do with the rites themselves:

> Perhaps also it is due to the very demands they place on the worshipper—one has to find ways of connecting with these rites, or indeed of allowing them to connect with us, because of their ritual complexity. Their multivalent nature has a particular value: it provides varying means of connection with Christ acting in the liturgy that perhaps better correspond to our differing temperaments and psyches.[26]

In my book *Noble Beauty, Transcendent Holiness*, I talk at one point about the effort involved in carrying out a traditional Tenebrae service at Wyoming Catholic College, and how many hours of practice and years of iteration it took to achieve a high level of singing: "The best and deepest things take time to assimilate, to understand, to perfect. When it comes to liturgy in particular, we have to fight tooth and nail against the modern spirit of immediate gratification and quick results."[27] Nowadays, prayer and liturgical services are prone to being shortened (perhaps "short-circuited" would be a better term), since the participants are either in a hurry to get to other business, or their span of attention is just too short. For Holy Week, the very highpoint

---

[24] Joseph Shaw, "*Evangelii gaudium* 3: open and closed worship," *LMS Chairman*, January 1, 2014; cf. chapter 23.
[25] For detailed discussions of the true and false meanings of *participatio actuosa* (actual or fully realized participation), see Kwasniewski, "How the *Usus Antiquior* Elicits Superior Participation" in *Noble Beauty*, 191–213; "A New (Old) Perspective on Active Participation" in *Reclaiming Our Roman Catholic Birthright*, 55–75; "How *Not* to Understand Active Participation" and "When Piety Is Mistaken for Passivity, and Passivity for Piety" in Kwasniewski, *Ministers of Christ*, 131–51.
[26] Gregory DiPippo, "*Beyond Pius V* by Andrea Grillo—Review by Dom Alcuin Reid," *NLM*, January 21, 2014.
[27] Kwasniewski, *Noble Beauty*, 185.

of the Church's year, one may observe in many new-rite communities that the customary procession of palms on Palm Sunday is omitted; the Reproaches on Good Friday are skipped, in spite of their immense antiquity, beauty, and spiritual power. The Novus Ordo liturgical books are characterized by the option of shortened versions of readings and prayers. The modern impatience with anything not immediately understood or gratifying extends even to (perhaps, especially to) pious activities. To this mentality, years before it reached its peak, St. Josemaría Escrivá made a pithy reply: "'The Mass is long,' you say, and I add: 'Because your love is short.'"[28] What a contrast may be found in old-rite communities that celebrate the Tridentine Holy Week! The pre-'55 liturgies for Palm Sunday, Maundy Thursday, Good Friday, Holy Saturday, can last for hours and hours, but no one complains—the rites are so beautiful, so solemn, so moving, one forgets all about time, one is carried beyond this passing realm into the eternal mysteries. Indeed, the very leisureliness of the rites makes it easier for laity to go out and come back in as the needs of little children demand.

A priest who discovered the liturgical tradition of the Roman rite and fell in love with it rhapsodizes:

> When you truly love God, you are not miserly in sharing your time with Him in prayer, in the Holy Mass, and other liturgical exercises, since He is constantly sharing His time with you, His beloved. Since youth, I had been accustomed to the Vatican II revisions of the liturgy. Thank God, through dear Pope Emeritus Benedict XVI's *Summorum Pontificum*, I came to discover the solemn beauty of the traditional Latin Mass and other Catholic practices. Yes, these are more demanding of our time, but if one *allows* them time to penetrate the depth of the soul, one will exclaim joyfully: "Lord, it is good for us to be here."

Now, everything we have discussed in this chapter pertains to the essential structure and rubrics of each of the two rites, old and new—not to the *ars celebrandi* or accidental features. In other words, there is no way to make the new rite do what the old rite does in the dozens of ways I've detailed. To adapt the words of a Gospel parable, between the one and the other is fixed a great chasm, so that they who would pass from hence to there cannot, nor from thence come hither" (cf. Lk 16:26). My contention is that, from the angle of "time for the soul to absorb the mysteries" as from so many other angles explored in this book, the old Mass isn't broken, and the new Mass can't be fixed.

---

[28] Josemaría Escrivá, *The Way*, no. 529.

⋈ I I ⋊
Discovering Tradition:
The Priest's Crisis of Conscience

THE FOLLOWING SETS OF LETTERS AND MY replies are real exchanges. Both priests kindly permitted the publication of versions in which identifying personal details were removed. I believe there are now many priests in a similar or even identical situation of conscience, and that reading these exchanges may help them to achieve greater clarity about what steps to take now and looking to the future.

Dear Dr. Kwasniewski,
    Today I write for a personal reason: I feel that I am in a battle for my very soul, which, because I am a priest, is synonymous with the battle fiercely being waged for the soul of the Church herself at the "crisis point" where it counts the most: the altar of God and the celebration of the Sacred Mysteries.
    I have been a priest for just over five years, and I celebrated my first Mass in the *usus antiquior* shortly after ordination. As a member of a religious community, I became progressively aware of many issues—running the veritable gamut of "issues" that can be faced in the Church today, but centering upon the Sacred Liturgy—which, although somehow "tolerable" for me as a religious brother, became *in*tolerable for me as a priest of Jesus Christ. My departure from my community of origin was not only a matter of moving *away* from what is harmful and/or what "falsifies" the faith, but also a hope to move toward something of greater truth and beauty. I say this not with any animus or anger, but simply as a matter of fact.
    The change in my soul upon the conferral of the priesthood brought with it an almost instantaneous clarity of vision and honing of conscience regarding the Holy Mass and all that flows from it. There are, simply speaking, things that, once you know them, you can't *not* know. This is the story of my priestly life, for the more I discover about the development of doctrine and praxis (particularly in the modern or "postconciliar" Church), the more I feel convicted to "do something" for the Church, my Bride, insofar as I am able, with an appropriate acceptance of my own limited role in the Mystical Body. More simply speaking, I can tell you that once I began to discover the Traditional Mass and

the way of life and "culture" that organically flow from it and lead to it, I was never able to truly "go back." This has cost me a great deal.

I have served in two "typical" parishes; in neither place did the Traditional Mass enter in any way into my public ministry, as I was *trying* to "lie low." However, I celebrated the Novus Ordo in a very traditional manner, preached on all of the important topics of our faith, and put a great deal of heart and time into marriage preparation, with a particular focus on the virtue of chastity and the sacramental life. I was loved by "the people," but very soon despised by the clergy who are in positions of power, and who are living very different priestly lives from what I was doing my best to live. I then experienced firsthand the very *un*-priestly and distinctly uncharitable ways in which priests who are favorable and faithful to "tradition" are treated by shepherds of the "new mercy."

I have taken some time away from parish ministry in order to heal, and to try to make sense out of the spiritually abusive way in which I have suffered at the hands of shepherds who are in fact commissioned to foster priestly life rather than to destroy it. My time apart has taken place in a religious community dedicated to the so-called "reform of the reform."

Although our conventual Mass and Divine Office are "traditional," all community members without exception "must" commit in some way to participation in the *Novus Ordo Missæ*. This in and of itself has created a significant pain of heart and matter of conscience for me, as my time here separated from the daily reality of "business as usual" in parish churches has reminded me of what exactly it is that I believe about Holy Mass and the concomitant care of souls; what I believe about the mystery of the Church and the "Marriage of the Lamb"; and how I am being drawn by Our Lord to stand in His Person as bridegroom in intimate relationship with the Church as my Bride, particularly in the celebration of Holy Mass. The "two forms" are presented as equally acceptable realities, almost like a liturgical café in which anything is a perfectly fine choice. This is supported by certain writings of Cardinal Sarah, along with Pope Benedict's *Con Grande Fiducia*, the pastoral letter accompanying *Summorum Pontificum*, which, although I once subscribed to it wholly (and still feel it to be one of his most beautiful and fatherly overtures as Supreme Pastor of the universal Church), I can no longer find adequate to the magnitude of the problem.

With all of this comes much ambiguity, stemming from liturgical visions. My brothers and I do share the desire for a "beautiful" liturgical life, but for me, this beauty is not a merely aesthetic matter. It is deeper, more philosophical, even ontological: it has to do with what is *there* in the rites of the Church—or not there. The brethren do share bonds of good will, and I thank God for that... but without an objective standard to which we are subject, how can a community grow in an ordered way? This, Dr. Kwasniewski, is my grief, not only for my community, but for our beautiful and ailing Church.

I face a critical "crisis question" as to whether or not I can, in good conscience, continue to celebrate the *Novus Ordo Missæ* at all. This crisis is not "new," nor has it been arrived at capriciously. It has mounted, slowly but surely, with each offering of a form of the Mass that I know to be a significant, vacuous, and even harmful departure from the Church's organic tradition, and thus from her integrity and her effective care of immortal souls, of which I, as a priest, am a steward.

In my early priestly life, I was "gung-ho" for the "reform of the reform" and believed that it was "the way forward" for the Church. I simply do not believe this anymore. A not insignificant contributor to my change in mind and heart has been the phenomenon of so often finding myself somehow more thwarted for endeavoring to "beautify" the New Mass than if I were simply to offer the Traditional Mass (!). It is as if the Novus Ordo was built for deconstruction and self-destruction. As Martin Mosebach says in the foreword to your book, *Noble Beauty, Transcendent Holiness*, "the Liturgy *is* the Church." This goes for any Mass that is celebrated, for "the Church" ritually embodied therein is "made present" through the *ars celebrandi* of the very *ritus et preces* of which the Mass of any rite is woven. I ask myself, and now, with great pain of heart: How I can continue to contribute to and perpetuate what I perceive as a lie — the lie of equivocation, artificiality, the spiritual crime of neglect and "malnutrition" of the faithful — knowing full well that I am "disfiguring" the Church by the offering of a "disfigured" Mass?

I have grown and developed in my thought on this subject with much time, study, and experience, and with the heartbreak of seeing all over the world the gaping chasm and bottomless lacuna that have opened up and are leaving souls veritably lost *because of* the Novus Ordo (even when "celebrated reverently") and all that goes with it. This last line is key for me: "all that goes with it." For although the problem centers upon the Mass, it is not "just" about the Mass. It is about the Church, my Bride, in her integrity and vital coherence. I am in a "battle for my soul," which is synonymous with the battle for the very soul of the Church.

Your perspective and "sense" of what I have shared — even your "checking" me on anything I have said that may be out of place, overstated, myopic, "extreme," or the like — would be most welcome. With great gratitude to you for your time and the promise of my prayer for you and your family,

Father N.

Dear Father,

Thank you for your words of appreciation, and for trusting me with the story of your trials. I am grateful every day for what the Lord is doing in His Church, as He leads many souls to see hard but liberating truths. He is making use of this undeniable crisis we are passing through as a giant alarm bell to awaken people to the deeper causes of our malaise.

Everything you described about your path from the Novus Ordo to the traditional Roman liturgy mirrors exactly my own experiences, thoughts, and feelings. As you must know from having read *Resurgent in the Midst of Crisis* and *Noble Beauty, Transcendent Holiness*, for twenty-five years I was in charge of providing music for both "forms" of the Mass and the Divine Office, directing choirs and scholas at each, and becoming intimately acquainted with the texts, rubrics, ceremonies, and music of each. Over the same period, I studied the history of liturgy as well as liturgical theology. Slowly, the conviction grew in me that the liturgical reform was not merely unfortunate in this or that point, but truly a disaster for the Church.

I went through all the usual phases. The first "naïve" phase is that the problem wasn't the reform in itself, but how it was implemented. The second "hopeful critic" phase was that the reform *does* have problems, but they can be mitigated by good practice and eventually reformed from on high. The third "realistic" phase is that the reform is flawed in its fundamental principles; it cannot be redeemed but must be rejected in favor of the classical Roman rite.

You know the arguments as well as I do, but it takes time to come to grips with the magnitude of the problem — time, much reading, much experience, much prayer, and a certain intuition, which I hardly dare to call mystical and yet which seems to be given from above: an immediate, unanswerable conviction of the *rightness* of the tradition and the *wrongness* of its modern replacement. As you say, one reaches a point where one cannot *not* know, and feel in the depths of one's soul and bones, that something is seriously wrong in the Novus Ordo, and seriously right in the traditional worship of the Catholic Church.

The Novus Ordo did not come to be in the way that living things are conceived, born, mature, and reach their apogee; it came to be as machines are built in the age of industry and technology. This helps explain why fabricated rites engender mysticism only with the greatest difficulty and offer scant nourishment to the contemplative life. Only real food and drink can satisfy our hunger and thirst, can produce healthy eyes, skin, flesh, bones. The Lord in His Divine Providence did not give His Church access to sacramental grace apart from sacramental signs; He did not give us signs apart from the rites that situate them; He did not give us rites apart from prayers, lessons, music, and ceremonies. All of this is necessary for a healthy diet, not just "the form and matter of the sacrament," as neoscholastic reductionism would have it. One might as well reduce a multi-course meal to protein powder and vitamin tablets.

"Rad trad" readers have sometimes stumbled over my tolerance for the Novus Ordo, an attitude that I admit can be found in the aforementioned pair of books. This benign toleration is now a thing of the past. It is just as you say with regard to *Con Grande Fiducia* and *Summorum Pontificum*: these are watershed documents for their place and time, considering the unofficial dogma of never questioning the Council or anything done in its name, but they are frightfully compromised by the constructivist assertion that there is no rupture, which is patently false, and by the liturgical relativism of multiple forms of a single rite, which mirrors the doctrinal and moral relativism characteristic of our times.

But now I am preaching to the choir, or at least to a cantor. What I had meant to say is that some readers have found my attitude towards the Novus Ordo troubling, because they, being quicker than I (as St. John was quicker in reaching the tomb than St. Peter), had already, possibly long ago, reached the conclusion that the new rites could not be endorsed and must be avoided. A philosophy professor from Europe once wrote the following to me:

> You expose the flaws of the Novus Ordo in a very compelling way. The whole thing has been a disaster and deprives too many souls of the good they'd receive for sure were they introduced to the traditional Mass. Now I was wondering: how is it that you still (according to what you write in *Noble Beauty*) work for the *Novus Ordo* with chants and music even though you repeatedly claim—and rightly so—that the whole Bugnini invention should disappear? I understand the idea of liturgical peace and allowing for people who attend the New Mass to get a glimpse of real sacred music and so on, but don't you think that this supports the surviving of what would best be dead and buried once and for all?

I answered:

> I have struggled with this question for decades. Up until recently, my responsibilities included directing music at both the *usus antiquior* and the *usus recentior*, but I found myself loving the former more and more, and hating the latter; serving the one, and despising the other. In fact, it became a psychological torture to attend the Novus Ordo. I knew that I should leave it behind forever. Now I am attending the old Mass exclusively and I am "in heaven"—at least in the liturgical reflection of heaven. For me, my work with the Novus Ordo was always practical or pragmatic in nature: it was

part of my job, and I wanted to do the best I could (for my own sake, too, not just for the congregation: the Gregorian chant made the Pauline Mass bearable to my psyche and my sensorium, if not to my intellect). But I agree with your general point, that it would be better to let this "banal on-the-spot fabrication" perish, and to put all of one's energy into worshiping the Lord in the way most worthy of Him and most perfective of us. That is what I am doing today, and my future books will clearly reflect this turn in my thinking.

The only substantive difference between your path and mine is that you came to see all these things through the grace of ordination and the daily round of priestly duties, while I came to see them as a musician, oblate, and liturgical theologian who couldn't help noticing "one thing after another." Your awakening reminds me of words spoken by the late Bishop Vitus Huonder in an interview:

> I have of course studied very closely the new rite and the traditional rite. This study has pointed out to me the significant differences: for example, that certain texts have been shortened, suppressed, such as the prayers that are very important for the priest. Now, I can live only on all these prayers in the traditional rite. It is clear that they fortify the priest, that they especially reinforce the faith, but also the gift of self during the Mass. One is truly before God, before Jesus and not simply in front of a community. All that, I can rediscover in the traditional rite; it is so precious and, let's say, so intemporal that I don't want to go back.... I no longer want to do it [the Novus Ordo]. I sense simply that I can no longer do it, because when you are immersed in the traditional Mass, you simply come to a point where you sense that you can no longer do anything else.[1]

Thus, I do not think you are "crazy," "extreme," "ideological," or whatever labels your enemies or your fears might put on you. Rather, you have been following in a serious way the instinct of faith, the movement of charity, the requirements of devotion, the demands of the virtue of religion—the need for total consistency among the *lex orandi*, the *lex credendi*, and the *lex vivendi*. Continual exposure to the traditional liturgy *with all that accompanies it*, as you rightly add, together with a willingness to absorb and ponder its lessons, will necessarily show the bankruptcy of the ersatz liturgy constructed by Pistoian rationalists, Protestant ecumenists, communist sympathizers, and probable Freemasons, the bankruptcy of the entire project of (as some call it, scorchingly but accurately) "neo-Catholicism."[2] It is a hard but salutary awakening.

---

[1] "An Interview with His Excellency Bishop Vitus Huonder," Society of St. Pius X, District of the USA, October 1, 2021, https://sspx.org/en/news/interview-his-excellency-bishop-vitus-huonder-26764.

[2] On the terminology, see Christopher Ferrara and Thomas E. Woods, Jr., *The Great Façade: The Regime of Novelty in the Catholic Church from Vatican II to the Francis Revolution* (Angelico Press, 2015), esp. 23–33.

Some traditionalist writers use the cultural meme "red pill" to describe this process of the scales falling from the eyes.

(I hasten to add that some traditionalists don't have the philosophical and theological education that would enable them to make distinctions and to draw only those conclusions that are demanded by the evidence. For example, seeing serious faults in the reformed liturgy, they draw false conclusions about its validity; seeing the repeated abuse of the papal office, they draw false conclusions about the incumbency of the see; attending to the elements of modernism in John Paul II, they draw the false conclusion that his entire life's work is to be rejected out of hand. One could multiply such examples indefinitely.)

We know that God can bring good out of evil, and this is why He can and does sanctify souls even with the instruments of an unholy reform, as He can raise up sons of Abraham from lifeless stones. Yet His ordinary *modus operandi* is to raise up sons from fathers, not from stones, and in like manner, He raises up the Church from its paternal tradition, at the hands of priests who are truly fathers in that tradition, handing down the family name and inheritance.

Many priests, religious, and laity have written to me over the years, saying, in essence, "This modern project is hollow and harmful, and I can't pretend to support it anymore; I don't want to lend it the slightest credibility, or even brush up against it." They wonder what in the world to do next: "Can I still go to Mass at my local parish?" "What order should I join?" "Can I even celebrate the new Mass again?"

The Lord gives us intuitions and convictions this powerful in order to move us to take suitable action for the glorification of God, our own sanctification, and the edification of the entire Body of Christ. In this sense, "riding it out," "getting along," or "offering it up" seem to be self-destructive options. Unless one is comfortable running the risk of spiritual schizophrenia, nervous breakdown, or the violation of one's conscience by turning away from God's inspirations, a decision eventually has to be made for or against traditional Catholicism.

Such decisions are fraught with peril and anguish. One priest who wrote to me had been transferred multiple times because he kept refusing to distribute Holy Communion in the hand or to use extraordinary ministers. Another priest who refused to distribute into people's hands was finally removed from ministry altogether; he now serves as a TLM supply priest, traveling to persecuted communities. Several priests I know of have been suspended for preaching against sodomy (this will happen more and more). A priest who had rediscovered the Faith via the charismatic movement joined up with a new religious order, and finally had to leave it when he learned how to celebrate the old Mass and saw, as if for the first time, the essence of the Mass as propitiatory sacrifice, as humble homage, as ardent supplication of the Most Holy Trinity, as the sovereign prayer both public and personal. A diocesan priest wrote to me in agony because his soul longs to celebrate the traditional Mass but he is stuck celebrating an English *versus populum* "Ordinary Form" for a congregation that hardly believes anything. There are even a few bishops about whom one could say all the same things.

You have accurately perceived the heart of the ecclesial crisis, which is the crisis of the liturgy and therefore also of the priesthood. We will remain in this crisis until the traditional liturgy is fully restored and the modern experimental liturgy is repudiated.

One cannot embrace both traditional and modern liturgy, since their principles are contradictory. One cannot believe that the Holy Spirit was guiding the Church all through the ages, and then take up with a liturgy whose fundamental premise is that the Roman liturgy, for centuries, was lacking many features it ought to have had and was chock-full of corruptions requiring removal. Indeed, Antoine Dumas, chief editor of the new orations, complained that the Collect of Easter Sunday transmitted a "Gregorian deformation."[3] One cannot praise the spirituality of the great saints, from the Desert Fathers to the Benedictines to medieval mystics to the Carmelite Doctors and beyond, while effectively contradicting them in liturgical and devotional practices.[4]

What is to be done? It seems to me that the only way forward is to join a religious community or society of apostolic life that is clear-sighted and courageous enough to celebrate exclusively a *traditional* liturgy, be it the Roman rite or a use specific to the order. Along this way lies peace of conscience and comfort of soul, light for the mind and warmth for the will. Along this way lies the most exacting and rewarding exercise of the gift of the priesthood, together with the most abundant fruit for faithful Catholics who are seeking God in the sublime mysteries of His love.

Do you know the book *In Sinu Jesu: When Heart Speaks to Heart—The Journal of a Priest at Prayer*? Here are three passages I would like to share with you, in which Our Lord speaks:

---

[3] See Lauren Pristas, "Theological Principles That Guided the Redaction of the Roman Missal (1970)," *The Thomist* 67 (2003): 157–95, at 170. As Yves Daoudal comments: "The neo-liturgy was manufactured in an openly anti-traditional way. It was necessary [claimed the reformers] to recover the purity of the liturgy of the first centuries, going beyond, as one of its principal manufacturers dared to say, the 'Gregorian deformation,' namely of Saint Gregory the Great. This is enough to deny any legitimacy to this 'reform.' Nothing in the Church can be done against tradition, especially when one pushes impiety to the point of speaking of a 'deformation' for which the principal codifier of the Latin liturgy, one of the greatest popes and doctors of the Church, would have been responsible." "Enough is Enough," *Rorate Caeli*, February 1, 2022.

[4] See my article "Sun, Moon, and Stars: Tradition for the Saints," *OnePeterFive*, February 3, 2021.

> I will not abandon or forsake you. I am faithful. I have chosen you and you are Mine. Why do you doubt My love for you? Have I not given you signs of My favour? Have I not shown you that My mercy has prepared for you a future full of hope? Did I not promise you years of happiness, of holiness, and of peace? My blessing is upon you and the designs of My Heart are about to unfold for you. You have only to trust Me. Believe that I will keep you as the apple of My eye. You are safe under My Mother's mantle. I hold you close to My wounded Heart. Trust that I will bring about all that I have promised you.
>
> Go forward in simplicity, free of fear and trusting in My merciful providence to prepare all things for a future full of hope. Leave the preparation of the future entirely in My hands. Your part is to remain faithful to the adoration I have asked of you.
>
> Offer the present to Me, and I will attend to repairing your past and to preparing your future.

I will raise up prayers for you to the Father of Lights, asking Him, by the intercession of Our Blessed Mother, St. Joseph, St. John Vianney, and your holy guardian angel, to send you the light you need to know your next steps and the strength to persevere in spite of all obstacles. The Church is passing through a crisis that can be surmounted only by heroic faith. Good people will be pummeled and shaken up, yet by this means the chaff will be drawn away and the fat of wheat prepared as a sacrifice to the Lord. This, too, is one of the works of Our Lady, through which she will bring to birth a purified clergy and a purified Church.

Your brother in Christ,
Peter Kwasniewski

A second exchange, with a different priest, follows.

LETTER 1

Dear Dr. Kwasniewski,

A mutual friend forwarded to me the letters between you and the priest entitled "Discovering Tradition: A Priest's Crisis of Conscience."

Just as a sort of prolegomenon, I came across the Traditional Mass in high school after a reversion experience. As so many do, I started researching the Old Mass and, as a result, began attending a local FSSP parish, where I learned how to serve. Later, after I had entered the diocesan seminary, I studied how to celebrate the TLM with the help of a Fraternity priest, and my first Mass (as celebrant) was in fact a traditional Low Mass. It was very important to me to signify in which liturgical/cultural "stream" I stood. Since then, I celebrate the Old Mass regularly—both privately and publicly. The traditional Mass has been the pillar of my priestly life. I cover my mouth with respect to the Novus Ordo...

No doubt, the death of an actually Catholic culture and a sense of the sacred/piety within the Church, the death of catechesis, the death of the capacity for deep prayer (both corporate and private), the death of a spirit of penance and the nobility of suffering (or, frankly, a sense of anything being noble at all), the neglect of the sacraments (especially confession), the preponderance of gay (or at least soft and emasculated) clergy, the ubiquity of sacrilege especially with respect to the Blessed Sacrament, show tunes at Mass and the death of the refined culture that grew out of the Mass of the Ages, Communion in the hand, the exchange of roles between clergy and laity, etc. . . . it all causes me grief and anguish.

And so, I do admit that most of what is said in that letter exchange has my empathy, but many of the problems discussed in the letters concerning the Novus Ordo are actually for me more reason *not* to "jump ship." When I joined the local seminary, the parishioners at a traditionalist parish cocked their heads and asked why I didn't just join a group like the FSSP, and my reason given then remains my reason for staying now: to put it briefly, I have problems with apparently retreating into the traditional "ghetto" and abandoning the sheep. I admit this is a problem and a suffering more peculiar to the priestly heart than the lay, but I'm sure you can understand. They really are sheep without shepherds, and even granting that some of the decay in the Church at large, as well as in the average parish, is perpetuated with malice, I would readily say that most of it is not. Most of it is simply ignorance, resulting from the spiritual abuse of bad priests neglecting to provide for, protect, and discipline their spiritual children.

Again, I am more than sympathetic to the sentiments of your interlocutor, and to be honest, the appeal of a traditional monastery is sometimes overwhelming. But my priestly heart breaks that another priest would apparently leave the sheep to the wolves of liberalism and modernism. It is beautiful that he has been given the grace to see the surpassing excellence of tradition, but how can I not be grieved when yet another foxhole around me is emptied because the man in it has apparently despaired of the cause? I am a priest in order that God may be glorified by the salvation of souls. Isn't it the Novus Ordo Catholics who *most need* the hand of good priests formed by sacred tradition to pull them out of the pit of hell, figuratively and literally?

I stay because my people are literally dying in their sins, because for sixty years they have scarcely been told that there *is* such a thing as sin. How can I not be disappointed to see another good priest running for apparently greener pastures, when "an enemy" has sown so much darnel and salt in the field of souls? I feel like St. Francis Xavier when he said:

We have visited the villages of the new converts who accepted the Christian religion a few years ago. No Portuguese live here—the country is so utterly barren and poor. The native Christians have no priests. They know only that they are Christians. There is nobody to say Mass for them; nobody to teach them the Creed, the Our Father, the Hail Mary and the Commandments of God's Law... Many, many people hereabouts are not becoming Christians for one reason only: there is nobody to make them Christians. Again and again I have thought of going round the universities of Europe, especially Paris, and everywhere crying out like a madman, riveting the attention of those with more learning than charity: "What a tragedy: how many souls are being shut out of heaven and falling into hell, thanks to you!"

I wish they would work as hard at this as they do at their books, and so settle their account with God for their learning and the talents entrusted to them. This thought would certainly stir most of them to meditate on spiritual realities, to listen actively to what God is saying to them. They would forget their own desires, their human affairs, and give themselves over entirely to God's will and his choice. They would cry out with all their heart: Lord, I am here! What do you want me to do? Send me anywhere you like—even to India.

I might add: "even to a Novus Ordo parish."

Thanks so much for your time and charity in reading what has inadvertently turned into a manifesto, and thank you even more for your time in responding, if you see fit to do so.

Sincerely in Christ,
A Priest in the Trenches

LETTER 2

Dear Father,

I well understand where you are coming from and why you are doing as you are doing. I myself directed choirs and scholas for decades in the Novus Ordo, and my goal was always to bring the riches of the Church's sacred music to the faithful in the pews—and to the clergy, too, who often appreciated it just as much or more, since it helped them pray the Mass better.

At the same time as I was providing music for the Novus Ordo, I was also leading music for the traditional Latin Mass. For almost that entire period, I attended both forms alternatingly. This gave me a close-up perspective on the differences and prompted me to think, over and over again, about what had been removed, changed, added, etc. I couldn't really avoid it, with my close involvement in planning and executing the liturgy. Plus, as an Aristotelian philosopher I always want to know *why*—why was this or that inserted, deleted, revised, made optional, etc., and I cannot rest with superficial answers. This led me to extensive research, which illuminated my experiences. I finally realized that there had been a profound rupture in the Roman liturgical tradition, and that this was going to have ripple effects until the end of time (or until the rupture is itself definitively canceled out). It would ripple into our attitude towards doctrine and dogma; our moral and social life; our asceticism and aesthetics; and obviously, *our sense of the basic good of tradition as such.*

Reflections like these prompted me to formulate my thesis: *reverence is not enough*; one needs to be united with the tradition as it developed under the guidance of Divine Providence. (I argue for this thesis in detail in my book *The Once and Future Roman Rite*.) As a result, I began to feel somehow complicit in perpetuating the rupture, again in spite of the obvious good of promoting sacred music and reconnecting laity piecemeal with their heritage.

Now, this is not to say that there should never be soldiers in the trenches, or even generals of armies, who make the best of a muddy, messy situation and press on towards eventual victory. There is much to admire in those who can do this, in spite of the constraints, imperfections, ignobility, incomprehension, resistance, and other problems encountered on the battlefield. Every wise soldier and especially every prudent general must nevertheless keep hold of his best weapons and use them whenever he can. So the priest who knows how to celebrate the old rite and appreciates its value must not only keep it at the heart of his own priestly life, but also share it with his people more and more. *Traditionis Custodes* has obviously obstructed this necessary work or rendered it more difficult, but good priests will find ways to work around it, looking ahead to a time when this unjust parody of law will be rescinded and replaced by a saner policy. Pope Benedict's recognition of the healing power of liturgical tradition remains as true as ever it was.

Thus, I urge you, as far as you can, for your own sake and for the poor sheep, to offer the traditional liturgy—not just the Mass, but baptism, penance, extreme unction, the divine office. The surprising resurgence of the old liturgy is a balm provided by God in our difficult times for those who are suffering the "grief and anguish" you so well describe. May Our Lord abundantly bless your care of souls, especially in its difficult moments.

Yours in Christ,
Dr. Kwasniewski

LETTER 3
(one year later)

Dear Dr. Kwasniewski

You may not remember that we had a brief exchange a while ago. I'm emailing again because I owe you something of an apology. When we last corresponded, I defended the position that priests sympathetic to tradition should remain where they are precisely because the situation is so desperate.

My thinking has developed, and I've come to the conclusion that the glory of God and the salvation of my soul are my first and most basic and most necessary work, and while the thought of what could be interpreted as leaving the flock to the wolves does cause me considerable distress, I do not believe that I can secure those primary objectives while remaining in my current situation. For that reason, I've begun looking for traditional orders to join.

I thought I would let you know, given our prior discussion. Thank you for your work generally, and your prayers for me personally, and know of mine for you.

Peace to you in Christ!
A Priest in the Trenches

LETTER 4

Dear Father,

It's good to hear from you again.

The realization you describe is becoming increasingly common. I am contacted regularly by priests, religious, and especially seminarians who are trying to figure out what to do when they see that the liturgical reform has opened a Pandora's Box that cannot be shut but must be buried (if we can alter the old myth that way). It is a veritable *abuse pandemic*, and the most subtle evil of it is that even a "reverent celebration" is a personal achievement of options tastefully chosen, within parameters negotiated between the expectations of bishops and the tolerance level of congregations. In other words, it's something like an auction at which the liturgy goes to the highest bidder.

It took me a long time to reach the conclusion that restoration is the only way forward; I resisted it pretty sternly for about ten years. I did my utmost as a choir director to promote the "hermeneutic of continuity" and to practice "mutual enrichment." I led chant and polyphony at the NOM, and encouraged the dialogue TLM.

But then my studies overtook my naivete and I realized, not without considerable anguish of spirit, that the problems were "baked in" to the reform, like the flour and sugar of a cake; they were (as the saying goes) features, not bugs. This fundamentally changes the objective nature of the gift of worship in both senses: a gift received from the Church's tradition and a gift given to God, who deserves the greatest and the best—and who deserves it *first*, prior to any human considerations.

The liturgical tradition of the Church reflects these lines of the psalmist: *Confiteantur nomini tuo magno: quoniam terribile et sanctum est: et honor regis judicium diligit. Tu parasti directiones.* "Let them give praise to thy great name: for it is terrible and holy: and the king's honour loveth judgment. Thou hast prepared directions" (Ps 98:3–4). The same psalm describes God as *ulciscens in omnes adinventiones eorum*, "taking vengeance on all their inventions" (Ps 98:8), that is, what they substitute for the right order He has established, the directions He has prepared. Elsewhere in the psalms we read: *Peccatori autem dixit Deus: Quare tu enarras justitias meas, et assumis testamentum meum per os tuum?* "But to the sinner God hath said: Why dost thou declare my justices, and take my covenant in thy mouth? Seeing thou hast hated discipline: and hast cast my words behind thee" (Ps 49:16–17). He makes the same reproach to us: Why, O reformers of the liturgy, do you repeat my Scriptures in your fat new lectionary, and enact my new covenant on your Cranmer tables? You hated the discipline I established in my Church over the course of two millennia; you have put my words—the developed liturgical expressions I inspired in her—behind you, into the memory hole. *Sacrificium laudis honorificabit me: et illic iter, quo ostendam illi salutare Dei.* "The sacrifice of praise shall glorify me: and *there* is the way by which I will shew him the salvation of God" (Ps 49:23). It is by the God-fearing sacrifice of praise, offered in accord with immemorial tradition, that God will be honored as He demands and deserves.

And yet, having seen this truth, my job obliged me to continue providing music for both Masses. I sought refuge in the Gregorian chants and tried to put all my concentration into them, using their beauty as a kind of psychological shield. This, ultimately, struck me as somewhat Pelagian: attending Mass became an ascetical effort in which my will had to conquer my intellect, and in which I had to force myself not to pay attention to certain grating aspects of Paul VI's rite. What was blocked, in any case, was precisely the kind of trustful surrender to the liturgy that one ought to be able to practice without even a second thought.

I loved the people I was working with, but the liturgical diet was, in one way, too sparse, and, in another way, too diverse and contradictory. I felt like I was being torn in two; that which should have been, in imitation of heaven, a place of "refreshment, light, and peace"—the *sacred* liturgy—was a source of discontentment, stress, and conflict. I reached a point where I needed to leave the schizophrenia of a "biformal" community and move to a "full service" traditional parish.

It's one thing to choose to be a Martha instead of a Mary; serving Christ actively can be legitimate, even if contemplative nuns and monks have chosen the better part. It's another thing to choose to be a Nicodemus who can visit Christ only at night, as it were. Eventually one has to "break ranks" with the party of the scribes (Consilium) and join the party of the apostles (Roman tradition).

Hence, I feel that I understand something of what you are going through. If there is anything I can do to help, please let me know.

Yours in Christ,
Dr. Kwasniewski

PART II

Did—Does—the Old Mass Need to Be "Reformed"?

12

The Liturgical Rollercoaster and the Temptation of Tinkeritis

IN PART I, I HAVE ARGUED THAT THE REFORM was fundamentally mistaken in its principles, causes, and elements. It unleashed a period of iconoclasm and mayhem that has denuded churches, desacralized worship, and depressed or driven away the faithful—and now its proponents even try to hunt down and eliminate any vestige of the old rite that might compete with it. The reform dreamt of by Annibale Bugnini, drawn up by the more progressive wing of the Liturgical Movement, and driven through by a pope bent on modernizing the Faith introduced a catastrophic rupture in Catholic liturgy that cannot be repaired from within the new rite, genetically deformed as it is. Assembling a committee of trigger-happy liturgical "experts" whose brains are stuffed with debatable scholarship and ideological agendas was not the way to improve *anything* that has been handed down to us by the Church. Of this one may be certain. The only sound response is the full restoration of the Roman rite in its bimillennial plenitude.

In the second part of this book, I will examine the other side of the coin: Did the old rite really need to be reformed? Or is it defensible, indeed preferable, just the way it is? Of course, as I shall discuss without mincing words, we need to hold ourselves to high standards, to what might be called "best practice": rubrics should be carefully followed, ministers well trained, choirs and scholas up to task with the appropriate music, the faithful taught from the pulpit and supplied with resources to use as they wish, such as handouts, chant booklets, or daily missals.

I am convinced, and will argue, that the Tridentine rite allows for the realization of the legitimate goals of *Sacrosanctum Concilium* better than the Novus Ordo does (even assuming Ratzingerian best practice for the latter, which, needless to say, seldom obtains).[1] Nor should it seem strange that this would be so. After all, most of the pioneers of the Liturgical Movement thought that the solution was not so much to change the Church's rites as to educate the people in the rites we have received as our inheritance. Even *Sacrosanctum Concilium* goes out of its way to say: "There must be no innovations unless the good of the Church genuinely and certainly requires them; and care must be

---

[1] The remainder of this subsection is adapted from Kwasniewski, *Noble Beauty*, 208–13.

taken that any new forms adopted should in some way grow organically from forms already existing" (*SC* 23). Yet as we saw in chapter 1, it was none other than Paul VI who, in a General Audience of November 26, 1969, openly endorsed and defended the ousting of Latin and the repudiation of Gregorian chant, in spite of manifest conciliar teaching to the contrary—teaching that he, in company with over 2,000 bishops, had approved only a few years earlier. This degree of contempt for an ecumenical council can hardly be found in the annals of Church history. With such flagrant disobedience in the shepherd, it is no wonder his pontificate was marked and marred by such disobedience in the flock. It could be seen as a form of divine poetic justice.[2]

One of the first objections raised against Catholics who love the traditional Latin Mass and labor for its broadest possible restoration is that we are viewing the past through rose-colored glasses and that, in reality, things were terribly bad before the Council and urgently needed changing. The problem with making this claim or refuting it is that the relevant historical evidence one might draw upon is vast and diversified, with many anecdotes and conflicting elements. Nevertheless, while admitting for the sake of argument that there were plenty of problems prior to the Council, I think it is safe to say there is one supremely obvious difference between the period before the heyday of liturgical rupture (ca. 1964–1972) and the period after.[3]

Before this period, Catholics around the world were known for their widespread attendance at Mass, and it seems that a great many people were trying to be devout, or at least respectful, at Mass. Worshipers praying the rosary or reading devotional books at Low Mass may not

[2] See my article "Paul VI: A Pope of Contradictions," *NLM*, December 10, 2013. Someone might be tempted to say: "The pope is, of course, above a council, and he need not follow a council's promulgated documents at all; indeed, their very meaning is so completely subject to his judgment that one could never say that a pope was rejecting or disobeying a council, since it has authority only by his consent and has meaning only by his interpretation, and he can withdraw that consent or change that interpretation." But such a view would be nothing other than an irrational ultramontanism that no Catholic who respects reason, tradition, the magisterium, or the papacy should ever countenance.

[3] Detailed evidence for the three claims I will make—(1) that there was a decline setting in already in the mid-'60s, before the new Mass was rolled out; (2) that prior to the Council, or prior to the end of it, Mass attendance was nonetheless still quite high, across the board; (3) that after the liturgical reforms began in the 1960s, and, in good measure, due to them, attendance dropped more and more precipitously—can be found in Bullivant's *Mass Exodus*. What preconciliar authors meant by "worrying pastoral indicators" looks like a dreamland in comparison to where things had already gone by the 1970s and 1980s, let alone now. For instance, Rahner in the 1950s sounded the alarm about most Catholics being "Sunday-only" Catholics, whereas now, sociologically speaking, it's only the hard-core who are even *there* on Sundays. A graph in Bullivant's book (267–69) illustrates the unrelenting decline from the mid-'60s onwards. For further data and analysis, see Shaw, "What Vatican II Did to the Church," in idem, *The Liturgy, the Family, and the Crisis of Modernity*, 101–18; cf. 215–37.

have exhibited the pinnacle of *participatio actuosa*, but then again, as the Liturgical Movement pointed out, many places had never implemented what St. Pius X had called for—namely, that Mass be sung, that the people sing the chants and dialogues of the Mass Ordinary, and that they become familiar with the actual prayers of the liturgy. Still, there was a distinctively Catholic thing that Catholics did every Sunday (and the more pious, more often than that); they knew that this was the Holy Sacrifice of the Mass, that Jesus was really and truly present in the Eucharist, and that you couldn't receive Him if you were in a state of mortal sin.

Mass attendance was already decreasing in the mid- to late sixties, for social and cultural reasons known to all, but after the liturgical rupture embodied in the Pauline missal, attendance fell precipitously. The situation we have on our hands today, with only a small percentage of the baptized still going to church at all, has its birth in this period of unprecedented liturgical insolence, experimentation, disruption, and confusion. A decline had already set in, to be sure, but it was the outrageous shock of substituting a new rite of worship for an age-old bearer and transmitter of Catholic identity that confirmed definitively the modernizing madness of the institutional church. To paraphrase Joseph Ratzinger, if this is how the Church treats her most valued possession, her mystical treasures, what other reversals or betrayals can be expected from her? Would anything remain stably in place? Could doctrine itself survive the onslaught?[4]

The unrelenting series of synods called by Francis—the family synods, the youth synod, the Amazonian synod, and the multi-year synod on synodality—are the logical continuation and completion of the conciliar process. The years during and after the Council were preoccupied with changing ritual and discipline as widely as possible, while doctrine seemed to be left untouched, but all along the modernists have been laying the groundwork for "renovating" the doctrine as well. Given the freedom to do so, there is almost *nothing* in the faith that they would not falsify or modify, in the same way that almost nothing in the Mass was left intact.

Sadly, even with a liturgy entirely in the vernacular, Catholics today *by and large* seem barely aware of those basic truths of the faith mentioned above—and again, it's not reasonable to say the problem is *merely* poor education. The very form of the liturgy doesn't convey those truths as effectively. If you don't hear aloud (or read in your

---

4 The original quotation: "A community is calling its very being into question when it suddenly declares that what until now was its holiest and highest possession is strictly forbidden and when it makes the longing for it seem downright indecent. Can it be trusted any more about anything else? Won't it proscribe again tomorrow what it prescribes today?" Joseph Ratzinger, *Salt of the Earth: Christianity and the Catholic Church at the End of the Millenium*, trans. Adrian Walker (Ignatius Press, 1997), 176–77.

missal) prayers indicating that the Mass is a true and proper sacrifice, then can we say that the Eucharistic liturgy is being true to itself, true to its very nature and purpose? In short, the reformed liturgy was as much a repudiation of *Sacrosanctum Concilium*'s principles as the traditional liturgy would have been the scene of their fulfillment if only patient formation had been pursued.

In this sense, I definitely concur with Dom Alcuin Reid that authentic liturgical formation is the golden key to *participatio actuosa*, and that without this formation, no amount of fiddling and fidgeting with the liturgy is ever going to make a real and profound difference in how the people participate.[5] They will be devout or semi-devout spectators at a TLM, bored or semi-bored spectators at a Novus Ordo. For this reason, too, a growing number today are of the opinion that the traditional liturgy, which carries within it so very much to participate in, is the ideal point of departure for the spiritual revitalization of Christian worship that Pope John XXIII seemed to have numbered among his objectives for Vatican II but that Paul VI thwarted with his myopic modernizations.

Does this mean there can never be change in the liturgy handed down by our forefathers? That conclusion would not seem to follow from anything I've argued; on the contrary, the liturgy should continue to develop organically, because that is both a sign and a cause of its vitality.[6] For example, it is good that the old missal can now accommodate some of the most beloved saints canonized after 1960, the vast majority of whom knew only the traditional Mass.[7] All the same, it is eminently understandable that, after the maelstrom of the past sixty years, change doesn't seem to be high on the list of desiderata for lovers of the sacred liturgy. Truly *organic* development takes time, plenty of time, and no one need be in a rush (though moderns typically are, and that is more than half their problem). The improvements most desperately needed in the Church today are those that will take place in our minds and hearts when we throw ourselves anew into the Church's treasury of worship and so learn how to be Catholic once more. Fundamentally, *we ourselves* are the ones who need reform, not the liturgy.

---

[5] See the following by Alcuin Reid: "'Thoroughly imbued with the spirit and power of the liturgy'—*Sacrosanctum Concilium* and Liturgical Formation," in idem, ed., *Sacred Liturgy: The Source and Summit*, 213–36; "Active Participation and Pastoral Adaptation," in *Liturgy, Participation and Sacred Music* (CIEL UK, 2006), 35–50; "In Pursuit of Participation—Liturgy and Liturgists in Early Modern and Post-Enlightenment Catholicism" and "Pastoral Liturgy Revisited," in idem, ed., *T&T Clark Companion to Liturgy*, 133–51 and 341–63.
[6] On true and false development, see Kwasniewski, *Once and Future Roman Rite*, 196–215.
[7] I will return in chapter 20 to the topic of "new saints in the old Mass."

Just when one thinks that one has stepped off the heaving, rickety train or storm-tossed boat of liturgical change, someone of an impeccably reformist mentality will come along and propose unleashing *Sacrosanctum Concilium* on the *usus antiquior*, or returning to 1965, or cobbling together a hybrid rite from the old and new books, or some other such monstrosity. So many of these issues have been thought through, fought over, re-thought and re-fought, that one would think we had safely entered a period of deep skepticism about further tinkering with the TLM's structure, prayers, ceremonies, and customs, which are found upon long acquaintance to be eminently fitting.

At *The Catholic World Report* on January 31, 2017, Fr. Peter Stravinskas published "How the Ordinary Form of the Mass Can 'Enrich' the Extraordinary Form." Before I comment on his fourteen suggestions, I will say that I appreciate Fr. Stravinskas's honesty in admitting that the Novus Ordo has little to do with what the Council Fathers believed they were agreeing to when they signed *Sacrosanctum Concilium*, even though we also know (as discussed in chapter 1) that Bugnini and Co. created enough loopholes in the document to drive a fleet of lorries through. That being said, it is perplexing that Fr. Stravinskas does not seem to have noticed that almost all of his suggestions have been the subject of many previously published articles critiquing the very "improvements" he advocates. I will now take up each of Fr. Stravinskas's suggestions for how the new rite can enrich the old and briefly explain why, on the contrary, they would do nothing of the sort.

1. ADOPT THE REVISED LECTIONARY

The traditional lectionary could have been gently expanded with additional ferial readings that had once actually existed in the history of the Western rites, without displacing the existing annual *cursus*. As I suggested some time ago,[8] readings for the feasts of particular saints could have been augmented without difficulty—e.g., St. Anthony of Egypt could fittingly have had an Epistle and Gospel perfectly reflective of his life and continued witness in the Church today: St. Paul about our struggle not being with flesh and blood, etc., and the Gospel that prompted his own conversion: "If thou wilt be perfect, go sell what thou hast, and give to the poor" (Mt 19:21). Unfortunately, the reformers after Vatican II opted to create a new multi-year lectionary that has almost nothing in common with historical Roman precedent[9] and conflicts in numerous ways with the genius of the Roman rite.

---

[8] See Peter Kwasniewski, *Resurgent in the Midst of Crisis: Sacred Liturgy, the Traditional Latin Mass, and Renewal in the Church* (Angelico Press, 2014), 124–38.
[9] See Gregory DiPippo's five-part series on the topic at *NLM*, published from November 17–December 11, 2013: "Did the Roman Rite Anciently Have Three Readings?"; "Is the

Quite apart from whether or not it can be seen as faithful to the Council's desiderata, the Novus Ordo lectionary is gravely flawed because of its unwieldy bulk, its omission of "difficult" texts, its watering down of key spiritual goods emphasized in the old readings, and its diremption from the sanctoral cycle. No human mind can relate to so great a quantity of biblical text spread over multiple years: it is out of proportion to the natural cycle of the year and its seasons; it is out of proportion to the supernatural cycle of the liturgical year. The revised lectionary does not lend itself readily to the sacrificial finality of the Mass but, inasmuch as it appears to serve a didactic function, sets up a different goal, quasi-independent of the offering of the Sacrifice. The use of the names "Liturgy of the Word" and "Liturgy of the Eucharist" underlines the problem: it is as if there are two liturgies glued together. They are seldom joined by the obvious connection of being related to one and the same *feast*, since the new lectionary prefers to ignore the saints in its march through the books of Scripture. Catholics who love the Roman rite should be unafraid to maintain and to argue that the traditional Mass possesses what is, in many ways, a superior lectionary. An attempt to replace it with the new lectionary would be an impoverishment, not an improvement, of the rite.[10]

2. INCORPORATE ADDITIONAL MASS FORMULARIES

The addition, to Paul VI's missal, of "historic euchological material"—that is, prayers drawn from ancient liturgical books or collections—was done in an utterly inorganic manner, as committees of archaeologizing experts met to discuss their favorite textual digs, and all the bones and teeth, jewels and plates they recovered—many, no doubt, in excellent shape, but not something to be grafted on *tout court* by executive fiat. In this "enrichment" there was also a huge amount of excision and progressive rewriting, in other words, a distortion of the *lex orandi*.[11] This has been thoroughly documented in Lauren Pristas's *Collects of the Roman Missals*, augmented by the yeoman's work of Matthew Hazell.[12]

Ambrosian Lectionary an Older Form of the Traditional Roman Lectionary?"; "Is the Ambrosian Liturgy a Source for the Modern Lectionary?"; "Is the Medieval Liturgy a Source for the Modern Lectionary?"; "*Sacrosanctum Concilium* and the New Lectionary."

[10] For arguments against the new lectionary's content and structure, see "Why We Use a One-Year Lectionary of Readings" in Kwasniewski, *Turned Around*, 133–61; Peter Miller, OSB, "Bible by the Pound: Would the Holy Spirit Agree that More Bible is Better at Mass?," in Kwasniewski, *Illusions of Reform*, 180–97.

[11] On the process of tearing up ancient texts and stitching the bits back together to create new texts, see Gregory DiPippo, "A Tradition Both 'Venerable' and 'Defective,'" *NLM*, February 3, 2015; idem, "The New Rite Prefaces for Advent," *NLM*, December 24, 2015.

[12] On the inherent problem of the scissors-and-paste method of "making liturgy," *regardless* of how good the material is, see Kwasniewski, "The Reign of Novelty and the Sins of the Times"; *Once and Future Roman Rite*, 1–77; *Noble Beauty*, 33–50.

3. EXPAND POSSIBILITIES FOR SOLEMNITY

While I agree with Fr. Stravinskas that sung Mass should be the norm or at least far more common, especially on Sundays and Holy Days,[13] the potential pitfalls of the new mix-and-match model of progressive solemnity need to be honestly reckoned with. One writer offers the following defense of the rule that *everything* must be sung in a sung Mass:

> One of the biggest liturgical shifts following the council was the breakdown of clear lines between the High Mass (everything audible sung) and Low Mass (nothing sung). Like many of the things that came as a part of the council's liturgical reforms, I think the shift was meant well, but in practice, it has failed spectacularly.
>
> I understand the concept of what it intended to do. In theory, it would enable a parish to have more liturgical singing—for example, a priest singing all the dialogues and his prayers, even if a choir or cantor could not be present. Or it could allow a congregation to chant the ordinary (in addition to the priest chanting his parts), even if a cantor capable of chanting Propers could not be present. It would allow the Sung Mass model (that is, the ideal) to be more widely used, in situations where it would have been otherwise impractical or impossible in the Extraordinary Form, where a sung Mass cannot be celebrated without a cantor capable of chanting the Propers of the Mass. In other words, Progressive Solemnity *should* enable Masses to be generally celebrated in a more ideal manner, bringing things higher and closer to the ideal of a sung liturgy.
>
> However, it has had the exact opposite effect in almost every case. Instead of allowing priests to bring things closer to the ideal and to sing more, it led to a widespread laziness where singing the actual Mass itself has become quite a rare thing. The allowance to sing every prayer or a minimal number of prayers has caused most priests to sing very minimally (if they follow the rubrics) or even none (if they ignore them), effectively annihilating the sung Mass from use in most parishes. Human nature being what it is, we often need rules to keep us on the straight and narrow.[14]

To this may be added a widespread experience on the ground: the challenge presented by the obligatory nature of singing at a High Mass, and the obvious coherence of that Mass when integrally sung, is a mighty incentive for everyone involved—celebrant, cantors, choir—to work hard to achieve the goal.[15]

---

[13] On the problem of the dominant Low Mass and the rare High Mass, see chapter 8 and Kwasniewski, *Noble Beauty*, 235–55.
[14] Anonymous, "All-or-Nothing vs. 'Progressive Solemnity': A Response," *NLM*, December 10, 2014.
[15] See chapter 21 for further discussion of progressive solemnity.

4. ELIMINATE DUPLICATE RECITATIONS

Fr. Stravinskas objects to the manner in which, at High Mass, the priest is required to repeat a number of texts that are being sung by other ministers. Yet this practice possesses a profound theological rationale and brings spiritual benefits, as I mentioned in chapters 9 and 10 and will discuss at greater length in chapter 15. Such a defense may readily be given of all the other supposedly "useless repetitions" that the liturgical reform purged from the Mass, such as the repeated Confiteors, the ninefold Kyrie, the sixfold *Domine, non sum dignus*, and the nearly daily use of the Gloria.[16]

5. RESTORE THE OFFERTORY PROCESSION AND PRAYER OF THE FAITHFUL

The "offertory procession" as it was fashioned by the Consilium bears little resemblance to any historical precedent in the West; it is a fanciful creation loosely based on the custom of people handing in bread and wine before the service began.[17] Its current form seems to be another method for giving jobs to lay people, like the Works Progress Administration for the unemployed in the Great Depression.

As for the Prayer of the Faithful (also termed the General Intercessions), one might well question their role. A motley collection of petitions, usually poorly written and even more poorly read,[18] disturbs the natural flow of the liturgy as it proceeds from the readings into the Profession of Faith, which is the natural response to God's revelation of Himself, then into the Offertory. The homily already threatens to disturb the liturgical flow because it represents more the temporal human axis of liturgy, but a good homily need not last for more than a few minutes, and if it is truly good, it has whetted the soul's appetite for the Bread of Life by pondering the Word of God. With the solemn chanting of the Creed, the eternal divine axis of the liturgy decisively reasserts itself, as the soul exercises the gift of faith in preparation for the offering of the elements that the Lord will transform into the gift of Himself. Seen from "above," looking at the structure and flow of the liturgical action, the intercessory prayers mark an awkward caesura.

It is different in the Good Friday liturgy because this liturgy is already radically different from the form that evolved for the other days of the

---

[16] See "Why We Repeat Ourselves in Traditional Worship" in Kwasniewski, *Turned Around*, 109–32.
[17] See Paul Bradshaw, "Gregory Dix and the Offertory Procession," *Theology*, vol. 120, no. 1 (2017): 27–33.
[18] There is no doubt that the intercessions can be done in an elevated style, and even chanted; once upon a time, I made a notable effort in this direction by providing model texts, which I myself had "test-driven" as a cantor. See my article "How Can We Elevate the Quality of the 'Prayer of the Faithful'?," *NLM*, May 11, 2015. However, this experience was not enough to convince me that the good of having such intercessions outweighs the difficulties mentioned above.

year. The public intercessory prayers have all the more power and force for being specially and solemnly recited on Good Friday, the day on which we recall the historical event of the Lord's sacrifice and death. One is almost knocked over by the power of the Good Friday liturgy; one only waters down its forcefulness by borrowing its custom of general intercessions and distributing them widely—albeit superficially—throughout the year.

It is unnecessary to establish a separate part of the liturgy for a Prayer of the Faithful as long as one uses the Roman Canon with its stately intercessions for the Church, the pope, the bishop, priests, and people, and, after the consecration, for the faithful departed. There is a pause at the *Memento, Domine, famulorum famularumque tuarum* for remembering those for whom we have promised to pray and "all those dear" to us. Once more, the *Placeat tibi* is intercessory, and rightly so: it brings to a full close the majestic action of the sacrifice begun at the *Suscipe, Domine* and tracing an arc whose apogee is the elevation and whose perigee, if I may so speak, is the *Domine, non sum dignus*, when the glorified Lamb of God, of infinite holiness, is besought to heal our souls, that he may enter and make His dwelling there. The end joins with the beginning in a cycle that is not Nietzsche's despairing eternal recurrence but the joyous certainty of faith: He who created the world at the beginning, He who re-created it by His Incarnation, will come again in glory to judge the living and the dead, and will give to His faithful servants the reward of everlasting happiness.

6. RE-ORDER THE DISMISSAL RITE

Fr. Stravinskas dislikes the TLM's placement of the final blessing after the *Ite missa est*. If, however, we understand the Mass to be the offering of the Holy Sacrifice, then *Ite missa est* is most appropriately said when the liturgical offering is complete, namely, after the Postcommunion: for it can mean "go, it [the sacrifice] is sent to God," as well as "go, the Mass is complete." The blessing of the people *is*, in that sense, an afterthought—a most welcome one, to be sure, as is the Last Gospel that recalls the mystery of the Incarnation, of which the liturgy just enacted is an extension.

After the people respond *Deo gratias* to *Ite missa est* (or to *Benedicamus Domino*), the priest turns around to pray a last private prayer, the *Placeat tibi*, which allows the congregation time to kneel in preparation for the blessing of the priest. I've grown to appreciate kneeling for that final blessing, which has habituated me to value a priest's blessing as something special, in the way that the traditional rite of blessing holy water teaches one to appreciate this sacramental more than a hasty pseudo-blessing from the *Book of Blessings*.[19]

---

[19] See the chapter "Priests Who Want Holy Water Must Use the *Rituale*—Despite Episcopal Prohibition," in Kwasniewski, *Bound by Truth*, 222–26.

7. MOVE THE "*FRACTIO*" FROM THE *LIBERA NOS* TO THE AGNUS DEI

Here once again, the reformers, by moving the breaking of the Host and the depositing of a particle of it in the chalice from the moment of the embolism immediately after the Lord's Prayer to the moment of the Agnus Dei after the sign of peace, went far beyond the mandate of the Council in disturbing a very ancient custom for no discernible good reason. The Agnus Dei is a later addition to the Order of Mass (and certainly a very worthy one) made by Pope St. Sergius I at the end of the seventh century.[20] The Fraction, on the other hand, is as ancient and universal as the Mass itself. The separate consecrations of the bread and wine, also an ancient and universal feature of all historical Christian rites, represents the shedding of Christ's Blood, which is to say, the separation of His Blood from His Body, and hence His death. The fraction ritual, at which they are reunited, represents the Resurrection.[21]

In accordance with the Western Church's ancient tradition, the priest from the Preface until the end of the *Libera nos* has thus far only addressed God the Father in prayer.[22] Only after the Fraction, the representation of the Resurrection, does he say (and the choir sing) the Agnus Dei, addressing the Son, the Lamb of God whom St. John sees in the heavenly court, acclaimed by the angels and saints: "The Lamb that was slain is worthy to receive power, and divinity, and wisdom, and strength, and honor, and glory, and benediction." And only after this has been accomplished does the celebrant invite the faithful into the peace of the risen Christ, after which the rite of the *Pax* begins. The old missal's addition of "always" to the celebrant's address to the people, "May the peace of the Lord *always* be with you," which occurs only here, emphasizes this vision of Christ in eternity.

The modern displacement of the fraction to the Agnus Dei has turned a crucial moment in the Mass into an afterthought, and something which is routinely not even noticed by the congregation, as they are busy shaking each other's hands. Indeed, the change is both theologically incoherent and, one may truly say, disrespectful to Christ, as Michael Foley points out:

> Placing the kiss before the fraction and before the commingling [as the NO does] blurs and confuses the figurative significance of this part of the liturgy.... Under the current arrangement, the sign of

---

[20] See Gregory DiPippo, "An Important Liturgical Reform of the Eighth Century," *NLM*, March 31, 2011. The reform mentioned in the article's title is Gregory III's addition of Thursday Lenten Masses in the early eighth century.

[21] See Claude Barthe, *A Forest of Symbols: The Traditional Mass and Its Meaning*, trans. David J. Critchley (Angelico Press, 2023), 127–31.

[22] A tiny handful of Secrets are addressed to the Son, all but one of them quite late additions; at most Masses, the priest has spoken to the Father since the beginning of the Offertory, apart from the prayer *Suscipe, Sancta Trinitas*.

the risen Christ's peace is now being exchanged *before* the sign that Christ is risen from the dead; the people of God are savoring the joys of the resurrection while Christ still lies mystically suffering and dying on the altar.[23]

Given "that the liturgy should be restored in such a way that its *texts and rites* express *more clearly* the *holy things* which they *signify*" (SC 21), this mutation is supremely ironic.

8. MAKE CLEAR THAT THE HOMILY IS A TRUE PART OF THE SACRED LITURGY

Rather: let us make it clear that the homily is *not* a part of the liturgy. Please! Although restricted to those whose ordination grants them authority (in principle) to preach, preaching is not part of the Church's public worship that is done by Christ the Head in union with His members. A beautiful symbol of the distinction between the priest as an individual man and the priest as *alter Christus*, image of the archetype, is the custom of the priest removing his maniple (sometimes also his chasuble)[24] before he ascends the pulpit to read the readings in the vernacular and preach on them or on some other suitable theme. After he is done, he descends, resumes the vestment(s), and continues the Holy Sacrifice at the altar.

Clearly this is a healthy distinction to make. In every other part of the Mass, it is Christ primarily acting, with the priest following His lead, conforming to His pattern—symbolized by the Latin language, the unchanging prayers, the appointed readings, the formality of every scripted action, the Canon or Rule which brings the entire people to the foot of the Cross on Calvary and communicates to them none other than the Body and Blood of the Lord Jesus Himself, the beloved Son in whom the Father delights, the unblemished Lamb offered as a sweet-smelling oblation. As Robert Lazu Kmita observes:

---

[23] Michael Foley, "The Whence and Whither of the Kiss of Peace in the Roman Rite," *Antiphon* 14 (2010): 45–94, at 76.

[24] In most places, the priest removes his maniple and places it on the missal before genuflecting and moving to the ambo for the readings and the homily, then resumes the maniple for the Credo. It seems that the original reason for removing the chasuble and/or maniple was that, back in the day, when homilies were much lengthier and more energetic affairs, the priest did not want to ruin the vestments' decorations by rubbing them too much against the pulpit's edges, and, at the same time, welcomed a break from wearing the additional garments (a far from negligible consideration in Mediterranean lands in summer). In any case, the maniple is worn only for the offering of the Mass; when, e.g., there is a procession after Mass, it is taken off. As I discuss in chapter 15, the original "literal" meaning of a certain action can legitimately become the basis for "spiritual" meanings, as occurred with the lifting of the chasuble at the elevation: originating as a way to assist the priest in lifting his arms beneath a heavy "bell" chasuble, it later became a symbol of the woman's touching of the holy garment of Christ in order to be healed. See my article "The Lifting of the Chasuble at the Elevations: Touching the Hem of Christ's Garment," *OnePeterFive*, November 9, 2022.

In the liturgical context, the particular person of the priest (that is, everything that gives him subjective identity — his ideas, opinions, feelings) no longer exists. The explanation goes as follows: in the context of sacred ceremonies, the priest merely conforms perfectly to everything he must perform. In front of the holy altar, he does nothing to highlight his own creativity, opinions, or ideas: for he must carry out a series of actions and gestures, all of which are precisely codified by the millennia-old Tradition of the Church. I repeat: *nothing* that the priest must do in the liturgical context is his own "invention." Everything is given, already established. Practically, he must "empty" himself in an act of perfect humility, allowing the High Priest (according to the order of Melchizedek), Jesus Christ, to accomplish through His divine power, together with the Holy Spirit, the Eucharistic sacrifice offered to God the Father for our forgiveness and the restoration of harmony between us and the Supreme Being.[25]

At the time of the homily, in contrast, it is the individual priest who comes to the fore and acts *in propria persona*, since his words, his actions, are no longer precisely those of Christ. His divestment of chasuble and/or maniple makes a symbolic statement that it is now *he*, as an individual, who is going to expound the Word of God, to the best of his ability. History proves countless times that a preacher can preach heresy or can otherwise fail in his duty; Christ, through the liturgy, never preaches heresy, and the priest, when acting as a living instrument of Christ, never fails to accomplish the work of the Master.[26]

9. MAINTAIN THE INTEGRITY OF THE SANCTUS

Fr. Stravinskas also protests against the separation of the Benedictus from the Sanctus by the choir in certain sung Masses, insisting that if a polyphonic setting of the Sanctus is so lengthy it cannot be sung straight through, then it stands condemned by *Tra le Sollecitudini*.

Fr. Stravinskas must be misremembering no. 22 ("It is not lawful to keep the priest at the altar waiting on account of the chant or the music for a length of time not allowed by the liturgy. According to the ecclesiastical prescriptions the Sanctus of the Mass should be over before the elevation, and therefore the priest must here have regard for the singers. The Gloria and the Credo ought, according to the Gregorian tradition, to be relatively short"), which, when read together with no. 8, which notes that a motet may be sung after the Benedictus in a Solemn Mass, implies that Pius X accepts the custom of splitting the Sanctus into two parts, with the Benedictus sung after

---

[25] Robert Lazu Kmita, "Sacred Gestures and Symbols: Why Communion in the Hand is Unacceptable," *The Remnant* online, September 20, 2024.
[26] For a fuller explanation, see my article "The Homily Is Not Part of the Liturgy," *The Remnant* online, January 15, 2021.

the consecration of the wine. One might argue that the more elaborate Gregorian settings of the Sanctus, and especially the best polyphonic settings, bring the Canon—insofar as the Canon really begins with the Preface—into that effusive mode of prayer that is not natively Roman but is characteristic of the East. A silent Canon enwrapped (as it were) by a Palestrina Sanctus fuses the Roman prosaicness and "legalese" of the text, heard though it be only by the priest, with a "doxological" element, making it a rather different total experience from the Canon as said by St. Leo the Great or in the early *Ordines Romani*.

How fitting it is when the choristers, singing a polyphonic Sanctus, stop after the first Hosanna, as if crying out to welcome the King entering into the Holy City; then kneel in silence to adore the Blessed Sacrament elevated, as if Christ were just that moment passing by their marveling gaze; and, standing again, resume their prayer with the fitting words: "Blessed is *He who comes* in the name of the Lord." Worthy is the Lamb, the Son of David, exalted on high in His glorified humanity and now really present upon the altar, to receive this resounding Hosanna!

In any case, a proposal that would require the Sanctus and Benedictus from Palestrina's *Missa Papæ Marcelli* and every other such work to be permanently discontinued except as concert hall specialties must have something deeply wrong with it.

10. ADOPT THE RUBRICS OF THE NOVUS ORDO FOR THE COMMUNION RITE

Our eager reformer wishes to see everyone chant the Lord's Prayer together. However, in the historical Western rites, the celebrant is the only one who chants the bulk of the *Pater Noster*, whether at the Divine Office or at Mass, in his capacity as minister of the High Priest and representative of the people. The antiquity of this practice is evident from the way St. Augustine of Hippo and St. Gregory the Great speak of it as a thing taken for granted in their day.[27] The shape of the plainchant tells a story, too: the tone dips down at *Et ne nos inducas in tentationem* (a distinctively priestly tone used also at the end of the Secret leading into the Preface), whereupon the people are cued to respond, *Sed libera nos a malo*. It is in the *bones* of the rite, so to speak.

As for saying the remainder of the prayers aloud, such as the embolism, this only adds verbosity. Everyone knows what the priest is praying for, and we can all fruitfully immerse ourselves in the intense silence. That short silence after the Lord's Prayer is much appreciated by the congregation, as it enables us to reflect on the transition from the worship of the Lamb to the partaking of the Lamb in Holy Communion.

---

[27] Kwasniewski, *Illusions of Reform*, 67–68.

11. FACE THE PEOPLE WHEN ADDRESSING THE PEOPLE; FACE GOD WHEN ADDRESSING GOD

In keeping with the mid-century reformers, Fr. Stravinskas thinks that the readings are solely meant as instructional moments for the people, and therefore demands that the minister read them facing the people. But the longstanding custom of doing the readings either eastward (for the Epistle) or northward (for the Gospel) has a rich history and theology supporting it.[28] We should recover our understanding of the symbols, not jettison them for rationalistic reasons.

12. UNITE THE OLD AND NEW CALENDARS

Fr. Stravinskas opines that the feast of Christ the King should be celebrated on the last Sunday of the liturgical year. Traditional Catholics beg to differ. Pius XI's intention in instituting the feast, as can be gleaned from his encyclical *Quas Primas* (no. 29), is to emphasize the glory of Christ as terminus of His earthly mission, a glory and mission *visible and perpetuated in history* by the saints. Hence the feast falls shortly before the Feast of All Saints, to emphasize that what Christ inaugurated in His own person before ascending in glory, the saints then instantiate and extend in human society, culture, and nations. It is a feast primarily about celebrating Christ's ongoing kingship over all reality, *including this present world*, where the Church must fight for the recognition of His rights, the actual extension of His dominion to all domains, individual and social. Indeed, there's also the obvious fact—unmentioned in *Quas Primas* but surely in everyone's mind when the feast was established—that the last Sunday in October had, for centuries, been celebrated as "Reformation Sunday." Pius XI's intention, consistent with the encyclical as a whole, was to insist on the rights of Jesus Christ *here and now*, and the corresponding duties of men and nations *on earth*: a Catholic counter-Sunday, reminding the world not only of the comprehensive Kingship of Jesus Christ (so often denied socially and culturally by various teachings of Protestantism) but also of the worldwide kingly authority of His Church. Paul VI replaced this feast with a feast of Christ, King of the Universe, placed at the end of the Church year to emphasize the eschatological fulfillment of the kingdom of God in the world to come. The texts of the feast were pruned of references to Christ reigning through the laws, arts, and institutions of Catholic states. In other words, as Archbishop Lefebvre memorably puts it, "they have uncrowned Him." We wish to have no

---

[28] See my pair of articles: "Why the Epistle Should Be Read Eastwards and the Gospel Northwards," *Tradition and Sanity* Substack, December 16 and 19, 2024. I return to this topic in chapters 16 and 17.

part in that rude marginalization of the Redeemer-King of mankind.[29]

Subsequent to the publication of Fr. Stravinskas's article, the Vatican itself (as noted above) made provision for the celebration of some of the more recently canonized saints.[30] Nevertheless, as we discussed in chapter 2, the Novus Ordo calendar as a whole is a disaster, with its loss of the Pentecost octave and Sundays after Pentecost, loss of correct days for Epiphany and Ascension, loss of Epiphanytide, loss of Septuagesima, loss of Ember Days, and on and on. The drastic mutilation of the temporal cycle removed from the Roman rite almost all of its characteristically Roman features.[31] The new calendar, the handiwork of a "trio of maniacs" as Bouyer calls them, needs to be scrapped, and the *usus antiquior* calendar reclaimed as the norm; regional and recent saints may then be carefully added to it, making generous use of commemorations rather than jettisoning long-honored saints already present.

13. MODIFY THE RUBRICS

Fr. Stravinskas repeats the call for removing "useless repetitions," without showing that he has even tried to grasp the practical or symbolic value of the repetitions in question. In chapter 15, I will delve into his example, the multiple signs of the cross in the Canon. There are many reasons not to reduce or remove repetitions, not the least of which is that they are not at all useless.[32] A modern mentality that dictates we should cut out anything not immediately and obviously useful should advocate tonsillectomies and appendectomies for everyone. A better comparison would be the difference between poetry and prose. The hard-nosed rationalist might say, "Surely, all that fancy language isn't really necessary for getting the point across in plain old prose," but poetry has special resources of its own, a distinctive voice or manner of speaking, that is by no means incidental to the poet's message but essential to its full expression and reception. We need to expand our notion of what is useful by thinking of what is noble and fitting, what transcends the merely utilitarian as it rises to the poetic and the mystical.

---

29 Those who wish to understand the shift in the *lex orandi* and all that it entails for the *lex credendi* and *lex vivendi* may consult my articles: "Should the Feast of Christ the King Be Celebrated in October or November?," *Rorate Caeli*, October 22, 2014; "Between Christ the King and We Have No King But Caesar," *OnePeterFive*, October 25, 2020; "May His Kingdom Come: Catholic Social Teaching, Part VII—The Kingship of Christ, Source and Summit of the Social Order," *Catholic Family News*, October 25, 2020; cf. Michael P. Foley, "A Reflection on the Fate of the Feast of Christ the King," *NLM*, October 21, 2020.
30 See chapter 20.
31 See Gregory DiPippo, "The Octave of Pentecost: A Proposal for Mutual Enrichment," *NLM*, June 16, 2011.
32 See the comparison of the rosary to the Mass in Kwasniewski, *Noble Beauty*, 257–62; cf. "Why We Repeat Ourselves in Traditional Worship" in Kwasniewski, *Turned Around*, 109–32.

14. RENAME THE TWO PRINCIPAL PARTS OF THE MASS

Fr. Stravinskas argues for retiring the division of the Mass into "Mass of Catechumens" and "Mass of the Faithful," a nomenclature we apparently owe to Dom Fernand Cabrol in the 1920s,[33] and for replacing it with "Liturgy of the Word" and "Liturgy of the Eucharist," as in the Novus Ordo. The classic division makes more sense. The first Christians saw in the Holy Eucharist the fulfillment of what the Jews read about in their Scriptures; thus, the liturgical connection between reading and offering sacrifice was understood to be much deeper than two back-to-back segments of ritual, one pertaining to "books" and the other to "sacraments" or "mysteries." From a Patristic perspective, one might say that Cabrol's division points to two aspects of the life of faith: the *approach* to Christ, as a Jew or Gentile called to salvation by confessing His name and receiving the rites of initiation, and the *abiding in Christ* as one who has already been incorporated into Him in the waters of rebirth, the anointing from above, and communion with His Body and Blood. Consequently, while there may indeed be some actual catechumens at Mass who are living the drama of being "on the outside looking in," so to speak, there is something in this distinction that pertains to all of us in our pilgrimage of faith to glory, as we repeatedly confess Jesus Christ as Lord—and, when we have fallen into sin, receive absolution through Confession, which renews our baptismal grace—and can now, at the threshold of the Holy of Holies, *reap the fruits* foretold in the Scriptures that are read aloud to everyone. Even in the midst of the most radical religious shift the world has ever seen within one religious tradition—from the Mosaic law to the grace of Christ, from the Torah to the Gospel, from the many sacrifices of the Old Covenant to the one all-holy and all-sufficient sacrifice of the New Covenant—the tradition teaches us continuity, not rupture and discontinuity. There was a transition not from letter to spirit, but from a cosmic catechumenate to an eternal fidelity, from one Mass to another Mass—or rather, a seamless transition from the outer chamber of expectant preparation to the inner chamber of loving communion.

On the other hand, the new terms are seriously misleading. Since the central and definitive "word" is Jesus Christ, the *Logos* or *Verbum* of the Father, made flesh for us men and for our salvation, the expression "Liturgy of the Word" should refer *par excellence* to the Holy Eucharist itself—or even more, to the Eucharistic *sacrifice*, because in this sacrifice the Word uttered by the Father is offered back to Him, thanks to His human nature, in a perfect self-offering, and it is this oblation of Christ

---

[33] On the terminology "Mass of the Catechumens/Faithful" and also "Liturgy of the Word/Eucharist," see Lynne C. Boughton, "An Imagined Past: Initiation, Liturgical Secrecy, and 'Mass of the Catechumens,'" *Antiphon*, vol. 25, no. 2 (2021): 161–210.

on the Cross that empowers us to become "hearers" and "doers" of the word of God. The problem, then, with the phrase "Liturgy of the Word" is that this Word is really and fully present most of all in the Liturgy of the Eucharist. A sign of the difference is that, while we offer incense to the Gospel in honor of Him whose Gospel it is, it would be sinful for someone to bow down and adore the lectionary, placing his faith and trust in it, and loving it above all things, whereas it is precisely this adoration or *latria* that must be given to most holy Eucharist; indeed, as St. Augustine says (and Benedict XVI often quotes him to this effect), we would be guilty of sinning were we not to adore It. Hence the Novus Ordo's division is more confusing than it is enlightening. It betrays a Protestant exaltation of the Bible as the principal Word of God and the basis of the Christian religion—a view no Catholic could hold.[34]

In any case, it is odd when an author claims that Pius XII's denunciation of "antiquarianism" would apply to those who wish to retain such a term as "Liturgy of the Catechumens," which was never more than an unofficial categorization about a century old, yet simultaneously indulges in just the kind of antiquarianism Pius XII *did* warn against by advocating the restoration of supposedly ancient but long-since-discontinued practices like an offertory procession or general intercessions modeled after those of Good Friday.

HANG UP THE HAMMERS AND SAWS

Thus, we have a grab-bag of proposals for fourteen putative "improvements" to the old rite—every one of which, on closer inspection, deserves to be dismissed. There could have been fourteen other suggestions—or 140, for that matter.

I do not wish to be seen as making a personal attack on the author of these proposals. I respect him for his priesthood and his admirable defense of Catholic orthodoxy over many decades. For present purposes, he stands in for an entire class of professional, semi-professional, and unprofessional liturgists and liturgical reformers who, over the decades, have presented their "laundry lists" of lamented defects and favorite improvements—lists that rarely coincide, often conflict, seldom edify, and never suggest that the author has stepped back to ask, in all humility, why centuries of great theologians and devout clerics never

---

[34] For more on this problem of nomenclature, see my article "Why the 'Word of God' for Catholics is not only the Bible, but more importantly, Jesus Himself," *LifeSiteNews*, August 29, 2019. Boughton points out that Cabrol's informal nomenclature was based on a view of the *disciplina arcani* and the dismissal of catechumens that has now been subjected to serious doubts. And yet, ironically, while Cabrol's division was never reflected in any official liturgical book (being limited to hand missals), the "Liturgy of the Word/Liturgy of the Eucharist" division, which is even more dubious, has been engraved by papal power into liturgical books—one more example of faulty scholarship enforced on the Church.

complained, never sought an overhaul of the Church's ceremonies, but instead commented lovingly on each and every detail of the rites they inherited. In chapter 4, I quoted St. John Henry Newman to the effect that no two men will ever agree on reforms, and if they proceed with some plan or other, everyone will be discontented with whatever happens.[35] That is exactly what has happened, and it suggests that our forefathers were wiser than we are in their stubborn conservatism.

But some people will never learn. Under the current Vatican regime—who knows how long it and its programs (I had almost said pogroms) will endure—there are campaigns under way to enforce liturgical "updates" on communities that have been accustomed to the peaceful use of the old rite. For the one thing that must never, ever be allowed is an untroubled continuation, in the present, of a life of worship rooted in the past. As we saw in Fr. Stravinskas's proposals, there will always be those who are so enamored of this or that "improvement" that they can barely sleep at night knowing that someone, somewhere, is not benefiting from it. Or worse, there are people so enamored of the cult of obedience that they cannot rest until everyone has been made to submit, on bended knee, to the latest desideratum from a dicastery's desk, even if it enforces less time on their knees in divine worship. Such authoritarians will cloak their plan to soften and ultimately liquefy conservative opposition under smiling expressions like "gestures of communion," "institutional solidarity," and "synodal discernment."

In a press release dated July 25, 2024, the Dominicans of the Holy Spirit, a community of nuns that celebrated the traditional rite for decades but was then ordered by the Vatican to begin adopting the Novus Ordo, announced that the Vatican had given them detailed stipulations as to how they should proceed in the future:

> From the beginning of the next liturgical year, on December 1, 2024, the Holy See asks us to follow the liturgical calendar currently in force in the Universal Church for the Roman rite [i.e., the Novus Ordo calendar]; it also asks that in our various houses, Mass be celebrated according to the Novus Ordo one week of the month, with the exception of Sundays, while the Vetus Ordo remains in use for the other three weeks and every Sunday. It specifies that the Mass readings for each day will be *those of the current Roman lectionary*, and that all the prefaces of the Paul VI Missal will be used for Masses according to the Vetus Ordo.[36]

That is the beginning of the end of this community, for they will be destabilized at the core of their vocation by a hodge-podge rite

---

[35] See pp. 73–74.
[36] "Communiqué du 25 juillet 2024," translated from www.dominicaines-du-saint-esprit.fr/fr/communique-du-25-juillet-2024/, emphasis added.

that has lost its integrity, being treated like a toy model whose parts can be switched around at will. The nature of the demands indicates a profound disregard, even contempt, for the structural principles of the old rite (and, for that matter, of the new rite), while the nature of the "obedience" indicates a vision of religious life no longer rooted in coherent tradition but tossed this way and that by the ideological commitments of current Roman leadership.

The Vatican here targets a vulnerable community of nuns, heavily reliant on the outside support of priests,[37] in order to pilot an experiment that it would like, if possible, to extend to all TLM institutes, such as the Priestly Fraternity of St. Peter, the Institute of Christ the King Sovereign Priest, the Institute of the Good Shepherd, the Fraternity of St. Vincent Ferrer, the Fontgombault monasteries, and so forth: namely, not to *suppress* the old rite, but to *hybridize* it with the Novus Ordo. Thus, the diktat might be issued that the old *Ordo Missæ* may be retained *but* the Novus Ordo calendar, lectionary, and prefaces must be used at all times, instead of the ones proper to the classical Roman rite.

This deconstruction by hybridization, and the resulting fractures in unity it would bring about in the traditionalist movement, would be the next and more subtle strategy for officials who have realized they cannot achieve direct and total abolition of the old rite. If you can't beat them, why not assimilate them in some fashion?

Such moves would, as noted above, undermine the integrity of the rite and make it a hodge-podge. As Joseph Shaw is especially good at explaining,[38] the old rite and the new rite each has its own "design principles," if one may use that expression. Each is consistent from start to finish in pursuing certain goals with certain means. In the old rite, the inflexibility of the rubrics, the separation of priest from people, the use of a hieratic language, the frequent periods of silent prayer, the exclusive use of the Roman Canon, the fixed, limited, and repeated texts, etc., form a phenomenological and theological unity. In the new rite, the compact order of celebration, the interaction with the people, the verbalization of nearly everything, the vernacular

---

[37] This trial run selected a vulnerable group of nuns who seem to be in the grip of a false conception of obedience. The visitor who acted as liaison was Henry Donneaud, OP, who, as it happens, wrote a critique of the French edition of my book *True Obedience*. John Lamont penned a refutation of his critique and of his entire theological orientation: "Dominican Theologian Attacks Catholic Tradition: Defending Kwasniewski against Donneaud's Positivist Reductionism," published at *Rorate Caeli* in four installments in September 2023; a PDF of the whole is available at https://bit.ly/4gSSqTz.

[38] See his books *The Liturgy, the Family, and the Crisis of Modernity* and *Sacred and Great*.

extroversion, the options, the looser movements, the ample portions of Scripture, the clerically controlled silences, and so forth, also form a phenomenological and theological unity.

I think that clergy and laity who are familiar with the two rites are well aware of the many profound differences between them. While the new rite presents itself as an assemblage of modules, a design feature that can be explained both by the manner of its genesis out of committees and by the intention of situational adaptability, the old rite is most definitely *nothing of the sort*, and it cannot be treated like a LEGO kit in which one can swap out blue pieces for yellow ones. Indeed, as we have seen in this chapter, almost every proposal for "improving" the old rite either rests on questionable antiquarian premises or betrays a faulty understanding of how the old rite works.

Anyone who knows about the hundreds of obvious and subtle differences between the old and new calendars will see immediately that combining the old rite with the new calendar is a non-starter. For one thing, the hagiocentricity so characteristic of the old rite will be instantly compromised.[39] For another, the symbolic and numerological patterns that fill the old calendar will be lost without a trace.[40] Of all the changes, the one that is most alarming is the forcing of the new lectionary into the old rite. Much has already been written on this topic, so we need not dwell on it here.[41]

The experiment in alternating between the old and new rites was already tried years ago by the monks of Norcia, who started as a "biritual" community that offered Mass in both the Novus Ordo and the Vetus Ordo, while singing the old monastic office. Over time, the incoherence of the alternating rites, the clashing of calendars, the lack of tight interaction between Mass and Office, and other inconveniences so pressed upon them that the monks unanimously chose a fully traditional way of life and worship, which instantly brought *"pax liturgica"*—the ability to rest in the liturgy of tradition, as countless monks, clerics, and laymen had done for centuries. And in *this* case, the cause of the monks' lack of peace wasn't a *hybridized* rite—God forbid!—but a mere *alternation* between old and new.

There is a phrase, "death by a thousand cuts." We learned recently that in Virginia, at three parishes that were given a further two-year extension for the TLM, the Novus Ordo is to be celebrated one Sunday

---

[39] See chapter 14.
[40] See my article "The Stigmata of Saint Francis, Appearing and Disappearing in the Liturgy," *NLM*, September 17, 2018, and the chapter "The Loss of Riches in the Sanctoral Cycle" in Kwasniewski, *Resurgent in the Midst of Crisis*, 124–38.
[41] In addition to points raised earlier in this chapter and in chapter 17, see the more extended treatment in Kwasniewski, *Turned Around*, 133–66.

per month (it was merely a "suggestion," but the bishop seized it eagerly; or perhaps he was told that it was an unusual kind of suggestion, namely, a requirement); this is the Cupich policy now applied to another diocese. In the case of the French nuns, a religious community may keep a mangled TLM, but once a week, they must use the Novus Ordo. First, one Sunday a month...then two.... One week a month...then two.... Those who could not obtain the total suppression of the TLM will attempt to subvert it in other ways. We could have predicted this, for the same methods have been used by the Vatican ever since the 1970s. Consider the monastery of Benedictines in Flavigny: they were "reconciled" to the Church on the condition that they take the Novus Ordo as their conventual Mass, although the monks individually offer the old Mass in the mornings.

If you don't want to die by a thousand cuts, do not offer your body to the first cut.

I feel genuinely sorry for the Dominicans of the Holy Spirit, as they now embark on the bumpy, cratered, agitating road of incoherence that wiser monks and nuns have left behind. A forced and clumsy attempt to fit new in old, and old in new, will make the resulting *neither-this-nor-that* liturgical life more self-conscious and wearisome. And to think they are making this shift *in 2024*—decades after the problems of the new rite have been exhaustively experienced and canvassed! After so many souls, responsive to the same Holy Spirit who raised up for us these noble apostolic rites in their millennial plenitude, have successfully disowned the "banal on-the-spot product" for good! Thus we see the devastating results of placing obedience to renegade authorities higher than obedience to any other principle, including the universal and unanimous acceptance of liturgical tradition that has characterized Western religious life from its dawn until the rise of hyperpapalism.

Nor is my concern limited to the current heads, more or less competent, of Roman dicasteries. For there are figures within the traditional movement who would gladly throw open the gates to the Trojan Horse of late Liturgical Movement innovations in order to maintain what they consider the core of their commitment. For example, in certain years on Pentecost Monday of the Chartres pilgrimage, the Epistle and Gospel have been read in French toward the congregation rather than being chanted in Latin while facing eastwards and northwards.[42] Apparently many French and German priests who offer the TLM believe that the readings should be given *in the vernacular only*, and facing the people.

---

[42] See chapters 16 and 17.

This mentality is a consequence of a fundamental failure to understand the role of the Word of God in the Eucharistic liturgy, reflecting widespread errors—largely rationalist in origin—about the exclusively or primarily "instructional" nature of the first part of the Mass.[43]

Imagine a future pope—let us call him Pius XIII, perhaps hailing from Africa or Asia—who, with all the good intentions in the world, wishes to end the "liturgy wars" and therefore decides to produce a hybrid missal for the "Roman rite" that combines what he, or a committee he appoints, decides are the best features of the old and new missals. With liturgical knowledge and praxis being as abysmal as they are in the second Dark Ages we are passing through, it is almost a foregone conclusion that such a hybrid rite, though it would doubtless begin from the old *Ordo Missæ*, probably in its 1965 Belvedere Torso form (where the head of the preparatory prayers and the feet of the Last Gospel are lopped off and only the bulk remains), would adopt the new lectionary because it is considered such a great success, indeed a necessary step of progress in the Church's relationship with the Bible.[44]

I have no inside information about what is being planned, but it's not difficult to connect the dots and to make projections. I say none of this to be a fearmonger or to promote anxiety. I simply wish to warn traditional clergy and faithful of the kind of maneuvers our antagonists have in mind, so that we can make sure we ourselves understand well the rationale behind every part of the traditional Roman rite and, on that basis, are prepared to offer respectful but firm resistance to any attempts at diluting or destroying its integrity. If or when the Dicastery for Divine Worship and the Discipline of the Sacraments (or the Dicastery for Institutes of Consecrated Life and Societies of Apostolic Life) issues the command to adopt the new calendar, the new lectionary, the new prefaces, etc., we must be ready to say: *Non licet. Non possumus.* It is not permitted. We cannot do it.

---

[43] It goes without saying that there *is* an instructional aspect, and that is why it has usually been the custom for the preacher to read the readings in the vernacular from the pulpit before his sermon. This is not a liturgical reading but a paraliturgical reading, for the benefit of those who do not know the Latin readings or have not followed them in a hand missal. Nor does it hurt to hear and read the readings twice, a point to which I will return later.
[44] For a refutation of this view, see Miller, "Bible by the Pound."

13

Just Say No to '65—and '62

THE POSITION THAT HAS DOMINATED THE traditionalist world for a long time is that we should be content with the 1962 missal (and accompanying liturgical books) as our point of departure for a healthy liturgical future. After all, the 1962 missal is the last *editio typica* prior to the upheavals occasioned by the Council; it is still in some recognizable continuity with the Tridentine rite; it was enjoined upon us by Church authority in the motu proprio *Summorum Pontificum*. Although that motu proprio's conciliatory policy has in recent years been sent into early retirement and replaced with an extermination campaign, some traditionalists, at least, will be inclined to hold on to its provisions.

Archbishop Thomas Gullickson, a retired Papal Nuncio, makes a rousing case for "pressing the reset button" on the Roman liturgy by abandoning a failed experiment and taking up again the traditional rites of the Catholic Church.[1] He offers a brisk version of what Joseph Shaw's book *The Case for Liturgical Restoration* provides in much greater detail. Then, with admirable candor, Archbishop Gullickson broaches the million-dollar question:

> I am avoiding the burning issue of setting a date for the reset. I used to think that going back to the 1962 Missal and to St. Pius X and his breviary reform was sufficient, but the marvels of the pre-Pius XII Triduum as we have begun to experience them leave me speechless on this point. Perhaps the teaching of Pope Benedict XVI on the mutual enrichment of the two forms will provide the paradigm for resolving the question of which Missal and which breviary. My call for a return to the presently approved texts for the Extraordinary Form, then, is inspired by a certain urgency to move forward, to further the process. I do not feel qualified to take a stance in this particular matter of where best to launch the restoration.

In a contrasting position, Dom Hugh Somerville Knapman urges that we must still take seriously the Constitution *Sacrosanctum Concilium* and that, accordingly, the 1962 missal will not pass muster:

> I still see a validity in a mild reform in the liturgy along the modest lines actually mandated by the Council: vernacular readings, setting aside the duplication of the celebrant having to recite prayers, etc., that were being sung by other ministers, a less obtrusive priestly

---

[1] See Gullickson, "Liturgy Summer Course 2019."

preparation at the beginning of Mass, etc. And the conciliar mandate for reform cannot be just forgotten as though it never happened: it must be faced and dealt with, either by reforming the reform made in its name, or by a specific magisterial act abrogating it.

That is why the interim rites interest me — OM65 [the *Ordo Missæ* of 1965] is clearly the Mass of Vatican II while also clearly being in organic continuity with liturgical tradition. It left the Canon alone as well as the integral reverence of the liturgical action. Even Lefebvre was approving of it. What distorts our perception of OM65 is that we have seen 50 years of development since, and cannot help but see OM65 as tainted by what came after it.

Moreover MR62 is a rather arbitrary point at which to stop liturgical tradition. For some committed trads this is an imperfect Missal, even a tainted one. Is a pre-53 Missal better? Or a pre-Pius XII one? Or maybe pre-Pius X? Why not go the whole hog and argue for pre-Trent — after all, Geoffrey Hull sees the seed of liturgical decay there? We end up in a situation in which each chooses for himself on varying sets of idiosyncratic principles. It is ecclesiologically impossible. The Catholic Church has a magisterial authority which establishes unity in liturgy. That this has been sadly lacking for some decades is not an argument for ignoring magisterial authority altogether. Then we may as well be Protestants.[2]

Dom Hugh is willing to admit that Bugnini and Co. were busy behind the scenes throughout the 1960s and early 1970s, plotting and eventually carrying out the rape and pillage of all that remained of the Western liturgical tradition. He nevertheless thinks that, in the world outside the Politburo, the 1965 missal was generally seen — and can still be seen today — as the reform that lines up with the Council's desiderata. *This*, then, should be where the reset button takes us.[3]

For a long time, I sincerely tried to understand, appreciate, and embrace *Sacrosanctum Concilium*. I assigned it to students every time I taught a course on liturgy, and in our discussions I leaned into its best Catholic content (for there are some veins of precious metal here and there). But it was not possible, after reading Michael Davies, and later Henry Sire's *Phoenix from the Ashes* and Yves Chiron's biography of Annibale Bugnini, to see in this document anything other than a carefully contrived blueprint for liturgical revolution.[4] It contradicts itself on several points and takes refuge more often than not in ambiguities put there deliberately (and this we know from documentary

---

[2] Hugh Somerville Knapman, "Saving the New Mass?," *Dominus Mihi Adjutor*, July 15, 2019.
[3] To brush up on what the 1965 missal was like, read Msgr. Charles Pope, "A Look at the 'Actual Mass' of Vatican II: the 1965 Missal," *Community in Mission*, January 28, 2015. Joseph Shaw discusses why it is a non-starter: "The Death of the Reform of the Reform, 5: 1965?," February 27, 2014.
[4] See chapter 1.

evidence examined in chapter 1—no need for conspiracy theories). When you delve into the history of this document—when you learn about the chicanery involved in its drafting, discussion, approval, and implementation—you have to get down on your knees to ask the Lord for the grace of faith, otherwise you will be in danger of losing it. Nowhere does the darkness of the human side of the Church appear darker than in the systematically dishonest dismantling of centuries (and in some cases, millennia) of religious ritual.[5]

For me, the evaporation of the honorable status of *Sacrosanctum Concilium* came from a deeper reflection on its abolition of the Office of Prime.[6] A document that would dare abolish a liturgical office received and practiced for 1,600 years—part of the sevenfold diurnal prayer offered to God by an innumerable throng of monks, nuns, friars, hermits, deacons, priests, and bishops—vitiates itself from the get-go. Since none of the documents of Vatican II contains *de fide* statements or anathemas, the charism of infallibility is not expressly involved. Given their contingent nature, a bunch of pastoral recommendations such as form the bulk of this Vatican II constitution can obviously be mistaken. As I have pointed out many times, a proposal for action is neither true nor false (although it is usually justified in light of certain truths and can be argued against in the same way). *A proposal for action is prudent or imprudent, wise or unwise, successful or unsuccessful.* Ever-mounting evidence indicates that the aims and means of the radical arm of the Liturgical Movement were grievously off-target; the corresponding assumptions of the Council about what "had to be done" to the liturgy ended up misreading the signs of the times. These aims, means, and

---

[5] I refer to "thousands of years" because the sacrificial rituals of the Hebrews and many aspects of temple worship inform traditional Catholic liturgy—and many of these features were abolished in the "reform." See, for instance, Gregory DiPippo's insightful seven-part series "Torah and Haftarah in the Roman Liturgy" at *NLM*, published from September 20–October 21, 2023: "Part 1: Torah and Haftarah in the Roman Liturgy"; "Part 2: The Ember Saturday of September"; "Part 3.1: The Ember Saturday of Lent"; "Part 3.2: The Ember Saturday of Pentecost, and Good Friday"; "Part 4: An Inheritance Repudiated"; "Part 5.1: The Easter Vigil"; "Part 5.2: The Easter Vigil, Concluded." See also Alisa Kunitz-Dick, "AUDI, ISRAËL: Jewish Feasts in the Propers of the Traditional Roman Rite," *Rorate Caeli*, August 31, 2021.

[6] A reflection prompted by Schrems, "The Council's Constitution on the Liturgy: Reform or Revolution?"; see chapter 1 above. As Matthew Hazell points out, the abolition of Prime was not originally part of Vatican II's liturgy constitution: it was only added to *Sacrosanctum Concilium* at a very late stage (October 21, 1963, to be precise: see https://archive.org/details/ASII.3/page/114/mode/2up). What had previously been described in the preparation of *SC* as an "extreme solution . . . contrary to the whole liturgical tradition" (https://archive.org/details/ADPIII.2/page/n43/mode/2up, p. 49) was sprung on the Council Fathers as a last-minute amendment, on the basis of only two cardinals and an unspecified "many" bishops (https://archive.org/details/ASII.3/page/132/mode/2up, pp. 133–134)—more evidence of the shenanigans perpetrated by the liturgical progressives, who could, and did, easily run circles around a behemoth of more than 4,000 prelates.

assumptions violated the axioms of religious anthropology, sociology, and psychology, not to mention those of dogmatic theology, moral theology, and ascetical-mystical theology. The proposals for reform bought into modern assumptions that have not stood the test of time; indeed, they had already been effectively criticized before and during the Council.[7] So it seems to me no feather in its cap that the '65 missal better reflects the conflicting and problematic ideas of the Council; that would be all the more reason to give it a pass.

Archbishop Lefebvre, like other conservatives at the Council,[8] had been naïve enough to believe in 1963 that only the modest reforms agreed upon in the conciliar debates and texts would be executed, and that there would be, a few years later, a partially vernacular, slightly simplified, but still recognizably Roman Catholic liturgy. The so-called 1965 missal, already an ugly enough duckling, was widely believed to be what the Council ordered. To take a notable piece of evidence, when the Abbot of Beuron sent the pope a copy of the latest postconciliar edition of the famous German Schott missal, the Cardinal Secretary of State Amleto Giovanni Cicognani sent a letter, *on behalf of Paul VI* and dated May 28, 1966, with the ringing affirmation: "The singular characteristic and primary importance of this new edition [of Schott] is that it reflects completely the intent of the Council's Constitution on the Sacred Liturgy"(!).[9]

The experimental previews of the 1967 *Missa Normativa*—basically, a rough draft of the Novus Ordo—were greeted with astonishment by many of the bishops who came to Rome that year. One of them was John Cardinal Heenan, archbishop of Westminster, later to be famous for his 1971 intervention with Paul VI that rescued the traditional Mass for England and Wales (the template for the worldwide "indult" later issued by John Paul II). Having witnessed Bugnini's *Missa Normativa*, Cardinal Heenan wrote: "At home it is not only women and children but also fathers of families and young men who come regularly to Mass. If we were to offer them the kind of ceremony we saw yesterday in the Sistine Chapel we would soon be left with a congregation mostly of women and children."[10]

---

[7] As can be seen, for example, in the reactions of the academic and cultural figures profiled in Shaw's *The Latin Mass and the Intellectuals*.
[8] Jerome Stridon, "The *Cœtus [Internationalis Patrum]*: Trad Godfathers at Vatican II," OnePeterFive, December 12, 2022.
[9] See my article "Seeking the Origins of 'Versus Populum' in the United States," *Tradition and Sanity* Substack, October 19, 2023.
[10] Quoted in Reid, *A Bitter Trial*, 102; the complete intervention of Cardinal Heenan at the 1967 Synod may be found on pp. 102–4. See the excellent commentary by Richard Cipolla, "The Devirilization of the Liturgy in the Novus Ordo Mass," *Rorate Caeli*, June 26, 2013.

In the same period—the exact year is not specified—Archbishop Lefebvre (then Superior General of the Congregation of the Fathers of the Holy Ghost) visited Rome for a meeting of Superiors General. He later reminisced about the indomitable influence Bugnini then enjoyed, as he enthusiastically lectured the gathering about a "new Mass" that would be radically different from what had been celebrated for centuries.[11] Once Lefebvre had seen up close the impresario of the circus, he would have realized that his signature was (to use an expression of another writer) "obtained through trickery."[12]

In any case, the idea that the 1965 *Ordo Missæ* represents the implementation of *SC* is hard to sustain in light of repeated statements by Paul VI (and other officials on his behalf) that what he promulgated in 1969 *is* the ultimate fulfillment of the liturgy constitution.[13] 1965 was presented publicly (though not always consistently) as an interim step on the evolutionary process away from medieval-Baroque liturgy to relevant modern liturgy.[14] The "moment of truth," I think, is when students of liturgy realize that the 1962 missal is extremely similar to that of 1965 in this respect: it, too, was an interim missal in the preparation of which Bugnini and other liturgists working at the Vatican had changed as much as they felt they could get away with. These liturgists had experienced a triumph of renovationism with the Holy Week "reform" of Pius XII—a dramatic makeover that deformed some of the most ancient and poignant rites of the Church, scattering novelties hither and yon—and they were rolling along with the momentum. The abolition under Pius XII of most octaves and vigils, obligatory additional Collects, and folded chasubles, *inter alia*, is part of this same sad tale of cutting away some of what was most distinctive and most precious in the Roman heritage.[15]

This is why the exclusivist 1962 and reformist 1965 positions are rapidly losing ground throughout the world, particularly as the internet continues to spread awareness of the ill-advised and sometimes calamitous "reforms" that took place throughout the twentieth century in various areas of the Roman liturgy, with Holy Week looming largest. Since I, too, disagree with the 1962 and 1965 camps, I would make the case for returning to

---

[11] The full account is quoted above on pp. 48–49.
[12] See my article "Prophets of Truth in a Decadent Age," *NLM*, May 18, 2015.
[13] See "Paul VI on liturgical reform, Part 6," *Pray Tell*, September 6, 2018, and Corrado Maggioni, "Fifty years of the Missal promulgated by Paul VI: A reform for the renewal of the Church," *Pray Tell*, April 17, 2019. I discuss the infamous addresses of 1965 and 1969 in *Once and Future Roman Rite*, 109–43.
[14] See Joseph Shaw, "The Mass of 1965: back to the future? Why it is not an option," *Rorate Caeli*, February 27, 2014.
[15] Archbishop Gullickson says, in the same address ("Liturgy Summer Course 2019"): "While we are at it: When it comes to calendar... isn't older better? From me you will get a resounding 'yes', especially if we are talking about vigils and octaves, and giving the proper denomination to times and seasons." See Kwasniewski, *Once and Future Roman Rite*, 333–75.

the last *editio typica* prior to the revolutionary alterations of Pope Pius XII: the *Missale Romanum* of Benedict XV, issued in 1920.[16] It is by no means arbitrary for traditionalists to land there. Except for some newly added feasts (the calendar being the part of the liturgy that changes the most), it is in all salient respects the missal codified by Trent. It is the Tridentine rite *simpliciter*. For those of us who believe that the Tridentine rite represents, as a whole and in its parts, an organically developed apogee of the Roman rite that it behooves us to receive with gratitude as a timeless inheritance (in the manner Greek Catholics receive *their* liturgical rites, which also achieved mature form in the Middle Ages), a pre-Pacellian missal gives us all that we seek, and nothing tainted.[17]

As we have seen, even to this day one will find people suggesting "improvements" that could or should be made to the old missal, or who believe that *Sacrosanctum Concilium* places on the Church an obligation to reform the old rite, such that it cannot be left in its traditional form. Those who have lived long and intimately with it are usually the last to be convinced that the suggested improvements would actually be anything of the sort.[18] We should flip the tables and ask: Why is a constitution from 1963 still believed to be in need of implementation? Yes, it stipulated some changes; but that was over sixty years ago, and just as we have reconsidered, modified, or sometimes quietly ignored things said in *Gaudium et Spes* that sound

---

[16] Needless to say, particular feasts that subsequently entered the calendar and met with a serene reception, such as that of St. Thérèse of Lisieux or of Christ the King, or the Preface added for the Sacred Heart, should be included, while Propers that may be controversial for one reason or another (e.g., the untraditional Common of Popes; the rewritten Assumption Mass; the Propers for Pius X that make use of the Bea psalter) should be relegated to an appendix for those who wish to use them.

[17] For a full argument arriving at this conclusion, see *Once and Future Roman Rite*, chapters 2 and 12. The Novus Ordo was the lightning rod on which modernism expended all its fury. In this way, the worst evils were deflected from the old liturgy, which was set aside in a condition only partially damaged by Pius XII's deformations, and these can easily be reversed—far more easily than the reform could ever be reformed. Bringing the Novus Ordo back into harmony with tradition would require changes as numerous and profound as those that were unleashed in the 1960s—and to what purpose? The authentic Roman rite is already to hand in the missals published between 1920 and 1948, though indeed for most days of the year *any* old-rite missal published in the past 400 years would suffice, so little has the content changed.

[18] The question of the reform of the Divine Office under Pius X is a separate can of worms. It is easy to see that the Church should restore some elements of the traditional Roman office that were lost, such as the *Laudate* psalms in Lauds, but it is by no means easy to see exactly how the old *cursus psalmorum* and calendar may be taken up again while privileging the recitation of the full psalter as often as possible. Indeed, probably the only way to resume the traditional (pre-Pius X) office is either to dissever the hours from the sanctoral or to make parts of the office optional for active clergy; both of these are, in their own way, radical changes. The situation with the Office is vastly more complex than the situation with the altar missal or the other sacramental rites. Fortunately, at least for members of the Benedictine family, an alternative already exists: taking up the 1934 *Antiphonale Monasticum*, which preserves an ancient heritage and lacks the worst aspects of Pius X's reforms.

dated or naively optimistic today, so, too, six decades of living with *Sacrosanctum Concilium* have exposed dubious assumptions, exploded theories, and reductionistic notions of "pastoral" that caused immense damage in their (mis)application and could easily cause new and gratuitous damage, or at least confusion and unrest, in any future (mis)application. If only the teaching of St. Pius X, Pius XI, and Pius XII on the faithful's *participatio actuosa* is implemented (as has been done in many traditional communities), the most important desiderata of the Council will already have been attained, and we can gratefully leave the more embarrassing bits—especially no. 34, reflective of a rationalistic mindset[19]—embedded in the annals of the 1960s.

It is pertinent to recall the very wise words of Fr. John Berg, Superior General of the Priestly Fraternity of St. Peter:

> There have always been a few voices which have advocated a "hybrid" missal, but this is unfortunately symptomatic of the liturgical age in which we live. These voices are often found among those who have no pastoral charge and look at the liturgy mostly as an object of study. The problem is that if you ask ten of them, each will give you a different point which needs to be changed. It also at times betrays a rather condescending attitude—experts who really want to help the "poor faithful" who would live the liturgy more fully, for example, "if only the priest read the Collect facing the congregation from the sedilia." In other words, no real connection with the actual prayer life of our faithful, and ultimately, I regret to say, not helpful. It is not the faithful in the pews each Sunday clamoring for such things.
>
> We have trained hundreds of diocesan priests, pastors, to offer the Mass according to the Missal of 1962 and, to the best of my knowledge, none of them have any interest in looking to change the Missal. They are just pleased to find a liturgy which is stable, where they do not have to make decisions, and choose options, and animate the congregation, and wonder how it could be improved.... It has always been the position of our Fraternity that now is not the time to make changes to the Missal, if indeed there were the need for such to be made, and that we need first to have a long period of time where the liturgy is simply lived rather than being constantly scrutinized and "tweaked."[20]

---

[19] *SC* 34 reads: "The rites should be distinguished by a noble simplicity; they should be short, clear, and unencumbered by useless repetitions; they should be within the people's powers of comprehension, and normally should not require much explanation." This description bears no resemblance to any apostolic liturgical tradition that we know of, Eastern *or* Western. The Pistoian rationalism of this paragraph has been the target of countless critiques since 1963—not surprisingly, since, as Aristotle once observed, no one can fail to hit a big target when aiming at it (*Metaphysics* II.1). On this strange provision of *SC*, see Kwasniewski, *Turned Around*, 109–32.

[20] "An Interview with Father Berg, FSSP," *The Latin Mass*, vol. 22, no. 1 (Winter/Spring 2013): 6–13, at 9–10, www.latinmassmagazine.com/pdfs/Berg-interview-LM-2013-1-WinSpr.pdf.

Interestingly enough, a not insignificant number of priests who belong to the Fraternity of St. Peter have gone over decisively to the pre-'55 Holy Week; this is already the default position for the Institute of Christ the King and the Institute of the Good Shepherd. Traditional Benedictine monks and nuns are either already pre-'55 or moving in that direction.[21] It is, in fact, impossible to follow the history of liturgical reform after World War II and not see it as a continuous process of demolition and reconstruction, initially cautious as the trial balloons were sent up, and later increasingly audacious as radical reformism took possession of the Holy See, experimental pastoralism pervaded the middle management, and hyperpapalism made possible a rupture that no Catholic in premodern history could have imagined, let alone consented to.

Without a doubt, no special permission is required to use the Tridentine rite as found in the liturgical books prior to the deformations introduced under Pius XII. The basis is nothing other (and need be nothing more) than the "*Summorum Pontificum* Principle": "What earlier generations held as sacred, remains sacred and great for us too, and it cannot be all of a sudden entirely forbidden or even considered harmful. It behooves all of us to preserve the riches which have developed in the Church's faith and prayer, and to give them their proper place." If the millennium-old Roman Holy Week does not count as one of the riches that developed in the Church's faith and prayer, what could possibly qualify? If earlier generations did not hold as sacred these august ceremonies at the core of the Church's year, was anything ever held sacred? The authentic Roman rite, in its pristine integrity, remains sacred and great for us too; there can be no question of its being harmful or forbidden. Let those who understand that right liturgy depends on tradition, on universal ecclesial acceptance and transmission, and not on arbitrary *diktats* that shift from one papal reign to another, be prepared to do the right thing: to receive the liturgy whole and then to transmit it intact to the next generation. *Tradidi quod et accepi.*

---

[21] While it is true that historically the SSPX has been staunchly against restoring the pre-'55 Roman rite, with Archbishop Lefebvre decisively intervening in the matter of "the Nine" who were expelled in March 1983 (largely for disobeying his instruction to cleave to the 1962 missal), I have received reliable reports that a growing number of Society chapels are returning to the traditional Holy Week ceremonies. May this good sense ultimately prevail in all individuals, institutes, and communities that adhere to the *usus antiquior*! At the moment, the prospects are admittedly mixed: the July-August 2024 issue of the SSPX's *Angelus* magazine raises the question and provides the official reply that the use of the pre-'55 ceremonies is absolutely out of the question, and, moreover, opines that the ex-Ecclesia Dei communities' openness to this discussion just shows that they have no principles and do what they do for personal, subjective reasons of taste.

14

Too Many Saints—
Too Many Intercessors?

ON JULY 12TH, THE CLASSICAL ROMAN RITE celebrates the feast of St. John Gualbert, Abbot, with a commemoration of Sts. Felix and Nabor, martyrs who were praised by St. Ambrose and enshrined by him in Milan. The Collect for the commemoration of the latter is noteworthy:

> Præsta, quæsumus, Domine: ut, sicut nos sanctorum Martyrum tuorum Naboris et Felicis natalitia celebranda non deserunt; ita jugiter suffragiis comitentur. Per Dominum... [Grant, we beseech Thee, O Lord, that just as the birthdays we are celebrating of Thy holy Martyrs Nabor and Felix never forsake us, so may they always accompany us by their prayers. Through our Lord...]

Nearly every time I praise a "lesser" saint's feast on the traditional calendar, inevitably I encounter resistance: "We should get rid of a lot of these obscure or territorial saints and leave more room for local or modern saints." The ones who make these comments may love the traditional liturgy, but they seem to agree with the rationale that led to the removal of over 300 saints from the general calendar in 1969.[1] I would like to suggest, in all kindness, that this gigantic overhaul was excessive, disproportionate, harmful, and uncharacteristic of liturgical history, which tends to prune rather than to purge, and which prefers to make room for more rather than to cut away. Yes, St. Pius V removed some saints from the calendar of the 1570 missal, but his cuts are trivial compared with those made by Paul VI—and besides, Pius V's successors pretty soon after began adding back saints that Pius had removed.[2] A university student once sent me this note:

> In my liturgy class, we discussed the calendar. What you wrote about St. Felix of Valois—"Who is this obscure saint, and why is he cluttering our calendar?"—was the exact mindset the professor

---

1 See Kwasniewski, "Sanctoral Killing Fields."
2 "In St. Pius V's reform of the Roman liturgical books, the feast of the Presentation is suppressed, along with those of SS. Joachim and Anne, precisely because they all derive from an apocryphal gospel. This went far too strongly against the grain of traditional piety, and all three feasts were swiftly restored, St. Anne's by Pius' own successor, Gregory XIII, in 1584, the Presentation by Sixtus V the following year, and St. Joachim by Gregory XV in 1622." Gregory DiPippo, "Liturgical Notes on the Presentation of the Virgin Mary," *NLM*, November 21, 2021. See my article "Polluting the Internet with Falsehoods," *OnePeterFive*, October 10, 2023.

strove to pound into students' minds that day. He described how over the centuries, "certain elements crept into the calendar" (his words), and these elements had clouded over the meaning of Sunday, plus many saints and feastdays held no meaning for us anymore and sometimes were mythological. But, he said, as if to clinch his point, "other popes have cleaned out the calendar before."

Thank you for being willing to defend the old calendar and its rich sanctoral cycle and prayers. Any time I've tried to defend the beauty of the traditional rites in class, the things I've pointed to have been declared "unnecessary for modern man." Well, to that I respond, the Mass should not have changed for modern man; modern man should have changed for the Mass.

"The calendar was too cluttered, it needed a lot of pruning." That's what all the modern liturgists said and still say. I used to think so, too — until I got to know the traditional missal well, over years of daily Mass-going, and came to love the richly-layered cycle of saints, famous and obscure, ancient and modern, and came to love, too, how they crowd into certain clusters, sometimes even forming "octaves" of a sort.[3]

My appreciation of the density of the old calendar grew still more during the year in which I attended Mass at an oratory of the Institute of Christ the King, whose clergy follow (somewhat inconsistently, but with growing conviction) a sanctoral calendar of circa 1948. In this calendar there are even *more* saints, and frequently double commemorations. I have to say: so far from seeming cluttered, it's like a big Catholic family with kids all over the place, and everyone happy. The multiple orations enrich the liturgy's prayerfulness and power, rather than detracting from a "simplicity" or "focus" conceived in rationalist

---

[3] See my article "The Stigmata of Saint Francis." Saints removed from the new calendar (or kept only as optional memorials and with generic prayers instead of the more specific ones given to them in the old missal) often turn out to be surprisingly "relevant" in light of more recent developments in world history, as I have shown in many places: see, *inter alia*, "Deliver Thy Church, O Lord, from a flawed liturgy," *Rorate Caeli*, November 20, 2018 (on St. Felix of Valois); "Two Collects Most Appropriate for Our Times," *Rorate Caeli*, February 10, 2018 (on St. John of Matha and St. Scholastica); "St. Catherine of Alexandria — broken on the Consilium's wheel," *Rorate Caeli*, November 24, 2017; "An Expansive Counter-Reformation *Lex Orandi* Retains Its Relevance," *NLM*, July 5, 2021 (on St. Anthony Mary Zaccaria); "A Saint — and a Mass — for Our Times: St. Camillus de Lellis," *Rorate Caeli*, July 17, 2020; "'The heathens have defiled Thy holy temple... Revenge the blood of Thy saints!': On the Thymotic Realism of the Traditional Latin Mass," *Rorate Caeli*, July 28, 2020 (on SS. Nazarius, Celsus, Victor I, and Innocent I); "A Collect Worthy of Royalty," *Rorate Caeli*, October 16, 2020 (on St. Hedwig); "Large Catholic families are promoted by the traditional liturgical calendar," *LifeSiteNews*, July 6, 2021 (on St. Felicitas and her seven sons, as well as Rufina and Secunda); "'Vera fraternitas': June, the month of brothers," *LifeSiteNews*, June 8, 2021 (on SS. Primus and Felician, Mark and Marcellian, Gervase and Protase, and John and Paul). Consider also how the Nativity extends out to Epiphany on January 6, forming four concentric circles of celebration: (1) Christmas, (2) the octave, (3) the twelve days, and (4) the forty days that end with Candlemas. See my article "Don't stop celebrating: After Christmas Day, Christmas continues," *LifeSiteNews*, December 24, 2019.

terms. Anyone who knows great works of art knows that they achieve their cumulative effect through multiple simultaneous means, and that their unity and coherence rely upon a carefully balanced harmony of many parts, including tiny and *seemingly* insignificant details. Multiplicity and complexity are not the problem; only pointless multiplication and a random or confused complexity are a problem. I am reminded of the insight of Martin Mosebach:

> It was the new Western way of perceiving the "real" sacred act as narrowed down to the consecration that handed over the Mass to the planners' clutches. But liturgy has this in common with art: within its sphere there is no distinction between the important and the unimportant. All parts of a painting by a master are of equal significance, none can be dispensed with. Just imagine, in regard to Raphael's painting of St. Cecilia, wanting only to recognize the value of the face and hands, because they are "important," while cutting off the musical instruments at her feet because they are "unimportant."[4]

Doubtless, we cannot say of the details of the sanctoral cycle that all are of equal importance; this claim would be easier to argue for the fixed Order of Mass. Nevertheless, we *love* our saints—especially that somewhat "arbitrary" group that our tradition, in its slow meandering, has put right in front of us in the missal. The combination of famous and obscure saints, and the concentration of martyrs and confessors of antiquity, is itself a resounding lesson: we do not pick and choose our saints at Mass to reflect our preoccupations or favoritisms; the saints pick us, as it were, by coming to us down through centuries of devotion. It is another expression of the "scandal of the particular" inseparable from the very essence of Christianity. No matter how wonderful a more recent or more local saint may be, this quality, in and of itself, does not justify the suppression of another saint who has been liturgically venerated by countless Christians for many centuries.

The solution we should favor is to let saints pile up on a given day, but decide which one gets the Mass and Office (so to speak) and which one gets the Commemoration. The main cause of the purge in 1969 was a positive dread of having more than one set of orations per Mass, since evidently Modern Man™ was deemed too stupid to follow more than one thread at a time. How differently things appear in an era of emails, texting, and social media!

And even if, as the liturgists say, calendric simplification has happened before in the history of the Roman rite, was it *necessary* between the mid-1950s and the early 1970s? Who was clamoring for it? The People of God? The parochial clergy? Truth be told, it was no one

---

4 Mosebach, *Heresy of Formlessness*, 185.

but the professional liturgists, lovers of "clear and distinct" Cartesian modernity, with its glassy, steely mien, as of hygienic instruments, silver aeroplanes, and whirring time-saving appliances. The lamentable empty-headedness of today's Catholics regarding their own heroes is, needless to say, not caused exclusively or even primarily by the loss of a rich sanctoral cycle, but surely we cannot avoid seeing a connection.

Consider the following exchange between two art historians, Martin Gayford and Philippe de Montebello:

> *MG*: Some would say that putting a religious work in a museum removes its most crucial meaning. It wasn't intended — or at least only intended — to be appreciated as a painting; it was made to be *prayed* before, to stand on an altar while a priest performed Mass.
>
> *PdM*: Well, the meanings are in danger of disappearing anyway. The modern public by and large no longer reads the Bible, no longer knows the stories represented in the pictures. The role of museums in re-educating people in sacred stories and doctrines is very large. One could almost make the case that museums fill a gap that the churches are increasingly leaving in teaching the lives of the saints, Christ, and the Virgin, plus the stories of the Old Testament. All of the pictures and sculptures in most museums carry a label briefly telling the story, something that you do not find in church.[5]

"The pictures and sculptures ... carry a label briefly telling the story, something that you do not find in church." Yet this is exactly what my *St. Andrew's Daily Missal* (reprint of the 1945 edition) and countless other hand missals did and still do for the laity: they tell us something about every saint and make them beloved companions of the journey.

Note that this postconciliar demotion of the *cultus* of saints goes hand in hand with the ecumenical downplaying of all that is distinctively Catholic, the pseudo-purity of "focusing on Christ" when even *He* is pushed away from the closed circle, and the utter ineffectiveness of the verbal didacticism of reading so much Scripture. The Catholics of old undoubtedly knew more about the saints and the stories of the Bible than modern believers, who are so much more "literate" and "educated." However many causes there are of the stygian vacuity of the modern Catholic mind, we can say without hesitation that the traditional Roman liturgy, by emphasizing the saints vastly more than the modern liturgy does, filled the minds of the faithful with the *cultus* of the Virgin and the saints. As Dom Guéranger writes in the general preface to *The Liturgical Year*:

> In order that the divine type may the more easily be stamped upon us, we need examples; we want to see how our fellow-men have realized that type in themselves: and the liturgy fulfils this need

---

[5] Martin Gayford and Philippe de Montebello, *Rendez-vous with Art* (Thames & Hudson, 2014), 110–11.

for us, by offering us the practical teaching and the encouragement of our dear saints, who shine like stars in the firmament of the ecclesiastical year. By looking upon them we come to learn the way which leads to Jesus, just as Jesus is our Way which leads to the Father. But above all the saints, and brighter than them all, we have Mary, showing us, in her single person, the Mirror of Justice, in which is reflected all the sanctity possible in a pure creature.[6]

I have to say, in passing, that the older Roman calendar reminds me much more of the Byzantine calendar, which expressly names saints in the liturgy *every day*. Of course, it works differently because the Byzantine daily liturgy is not nearly as shaped and "governed" by the saint as the Roman one is—there is no concept of a "Mass of a Virgin" or a "Mass of a Confessor" in the Divine Liturgy: it has a few special antiphons sprinkled throughout for the saint, and then the rest is generic or seasonal. Still, the Eastern and Western traditions bear witness to the *norm* throughout Christian history until the Protestant revolt: "the more saints, the merrier." The presence of saints on the calendar is seen as augmenting the glory of Christ rather than detracting from Him, as indeed the original placement of the feast of Christ the King right before the feast of All Saints underlines.

Twenty-five years of working under both Roman calendars, old and new, gave me a vivid experience of the truth of Louis Bouyer's acerbic estimation of the reform:

> I prefer to say nothing, or little, about the new calendar, the handiwork of a trio of maniacs who suppressed, with no good reason, Septuagesima and the Octave of Pentecost, and who scattered three-quarters of the Saints higgledy-piggledy, all based on notions of their own devising! Because these three hotheads obstinately refused to change anything in their work and because the pope wanted to finish up quickly to avoid letting the chaos get out of hand, their project, however insane, was accepted![7]

To return, then, to our starting point, Sts. Nabor and Felix. For many centuries the Church at prayer told her Lord that the birthdays of these martyrs "never forsake us" and saw this recurring date as a promise that their intercession, too, would always be ours. Every time I encounter these "obscure" saints, I thank God for making them part of my life, for connecting me to the memory of their triumph and the power of their living intercession. Nor will this grand old calendar of saints ever cease to be followed within the Catholic Church, notwithstanding the feeble fulminations of faded flower-children.

---

[6] Prosper Guéranger, OSB, *The Liturgical Year*, trans. Laurence Shepherd (The Newman Press, 1948), vol. 1, "Advent," 17.
[7] Bouyer, *Memoirs*, 222–23.

ASK, AND IT SHALL BE GIVEN YOU

In the modern missal of Paul VI, first issued in 1969, an entire celebration of the Holy Mass, using licit options, can take place without even once directly asking the saints to pray for us or without asking the Lord to grant us that the saints would pray for us. If, however, the Confiteor is used, as well as the Roman Canon, then at least twice we do ask for the help of their prayers or directly ask them to pray for us. But it is rare for the Confiteor and the Roman Canon to be chosen in the same celebration, and, depending on the celebrant's habits, neither of them may ever turn up.

Here is a synthesis of some of the teaching, in the modern missal's Ordinary of the Mass, on the intercession of the saints. By their intercession, we receive sure support. Their fervent prayers sustain us in that all we rightly do. Their merits and prayers can gain us the constant help and protection of God. We rely on their constant intercession in the presence of the Lord for unfailing help.[8] So the postconciliar missal *recognizes* the great help that can be obtained by the People of God through the intercession of the saints. And yet it very often, according to the options made use of, does not *ask* for this intercession.

In Eucharistic Prayer II it says:

> Have mercy on us all, we pray, that with the blessed Virgin Mary, Mother of God, with blessed Joseph, her Spouse, with the blessed Apostles, and all the saints who have pleased you throughout the ages, we may merit to be co-heirs to eternal life, and may praise and glorify you...

The mercy requested is that we, the faithful, would merit to be with the saints in eternal life — but their intercession is not asked for.

In Eucharistic Prayer III it says:

> May he make of us an eternal offering to you, so that we may obtain an inheritance with your elect, especially with the most blessed Virgin Mary, Mother of God, with blessed Joseph, her Spouse, with the blessed Apostles and glorious Martyrs and with all the Saints, on whose constant intercession in your presence we rely for unfailing help.

Although it is praised, the intercession of the saints is not explicitly requested.

It is an important thing in the "economy of salvation," the Lord's household arrangement (so to speak), that we *ask*. "For every one that

---

[8] Exact phrases: "By their intercession, sure support" (Preface I of the Saints); "their fervent prayers sustain us in all we do" (Preface II of the Saints); "their merits and prayers [can] gain us [God's] constant help and protection" (Eucharistic Prayer I); "[the] constant intercession in your presence [of the saints] [can give us] unfailing help" (Eucharistic Prayer III).

asketh, *receiveth*" (Mt 7:8), Our Lord taught us. This implies that whoever does not ask, does not receive—or at least, does not receive as much as he might.

The saints are constantly interceding for us. Their merits and prayers are efficacious and operative in the flow of divine grace to us, in the communion of saints. But they could do so much more for us if only we were to ask for their intercession and help.

Here we can see one of the ways in which the traditional Roman missal is superior to the postconciliar one, as regards both the welfare of the Church militant and the salvation of the entire world. In the traditional *Ordo Missæ*, the intercession of the saints is requested *seven* times. In a very common and perfectly licit variation of the modern Mass, the intercession of the saints is requested *zero* times. What difference might this make in the life of the Church on earth?

But that is only the first level of the issue. As my friend Hilary White likes to say, one reaches what one thinks is the bottom, and then a trap door opens, and one realizes that the bottom is further down. "Have we hit rock bottom yet?" is, in liturgical discussions, by no means a frivolous question. So, when we discover that even the 1962 missal, as much better than the Novus Ordo as it is, is vastly inferior to the practices of the pre-'55 missal as regards precisely this point—the intercession of the saints—we realize that the Novus Ordo was not a sudden departure but rather continued, more radically of course, a process of denudation, evisceration, and suppression that was already underway *prior* to the Council, and which appeared to legitimize the direction in which the Consilium acted.

As I discuss in the last chapter of *The Once and Future Roman Rite*, for centuries it was the custom for priests to say or to sing more than one set of orations (Collect, Secret, Postcommunion) at Mass. The rubrics told the priest which additional prayers to use. For example, in Advent, from the first Sunday, the missal prescribed the addition of a second set of orations beseeching the aid of the Blessed Virgin Mary and a third set praying either for the Church or for the pope, although if there were saints to be commemorated, *their* prayers would be used instead.

Here, for example, are the orations that were added "to implore the intercession of the saints" in the time between Purification and Ash Wednesday and during the time after Pentecost:

> *Collect.* Defend us, we beseech Thee, O Lord, from all dangers of mind and body; and through the intercession of the blessed and glorious ever Virgin Mary, Mother of God, together with blessed Joseph, Thy blessed apostles Peter and Paul, blessed *N.* [titular saint

of the church], and all the saints, mercifully grant us safety and peace, that all adversities and errors being overcome, Thy Church may serve Thee in security and freedom. Through the same Lord Jesus Christ Thy Son...

Secret. Graciously hear us, O God our Savior, and by the virtue of this sacrament protect us from all enemies of soul and body, bestowing on us both grace in this life and glory hereafter. Through our Lord Jesus Christ...

Postcommunion. May the oblation of this divine Sacrament both cleanse and defend us, we beseech Thee, O Lord, and, through the intercession of the blessed Virgin Mary, Mother of God, with blessed Joseph, Thy blessed apostles, Peter and Paul, blessed *N.* [titular saint of the church], and all the saints, render us at once purified from all perversities and freed from all adversities. Through our Lord Jesus Christ...[9]

A large number of the required additional orations had precisely this character of invoking the intercession of the saints. "Ask, and it shall be given you" (Mt 7:7).

On Sundays, too, saints would be commemorated instead of simply ignored. In late June it would be quite possible to have a situation where the Third Sunday after Pentecost fell within the Octave of the Sacred Heart and of the birth of Saint John the Baptist. The priest at Mass would say or sing Sunday's oration, followed by those of the Sacred Heart and of Saint John the Baptist. *Ask, and it shall be given you, grace upon grace.*

Prior to 1955, the maximum number of orations at a Low Mass on simple days was five or seven (depending on circumstances). In 1955, this number was reduced to three, and mandatory prayers of the season were abolished. In 1960, the possibility of additional orations was reduced still further, and, for most Sundays of the year, done away with altogether. *Ask not, receive not.*

Think about this: *thousands* of priests were praying for these intentions *daily* at the altar, in the voice of the Church, in the name of Christ—the prayer most pleasing, most acceptable, most heard... and then suddenly, all these long-established, saint-saturated prayers... GONE.

If we believe in the power of prayer—if we believe that liturgical prayer is the highest form of it, being offered to the Lord by His Bride and Mystical Body—then wouldn't this gaping omission have some consequences? Is it possible to believe that the sudden abandonment of praying for the pope with quite specific and "demanding"

---

[9] Translation from the *St. Andrew Daily Missal*, 1945 edition, p. 1712.

intentions in thousands of Masses, or the sudden abandonment of pleading for various needs with the Virgin Mary, local patron saints, and even *all* of the saints day by day from the altar, could have *no effect* in the spiritual order, no effect in the Church on earth? Is it possible to believe this and still be a believer in the reality of God and the efficacy of prayer?

It is not fanciful to think that there is at least *some* connection between the official abandonment of liturgical prayer asking for the intercession of the saints, the strengthening of the pope, and other such intentions, and the grievous afflictions of the Church on earth since about the time when these orations were systematically canceled. It hardly seems coincidental that neo-modernism slithered out of the shadows and injected its venom into the Church's bloodstream starting in the pontificate of Pius XII, who dared to bring scissors and white-out against the Tridentine missal.

15
Allegory as a Key to Understanding Traditional Liturgy

IN DISCUSSIONS OF THE LITURGY, ONE OFTEN hears something like the following: "Granted, the changes may have gone too far, but you have to admit that there *were* some things in the old Mass that needed to be changed. *Sacrosanctum Concilium* was asking for changes, and it did issue some real (though modest) directives—and perhaps in a future revision of the traditional Roman Missal, these improvements could be made."

Nowadays I always want to ask (and if I am on the scene, I *do* ask) exactly which changes the person has in mind and why he thinks they would be improvements. With few exceptions, arguments in favor of changes to the missal's texts, rubrics, or ceremonies do not carry conviction with those who understand (and therefore love) the *meaning* of those texts, rubrics, or ceremonies, as we saw in chapter 12 when evaluating Fr. Stravinskas's fourteen proposals. At this point in my life, after many decades of experience with the traditional liturgy, knowing and loving its purity of doctrine, poetic expressiveness, poignant symbolism, effortless integration of clergy, people, and musicians, and (not least) unerring psychology and pedagogy, I tend to have the most serious misgivings about any of the proposed "improvements" that people suggest. Such "improvements" would be obtained at the cost of harming the integrity of the liturgical rite—a cost too high to pay for debatable gains.

THE PRIEST RECITING ALL TEXTS, EVEN AT HIGH MASS

My view was not always thus. There was a time, years ago, when I thought that the old Mass could be improved in this way or that. For example, I once believed it was self-evident that the priest should not be repeating the antiphons, prayers, and readings that the schola and other ministers were already singing. I had read liturgical scholars who pointed out that this had resulted from the backwards influence of the Low Mass upon the High Mass and who judged it to be a superfluous redundancy, a sort of subtle clericalism that required the priest to cover all the roles or else "his Mass" would not be complete. I remember arguing in a forum that during the Gloria and the Credo, the priest should not recite the text and then sit down, but sing it along with the people, standing all the while with them.

But I no longer agree with the so-called experts. I have come to see beauty and wisdom in the development that led to the priest's personal recitation of all the texts in an *usus antiquior* High Mass. Because the priest stands at the altar *in persona Christi*, he stands in the person of the "whole Christ," head and body. He performs gestures and recites prayers both in the direction of Christ to the faithful, the downward mediation of sacred things, and in the direction of the faithful to Christ, the upward offering of gifts and prayers. The moment of perfect assimilation to Christ the High Priest comes at the moment of consecration, when the priest speaks as if he were none other than Christ Himself, whose living icon and instrument he indeed is: *Hoc est enim Corpus meum... Hic est enim Calix Sanguinis mei...*

The ministerial priest's identity is thus consumed by and hidden within the singular, all-perfect ontological priesthood of Jesus Christ. But when the priest says out loud *Nobis quoque peccatoribus*, there he is representing the people, the members of Christ's mystical body—for in the head of this body there is no sin, while in its members there are imperfections that must be overcome to make their incorporation all the more definitive. Hence, in his very sacramental identity, the priest represents the whole Christ, head and body, and it is fitting that he maintain this role of complete representation from start to finish—from the beginning of the Mass, bowing before the altar in humility and confession, until the very end, blessing the people and reminding them of the sublime Incarnation of the Word, *plenum gratiæ et veritatis*. The dramatic symbolism of the liturgy admits of no interruption, no mixed messages.

With this truth in mind, it becomes clearer why, under the hand of Divine Providence, the custom developed that the priest recites *all* of the Propers, readings, and prayers, even when subordinate ministers, a schola, or the people are reciting or singing some of them. When the priest recites the Introit, he is standing in the person of Christ the prophet, announcing some mystery that has been accomplished in the Lord's earthly mission. When the priest recites the threefold Kyrie with its quiet, somber rhythm, he is beseeching the mercy of almighty God, again acting visibly in the person of the one High Priest who offers sacrifice on behalf of sinners. When he intones the Gloria, he acts as representative of the people, the members of Christ, who worship the triune God; this, too, is a priestly act, one that belongs to all the faithful but is nevertheless most proper to *him*, in virtue of his possession of Holy Orders. When he reads the Gospel, it is as the living image of Christ that he reads it. None of this downplays or dilutes the roles that other ministers or singers or the people themselves have and should have; instead, it merely draws into maximal unity the liturgical action by having it flow from and return to the same Alpha and Omega, Christ Himself, whose unity of being and operation is represented to our senses by the one and only celebrant: *Tu solus Altissimus...* Apart from the Mass of a priest's ordination, which is partially concelebrated, in the TLM there is never concelebration but always an emphasis on the one priest offering in the likeness of Christ our High Priest, with everyone else occupying subordinate positions, even if they too are ministerial priests. It was both natural and right that, over time, this sacerdotalist gravity should draw to itself all the texts of the Mass, without, however, depriving anyone else of his proper task in the hierarchical execution of the rite. Thus, in the Roman rite there developed a unique combination of absolute Christic primacy, refracted hierarchy, and gratuitous redundancy that reflects the way things actually are in the kingdom of heaven.[1]

Many such examples can be given from the liturgy. The priest performs gestures and recites prayers that are fitting not only to the head, Christ as High Priest, but also to the members of Christ's body, the Church, bone of His bone and flesh of His flesh. To repeat, as he represents the *whole* Christ, head and members, so it is eminently fitting that he, who has been fashioned to the image and likeness of the Mediator between God and man, should ever have on his lips and in his heart the prayer of the head as well as the responding prayers of the members.[2]

True it is, and a wonderful mystery, that *all* Christians share in the priesthood of Christ: each of the faithful is baptized a priest, prophet, and king. The sacramental character indelibly imprinted upon the soul at baptism is a title to worship the true and living God, bestowing the right to partake of the other sacraments and, ultimately, to receive their fruit, eternal life. The baptismal character empowers the Christian to receive further gifts of grace, to offer pleasing worship, and, above all, to receive the precious Body and Blood of Christ. This is classic doctrine, taught by St. Thomas Aquinas, many other doctors of the Church, and the Magisterium itself. So it is no less right and fitting that the

---

[1] When I say "refracted" I mean that all ministries and participations whatsoever, from that of the bishop down to the lowliest baptized child, are all precontained in Christ the High Priest and derived from Him in the form of diverse capacities, actions, and offices.
[2] This should not be taken to imply that the properly dialogic parts of the Mass, such as the prayers at the foot of the altar or the Preface dialogue, ought not to be conducted *as* dialogues with other ministers. It is merely to say that it is appropriate for the priest to "shuttle," as it were, between Head and members, as a mediator does by definition — as when St. Augustine says that Christ, as Son of God and son of man, prays the psalms sometimes in the person of God and sometimes on behalf of sinful man.

faithful sing those parts of the High Mass that pertain to them, such as the Ordinary—the dialogues, the Kyrie, Gloria, Credo, Sanctus, Agnus Dei, etc.—and that they perform the bodily actions called for by rubric or custom, and join their fervent silent prayer to that of the priest who represents them. In so doing, they exercise their priestly office. Each does that which is proper to him to do, and is united in spirit to all the others, under the headship of Christ.

This, truly, is a vision of order, harmony, peace, and wisdom. It is the order we see in germinal form in the New Testament, manifested in the epochs of Church history, inherent in Catholic Tradition, unfolded in the organic development of the liturgy. As hellbent as the liturgical reformers and radicals were (and still are) to overthrow this natural and supernatural hierarchy, they are kicking against the goad, like Saul, and might as well kick against an immovable rock. It is our privilege as Catholics to be the many and varied members of the Mystical Body and to find our sanctity in serving humbly in the place to which we have been summoned by Divine Providence. This includes, of course, the priest serving to the maximum in his priestly role, without embarrassment, attenuation, or dispersion.

My argument is founded on objective facts about the very nature of the liturgy and the priesthood—an objectivity that is beautifully symbolized and enacted by the customary practice under discussion, and therefore duly impressed upon the faithful who attend the Mass. Yet there is a further dimension I have not touched on: the subjective or personal devotional value of the celebrant's recitation of these antiphons, prayers, and readings.

Many priests who celebrate the *usus antiquior* find the opportunity to "work through" the entire Mass to be a precious help to their own *participatio actuosa* in worshiping the Lord. The reason is not far to seek: given the traditional practice of "parallel liturgy," in which multiple things are happening at the same time, the priest, if he did not recite everything in order, would frequently miss the opportunity to attend to a certain part of the Mass and take it into his mind and heart as the rite proceeds. For example, since the choir is singing the Introit while the priest is reciting the prayers at the foot of the altar, he would miss the benefit of reflecting on the Introit, which sets the tone for the day's Mass, if, after ascending to and kissing the altar, he did not take a moment to recite the Introit himself. The same applies to all the different moments of the celebration. Indeed, it would be bizarre if the priest could enjoy the benefit of reading the entire Mass when offering a Low Mass but be deprived of that spiritual nourishment when offering a High Mass; that would make the High Mass, from the point of view of the priest's devotional engagement with it, inferior to a lower grade. The integrity and "flow" of his liturgical act would thus be broken and impoverished.

The wisdom of Catholic tradition ensured over time that everything a priest does in the Low Mass is replicated in the High Mass, yet without detriment to any of the High Mass's peculiar perfections. A fusion of High and Low was thus brought about, uniting the personal piety of recitation to the ceremonial splendor of diversified roles. One might almost apply to this happy solution the expression used in an Alleluia verse for Our Lady: the Mass reconciles in itself the lowest with the highest.[3] No one loses out; no crumbs, so to speak, are lost.

THE MINISTERS' SITTING DOWN AFTER READING THE GLORIA OR CREDO

Purists may be willing to accept the above account, but they generally balk at the custom of the minister(s) sitting down during the singing of the Gloria and Credo after having recited those texts quietly at the altar. In discussions of the classical Roman rite and the twentieth-century liturgical reform, one example that always comes up of "something that just *had* to change" is the custom whereby the ministers—the priest at a *Missa cantata*, the priest, deacon, and subdeacon at a *Missa solemnis*—return to their seats for the duration of the sung Gloria and Credo after they have recited the text themselves at the altar.[4] The reform-minded will protest against both the "duplication" of the text and the alleged oddity of everyone sitting during the singing of these parts of the Mass Ordinary. Shouldn't the clergy sing the texts together with the people, and everyone remain standing?

Here I will not comment on *practical* reasons for sitting, such as giving older or infirm clergy a chance to rest, or giving clergy of any age a suitable way to wait for the completion of a lengthy piece of polyphony. I would also not dispute that the custom I have sometimes seen at Benedictine monasteries, where the ministers remain standing during the entirety of the Gloria and the Credo, can be fitting for the relatively short duration of chanted Ordinaries. I do not maintain that the ministers should sit down *as a rule*. The rubrics do not state that they *must* sit down; sitting is permitted as a concession. They may remain standing the whole time, a posture that will always retain its resurrectional significance, as it does to this day in the Eastern tradition.

---

[3] Cf. Alleluia verse for the Mass *Salve* from the Purification until Shrove Tuesday: "*in se reconcilians ima summis*," "reconciling in Himself the lowest with the highest."
[4] I have decided not to address here the question of the (likewise optional) sitting of the clergy during the Kyrie, although the enterprising reader will find it pleasant to meditate on the allegorical interpretations that might be proffered.

Rather, taking it for granted that there are theological reasons for duplicating and practical reasons for sitting, I would like to consider some theological connections that have occurred to me over the years as I have watched this custom and thought about it. The contemplative atmosphere of the classical Roman liturgy has nurtured in me a patient, open-minded, speculative disposition towards texts, music, and ceremonies. My habit of mind is now to ask, in accord with the allegorical method of our ancestors: "What meanings can I glean from the liturgy *as it exists in front of me*?" rather than "How could it be improved according to my own ideas?"

It was the Solemn High Mass that drew my attention to the Christological meaning of being seated. I can honestly say that I had never pondered the mystery of the "session" or seatedness of the Son of God until I had seen ministers at the High Mass and Solemn Mass moving from the altar in a liturgically dignified manner and sitting down ceremonially. Until then, "sits [or is seated] at the right hand of the Father" had been no more than a line rattled off when reciting the Apostles' Creed or the Niceno-Constantinopolitan Creed. Yet it is a mystery important enough to receive many mentions in the New Testament[5] and in liturgical texts. In the Gloria itself: *Qui sedes ad dexteram Patris, miserere nobis*: "Thou who art seated at the right [hand] of the Father, have mercy on us." In the Credo: *Et ascendit in cælum, sedet ad dexteram Patris*: "And He ascended into heaven, [and] is seated at the right [hand] of the Father."

At the time of the Creed, the three major ministers line up in their usual order, the priest at the altar, the deacon behind and below the priest, and the subdeacon behind and below the deacon. The priest chants the incipit, *Credo in unum Deum*, with all three ministers bowing their heads, and the schola, with the people, takes up the rest of the chant. The deacon and subdeacon step up on either side of the priest and the three of them recite the remainder of the Creed together. At *Et incarnatus est de Spiritu Sancto ex Maria Virgine: et homo factus est*, they genuflect.[6] This being completed, they rise and return to the sedilia at the side of the sanctuary. The priest, who primarily represents Christ in the offering of the Mass, is seated, and together with him,

---

[5] See Mk 16:19, Acts 7:55, Rom 8:34, Heb 1:3, Rev 3:21.

[6] This genuflection is *required* by the rubrics on the Annunciation and for the three Masses of Christmas. On other days, the ministers are in fact free to return directly to the sedilia after they finish reciting the text of the Creed. Once there, they would remove their birettas and bow their heads at the *Et incarnatus est*. Alternatively, if the ministers will not be seated during the Creed, then, at the *descendit de cælis*, they go down to the top step, kneel at the edge of the footpace, and genuflect for the *Et incarnatus est*; then, returning to the altar, the deacon goes to retrieve the corporal in the burse and spreads it out, the celebrant and subdeacon moving aside a little.

the people sit down.⁷ Around this time, the schola (and in some places the people too) are likely to be singing the words: *passus et sepultus est*—Christ, having suffered, was laid in the tomb. The Creed almost suggests this natural moment of rest as it mentions the lowest and humblest point of the Savior's descent among us. At the same time, the subdeacon remains standing beside the priest while the deacon receives the burse from the MC and, accompanied by him, brings it to the altar to set forth the corporal. During this time the cantors are usually singing *Et resurrexit tertia die, secundum Scripturas, et ascendit in cælum*. The reason we can turn from the primarily Scriptural part of the service to the Eucharistic sacrifice proper is that Christ is indeed risen from the dead, and death hath no more dominion over Him. Because He is glorified, no longer subject to mortal limitations, He is able to renew His sacrifice among us in sacramental form and to bestow on us His divine life. By His Passion, Resurrection, Ascension, session at the right hand, and pouring forth of the Spirit, He opened the sevenfold font of sacramental grace that brings us to heaven.

The Creed then acknowledges the seating of Christ at the right hand of the Father, and His return in glory: *sedet ad dexteram Patris: et iterum venturus est cum gloria*. Call it accidental, if you wish, but I find it very beautiful that as this Christological confession is sung, the principal minister, icon of Christ, occupies his seat or throne as does Christ the Lord in heavenly glory, while the deacon, also bearing His image, prepares the altar for the "return" of the King, and the subdeacon stands at attention. Shortly after, the deacon returns to the side, and both he and the subdeacon take their seats. In this way, the various intertwined mysteries the Creed mentions at this point— around the Resurrection, Ascension, and Session—are all somehow put on display, as if being acted out before our eyes.

Then, when the schola sings: *Et vitam venturi sæculi*, "[and I believe] in the life of the world to come," all make the sign of the cross, the ministers rise, and the people rise as well. This final strophe of the Creed has just mentioned the general resurrection (literally, standing up again) of the dead and the life without end in heaven, when all the blessed will share the glory of the risen Lord. How appropriate that the "general rising" takes place right at this point in the Creed!

It is as if we are permitted to "act out," in a sense, certain of the mysteries confessed, even as the priest during the Canon "acts out"

---

7 Customs vary as to when the congregation sits down. At many places, everyone waits until the deacon has finished setting up the altar. There are no rubrics that govern the people at the TLM, but I would say this custom doesn't make sense. The priest is the *only celebrant*, and when he sits, everyone should sit. The ministers can continue doing what they need to do.

some of Christ's gestures, as Michael Fiedrowicz describes:

> The traditional rubrics of the Roman Canon call for a "reenacting" of Christ's actions through the celebrating priest. He not only reads aloud the words of institution, but copies Christ's gestures as they are described: at the moment of the *accepit panem/calicem* he takes the offerings in his hands, which were anointed by the blessing [in the old rite of ordination] (*in sanctas ac venerabiles manus suas*), lifts his eyes (*elevatis oculis*), gratefully (*gratias agens*) bows his head, makes a sign of the Cross at the *benedixit*, and in a humble attitude completes the transubstantiation, with his arms touching the altar, once more emphasizing the union with Christ.[8]

Years after the above "picture" was formed in my mind, I decided to consult Bishop William Durandus, whose *Rationale Divinorum Officiorum* had recently entered my library. Sure enough, he had beat me to the main point, once more demonstrating that "there is nothing new under the sun" (Eccles 1:9). Book IV, chapter 18 concerns "Of the Seating of the Bishop or the Priest and the Ministers," of which the following lines are apropos:

> He is seated in a prominent place, so that just as the vinedresser cares for his vineyard, he cares for his people; for the Lord, seated in the highest heavens, guards His city (cf. Ps 126:1).... Sitting down after the prayer signifies the seating of Christ at the right hand of the Father after His Ascension, for the seat naturally goes to the victor. Thus, the seating of the priest designates the victory of Christ.... The seating of the ministers signifies the seating of those to whom it is said: *You shall also sit on the twelve thrones, judging the twelve tribes of Israel* (Mt 19:28): namely, those who now reign in heaven; those who labor in the choir signify those who are as yet pilgrims in this world.... Some ministers sit with the bishop, through whom is understood that the members of Christ at last have repose in peace, about which the Apostle says: *He seated us together in heaven, in Christ* (Eph 2:6), or else those who judge the twelve tribes of Israel; others remain standing, through whom is understood those members of Christ who continue with the struggle in this world.[9]

We should also bear in mind that in a church with no pews in the nave (as was the case for the better part of Church history),[10] the sitting of the clergy would more obviously accentuate their special role in the liturgy. St. Thomas Aquinas quotes St. Gregory the Great: "It is the judge's place to sit, while to stand is the place of the combatant or helper."[11]

---

[8] Fiedrowicz, *The Traditional Mass*, 274.
[9] William Durand, *Rationale IV: On the Mass and Each Action Pertaining to It*, trans. Timothy M. Thibodeau (Brepols, 2013), 168–69.
[10] See my article "Are Pews in Churches a Problem?".
[11] *Summa theologiæ* III, Q. 58, art. 1, ad 3, citing *Hom. xxix in Evang.*

IN DEFENSE OF ALLEGORICAL INTERPRETATION

Allegorical interpretation of the liturgy, illustrated by my presentation of the sitting of the ministers, was totally rejected during the period of liturgical reform, and even earlier by liturgists who tended towards rationalistic or reductionistic explanations (Fr. Adrian Fortescue comes to mind, although he was fortunately inconsistent in his error). Here's the kind of argument I mean: "We know that the lifting up of the chasuble by the deacon and subdeacon, or the servers, at the elevation of the host and the chalice was only because the Gothic chasuble was made of heavy material and ornament, and the priest needed help getting his arms up high." The implication is: "And therefore it can't have anything to do with the story in the Gospel about the woman with a flow of blood who touched the garment of Christ in order to be healed. That's just a willful, arbitrary connection some ignorant person made in a devotional book, and then it got spread around."

This, as can be plainly seen, is no more than a Catholic version of the modern tendency that C. S. Lewis called "nothing buttery," namely (in the words of George Gilder) "dismissing non-material qualities as 'nothing but...' some lower physical property."[12] Life is "nothing but" chemical processes; mind is "nothing but" firing neurons; love is "nothing but" hormones; and so forth. The liturgical equivalent is easy to recognize. The subdeacon's use of the humeral veil for the paten is "nothing but" a holdover from the early Roman *fermentum* rite. The conclusion, whether stated or implied, is always: "And therefore it should be abolished." Which, indeed, is what the reformers did: they stripped away nearly everything that no longer served an immediate practical function or had lost its original (known or hypothesized) purpose.[13]

Those who study the history of the liturgy often discover that certain practices later held to be richly symbolic had or may have had quite prosaic, practical, or accidental origins—origins in which their later symbolism played no part whatsoever. Yet this makes no difference at all to the validity of allegorical interpretations, for the simple reason that any given practice (construed broadly to include minister, object, action, cessation of action, etc.) presents itself to the worshiper *now* as part of an ensemble of ceremonial and symbolic actions, thereby acquiring, as if magnetically, new meanings, new interpretations, new resonances. In its fine texture of details, the traditional liturgy speaks both the same messages and new messages to each generation. Like an ancient epic poem, the same text reads differently in this or that age, without losing

---

[12] George Gilder, "The Materialist Superstition," *The Imaginative Conservative*, September 8, 2012.
[13] For a notable example, see "The Displacement of the *Mysterium Fidei*" in Kwasniewski, *Once and Future Roman Rite*, 263–77.

its remarkable ability to transcend them all. The most potent and transformative signs are not those that are limited to a single definite meaning, but those that are, to use a favorite word of Dante's, "polysemous," turning this way and that, accumulating layers of associations.

As with patristic and medieval exegesis of Scripture, it simply does not matter if we "read into" the liturgical rites an intention that was not present in the human author's or initiator's mind, and this for two reasons. First, the ultimate author is God, the First Cause, who sees further and intends more than His created agent is capable of seeing and intending. For example, it was no surprise to Him that the number of signs of the cross made in the Solemn Mass would achieve, after many centuries, the numerological perfection of $7 \times 7 + 3$. Second, even subjective or arbitrary interpretations can be essentially in harmony with the objective referent, as meditating on the mysteries of the rosary can be essentially in harmony with the re-presentation of these mysteries in the Mass,[14] and, moreover, can be personally helpful to the one who "indulges" in them. It is like St. Augustine's rule for Scripture: any interpretation or application that is not contrary to the Church's faith or to the sovereign rule of charity is legitimate—indeed, was already known to God from all eternity, even if some interpretations are superior to others in their contextual fidelity, applicability, nuance, or depth.

This ancient-medieval exegetical freedom, exercised on the traditional rites given to us by the same ancient and medieval Church, has very often led me to notable breakthroughs in my understanding of the mysteries of the Christian faith and how to live my life—in ways that I don't recall happening with the Novus Ordo. There are several reasons for this difference, but for my present purposes, the key difference is that the Novus Ordo was fashioned by its architects to be *immediately understandable and understood*: "what you see is what you get." It tends to "make sense" immediately and without remainder, and that is precisely why it is boring, and why people have to write books and articles about how to make Mass not a boring experience, or why one should embrace its boringness as a virtue.[15] In contrast, the old liturgy has accumulated

---

[14] See Pius XII, *Mediator Dei*, no. 108.
[15] See, for example, Timothy P. O'Malley's *Bored Again Catholic: How the Mass Could Save Your Life* (Our Sunday Visitor, 2017). O'Malley does not, of course, expressly admit that the Novus Ordo is boring, but many of the aspects of Mass that he identifies as difficult for modern people are in fact bound up with the new liturgy's verbosity, horizontality, dullness, banality, sentimentality, and so forth; nor does he grapple seriously with the old liturgy's power of attraction for very diverse and young congregations, who apparently do not find it boring. For numerous testimonials, see Reyers Brusoe, ed., *The Latin Mass and the Youth* (Cruachan Hill Press, 2024); David Dashiell, ed., *Ever Ancient, Ever New: Why Younger Generations Are Embracing Traditional Catholicism* (TAN Books, 2022); Jesse Romero, *What Attracts Men to the Sacred Liturgy—and Why* (Sophia Institute Press, 2024).

so many features over the centuries that, like a vast rambling mansion that seems never to run out of rooms, closets, attics, passageways, gardens, fields or forests to explore, one never really "sees it all" or "gets to the bottom of it." It is more of a closed book than an open book, yet a book that is freely offered to be opened and pondered *ad libitum*.[16]

The analogy between the Bible and traditional liturgical rites deserves to be underlined: on the one hand, a book that was written by a single divine author and as many as a hundred inspired human authors, coming together over a period of 1,300 years (from ca. 1200 BC to AD 100); on the other hand, Christian rites that were guided by a single Holy Spirit, built up into their mature form by apostles, bishops, popes, and other saints over a similar span of time (the period from the apostolic age to the high Middle Ages). With similar gestations, guiding principles, and aims, it seems probable, at very least, that Scripture and Liturgy ought to be susceptible to the same spiritual creativity in tandem with fixity of content.[17] A negative confirmation is found in the fact that biblical modernism rejects the spiritual senses just as liturgical modernism rejects liturgical allegory. Yet the spiritual senses of Scripture are patently evident in Scripture itself: St. Paul in 1 Corinthians 10:11 says "these things [from the old covenant] happened in figure [*tupikōs*]" and Galatians 4:24 relates how the things said about the two sons of Abraham are said "by an allegory [*allēgoroumena*]." Christ reads the Old Testament mystically, as when he refers to the "cornerstone" of Psalm 117:22 and the "sign of Jonah." Nor is the principle of a mystical reading of the liturgy a peculiarity of Western Christianity. Nicholas Cabasilas's *Commentary on the Divine Liturgy* notes how the Byzantine rite works on two levels simultaneously: its prayers address God and help us, while its ceremonies represent "Christ and the deeds he accomplished and the sufferings he endured."

Therefore, lovers of the liturgical tradition: do not be afraid to attach meanings to ministers, objects, or actions, or to adopt the meanings given in devotional literature, if they help you to pray.[18] One sign of a great work of art is that it has the wherewithal to provoke, and the capacity to support, many responses, all more or less closely tied to its ingredients and offering diverse paths of access into it. The Mass is the greatest work of art the West has ever known, exceeding all others in

---

[16] See Kwasniewski, *Turned Around*, 191–212.
[17] As Claude Barthe notes in his introduction to a mystagogical classic, "The search for the spiritual sense hidden beneath the letter of the ceremony is an extension of the search for the spiritual sense hidden under the letter of the books of Sacred Scripture... and, like that sense, is inexhaustible and even infinite, as St. Gregory remarked." Jean-Jacques Olier, *The Mystical Meaning of the Ceremonies of the Mass*, trans. David J. Critchley (Angelico Press, 2024), xx.
[18] I will recommend some literature at the end of the chapter.

its intelligible density and its fertility of cultural power. Reading off "spiritual senses" from its literal sense is no less natural and fitting than doing the same with the narrative of Israel in the Old Testament or the narrative of Christ in the New.

THE MANY SIGNS OF THE CROSS: USELESS REPETITION OR RECURRENT MNEMONIC?

On the first page of his beloved introduction to the Mass,[19] Dom Prosper Guéranger utters these decisive words: "The Sacrifice of the Mass is the Sacrifice of the Cross itself; and in it we must see our Lord nailed to the Cross; and offering up his Blood for our sins, to his Eternal Father." Throughout the work, Guéranger lovingly comments on the significance of each of the many signs of the cross that the priest makes, upon himself, over the people, over the host and chalice, with the host and chalice, etc. It never once occurs to him to criticize or to express perplexity about the number of these signs. He takes it for granted that they are present because they are meaningful, and it is our task to understand their meaning.

Fiedrowicz speaks thus of Frankish developments in the Roman Canon: "The Canon, which was meanwhile being prayed in silence, was embellished by means of many gestures, bows, and signs of the Cross, to become a vivid action of the priest (*actio*)."[20] The 1243 Franciscan edition of the Roman Curia's *Ordo Missæ* was the first to incorporate detailed rubrics for "genuflections, bows, signs of the Cross, and other gestures," which "became a firm element of the Roman rite through such exact recording, later continued (1498; 1502) by the papal Master of Ceremonies Johann Burchard of Strassburg with minute arrangement of even the smallest gestures."[21]

Fiedrowicz later expands on a particular aspect of this rituality:

> The signs of the Cross, which in various forms accompany many prayers or are accompanied by them, emphatically connect the sacrifice on the Cross, which obtained forgiveness of sin and eternal life, to particular parts of the celebration of the Mass, e.g., the request for forgiveness after the Confiteor (*Indulgentiam, absolutionem, et remissionem peccatorum*), the close of the Credo (*et vitam venturi sæculi*), and the reception of Communion (*Corpus Domini nostri Jesu Christi custodiat animam tuam in vitam æternam*). The sign of the Cross made at the close of the Sanctus during the words *Benedictus qui venit in nomine Domini* recalls that the entrance

---

[19] Originally entitled *Explanation of the Prayers and Ceremonies of Holy Mass: Taken from Notes Made at the Conferences of Dom Prosper Guéranger, Abbot of Solesmes*, it has been republished as *The Traditional Latin Mass Explained* (Angelico Press, 2017).
[20] Fiedrowicz, *The Traditional Mass*, 20.
[21] Fiedrowicz, 23–24.

into Jerusalem began Our Lord's Passion, to which, as a mystery to be realized, vivid witness is given again and again on the altar with profound numerical symbolism, above all by the numerous signs of the Cross made over the bread and wine, or the Body and Blood, respectively, during the prayers of the Canon. Even in the slightest gestures, for instance the thumbs crossed over each other in a cross at the spreading of the hands over the Eucharistic offerings (*Hanc igitur oblationem*), the sign of salvation is present in order to indicate Christ as the sacrificial lamb.[22]

Later in the book he enters into this matter more deeply:

> The sacrificial character of the Canon is emphasized also by the multiple signs of the Cross that accompany it in ornate arrangement, functioning as either effective blessings or symbolic illustrations. Before the consecration they possess a sanctifying function of preparing for the Eucharistic transubstantiation: *benedicas hæc* ✠ *dona, hæc* ✠ *munera, hæc* ✠ *sancta sacrificia* (*Te igitur*); *benedictam* ✠, *adscriptam* ✠, *ratam* ✠ (*Quam oblationem*); *benedixit* ✠ (*Qui pridie*; *Simili Modo*). Equally before and after the consecration they partly illustrate and intensify terms of blessing and sanctification—*sanctificas* ✠, *vivificas* ✠, *benedicis* ✠ (*Per quem hæc omnia*)—and partly identify and distinguish particular words as being sacred: *corpus* ✠ *et sanguis* ✠ (*Quam oblationem*); *hostiam* ✠ *puram, hostiam* ✠ *sanctam, hostiam* ✠ *immaculatam, panem* ✠ *sanctum vitæ æternæ et calicem* ✠ *salutis perpetuæ* (*Unde et memores*); *sacrosanctum Filii tui* ✠ *corpus* ✠ *et sanguinem* ✠ (*Supplices te rogamus*). The signs of the Cross witnessed since the eighth century were in part originally rhetorical pointing gestures that, according to ancient custom, accompanied the spoken word and were gradually stylized into a cross. The twenty-five signs of the Cross *in toto* thus continually refer to the sacrifice of the Cross.[23]

A short digression is in order as to the antiquity of these signs. Fr. Barthe notes:

> So far as concerns the numerous signs of the cross made during the Canon, if one agrees that the first of the *Ordines Romani*, "*Ordo I*" (a *ceremoniale*, or book of rites and ceremonies, for the Papal Mass on Easter morning, dating to the eighth century), is evidence of a Roman ritual tradition several centuries older, then its attestation of the repetition of these gestures during the Canon would confirm that they originated in the Late Antique period.[24]

One would think their antiquity would have won them protection from the supposed champions of returning to earlier and "purer" forms of

---

[22] Fiedrowicz, 208.
[23] Fiedrowicz, 281. Usually, twenty-six signs of the cross are counted.
[24] Barthe, *Forest of Symbols*, 108.

worship. But just as we know that today's loudest proponents of synodality are the most autocratic and the least collegial, so too yesterday's loudest proponents of "recovering the way the early Christians prayed" turned out to be the most modern in their assumptions and the least respectful of unbroken customs whose origins are lost in the mists of time. One begins to sense a pattern...

Fiedrowicz cites St. Thomas[25] in support of Passion-symbolizing crosses, eloquently summarizing:

> The multiple signs of the Cross are always and everywhere signs of remembrance, which refer to the Passion of Christ and identify the Mass as the realization of the sacrifice of the Cross. Moreover, the signs of the Cross before and after the consecration are also symbols of the blessing and grace that are contained in the Body and Blood of Christ and are to flow out over Christ's mystical body. Especially after the consecration, the signs of the Cross emphasize the identity of the Eucharistic species with Christ's Body and Blood, offered up on the Cross.[26]

In his 1955 book *The Great Prayer: Concerning the Canon of the Mass*, the convert historian Hugh Ross Williamson noted:

> During the Canon of the Mass, the sign of the cross is made twenty-six times. It is almost as if the Church were determined that, however attention may wander and words become a mechanical repetition, however dry the devotion or lazy the intellect, the body at least shall focus the meaning.... Yet the signs are not repetitive. The twenty-six fall into six separate groups each having its own particular significance.[27]

Williamson proceeds to connect the first three with the Trinity, the second five with the wounds of Christ, the two at the consecration with the twofold blessing narrated in the Last Supper, and so forth, in keeping with the allegorical tradition best summarized in Barthe's *Forest of Symbols*. In short, the plethora of carefully numbered signs of the cross throughout the Mass and particularly in the Roman Canon is part of the Catholic Church's *lex orandi* that reveals her *lex credendi*.

A sign that this was once a widely understood fact may be seen in the attitude of Protestant reformers. In his scorching 1969 pamphlet *The Modern Mass: A Reversion to the Reforms of Cranmer*—a crucial precursor to Michael Davies's far better-known book *Cranmer's Godly Order*—Williamson reminds us: "Cranmer forbade the Crosses [i.e.,

---

25 *Summa theologiæ* III, Q. 83, art. 5, ad 3.
26 Fiedrowicz, *The Traditional Mass*, 282.
27 Hugh Ross Williamson, *The Great Prayer: Concerning the Canon of the Mass* (Gracewing, 2009), 22.

the signs of the cross] and the Elevation but kept an approximation to the words, which now meant something quite different, to give the illusion of continuity."[28] The removal of these signs of the cross is one of several vivid differences between the *lex orandi* of the venerable Roman Canon and that of the so-called "Eucharistic Prayer I" of Paul VI's modern missal.[29]

Back in high school, I went on a youth retreat (pretty useless and annoying, as I recall) in which I remember an older priest making fun of the old Latin Mass, which at that time I did not know at all, like the infant Samuel "who did not know the Lord" (1 Sam 3:7). This priest said, with a slightly mocking laugh: "We used to have to make *so many* signs of the cross, it was like... we were brushing flies off, or something!" That stuck with me for some reason.

Later, when I discovered the old Mass, I noticed how the new generation of clergy offering it did these signs much more reverently — they *took care* in how they did them. Some still rush a bit, human weakness being what it is, but most of the clergy trace out deliberate signs of the cross in order to put themselves in mind of what they are about. They would agree with the opinion of François Cassingena-Trévedy:

> Provided that it is really lived with love, and no longer performed in a cranky and mechanical way, the richness of gestures in the Tridentine celebration, with its signs of the cross, its kisses, its genuflections, eminently favors, in the deepest sense of the term, the commitment of the celebrant in the act he carries out: in a movement at once gymnastic and spiritual, it draws the gift of his own body, the real presence of his body (that is to say, of his whole being) to the Body he presents; gesture after gesture, sign after sign, it sews and binds the celebrant to the altar of the Lord and recalls his body to the Body.[30]

To my surprise, years later I came across another reference to flies in relation to the sign of the cross. It was in a short text called *The Nine Ways of Prayer of St. Dominic*, a description left to us of how the great saint was accustomed to praying. How could I fail to be struck by the description given of the ninth?

> While he prayed it appeared as if he were brushing dust or bothersome flies from his face when he repeatedly fortified himself with the Sign of the Cross. The brethren thought that it was while praying in this way that the saint obtained his extensive penetration of Sacred Scripture and profound understanding of the divine words, the

---

[28] Hugh Ross Williamson, *The Great Betrayal: Thoughts on the Destruction of the Mass* (Arouca Press, 2021), 35.
[29] Additional differences are detailed in chapters 8 and 9 of Kwasniewski, *Once and Future Roman Rite*.
[30] Cited in Fiedrowicz, *The Traditional Mass*, 205 n36.

power to preach so fervently and courageously, and that intimate acquaintance with the Holy Spirit by which he came to know the hidden things of God.[31]

Did St. Dominic in his passionate embrace of the Cross, in his repeated action of crucifying himself (as it were), know something that the polite, efficient, apathetic managers of the Consilium did not? Yes. Though to the frivolous observer he seemed to be "brushing dust or bothersome flies from his face," he was in reality communing with the Cross, with which he "repeatedly fortified himself." He knew the secret of the lover of Christ. One who loves the Lord as he did will not complain but rather rejoice to find this primary symbol of His love and of our response to His love everywhere in the Mass, with its signs of the Cross that He bore for us, and that we take up in order to follow Him.

This is the sort of difference between the old rite and the new rite that is at once subtle and overpowering. It is subtle enough that a layman may not notice it for a long while, especially when first assisting at the *usus antiquior*. But soon enough, the attentive will perceive the *cruciform liturgy*; he will begin to sense how the priest is chained and configured to it; he will catch notice of the shining *mysterium fidei* sunk within the chalice of blood—and one *sees*, one *knows*, that this is the Mass of the Holy Sacrifice.

In the Canticle of Canticles, the lover wishes to lavish all the expressions of love he can upon the beloved, and she wishes to reciprocate. We see the same exchange of love in the intense mysticism of the traditional Mass. No wonder fervent young people, and above all, priests, are so strongly drawn to it and affected by it. The difference between old and new rites is the difference between the "drunken madman"[32] who, falling under the fascination of God, seeks the Divine Lover's face, and the sober bureaucrat who makes eye-contact with others, seeking their approval.

LOST AND FOUND IN THE FOREST

As Barthe points out (using an evocative phrase from Baudelaire), for over a thousand years the Roman Mass was approached as a "forest of symbols." Every part of the rite, every ceremony, down to the smallest sign of the cross or movement from left to right or incensation pattern, was eagerly mined for meaning. Yes, one might say these meanings were

---

[31] This work was written by an anonymous Bolognese sometime between 1260 and 1288. The text may be found at www.fisheaters.com/stdominic9ways.html.
[32] See my essay "Divine Drunkenness, Mystical Madness," *Tradition and Sanity* Substack, May 25, 2023.

imposed, but one could also say they were *discovered*, elicited from the rite itself, due to the extreme ease or naturalness with which our forefathers saw spiritual meanings in all kinds of things, above all in Scripture. They extracted the full juice of the grape and allowed it to mature into rich wine.

So far from this being "eisegesis" (i.e., reading into something what can't possibly have been intended to be there), it is a form of spiritual *exegesis* based on the belief that God has communicated something of His infinite depth of truth to all that He has made or caused, which thereby serves as some revelation of Himself—including the liturgy that emerged from the Age of Faith. Yes, human authors and architects may not have been thinking of all that is present in their writings or their works, but *God* knows, and *wills*, deeper meanings than His human instruments can fathom. This is taken for granted by our ancestors, and one who reads St. Bernard of Clairvaux's sermons on the Song of Songs or William Durandus's commentary on the Mass can readily see how fruitful this assumption is, as they discern layer after layer of significance in what might have seemed purely functional or historically conditioned or even initially arbitrary. Barthe:

> The Christian liturgy—and the Roman liturgy in particular—developed and thrived within a tradition of commentary and meditation that was fundamental for its understanding, running parallel with the same way of approaching Scripture. The rationalist influences that led to the decline and eventual rejection of the mystical or spiritual senses of Scripture in favor of a narrowly-conceived literal sense led to a narrowing of liturgy as well, which was reduced to its material parts and their various functions. While in recent decades the importance of the spiritual sense of Scripture has been reclaimed, its liturgical equivalent remains in shadow.[33]

Reading Barthe, I was struck once again by the transformation of mind that occurs when a person comes to appreciate the inner continuity and coherence of the Roman rite (by which I mean, of course, the *usus antiquior*, the only *Roman rite* there is). When you *understand* the Mass in each of its parts, down to the grainiest detail, you see that everything is in the right place: it all makes sense, fits together, and nourishes meditation. The sterility of the academic rationalism that rejected the allegorical approach was the necessary precondition for the violent dismantling and reconstruction of liturgy that took place in the twentieth century, much as the mechanistic assumptions of modern materialistic medicine are the precondition for sex changes, which treat organs like computer components.

---

33 From the back cover of Barthe's *Forest of Symbols*.

To skeptics, Fr. Barthe makes the unanswerable rejoinder that

> this spiritual commentary on the liturgy is already at work in the New Testament, particularly in the Apocalypse, but also in the Epistle to the Hebrews and in the Gospel according to St. John. The Apocalypse itself proceeds in this way to complex mystical interpretations of cultic objects that will go on to serve as models for patristic and medieval authors: the seven lamps are the seven spirits of God (4:5); the gold cups full of perfume represent the prayers of the saints (5:8 and 8:3–4); and the fine linen with which the Spouse is clothed signifies the virtues of the saints (19:8).[34]

The introduction is a marvelous compact history of the allegorical reading of the Mass. He says, for example, concerning Amalarius of Metz (c. 780–850):

> One of Amalarius's principal ideas, which he acquired as part of an already well-established tradition and which became a key element in the spiritual interpretation of the Eucharistic sacrifice, is that there is a link between the unfolding of the Mass and the history of salvation: the Mass represents the mission of Jesus Christ, from the proclamation of his arrival on earth, to which the *Introit* corresponds, sung by the choir, who in their turn represent the choir of prophets who foretold Christ's arrival, up to his Ascension, to which corresponds the *Ite missa est*, the dismissal of the faithful (we will return to this), with which those assisting at the Mass are dismissed just as Christ dismissed his apostles on the Mount of Olives.[35]

One of the finest fruits of Barthe's study is a revitalized appreciation of the normativity of the Solemn Mass, since the rich symbolism unfolded in the sources is very much keyed to the presence of all the ministers doing all that belongs to them:

> The special characteristic of a Solemn Mass is that it revolves around the actions of three sacred ministers: the priest, the deacon, and the subdeacon, who all belong to the major orders. And the three of them, from one point of view, are simply one; and when a single bench without a back (called the sedilia) is available, they all sit on it together. This is because the three ministers of the Solemn Mass all represent the same Jesus Christ in three different states: yesterday, today, and world without end.
>
> The subdeacon represents the Old Testament, Jesus Christ yesterday, who was proclaimed partly in the sayings of the prophets, and partly in figures by the saintly individuals who preceded his coming. As is appropriate, the subdeacon always occupies the lowest rank, that of incompleteness....

---

34 Barthe, *Forest of Symbols*, 10.
35 Barthe, 14.

The deacon represents the New Testament, Jesus Christ today, proclaimed in his fullness by the apostles and their successors, the bishops, who are the propagators of the Gospel....

The celebrant himself is most fully identified with Jesus Christ today and world without end, as he presently is and always will be, in glory in heaven. The celebrant is the instrument and the representative of Christ glorious and victorious, the Christ who makes himself really present on the altar in the elements of bread and wine in order to accomplish there his sacrifice for the remission of sins and to the glory of his Father. The priest who celebrates at the altar is the image of Jesus Christ priest and victim, but an unbloody victim in his heavenly state.[36]

Particularly illuminating is Barthe's discussion of the Offertory of the Mass. Modern liturgists denounced with increasing clamor the Roman rite's "doublets," namely, elements that seemed to them redundant or uselessly repetitious. Adhering to the odd and ahistorical belief of Romano Guardini that devotion is characterized by repetition but liturgy by linear singularity,[37] they claimed in the twentieth century that the medieval Offertory needlessly and confusingly anticipated the Canon and therefore needed to be radically modified. As mentioned in chapter 10, their solution was to jettison nearly all of the existing Offertory and to replace it with a *faux*-Jewish "workerist" blessing of bread and wine, surely one of their most infamous and audacious acts.[38] It is hard to evade the impression that such reformers were like the Enlightenment and Victorian critics who complained of obscurities, infelicities, and improprieties in Shakespeare's plays and therefore felt themselves justified in diligently "correcting" them for modern readers. Looking back today, we can only marvel that otherwise literate and competent people should be so blind to the extraordinary perfection of the Bard's works, as he achieved his goals with full mastery of materials. A far greater perfection belongs

---

[36] Barthe, 24–25.
[37] See Romano Guardini, *The Spirit of the Liturgy*, trans. Ada Lane (Crossroad, n.d.), ch. 1, note 10, pp. 30–31.
[38] Oxford Dictionaries defines "workerism" as "a theory or view of society that (excessively) emphasizes the importance or centrality of the working class. Also more generally: any theory, policy, or view that supports workers and their rights and interests." After World War II, this view gave birth to the experiment of "worker-priests" who would dress in lay clothes and work in factories in order to be in solidarity with the proletariat; the socialist and even Marxist overtones brought discredit on the experiment. The Liturgical Movement displayed a milder form of workerism that highlighted the contribution of man to the rite, the dignity of work, the labor of harvest; its poster-child might be the institution in 1955 of a feast of "St. Joseph the Worker" on May 1, an explicit attempt to "baptize" the International Workers' Day of Communist fame. The replacement of the medieval Offertory formulas with labor-themed blessings belongs to the same mentality.

to the Mass, which has been called the greatest work of art in Western civilization. Though the missal and other liturgical books are the patient work of many minds over many centuries, they, too, achieve their goals with full mastery.

Barthe guides us to see the meaning, so poorly grasped by reformers, of the intentional parallelism between the Roman Offertory and the Roman Canon.[39] So far from this being an example of useless repetition or incoherent anticipation, it is a glowing example of how the liturgy proceeds by way of preparation and reinforcement, building a system of cross-references that allow the fullest meaning to be grasped—much as men have two eyes and two ears in order to see and to hear a single reality better, or as a train rides on two parallel tracks in order to remain stable and not veer to the left or right. Indeed, just about every cognitive process involves multiple sources that are compared with and complete one another. What would be strange is reducing the approach to truth to a single line, unaccompanied and unrelational; nor is it at all surprising that no divino-apostolic liturgical rite exhibits this rationalist flaw. Drawing on premodern wisdom, Barthe defends precisely the *sacrificial* Offertory:

> Here we enter the Offertory, strictly speaking, a term that must be understood in the strong sense of a "sacrifice." The oblations that will shortly be consecrated are brought to the altar and unveiled. All the Christian liturgies, in a spiritual pedagogy married to the very rhythm of the Incarnation—"when he cometh into the world, he saith: Sacrifice and oblation thou wouldest not: but a body thou hast fitted to me.... Then said I: Behold I come: in the head of the book it is written of me: that I should do thy will, O God" (Heb 10:5–7)—proceed to a sort of pre-consecration. At once, the liturgical sequence is upset: the Offertory anticipates the act that is going to reproduce the sacrifice of the Cross, just as Christ anticipated the offering of the Passion.
>
> Allegorically, this moment of the Mass therefore recalls those moments in Christ's life in which more than elsewhere he offers himself in an anticipation of his Passion: the offering of Christ to the Father, as we have just seen, when he came into the world and entered the womb of Mary; the offering of Christ in the Temple, at the Presentation; and the offering during the Agony in the Garden of Gethsemane, which is recalled particularly when the priest invites the ministers to pray (*Orate fratres...*), an invitation like that of

---

[39] See Barthe, *Forest of Symbols*, 84–88 for all the texts, which are also given online in my article "Defending So-Called Doublets by Understanding Parallelism," *NLM*, September 30, 2024. For more on how the Roman Offertory deliberately anticipates the sacrifice of the altar through a figure of speech called "prolepsis," see Kwasniewski, *Once and Future Roman Rite*, 158; Gregory DiPippo, "The Theology of the Offertory—Part 6: Prolepsis in the Offertory," *NLM*, June 26, 2014.

Gethsemane (Lk 22:40), and when the priest prays in silence, recalling the solitary prayer of Christ on the Mount of Olives.

At this point we must emphasize the traditional comparison of the Offertory of the Mass with the Presentation of Jesus in the Temple. Surely that Presentation was above all a liturgical action? This rite applied to firstborn males, forty days after their birth. It was when parents really repurchased their male firstborn, for whom in substitution they gave the animals offered in sacrifice. The rite reflected the preservation of the firstborn of the Hebrews during the tenth of the plagues of Egypt, and the sacrifice of Isaac demanded of Abraham his father. Firstborn male children and Abraham's firstborn son are both figures of Christ, the sacrificed Son of God: figures that were not yet fully realized, since the firstborn of the Hebrews had been spared, as had Abraham's only son.

By this act Jesus showed what he had come into the world to accomplish: his self-offering on the Cross and for eternity. He did this first on the altar and in the temple formed by the womb of his mother. He next demonstrated it on the day of the Presentation in the Temple at Jerusalem. He finally repeated it in the Garden of Gethsemane.... At the Presentation Mary offered her Son in advance as a sacrifice as she would one day have to offer him to God on Calvary, in the manner of a priest who, at the Mass, offers in advance the oblations that he is again going to offer (in the sacrificial sense of the word) at the consecration. Mary also lifted up Jesus in her hands to put him in the hands of Simeon, who represents the eternal Father, in the same way that the priest lifts up a little above the altar the host and the chalice that he offers. By this offering in the Temple, Jesus Christ was made ready to be offered in his entirety, in the same way that the oblations are prepared for the perfect offering that takes place at the consecration.[40]

Proceeding to show that the many other "doublets" of the Roman rite are equally carefully contrived to bring out the fullest depth of theological meaning, as are the equivalent doublets in the Byzantine rite, Barthe helps us to see, from new perspectives, the profound analogies between East and West that the liturgical reform almost obliterated and that the Roman rite in its classical integrity preserves as a witness to catholicity.[41]

Did not all these rites take their cue from the Word of God, in which repetition and parallelism are key features? Hebrew poetry cannot be understood unless one grasps its use of parallel phrases that echo one another in a sort of conceptual rhyme. And who could forget the thunderous verse in chapter seven of the prophet Jeremiah?

---

[40] Barthe, *Forest of Symbols*, 76–79. A small correction: the firstborn were redeemed at a price, not by animal sacrifice (that was for the mother's purification).
[41] See Kwasniewski, *Once and Future Roman Rite*, 279–311.

"Trust not in lying words, saying: The temple of the Lord, the temple of the Lord, it is the temple of the Lord" (Jer 7:4). As if to say: it is not enough to have a consecrated building; one must live as a consecrated people, receiving humbly and gratefully all that the Lord wishes to give. It's not enough to have a "valid Mass"; one must have the fullness of tradition, which is the fullness of validity: valid from and for a people the Lord has made His own, in a grand spousal love announced, anticipated, achieved, and fulfilled, renewed upon our altars and eternalized in heaven.

The foregoing are characteristic examples of the insights Fr. Barthe has gathered by his assiduous labors in the vast treasury of the allegorists. How ironic it is that, at the very time when the Roman rite is under renewed papal and episcopal attack, the traditional movement is producing a mighty literature on this rite's beauty, fittingness, and orthodoxy, compared with which the reformed rite's promotional literature is limp, untruthful, and uninspiring. Such a thought brings both comfort and confidence.

In addition to the work from which we have been quoting—Fr. Claude Barthe's *A Forest of Symbols: The Traditional Mass and Its Meaning*—new publications in the same vein include Honorius Augustodunensis's *Jewel of the Soul* (Harvard University Press, 2023);[42] Pope Innocent III's *The Mysteries of the Mass* and *The Four Kinds of Marriage* (Angelus Press, 2023); William Durandus's *Rationale Divinorum Officiorum* (Paschal Light, 2019–2021);[43] Urban Hannon's *Thomistic Mystagogy: St. Thomas Aquinas's Commentaries on the Mass* (Os Justi Press, 2024); Abbé Franck Quoëx's *Liturgical Theology in Thomas Aquinas: Sacrifice and Salvation History* (Catholic University of America Press, 2023); Jean-Jacques Olier's *The Mystical Meaning of the Ceremonies of the Mass* (Angelico Press, 2024); and Pierre Lebrun's *The Mass: A Literal, Historical, and Dogmatic Explanation of Its Prayers and Ceremonies* (Ubi Caritas Press, 2024).

This renaissance in spiritual commentary on the traditional rites responds to a deep hunger, in our deracinated postmodern West, for the inherited wisdom of the ages. Far from discarding this wisdom as did haughty reformers of yesteryear, Latin-rite Catholics should receptively immerse themselves in its light and embrace its works as their rightful inheritance.

---

[42] Many excerpts from this work may be read in my review, "Adorning the Soul with Allegorical Gems," *OnePeterFive*, July 19, 2023.
[43] This translation in nine volumes was done by Janet Gentles. The Prologue and Books 1 through 4 were also newly translated by Timothy Thibodeau, but those volumes seem to be out of print at this time.

16

The Importance of Understanding and Abiding by the Rubrics

FOR OVER 1,600 YEARS, THE CHURCH IN THE West has sung her readings at Mass in the Latin tongue. Having grown up with the texts, their chant tones clothe them to perfection. For a long time now, she has read the Epistle towards the east and the Gospel towards the north, offering them up as part of the high-priestly sacrifice of the Mass, for the glorification of God and not merely for the instruction of the people (as the Protestants would maintain). When it was thought desirable to convey the readings also in the vernacular, Holy Mother Church, in imitation of Our Lady, "*kept* these things and pondered them in her heart": she did not abolish the chanted Latin readings but gave permission for them to be read aloud in the vernacular afterwards, from the ambo or pulpit.[1] There is absolutely no reason to change the Catholic practice of chanting the Epistle and Gospel in Latin, and every reason to conserve it for the theological and spiritual patrimony it transmits.

A friend shared with me a video of the Pontifical Mass celebrated by Robert Cardinal Sarah at the end of the Chartres pilgrimage on May 21, 2018. The liturgy was going along magnificently, as one would have every reason to expect—until the Lesson and the Gospel. At this point, the subdeacon faced the people rather than the East, chanted *only* the title of the reading in Latin, and proceeded to speak aloud a French translation. The Latin reading was never chanted *ad orientem* in its ancient and thrilling tone. Then along came the deacon, and instead of chanting the Gospel in Latin facing northward, he again faced the people, and after singing the title, proceeding to read the Gospel in French, omitting to sing it in Latin.

This practice is contrary both to the spirit of the ancient Roman liturgy and to the rubrics that govern its celebration. As to the rubrics, the case is easily made. The 2011 Instruction *Universæ Ecclesiæ* of the Pontifical Commission Ecclesia Dei states in no. 26: "As foreseen by

---

[1] In fact, the tradition of reciting the readings aloud in the vernacular *outside* their liturgical proclamation in Latin traces back to the tenth century, at least in the English-speaking world. See Nico Fassino, "The Epistles & Gospels in English: A history of vernacular scripture from the pulpit, 971–1964," *Hand Missal History* (https://handmissalhistory.com/Feature-Epistles/), 2023.

article 6 of the Motu Proprio *Summorum Pontificum*, the readings of the Holy Mass of the missal of 1962 can be proclaimed either solely in the Latin language, or in Latin followed by the vernacular or, in Low Masses, solely in the vernacular."

Only in a Low Mass, therefore, is it permitted to substitute vernacular readings for Latin—and note, it is *permitted*, not required or recommended. In fact, for reasons I shall discuss below, it is always better to read the lections in Latin first, and then read them in the vernacular from the pulpit just before the homily, if it is judged pastorally wise. But at a sung Mass, *a fortiori* a Solemn High Mass, *a fortiori* a Pontifical Mass, the readings are always to be sung in Latin, with the correct ceremonial and directionality. What happened in the Chartres Mass is a liturgical abuse, no different in kind from the host of abuses with which the Novus Ordo is plagued.

This violation of rubrics was no doubt intended as a "pastoral adaptation" or "accommodation." Nevertheless, it is an example of exactly what we must be careful *not* to do. Many of the worst aberrations and deviations in the 1960s, when the old Mass was already being subjected to torture and dismemberment, and subsequently the ruinous missal of Paul VI, arose exactly from such supposedly "pastoral considerations." Fr. Louis Bouyer, who, as we discussed in earlier chapters, toiled at the Bugninian abattoir before regretting his complicity, already caught the whiff of a weird pastoralism in the 1950s that wanted to change everything in the name of "relevance" and "outreach." In opposition, Bouyer taught that liturgy is first of all "given, a *traditional given*."

> From a material point of view it is a precisely circumscribed object: the whole of the rites and ceremonies, of readings and prayers that are written down in the books called the Missal, the Breviary, and the Ritual. It is something we can desire to enrich, as every living Christian generation enriches Christian spirituality, Christian morals, even dogma; but it is something that has first to be *received*, received from the Church.[2]

A major difference between the theology of the Roman rite and that of Paul VI's modern rite is the difference in how readings are understood. For the former, the readings at Mass are not merely instructional or didactic; they are an integral part of the seamless act of worship offered to God in the Holy Sacrifice. The clergy chant the divine words in the presence of their Author as part of the *logike latreia*, the

---

[2] "Après les journées de Vanves. Quelques mises au point sur le sens et le rôle de la Liturgie," in *Études de pastorale* (Cerf, 1944 and Abeille, 1944), 383, cited in John Pepino, "Cassandra's Curse: Louis Bouyer, the Liturgical Movement, and the Post-Conciliar Reform of the Mass," *Antiphon* 18.3 (2014): 254–300, at 270.

rational worship, we owe to our Creator and Redeemer. These words are a making-present of the covenant with God, an enactment of their meaning in the sacramental context for which they were intended, a grateful and humble recitation in the sight of God of the truths He has spoken and the good things He has promised, and a form of verbal incense by which we raise our hands to His commandments, as the great Offertory chant has it: *Meditabor in mandatis tuis, quæ dilexi valde: et levabo manus meas ad mandata tua, quæ dilexi*, "I have meditated on Thy commands, which I have greatly loved: and I have lifted up my hands to Thy commandments, which I have loved."

The chanted Latin reading is an expression of adoring love directed to God *before* it is a communication of knowledge to the people, and the form in which it is done should reflect this primacy. In the ancient liturgy, always and everywhere God enjoys primacy. Nothing is done "simply" for the people. Holy Communion, which is manifestly for the benefit of the people, is nevertheless treated with adoration, reverence, care, and attentive love, being distributed exclusively by the hands of the ordained, on the tongues of the kneeling faithful, with a paten held underneath. All eyes are thus fixed on the Eucharistic Lord, giving Him the primacy that is His due. It should be no different with the utterance of the divine words, in which we find a symbolic incarnation of the Word of God that nourishes our souls in preparation for the divine banquet of the Most Holy Sacrament.[3]

Vernacularization and mere recitation of the readings at High Mass betrays the telltale rationalism, utilitarianism, and minimalism of the Synod of Pistoia, whose proposals for liturgical reform were repudiated by Pope Pius VI. So far from being solely instructional, the chanting of the Word of God is a quasi-sacramental action in and of itself, as Martin Mosebach argues with regard to the use of incense, candles, and the prayer *Per evangelica dicta, deleantur nostra delicta* (which, to translate quite literally, would be "through the gospelish things read, may our sins be wiped away").[4] Another confirmation is found in the traditional rites for the ordination of deacons and subdeacons:

> After the bishop vests the new deacon in the stole and dalmatic, he presents the Gospel book and says: "Accipe potestatem legendi Evangelium in Ecclesia Dei, tam pro vivis, quam pro defunctis. In nomine Domini." "Receive the power of reading the Gospel in the Church of God, both for the living and for the dead. In the name of the Lord." The part about reading the Gospel for the dead would be nonsense if the reading were merely a practical instruction for

---

[3] For a more extensive treatment of this topic, see the next chapter.
[4] See Mosebach, *Heresy of Formlessness*, 98; 118; 130. See also Michael P. Foley, "The *Per Evangelica Dicta*," *NLM*, October 18, 2024.

those members of the Church Militant who happen to be present at a particular Mass. The rite for subdeacons has a similar formula with the Book of Epistles, with reference to power to read them both for the living and for the dead.[5]

The chanting of the reading is truly part of the activity of *worship*, and, like the other prayers of the Mass, it should be distinguished by words of a sacral register, hallowed by tradition. No one will complain if this formal liturgical chant, which takes only a few minutes in any case, is followed up with a recitation of the vernacular text before the homily. But the latter should never be substituted for the former.

I have learned about priests in France and Germany who, in keeping with this cavalier pastoral attitude, also change the *Ecce Agnus Dei* and *Domine non sum dignus* into the vernacular. Seriously: has it ever really caused difficulty for the faithful to understand what is meant by these phrases, which are repeated at every Holy Mass? Additionally, some clergy in Germany, who have apparently learned nothing from the past sixty years, persist in recycling the old saccharine German paraphrase-Masses,[6] which they fob off on the people instead of sharing with them the riches of Gregorian chant, as every pope, especially in the period from 1903 to 2013, has urged should be done.[7]

Then there are practical concerns, based on those stubborn little things known as facts. Congregations who attend the *usus antiquior* today are often made up of faithful of diverse linguistic backgrounds, because in many locales only a single Latin Mass is available, and all the people of the surrounding territory gather for it. On a visit to St. Clement's in Ottawa, I learned that about 40% of the faithful are Francophone and 60% are Anglophone; Latin serves as the common liturgical language that unites them. In the United States, when Hispanic Catholics attend a Latin Mass, the Latin is closer to their native tongue than English would be. Another city parish of which I am aware draws a diverse linguistic

---

[5] A comment left at "Why We Say the Black and Do the Red," *Fr. Z's Blog*, June 11, 2018.
[6] The most famous of these is Schubert's *Deutsche Messe*, a work in nine movements written in 1827 and originally intended for Catholic services, although approval was denied at the time; it came into its own later, in the twentieth century. The movements are poetic paraphrases of parts of the Mass, not actual translations of the liturgical texts. Prior to the Novus Ordo, they would have been sung by a congregation while the priest at the altar said the Mass according to the missal. However, after Vatican II, the paraphrases have been completely substituted for the texts in the missal. I experienced this firsthand at the local German Mass in the village in Austria where I lived for seven and a half years.
[7] I do not object to vernacular hymns being sung before and after High Mass, that is, during the procession of ministers and at their departure, since these lie outside of the liturgy proper. Singing hymns in the vernacular once the Mass has started seems extremely unfitting, as it shatters the "sonic iconostasis" of Latin. To supplant what is liturgical with what is non-liturgical is Protestant, not Catholic or Orthodox.

mix of families: English, Romanian, Polish, Russian, Czech, Italian, and Spanish. Quite apart from fidelity to the rubrics, such situations present a *genuine* pastoral reason for the consistent use of Latin!

In this respect, the Chartres Mass afforded us a spectacular lack of pastoral common sense. This is an international pilgrimage of people. Even if French is the language of the majority, there would be plenty of attendees for whom it is not a first language, and a sizable number who do not speak it at all. To read the lections in French alone reveals a nationalist, regionalist, and culturally imperialist attitude.[8] As Pope John XXIII noted in *Veterum Sapientia*, only the use of the venerable and universal Latin tongue is exempt from such problems: no longer the language of a nation or empire, it belongs equally to all.[9]

It would be opportune for religious congregations and societies of apostolic life that utilize the *usus antiquior* to monitor such liturgical abuses and correct them before they spread. How can clergy expect the faithful to show due obedience to their fathers in Christ, if these same fathers are not faithful to the inherited liturgy? Is it too much to ask that priests follow the spirit and the letter of the Roman rite as it has been passed down to us, without introducing the deviations and creative adaptations of the Liturgical Movement? We have seen where those ended up: the Novus Ordo.

To my amazement, there are voices in the traditional Catholic world that consistently support liturgical irregularities. With surprise and disappointment, I learned that one of these voices belongs to a German member of the Priestly Fraternity of St. Peter, who on June 28, 2018, published a column in the major Catholic newspaper *Die Tagespost*, entitled "Zeit, 'danke' zu sagen" ("Time to Say Thanks"), in which, after expressing his confidence in the rightness of the founding of the FSSP in 1988 and its peaceful role within the Church, he veers into an attack on a perceived type of traditionalist:

> I see an unexpected danger for the traditional movement somewhere else in the Church, that is to say, in a hyperliturgization [*Hyperliturgisierung*]. Despite all the theological narrowness of which

---

[8] Let one example suffice to make the point: "Vernacular liturgy in Africa for a great number of Africans is, in reality, liturgy not in their mother tongue, but in a second language, often the former colonial language.... The practical result is a very widespread use of the former colonial languages in the liturgy, and a concomitant increase in those languages' perceived prestige.... Latin does not belong to any particular tribe, nor is it the language of any colonial power; furthermore, it is not the language of contemporary European or American cultural influence." Shaw, *The Case for Liturgical Restoration*, 271–72.

[9] In the words of Pope John XXIII, "Of its very nature Latin is most suitable for promoting every culture among diverse peoples, for it gives no rise to jealousies, it does not favour any one group, but presents itself with equal impartiality, gracious and friendly to all." Apostolic Constitution *Veterum Sapientia* (1962), no. 3.

one might accuse Archbishop Lefebvre, he had the zeal of a true shepherd who is concerned with the salvation of souls. To him, the preservation of the liturgy was not an aesthetic end-in-itself. Far more, he saw the liturgical crisis as part of the crisis of faith that was endangering the salvation of many souls. His intention was highly pastoral, in the full Catholic sense of the word. He was not concerned with rubrics, that is, with the letter of liturgical rules, but with their spirit. He was not altogether against reforms, but only against reforms that cloud over the spirit of the liturgy.

In my first year as a priest in the Society of St. Pius X, on Sundays I served at a chapel where they sang, on alternating weeks, Gregorian chant and Schubert Masses [i.e., Mass paraphrases in German]. No one had thought anything of that. The phenomenon of a liturgical purism that despises German songs in the liturgy, rejects the direct reading of Epistle and Gospel in the vernacular [i.e., without their having been first read or chanted in Latin], and cultivates an excessive rubricism to the point of a missionary self-gagging, crossed my path much later, especially in lay circles. Thus [outside] critics of the traditional liturgy are offered a target, while newcomers have a more difficult start. One enters upon an oblique path at the end of which liturgy appears to be the hobby of an exclusive club of exotic aesthetes.

I am grateful to Cardinal Sarah that, at the concluding Mass of the Chartres pilgrimage, he set a sign and gave a reminder about the correct measure of the way one ought to celebrate: "with a noble simplicity, without useless additions, false aestheticism, or theatricality, but with a sense of the sacred that first and foremost gives glory to God."[10]

Consider the eerie similarity between the way this priest is arguing today and the way that Annibale Bugnini and his liturgist comrades were arguing about the "urgent need" to modify the old Mass. Chiron's biography of Bugnini details just how willing were the liturgical "experts" of the 1940s, '50s, and '60s to experiment with the liturgy, as if it were their personal possession. No established rubrics could hold them back, in spite of nearly constant warnings and reproofs from the popes, the Sacred Congregation of Rites, and other curial officials. The attitude seemed to be: "If we have a good enough reason to break the rubrics to try something new that we think is a pastoral improvement, then we have sufficient justification." This attitude was the acid that dissolved any notion of a received, inherited rite to which we are humbly subject, by which we allow ourselves to be shaped and guided.[11]

---

10 Translation mine; at the end, the priest is quoting from Cardinal Sarah's homily at Chartres.
11 See "Why We Follow Inherited Rituals and Strict Rubrics" in Kwasniewski, *Turned Around*, 79–108.

Once this erroneous attitude had established itself, it was relatively easy to discard the entire rite in favor of a fabricated one. Why not? It's all about what *we* want to do. The Novus Ordo was simply the crown placed on decades of liturgical experimentation rooted in rationalism, voluntarism, and pastoralism. In some ways, it was the archetypal expression of a council that claimed to be not dogmatic but pastoral, a council that was content with rambling texts that tack to and fro like a sailboat trying to catch the wind, even as the Tridentine rite in its majestic solidity and stability is the perfect expression of the genuine pastoral concern and luminous dogmatic teaching of the Council of Trent, valid for all time, all places, all cultures.

In their myopia, partisans of the later phase of the Liturgical Movement thought that *they*, and not the providentially unfolded tradition of the Church, knew best what Modern Man™ needed. To them, it was evident that he needed *as much vernacularization as possible.* That is why Latin was eventually thrown out of the window completely. They also thought nearly everything needed to be *simplified*, so they sought greater and greater simplification—be it in vestments (away with the amice and maniple and biretta), in furnishings (away with six candles, antependia, and reliquaries), in the texts of the Mass (away with the Propers, second or third orations, Psalm 42, Prologue of John, Leonine prayers), in the ceremonies of the Mass (away with osculations, signs of the cross, genuflections, *ad orientem*), or in its music (away with ancient chant).

It never seems to have occurred to the Liturgical Movement that quite possibly what an increasingly secular and materialist age needed was precisely a movement in the *opposite* direction—towards *greater* liturgical symbolism, a *richer* pageantry of ritual, a *fuller* immersion in Gregorian chant with its incomparable spirituality, all of which was already on offer in the Roman rite. What Modern Man needed most of all was to be rescued from the prison of his own making, namely, the rationalist anthropocentrism of modernity. To our shame, the Catholic Church freely stepped into this prison through the liturgical reform, in its many intended and unintended consequences. In this sense, the proposed cure turned out to be more of the same disease, which is why, predictably, it has made the patient worse, not better.

The accusation of "hyperliturgization" is therefore ironic. Clergy who defend departures from the rubrics—often nationalistic departures from the universal Roman tradition—are the ones who deem themselves competent to make improvements or adjustments to the liturgy. *They* are the hyperliturgists. Those who wish to attend a Roman Mass that, at least as regards what is specified in the liturgical books, is the same everywhere in the world, even as the Catholic faith is the same, are not hyperliturgists; they are not even liturgists. They are faithful Catholics. They are Catholics who believe that what the longstanding tradition of the Church offers them, such as the chanting of the readings in Latin, is going to be spiritually superior to some "adaptation" or "inculturation" that this or that priest, or group of priests, may happen to think is better.[12] We are called to dwell in the house of the liturgy as grateful guests, not to re-engineer it as project managers.

Those who make changes like this in the liturgy are no doubt acting in good faith. But they are not acting with humble trust that there are always many layers of meaning in the liturgy that go beyond what we, with our necessarily limited understanding, might perceive to be the purpose of some ceremony or text or music or vestment. They are acting, in short, by their own lights. But what we must do, especially today, is to act by the light of Catholic tradition, until we have learned again, like children in grammar school, why it developed in the first place. We need to learn our ABCs again before we dare to make our own contributions, whatever those might be (and may God preserve us from "creativity").

What about the charge of "rubricism," flung in the face of those who cite *Universæ Ecclesiæ* 26 or any other binding prescription? The charge is quite misplaced. The phenomenon of rubricism occurs when the liturgical or theological rationale for a given practice is forgotten, and all that one has to stand on is a rubric, a prescription of positive human law. If one cannot say why a practice is right and fitting but simply shouts "That's the rubric and we must follow it!," or if one breaks out into a cold sweat at three o'clock in the morning because one suddenly realizes that four manuals disagree about how many inches apart the items on the credence table should be, then perhaps one might merit being called a rubricist. But my defense of the rubrically correct way of doing the readings at a High Mass expressly refers to the liturgical-theological rationale behind the rubrics.

Rubrics are good when the practices they guarantee are themselves good and right and fitting. It is not the other way around, namely, that something is good because the rubrics dictate it. That is legal positivism. The Church under the guidance of the Holy Spirit learns the best way of doing something—best either in practical terms, or for theological/spiritual reasons, or both—and *then* she formulates it as a rubric and enforces its observance. For example, the priest's holding thumb and forefinger together after consecration arose as a custom, gradually

---

[12] While rubrics and reverence for tradition prevent the priest from changing the liturgy as such, local custom can have a real effect on the actions and postures of the laity during Mass, as we will see in chapter 23.

spread, and was finally taken up into the rubrics enjoined on all.[13] That is usually how such things develop. A great problem of twentieth-century Catholicism was that rubrics had become a cottage industry. The Sacred Congregation of Rites, followed in turn by the Consilium, followed by the Congregation for Divine Worship, were cranking out new rubrics year by year, leading to a weariness and annoyance with the whole business. Forgotten was the theological and spiritual meaning of the rubrics, the reason they developed in the first place.

A rubricist is one who insists on the rubrics *for their own sake*. A traditionalist insists on the rubrics because they protect and promote something important—something that one *first* has to understand theologically and spiritually, after which the rubrics are seen to be right. Rubrics have legal force because they are promulgated by legitimate authority, but they have their intrinsic force from the nature of the thing itself.[14]

"Pastoral" priests who ignore or contradict the sound rubrics of the old missal are demonstrating not "flexibility within rules," but an antinomian mentality characteristic of the modern period, with its habit of calling traditions into question and giving first place to utilitarian and pragmatic considerations. When a priest sees a traditional rubric not as the guardian of a theological or spiritual truth but as an arbitrary dictate of law, he will be all the more willing to violate it whenever he thinks he has a better idea.

This whole question of how readings are to be done is more important than it may seem at first blush, because it is not an isolated issue. It is one among several backdoors through which selfless and tireless reformists may enter the traditional movement and turn it—or at least geographical portions of it—into a recapitulation of the Consilium's descent into insatiable tinkering, modifying, expurgating, reinventing, archaeologizing, and ultimately transmogrifying the liturgy, always in the name of "pastoral improvements." This, and not loving care for the traditional *ars celebrandi*, will be the "self-gagging" we need to avoid.

---

[13] See my article "'The Fingers that Hold God': The Priestly Benefits of 'Liturgical Digits': Historical, Theological, and Liturgical Conclusions," *NLM*, March 8, 2018.

[14] This is why a traditionalist is consistent in saying that rubrics ought to be followed, but also that some rubrics are better than others, because of *what* they require and *why* they require it; and, indeed, that some rubrics are bad, such as the Novus Ordo rubric that during Mass no one should genuflect to Our God and Lord Jesus Christ, really present in the tabernacle, even when passing in front of Him. The abolition of genuflection in a rite in which genuflection was the rule for centuries is stupid and wrong. It is an act of anti-reverence, of irreverence. It is "on the books," but much in the same way that any bad law is on the books, and deserving of as much observance. As we saw in chapter 10, Fr. Ray Blake observed that the Novus Ordo does not seem to be concerned very much with *latria*, except in words (sometimes). This, of course, is pertinent to the tendency to see the readings as having only a didactic value, without a latreutic function within the liturgy.

The faithful deserve and have a right to a traditional Mass offered in accordance with the wise slogan "Say the Black, Do the Red," sourced from the purest springs of the Tridentine inheritance. After decades of confusion, the Church is being given an unparalleled opportunity to restart the celebration of the liturgy with a correct attitude and praxis. If we mess it up this time with short-sighted pastoral adaptations, we will have no one to blame but ourselves when we slide into a second "liturgical reform" from which Divine Providence may not rescue us.

It would be irresponsible for me to leave this topic without a final admonition. The readings are a form of worship offered up, certainly; yet they are not *latria* alone, but a pronouncing of God's words to men, in the presence of the *ecclesia*: they are a speech-act to human hearers simultaneously with being raised up to God in praise. For this reason, it is imperative that the subdeacon, deacon, and priest, when chanting texts, should enunciate the words intelligibly, with distinct articulation of syllables, no impression of unseemly haste or garbled vocables, and a good command of the tones to be sung. A layman familiar with Latin should encounter no difficulty in following the chanted readings. To be sure, it requires some effort to chant loudly and distinctly, but when it is done, the effect is edifying, as the word rises aloft on wings, taking possession of the space and of the ears.

THE PRICE OF DISREGARDING THE RUBRICS

It had never occurred to me to think of certain liturgical abuses I often saw when younger, such as priests ad-libbing prayers, people clapping during Mass, and casual behavior on the part of one and all, as potentially mortal sins until I stumbled across a couple of texts in St. Thomas that awakened me to this real possibility. For some reason, such abuse had seemed to me — to the extent I'd given the matter any thought — a venial sin, more of a nuisance, an inconvenience, an offense to the faithful in the pews who deserve better, but not a severance of the friendship of charity with God. And yet, as I ponder the matter more carefully, it seems to me that there is, after all, something very serious happening whenever a minister *knowingly* departs from the Church's rule of worship as expressed in the texts and rubrics of the liturgy (which, of course, he is required to be familiar with; ignorance is no excuse). The disregard or violation of text or rubric is an expression of contempt towards Christ and the authorities He has established to rule in His name.

Here is what St. Thomas says in an article of the *Summa theologiæ* on the sin of the fallen angels:

Mortal sin occurs in two ways in the act of free-will.

In one way, when *something evil* is chosen — as man sins by choosing adultery, which is evil of itself. Such sin always comes of ignorance or error; otherwise what is evil would never be chosen as good. The adulterer errs in the particular, choosing this delight of an inordinate act as something good to be performed now, from the inclination of passion or of habit; even though he does not err in his universal judgment, but retains a right opinion in this respect. In this way there can be no sin in the angel; because there are no passions in the angels to fetter reason or intellect... nor, again, could any habit inclining to sin precede their first sin.

In another way, sin comes of free-will by choosing *something good* in itself, but not according to proper measure or rule; so that the defect which induces sin is only on the part of the choice which is not properly regulated, but not on the part of the thing chosen — *as, for example, if one were to pray, without heeding the order established by the Church*. Such a sin does not presuppose ignorance, but merely absence of consideration of the things which ought to be considered. In this way the angel sinned, by seeking his own good, from his own free-will, insubordinately to the rule of the divine will.[15]

What I find striking about this text is that, when St. Thomas wishes to find an example of a human sin to which he can fitly compare the kind of sin Satan and the other malicious angels committed, he chooses praying without heeding the order established by the Church! In the heavens there is a rule to which the angels must submit in their pursuit of their own good, and likewise on earth, there is a rule to which men must submit in their pursuit of the good of holiness. A failure to consider the established order in the macrocosm of the universal society of intellectual and rational creatures is reflected in a failure to consider the established order in the microcosm of ecclesiastical society; the latter is a miniature fall from grace, that is, a fall from the divine will, which manifests itself to us as an order into which we can freely insert ourselves, or against which we can freely revolt.

It is, in other words, not the choice of something *bad* in its very definition that characterizes the fallen angel, but the choice of something good, yet in a perverted way. Those who offer the Church's prayer, which is man's noblest and best act as a creature, but violate or mutate the rubrics according to their own whims and wishes, are offering a gift vitiated, to some extent, by a will insubordinate to the rule of the divine will. This need not necessarily detract from the objective value of the gift, but it will certainly affect the subjective benefit of the offering for the offerer and possibly for those who share in it.

---

[15] *Summa theologiæ* I, Q. 63, art. 1, ad 4.

Indeed, St. Thomas in a different text seems to say that those who knowingly consent to liturgical abuses deprive themselves of the grace of the sacrament. As long as they *know* that the Church calls for a certain way of acting and speaking, and they *know* that a celebrant is deviating from this, they must either consent to it or internally reject that deviation. It makes no difference if they think that these violations of the rubrics are warranted by some political agenda or perceived "pastoral need," since the liturgy, the ministers, and the faithful are all subject to the Church's judgment and law. Here is how his argument reads:

> Sometimes the one who celebrates a sacrament differently [than prescribed] does not vary the things that are essential to the sacrament [i.e., the form and matter], and in that case, the sacrament is indeed conferred; but the recipient does not obtain the reality of the sacrament unless he is immune from the fault of the one celebrating it that way.[16]

That is an astonishing claim: one does not receive the *res sacramenti*, the very grace the sacrament was instituted to give us, if one embraces the fault of the minister who unlawfully varies even things that are not essential to the conferral of the sacrament.[17] Such a claim brings into sharp relief the seriousness with which St. Thomas took the liturgical law of the Church, a perspective widely shared by his contemporaries. It is a perspective that, while slowly reviving among us, still has many converts to win.

Sometimes the itch to be creative or experimental or spontaneous or informal with the liturgy comes from a mistaken view that this is somehow more humble, more "authentic," more in keeping with the needs of the moment or the locale. But, as we saw earlier, C. S. Lewis puts his finger on what's really happening here (and a line like this is well worth repeating): "The modern habit of doing ceremonial things unceremoniously is no proof of humility; rather it proves the offender's inability to forget himself in the rite, and his readiness to spoil for every one else the proper pleasure of ritual."[18]

With his usual perceptiveness, Lewis is pointing to a peculiar sort of pride or vanity or vainglory that consists in *not* abandoning oneself to the structure and content of the rite, in having to be the one who constructs it in midair, who cleverly (or not so cleverly) adapts it, who

---

[16] *In IV Sent.*, D. 4, Q. 3, art. 2, qa. 2, ad 4: "Ad quartum dicendum, quod aliter celebrans quandoque non variat ea quæ sunt de essentia sacramenti, et tunc confertur sacramentum; sed non consequitur aliquis rem sacramenti, nisi suscipiens sacramentum sit immunis a culpa aliter celebrantis."

[17] I interpret St. Thomas to mean that when the attendee *consents* to an abuse he would be guilty of fault, but if he did not know it or notice it, or having noticed it, rued and spurned it, he would not be guilty.

[18] Lewis, *Preface to Paradise Lost*, 17.

produces it as if he were its author—all the while inserting his ego into every nook and cranny. By not surrendering to the rite and its ceremonial demands as established by rubrical law, such a man cannot forget himself—and he cannot allow others to forget him, either. It is as if the attention that God rightfully demands is compromised, our attention being split between the transcendent object of the ritual as ritual, and the immanent object of the performance before us. A sign of this split is that the "proper pleasure of ritual" is either not experienced by the worshiper or experienced in a muted and unsatisfactory way.

Although examining this claim would take us far afield, it is worth remembering that St. Thomas holds that virtuous action is accompanied by its own proper pleasure and that taking delight in the good is a sign of moral maturity. So we *ought* to enjoy our worship of God—not the way we enjoy God Himself, obviously, but in a way that recognizes our need (and God's provision for our need) to emerge rejuvenated, enlightened, consoled, strengthened. This, I think, is what Lewis has in mind, and his assessment of the pride of the minister as well as the injury inflicted on the faithful helps us better understand how St. Thomas can compare violation of liturgical order to the pride of the fallen angels and how he can see consent to such violations as a form of self-deprivation of the sacrament's grace. But we may also think about the magnitude of the crime incurred by the revolutionaries who overturned the entire liturgical order of the Latin Church and opened the floodgates to abuses great and small that continue to our day like a generational curse. The only way out is to step away from the constant tinkeritis that seized hold of the Church after World War II, and to take up again, humbly and gratefully, the Roman patrimony embodied in the last *editio typica* of the integral Tridentine rite.[19]

TWO "DISOBEDIENCES" COMPARED

The analysis offered here of obedience to rubrics helps us to see their role more clearly. They are not the most important thing, for they presuppose a context that makes sense out of them—let's call it customary good practice, itself shaped by spiritual and theological reasons. If, thanks to a hypertrophic development of legal positivism, rubrics become detached from tradition and reason, they could also become impediments to the right offering of the liturgy. Conversely, the removal of sound rubrics thanks to a revolutionary spirit brings with it a host of evils, ranging from looseness and distraction to irreverence and profanation.

---

[19] See my article "The Centenary of the Last Integral *Editio Typica* of the *Missale Romanum*," NLM, July 25, 2020; cf. *Once and Future Roman Rite*, ch. 12.

Well-informed young priests of today are aware of these problems. Thanks to studying Benedict XVI and other authors, they know that the Novus Ordo has serious flaws and lacunae to which the TLM can supply remedies, for it is the refined expression of centuries of practice and reflection. Plus, Benedict encouraged them to think in terms of "mutual enrichment"—although the enriching tends to flow in one direction. So, they set about fixing what is broken. Some try to fix it on a modest scale by wearing an amice and maniple (not required, but then again, not forbidden), observing canonical digits, incensing in the elaborate old manner, and keeping their eyes down when looking toward the congregation. In addition, they choose what is already allowed, such as using Latin and chant, praying *ad orientem*, and giving Communion on the tongue to kneeling faithful.

Others go further, introducing major "Tridentinisms": they add back certain silent prayers, such as those at the Offertory; they genuflect after the consecration rather than only after the elevation; they say the Canon almost inaudibly; they receive the Eucharist prior to turning around and showing It to the congregation. The epitome of this Tridentinizing approach may be seen in Fr. Richard Cipolla's "A Primer for a Tradition-Minded Celebration of the OF Mass," published at *New Liturgical Movement* on September 14, 2017.[20] The trouble with this last approach (and, indeed, with some of the earlier, more modest examples) is that, strictly speaking, none of it is allowed. It is against the Novus Ordo's rubrics and the Vatican directives that interpret them. The journal *Notitiæ*, which has provided official guidelines for the Novus Ordo for decades now, stated repeatedly that elements from the old missal were never to be incorporated into the new, and that the celebrant should not do so; nothing beyond what is specifically mentioned in the new rite may be done. This was back in the days when the rupture was plainly admitted, before it became politic for a time to deny there was a rupture. We are, of course, right back to the same spot:

> It must never be forgotten that the Missal of Pope Paul VI, from the year 1970, has taken the place of that which is improperly called "the Missal of St. Pius V" and that *it has done this totally, whether with regard to texts or rubrics*. Where the rubrics of the Missal of Paul VI say nothing or say little in specifics in some places, it is not therefore to be inferred that the old rite must be followed. Accordingly, the many and complex gestures of incensation according to the prescripts of the earlier Missal (cf. *Missale Romanum*,

---

20 I defended this approach in my article "Two Attitudes toward Ordinary Form Rubrics: Kantian Duty and Aristotelian *Epikeia*," NLM, January 8, 2018. At this point I would distance myself from the opinions expressed in that article and in Fr. Cipolla's from 2017.

T. P. Vaticanis, 1962: Ritus servandus VII et Ordo Incensandi, pp. LXXX-LXXXIII) are not to be repeated.[21]

As it was said in response n. 2 of the Commentary *Notitiæ* 1978, p. 301: where the rubrics of the Missal of Paul VI say nothing, it must not therefore be inferred that it is necessary to observe the old rubrics. The restored Missal does not supplement the old one but has replaced it. In reality, the Missal formerly indicated at the Agnus Dei [the rubric] "striking the breast three times," and in pronouncing the triple *Domine, non sum dignus*, "striking the breast...[he] says three times." Since, however, the new Missal says nothing about this (OM 131 and 133), there is no reason to suppose that any gesture should be added to these invocations.[22]

As generally happens, it [the manner of a priest's raising hands and joining them at the Preface or at the final blessing] is a matter of a habit which comes from the rubrics of the former Missal. The indications of the OM, however, should be observed... Thus the ancient rite should not be retained...[23]

While I am fully prepared to call into question the credibility of the Congregation or Dicastery of Divine Worship and even the canonical standing of its decisions, there is no doubt that such quotations well express the dominant intention of liturgical severance that has animated the Vatican from 1969 onwards, with a short and partial reprieve under Benedict XVI. What I do *not* see room for is a gradual "Tridentinization" of the new rite, because, as I argued in Part I, this is neither consistent with its rubrics nor ultimately possible given its extensive genetic mutations (nor, as discussed in chapter 8, compatible with its spirit of simplicity and immediate comprehensibility). The Eucharistic species may be the same, but the liturgical species is different, and there is no evolutionary path from the one to the other.

So, the Tridentinizing new-rite priests, though undoubtedly actuated by the best motives, are choosing to be disobedient in the name of a higher obedience to what their conscience dictates as *"dignum et justum"* for the celebration of the Holy Sacrifice. They may not feel it to be unsustainable, they may even believe it to be required of them, but they cannot deny it involves a conflict of principles.

In reaction to this insoluble difficulty with the Novus Ordo, *other* priests reach a point where they realize: "All that I'm doing is trying to turn the new rite into something rather like the TLM or at least with its best features. This is ultimately impossible and, in any case, a thankless and pointless task. *Why not just take up the TLM and be done with it?*" It should hardly surprise anyone that many priests

---

[21] *Notitiæ* 14 (1978): 301–302, no. 2, emphasis added.
[22] *Notitiæ* 14 (1978): 534–535, no. 10.
[23] *Notitiæ* 14 (1978): 536–537, no. 12.

who used to offer a "fancy" Novus Ordo switched over at some point to the "real McCoy." The traditional elements themselves have a way of pushing one in that direction, since they all came from the great liturgical tradition and readily cohere *in their proper context*, namely, the old rite. While there is, for instance, something exceedingly awkward about a Latin Gradual chant in the NO, it fits smoothly and elegantly into the TLM. Such examples could be multiplied by the dozens.[24]

The quest for the "perfect Novus Ordo" is about as elusive as the hunt for Red October—actually, more so. Once one realizes that every "good" instantiation of it is the result of about a hundred moving pieces having been put together in "just the right way" by several individuals (all of whom could change at a moment's notice), and once one intimately experiences the old Roman rite as something permanent and beyond messing with, then one is brought to the certain knowledge that the former path is a dead end, the latter, a highway for our God. Some priests will, in due course, arrive at an unshakable moral certainty: "I can't abide that travesty, and I'm not leaving this treasure." They find in the old rite exact, detailed rubrics that leave nothing to chance or whim; all is done in a manner most fitting, serene, reverent, and symbolically apt. Although it is a great challenge at first, mastery of the rubrics, when it becomes second-nature, allows the priest to pray the Mass fervently, without distraction, forgetting himself in his focus on Christ. As Mosebach eloquently observes:

> The great mystics of the past never felt rubrics to be a burden. Even the twentieth century had a great mystical saint, Padre Pio, from Apulia, who was given the stigmata and, with his five bleeding wounds, read the Mass in iron submission to the rubrics. Formerly, seminarians learned rubrics so well they could perform them in their sleep. Just as pianists have to practice hard to acquire some

[24] It's true that some celebrations of the Novus Ordo are more aesthetically appealing than others. As mentioned earlier, for over twenty-five years I served as a choir director doing my utmost to elevate the NO with chant and polyphony (I did this simultaneously with providing music for the TLM). The difficulty is that the "smells and bells" dimension is only one layer, the first and most obvious. The second layer is the very content of the rites, in their texts and rubrics. At that second level, a profound discontinuity appears between the old and new forms of the Mass, to the point of making it impossible to maintain they are just two versions of the same Roman rite (in spite of Benedict XVI's pacifying innovation in declaring them to be so). When a person realizes that the Tridentine rite has *authenticity* (which I would define as remaining in manifest and substantial continuity with its well-established and perfected historical form, derived and developed out of its apostolic root) and the Novus Ordo does not (since it originated quite obviously with the Consilium in the period 1963–1969, with 46 committees of experts through whose filter everything had to pass), he loses whatever appetite he may have had for the reform of the reform. Or, to put it more succinctly: When you celebrate the old rite, you are lifted up by the work of anonymous geniuses. When you celebrate the new rite, you are weighed down by the work of well-known mediocrities.

technique that is initially a pure torture, but ultimately sounds like free improvisation, experienced celebrants used to move to and fro at the altar with consummate poise; the whole action poured forth as if from a single mold. These celebrants were not hemmed in by armor-plated rubrics, as it were: they floated on them as if on clouds.[25]

In the era of *Traditionis Custodes*, these priests are likely to be told at some point that they are "not allowed" (or no longer allowed) to say the traditional Latin Mass. But they know that the war against the TLM stems from ill will and lacks legitimacy, and that no pope or bishop on earth has the authority to abolish or prohibit what was, and cannot cease to be, the immemorial liturgical rite of the Church of Rome.[26] So these priests will continue to say the TLM, *come what may*. They will be blamed for their "disobedience," even as all conscientious objectors are blamed for resisting structures of sin, but they know in their consciences that they are acting in the name of a higher obedience to the common good of the Church and of the People of God, which is inseparable from the offering of the Holy Sacrifice of the Mass and of the other sacramental rites in the way that is *dignum et justum*.

Let us now compare these two scenarios.

Is not the second "disobedience" more coherent and more defensible than the first? The first, which makes a custom house-blend of *novus* and *vetus* elements, is hard to justify within the context of a liturgy already non-liturgical in its "optionitis," the sport of ideological innovators and political abusers. The second, however, is easy to understand and to justify, because it is founded on the solid rock of a praiseworthy, supremely venerable *lex orandi*.

There is a certain willfulness or arbitrariness in the first scenario that is absent in the second. In the first, one could ask a priest: "By what authority do you make this or that modification to Paul VI's missal?," and any answer he might give would sound subjective; there is no objective way to know if a Novus Ordo has become "traditional enough" or "reverent enough" or "Roman enough." In the second scenario, one could ask him: "By what authority do you offer Mass with the old missal?" The answer: By its inherent goodness, rightness, fittingness, authenticity; due to its continual reception and approval by the Church of every century in the course of its gradual growth, culminating in the missal St. Pius V "canonized" in *Quo Primum* — a missal (and a mentality) that was handed down faithfully through the

---

[25] Mosebach, *Heresy of Formlessness*, 132.
[26] See Kwasniewski, *True Obedience*; *Bound by Truth*; *From Benedict's Peace to Francis's War*.

1920 *editio typica*. This answer would be as objective and stable as the endless Tridentinizing experiments are subjective and unstable.

A curious passage recorded only in the Gospel of Mark (8:22–25) may help illustrate the difference between these two scenarios. We see a blind man being healed by Jesus, who, instead of healing him all at once, as He often does on other occasions, carries out the healing in stages:

> Some people brought to him a blind man, and begged him to touch him. And he took the blind man by the hand, and led him out of the village; and when he had spit on his eyes and laid his hands upon him, he asked him, "Do you see anything?" And he looked up and said, "I see men; but they look like trees, walking." Then again he [Jesus] laid his hands upon his eyes; and he looked intently and was restored, and saw everything clearly.

It was only when Our Lord laid His hands upon the man's eyes a second time that the man's sight was fully restored. The initial cure was partial; the definitive cure took another round of divine work. This parable could be and has been given many possible (and compatible) interpretations, but it strikes me as an apt allegory for the two stages described above.

The man in need of healing is the modern Catholic, and especially the modern cleric: blind to Tradition, to reverence, to beauty, to continuity—even, at times, to truth itself. The Lord begins to heal this blindness, but what is often the first step—conservatism—is still a topsy-turvy world, where things are not as they seem; where, for example, a novel liturgy, the modern product of a modern committee, is treated as if it were traditional and in continuity with Tradition.

With the patience of divine pedagogy, the Lord completes the healing. At last, the man "looks intently"; he is "restored"; he "sees everything clearly." Such is the priest, such the layman, who is given the grace to look intently at the ways things really are; who is restored to his own inheritance, which he then seeks to restore for others; who sees clearly where the call of obedience should, and should not, take him.

17

In Defense of Readings in Latin

AS THE LAST CHAPTER RECALLED, THE MOTU proprio *Summorum Pontificum* made allowance for doing the readings solely in the vernacular. Although this permission was said to apply to Low Masses alone (in sung Mass the readings must be chanted in Latin), and although it is only an option that need never be chosen, the very mention of the idea has prompted proponents of a "modified" *usus antiquior* to suggest that in the future we should simply drop Latin readings altogether and replace them with vernacular versions, in keeping with their understanding of the desire of the Second Vatican Council to make the Mass more "accessible" to the people.[1]

Needless to say, changing the readings of the *usus antiquior* into the vernacular *as a rule* would be a major change in the manner in which this form of the Roman rite is celebrated; it would mark a rupture in the way the Mass has come down to Catholics of the Latin rite for well over 1,600 years. In this chapter, I would like to reflect on some of the many reasons why we should stalwartly resist such a vernacularization of the readings.

THE SACRED LANGUAGE OF THE WESTERN CHURCH

With the passing of ages, and even with considerable organic development in the various rites and uses of the Holy Sacrifice of the Mass, the Catholic Church never jettisoned the mother tongue of the Roman rite. Latin became a sacral and hieratic language, and served a role that has been compared with that of ancient Greek for the Greek Orthodox, of Hebrew for the Jews, of Quranic Arabic for the Moslems, and of Sanskrit for the Hindus. Such languages are not simply exchangeable with a vernacular, as if the two stand on the same level, or as if any translation offered to the people could be said to convey the full meaning of the original religious text, which serves as a perennial gravitational

---

[1] Some have gone so far as to advocate that the *entire TLM* should be translated into the vernacular, suggesting that this might be a mutually acceptable way of ending the "liturgy wars." They do not recall that for a few short years in the mid-sixties, something like this was done — and it was still rejected as inadequate by the liturgists of the day as well as by Paul VI. While one might say that the Anglican Ordinariate offers something akin to this possibility, the proposal is a non-starter until progressive liturgists are gone for good. All the same, the arguments that I will make in this chapter on behalf of keeping the readings of the TLM in Latin can easily be extrapolated to a defense of Latin for the entire rite from start to finish — a case I have made at greater length in "Why We Pray in Latin" in *Turned Around*, 167–90.

center that keeps the forces of diverse cultures and circumstances from assuming control.

Put differently, doing the readings in Latin is not equivalent to doing them in the vernacular, because the former, as perfected and fixed over time, is for us the very language of formal liturgy, while the latter is a diverse and ever-changing medium of ordinary communication. It is a rationalist fallacy to think that languages are all equal to one another, so that it is a matter of indifference whether readings are given in Latin or in a vernacular language. Every language is a bearer of cultural, aesthetic, and even political values; every language flows from, evokes, and reinforces a certain "domain," greater or smaller, older or younger. It is therefore *not the same experience* to give or to hear readings in Latin and to give or to hear them in (say) English or Spanish. The one vehicle is universal, tied down to no particular people or nation or age, redolent of the ages of faith, suited to the sacred ambiance of the church. The other, whatever its merits, does not have the same qualities.

SEAMLESS GARMENT OF THE LORD

Another argument in favor of preserving Latin for the lections at Mass—and by no means a negligible one, given the sanctifying function of the liturgy—comes from the experience of worshipers accustomed to the unity and coherence, formality and dignity of the traditional Roman rite.

Akin to the seamless garment of the Lord, this rite is woven of ecclesiastical Latin from top to bottom, with Greek and Hebrew trim. To shift from Latin dialogues and orations to vernacular readings is experienced as a jarring disruption, an awkward movement away from theocentric focus and ceremonial formality. One steps outside of the realm of the liturgical action, which is primarily oriented towards the adoration of God, into a didactic mode directed exclusively to the people at hand.

There is a time and place for such instruction, namely, the homily; and it is neither inappropriate nor surprising that in many places the readings are read in the vernacular from the pulpit prior to the homily. The inclusion of such vernacular readings is *not* considered to be part of the liturgical action, and for good reason: it is a moment of teaching the people, and is not directed to God *per se*. In the classical Roman rite, in contrast, the readings, whether spoken or chanted, are offered up to God as a kind of verbal incense, a spiritual offering of the word to the Word before whom we come in adoration. The words here are a prayer of praise and petition. They do *teach* us (how could they not?), but their function in the Eucharistic liturgy goes far beyond conveying a doctrinal message.

At the time of the homily (and, where it is customary, reading out the lections in the vernacular), it is the ministerial priest who comes to the fore and acts *in propria persona*. The priest's acting *in persona Christi*, on the other hand, is symbolized, as mentioned in chapter 12, by the use of Latin throughout the rest of the Mass for the appointed prayers, readings, and Canon. The integrity of the parts of the Mass—that fact that many disparate elements come together in one great offering of worship—is strongly brought home to the worshiper by the use of this noble, ancient, and worshipful language. The whole is a flowing river, a seamless garment, a landscape in which the various distinct objects are gathered together into a natural unity of environment. Think of mountains covered with pine trees—one can see many individual items, but the whole view is utterly *one*. In a Latin liturgy, there is no awkward transition or lack of transition from part to part; there is simply the flow of one great action of Christ the High Priest, teaching, ruling, sanctifying.

SYMBOLISM OF SOLEMN READINGS

One may not, of course, deny that the word of God is the word of God regardless of what language it is in. The point is rather a symbolic one, at least as regards the lections at Mass. It should be readily apparent that symbolism is not something incidental to the liturgy but is rather a constitutive dimension of the entire sacramental system. Put differently, *how* we do the readings, how we treat the book in the handling of it and the chanting of it, is just as important as—and in some ways more important than—the specific message delivered in any given set of readings. The special way Scripture is treated in the classical Roman rite is already a powerful formation of the soul of the believer.

Among the most moving and beautiful signs of the latreutic or adorational function of the readings in the *usus antiquior* are those moments strewn throughout the course of the liturgical year when the priest, ministers, and faithful genuflect *during* a reading or Proper, as described below in chapter 19 (see page 308). Sadly, in the new liturgy, this passionate yet peaceful gesture is done only twice a year, at the moment of the narration of the death of our Lord on Palm Sunday and Good Friday. One might compare this reduction to the parallel reduction of the number of times the faithful genuflect at the *Et incarnatus est*. When worshipping in the old rite, the faithful kneel for that statement *every time* the Creed is recited or sung, in a poignant reminder that the

Incarnation of the Son of God is the center of all time and indeed of all reality (and the Creed, be it noted, is appointed to be said or sung more often in the TLM than in the NO); in Paul VI's new Mass, the rubrics call for kneeling at the *Et incarnatus est* exclusively on Christmas and the Annunciation, and in practice, such kneeling causes confusion when attempted, through lack of familiarity. In the *usus antiquior*, exactly parallel to the kneeling at the *Et incarnatus* is the kneeling at *Et Verbum caro factum est* of the Last Gospel.

In these and many other instances, we see how the traditional Mass literally *embodies* our faith by bringing into play not only man's mind or voice, but his entire body—as befits a religion founded on the Word-made-flesh.

THE SACRALITY OF THE ACT OF READING

One way in which the ancient Mass sets apart the word of God for special veneration and allows the faithful to *perceive* its unique character is by treating it in a way that mere profane texts are never treated, namely, by chanting it in its entirety at any sung Mass. Right away, we are catapulted into a different world, the world of God, in which his holy words, so beautiful and so beloved, must be lovingly lingered over, savored and reverenced, lifted up in a solemn sacrifice of song. One cannot overestimate the formative power of the chanted readings to communicate immediately to the faithful that we are plunged into God's holiness when we encounter His revelation.

This liturgical action of reading puts us in contact with the source of sanctification, and does so in a way that deserves a treatment no less noble than that which any part of the Ordinary (Kyrie, Gloria, Credo, Sanctus, Agnus Dei) or the Preface of the Mass receives. How strange it would be to chant so many other prayers, written by holy men but not equivalent to the revealed word of God, and yet to leave unchanted the very words of God himself! If it is only the lover who sings, according to St. Augustine, should not the lover of God sing most of all the words of God?

With this theological background in mind, it is fair to say that the chanting of the lections would suffer considerably from a sudden and rash shift to vernacular readings. The chanting tones for the various classes of readings are ancient, solemn, noble, and perfectly fitted to the Latin language. Although vernaculars *can* be sung with adapted tones, the Church of the Roman rite had never done this historically, and so an organic opportunity for developing well-sung vernacular chant never occurred. In any event, the very worst thing that could happen would be the loss of chanted readings right at a time when this magnificent custom has reentered the life of the Church thanks to the sung and solemn celebrations of the *usus antiquior*.

In the Low Mass, by contrast, when the Epistle and Gospel are merely spoken, proper reverence for the word of God is assured by the priest reading it *at the altar*, signifying two things: first, that this word of Scripture is *derived from* and *ordered to* the primal Word of God, Jesus Christ the High Priest, the Lawgiver, the very *life* of the word; second, that this word of Scripture is so sacred that it is not treated like any other word (e.g., announcements or homily), but is reserved to the spiritual domain symbolized by the altar of divine sacrifice. This is a guarantee that the uniquely *sacred* character of the text will be appreciated and respected. There is ample room in the homily to *apply* the word of God to the lives of the faithful, so there is no need to fear too great a "separation" between the domain of the spiritual and the domain of life in the world. The word of Scripture should never be severed from its home—the Word, the font of life, the fire of love, the pleasing and acceptable sacrifice of holiness.

That is why it is not only *not* confusing for the priest to chant or read the readings at the altar, but eminently *fitting* for him to do so whenever the liturgy is not of a more solemn character, with a greater diversity of hierarchical ministers. The more solemn the liturgy, the more appropriate it is to separate out its elements and give each of them greater prominence. The chanting of the readings (as with the celebration of the rest of the rite) in a direction other than towards the people symbolizes that *conversio ad Deum* or turning to God which is the entire purpose of both Scripture and the Holy Sacrifice.

WIDESPREAD LITERACY

Lastly, in this age of widespread literacy and hunger for the sacred, there is no pressing need for the change from Latin to vernacular. In the words of *Sacrosanctum Concilium*, "there must be no innovations unless the good of the Church genuinely and certainly requires them" (*SC* 23). It is clear to all who are involved in the movement to recover traditional worship in the Roman rite that the Latin language is a dearly loved and particularly beautiful sign of the unity of the Catholic Church and the grandeur of our bimillennial history. As far as *participatio actuosa* is concerned, either the readings can be given in the vernacular *after* they are read or chanted in the Church's mother tongue (such as right before the homily, as is done in many places); or today's faithful can follow along in their daily missals, pick up a printed sheet at the entrance of the church, or even glance at a TLM smartphone app (of which there are a dozen at least, and in every major language).

No one goes to the traditional Mass in order to "hear Scripture," much less to gain biblical expertise, since that is hardly the purpose of the Holy Sacrifice; we go to worship God and be nourished by His word and His flesh, and to this profound and specific purpose the modest but well-chosen selection of Scripture passages in the classical Roman rite makes a decisive contribution.[2] It is my conviction, and that of many of my fellow Catholics in the traditional movement, that the Latin language makes a similarly decisive contribution—one that deserves to be understood, cherished, and preserved for all future generations.

BUT WHAT ABOUT *TRADITIONIS CUSTODES*?

The Apostolic Letter *Traditionis Custodes* is illicit on numerous grounds and should be ignored or resisted rather than accepted and implemented. However, here is not the place to make this case, which I together with many others have made elsewhere.[3] Besides, whatever we may think of the motu proprio, it is (as of writing) still "on the books," and we cannot stop some people from treating it as law, until a future pope rescinds this act of violence so contrary to the Church's common good. Thus, we must be prepared to deal with certain problems that may arise, problems caused in part by what appears to be an almost total ignorance on the part of the document's drafters of how the traditional Latin Mass actually functions in practice.

A case in point is Article 3 §3, which states: "In these celebrations the readings are proclaimed in the vernacular language, using translations of the Sacred Scripture approved for liturgical use by the respective Episcopal Conferences."

1. Note that the formulation does not prohibit (nor could it) the reading or chanting of the readings *in Latin*, as included in the official liturgical books of the *Missale Romanum* of 1962 (and preceding years), following immemorial tradition. Thus, the Epistle and the Gospel may still be read or chanted *in Latin*, and ought to be—not least because of the pastoral expectations of the people, who have come for the Church's official and venerable liturgy, not for substituted vernacular readings.

2. What this statement would require, strictly speaking, is that in celebrations according to the old missal, readings shall be proclaimed in the vernacular language at some point. In keeping with longstanding custom, this can surely be from the pulpit before the homily (when there is a homily). But it is always understood, as in the liturgical legislation for the Novus Ordo, that an extra step like this may, "for

---

[2] See Miller, "Bible by the Pound," in Kwasniewski, *Illusions of Reform*, 180–97.
[3] See Kwasniewski, ed., *From Benedict's Peace to Francis's War*; Kwasniewski, *True Obedience* and *Bound by Truth*; Rivoire, *Does "TC" Pass the Juridical Rationality Test?*

appropriate pastoral reasons," be omitted. In the English text published by the Vatican, the *motu proprio* says "the readings are proclaimed," not "the readings *must be* proclaimed." The former phrase indicates a general state of affairs that would be compatible with something not being done every time, as if one were to say "the passengers are seated," though a few might be standing or walking; the latter stipulates a sole way of doing a thing, as in "the passengers must be seated."

3. The classical Roman rite has its own official liturgical books for the chanting of the Epistle by the subdeacon and the Gospel by the deacon at the Solemn Mass. Since it is a non-negotiable principle that liturgical texts should be read in their integrity using the appropriate liturgical books as per the rubrics, in a Solemn Mass it is clear that the Epistle and Gospel must be chanted in Latin. Similarly, the altar missal used by the priest at Low Mass or at a *Missa cantata* has the proper readings printed in it as integral parts of the texts of the day's Mass, and therefore they too should be read or sung at the appropriate time from the missal (or from a book that exactly reproduces the readings of the missal), *not* read or sung in translation. A translation may be read later from the pulpit.

4. Translations into modern vernacular languages currently approved for the Novus Ordo do not match the readings printed in the *Missale Romanum* of 1962 or earlier years. The vocabulary of the old Vulgate and the new translations based on (sometimes questionable) modern biblical scholarship are sufficiently different that one would be hard-pressed to maintain their exact equivalency. For example, the New American Bible significantly departs from the Vulgate in the psalms and in verses like the Johannine Comma read on Low Sunday, which is altogether absent from the NAB. Someone who read *only* from the NAB would therefore be violating the spirit and the letter of the liturgical celebration, contrary to liturgical laws of universal application.[4] Furthermore, the NAB as used at the Novus Ordo is not the same as what is sold by publishers, nor is it what will be used in the new translation of the Liturgy of the Hours and the new edition of psalms for the lectionary, which have been revised. In other words, at least in the USA, matching a currently approved vernacular edition to the lections of the traditional *Missale Romanum* would be to some extent impossible, and in any case a complicated business and pastorally inopportune.

5. Prior to the liturgical reform, the Church had already approved translations for liturgical use that actually correspond to the content of

---

[4] See, for more details, Matthew Hazell, "Demanding the Impossible: *Traditionis custodes* and Vernacular Readings," *Rorate Caeli*, July 20, 2021.

the old missal, such as the "Confraternity Bible" produced under the auspices of the Confraternity of Christian Doctrine between 1941 and 1969, and based on the Vulgate and, to some extent, the Douay-Rheims. To read from the Confraternity edition would technically be to read from a version that won the approval of the US bishops at the time that corresponds to the missal in question. There may be other versions printed in hand missals that would be suitable for use in the pulpit.

6. There are many ironies in *Traditionis Custodes*. One of them is that Article 3 §3 seems to wish to require for the old Mass something that is not even required in the new Mass. It is a perfectly licit option, although exceedingly rare, for the readings at the Novus Ordo to be done entirely in Latin (said or sung), with no translation being given. Indeed, according to its governing rubrics, one could licitly celebrate an entire Mass in English but do the readings in Latin. Needless to say, no one does this, but it is compatible with the rubrics and the pertinent canon law. It seems strange to require at the old Mass something that is not even obligatory for the new.

In reactions to the motu proprio, on occasion one sees a disturbing lack of imagination and flexibility among some who do not seem to understand the nuanced reading one must bring to every piece of legislation. In particular, they seem to think that it is not a great loss to substitute vernacular readings for Latin ones. This, however, would be both a mistaken reaction to the motu proprio and a mistake in liturgical praxis itself. It is crucial, whatever we do, not to lose the tradition of reciting or chanting the readings *in Latin* in the Mass of the Roman rite. This is a non-negligible and non-negotiable part of our Catholic heritage, an element in the integrity of the *Missale Romanum* that is fraught with theological meaning. We would do well to rediscover this treasure and to protect it from extinction, rather than joining forces with geriatric iconoclasts who want to smash it before they expire.

AGAINST VERNACULAR READINGS IN THE TRADITIONAL MASS

As we have seen, *Traditionis Custodes* reignited the debate over doing readings at the TLM exclusively in the vernacular—a possibility that *Summorum Pontificum* had already opened up for Low Masses. Since traditionalists tend to understand that the readings are an integral part of the missal and of the act of worship and that continuity ought to be maintained among all elements of the liturgical action, that option was, thankfully, seldom used. In many places, readings were already being given in the vernacular from the pulpit prior to the homily, and most of the faithful have translations in their hand missals (or on their phones — not a method I approve of, for reasons I will not go into here). By and large, it is a non-question and a non-starter within the TLM world, and this latest assault on the integrity of the Latin liturgical tradition has met with a resistance both principled and pragmatic.

Nevertheless, this topic deserves to be revisited from time to time in order to understand better the rationale for sticking with the tradition, particularly as one does occasionally encounter traditionalists who seem bent on recapitulating the phylogeny of the Liturgical Movement. Here's what a friend who is quite sympathetic to the TLM wrote to me:

> I personally find that one of the best things about the Novus Ordo is vernacular readings. I take a *via media* approach; I don't believe "pastoral" adaptations should be made in the liturgy, but I do enjoy how, in the Novus Ordo, the Word is proclaimed in the vernacular. When I have been at Latin Masses, I love the chanting of the Epistle & Gospel, but then when the priest goes and reads it from the pulpit before the homily, it is often done in a rushed, sloppy, and awkward manner. What is the justification for retaining the readings in chanted or spoken Latin? Like I said, I think it's beautiful, but in my idealized liturgy which I imagine to be the fruit of a Third Vatican Council called for by Cardinal Sarah-turned-Pope Benedict XVII, it largely looks like the 1962 Missal but with vernacular readings.

This is indeed a complex question. There are two aspects of the issue. First, what is the purpose of the reading of Scripture at Mass? And second, how can we practically overcome the language barrier that Latin presents to most?

In terms of the first aspect, there is no doubt that the traditional liturgy views, and treats, every component as primarily doxological and latreutic; nothing is merely didactic or informative. (This is why, as Martin Mosebach points out, the homily comes across as an interruption in the action: it is certainly *merely* didactic and informative, and therefore doesn't smoothly harmonize with the rest of the liturgy, which is a ritual of worship, a sacred action.) Because of this fundamental orientation to God, the readings are chanted like prayers, incense is used, a ceremonial procession is formed. The Novus Ordo, in contrast, was unfortunately composed at a time when it was all the rage to think of readings at Mass as a sort of communal Bible study, and that is why the Liturgy of the Word is so dreadfully verbose, static, and anthropocentric. Everything is read (almost never sung), towards the people, from the ambo, and without a sense that this Word is being offered up to God and raising the minds of the faithful up to Him in prayer.[5]

---

[5] See my articles "Homogeneity vs. Hierarchy: On the Treatment of Verbal Moments," *NLM*, October 16, 2017 and "'Moments of Liturgical Action': Recovering the Sacramentality of Biblical Lections," *NLM*, January 24, 2022.

At the Latin Mass, everything is done primarily *for God* and only secondarily for the people: nothing is "just for the people," as if we're turning our backs on God and saying: "Pardon us, we have some business of our own to take care of now; we'll come back to You later." The phrases customarily used to describe the two main parts of the Mass—"Mass of the Catechumens" and "Mass of the Faithful"—each speaks of a *missa*, and this, not only because it was thought that certain categories of people were "sent away" (first, the catechumens after the readings, and then the faithful after the final thanksgiving), but also because, as the medieval commentators explain, *missa est* means "it is sent": our offering to God is sent up to Him by the hands of angels! In ancient Israel as in the Church, much of our worship consists in offering words up to God as a verbal sacrifice, parallel to our offering up of incense to Him. "The priests of the Lord offer incense and loaves to God," says Leviticus 21:6—repeated in the Offertory antiphon of the feast of Corpus Christi. As incense pervades the church but also rises up, so too does the Word of God: it is not shot forth to the people (as if they are the pupils drilled by a teacher), but exalted so that it may rain down on them. Yes, there is something sacramental and mystical in this descent: there is a blessing in the repetition of the hallowed words of the liturgy that goes beyond their rational content. In the *Liber specialis gratiæ*, St. Mechtild of Hackeborn says that Christ spoke to her these remarkable words:

> You shall understand that when you say any psalm or prayer which any saints prayed when they were alive on earth, then all of those saints pray to me for you. Additionally, when you are in your devotions and speak with me, then all of the saints are joyful and worship and thank me.

It is surely no small thing for us to be reciting and singing the very same words that most of the saints of the Western half of the Church had on their lips across all the centuries. These are words of diachronic unity, reverberating harmony, and revelatory power.

In terms of the second aspect mentioned above, it seems there are better ways to accomplish the good of comprehension than chucking out a stable practice of over 1,600 years' duration and replacing it with the use of embattled compromise translations that please no one, being (depending on who you are talking to) dated, too casual or too formal, too prosaic or too poetic, too loose or too literal, etc. Most modern Westerners are still literate enough to find following along in a missal no difficulty, and since the translations in the missals are not official, they can vary in style. I have come to prefer this multi-sensory and more *laissez-faire* approach. If the reading from the pulpit is done well, it reinforces the proclamation. On most Sundays I engage with the reading multiple times: at Mass when I hear it in Latin and possibly read it; again when it's read from the pulpit; and then in the parts that come up in Vespers. The old approach in fact saturates you slowly in Scripture rather than hosing you from the fire hydrant.

We can and should also make a concerted effort to teach Latin to all Catholics, both children and adults. Any serious religion teaches serious stuff to its followers: the Jews teach Hebrew, the Moslems teach classical Arabic, etc. If we cared about our heritage, you can bet that every schoolchild would be translating passages from the Vulgate, which is a more enormously consequential text in the history of the West than Homer, Virgil, Dante, Shakespeare, or [insert name of favorite famous author].

I deliberately place the next consideration after the foregoing points to avoid the accusation of aestheticism. However, it is quite true, and rather obvious, that the Tridentine liturgy possesses a colossal unity of form and substance—a unity to which the use of Latin makes a significant contribution. Like the foreigner who (according to Samuel Johnson) "tells part of his meaning by words, and conveys part by signs,"[6] the liturgy makes use of both: the words alone are not enough, nor are the non-verbal signs, but together they constitute a whole that is greater than its parts. We understand the uniqueness and the divine authorship of the words of Scripture better when we hear them read or chanted in Latin than if we heard them only in the vernacular; but their exalted status is no less emphasized by the elaborate treatment accorded to the book, the kissing of it, the incensing of it, the processing with it. We don't *do* that kind of thing with ordinary books.

It is often said that a major driving force in the Catholic liturgical reform was the secret Protestantizing sympathies of many of the liturgists and their not-so-secret obsession with lowest-common-denominator ecumenism. That seems to be true in all kinds of ways.[7] We should not forget, all the same, that most of the early Protestants were a good deal more conservative, more "traditional" in their instincts, than the Catholic liturgists of the 1960s or their ragtag sympathizers today. I wrote about this elsewhere in connection with the manner of receiving Holy Communion,[8] but here is a passage in which Martin Luther expresses a desire to preserve the ancient languages in worship:

---

[6] Samuel Johnson, On the "Epitaph to James Craggs," in *The Works of Samuel Johnson* (J. Nichols and Son, 1810), vol. 6, "Life of Pope," 206.
[7] See chapter 5 and Kwasniewski, *Once and Future Roman Rite*, 208–15.
[8] See my article "What modern Catholics can learn from Eastern Christians and Protestants about reverent Communion," *LifeSiteNews*, May 18, 2021.

Now there are three different kinds of Divine Service. The first, in Latin, which we published lately, called the *Formula Missæ*. This I do not want to have set aside or changed; but, as we have hitherto kept it, so should we be still free to use it where and when we please, or as occasion requires. I do not want in any way to let the Latin tongue disappear out of Divine Service; for I am so deeply concerned for the young. If it lay in my power, and the Greek and Hebrew tongues were as familiar to us as the Latin, and possessed as great a store of fine music and song as the Latin does, Mass should be held and there should be singing and reading, on alternate Sundays, in all four languages — German, Latin, Greek, and Hebrew. I am by no means of one mind with those who set all their store by one language [in context, this seems to mean German].⁹

Of course, I wouldn't say we should do anything, or keep something, because Luther said so or did so. Rather, the point is that the "Catholic" liturgical reformers and implementers — including Paul VI — were, in certain ways, more Lutheran than Luther himself. That's why the pope's good friend Jean Guitton was right to say in an interview that Paul VI's intention was "to bring the Catholic Mass closer to the Calvinist Mass."¹⁰

Meanwhile, the truly universal or catholic, and dare I say Pentecostal, attitude of the Catholic Church was well expressed by Maisie Ward in 1937, in sentiments that have been echoed and reechoed by countless laymen and clergy down through the centuries: "This union of localization and universality finds expression in the miracle of tongues on Whit Sunday and to-day in the language and liturgy [viz., the Latin Mass] which unites, at one altar, men severed by national languages and national interests."¹¹ With gratitude to their ancestors, with love for their descendants, the heirs of the Judaeo-Greco-Roman civilization in its Western and Latin sphere owe it to themselves and to the Church as a whole to pass on enthusiastically what they have humbly received and gratefully enjoyed.

---

9 B. J. Kidd, ed., *Documents Illustrative of the Continental Reformation* (Clarendon Press, 1911), 195.
10 See Kabel, "Catholic fact check: Jean Guitton, Pope Paul VI, and the liturgical reforms."
11 Maisie Ward, *The Wilfrid Wards and the Transition*, vol. 2: *Insurrection versus Resurrection* (Sheed & Ward, 1937), 7. For particularly insightful defenses of the role of Latin in the liturgy and in the Catholic Church more generally, see Shaw, *The Case for Liturgical Restoration*, 139–68; idem, *The Liturgy, the Family, and the Crisis of Modernity*, 57–85; idem, ed., *Latin Mass and the Intellectuals*, 18–30, 43–47.

The Truthfulness of the Pre-1955 Good Friday Prayer for the Jews

JESUS THE CHRIST SAYS OF HIMSELF THAT HE was sent "only to the lost sheep of the house of Israel" (Mt 15:24), among whom He inaugurated His visible mission "to seek and to save the lost" (Lk 19:10). There is, then, something peculiarly ludicrous, not to say impious, in the embarrassment of modern churchmen over the Church's permanent and inescapable mission to convert the Jews, the children of Israel, among whom Our Lord was born. They are still the lost sheep; they are lost and must be sought, won over, baptized in the life-giving waters of salvation. Their lack of faith in the Messiah sent into the world *from* and *for* them cannot be shrugged off as an unfortunate difference of opinion when, in reality, it is a crippling spiritual defect and a cause of condemnation. Thus, it is entirely right and just that Catholics pray for the Jews as follows:

> Let us pray also for the faithless Jews [*perfidis Judæis*]: that Almighty God may remove the veil from their hearts; so that they too may acknowledge Jesus Christ our Lord. [No instruction to kneel or to rise is given, but immediately is said:] Almighty and eternal God, who dost not exclude from Thy mercy even Jewish faithlessness [*Judaicam perfidiam*]: hear our prayers, which we offer for the blindness of that people; that acknowledging the light of Thy Truth, which is Christ, they may be delivered from their darkness. Through the same our Lord Jesus Christ, who liveth and reigneth with Thee in the unity of the Holy Spirit, God, for ever and ever. Amen.

That is the formulation found in the pre-1955 Mass of the Presanctified on Good Friday.

Fr. Henri de Lubac—no traditionalist, to be sure—devotes an entire chapter of his famous work *Medieval Exegesis* to the meaning of the word *perfidus* in patristic literature, and (surprise!) it turns out that it does *not* mean "perfidious" as this word is used in modern parlance, according to which it means "treacherous" or "malevolent." In Christian vocabulary, it is the right word to designate the idea of being unfaithful to a commitment one had undertaken. The Israelites accepted the old covenant, which was ordered to accepting the Messiah. By not having received Him when He came, they were guilty of infidelity to the Lord. Thus, the phraseology is absolutely correct. *Perfidus* and its derivatives occur twenty times in the traditional Hispano-Mozarabic missal: once against those who stoned St. Stephen, a few times against pagans, sometimes against heretics, and at other times against irreligious sinners without further distinction—all correct usages.

In 1955, Pius XII introduced the first unnecessary change to this venerable Good Friday prayer by inserting the standard instruction for kneeling and standing. John XXIII yielded to political pressure by removing the words *perfidis* and *perfidiam*. The rite of Paul VI simply jettisoned the traditional prayer altogether, replacing it with a typically Hallmarkian text. It was a final misstep for Benedict XVI, in "rehabilitating" the *usus antiquior*, to replace the John XXIII version with a brand-new prayer of eschatological rather than evangelical orientation, which makes it inferior, *as* Christian prayer, to the ancient prayer. For comparison's sake, here are Paul VI's and Benedict XVI's versions:

> [*Novus Ordo*, 2011 translation:] Let us pray also for the Jewish people, to whom the Lord our God spoke first, that he may grant them to advance in love of his name and in faithfulness to his covenant. [Prayer in silence. Then the priest says:] Almighty ever-living God, who bestowed your promises on Abraham and his descendants, hear graciously the prayers of your Church, that the people you first made your own may attain the fullness of redemption. Through Christ our Lord. Amen.

> [Benedict XVI substitution in the 1962 missal:] Let us pray also for the Jews: may our God and Lord enlighten their hearts, so that they may acknowledge Jesus Christ, the savior of all men. (Let us pray. ℣. Let us kneel. ℟. Arise.) Almighty and everlasting God, who desirest that all men be saved and come to the knowledge of truth, mercifully grant that, as the fullness of the Gentiles enters into Thy Church, all Israel may be saved. Through Christ our Lord. ℟. Amen.[1]

This succession of changes seems to concede the anti-Catholic argument that there really was something "antisemitic" about the old prayer, when it does no more than translate the teaching of the New Testament into the *lex orandi*. Balking at this *lex orandi* is a backhanded way of balking at divine revelation. Ironically, those who show themselves to be guilty of *perfidia* are the Christians who cease to pray and work for the conversion of all, including the Jews.

Catholics who make grateful use of the pre-'1955 Holy Week liturgy should be in a position to defend the classic prayer rather than accept the false premise that there was something wrong with it. On the now-defunct *Foretaste of Wisdom* blog there was a fine piece entitled

---

[1] This English translation is taken from *The Campion Missal and Hymnal*, courtesy of Corpus Christi Watershed. Benedict XVI promulgated the text in Latin only, since that is the version to be used on Good Friday in the *usus antiquior*—for those who have not confidently returned to the pre-55 Holy Week.

"St. Thomas Aquinas on the Relationship between Christianity and Judaism after Christ," which gathered the following quotations.

1. *Christianity is the continuity (fulfillment) of the faith of the Judaism of the Old Covenant.*

> As regards the substance of the articles of faith, they have not received any increase as time went on: since whatever those who lived later have believed, was contained, albeit implicitly, in the faith of those Fathers who preceded them.[2]

2. *Judaism after Christ is* not *the continuity of the faith of the Judaism of the Old Covenant.*

> Accordingly we must say that if unbelief be considered in comparison to faith, there are several species of unbelief, determinate in number. For, since the sin of unbelief consists in resisting the faith, this may happen in two ways: either the faith is resisted before it has been accepted, and such is the unbelief of pagans or heathens; or the Christian faith is resisted after it has been accepted, and this either in the figure, and such is the unbelief of the Jews, or in the very manifestation of truth, and such is the unbelief of heretics. Hence we may, in a general way, reckon these three as species of unbelief.[3]

3. *The Old Law was a step, a bridge from the law of nature to the New Law of the Gospel. It is inherently temporary and ordered beyond itself.*

> Hence, the New Law is called a law of love and consequently is called an image, because it has an express likeness to future goods. But the Old Law represents that image by certain carnal things and very remotely. Therefore, it is called a shadow (as in) Colossians 2:17: "These are but a shadow of the things to come." This, therefore, is the condition of the Old Testament, that it has the shadow of future things and not their image.[4]

> In the present state of life, we are unable to gaze on the Divine Truth in itself, and we need the ray of divine light to shine upon us under the form of certain sensible figures, as Dionysius states (*Cœl. Hier.* i); in various ways, however, according to the various states of human knowledge. For under the Old Law, neither was the Divine Truth manifest in itself, nor was the way leading to that manifestation as yet opened out, as the Apostle declares (Heb 9:8). Hence the external worship of the Old Law needed to be figurative not only of the future truth to be manifested in our heavenly country, but also of Christ, Who is the way leading to that heavenly manifestation. But under the New Law this way is already revealed: and therefore it needs no longer to be foreshadowed as something future, but to be brought to our minds as something past or present:

---

[2] *Summa theologiæ* II-II, Q. 1, art. 7.
[3] *Summa theologiæ* I-II, Q. 10, art. 5.
[4] *Super Heb.* X.1, no. 480.

and the truth of the glory to come, which is not yet revealed, alone needs to be foreshadowed. This is what the Apostle says (Heb 11:1): "The Law has a shadow of the good things to come, not the very image of the things": for a shadow is less than an image; so that the image belongs to the New Law, but the shadow to the Old.[5]

4. *That the Old Law is said to be "everlasting" and that the call of God is "without repentance" does not establish that the Old Law remains in force as such or that it was not God's intention to bring it to an end in the fullness of time.*

The Old Law is said to be "for ever" simply and absolutely, as regards its moral precepts; but as regards the ceremonial precepts it lasts for ever in respect of the reality which those ceremonies foreshadowed.[6]

In this way one avoids the opinion of the Jews, who believe that the sacraments of the Law must be observed forever precisely because they were established by God, since God has no regrets and is not changed. But without change or regret one who disposes things may dispose things differently in harmony with a difference of times; thus, the father of a family gives one set of orders to a small child and another to one already grown. Thus, God also harmoniously gave one set of sacraments and commandments before the Incarnation to point to the future, and another set after the Incarnation to deliver things present and bring to mind things past.[7]

5. *Professing "Judaism" after the time of Christ — that is, holding on to the Old Covenant in its oldness after it has been fulfilled — is objectively a grave sin based on a grave theological error.*

All ceremonies are professions of faith, in which the interior worship of God consists. Now man can make profession of his inward faith, by deeds as well as by words: and in either profession, if he make a false declaration, he sins mortally. Now, though our faith in Christ is the same as that of the fathers of old; yet, since they came before Christ, whereas we come after Him, the same faith is expressed in different words, by us and by them. For by them was it said: "Behold a virgin shall conceive and bear a son," where the verbs are in the future tense: whereas we express the same by means of verbs in the past tense, and say that she "conceived and bore." In like manner the ceremonies of the Old Law betokened Christ as having yet to be born and to suffer: whereas our sacraments signify Him as already born and having suffered. Consequently, just as it would be a mortal sin now for anyone, in making a profession of faith, to say that Christ is yet to be born, which the fathers of old said devoutly and truthfully; so too it would be a mortal sin now to observe those ceremonies which the fathers of old fulfilled with

---

[5] *Summa theologiæ* I-II, Q. 101, art. 2.
[6] *Summa theologiæ* I-II, Q. 103, art. 3 ad 1; see also the *corpus* in full.
[7] *Summa contra gentiles* IV.57, 2.

devotion and fidelity. Such is the teaching of Augustine (*Contra Faust.* xix, 16), who says: "It is no longer promised that He shall be born, shall suffer and rise again, truths of which their sacraments were a kind of image: but it is declared that He is already born, has suffered and risen again; of which our sacraments, in which Christians share, are the actual representation."[8]

6. The Old and New Laws are not parallel; the Old Law was a step in God's divine economy, in which the New Law is the goal.

Accordingly, then, two laws may be distinguished from one another in two ways. First, through being altogether diverse, from the fact that they are ordained to diverse ends: thus a state-law ordained to democratic government would differ specifically from a law ordained to government by the aristocracy. Secondly, two laws may be distinguished from one another, through one of them being more closely connected with the end, and the other more remotely: thus in one and the same state there is one law enjoined on men of mature age, who can forthwith accomplish that which pertains to the common good; and another law regulating the education of children who need to be taught how they are to achieve manly deeds later on. We must therefore say that, according to the first way, the New Law is not distinct from the Old Law: because they both have the same end, namely, man's subjection to God; and there is but one God of the New and of the Old Testament, according to Romans 3:30: "It is one God that justifieth circumcision by faith, and uncircumcision through faith." According to the second way, the New Law is distinct from the Old Law: because the Old Law is like a pedagogue of children, as the Apostle says (Gal 3:24), whereas the New Law is the law of perfection, since it is the law of charity, of which the Apostle says (Col 3:14) that it is "the bond of perfection."[9]

In all of this, St. Thomas shows himself to be the faithful interpreter of Tradition, as this quotation from St. Augustine shows:

For we see that [the] priesthood has been changed; and there can be no hope that what was promised to that house may some time be fulfilled, because that which succeeds on its being rejected and changed is rather predicted as eternal. He who says this does not yet understand, or does not recollect, that this very priesthood after the order of Aaron was appointed as the shadow of a future eternal priesthood; and therefore, when eternity is promised to it, it is not promised to the mere shadow and figure, but to what is shadowed forth and prefigured by it. But lest it should be thought the shadow itself was to remain, therefore its mutation also behooved to be foretold.[10]

---

[8] *Summa theologiæ* I-II, Q. 103, art. 4.
[9] *Summa theologiæ* I-II, Q. 107, art. 1; see also the responses to the objections.
[10] *City of God*, XVII, 6. Translated by Marcus Dods, from *Nicene and Post-Nicene Fathers, First Series*, vol. 2, ed. Philip Schaff (Christian Literature Publishing Co., 1887), rev. and ed. for New Advent by Kevin Knight, www.newadvent.org/fathers/120117.htm.

In light of this rock-solid teaching from the Church's Common Doctor, it is impossible to maintain that the traditional (pre-1955) version of the prayer for the conversion of the Jews on Good Friday constitutes an "antisemitic" attack on them. Rather, it expresses accurately, elegantly, and charitably the teaching of the New Testament and of the Church, ordered to the salvation of all mankind in Christ—especially the people chosen in view of the Christ, the true and natural Son of God.

I should like to close with a quotation from an article published in (of all places) *Theological Studies* in the year 1947, by John M. Oesterreicher, "*Pro Perfidis Judæis*":

> To conclude with a proposal made from time to time: that the Church should modify the expression *perfidia Judaica* and restore the ancient order for the Good Friday prayer, I should like to venture an opinion. The Church will hardly alter the words *perfidia Judaica*, which, as we have shown, are not intended to dishonor the Jews, and this because she may not and will not forget Christ's claim for recognition from His own people. She, the custodian of truth, must call things by their proper names; thus, Israel's resistance to Christ, unbelief. Indeed, she would be an enemy of the Jews did she conceal from them the source of their unrest.[11]

In 1947, it was still possible for a scholar naively to say: "The Church will *hardly alter* the words..." and that "she may not and *will not* forget Christ's claim for recognition from His own people." It has, alas, been much too long since the statement "the custodian of truth must call things by their proper name" has been obviously and undeniably true; on the contrary, it often appears as if the very last thing the Church will do today is call *anything* by its proper name, least of all sins. Caught up in the spirit of the times, our author Oesterreicher later took to "Judaizing" opinions himself, and no doubt abandoned these earlier perfectly Catholic judgments of his.

After the reformatory carnage through which we have passed since then, we are in a position to learn a lesson from our mistakes as we work to restore the traditional Roman rite.[12] The lesson is: never be embarrassed by the traditional *lex orandi*. Pray it; seek to understand it; defend it. The Church's prayer is our guide in the spiritual and intellectual life, not the prey and sport of the latest cultural fads, philosophical sects, or secular crusades.

---

11 John M. Oesterreicher, "*Pro Perfidis Judaeis*," *Theological Studies* 8 (1947): 80–96; online at https://scholarship.shu.edu/cgi/viewcontent.cgi?article=1007&context=oesterreicher.

12 For further reading on this topic, I recommend Brian Harrison, "The Liturgy and 'Supersessionism,'" *CatholicCulture.org*, item 9168; "The Good Friday Prayer for the Jews," in Shaw, *The Case for Liturgical Restoration*, 275–91; John Hunwicke, many articles at https://liturgicalnotes.blogspot.com/search?q=jews.

19

The Grace of Stability: How Liturgy Forms the Christian Soul

CATHOLICS WHO ASSIST AT THE TRADItional liturgy of the Church quickly come to love one monumental fact about it: its stability, regularity, and constancy.[1] With a few exceptions due to local calendars or unannounced votive Masses, one can come to any Tridentine liturgy and know within moments which Mass in the missal is being celebrated—and then know exactly how that Mass will unfold for the remaining half-hour or hour, since everything is fixed in place. What a consolation to know that the celebrant is not being asked to exhibit the state of his mind in extemporaneous remarks, or his pastoral judgment in choosing from dozens of options in a row! *The Mass is simply the Mass*—older, greater, stronger, and steadier than any of us mere mortals. We can gratefully entrust ourselves to its lofty spiritual pedagogy and accumulated wisdom. We are not the drivers but the passengers. The driver is Christ our Lord, and never once in the liturgy (except perhaps in a homily gone awry) are we confronted with a jarring disjunct between the principal Celebrant and His intelligent instrument.

People who have practiced *lectio divina* or the prayerful reading of the Bible know that it works best with the slow assimilation of a chosen text. One must mortify the desire to read too much or to skip all over the place. One often has to read and re-read a passage before it penetrates the mind and, even more, the heart. In just the same way, the great strength of the one-year lectionary contained in the traditional *Missale Romanum* is that it affords the worshiper time to absorb a certain set of luminous biblical passages, extremely well chosen for their liturgical purpose. Meeting these texts repeatedly, one puts them on like a garment, or assimilates them like food and drink. One begins to think and pray in their phrases. What happens with the lectionary happens, in turn, with the entire liturgy. The fixity of the TLM from top to bottom, from Collect to Postcommunion, from Psalm 42 to the Prologue of John, facilitates a liturgical *lectio divina* that can range over the words of the entire missal, in both its repeated and changing parts, that is, the Ordinary and the Propers.[2]

---

[1] This section includes material drawn from Kwasniewski, *Noble Beauty*, 228–32.
[2] For an exquisite example from a Jesuit writing in 1932, see C. C. Martindale, *The Words of the Missal* (Os Justi Press, 2023).

To have the light and warmth of contemplation, you first need the fire of prayer; to fuel prayer, you need the wood of meditation; and to have meditation, there has to be *reading*. Reading presupposes something fixed and stable to be read, internalized, remembered, pondered. Any improvisation at this level, or any overwhelming quantity of text or a constantly changing text, will tend to thwart the slow and steady building of memory, the shaping of the imagination, and the fertilizing of the intellect. If you throw too much wood on the fire, you put it out. If the wood is green, the fire smokes. And if there is no kindling and no match, the fire can't be started. *All* of these things have to be in place: the right ingredients in the right order, with the right proportions and the right timing. More than fifteen hundred years of slow and highly conservative liturgical development produced the right content, the right order, the right proportions, and the right timing.³ Because the new liturgy has vastly more text and the way things play out is subject to the choices of celebrant and musicians, the content and proportion of parts is quite malleable and liable to enormous imbalance, and the pacing or feel of the liturgy is not invariable and focused.

This, then, is the fundamental problem with *praying* the new liturgy: it is too pluriform, too gigantic, and too mutable to sustain a meditative engagement or *lectio divina* with its texts, music, and gestures. One cannot simply surrender to it and take on its own identity, since the wills and intellects of various secondary agents are too much in play, making its identity like the chameleon's color. One might well ask the question: "Will the real Novus Ordo please stand up?"⁴ It would be hard to deny that there are correlations between the character of the revised liturgical books, the customary crowd-oriented *ars celebrandi*, the lack of ascetical-mystical life among so large a part of the clergy, and the shallowness, if not heterodoxy, of preaching. All these things reinforce one another; there is little to oppose them from within *the form of the liturgy* itself.

In the traditional liturgy, the daily stability of the Mass and its relatively limited selection of readings, together with the recurrence of the psalms in the weekly cursus of the Divine Office, strongly supports a liturgical *lectio divina* that is decisive in deepening the spiritual life of clergy and laity. In particular, one profits from the powerful correlation of the antiphons and readings of the Office with those of the

---

3 This is not to say that there is only *one* ideal combination of content, order, proportions, and timing for the entire Church; each of the traditional liturgical rites of East and West has developed its own combination that reflects its own "genius." The point is that a successful recipe requires a proper balance among all these factors, which is noticeably absent from the Novus Ordo.
4 See chapter 4.

Mass. I speak here from personal experience. Although I had already begun to attend the *usus antiquior* Mass at Thomas Aquinas College, I came to know it well when, at the International Theological Institute in Austria, I was able to attend a daily 6:00 a.m. Low Mass over a period of several years. Going through that cycle day by day profoundly formed me and won me over to the old prayers and calendar. I believe it would win over any serious Catholic who was given the grace of such consistent exposure. Later on, as I began to pray the old Divine Office, the numerous connections between the Mass and the breviary were a cause of continual delight and strengthened my life of prayer.

Moreover, the overwhelming fixity of traditional liturgical forms makes the times when there *are* differences in the prescribed liturgy so much more striking. The omission of Psalm 42 and the doxologies during Passiontide makes us feel we are being stripped and humiliated with Christ. The *dona eis requiem* of the Agnus Dei at the Mass for the Dead reminds us (as do so many other details of the Requiem Mass) that we are offering up our prayers primarily for the repose of the souls of the faithful departed.[5] One thinks of those times in the year when a genuflection is stipulated for a certain verse of Scripture that *cries out* for the total response of the believer, in body and soul (I am speaking here of passages *other* than the final verses of Prologue of John at which we genuflect in nearly every Mass). On Epiphany and during its octave, when the priest reads or chants the Gospel of the Magi falling down and worshiping the Christ-child, the priest and everyone along with him bends the knee in silent adoration. In Lenten Masses, the priest kneels at the Tract *Adiuva nos*; on Palm Sunday, the Finding of the Holy Cross, and the Exaltation of the Holy Cross, at the Epistle (*ut in nomine Jesu omne genu flectatur*); and on a number of other occasions, such as the third Mass of Christmas, when the Prologue of John is read; at the end of the Gospel for Wednesday of the Fourth Week of Lent (Jn 9:1–38); during the Alleluia before the *Veni, Sancte Spiritus* Sequence; and at votive Masses of the Holy Spirit, the Passion of the Lord, and Deliverance from Mortality.

Discrepant moments like these, in an otherwise monolithic and highly determined pattern of prayer, have a definite psychological effect: it is like a great composer who knows how to use a touch of

---

[5] This, in contrast to postconciliar funerals and Masses for the dead, which are almost entirely focused on the living who are present, due to the assumption (often stated explicitly) that the deceased is already rejoicing with all his friends and relatives in heaven and thus requires no prayers. In a severe manner, the traditional Requiem Mass orders the entire service to the benefit of the deceased soul, which is no doubt why it was particularly loathed by reformers both of the sixteenth century and of the twentieth. See Phillip Campbell, "Two Deaths and Two Masses: The Healing Power of the Requiem," *Unam Sanctam Catholicam*, September 13, 2024.

sharp dissonance that makes the prevailing consonance all the more powerful, or a great painter who adds a touch of bright red to an otherwise subdued canvas. The old liturgy has a masterful grasp of how human psychology works. We must have things *mostly* the same in order to pray well; yet we must have occasional differences to keep us from becoming rote and robotic. The old rite's blend of the same and the different is exquisitely balanced.

The rationalistic instinct that multiplied the new rite's quantity of texts also abolished almost all the unique features and differentiations found in the old rite: there was a simultaneous *flattening* of rites into uniformity and an uncontrolled *expansion* of material in the lectionary and missal. Sadly, we can note that both the uniformity and the expansion are characteristic of industrial methods of mass production. Indeed, the word "mass" in contemporary English has two meanings: the density of matter and a widespread group of similarly-minded individuals. The modern Mass exhibits excess of material as well as a democratic leveling of differences within that material. This phenomenon can be seen in the multi-year lectionary, which, although many times larger than the traditional one-year lectionary, nevertheless contains less of the total breadth of Scripture's actual message because of its studied avoidance of passages that could "offend" modern readers or be "misunderstood" by them.[6]

THE PROVIDENTIAL PATH FROM EXTEMPORANEITY TO FIXITY

Catholics who worship with the Church's traditional rites see the fixity, stability, and relative compactness of sacred formulas as supremely fitting to the nature of the liturgy and as helpful for the laity's fruitful participation. At work here is an ironclad law. In the words of Belgian philosopher Marcel De Corte, writing in 1977:

> Because the soul of each member of the faithful is oriented towards God, the unchanging [traditional] Mass realizes the union in God of all those who take part. Each goes according to his or her personal disposition, and according to the grace of God that sustains them. Some unite themselves to God in this or that part of the Mass, this or that phrase, this or that formula; others do so in others. Even those who are present only in body take part in the Mass to a degree that is not nil. The Tridentine Mass is the only one that is truly "personal *and* communal."
>
> For the Mass to be attended and participated in with such analogical degrees, it must always remain the same in its meaning and signs. Any change introduced disrupts the accustomed

---

[6] See my article "A Tale of Two Lectionaries: Quality versus Quantity," *NLM*, January 16, 2017.

momentum of the soul as it rises to God above the vicissitudes of this world. Any change breaks the cohesion of the faithful. The mere fact of having allowed different Eucharistic Prayers can only disperse attention, diminish it, extinguish it. Because it's always the same, the Tridentine Mass creates habits (in Latin, *habitus*) — stable qualities that perfect the faithful's faculties, their being and their actions. Regularly repeated physical exercise strengthens the limbs. Regularly repeated religious practice brings the action of the supernatural ever more deeply into the soul. God does not despise this psychological law, which He Himself created, and which the most rudimentary experience of human life reveals to the most untrained eye. In order to live, and above all to access the spiritual life, man urgently needs all those earthly substitutes for eternity: identity, permanence, repetition, refrains, accumulation of synonymous expressions, etc.[7]

At this point, conventional liturgical scholarship will object: "Liturgy in the earliest centuries of the church was extemporaneous, improvised, full of variety. Only later on did it ossify, petrify, and fossilize into medieval and Baroque forms." (They love to use verbs like that, which express their utter disdain for things that don't change over the centuries: they are "ossified, petrified, fossilized.") But are the liturgists correct? Not really. Let's consider how and why the Church moved from liturgy-in-a-state-of-flux to fixed and stable liturgy.

For starters, in their gatherings for worship, ancient Christians do not seem to have practiced "casual" or "informal" prayer in the way in which the relaxed Christians of today practice it. All the records we have indicate *set prayer forms* not only among the Jews whose Scriptures are full of formulaic prayers but also among the earliest Christians, several of whose hymns are preserved in the New Testament and in Patristic literature.[8] Gregory Dix, Adrian Fortescue, Paul Bradshaw, and other scholars note that the prayers of the Christians, offered up by their leaders in a spontaneous but tradition-informed manner, acquired consistent formulaic patterns over time and settled into repeatable rites and ceremonies.

---

[7] Marcel De Corte, "Sur les variations du clergé catholique," *Itinéraires* 210 (February 1977): 92–104; translation mine.

[8] This is not to say that every passage in the NT that is *styled* a hymn by scholars was, in fact, utilized as a hymn; many false claims have been made in this regard. See Matthew Hazell, "'Expert Consensus' in the Post-Vatican II Liturgical Reforms: More Half-Truths and Dated Scholarship," *NLM*, August 24, 2024. The difference between the supposed "Christ hymns" in Colossians and Philippians and the "hymns" in the book of Revelation is that we are specifically told some of the texts in Revelation are sung by the angels and/or saints (5:9ff.; 15:3ff.). There is thus a hymnic quality to them, regardless of how well they fit into the genre of hymn. Further, although one can question whether texts like the *Magnificat* were originally composed as hymns, there is very clear evidence that they were quickly taken up as such by the early Christians.

After a few centuries of ever-solidifying praxis, improvisation ceased to be a feature of the liturgy—and this, for obvious reasons. Christianity is a religion with deeply conservative instincts: we are holding on to what has been given to us once for all in the revelation of Jesus Christ, the *depositum fidei*.[9] From the very beginning, St. Paul exhorts the Thessalonians, and by extension all Christians, to "stand firm and hold to the traditions" that he and others taught them (2 Thess 2:15)—which undoubtedly included liturgical traditions. A devout bishop who celebrated the Eucharist would arrive at satisfactory ways of speaking to which the people became habituated,[10] and his successor, drawn from the local clergy, would naturally wish to follow in his footsteps and model his own liturgical prayer after that of his father in Christ. As Michael Davies observes, when a community had a holy bishop who was accustomed to praying in certain ways, his successor would have every reason to imitate him, and the people every right to expect that continuity. Otherwise, how would the ancient sacramentaries—manuscripts full of carefully formulated orations—have ever developed to begin with?

The eloquent and polished prayers we find in the oldest extant liturgical books did not suddenly drop down from heaven; they are the faithful reflection of the actual practice of Catholic communities gathered around their God-fearing bishops. In this way it was normal, one could say inevitable, that fixed anaphoras, readings, Collects, antiphons, etc., would develop and stabilize over time. Thus, it should come as no surprise to find, no later than the seventh century and possibly as early as the fifth, a complete cycle of Propers for the Roman rite. Gennadius of Massilia (fifth century) says of St. Paulinus of Nola,

---

[9] Indeed, this is what the Son of God Himself did, to set us an example: "Our Lord Jesus Christ was accustomed to this kind of [ritual] worship—indeed, when he joined his parents and fellow Jews in weekly worship, he entered into the ritual. No one had ever heard of spontaneous public worship. The early Church, in great wisdom, realized that this is a principle that goes to the root of the mystery of our being. Spontaneity is a good and precious thing. The Lord loves any lisping, stammering, broken, and halting words we can offer to him, as he loves the buzzing of bumblebees and the braying of donkeys. But when we come together for the particular act of offering our corporate, regular, recurring adoration of him, then we need a form.... The worship of the ancient Church is far from being a matter of endless tinkering, experimenting, and innovating. The entire mystery of revelation and redemption is unfurled for us in the Church's liturgy. That liturgy is here in all of its plenitude, majesty, and magnificence, judging us" (Howard, *The Night Is Far Spent*, 255, 266).

[10] Funnily enough, we see this even today among well-practiced Protestant preachers when they are offering public prayers, for which they have developed their own vocabulary and formulas. The result is not random but carefully channeled, even predictable. Thomas Howard frequently comments on this phenomenon, which he considers a natural testimony to the human need for rituality: see *The Night Is Far Spent*, 175–83, 227–28, 254–55. I have encountered the same thing in the Catholic Church. For example, in a certain diocese, almost every "spontaneous" prayer I ever heard began: "Good and gracious God..." I don't know who introduced this alliterative and rhythmic phrase, but it reproduces successfully in the wild.

fecit et sacramentarium et hymnarium, he made both a sacramentary and a hymnal (*De viris illustribus*, XLVIII). There is an account in St. Gregory of Tours of a bishop who, from repetition, had everything memorized, and when on one occasion the altar book was missing (it had been maliciously stolen), he was able to do his part from memory.

In short, improvisation has not been a characteristic of the liturgy for 1,500 years or more. The evidence we have points to the relatively rapid development of fixed forms. The early Church was in a divinely-willed state of formation, and had wider and freer powers precisely because she was in an embryonic condition, growing rapidly and establishing her institutions under the guidance of the Holy Spirit.[11] The same Spirit guides her gently and gradually into set forms, which are the fairest flowers of those early developments. He prunes what is less worthy and nourishes what is more worthy. We should therefore expect, as time goes on, that the liturgy will become more and more solid, definite, fixed, and perfected. It will be handed down increasingly as a *family inheritance*, an approved profession of the Church's one faith. It is absurd to think that the Holy Spirit did not intend this consolidation of formulas as a positive good, or that the Church erred in remaining a jealous guardian of the spelled-out content of inherited liturgical books. It would be no less ridiculous to assert that the same Spirit, after having willed such a state of affairs for 1,500 years, would suddenly will its dissolution, dilution, or replacement. So much for improvisation—or optionitis, which might be called a soft version of improvisation.

The development of liturgy parallels the development of dogmatic determinations in the early councils, with their ever more precise creeds that cut off all heretical depravity. Just as we do not have the "freedom" to go back to the looseness and ambiguity of the early centuries, although modernists seem to wish they could do so, we do not have the freedom to toss out matured prayer and replace it with our own "on-the-spot fabrications." Catholics who live later on in history enjoy the immense blessing and privilege of carrying *more* refined and *more* precise formulas on their lips. Those who live after an Ecumenical Council (except for the last one) are at a decisive advantage compared with those who lived before it, since they can now profess their faith in the Lord and confess His holy Name using a more perfect expression of the truth, and with less danger of lapsing into error about the highest, best, and most difficult things. Those who live after 1570

---

[11] One may consider what Charles Cardinal Journet said about the difference between the apostolic period and the succeeding ages (*The Theology of the Church*, trans. Victor Szczurek [Ignatius Press, 2004], 116–22, 156–57) and apply it analogously to the early age of worship in contrast with later ages of worship. See also "Formulating laws of organic development" in Kwasniewski, *Once and Future Roman Rite*, 51–61.

enjoy the blessing and privilege of worshiping in a received rite that has been solemnly acknowledged as a veritable ark or bastion of the Catholic faith.

The development of the liturgy in this respect is much like the development of languages. Yes, a language such as French or German or English is ever developing, but it is much more *the same* than *different* from decade to decade and even, as time goes on, century to century. English as we write it today is much the same as that which was written 300 years ago; any literate person can pick up Samuel Johnson and read him without much difficulty (perhaps looking up a word here or there).

Yet a notable difference obtains between vernacular languages and "hieratic" languages — those that, having attained a certain richness or fullness of development, were then taken up into religious practice as tongues dedicated to the invocation and evocation of the sacred. The hieratic languages — e.g., Hebrew, ancient Greek, ecclesiastical Latin, Church Slavonic — are, as regards their use in divine worship, unchanging and unchangeable. They do not *need* to develop any more, since they are perfect at expressing what their respective liturgies need them to express. Only if, *per impossibile*, revelation itself were to change would the long-received and unanimously accepted language conveying it need to change. A hieratic language becomes an external sign of the internal stability, consistency, and timelessness of the religious truths conveyed through it. It does not deviate to the left or to the right in its unerring delivery of the message. Its linguistic completeness not only participates in divine attributes but helps bring about our participation in these attributes. In this way, a sacred language has a *sacramental function*.[12]

A vernacular language, on the other hand, is intended to be the medium of daily discourse, the supple tool of life in the world, which is rife with change. The vernacular will never be done changing, reflecting the hustle and bustle of the people who use it — which is exactly how the Novus Ordo was intended to fluctuate according to some of its

---

[12] As Fr. Matthew McCarthy, FSSP, once preached: "Only because of piety can there be a tradition, stability from generation to generation, like the same piece of land passed on as an inheritance. St. Paul writes: 'I preached to you the gospel, which you received, in which you stand, by which you are saved, if you hold it fast... for I delivered to you as of first importance what I also received' (1 Cor 15:1–3). The meek and pious transcend the present moment. Formed by venerable tradition, they reap the wisdom of the ancients and begin to participate in the eternal wisdom, in the eternal stability — in the very eternity — of God. In contrast, putting aside the wisdom of the ages, the impious live by their own myopic insights. Drawn this way and that by *rerum novarum cupidine* — the lust for novelty — imprisoned by the spirit of the age, they are condemned to instability. Neither they nor their followers will ever achieve rest." Text shared with author.

leading architects, as we saw in chapter 5. It is to escape this mutability and instability that the religious instincts of *all* peoples have enshrined their highest forms of worship and doctrine in hieratic or classical languages. The vernacular is for this world of change, of Heraclitean flux; the hieratic is for the eternal world that always abides, like Parmenidean Being, penetrating in the form of dogma and doxology through the shifting veils of this world.

Although some Eastern Christian liturgies are celebrated in the vernacular, the spirit of these rites is extremely conservative. The Eastern priest might add a personal intention during the litanies, but the fixed prayers are exactly that: fixed, finalized, admitting of no improvement. It would be a species of arrogance to tamper with inherited prayers attributed to great saints like St. John Chrysostom, St. Basil, St. Gregory, St. James, St. Romanus the Melodist. That, too, was the attitude of the Latin Church towards the pillars of the liturgy: the antiphons, the readings, the Offertory, the Canon, the calendar, the use of certain psalms at certain times of the day or in certain seasons. We might have augmented, extrapolated, enhanced, ornamented, even occasionally pruned the dense growth, but in no sense did we throw off what earlier generations held to be sacred and great.

The limits of translations into the vernacular are evident when we consider the more than ten-year-long saga over the 2011 English translation of the modern "Roman Missal." After so much ink spilled, so many versions and revisions haggled over, such bitter partisan polemics, so much anticipation and emotion, uncomfortable facts remain: this new translation is very uneven, in some places theologically problematic;[13] above all, it is still a translation of texts that are objectively flawed and represent discontinuity, as Lauren Pristas and Fr. Cekada have amply demonstrated. So much fuss—for an inherently flawed missal. At present, years of effort are being poured into retranslating the Liturgy of the Hours, when this is even more of an irremediable disaster than the missal (and that's saying something).

Consider, on the other hand, the situation in any parish or chapel that celebrates the old rite. The prayers are the classic prayers that have piously addressed the Lord and formed faithful sons of the Church for

---

[13] For many examples of mistranslations, including a few that contain outright theological error, see Ansgar Chupungco, *The Prayers of the New Missal* (Liturgical Press, 2013). A summary is given by Michael Joncas, "An Issue for Future Liturgical Translation (I): Correcting Already-Approved Mistranslations," *Pray Tell*, October 16, 2017. It goes without saying that many things to which progressive "liturgical experts" object in the 2011 ICEL translation are, in fact, improvements both on what preceded it (1973) and on what was going to be (1998)! In that sense, my citing of Chupungco and Joncas is in support not of better translations, but of abandoning the Sisyphean project of vernacularity.

centuries. And the people in the pews have hand missals with noble, traditional translations of the prayers. Sometimes these translations aren't fully accurate, either—but it doesn't matter as much, because the worship being offered to God is not the translation, it is the altogether reliable Latin in the missal. When we use the Church's mother tongue and follow her time-honored tradition, we find peace, security, stability: no decades-long battles about what register of language to use, no disappointments about opportunities lost. The old rite abides far beyond all that nonsense; it is serious about worshiping God, and it does so without fuss, without cutting corners, without compromises. Once again, the future of the Roman rite is the Roman rite in its slowly developed perfection, not the version that resulted from some weird experimental editorial hack-job intended for that most unstable of targets known as "Modern Man."

"Thou shalt hide them in the secret of thy face, from the disturbance of men. Thou shalt protect them in thy tabernacle from the contradiction of tongues" (Ps 30:21), or, as another translation has it, "In the covert of your presence you will hide them from the plottings of man. You will keep them secretly in a pavilion from the strife of tongues" (Ps 31:20 ASV). Yes: we are weary of the plottings of liturgists and the strife of vernacular tongues; we seek the secret pavilion of tradition, the covert of God's holy presence. There we dwell in His ineffable peace, in the fear of His greatness and the love of His glory.

THE DIFFERENCE BETWEEN US AND THE FIRST CHRISTIANS

Hence, the essential response to the objection "Wasn't liturgy in the earliest centuries of the church extemporaneous and improvised?" is at once simple and profound: *we are not in the same position as the early Christians.* They had the first contact with Christ's life, death, and resurrection; they had the guidance of the Apostles and the Apostles' immediate successors; they had to develop for themselves a liturgy out of Jewish precedents and apostolic oral tradition. It was a unique situation. The need to design or write a liturgy is, in fact, a sign of *im*perfection, because it belongs to a phase of institutional immaturity. On the other hand, because of how central the liturgy is and will be for all future generations until the end of time, the writing of liturgy requires a special charism of the Holy Spirit—a profound spiritual maturity, discernment, and inspiration on the part of anyone who would dare to write liturgical texts or chants.[14] According to St. John Henry Newman, it follows that liturgical rites already elaborated possess an inherent sanctity and nobility that will not and cannot be surpassed

---

[14] See Fiedrowicz, *The Traditional Mass*, 181–82.

by later generations.¹⁵ Since, as time went on, such rites became more stable, refined, explicit, and expressive of their sacred content, Christians received them accordingly with reverence, as gifts handed down from their forebears. This process of development—which is at the same time a process of explicitation and solidification—must be held to be a work of the Holy Spirit, as Pope Pius XII reminded the Church in his encyclical *Mediator Dei* of 1947.¹⁶

After 1,500 or 2,000 years have passed, the situation *is not and could never be the same* as it was for the early Christians in the decades and centuries immediately after Christ. The reformers' argument from antiquity is invalid from the word "go." Nor has this argument the wherewithal to be taken seriously. Henry Sire demonstrates in *Phoenix from the Ashes* that the twentieth-century reformers invoked antiquity as an excuse for their modernist agenda, since as a matter of fact (1) they did not restore much that was ancient; (2) they abolished many things that were known to be ancient; (3) and they invented much that was utterly novel. How such people, whose motley work is clear for all to see, can expect us to credit their affected motives is quite beyond me.

The main argument of the postconciliar reformers, expressed in countless pamphlets and publications, boils down to this: "We are now celebrating the Mass as the early Christians did, and dropping away all the 'accretions' that accumulated like soot over time and obscured the original purity of worship." But there are devastating flaws in this argument.

First, we have exceedingly few details about what the early Christians did, so most arguments are based on imaginative reconstructions, in the way that a scrap of ancient pottery might be extrapolated into a full vase or a tooth found in Africa into a hypothetical prehistoric human. Evidence from cultural anthropology suggests that early Christian worship, so far from being a simple, homey affair, was probably quite elaborate—as elaborate as it could be, given the restrictions imposed by persecution. An unanswerable proof is the fact that the moment Christianity became legal in the early fourth century, its churches and liturgy rapidly blossomed into grand architecture and ceremonial. This would only have happened if there had been a pent-up dynamism in that direction all along.

---

¹⁵ See quotation on p. 44; for more such passages, see *Newman on Worship, Reverence, and Ritual*, ed. Kwasniewski, 1–6, 69–80, 95–96.

¹⁶ Pius XII insists that even liturgical rites that developed as late as the medieval and Baroque eras "owe their inspiration to the Holy Spirit, who assists the Church in every age even to the consummation of the world (cf. Mt 28:20)" (*Mediator Dei*, no. 61). Consequently, to question the inherited forms in the radical way they were questioned in the 1960s was a kind of sin against the Holy Spirit; see Kwasniewski, *Once and Future Roman Rite*, 61–72.

Second, many arguments based on antiquity have subsequently been proven false, such as the claim that St. Peter's Basilica was built with the sanctuary at the western side and the priest standing behind the altar facing the nave so that celebration "toward the people" could be carried out, which was then taken as ancient precedent for "restoring" the *versus populum* stance at Mass. Yet the shrine was built in this exceptional manner due to unavoidable geographical constraints, and the priest faced as he did precisely in order to be *ad orientem*. The disposition of the people was not a consideration. The work of Stefan Heid in this regard has been decisive: he has demonstrated that eastward orientation was taken as a given by the early Christians, who would have been quite surprised to hear about any other practice.[17]

In conclusion, Pius XII taught in *Mediator Dei* that we must believe that the Church is guided by the Holy Spirit throughout the ages and that the developments that occur are part of God's plan. The liturgical developments of the Middle Ages and the Counter-Reformation period are — if not in every last detail, yet at least in the main — providential. To cast them away in favor of a questionably reconstructed "primitive church model" is not only to exalt mere hypotheticals over real facts, it is an assertion that the Holy Spirit guides the Church *less and less as time goes on*, and that we must strip away what each age has added in order to return to the purity of our origins. This is Protestantism; this is liberal "higher criticism"; this is modernism. All of it was rightly condemned by the Church, once and for all.[18]

HOW "FORMS" DEFINE RELIGIOUS BELIEF — OR UNDERMINE IT

Let's take a small concrete example of a liturgical custom that developed for good reason and endured for centuries before being unceremoniously discarded by the revolutionaries. For a thousand years, priests offering Mass in the Roman rite observed canonical digits, the rule that they should hold their thumb and forefinger together from the time of the consecration until the ablutions (a rule still observed, of course, wherever the traditional Latin Mass is celebrated). This custom reflects the Church's faith in the Real Presence. After the consecration, Our Lord is really, truly, substantially present wherever the outward appearances of bread and wine are present, which means: *every last particle of the host*. For this reason, the priest should not casually handle other things after touching the host, but keep those two fingers together (except, of course, when handling a consecrated

---

17 See Heid, *Altar and Church*; cf. Lang, *Turning Towards the Lord*.
18 See my article "The Acorn and the Oak Tree: In Defense of Liturgical Growth and Maturation," *Tradition and Sanity* Substack, January 23, 2025.

host) until he is able to wash them in the ablutions. In this way, the priest is continually reminded of the awesome mystery he is handling with his fingers—and so are the laity.

As a layman, it bothered me that this longstanding and sensible custom had disappeared in the new rite, so I decided to pose a number of questions to a sizeable group of priests who celebrate the *usus antiquior*, primarily to learn the importance they themselves attach to the custom. The results were published at *New Liturgical Movement* in five installments, with a concluding reflection.[19] One priest responded to the series with the following account:

> At the Mass in which I was ordained a deacon, the Eucharist was "served" from a glass dish of sorts.... I purified it with great care after Holy Communion; it required a rather noticeable period of time to do so, which was obviously more than local clergy and people were used to. After that Mass both the vocation director and the ordaining bishop "corrected" me on this matter, with the bishop reminding me that the purification was only a "ritual purification" and that such care was not needed in carrying it out, since a sacristan would wash everything after. (A totally incoherent position.)
>
> This was my introduction—and a rather painful one, at that—to the practical lack of faith on the part of the clergy in the Real Presence, which I have witnessed and experienced many times in the eleven years since then. I say "practical," because few would deny the Real Presence [in theory] and most would even defend it quite eloquently. *But the way they actually handle the Eucharist betrays their lack of understanding and/or belief.* This is particularly the case with how they handle the Precious Blood, the purificator, etc.
>
> Therefore, when I began to study the *usus antiquior* and learned about the detailed and systematic process of purification, which really leaves little room for error, and of the practicalities such as holding the consecrating digits together until purification, my faith was confirmed. And, although knowledge of the Church's historic practice served, perhaps, to heighten my awareness of just how bad things generally can be now, and thus heightened my sense of pain, yet at the same time, it was a consolation to know that I was on the right track.

This author has put his finger (if I may say so) on the nub of the problem. The Catholic faith is not something purely abstract that we learn and assent to as an intellectual exercise. We learn our faith and discern its meaning *through practice*, through what we do with or to the words, things, and persons that embody this faith. How we speak to, or about, Our Lord; how we handle the sacramental signs and, above all, His all-holy and life-giving Body and precious Blood; how we treat

---

[19] See my article "'The Fingers that Hold God.'"

our priests, and how they treat their people: *this* is where we will find out, experientially, day after day, whether or not the Catholic religion is believed and lived, or if a rival system of belief may have supplanted it.

In how we practice, we teach ourselves; by our example, we teach those around us, especially children. This is where modern liturgy has grievously failed, in numerous ways and as a matter of practice, through its repudiation of the meaning of vital forms of expression—forms that convey the essence and purpose of the Mass. What is at stake in the escalating tensions between divergent liturgical "sensibilities" is not just mere "form" (as if we were talking about matters of taste or fine art), but rather, the meaning inherent in form and expressed by it—that is to say, *truth*. And not truth alone, but justice, since, by the virtue of religion, we are required to give to God and the things of God that which they rightly demand and which we owe as His creatures and dependents.

The reverent forms and practices of the traditional liturgy point to and express vital truths about the Holy Sacrifice of the Mass; the numerous casual practices that permeate Novus Ordo liturgies are not coherent with the meaning and purpose of the same. Some Novus Ordo proponents criticize those who adhere to the traditional liturgy as people fixated on form; in reality, it is impossible *not* to care about form, since there is no truth accessible to us humans without the clothing of form. Every liturgy comes to us as a concrete set of meaning-bearing forms, and the meaning borne will be either full, rich, accurate, and nourishing of orthodoxy, or banal, impoverished, ambiguous, and inadequate to our needs. In this sense, *everyone* is fixated on form because human language and spiritual activity are formal things, through and through. The primacy of form, and the corresponding duty and priority of getting it right, are inescapable; there is no "essential thing," independent of form, that is "enough" for us. No doubt, truth is known by the divine intellect apart from any created form; but men know the truth as *expressed* in a definite way, under sensible and intelligible signs.[20] Some signs are well suited to the truth they signify, and others are not. For example, solemnity is compatible with, indeed required by, the notion of the sacred, while casualness and spontaneity are not.

Martin Mosebach's book *The Heresy of Formlessness* illuminates the folly (and ugliness) of imposing on ourselves the modern faith in an abstract society in an abstract world with abstractions reigning globally and governing relationships individually, as opposed to the real

---

[20] See "The splendor of the truth" in Kwasniewski, *Once and Future Roman Rite*, 24–27.

spiritual vitality that can be found in things—*real* things with a place and a history—that resonate in the spiritual realm.[21] This sensitivity to material reality is something our society has lost—not only the idea that there *is* a spiritual reality encompassing the material world, but also that we touch the spiritual through what we do with matter, or, in other words, that the forms of things and what we do with them matter in the life of the spirit. One sees the same Cartesian contempt for the flesh in the liturgical reform, which stripped bare the inherited treasury of forms in order to present as purely verbal and conceptual a worship as is still consonant with public human activity.[22]

Modernity fears the Catholic religion because Catholicism reminds it—reminds *us*—that reality includes the supernatural, that which encompasses and penetrates the natural with mysterious powers that reason can approach, but only through faith and analogy. This approach requires a surrender to the divine and an acceptance of tradition that modern epistemology in its egocentric rationalism and promethean voluntarism cannot tolerate. Like liberalism, a halfway house between Catholicism and atheism in Newman's analysis, the Novus Ordo is a halfway house between a time-embracing, time-transcending Tradition and a Modernity trapped in its own death spiral.

HUMILITY OF SERVICE IN FIXITY OF FORM[23]

According to St. Benedict in chapter 5 of his *Holy Rule*, the root of humility is that a man must live not by his own desires and passions but by the judgment and bidding of another: *ambulantes alieno judicio et imperio*. When St. Benedict sets about ordering the monastic liturgy, he doesn't speak like a man who is making things up as he goes along, or setting up a committee to produce the order of worship. Rather, he continually looks to how things are already being done elsewhere. He carefully enumerates the psalms as prayed by the monastic fathers before him; he mentions the Ambrosian hymn and the canticles used by the Church in Rome. Even when fashioning his monastic cycle of prayer, he is constantly looking to existing models. In like manner, chapter 7 warns us against "doing our own will," lest we become corrupt and abominable. This is the true spirit of liturgical conservatism, piety toward elders, and the imitation of Christ. We are not the ones who determine the shape of our worship; we receive it in humility as an "alien judgment" that we make our own. To do otherwise is to put the axe to the tree

---

[21] Dietrich von Hildebrand expounded similar insights in his magnificent work *Liturgy and Personality*.
[22] See Morello, *Mysticism, Magic, and Monasteries*, 13–39.
[23] This section was adapted from Kwasniewski, *Turned Around*, 91–93, 99–102, 104–5; there the points are developed further.

of humility.²⁴ Liturgical prayer has always been the foremost way of inculcating submission to Christ and His Church, so that we can learn *His* ways, and assimilate *His* prayer, and drink of *His* wisdom—which will certainly not be something we ourselves could have "cooked up" on our own. Thus, we take *His* yoke upon us... the yoke of tradition.

Prior to the middle of the twentieth century, it was uncontroversial in Catholic circles to believe that the sacred liturgy's being fixed, constant, and stable is a special *perfection*, enabling it to serve as an immovable rock on which to build one's spiritual life. The liturgy's numerous and exacting rubrics were understood as guiding the celebrant along a prayerful path of submissive obedience, in which he could submerge his personality into the Person of Christ and merge his individual voice with the chorus of the Church at prayer. The formal, hieratic gestures transmitted an eternally fresh symbolism while limiting (if not eliminating) the danger of subjectivism and emotionalism. The priest or other minister was conformed to Christ the servant, who came not to do His own will but the will of Him who sent Him. He is commanded what to speak and what to do; he never speaks of himself.²⁵

Even as the Son was "emptied of glory" in taking on the form of a slave, so, too, is the priest who enters His *kenosis*, sharing the hiddenness, humiliation, passion, and death of Christ. Our Lord, the great High Priest of the New Covenant, said: "I cannot do anything of myself" (Jn 5:30). Here we have perhaps the most radical justification of the priest's being tethered to the liturgy by unchanging texts and comprehensive rubrics. It is a tethering so complete that he may truthfully say: "I *cannot* do otherwise." If he thinks or acts otherwise, he has not yet become a slave, in imitation of the One who assumed the likeness of a slave. Worse, if he is *encouraged* to do otherwise by a liturgical book, that book is a smudged and fractured mirror that does not reflect the Word.

This is why we ought to find disturbing one of the major novelties of the postconciliar liturgical books, namely, that the celebrant is given many options among which he may choose as he wishes, as well as opportunities for crafting his own speech: "in these or similar words."²⁶ Confronted with such a phrase, one might legitimately ask:

---

24 St. Benedict allows for a redistribution of the psalms, *as long as* monks rigorously hold to the principle of praying the full psalter in one week. It would not conflict with humility for a monastic community to make *some* adjustments to the cycle of psalms, yet it would smack of temerity to reject the most ancient and stable pillars of the office, such as praying the whole psalter each week and using Psalms 109–112 for Sunday Vespers and Psalms 66, 50, 117, 62, and 148–150 for Sunday Lauds.
25 See John 5:30, 8:28, 12:49–50, 14:10, etc.
26 See Paul Turner, *In These or Similar Words: Praying and Crafting the Language of the Liturgy* (World Library Publications, 2014). A synopsis may be found at http://paulturner.org/wp-content/uploads/2015/01/ml-in-these-or-similar-words.pdf. As to

"How similar is similar?" In reality, the word of the liturgy and the word of the minister ought to be *homoousios*, of one and the same substance, not *homoiousios*, of a similar substance. In the action of selecting options and extemporizing texts, the celebrant no longer perfectly reflects the Word of God who, as the perfect Image of the Father, receives His words and does not originate them, who does the will of another and not His own will. The elective and extemporizing celebrant does not show forth the fundamental identity of the Christian: one who receives and bears fruit, like the Blessed Virgin Mary; one who conceives with no help of man, by the descent of the Spirit alone.[27] Instead, he adopts the posture of one who originates; he removes this sphere of action from the master to whom he reports; he carves out for himself a zone of autonomy; he denies the Lord the privilege of commanding him and deprives himself of the guerdon of submission. For a moment, he leaves the narrow way of being a tool and steps on to the broad way of being somebody. He becomes not only an actor but a playwright; his *free choice* as an individual is exalted into a principle of liturgy. He joins the madding crowd that says, in the words of the Psalmist: *linguam nostram magnificabimus, labia nostra a nobis sunt; quis noster dominus est?* "We will magnify our tongue; our lips are our own; who is Lord over us?" (Ps 11:5).

But since free choice is antithetical to liturgy as a fixed ritual received from our ancestors and handed down to our descendants, choice tends rather to be a principle of distraction, dilution, or dissolution in the liturgy than of its well-being. The same critique may be given of all of the ways in which the new liturgy permits the celebrant an indeterminate freedom of speech, bodily bearing, and movement. Such voluntarism strikes at the very essence of liturgy, which is a public, objective, solemn, and common prayer, in which all Christians are equally participants, even when they are performing irreducibly distinct acts. The prayer of Christians belongs to everyone in common, which means it should belong to no one in particular. The moment a priest invents something that is not common, he sets himself up as a clerical overlord vis-à-vis the people, who must now submit not to a rule of Christ and the Church, but to the arbitrary rule of this individual.

In the liturgy *above all*, we must never speak "from ourselves," but only from Christ and His beloved Bride. The deepest cause of the missionary collapse of the Church in the Western world is that we have lost our institutional and personal subordination to Christ the High Priest, the principal actor in the liturgy, the Word to whom we

---

the very limited options available to the priest offering the old Mass, see note 31 on p. 41 and the next chapter.
[27] See Kwasniewski, *Noble Beauty*, 53–87.

lend our mouth, our hands, our bodies, our souls. For the past sixty years it has *not* been perfectly clear that we are ministers and servants *of another*, intelligent instruments wholly at His disposal. On the contrary, the opposite message has been transmitted over and over again, whether in words or in deeds: we have "come of age," *we* are shaping the world, the Church, the Mass, the entire Christian life, according to our own lights, and for our own purposes. It is not difficult to see that this is an inversion of the preaching of Christ and of the tradition of the Church. We see here an exact parallel to what has happened with marriage: when so-called "free love" entered into the picture, out went committed love and heroic sacrifice, and in came lust, selfishness, dissatisfaction, and an unspeakable plague of loneliness. "Without me, you can do nothing" (Jn 15:5). In the realm of sexual morality as in the realm of liturgical morality, we have been permitted to see what we can accomplish without Christ and without His gift of tradition — namely, nothing. This is why we must begin again humbly, like little children ready to memorize lessons taken from absolutely reliable sources.

OFFERING MASS FROM THE MISSAL OF THE HEART

As priests know better than anyone else, the smooth celebration of the *usus antiquior* requires the memorization of a significant number of prayers ahead of time, so that one need not be squinting at cards, or surrounded by servers with cheat-sheets, or embarrassed by long delays while one looks for the elusive page in the altar missal. These prayers include (depending on the design of the altar cards on which they typically appear):

- Psalm 42
- Confiteor
- absolution and short dialogue
- *Aufer a nobis* and *Oramus te*
- blessing of incense
- *Munda cor meum* and *Jube Domine*
- *Per evangelica dicta*
- *Orate fratres*
- *Supplices te rogamus*
- *Ecce Agnus Dei*
- formula for Communion
- *Benedicat vos*

This requirement of memorization, far from being a mere guarantee of efficiency, has its own profound value: it is one more way in which the ancient liturgy demands that the celebrant "put on the mind of Christ" — or better, enter into His Heart — by means of "knowing *by heart*" certain prayers of the Church that mold him into the image of their sentiments. Prayers run the risk of remaining external to the celebrant as long as they are merely written in the missal, because their location is an external book. Memorized prayers, on the other hand, are already internal(ized) and, as such, are available as a wellspring of piety within. The heart has become the book, the living book from which the Mass is celebrated.

In one of the many letters that J. R. R. Tolkien wrote to his son Christopher when the latter was in the Royal Air Force during World War II, we read:

> If you don't do so already, make a habit of the 'praises'. I use them much (in Latin): the Gloria Patri, the Gloria in Excelsis, the Laudate Dominum; the Laudate Pueri Dominum (of which I am specially fond), one of the Sunday psalms; and the Magnificat; also the Litany of Loretto (with the prayer Sub tuum præsidium). If you have these by heart you never need for words of joy. It is also a good and admirable thing to know by heart the Canon of the Mass, for you can say this in your heart if ever hard circumstances keep you from hearing Mass.... Less doth yearning trouble him who knoweth many songs, or with his hands can touch the harp: his possession is his gift of 'glee' which God gave him.[28]

In the famous book *He Leadeth Me*, Fr. Walter J. Ciszek, SJ, describes what he did to avoid going insane in his solitary confinement: "After breakfast, I would say Mass by heart—that is, I would say all the prayers, for of course I had no way actually to celebrate the Holy Sacrifice."[29] Elsewhere he recounts how he and his fellow missionaries had prepared themselves in a lumber camp in the Urals for the hardships to come: "Over and over again in the evenings, when others were chatting or reading or playing cards, we would repeat to each other the prayers of the Mass until we had learned them by heart."[30]

The culture to which J. R. R. Tolkien and Fr. Ciszek bear witness is a culture of sacred text, stability, repetition, memory, and inexhaustible meaning, even in the midst of the most barbaric conditions of war or imprisonment.

Fast forward to the optimistic post-War world of the 1960s, where sacred and secular are blurring together, stability is misidentified as fossilization, memory is written off as nostalgia, morals are loosening,

---

[28] Letter no. 54, dated January 8, 1944, in *The Letters of J. R. R. Tolkien*, revised and expanded edition, ed. Humphrey Carpenter and Christopher Tolkien (HarperCollins, 2023), 95. The last line is J. R. R.'s translation of Anglo-Saxon verses from the Exeter Book, which he had just quoted in their original form.
[29] Walter J. Ciszek, SJ, with Daniel Flaherty, SJ, *He Leadeth Me* (Ignatius Press, 1995), 54.
[30] Ciszek, 124.

and the givenness of tradition—in reality, a weight of glory—is felt as a chafing burden. With its programmatic variability, large number of texts, and paucity of obligatory prayers in the Mass ordinary, the missal of Paul VI strikes at the root of this age-old disciplining, stocking, and shaping of memory (and therefore of man's mind and heart) by fixed liturgical formulas. Its novel instruction to speak "these *or similar* words" interferes with the ritual subjugation of the individual ego to the common voice of the Church.[31] The fact that certain words are not fixed—not deemed worthy of being fixed and of being committed to memory forever—shows that the real appeal is to *imagination*, the power of constructing, rather than to memory, the power of conserving and contemplating.

When a priest knows and says the same thing at certain moments in the liturgy, he unites in this act with all the other worshipers who know (or can easily know) the same prayer. They are brought together even if the priest is praying silently and not facing them. Paradoxically, when a priest instead uses his imagination to say out loud a new formulation of words, this content from *his* mind is necessarily going to be different from what might be in *your* mind. Thus, when the priest "uses similar words," he becomes, by that very fact, *dissimilar* from you, and so, *over against you* in his distinctiveness, rather than together with you in a common discipleship to the given liturgy. Memory and fixed forms draw us together and make of us one body with a shared past and a shared future. Imagination and loose liturgical forms, on the other hand, assemble us temporarily into a *sui generis* body that links up with no past and no heritage, which intends no future and no permanence. It is like the difference between carving stone or wood, and drawing pictures in the sand; or better, like the difference between lifelong matrimony and a weekend fling.

Our identity comes from our "collective memory," the continually renewed remembrance of who and what we have been, and all the cultural forms that embody it. This remembrance is not primarily conceptual or intellectual but dwells in concrete, visible, audible, tangible expressions that serve as prompts for significant feelings and actions.

Jeremy Holmes describes how every civilization known to history develops a literary canon of some kind, made up of myths told in epic and lyric form, histories of heroes, law codes, sagacious adages, and the like. The artists of this culture see the all-pervasive presence

---

[31] Another indication of the Enlightenment pedigree of the Novus Ordo. "Rousseau also anticipated the contemporary hostility toward memorization. 'Emile,' he decreed, 'will never learn anything by heart'—thus reversing at a stroke an educational tradition that began with Plato's Academy, one that made possible the vast accumulation of knowledge in medieval society." Scruton, "Rousseau and the origins of liberalism."

of the canon not as a burdensome limitation to their creativity but as the necessary condition for their own fruitfulness, a perpetual source of inspiration and direction that channels and intensifies their powers. They so internalize the canon that it becomes less like an object external to them and more like their own eyes and hands, through which they see and feel the world. The canon equips them with tools that nature could not have supplied, a vast vocabulary surpassing what any individual could arrive at by himself.[32]

The traditional Roman liturgy was just such a literary canon for the clergy, for intellectuals and artists, for the pious folk who flocked to it and were shaped by it, century after century, father and son, mother and daughter. It was the internal linguistic form of the Western Church that gave her her very identity; it was the eyes and hands through which she saw and felt creation. The liturgy was the core of the Church's collective memory, since it was the one reality that concerned everyone, all the time, drawing the many parts into unity and imparting a definite character to the whole. All this happens when there is a stable sacred text of inexhaustible meaning that permeates the memory of man. It still happens wherever the authentic Latin liturgy lives on.

I think here of my experience learning the server's responses at Mass as a young adult. I printed a tiny card for myself with the prayers at the foot of the altar and so forth, and used to keep it tucked into my sleeve when serving. After a time, the prayers had become so internalized that the card was no longer needed. This felt like a new step into freedom: those prayers of the Mass were now completely within me. One night, when I had trouble falling asleep, I found myself running through the prayers at the foot of the altar, reciting Psalm 42 and all that comes after. It draped a wonderful peace over my soul. When my mind is racing or I am suffering from stress, I begin to recite Psalm 42 slowly, and, comforted by its words, I become calm.

---

[32] Holmes, *Cur Deus Verba*, 62–68, 166, 226–27, 238–40. It is for the same reason that we should cleave to a venerable translation of Scripture, made in a sacral register. Such a translation is more memorable precisely because it is poetic, striking, resonant, and oft-repeated over the course of centuries, giving its phrasings cultural weightiness. This is why the New American Bible—written in what Anthony Esolen dubbed "Nabbish," a "bumping boxcar language"—is a translation built to fail, one that will never be the inspiration for any high culture. Moreover, the changing translations of Scripture and liturgical texts used in the Novus Ordo, such as the psalms and hymns, make it far more difficult for the sacred formulas to find a place in the heart. The text of the Gloria in Latin—that marvelous hymn that has been set to great music countless times, in chant, in polyphony, in homophony, in every style—*has not changed since the fourth century*. Meanwhile, the vernacular translations of it will never be stable for more than a few decades, and their musical settings are appropriately transitory. If we value divine, eternal, essential truth (as we claim to in our catechisms), then we ought to take more seriously the potent counter-message that is being uttered by our liturgical habits.

Disciplined internalization of traditional ecclesial prayer leads to freedom, peace, and joy. For the one who attends to what he is saying, it opens ever more layers of meaning and levels of self-surrender. For the entire Church, it provides the inspiring example of the fusion of a person and his office, or better, the submersion of a person in his office, and weans us from the distinctively modern temptation of originality, a quality that is proper to God alone. Pope John Paul II recognized that something analogous was true about catechizing the young:

> At a time when, in non-religious teaching in certain countries, more and more complaints are being made about the unfortunate consequences of disregarding the human faculty of memory, should we not attempt to put this faculty back into use... in catechesis, all the more since the celebration or "memorial" of the great events of the history of salvation requires a precise knowledge of them? A certain memorization of the words of Jesus, of important Bible passages, of the Ten Commandments, of the formulas of profession of the faith, of the liturgical texts, of the essential prayers, of key doctrinal ideas, etc., far from being opposed to the dignity of young Christians, or constituting an obstacle to personal dialogue with the Lord, is a real need, as the synod fathers forcefully recalled. We must be realists. The blossoms, if we may call them that, of faith and piety do not grow in the desert places of a memoryless catechesis.[33]

CONCLUSION

The past sixty years of liturgical praxis have taken a serious toll on the life of faith in our communities. The Novus Ordo perspective fixates on validity and fails to recognize the deep connection between form and meaning, that is, praxis and truth. The consequences of this error are now unmistakable. According to Bishop Robert Barron, for every new Catholic, six are leaving the Church. Surveys indicate that large numbers of Catholics do not believe in the Real Presence.[34] The Covid pandemic only accelerated the already glaring differences between the traditional practice of Catholicism and its modern substitute, wherein Mass can be treated as a "non-essential service." The loss of faith evidenced statistically is understandable, even predictable,

---

[33] John Paul II, Apostolic Exhortation *Catechesi Tradendæ*, no. 55.
[34] The Pew Research Center survey of 2019 and the Vinea Research survey of 2022 reached different conclusions, but questions about the accuracy of both surveys continue to be asked. The survey results of the Real Presence Coalition (https://realpresencecoalition.com/), based on 12,680 completed responses, should also be taken into account. Undoubtedly there is a crisis of faith, reflected in poor Mass attendance, indiscriminate reception of Holy Communion regardless of mortal sins or irregular marital status (with little use of Confession), the notable disjunct between supposed belief and actual behavior, and so forth.

given that *the main source of catechesis for most Catholics is the Mass.* A concerted return to the traditional liturgy is, therefore, not simply beneficial but necessary for the continued life of our churches. Bishops who do not grasp this in time will preside over the white-chasubled, alleluia-saturated funerals of cremated dioceses.

Nevertheless, we have reason today to be of good cheer, for the problems noted in this chapter are more and more widely acknowledged, and the only sensible solution to them is the restoration of the fullness of traditional Catholic worship, whose appeal to the young who encounter it is by now so obvious that all the major secular newspapers are talking about it. The goal of restoration is currently very much *out* of favor in Rome, but the enemies of tradition are predominantly very old and have little time left to implement their agenda, nor have they much support at the grassroots level. What will happen when the last barriers fall down in the coming years is not difficult to predict. A liturgy as ideal for the life of prayer as is the classical Roman rite — that life of prayer to which we are all called by God, and to which our baptism invisibly impels us — is bound to regain ascendency when the revolution expires.

In the cycles of history, including the history of salvation unfolded for us in Scripture, we see times of exile, and in those times, the varied responses people make to their exilic condition. It seems that we are living in a peculiar time marked by institutional self-exile, as if churchmen had become Pharaohs and Pontius Pilates. That is no excuse for failing to do what we can and must as sons of Abraham, children of Israel, and disciples of Christ; rather, it is the perfect opportunity to pray for and seek a return to Catholic tradition, having at its heart a liturgy that is worthy of — and truly *communicative* of — the most important work the Church does: offering to the Lord the holy oblation in peace, ourselves united, in faith and love, with the spotless Lamb.

20

The Minor Options of the Old Rite and How They Avoid Optionitis

THIRTEEN YEARS AFTER POPE BENEDICT XVI mentioned in 2007 that the old missal might be expanded by new prefaces and new saints' feasts, the then-Congregation for the Doctrine of the Faith, in its capacity as the successor to the Pontifical Commission Ecclesia Dei, issued two decrees on March 25, 2020 concerning the 1962 *Missale Romanum* (MR1962). The one, *Quo Magis*, adds seven prefaces, while the other, *Cum Sanctissima*, makes provision for celebrating Mass in honor of saints canonized after 1960.[1] The provisions bend over backwards to avoid stomping on anything already in the MR1962 general calendar. The principle of commemorations is generously applied (that is, no saint or feast or vigil will ever get "dropped," and a lengthy list of 3rd-class feasts are declared inviolable). Put simply: no saint is removed from the calendar or bumped out by any other saint.

The celebration of saints canonized post-1960 is *optional*: the Vatican is not requiring but permitting (e.g.) St. Pio of Pietrelcina, St. Teresa Benedicta of the Cross, or St. Elizabeth of the Trinity to be celebrated or commemorated on their feastdays.[2] We have to bear in mind that a very great number of saints canonized after 1960 lived, in fact, decades or centuries before the liturgical reform and are as much "saints of the Tridentine Mass" as any of the saints currently honored in the old general calendar. Indeed, Padre Pio was vehemently opposed to the liturgical reform as it played out in the 1960s until his death in 1968.[3] As I discussed in chapter 14, the calendar of the traditional Roman rite is extremely "saint-friendly" and has always heartily accumulated feasts and commemorations, in contrast to the tradition-scorning,

---

[1] For a summary of these documents, with apposite quotations, see Gregory DiPippo, "New Prefaces and Feasts for the EF Missal," *NLM*, March 25, 2020.

[2] *Cum Sanctissima* lists the Class III feasts that cannot be impeded, so if a saint canonized after 1960 has a feastday that falls on any other Class III or IV day, that saint can be celebrated using the appropriate Common in the missal. Thus, St. Pio of Pietrelcina's feast of September 23, St. Teresa Benedicta's on August 9, and St. Elizabeth of the Trinity's on November 8 could all be celebrated (with, respectively, commemorations of St. Linus, St. Romanus or the Vigil of St. Lawrence, and the Four Holy Crowned Martyrs).

[3] See Alessandro Gnocchi and Mario Palmaro, *The Last Mass of Padre Pio: The Secret Soul of the Stigmatic Saint*, trans. Marianna Gattozzi (Angelus Press, 2019); Phillip Campbell, "The Obedience of St. Padre Pio," *Unam Sanctam Catholicam*, July 29, 2023.

saint-suppressing mentality reflected in the general calendar for the Novus Ordo rolled out by Paul VI in 1969, from which over 300 saints had been removed.[4]

Admittedly, the thought of a well-meaning young priest who knows no better commemorating "St. Paul VI" at the TLM is enough to make one's *viscera* twist and one's flesh crawl, but it is hard to imagine any well-informed priest who has the "pulse" of his traditional congregation even considering the offering of a TLM in honor of controversial saints of more recent times, let alone actually doing it.[5]

Seven new prefaces have been added, but of these, three are neo-Gallican prefaces already found in many editions of the *Missale Romanum* 1962, with their use now being unrestricted (oddly, the fourth neo-Gallican Preface, the one for Advent, is not listed, yet it would remain permissible according to earlier legislation that has not been rescinded, namely, the Ecclesia Dei Ordo), while the other four are based on ancient sources, albeit somewhat modified.

Reception of the decree allowing seven more prefaces has been decidedly more ambivalent. While no one questions the legitimacy of adding a preface from time to time, in practice the Roman rite has been characterized for many centuries by a limited number of prefaces and an extremely conservative mind when it comes to expanding the repertoire. Adding seven at once is an upward bump with no historical parallel. Moreover, several of the texts have been tampered with in comparison to their actual ancient sources.[6] It seems to me that the use of the prefaces will have to be a matter of ongoing theological and pastoral discernment. In any case, the utmost caution may be recommended: it would not do to take all of the prefaces on board at once, and whenever any such preface is to be used, it seems advisable to make the Latin text with a translation available as a handout, incorporate it into a worship aid, or print it in the bulletin.

It took thirteen years to reach these decisions. In the decrees transmitting them, the possibilities are repeatedly said to be *optional*. This is how liturgical reform should be done: as Gregory DiPippo likes to say, "run the flag up the flagpole and see who salutes; if no one salutes, take it down." This is a far cry from the slap-dash draconian imposition of the Novus Ordo under Paul VI. In fact, one might say the decrees represent a gentle encouragement for organic development. They effectively say, "Here are possibilities; use as they may be helpful,"

---

[4] See Kwasniewski, "Sanctoral Killing Fields."
[5] See Kwasniewski, "Animadversions on the Canonization of Paul VI."
[6] Gregory DiPippo has published a study of each of the new Prefaces at *NLM*; all the links are gathered in my article, "Roundup on the CDF Decrees on New Saints and Prefaces for the TLM," *NLM*, July 13, 2020.

thereby removing the reproach that the MR1962 is frozen in pack ice. From this point of view, the new provisions fit well with the worldwide movement to recover the pre-'55 Holy Week and other glories of the old rite that were damaged under Pope Pius XII. We are looking at a living liturgy, not something that exists only in books printed in a certain arbitrary year, reflecting (as MR1962 does) the mentality of the liturgists of that period.

The decree about saints subtly notes that, on the one hand, it is to be left to the discretion of superiors (*not* to the celebrant on the spur of the moment) which provisions will be utilized; and on the other hand, that the traditional Roman rite has seen optional sanctoral and devotional Masses in the past: "Throughout the post-Tridentine period, and up till the rubrical reform carried out by Pope St. Pius X, the calendar included no less that twenty-five such so-called *ad libitum* feasts."

The most frequently repeated criticism of the 2020 decrees has been that they introduce, or risk introducing, into the celebration of the *usus antiquior* an unwelcome and indeed uncharacteristic spirit of "optionitis." Critics will say that the classical Roman rite is known and loved for its objectivity, stability, and fixity—these being the qualities of any perfected liturgical tradition—and that the clergy should not have options at their disposal.

While I agree that the classical rite has these desirable qualities,[7] I think we should be careful not to overstate our case by speaking as if options have never had a place within it—a highly circumscribed place, to be sure, and one that does not threaten the integrity and "predictability" of the rite, but still, at the end of the day, options. I will look at several examples: alternative readings; votive Masses and Masses *pro aliquibus locis*; multiple orations; some minor matters; and, paraliturgically, the style of vestments.

ALTERNATIVE READINGS

Unlike the new lectionary, the old lectionary, built into the missal, almost never gives an option as to what reading is to be used on any given day or for any given Mass formulary. However, in the Commons there are a few instances of "alternative readings." For example:

- in the Mass *Me exspectaverunt* for virgin martyrs, the Gospel is Matthew 13:44–52 *or* Matthew 19:3–12;
- in the Mass *In medio ecclesiæ* for doctors of the Church, the Epistle is 2 Timothy 4:1–8 *or* Ecclesiasticus 39:6–14;
- in the Mass *Salus autem* for several martyrs, the Gospel is Luke 12:1–8 *or* Matthew 24:3–13.

---

7 See the preceding chapter.

It gets really interesting with the Mass *Lætabitur justus* for a martyr not a bishop, where *three* Epistles are listed: 2 Timothy 2:8–10 and 3:10–12; James 1:2–12; and 1 Peter 4:13–19, as well as *two* Gospels: Matthew 10:26–32 and John 12:24–26.

There is a rubric in the Commons section of the missal—first appearing, I think, in the 1920 edition—that states that the Epistles and Gospels printed within one of the Commons can be used *ad libitum* for the Mass of a saint, unless the Mass formulary directs otherwise. In the Sanctorale, there is either the minimal instruction to follow the Common or, more rarely, the additional direction to use a specific Gospel. A rubrical expert I consulted had never seen preconciliar diocesan *ordines* specifying these in any way; he has a collection of about fifty which, though differing greatly in style and content, make no reference to the choice of pericopes where several are given. We should see this as a small example of liberty within the otherwise (blessedly) monolithic old missal.

In my admittedly limited experience over the past few decades, priests rarely avail themselves of these alternative readings. It seems they follow the principle articulated by a friend of mine: "Whatever text will be the least trouble to read is the one that is most likely to be read." (He initially came up with this principle to explain why, when it comes to the new lectionary, priests so rarely break out of the mold of the *lectio continua* that plods along from day to day, even though for almost any of the saints they could choose a more appropriate reading if they wished.) Yet hand missals always print these alternative readings right alongside the other readings for the Common, so it is hard to see why they should not be used. This is a case where admirable Scripture readings already given in the old missal are being neglected in practice.

VOTIVE MASSES AND *MISSÆ PRO ALIQUIBUS LOCIS*

We take it for granted that any time there is a feria, when the Mass of the preceding Sunday could be said again, a priest is also free to make a choice of any of the Votive Masses contained in the missal. There is a longstanding custom of using the Mass of the Most Holy Trinity on Monday; that of the Holy Angels on Tuesday; that of St. Joseph, the Holy Apostles Peter and Paul, or All Holy Apostles on Wednesday; that of the Holy Ghost, the Blessed Sacrament, or Jesus Christ Eternal High Priest on Thursday; that of the Holy Cross or of the Passion of Our Lord on Friday; and that of the Blessed Virgin Mary on Saturday—but, apart from the Saturday Mass of Our Lady, this association of themes and days is merely a recommendation and does not have any obliging force.

Beyond these popular Votive Masses are a host of others that some priests use quite regularly and others seem strangely unfamiliar with or uninterested in: Mass for the Sick (I have never actually been present when this formulary has been used!); Mass for the Propagation of the Faith (interestingly, this one has an alternative Epistle, 1 Timothy 2:1–7; the Epistle listed first is Sirach 36:1–10, 17–19); Mass Against the Heathen; Mass for the Removal of Schism; Mass in Time of War; Mass for Peace; Mass for Deliverance from Mortality or in Time of Pestilence; Mass of Thanksgiving; Mass for the Forgiveness of Sins; Mass for Pilgrims and Travelers; Mass for Any Necessity; Mass for a Happy Death. (I would add that when a priest is going to celebrate with one of these formularies, he should somehow announce it to the people, either in the bulletin if he has decided it in advance, or on a sheet posted near the inside church door, or in a brief mention after emerging from the sacristy and before starting the prayers at the foot of the altar.)

Moreover, altar missals usually feature a section towards the back called *Missæ pro aliquibus locis*, Masses for certain places. Like Votive Masses, these too may be chosen under certain conditions. My 1947 Benziger altar missal, with a commendatory letter signed by Cardinal Spellman, has quite a substantive "M. P. A. L." section: page (131) to page (196). It includes such worthy feasts as The Translation of the Holy House of the Blessed Virgin Mary on December 10, the Expectation of Our Lady on December 18, the Espousal of the Blessed Virgin and St. Joseph on January 23, the Flight of Our Lord Jesus Christ into Egypt on February 17, the Feast of the Prayer of Our Lord Jesus Christ on the Tuesday after Septuagesima, and many others.[8]

All of these feasts share in common the trait that they are not normally prescribed but allowed to be used when there is no impediment. They must be chosen in order to be used; they are, in that sense, options and meant as options.

MULTIPLE ORATIONS

One of the worst casualties of the 1960 rubrical revisions was the loss of multiple orations at Mass (Collects, Secrets, and Postcommunions) and at the Divine Office (Collects). This runs contrary to the Roman tradition in the second millennium, when multiple orations were a universal feature. The history of the question of how many orations

---

[8] Prior to the 1962 missal, the use of these Mass formularies was restricted to the places where the feasts were celebrated. "The Mass of a Saint given among the Masses for Certain Places may not be used as a votive Mass, except where the feast is celebrated by apostolic indult; otherwise, a votive Mass of the Saint must be taken from the appropriate Common." Joseph Wuest, *Matters Liturgical (the* Collectio Rerum Liturgicarum*)*, trans. Thomas W. Mullaney (Frederick Pustet, 1956; repr. Angelus Press, 2023), no. 254, f, pp. 468–69. This would be one of those rare instances where a post-'54 rubric is superior.

were allowed is quite complex. Here it suffices to speak of the period after 1570, when it was normal for the priest to say the oration of the day, followed sometimes by a commemoration of a saint, other times by a required seasonal oration or required prayer (*oratio imperata*), and concluding with a third oration at his choice (*ad libitum eligenda*).[9] There is a magnificent corpus of orations printed in the Tridentine missal for precisely this reason, too few of which have remained in use after the asphyxiating limitations imposed by John XXIII's rubrical reform.

We can see here, once again, that Holy Mother Church recognized a certain "ordered liberty" on the part of the celebrant, who was thus able to pray liturgically for his own needs, for those of the local community, or for those of the larger world.

MINOR MATTERS

Five other areas in which a choice is required are:

1. Whether to precede the Sunday High Mass with the *Asperges*, or to start with the entrance procession accompanied by the Introit antiphon;[10]

2. Whether to remain standing or to sit down during the Kyrie, the Gloria, and the Credo;

3. Which tone to use for the orations, readings, and Preface;

4. Whether or not to use incense at a *Missa cantata*;[11]

5. Whether to observe an "external solemnity" for the Sacred Heart of Jesus or the Most Holy Rosary, to enable the maximum number of faithful to participate in the celebration of these feasts.[12] It is important

---

[9] To be more precise: Sometimes there is a choice only between the prayer for the pope and the prayer for the Church (from Advent until the Purification); sometimes it is *ad libitum* (after Candlemas until Ash Wednesday; the time after Pentecost); during Lent, the prayers are fixed. On days (i.e., Semidoubles and Simples) that call for a minimum of three orations and leave the third to the celebrant's choice, the celebrant does *not* have the option to omit a third prayer. He still must choose some set of orations to fill the third slot.

[10] The *Asperges* is mandatory only in cathedral and collegiate churches where the Office is sung, to be done after Terce and before the Sunday conventual Mass. In parochial churches, the *Asperges* is optional, except where custom would demand the practice. The *Asperges* can be done only once per Sunday; thus, if there is more than one sung Mass on a Sunday, a decision has to be made as to which is the principal Mass (fittingness suggests the one closest to the time when Terce would be prayed). See Wuest, *Matters Liturgical*, no. 401, p. 799.

[11] It is worthy of note that the Code of Rubrics promulgated by John XXIII in 1960 added options to the actions of the celebrant and other ministers. For example, no. 399 allows the celebrant who offers more than one Mass on All Souls to omit the sequence at all but the principal or first Mass; no. 523 allows for sitting at sung Masses during the singing of the Sequence in addition to during the Kyrie, Gloria, and Credo as allowed in the 1920 General Rubrics; no. 426 allows the use of incense in all sung Masses that are not solemn (prior to the 1960 Code, the use of incense in a non-solemn Mass was allowed only where a papal indult had been granted to a diocese or country, and even then it was limited to Doubles of the First and Second Class).

[12] Whether or not to have an external solemnity for Corpus Christi is in some places a free decision but in the USA and certain other countries, this feast must be both celebrated on its proper day and observed on Sunday.

to recognize that here we are looking not at an obligatory transferral, where the feast is simply packed up and *moved*—an aberration possible only in the Novus Ordo—but at a *separate additional* celebration of some feast, which has already been celebrated on the proper day.[13]

It is true that the foregoing choices are limited and the things being chosen are entirely defined; there is no room for creativity or extemporization. Nevertheless, they constitute options.

STYLE OF VESTMENTS

While this final example does not concern something in the liturgical rite as such but only something associated with it, it is (oddly) one of the most controversial among traditionalists: I refer to the simple fact that the celebrant has, in theory, the option of wearing either Gothic vestments or Roman vestments. (I say "in theory" because not every sacristy is equipped with both kinds.)

In the Western tradition, the original vestments received their aesthetic perfection in the so-called Gothic period, but, over the course of the Renaissance and the Counter-Reformation, a strikingly different style emerged, known (more or less accurately) as the Roman style. The difference between a Gothic conical chasuble and a Roman "fiddleback" chasuble could not be more pronounced.[14] Some, especially Liturgical Movement enthusiasts who first sipped the chalice of medieval romanticism before drowning in the cups of modern rationalism, insisted that the Roman style of chasuble was an outrageous corruption; for others of a reactionary bent, it has become a shibboleth of Tridentine identity. One still occasionally hears a traditionalist layman explaining to his neighbors at the coffee hour that "at the Novus Ordo the priest wears this full draping kind of chasuble, but at the Latin Mass he wears the old-fashioned Roman fiddleback." If I overhear something

---

[13] See Gregory DiPippo, "A Note on External Solemnities in the EF," *NLM*, April 27, 2016.

[14] The Eastern Christian equivalent to the chasuble, the phelonion, also evolved in a parallel way to the Western chasuble. How often one hears Eastern Christians (whether Catholic or schismatic) say something like the following: "In the West, you kept on changing over time, but in the East we always retained the ancient ways. Our liturgy, our churches, our vestments, always the same, while yours evolve." Well... one learns through study that this isn't so. Relatively speaking there may be less change and more continuity in the East, but there are still developments: the texts and ceremonies of the liturgy were elaborated over time and reached maturity well after the period of the Church Fathers; the layout and decoration of churches have seen multiple variations; and the vestments have seen modification too. In the West, the chasuble was shortened and the sides were cut off; in the East, the phelonion was shortened and the front was cut out. Both were practical responses to an originally fairly impractical vestment. See Shawn Tribe, "The Development of the Shape of the Eastern Phelonion (Chasuble) and Its Parallels to the Same in the Latin West," *LAJ*, November 18, 2024.

like that, I share with them photographs of glorious traditional Masses from Australia, where Gothic is practically the only thing in existence, whether architecturally or vesturally.

I think there is room for both styles. Noble vestments have been created along the entire spectrum; aesthetic preferences are not only allowed but inevitable. Again, to my knowledge, the Church has never specified that one or another style of vestments must be used, as long as every essential piece is present (including the amice and maniple); she again allows an ordered liberty of choice.

AVOIDING THE WORSHIP OPTION

The decree *Cum Sanctissima* permits, among other things, the observance of saints during Lent whose feasts were always impeded and reduced to commemorations by the 1960 code of rubrics' insistence on privileging every feria of Lent. No one disputes that the Lenten ferias are absolutely wonderful, and they deserve their prominence. But it was poor thinking that allowed for no flexibility with regard to celebrating, even during Lent, feasts of saints who enjoy a particular prominence in this or that community. Surely for Catholic schools, St. Thomas Aquinas may get his full due on March 7; surely for religious communities, St. Gregory the Great on March 12; surely for the Irish, St. Patrick on March 17. The CDF decree restores a reasonable flexibility, with the feria always commemorated. (The Novus Ordo runs into intractable difficulties because it has abandoned the wisdom of commemorations, which prescribes that when two things conflict, both should somehow be liturgically present, rather than one of them simply being dumped. The same problem, it must be admitted, already affects the 1962 missal to a large extent, especially with sung Masses — yet another reason to return to the 1920 *editio typica*.)

In regard to the foregoing examples, I would say that clergy and laity are so accustomed to the choices involved that perhaps they do not even notice that a choice *is* involved. What I mean is that we expect a priest to have the freedom to choose a Votive Mass on a feria, and everything else about the Mass is so predictable that it all seems inevitable; but a major choice was made beforehand to do the Votive instead of repeating the prior Sunday. It's like a skier considering various trails to descend — once he commits himself to a trail, he is committed to the whole of it until he exits at the bottom. The choice is *pre*liturgical, so to speak, rather than *intra*liturgical.

Not every choice need be construed as, or need have the psychological and pastoral effect of, the deservedly decried optionitis of the Novus Ordo. In the Tridentine rite, all options are safely folded within the dominating unity of its architecture and the exacting prescriptions of its rubrics, and therefore acquire the same rituality. In the Novus Ordo, in stark contrast, the options are so numerous and concern such basic elements of the liturgy—its opening rite and penitential rite, the readings of the day vs. those of the Commons, whether the Offertory is said aloud or silently, which Eucharistic prayer to use[!], what and when to sing, etc. etc.—that the rite itself can barely hold on to its rituality and becomes, in a sense, a giant Worship Option. This, it seems to me, is the fundamental difference between the Vetus Ordo, even with the few options placed at its disposal, and the Novus Ordo.

WHEN DISPUTES BECOME FATAL

The preceding list of a small number of strictly-controlled options in the old rite allows us to appreciate all the more a colossal fact: the disagreements that occur within the realm of the Novus Ordo belong to an entirely different order of magnitude from those that occur within the realm of the traditional Latin Mass. In the world of the *usus antiquior*, we find disagreements like the following:

- whether orchestral Masses (e.g., Mozart's) should be performed, or whether they run contrary to the spirit of the liturgy;
- whether to follow exactly the Solesmes rhythmic markings or to incorporate the findings of chant paleography;
- whether the people should sing the Mass Ordinary together with the choir, or the choir alone should sing;
- whether a Gothic chasuble is better than, worse than, or equal to, a Roman fiddleback;
- whether to remove the chasuble before preaching, or only the maniple;
- whether buckled shoes are worth reviving or may be considered an affectation;
- whether *this* much lace is *too* much lace.

Such disagreements, I think all would agree, are, in the grand scheme of things, about relatively minor matters. At their fiercest, such disputes might be compared to boxing or wrestling; at their mildest, to chess or culinary tastes. Everyone agrees about the essentials: the Mass is a true and proper sacrifice; the universal tradition of *ad orientem* worship and the Western tradition of the Latin language are ever to be retained; the Ordinary and Propers of the Mass are always to be recited or sung, and if sung, normatively in Gregorian chant; the Roman Canon is the heart of our central act of worship, and like the heart's beating, it takes place in silence, hidden within; the sanctuary, which represents the Holy of Holies and the court of heaven gained by Christ the High Priest, is off limits to all but ordained ministers and the men or boys deputed to substitute for them; the awesome mystery of the Holy Eucharist is to be received kneeling, on the tongue, in an attitude of utmost humility and adoration, from hands specially anointed for the purpose of consecrating, carrying, and giving the Lord.

We might compare such differences as there are to the performance of a stately piece of Baroque music, where musicians ornament the music in diverse ways, but according to the conventions of the period and the indications of the figured bass. Two performances of Bach's *St. Matthew Passion* or Handel's *Messiah* may vary in many details, but the music in both cases is still obviously the same, with the same words, in the same order, and with largely the same impact.

In the world of the Novus Ordo, we also find disagreements—indeed, quite a number of them. Here are examples:

- whether the Mass is primarily to be understood and enacted as a sacrifice or as a meal;
- whether the language used should be the age-old Latin, a "sacral" vernacular, or a contemporary vernacular;
- whether traditional sacred music should be employed a lot, a little, or never, with modern popular styles in its place;
- whether the priest in accord with bimillennial tradition should offer the Mass facing eastwards, or rather facing the people;
- whether the priest should pray the only traditional Roman anaphora, the Roman Canon, or choose another one from the menu;
- whether Mass should be recognizably the same throughout the world or radically inculturated;
- whether women should serve in as many liturgical ministries as possible, or the tradition of men only in the sanctuary should be retained;
- whether lay people should handle the true Body and Blood of Christ, or whether only ordained ministers—bishops, priests, and deacons—should do so;
- whether this sacrosanct, august Mystery of the Flesh and Blood of God should be placed on the tongues of kneeling faithful, or into the hands of people standing in line.

It is not difficult to see that the number, nature, and magnitude of disagreements in this realm vastly exceed those found in the traditional realm. These disagreements—let us be honest about it—are more like warfare between countries. The sides are embedded in their trenches; they fire away with belligerence and take no hostages. Indeed, if someone in 1950 had been given a list of the disputed points above, he would have reasonably assumed that it was an accurate statement of disagreements separating Catholics from Protestants, or believers from modernists.

This monumental contrast between the two worlds should give us pause and prompt serious reflection. How does this welter of deep disagreements across the board about the *lex orandi* of Paul VI (and, therefore, inevitably, about the *lex credendi* of the People of God) square with the consistent teaching and practice of Paul VI's eponym? The Apostle Paul placed much emphasis on unity, not only in matters of doctrine but also in matters of practice, where he urged conformity with tradition: "The things which you have both learned, and received, and heard, and seen in me, these do ye, and the God of peace shall be with you" (Phil 4:9). "We charge you, brethren, in the name of our Lord Jesus Christ, that you withdraw yourselves from every brother walking disorderly, and not according to the tradition which they have received of us" (2 Thess 3:6). "Fulfill ye my joy, that you may be of one mind, having the same charity, being of one accord, agreeing in sentiment" (Phil 2:2). "Now I beseech you, brethren, by the name of our Lord Jesus Christ, that you all speak the same thing, and that there be no schisms among you; but that you be perfect in the same mind, and in the same judgment [*in eodem sensu, et in eadem sententia*]" (1 Cor 1:10). Or, in the words of St. John: "Remember then what you received and heard; keep that, and repent" (Rev 3:3).

Which of the two worlds we have discussed better embodies the apostolic advice to receive the tradition gratefully and wholly, and thereby be at peace; to withdraw from the disorderly who walk not according to tradition; to have one mind, in one accord, speaking the same thing, walking by the same judgments?

The same teaching is consistently given from the early Fathers through the Middle Ages down to the modern period. The Council of Trent says:

> This holy Synod with true fatherly affection admonishes, exhorts, begs, and beseeches, through the bowels of the mercy of our God, that all and each of those who bear the Christian name would now at length agree and be of one mind in this sign of unity, in this bond of charity, in this symbol of concord; and that mindful of the so great majesty, and the so exceeding love of our Lord Jesus Christ, who gave His own beloved soul as the price of our salvation, and gave us His own flesh to eat, they would believe and venerate these sacred mysteries of His body and blood with such constancy and firmness of faith, with such devotion of soul, with such piety and worship as to be able frequently to receive that supersubstantial bread...[15]

---

[15] Council of Trent, Sess. XIII, ch. 8.

In the culminating lines of Pope Pius XII's famous encyclical on the liturgy, *Mediator Dei*—which makes for eye-opening reading, as one sees how brazenly the teaching on almost every page has been contradicted by the course of events—the pontiff declares:

> May God, whom we worship, and who is "not the God of dissension but of peace" (1 Cor 14:33) graciously grant to us all that during our earthly exile we may with one mind and one heart participate in the sacred liturgy which is, as it were, a preparation and a token of that heavenly liturgy in which we hope one day to sing together with the most glorious Mother of God and our most loving Mother, "To Him that sitteth on the throne, and to the Lamb, benediction and honor, and glory and power for ever and ever" (Rev 5:13).[16]

This is from 1947, one year before Annibale Bugnini, joining the Vatican's commission for liturgical reform, began his slow ambitious climb to prominence and ultimate hegemony over the Hamletesque Montini.

A reader once wrote to me:

> People wedded to the new liturgy have narratives and they become invested in them, especially as they get older. To concede the superiority of the traditional liturgy would mean having to rethink more aspects of that narrative than they are ready to do, especially as it would involve admitting to being wrong for a long time about things of great importance. It is a shame, because the traditional Roman rite is fully the heritage of every Catholic, yet so few avail themselves of it.

When all is said and done, the *only* narrative that can make sense for a Catholic is continuity with his own heritage, with stronger allegiance to that which has been of longer use. Received forms and practices have intrinsic value, according to the mind of Christ and the Church; they enjoy the privilege of seniority, settled reception, and proven efficacy. So, while one might be wrong in one's "take" on this or that aspect of one's heritage (I refer to the disputed questions listed at the head of this section), one will never be mistaken *in principle* by adhering to tradition. Whereas the moment one abandons this compass, one is in a ship afloat at sea, with no established route and no guarantee of arrival, confined with passengers who are confused, restive, and strongly at odds about what to do next. It should come as no surprise that Catholics wish to be passengers on a ship that knows whence it comes and whither it goes, and has all the means for a safe and speedy journey—with amicable differences of opinion along the way, yet with the guarantee of fraternal harmony in all that matters most.

---

[16] Pius XII, *Mediator Dei*, no. 209.

❧ 21 ❦
Progressive Solemnity: Traditional Interpretations and Methods

As we saw in the previous chapter, adaptability and variability are certainly possible with the TLM. However, they are not the result of parish committees or inculturation workshops. Rather, they derive from the possibilities inherent in the rite itself, according to its millennial development, and involve choices from among many legitimate incidental features. In this chapter, I will explain the possibilities and choices we have available to us for differentiating our celebrations, beyond the priest's choice of formularies for the day.

In the world of the postconciliar liturgy, one encounters a concept of "progressive solemnity" that has little to do with the Latin liturgical tradition. Basically, the idea is this: start with a spoken Mass as your baseline, and then add things on to it *ad libitum*: for an ordinary day, sing the "presidential" parts; on a feast, add the Propers; on a very special day, bring on the incense and chant the Introit, etc. In practice, at least in my experience, it ends up being a random series of steps: on weekdays we sing the Alleluia but nothing else; on feasts, we sing maybe the Gloria and the Alleluia; on Sundays we do the four-hymn sandwich and the celebrant sings his parts. Since there is much confusion about what rubrics, if any, govern these sorts of decisions, just about any mix-'n'-match combination can happen.[1]

With the traditional Roman rite, this confusion is simply not possible: a Mass is either a Low Mass or a *Missa cantata* or a *Missa solemnis*, etc., and each has strict requirements about what is to be sung (or not sung). As a result, followers of the traditional rite tend to use the *forms* of Mass as a way of distinguishing calendrical solemnity: ferias or low-ranking feasts will be Low Masses; high-ranking feasts are *Missæ Cantatæ*; Sundays and Holy Days are Solemn High Masses, if the ministers for it are available; and a bishop may be invited in for a Pontifical High Mass on the most special occasions of all.

While this is understandable for practical reasons (bishops are not commonly available to pontificate, and even a deacon and subdeacon can be hard to come by), we should recognize that it is not the *primary* way

---

[1] See Fr. David Friel's critique of the notion of "progressive solemnity" in the article of that name at *Views from the Choir Loft*, December 21, 2014.

in which the liturgical tradition of the Church distinguishes degrees of solemnity. In a church sufficiently well equipped with ministers, such as a monastic community or a cathedral with canons, the liturgy will be sung every day; it could be solemn every day. The normative—in the sense of fundamental and exemplary—form of liturgy will always be the Pontifical Mass chanted by a bishop or an abbot, or the nearest thing to it, the *Missa solemnis*.

On one of my visits to the Benedictine monastery of Norcia, I remember how beautiful it was to attend Solemn Masses all week long. It showed me that this can indeed be a norm rather than an exception. Moreover, since the monks were so skilled in liturgy and chant, and there was no homily, Solemn Mass took less than an hour. Each day nevertheless had a distinctive feel to it because of the intelligent use of other ways of distinguishing ranks of feasts and ferias that Catholic tradition has developed over the centuries. Taking the solemn *form* as normative does not mean placing everything at the same level of solemnity. The solemnity is distinguished rather by the accidents, the *manner* or *mode* in which the elements of the liturgy are configured.

Liturgically speaking, "solemn" refers first of all to a Mass with priest, deacon, and subdeacon, or to a pontifical Mass with bishop, archpriest, deacon, and subdeacon. However, by extension, "solemn" refers to all that enhances the grandeur or splendor of the liturgical rite, underlines its seriousness, and magnifies its festal character. Having a priest, deacon, and subdeacon is what gets you *solemn ceremonies*; but even if one were to do this on a daily basis or fairly regularly, there are still ways to differentiate between ferias and feasts. That is what I am primarily concerned with in this chapter: the "phenomenology" of solemnity, not the rubrical and juridical definition of it. There is ritual or ceremonial solemnity, where one has the full complement of ministers and ceremonies, and then there is something that might be called calendrical solemnity, observing the ranks of feasts. A first-class feast should not be celebrated in altogether the same manner as a fourth-class feast (in normal circumstances; there might be a peculiar reason to do otherwise). How do we make the differentiations in the calendar line up with the differentiations in the liturgy? My proposal is that we should *not* do this solely by the use of low, sung, or Solemn Mass, even if that's going to be the way it's done in most places, for pragmatic reasons.

GRADATIONS IN CHANT

While every liturgy should ideally be chanted, there are notable distinctions within the repertoire of chant itself. Fr. Dominique Delalande, OP, observes:

It is too obvious to be denied that a celebration sung in the Gregorian manner is more solemn than a celebration which is merely recited; but this statement is especially true in the modern perspective of a celebration which is habitually recited. The ancients had provided melodies for the most modest celebrations of the liturgical year, and these melodies were no less carefully worked out than those of the great feasts. For them the chant was, before all else, a means of giving to liturgical prayer a fullness of religious and contemplative value, whatever might be the solemnity [i.e., rank] of the day. Such should also be our sole preoccupation in singing. As long as people look upon the Gregorian chant solely as a means of solemnising the celebration, there will be the danger of making it deviate from its true path, which is more interior.[2]

Put differently, Fr. Delalande is saying that chant is integral to the expression of the liturgy, not a mere ornament tacked on, like a bow on a Christmas present, and that we do well to utilize the different *spheres* of chant rather than merely toggling back and forth between recited and sung.

Ordinary. For example, the Mass Ordinary given in the *Liber Usualis* for ferias is short and simple, while the Ordinaries suggested for Solemn Feasts (Mass II, *Kyrie fons bonitatis*, or Mass III, *Kyrie Deus sempiterne*) are melodically elaborate and grand in scope. Five Ordinaries (III–VIII), of varying complexity and length, are suggested for Doubles. Simpler feasts of Our Lady, e.g., the Holy Name of Mary on September 12, might use Ordinary X, *Alme Pater*, while loftier feasts such as the Immaculate Conception or the Assumption could use the great Mass IX, *Cum jubilo.*

Creed. Similarly, the *Liber* makes available six settings of the Creed (and a few other chant settings are in circulation as well),[3] which vary considerably in their ornateness or "tonality." Once again, the choice of a Creed melody can reflect something of the nature of the feast or occasion or season.

Preface. The missal offers three tones for the Prefaces: simple, solemn, and more solemn (*solemnior*). For a ferial Mass, a Requiem, or a lesser feast, the simple tone should be used; for a higher-ranking feast, such as that of an apostle or doctor, the solemn tone could be used; for the highest feasts, such as Christmas, Easter, Ascension, Pentecost,

---

2 "Le chant grégorien," in *Initiation théologique*, v. 1: *Les sources de la théologie* (Cerf, 1950), 255–56, cited in Marc-Daniel Kirby, "Sung Theology: The Liturgical Chant of the Church," in *Beyond the Prosaic: Renewing the Liturgical Movement*, ed. Stratford Caldecott (T&T Clark, 1998), 148 n62.

3 Thus, *The Our Lady of Mount Carmel Hymnal* (Os Justi Press, 2023) has a total of eleven settings: the six standard ones plus a seventh in wide circulation; the Ambrosian; and three from Du Mont: *Missa Regia*, *Missa secundi toni*, and *Missa sexti toni*.

Corpus Christi, the Sacred Heart, the Immaculate Conception, or the Assumption, the more solemn tone would be highly appropriate. (In an oft-repeated anecdote, Mozart is said to have claimed that he would gladly exchange all his music for the fame of having composed the Preface tone. If he said this, he would doubtless have been thinking of the more solemn tone, which is indeed of rare beauty.)

Propers. The Proper chants should be sung in full in any case, but for a special occasion with incense and more ceremonial, a verse from the *Offertoriale Triplex* might be used, and at Communion time, verses and a doxology to go with the antiphon.

Beyond the chant, there are other obvious and subtle ways to elevate or lower the solemnity of a particular day on the calendar, so that ferias do not seem the equal of feasts of saints, and feasts of saints the equal of feasts of Our Lady, and these, in turn, the equal of those of Our Lord. It is true that many of the following presuppose a well-stocked sacristy, the contents of which have been assembled over a long period of time by people with good taste who understand that there is symbolic value in having more than one kind of any given item.

IN THE REALM OF SIGHT

Since, as Aristotle says, the sense of sight is the one that gives us the most information about things, it is not surprising that the largest number of modes for signaling solemnity pertain to the visual domain.[4]

Copes, chasubles, dalmatics, tunicles. It is obvious that plainer vestments should be used for ferias, more decorative ones for feasts, and over-the-top ones for solemnities. There are churches that have special sets used only at Christmas and/or Easter, or for a patronal feastday, etc.

Other vestments. For a feria, the alb can be plain; for a feast, it can be patterned; for a solemnity, with lacework. When worn with a Roman chasuble, the design of the alb becomes an important aesthetic element in itself. Similarly, the surplices of acolytes can be plain white or with worked borders; the cassocks can be black throughout the year but red for Christmastide and Paschaltide.[5]

---

[4] "The senses which operate through external media, viz., smelling, hearing, seeing, are found in all animals which possess the faculty of locomotion.... But in animals which have also intelligence they serve for the attainment of a higher perfection. They bring in tidings of many distinctive qualities of things, from which knowledge of things both speculative and practical is generated in the soul. Of the two last mentioned, seeing, regarded as a supply for the primary wants of life, is in its own right the superior sense; but for developing thought, hearing incidentally takes the precedence." *Sense and Sensibilia*, ch. 1, 436b18–437a6, trans. J. I. Beare, in *The Complete Works of Aristotle*, ed. Jonathan Barnes (Princeton University Press, 1984), 694.

[5] I suggest readers become intimately familiar with the online *Liturgical Arts Journal*, which thoroughly covers vestment periods, styles, colors, and manufacturers, not to mention every other liturgical artifact known to man.

Chalice, paten, and other vessels. It is obvious that these can be of simple or ornate design; in gold or silver or a combination thereof; with or without stones; taller or more squat, Romanesque, Gothic, or Baroque; engraved or plain; etc. This is one detail that is particularly noticed by the faithful, because of the custom of gazing upon the chalice as it is elevated and praying: "My Lord and my God!"[6]

The Processional Cross. This can be of silver or of gold; a simple design or an ornate design; smaller or larger.

Candles and candlesticks. There are many ways to use candles in relation to varying degrees of festivity or solemnity. The most obvious are: to use gold or gold-and-marble candlesticks for Sundays and feasts; to light "the big six" above the altar for sung Masses, versus lighting two smaller candlesticks on weekdays for Low Mass; to have a special elaborate set for the highest occasions; to use silver or wooden candlesticks with unbleached candles for Requiems and Good Friday.

Reliquaries. Most churches will display reliquaries throughout the year except during Eucharistic Adoration or at a Requiem. However, a church with enough reliquaries can vary the relics placed out. Obviously when a saint's feast arises, his or her relics should be present. But a nobler occasion can call for the most ornate reliquaries to be displayed, and in some places, *all* relics are brought out on November 1. This is another small way of lifting minds and hearts to God, who is glorious in His saints. The same observation can be made of monstrances: a simpler one might be used for First Fridays, a more elaborate one for Corpus Christi or other feasts of the Lord.

Flowers. An obvious advantage of a traditional high altar is the perfect accommodation it makes for floral arrangements on the gradine or ledge above the mensa. Anyone who has seen a well-decorated high altar knows that flowers add the finishing touch of natural beauty to a supernatural environment. The arrangements can be modest, of one or two colors or types of plant, or lavish, large, and in many colors and varieties of plant; there can be two or four arrangements (one or a pair for the Epistle side and one or a pair for the Gospel side), or even additional vases on stands, as long as symmetry is always preserved. The vases, too, can be varied, made from glass or different metals, in diverse colors or styles. Needless to say, the flowers or foliage put into the vases should always be *cut*; potted living plants are not to be used.[7]

Altar cards. Instead of having only one set of prefabricated altar cards, multiple sets may be obtained, of different designs in different

---

[6] See my article "We, Too, Are the Sacrifice We Offer," *OnePeterFive*, June 17, 2020.
[7] See my article "The Beautiful Death: Why We Favor Cut Flowers in the Sanctuary," *NLM*, May 1, 2023.

kinds of frames, with the larger and more elaborate for feasts and the simpler for weekdays. Sometimes sacristies will have a very plain set for Lent, to contrast it with the rest of the year; and a distinct set for the Requiem Mass, in sober black and white and silver, is highly to be recommended (not least, because the texts and rubrics of the Requiem are somewhat different from those of any other Mass). If possible, commission a calligrapher to prepare altar cards that will be unique to your church, and if this isn't within reach, at least obtain a high-quality reproduction of a more elegant set than the mass-produced options.[8]

Altar frontals (antependia). Since the altar itself represents Christ the High Priest, the custom arose long ago of robing it in a vesture of colored cloth hung over the front, much as a cope or a chasuble covers a priest. This covering, its color determined by the liturgical color of the day, highlights the prominence of the high altar and amplifies the impact of the feast or season. Frontals come in all levels of formality, from simple designs of a single color with perhaps a couple of bands of contrasting color (say, white and gold) to elaborate designs with multiple colors, orphreys, and appliqués. One sees here the possibility of distinguishing the levels of feasts and seasons by having more than one set of antependia in a given color, even as sacristies will have different sets of vestments of the same color.[9]

Missal stand. The "workhorse" of the altar, the missal stand is seldom considered an artistic object, but all it takes is some exploring to see how many different designs are available: with latticework or with solid surfaces, in silver or in gold, with or without semi-precious stones. A wooden stand is appropriate for Requiems or penitential occasions. Before there were missal stands, there were cushions, and these ought to be rescued from their oblivion.[10] Done in liturgically colored fabrics, they complement well the rest of the ensemble. The stand can also be covered: "It is fitting that the missal-stand should be draped with a covering of the same color as the vestments of the celebrant, unless the stand is out of the ordinary by reason of its precious material or beautiful workmanship in which case the veil may be dispensed with."[11]

Wall hangings. To mention this idea is to risk rolled eyes in American readers, who might have nightmares of banners produced in the

---

[8] See, e.g., Shawn Tribe, "Hand Illuminated Altar Cards by Pelican Printery House," *LAJ*, June 9, 2021; Daniel Mitsui, "New Illuminated Altar Cards," *LAJ*, November 24, 2017; idem, "Altar Cards for the Requiem Mass," *LAJ*, April 15, 2021; John Paul Sonnen, "Requiem Mass Altar Cards," *LAJ*, December 9, 2020.
[9] For a detailed treatment, see Shawn Tribe, "The Historical, Theological, Liturgical and Artistic Case for Altar Frontals," *LAJ*, November 16, 2017.
[10] See Shawn Tribe, "The Missal Cushion," *LAJ*, February 4, 2020.
[11] Wuest, *Matters Liturgical*, no. 157, h, p. 266.

CCD First Communion class: "a darkness so thick it could be felt," to borrow a phrase from Exodus 10:21. But here I am referring to the elegant red banners lowered from the ceiling to add a bright note for festal occasions.[12] In central Europe I have seen ribbons of white and gold festooned over the sanctuary during Paschaltide; I'm sure there are similar customs in many Catholic cultures. A similar function could be allotted to processional banners, which might be put out, upright in their stands, on occasions referenced by the banner artwork (e.g., for the feastday and octave of the Sacred Heart, a banner depicting that object of veneration). If done tastefully (and that proviso applies to every item in my list), these things give prominence to the day or the season, which in turn helps make us aware of its message, without the need for tedious verbiage.

IN THE REALM OF SOUND

Chant variations. I have already discussed the considerable diversity within the corpus of Gregorian chant. Beyond that, one should take into account the use of isons or drones, organum, and alternatim with men and women (or monophony and polyphony)—always bearing in mind that, as with spices, too much of a good thing is distasteful.[13]

Ad libitum chants present other ways of marking levels of solemnity. For a ferial Solemn Mass, one might simply let there be silence after the Offertory and Communion antiphons. (I never tire of reminding musicians that the belief that every moment must be filled with music is a form of psychological insecurity called kenophobia.[14]) For a feastday, one could choose a votive chant from the *Liber* or another Solesmes book.

Polyphony. For greater occasions, equal voice or mixed choir motets would be most appropriate, as polyphony already stands out from chant as more splendid or majestic, although certainly no more perfect qua liturgical music. When the choral forces are equal to the challenge, music scored for double choir or for small and large ensembles, or choral music with instruments, can make a feast unforgettably grand.

Pipe organ. It goes without saying that the pipe organ has much to contribute in regard to levels of solemnity. In a church with a fine

---

12 See, for an example, John Paul Sonnen, "The Custom of Festive Hangings in Rome: The Chiesa Nuova," *LAJ*, January 1, 2025.
13 See Kwasniewski, *Good Music*, 103–4; Joseph Ahmad, "Droning at Mass," *NLM*, January 3, 2020; idem, "Singing Upon the Book: Further Methods of Chant Harmonization," *NLM*, October 7 and 8, 2020; David Clayton, "Using Drones as Harmony—A Simple Way to Add to the Spiritual Effect of Sacred Music," *The Way of Beauty* blog, December 27, 2017.
14 See "'Where Has God Gone?' The Pressure of *Horror Vacui*" in Kwasniewski, *Good Music*, 276–82.

organ, its very silence already says that we are at a lower level. When, on the other hand, all stops are pulled for a processional or a postlude, we feel in our bones that we are present for the coming or the departure of the King.[15]

Bells. Among the rarest "fine touches" is that of having one set of sanctuary bells for weekdays and another for Sundays or other solemn occasions. The effect is instant: the very difference in the sound of the tinkling bells transmits an immediate message about the occasion. Churches with bell towers may ring the large bells during the consecration. This, again, can be an excellent distinction between ferias and feasts, or weekdays and Sundays: ringing or not ringing the big bells. (Where I lived in Austria, however, they rang the tower bells every day at consecration; nor would I say that this is inappropriate!)

IN THE REALM OF SMELL

Incense comes in a wide variety of types, so we can vary the type used according to the liturgical calendar, with this scent for Christmas, that one for Lent, that other one for Paschaltide, and so forth.[16] Most well-stocked sacristies settle into a routine along these lines, but it is worth giving some thought to it. We know how powerful the sense of smell is for memory associations. Think of what it would be like if families attending the same church for decades always smell a certain Ethiopian incense at Christmas, and a certain Somalian one at Easter, just as they might be accustomed to smelling turkey and pumpkin pie at Thanksgiving or lamb with mint jam at Easter. In church their noses will instantly draw them into the feast even before their minds have had a chance to process the words being sung. At the Incarnation, the Word assumed our senses, not just our mental faculties. The Lord, too, had his favorite scents at home, the ones that perhaps He most associated with His mother and foster-father.

IN THE REALMS OF TASTE AND TOUCH

This, admittedly, is a more difficult area to speak about, because the liturgy *as such* communicates mostly through man's noblest and most rational senses, sight and hearing, with smell coming in third. For taste and touch, there is not much more to discuss than furniture and the type of altar bread used.

---

[15] See Kwasniewski, *Good Music*, 234–38. On all these questions of music (chant, polyphony, organ), see Patrick John Brill, *The Great Sacred Music Reform of Pope St. Pius X: The Genesis, Interpretation, and Implementation of the Motu Proprio* Tra le Sollecitudini (Os Justi Press, 2025).

[16] See my article "Benedictine Monks on Incense: Sourcing It and Making It," *NLM*, February 10, 2020.

Nevertheless, even here there is room for a judicious variety. At least for the priest, different large hosts could be used for different seasons, as some of them are plain while others have imprints of the crucifixion or a lamb, and different wines might be assigned, such as a drier wine for Lent and a sweeter wine for Paschaltide. The accidents, after all, are meant to point to the reality commemorated, and since sensibles are mutually exclusive (by which I mean, the same wine cannot be dry and sweet at the same time and in the same respect), the accident of taste is not excluded from symbolism. Certainly there is a notable difference in taste between a pure white host and a more wheaten host.

As for the lowliest sense in Aristotle's hierarchy of sensation, touch: if the altar servers are accustomed to using portable kneeling pads, or if the people have a detachable kneeling pad along the Communion rail, such pads could be removed during penitential seasons. The knees, at least, would register the difference right quick. A layman could also choose to kneel straight on the floor for Mass rather than using the retractable kneeler.

CONCLUSIONS

The point of the foregoing overview is not to suggest that *all* of these different things should be done all at once, much less to imply that all of them are equally important, but merely to give lots of ideas of how the Catholic tradition, especially through the fine arts, has offered us a plethora of ways to differentiate levels of solemnity[17]—*even if every Mass offered were to be a Solemn High Mass.*

All these things pertain to the execution of liturgy, but the laity for their part could mark the difference in days with how formally they dress, which rosary they bring to Mass, which daily missal or devotional book they use. It happens rather often, for example, that women have different veils, some simple, some more elaborate, for different occasions; some will use a white chapel veil during Christmastide and Eastertide and black the rest of the year, or will have veils in darker shades of the liturgical colors. Perhaps even more popular for festive occasions is the wearing of hats or bonnets.

I am the first to admit that none of these things is "essential," but that is also somewhat beside the point. What is essential in the liturgy, at least in a canonical mindset, is relatively minimal. The fullness of liturgical life should go well beyond the minimum to embrace all the ways in which human beings, as creatures of flesh and blood, can communicate about invisible mysteries through sensible means.

---

[17] See Shawn Tribe, "Keeping Feasts with Greater Festivity," *LAJ*, July 5, 2019.

❧ 22 ❧
Modest Proposals for Improving Low Mass

WITH THE LARGE NUMBER OF MASSES NOW being offered in the *usus antiquior* worldwide, it is fair to say that Catholics are experiencing some of the same problems that were pointed to as reasons for the liturgical reform prior to the Council. While the list of such problems is lengthy, none of them in fact justified the liturgical reform as it actually played out. Nevertheless, one would hope that the traditional movement could learn from past mistakes and make a special effort to avoid the same in the current fraught ecclesiastical situation. Since the manner of carrying out the Mass redounds immediately to either the edification and devotion of the priest and people or to their distraction and frustration, it behooves us to take it seriously. For indeed, nothing could be more serious than the sacramental re-presentation of the Sacrifice of the Cross.

In this chapter, I will look at three common problems: inaudible, inarticulate muttering of servers at Low Mass; rapid-fire delivery of the Latin prayers by the priest, as if he were in a race against time; and a celebrant violating the *clara voce* rubrics by treating a parochial Mass as if it were a silent monastic Mass, thereby depriving the people of the opportunity to hear those parts of the Mass that, according to centuries-old rubrics, Holy Mother Church wishes them to hear. It is important to note that none of my proposals requires changing the predetermined rubrics or structure of the Mass itself. In the spirit of the initial phase of the twentieth-century Liturgical Movement, they merely call upon priest and servers to observe more closely the existing rubrics, which will in turn augment the reverence of the sacrifice and the laity's understanding of and unity with it.

THE DIALOGUE BETWEEN PRIEST AND SERVERS

While it would be ideal to have liturgy served by clerics in minor orders, religious brothers, or seminarians, most of the time Catholics have recourse to "altar boys" filling in for acolytes. And I have no complaint about the institution of altar boys as such, provided they are tall enough and serious enough to fulfill their functions in the sanctuary. There are many social and spiritual benefits for the boys, not least the opportunity given to them of learning the liturgy up-close, acquiring habits of discipline, and actively discerning a priestly vocation.[1]

However, as we learn from the High Mass, which is the real template of the Low Mass, the servers may be seen as making responses on behalf of the entire body of the faithful. At High Mass, we all sing *Et cum spiritu tuo*, and at Low Mass the servers speak the same words (in this chapter I am purposefully not discussing the Dialogue Mass, a twentieth-century aberration). Moreover, as the Roman rite developed, the preparatory prayers or prayers at the foot of the altar ceased to be purely private prayers for the priest and ministers; they belong to the faithful, too, who treasure them, follow them in their missals or from memory, and wish to *hear* them at Low Mass. As if in tacit acknowledgment of this fact, nearly all of the priests whose old rite Masses I have heard over the past thirty years utter Psalm 42 and the additional prayers prior to the *Aufer a nobis* with a level of voice that can be readily heard throughout the church.

It is therefore asymmetrical and irritating when the servers mumble, swallow, or whisper their responses to the priest's well-articulated phrases. It is the liturgical equivalent to someone walking with one normal leg and one peg-leg. Here is how it comes across to the faithful in the pews:

Priest. In nómine Patris, et Fílii, ✠ et Spíritus Sancti. Amen. Introíbo ad altáre Dei.
Servers. Ad Deum qui lætíficat juventútem meam.

P. Júdica me, Deus, et discérne causam meam de gente non sancta: ab hómine iníquo, et dolóso érue me.
S. Quia tu es, Deus, fortitúdo mea: quare me repulísti, et quare tristis incédo, dum afflígit me inimícus?

P. Emítte lucem tuam, et veritátem tuam: ipsa me deduxérunt, et aduxérunt in montem sanctum tuum, et in tabernácula tua.
S. Et introíbo ad altáre Dei: ad Deum qui lætíficat juventútem meam.

P. Confitébor tibi in cíthara, Deus, Deus meus: quare tristis es, ánima mea, et quare contúrbas me?
S. Spera in Deo, quóniam adhuc confitébor illi: salutáre vultus mei, et Deus meus.

P. Glória Patri, et Fílio, et Spirítui Sancto.
S. Sicut erat in princípio et nunc, et semper, et in sæcula sæculórum. Amen.

P. Introíbo ad altáre Dei.
S. Ad Deum qui lætíficat juventútem meam.

P. Adjutórium nostrum ✠ in nómine Dómini.
S. Qui fecit cælum et terram.

And so forth, throughout the liturgy. The dialogue is often so unequal that the priest might as well be the only one speaking, in a bizarre,

---

[1] See my article "Ordained, Assistants, and Faithful: On Hierarchical Participation in Three Spheres," *OnePeterFive*, February 23, 2022.

vivisected conversation, somewhat like overhearing a telephone call. If such servers are representing *us* at the foot of the altar, they are doing a poor job of it. Why don't they speak up a bit—"enunciate and articulate!," as my high school rhetoric teacher used to say? Again, this is not about using a *loud* voice. It is simply about using a normal audible voice and not rushing through the words. They are, after all, *prayers*, and prayers are worth taking the time to pray. *Deo gratias* after the Epistle should sound like it means "Thanks be to God," and the same with *Laus tibi, Christe*, "Praise to Thee, O Christ."

Am I asking too much of these well-meaning and sometimes clueless boys? No. I believe that those who train altar boys should teach them what the words mean, and teach them how to enunciate them and articulate them at a normal volume and a walking, not running, pace. Not:

> *P.* Kyrie eleison.
> *S.* Kyrie eleison.
> *P.* Kyrie eleison.
> *S.* Christe eleison.
> *P.* Christe eleison.
> *S.* Christe eleison.
> *P.* Kyrie eleison.
> *S.* Kyrie eleison.
> *P.* Kyrie eleison.

Above all, at the end of the Offertory, these words should be distinct and audible at Low Mass:

> Suscípiat Dóminus sacrifícium de mánibus tuis ad laudem et glóriam nóminis sui, ad utilitátem quoque nostram, totiúsque Ecclésiæ suæ sanctæ.

And moving into the Preface dialogue, it is totally unfitting to hear the following:

> *P.* ... per omnia sæcula sæculorum.
> *S.* Amen.
> *P.* Dóminus vobíscum.
> *S.* Et cum spíritu tuo.
> *P.* Sursum corda.
> *S.* Habémus ad Dóminum.
> *P.* Grátias agámus Dómino Deo nostro.
> *S.* Dignum et justum est.

The priest is inviting us, in one of the most beautiful phrases of the Roman liturgy, to "Lift your hearts on high!," and the response should be in earnest: "We have lifted [them] up to the Lord!" Then, in a phrase rich with Eucharistic meaning: "Let us give thanks unto the

Lord our God." To which the response must be equally meaningful, as if the servers are senators speaking for a holy nation: "It is worthy and just." These are not phrases to be rattled off under one's breath; they are to be sounded forth in public.

The inaudibility of the servers, the disharmony it creates with the priest, and the lack of "purchase" it offers the congregation are matters that deserve to be taken seriously by the adult trainers who prepare the servers and by the MCs who regulate the teams. This is not a difficult problem to correct, but it does require awareness, attentiveness, and follow-through, together with positive reinforcement ("Johnny, it was great how you spoke your responses so clearly today. Keep it up!").

HASTE IN CLERICAL RECITATION OF TEXTS

A related matter of concern is the post-*Summorum* reappearance of clergy who habitually rush through the Low Mass. As far as I can tell, we are dealing in most cases with genuinely good men who intend no disrespect to Our Lord and no disedification to the faithful. Nevertheless, machine-gun Latin —

> Paternoster,quiesincælis:Sanctificéturnomentuum:Advéniatregnum tuum:Fiatvolúntastua,sicutincælo,etinterra.Panemnostrumquotidiánumdanobishódie:Etdimíttenobisdébitanostra,sicutetnosdimít timusdebitóribusnostris.Etnenosindúcasintentatiónem.
>
> AgnusDei,quitollispeccátamundi:miserérenobis.AgnusDei,quitollis peccátamundi:miserérenobis.AgnusDei,quitollispeccátamundi:dona nobispacem.
>
> Dómine,nonsumdignus,utintressubtectummeum
> Dómine,nonsumdignus,utintressubtectummeum
> Dómine,nonsumdignus,utintressubtectummeum

— does not carry any conviction of being speech truly addressed to the face of a living Person with whom one is communicating, as two friends would talk to one another, nor, for this reason, can it in fact increase the devotion of the speaker or of the listeners. It seems, on the contrary, to be a lost opportunity on the part of both priest and people for the intensification of acts of adoration, faith, humility, contrition, and other virtues. In spite of the daily repetition of the Mass, we could truthfully apply to its celebration the familiar words of the Quaker who said: "I shall pass this way but once; any good that I can do or any kindness I can show to any human being, let me do it now. Let me not defer nor neglect it, for I shall not pass this way again." This particular Mass will never be repeated, nor will this particular congregation assist at it, at least in this moment of their lives. And as we know from the dogmatic theologians, the subjective devotion of the priest and of the people have a role to play in the spiritual fruitfulness of the Mass.

Perhaps the most germane statement made on this subject is that of St. Francis de Sales: "Beware of haste, for it is a deadly enemy of true devotion; and anything done with precipitation is never done well. Let us go slowly, for if we do but keep advancing we shall thus go far."[2]

Dom Chautard, author of *The Soul of the Apostolate*—one of the few truly essential spiritual books written in the past century—has a lot to say on this subject. The author spends several pages unpacking the meaning of the prayer said before the Divine Office, in which the cleric asks for the grace to recite it *digne, attente, devote*, worthily, attentively, devoutly:

> *DIGNE.* A respectful position and bearing, the precise pronunciation of the words, slowing down over the more important parts. Careful observance of the rubrics. My tone of voice, *the way in which I make signs of the Cross, genuflections, etc.; my body* itself: all will go to show not only that *I know Whom I am addressing, and what I am saying*, but also that *my heart is in what I am doing*. What an apostolate I can sometimes exercise [this way]!...
>
> *DEVOTE.* This is the most important point. Everything comes back to the need of making our Office and all our liturgical functions *acts of piety*, and, consequently, acts that come *from the heart*.
>
> "Haste kills all devotion." Such is the principle laid down by St. Francis de Sales in talking of the Breviary, and it applies *a fortiori* to the Mass. Hence, I shall make it a hard and fast rule to devote around *half an hour to my Mass* in order to ensure a devout recitation not only of the Canon but of all the other parts as well. I shall reject without pity all pretexts for getting through this, the principal act of my day, in a hurry. If I have the habit of mutilating certain words or ceremonies, I shall apply myself, and go over these faulty places *very slowly and carefully*, even exaggerating my exactitude for a while....
>
> O my Divine Mediator! Fill my heart with detestation for all haste in those things where I stand in Your place, or act in the name of the Church! Fill me with the conviction that haste paralyzes that *great Sacramental*, the Liturgy, and makes impossible that spirit of prayer without which, no matter how zealous a priest I may appear to be on the outside, I would be lukewarm, or perhaps worse, in Your estimation. Burn into my inmost heart those words so full of terror: "*Cursed be he that doth the work of God deceitfully*" (Jer 48:10).[3]

---

[2] See the reflections of Archbishop Gullickson: "Velocity: Haste as Liturgical Abuse," *ad montem myrrhae*, January 12, 2020, https://admontemmyrrhae.blogspot.com/2020/01/velocity-haste-as-liturgical-abuse.html.

[3] Jean-Baptiste Chautard, OCSO, *The Soul of the Apostolate*, trans. A Monk of Our

St. Leonard of Port Maurice counsels the priest in the following words:

> Use all diligence to celebrate with the utmost modesty, recollection, and care, taking time to pronounce well and distinctly every word, and perfectly to fulfill every ceremony with due propriety and gravity; for words ill articulated, or spoken without a tone of meekness and awe, and ceremonies done without decorum and accuracy, render the divine service, instead of a help to piety and religion, a source of distress and scandal. Let the priest keep the inner man devoutly recollected; let him think of the sense of all the words which he articulates, dwelling on their sense and spirit, and making throughout internal efforts corresponding to their holy suggestions. Then truly will there be an influx of great devotion into those assisting, and he will obtain the utmost profit for his own soul.[4]

There is no question that a reverent Low Mass can be offered in thirty minutes by a priest whose Latin flows well, who is extremely adept at the ceremonies, and who knows many of the prayers by heart. It is also true that sometimes Low Mass takes longer than it should because the celebrant is still learning the ropes and has not yet "mastered" the liturgical form. But regardless of the total duration, any appearance of rushing in words or gestures is never edifying and always detracts from the dignity and beauty of the celebration—and consequently from the prayerfulness it is meant to induce as well as the spiritual fruit likely to be derived from it.

Small things make a difference in the spiritual life; why would it not be the same in the greatest act of worship we can offer to God, the Holy Sacrifice of the Mass? For a long time, Catholics have fought simply to have access to the old Mass, an immense reservoir of grace, doctrine, and godly piety. We should not stop fighting for that access if we do not yet enjoy it or if it has been discontinued in our area, but now that we are some years down the road from the Mass's reintroduction on a wider scale, it is time to correct bad habits into which we may have inadvertently slid.

Some may be wondering: Why should we concern ourselves with such tiny matters when the Church on earth seems to be falling apart in front of our very eyes? My view, however, is quite the opposite. The crisis we are living is one of worldliness, lukewarmness, infidelity, and apostasy. The ultimate solution to it is not investigations (however necessary), proclamations of doom and hand-wringing (however correct and satisfying), or a flurry of activism (however tempting).

Lady of Gethsemani (TAN Books, 2008; originally published in 1927), 266; 268–69.
4 Leonard of Port Maurice, *The Hidden Treasure: Holy Mass* (TAN Books, 2012), 51.

The solution begins and ends with drawing near to the Father and joining with the citizens of the fatherland. Now is the very best time to attend to the service of Almighty God in His holy sanctuary and to do what is right, *because* it is right, for the love and glory of God. Fidelity in little things is rewarded with greater blessings, and infidelity in little things leads to blessings being taken away. This is the teaching of Our Lord Himself.[5]

THE PARISH LOW MASS IS NOT A "SILENT" MASS

One Pentecost octave, I happened to be visiting a big city and decided to go to a nearby Latin Mass on the Ember Friday. I invited two acquaintances to come with me.

I was surprised when Mass began and I could hear *nothing* of the dialogue of priests and servers. "Perhaps this is just — for some reason — how they do the prayers at the foot of the altar," I thought to myself. The priest mounted the steps and went to the missal to recite the Introit. Again, total silence. My bewilderment turned to frustration and disappointment as the entire Mass continued, with hardly a single word of it being audible. The only thing recited *clara voce* was the *Domine, non sum dignus* before the Communion of the faithful.[6]

Since I was traveling, I did not have my *St. Andrew's Daily Missal* with me, and my two guests, who are not regular attendees, had no access to the Propers either.[7] I wasn't expecting this lack of a missal to be a problem, as I can follow the Latin to a great extent if I can just hear the words. Hearing nothing, I was simply watching a priest say his private Mass. The motions are beautiful and the silence is prayerful, but I still felt deprived of access to the parts of the Mass that the Church intends the faithful to hear. Even aside from verbal comprehension (which, I recognize, is often overrated nowadays), it is comforting to hear the Latin words floating through the church at the appropriate times. There is benefit in *hearing* the Gloria, the Credo, the Sanctus, the Agnus Dei.

Evidently my guests felt a similar perplexity, since they both said to me afterwards at breakfast: "Is the old Mass always so completely

---

[5] Lk 16:10–12; Lk 19:12–27; Mt 25:14–30; cf. Kwasniewski, *Turned Around*, 79–108.
[6] In my consternation, I tried to come up with excuses for the priest and server: "The church is so large, perhaps the priest simply couldn't speak in a way that the faithful could hear" (I am, needless to say, opposed to rigging up a lapel mic or an altar mic connected to loudspeakers); but then the easy audibility of his voice when he *did* speak up made me realize that the silence for the rest of the time was a chosen policy.
[7] No one is required to use a missal, of course; but for the priest to say silently that which is supposed to be said aloud — again, not according to my personal opinion, but according to the requirement of the rubrics — is for him to impose his personal devotional preference on the rest of us in the congregation.

silent?" I had to respond: "No, it's not supposed to be. When I attend Mass elsewhere—with the Fraternity of St. Peter, or the Institute of Christ the King, or a diocesan priest—one can hear most of the Mass of the Catechumens, and some parts of the Mass of the Faithful."

The rubrics of the *usus antiquior* stipulate unambiguously which parts of the Proper and Ordinary of the Mass are to be recited in an elevated tone of voice. A traditional *Missale Romanum* contains at its head the *Rubricæ generales Missalis*, rubrics telling the celebrant what to do and say, and how to do it and say it. Let's take a 1920 *editio typica* as our reference point. Chapter XVI concerns *De his quæ clara voce, aut secreto dicenda sunt in Missa*, or "Concerning things that are to be said in the Mass with an audible voice or silently." Here is my translation of the pertinent paragraphs (underlining for emphasis):

> In a private Mass the following are to be said *clara voce*: the antiphon and psalm before the Introit, the Confession and that which follows (except *Aufer a nobis* and *Oramus te*); again, the Introit, Kyrie, Gloria, *Dominus vobiscum*, *Oremus*, *Flectamus genua*, *Levate*, Collect or Collects, Prophecy, Epistle, Gradual, Alleluia, Tract, Sequence, Gospel, Creed, Offertory antiphon, *Orate fratres* (just those two words), Preface, *Nobis quoque peccatoribus* (just those three words), *Per omnia* &c. with *Pater noster*, *Per omnia* &c. with *Pax Domini*, Agnus Dei, *Domine non sum dignus* (just those four words), Communion antiphon, Postcommunion or Postcommunions, *Humiliate capita*, *Ite missa est* or *Benedicamus Domino* or *Requiescant in pace*, Blessing, and Last Gospel or other Gospel. All the rest is to be said *secreto*.

Of great interest is the next paragraph, which specifies that *clara voce* means spoken in such a way that those around may hear and follow:

> The priest ought to take the utmost care that things which are to be said *clara voce* are pronounced distinctly and appropriately—not very quickly, so that he can pay attention to what he reads, nor exceedingly slowly, lest the listeners be afflicted with tedium; neither with a voice excessively raised, lest others be disturbed who perhaps might be offering Mass in the same church at the same time, nor with one that is too faint [*submissa*], lest those gathered around be unable to hear, but in a moderate and earnest tone, that it may both stir up devotion and be accommodated to the listeners that they may understand what is read.[8] Those things, on the other hand, which are to be said *secreto* should be pronounced in such a way that only the priest himself may hear them, and they are not heard by those gathered around.

---

[8] I take this to mean that those who know Latin should be able to follow the *clara voce* portions without the use of a hand missal—which makes sense, since hand missals were not widely and easily available prior to the twentieth century.

The "marching orders" contained in this rubric, however flowery its expression, are not especially hard to grasp and put into practice. While it is true that some churches are so vast that even a priest speaking *clara voce* might not be able to be heard or understood by those sitting far away, I have found that it depends not so much on the size of a church but on its architecture, and on such factors as whether the heating or air conditioning is blowing, or fans are running, or other ambient noise is coming in. At the church I visited on that Ember Friday of Pentecost, it was not difficult to hear the priest when he did speak up. Despite the great volume of space, the Latin was perfectly comprehensible; the acoustics would be excellent for a *Missa recitata* or *Missa lecta*.

It seems to me important to recognize an unofficial distinction not discussed in the rubrics. There is a difference between a publicly scheduled Mass offered at the high altar in the expected presence of a congregation of people, and a "private" Mass of a monk at a side altar in a monastery, adjacent to a dozen other monks simultaneously offering Masses. At Clear Creek, Le Barroux, Norcia, Silverstream, and other such places, those whispered early morning Masses—with the faithful seldom more than a few feet away from their chosen side chapel—seem like quite a different affair from a scheduled public parochial Mass at a high altar in the main church, with the *circumstantes* standing dozens or possibly hundreds of feet away. The latter scenario demands more care on the part of the priest to ensure that the audible parts are indeed audible.

I was grateful to be able to assist at Holy Mass during the Pentecost octave, immerse myself in prayer, and rejoice in the beauty of God's house; I was even more grateful to receive Our Lord in Holy Communion. Nevertheless, it disturbed me to be cut off from the antiphons, orations, and readings that Holy Mother Church wishes the faithful to be able to hear with their ears. It seems to me that priests, if any may have fallen into bad habits in this regard, ought to bear in mind that speaking those parts of the Proper and Ordinary *clara voce*, as specified in the rubrics, is a way of showing respect and consideration to the faithful who come to church to drink from the greatest source of prayer we enjoy as Catholics: the sacred liturgy.

"REACTIVE PARTICIPATION"

As we have seen, the paragraphs that call for *clara voce* really do exist and really do govern the celebration of Mass. They are not "a personal preference," or an attempt at quashing legitimate diversity, or a Trojan Horse for the Dialogue Mass or the Radical Liturgical Movement, since they have been in the missal for a very long time—for centuries, in fact.

Let's review what was said. (1) Priests should observe the rubrics of the missal. (2) This is even more the case if the rubric is designed to ensure that the public prayer of the Church is shared with the public. (3) It is a good thing to be able to hear the prayers of the Mass that are meant to be said or sung aloud, regardless of whether one has a daily missal to hand or not. Indeed, if one likes to follow the Proper of the Mass but happens to be *sans* missal, audibility becomes still more important.

And let's review what was *not* said. (1) There should never be any silence at all for meditating or for praying the rosary. (2) Everyone should be saying everything at Mass—"dialogue till you die!" (3) A silent monastic Mass is evil and should be abolished. (4) My personal preferences should be those of everyone else. (5) Everyone should have his eyes or nose glued into a hand missal.

Here are five pieces of advice for critics of the *Missa recitata*:

1. Learn to read the rubrics. They are quite interesting, have a rich history, and are there for a good reason. At least, this can be safely assumed until the reform—at first tipsy, later intoxicated—gets into full swing in the 1960s.

2. *Abusus non tollit usum.* The deformation of right principles by 1960s reformers does not diminish the rightness of said principles. For example, the reformers wanted the liturgy to be within the hands and hearts of the faithful. Fair enough. Then they slashed and burned the inherited liturgy, with its immeasurable treasures, and built a sleek new liturgy that reflected their modern prejudices, all in order to put *their* ideas into the hands and hearts of the faithful. Bad business; nothing short of a betrayal of right principles. Yet the desideratum did not cause the disaster, since the same desideratum is entirely compatible with a different state of affairs.

3. Slippery slope arguments are amongst the weakest. "If you think the priest should speak up, or the faithful join their prayers to the Church's, then—then—it's only a matter of time before you'll want—the *vernacular*! and Communion in the hand! and altar girls! and ... " Really?

4. A Low Mass offered according to the rubrics will still have plenty of silence in it, during which the faithful may pray a rosary or meditate in some other manner. No one in the traditional movement wants to do away with the silent Canon that we all dearly love. By this time, we have learned a thing or two from the dark years of autodemolition.

Why have some people arrived at the idea that a stone-silent parish Low Mass, *contra rubricas*, is either ideal, or at least a form of legitimate diversity? (Again, read carefully: I am speaking of a regular parish Mass intentionally offered in the presence of a congregation, not a monastic side-chapel Mass at 6:00 a.m. with a couple of overachieving scouts on their knees in the shadow of the arch.)

1. The *Missa murmurata* was a highly useful precaution against English soldiers combing through the hedges and bogs to arrest Irish priests. Noise attracted danger. It is thus the safer option.

2. The *Missa murmurata* is also as remote as possible from the Novus Ordo and all its pomps and works. One gets to relish a nice chunk of quiet personal prayer, while leaving "that liturgy business" to the priest, and then one can receive Communion. In short: *the ideal Communion service!* (And people wonder where the abuses of the postconciliar period came from? Hint: they were already in place, albeit less offensively!) This is what I like to call "reactive participation": anything at all that has a parallel in the Novus Ordo, such as the congregation singing, or the priest speaking audibly, or preaching based on the Scripture readings, should *never* be done in the old Mass.

While skittishness about repeating abuses ushered in by the Novus Ordo—above all, the reformers' faulty notion of what constitutes "active participation"—is fully understandable, one ought not to allow such a fear to cloud one's better judgment. Likewise, while the practice of silent Masses was prudent in Ireland under English oppression (one thinks of the famous painting *Mass in a Connemara Cabin* by Aloysius O'Kelly) and indeed testifies to the heroic fortitude of a great Christian people under trying circumstances, it hardly constitutes an exemplar of the best we can do in a time of freedom.

Priests who remember starting up the TLM again after its near extinction remember what it was like in those bumpy days. Any movement towards having the people participate, any hint they should do something besides flipping pages in the red booklet or suppressing noisy kids, was met with "You don't mean the *Dialogue Mass*, Father?" In other words, anything but Cleveland circa 1956 was perceived as stepping onto the slippery slope.

Now, one need have no bone to pick with Cleveland or with 1956 in order to have a fundamental objection to the notion that the public side of the Church's prayer should be given to God in a *non*-public manner that the faithful, even if they wish to do so, cannot internalize in the normal way in which speech is heard and pondered. The very texts of the old Mass are full of ageless wisdom and burning charity.[9] This is our common possession as members of the Mystical Body of Christ, and some of it—the parts, namely, specified in the rubrics

---

[9] This is why I agree with Fr. Joseph Kreuter's sermon on the use of the missal. See p. 154.

under discussion—is meant to be prayed *in common*, in such a way that those who either have a missal or have learned Latin can follow and internalize those antiphons, prayers, and readings *if they wish*. Outside of individual higher states of prayer, which in any case go beyond words, people have a normal human expectation to hear and grasp the words of the liturgy. After all, it is not, *as such*, a private ineffable ecstasy, but a verbal sacrifice of praise.

The admiration for St. Pius X is surely well-deserved. It was this Pope who not only encouraged frequent Communion but also urged Catholics to "pray the Mass, not merely pray *at* Mass."[10] There is more than one way to carry out this advice, and indeed, as Pius XII famously said, not even the same person always wants or needs to pray the same way.[11] Some days we look at a missal, other days we don't; some days we might pray the Sorrowful Mysteries and meditate on the Crucifixion during the Canon, other days we might sit there quietly, watching, listening, silently absorbing the gestures that are a sublime form of prayer unto themselves. The rubrics of the Church are meant to guard and foster *all* these ways of participating, not to dictate only one way to the laity; and yet, allowing for slight differences, there must be a correct way for the *priest* to offer the Mass if our worship is not to explode into as many different liturgies as there are celebrants. This incoherent pluralism is just what the Novus Ordo has unleashed upon the Church, and we can see the fragments of faith and innocence scattered about, past all hope of recollection.

In short, there ought to be an objective stability in how Mass is offered so that the faithful know what to expect, know what Holy Mother Church is sharing with them to nourish their prayer, and may accordingly conform themselves to the liturgy in order to pray as best they can, in their several ways.

---

10 See "When Piety Is Mistaken for Passivity, and Passivity for Piety" in Kwasniewski, *Ministers of Christ*, 141–51.
11 Pius XII, *Mediator Dei*, no. 108: "The needs and inclinations of all are not the same, nor are they always constant in the same individual."

↭ 23 ↮
Should the Postures of the Laity Be Regulated, Legislated, or Revised?

O VER THE YEARS, I HAVE NOTICED AN interesting group of people who are passionate about the subject of the postures of the laity at the traditional Latin Mass. They sometimes have the zeal of crusaders warring against a stubborn enemy, be it *indifference* (laity who couldn't bother to care who's kneeling or standing or sitting, when, or why), *diversity* (varying customs from country to country or even church to church), or *disorderliness* (lack of uniformity at the same Mass). To them, it is very important that a consistent rubric derived from custom or argument be created and implemented. Editors of missals and missalettes likewise often provide directives on when to kneel, sit, or stand; the Baronius missal comes with a nicely-printed insert in two colors, with columns for High Mass and Low Mass.

One sympathizes with them. We all know about the mayhem that can occur inside a church when the congregation is made up of a mix of regular attendees and newbies who are clueless about what's going on in the TLM. At various moments, certain decisive individuals kneel decisively, and people look around sheepishly as if to figure out what they're supposed to do. Sometimes you have a visiting European, or perhaps an American who intensively studies Liturgical Movement brochures, who follows a different set of customs; the confusion multiplies. One can understand, from a purely pragmatic point of view, why a common rubric might be helpful.

This is the perspective offered by a friend who sent me the following letter:

> Ever since I started attending the Latin Mass last year, I have wondered about the physical gestures done by those around me. For example, making the sign of the cross during the prayer after the Confiteor, during the Gloria, and during the Sanctus, as well as striking the breast during the consecration. I am not sure if I am supposed to be doing all these or not (or even what all of them are—is there a list somewhere?).
>
> Having grown up in the Novus Ordo, I have been accustomed to seeing people all doing the same thing, and I had always been told that it was wrong when certain individuals did their own thing (e.g., kneeling during the Agnus Dei), on the basis that "since the

Church doesn't say we're supposed to do these gestures, we're not supposed to do them." Am I mistaken in thinking that a gesture of the people must be approved or instructed to be done by the *General Instruction of the Roman Missal*? Would this assumption only apply to the Mass of Paul VI?

I suppose my inclination toward uniformity in gestures comes from a desire to have the "say the black, do the red" consistency of the Tridentine Mass *equally present* for both the priest and the people. I want to go to Mass and (to quote one of your books) "know what I am going to *see* and hear. The same texts, *the same gestures*, the same ethos, the same Catholic religion."[1] Am I misguided in desiring that consistency among the congregation?

In one way, I lean toward desiring to perform more gestures as a layperson. I'm not sure why, but it seems like a more wholly immersive experience if my arms are symbolizing a truth of the liturgy in addition to my legs (kneeling and standing). On the other hand, my desire to "do" more might just be a symptom of the late Liturgical Movement's faulty desire to create more opportunities for "active participation," as if my standing there in reverent, attentive participation isn't enough. I am torn and don't know what to do, in both the old and new Mass.

My response was as follows.

You raise a great question about bodily participation. The wonderful thing about the old Mass is that the laity's bodily postures and actions *were never regulated*. For nearly 2,000 years, and even now, there are no rubrics that govern what the laity do. Whether they stand, sit, kneel, beat their breasts, make the sign of the cross — all of this is up to them.

The liturgical reformers, who were often of a bureaucratic and even fascist mentality,[2] were disturbed about this lack of uniformity, which struck them as devotionalistic if not dissolute, and succeeded in creating, in the Novus Ordo, a totally regulated set of actions for the congregation (as you surmised, the *General Instruction* pertains only to the modern missal). The problem is, what they agreed on is rather minimalistic, so that one ends up with the surprising paradox that the old rite tended, in the customs that grew up around it, to promote *more* bodily activity during the Mass, while the new rite tends to encourage something more cerebral and passive. Elsewhere, I document the wide variety of actions that are often seen at the TLM (note: as customs, not as requirements).[3]

I suggest that you relinquish the very modern idea that everyone should be doing the same thing at the same time. It may be *fitting* to

---

[1] See Kwasniewski, *Reclaiming Our Roman Catholic Birthright*, 125, emphasis added.
[2] See James Baresel, "The Liturgists and the Fascists," *Rorate Caeli*, August 3, 2023.
[3] See "How the *Usus Antiquior* Elicits Superior Participation" in Kwasniewski, *Noble Beauty*, 191–213.

make certain physical gestures, but they simply can't be imposed or demanded. It seems better that books (or occasionally homilies) should explain to the faithful how their discreet imitation of some of the priest's gestures can be a way to make their prayer more holistic, more "whole-person," and more likely to elicit real prayer—without any of it being required. Basically, if it helps, do it; if it doesn't, no bother.

To my mind there is a judgment call with the Novus Ordo. If you attempt to do *all* of the old gestures at it, you will probably become a distraction to others, and perhaps to yourself as well. If, on the other hand, you're far back in the nave with a pew of your own and no one is likely to notice you, why not do some of the same gestures that one would do during the old Mass? It may be a form of that "mutual enrichment" Benedict XVI called for. When I was still attending the Novus Ordo, I found myself making all sorts of "extra-rubrical" signs of the cross, kneeling when I wasn't "supposed" to, and so forth. I could get away with it easily enough because I basically lived in the choir loft!

To this, my intrepid friend responded:

> My experience, together with your writings, has convinced me that active participation is more perfectly present in the TLM. I am, however, still left with some confusion.
>
> You said that I should relinquish the modern idea that everyone should be doing the same thing. I can see why this idea is wrong when it is motivated by bureaucratic and fascist intentions, but I do not understand what could be wrong with it when it springs from an authentic desire for liturgical unity among the laity, consistent with the precise liturgical unity demanded of priests during the Mass. If it is demanded down to the last detail that the priest have specific physical gestures, why is it unreasonable to similarly demand specific physical gestures from the laity?
>
> It seems like such a demand would promote the liturgical unity and consistency you so often extol. I remember you telling me once about why the rubrics of the traditional Latin Mass were originally "nailed down": years of regional liturgical variances had resulted in a certain anarchy within Catholic worship. To recover liturgical unity in the face of the Protestants, the Church demanded that priests adhere to the rubrics she put forth, which were not novel but had organically developed through the centuries.
>
> The situation with the laity seems similar to me. Even if distraction by what others are idiosyncratically doing during Mass is the sole detrimental result of the lack of gestural unity, that lack itself seems to contradict the marvelously regimented spirit of the old Mass. Would it not be helpful for the Church to put forth a set of TLM rubrics that definitively list the physical gestures she wants the people to follow, as long as the gestures on the list are the ones that have organically developed through centuries of tradition?

Perhaps I am misunderstanding the shortcomings of a regulated set of actions created by the liturgical reformers. In order to avoid the danger of minimalism, doesn't it seem better to establish a more thorough and rightly-ordered rubric?

Your advocacy of "extra-rubrical" gestures in the Novus Ordo surprises me, considering what the *General Instruction* says in no. 42 (2011 ed., USA): "The gestures and bodily posture of both the Priest, the Deacon, and the ministers, and also of the people, must be conducive to making the entire celebration resplendent with beauty and noble simplicity, to making clear the true and full meaning of its different parts, and to fostering the participation of all. Attention must therefore be paid to what is determined by this *General Instruction* and by the traditional practice of the Roman rite and to what serves the common spiritual good of the People of God, *rather than private inclination or arbitrary choice. A common bodily posture, to be observed by all those taking part, is a sign of the unity of the members of the Christian community gathered together for the Sacred Liturgy, for it expresses the intentions and spiritual attitude of the participants and also fosters them.*"

The part I put into italics sounds reasonable to me; am I barking up the wrong tree?

In response, I wrote:

There is something indescribably beautiful about people being allowed to pray in their own way, and peacefully. Now, obviously, some large-scale postures can be expected of everyone: this is consistent with piety, and who would complain? We all stand at both Gospels (the Gospel of the day and the Last Gospel); we all kneel at the *Et incarnatus est* and during the Canon. There are some other widespread customs.

But the moment one tries to legislate details such as "everyone makes the sign of the cross at these eight times, and everyone beats their breasts at these four times, and everyone should bow their heads at these five times," etc., it becomes extremely difficult to implement and enforce, and also turns into an occasion for policing and hectoring. It's too complicated to ask it of everyone all the time; *I* don't even do quite the same thing each time I attend Mass! As you know, it depends at least in part on how slowly or quickly the priest is celebrating it and how well one can hear the priest and servers.[4]

To achieve total uniformity, one would have to "put people through their paces," like a marching band or a squadron of soldiers. In addition, one would practically be forced to simplify to a minimalist extent, as has indeed occurred with Novus Ordo rubrics for the laity. The very thought of it makes me cringe. I honestly don't think it's either possible

---

4 See chapter 22. Cf. John Zuhlsdorf, "Excessive pious gestures during Mass," *Fr. Z's Blog*, January 12, 2019; Kwasniewski, *Ministers of Christ*, 141–51.

or desirable to nail down every last detail for an entire congregation. Obviously it is different for the priest: he is the one offering the awful and sublime Sacrifice, *in persona Christi capitis*, and for him there must be rigid and rigorous rubrics in order to avoid accidents, excesses, defects, arbitrariness, confusion, scandal, etc. There are relatively few ministers in the sanctuary compared to the number of faithful who might be assisting in the nave; and the major ministers spend years in training, becoming true masters of their holy discipline. For the laity, it suffices to have broad agreement on major postures and then to enjoy a broad latitude about everything else.

Even when it comes to the major postures, customs differ from country to country. Why should the bishops or liturgists of the USA or Canada, the United Kingdom or Ireland, Poland or Germany, etc., get to be the ones who decide how the rest of the world will behave?

Jacques and Raïssa Maritain were convinced that Rome was the friend of liberty in this regard—even as late as the years just before the Second Vatican Council; and perhaps, indeed, she once was. Here is what they say in a book published in French in 1959 and in English in 1960:

> Against the pseudo-liturgical exaggerations it behooves one to defend the liberty of souls.... Rome has always been vigilant in opposing any attempt to regiment souls. She knows that the spirit of the liturgy requires respect for the Gospel liberty proper to the New Law. On the contrary, in holding as valid one single form of piety, that in which each one acts in common with the others, and in demanding of all that by word and gesture they obey the liturgical forms with a military precision; in challenging or putting in question private devotions, nay even the adoration of the Blessed Sacrament outside of Mass, those who confuse liturgy and pseudo-liturgy impose on souls rigid frameworks and burden them with external obligations which are of the same type as the observances of the Old Law.[5]

So, in a truly Catholic spirit, we should let the French kneel throughout Mass if that is how they pray best, let the Germans stand a lot instead, and let the Americans alternate between kneeling and sitting; let the people in some countries or chapels make all the Mass responses, while others say a few, or none at all. Catholicity involves both holding the most important things in common, and having a wide variation and flexibility in how things that are not matters of natural or divine law are conducted. I am reminded of the old saying, which is no less true for being vague and overused: *In necessariis unitas, in dubiis*

---

[5] Jacques Maritain, *Liturgy and Contemplation*, trans. Joseph W. Evans (P. J. Kenedy & Sons, 1960), 88–90.

libertas, in omnibus caritas — in necessary matters, unity; in doubtful matters, liberty; in everything, charity. I think one would be extremely hard-pressed to argue successfully that a regulated uniformity of lay postures and gestures during Mass is something essential to our fruitful participation in the liturgy. As Fiedrowicz writes:

> In typical Catholic vastness, a great variety of individual possibilities for participation accompany the rubrical strictness of the rite that do not need to be regulated in any way, but should be respected. Even being silently present and merely watching do not necessarily indicate a lack of interior involvement. The very act of listening, be it with the ears or with the heart, is assuredly a form of active participation.[6]

I would hazard to guess that most traditional Catholics prefer it when everyone is doing the same things in regard to the major actions of standing, sitting, and kneeling, as it removes occasions of confusion and distraction and assists in prayerful engagement with the liturgy. But this much has become clear to me from my travels: whenever I am somewhere unfamiliar, I don't sit in the front row but rather towards the back, and, keeping my wits about me, I look at what the majority are doing and follow the local custom, as St. Augustine recommended long ago in his Letter 54 to Januarius. Few things are worse than the stranger who acts like an angel sent by God to correct singlehandedly the waywardness of backwater yokels. If it matters much to you to keep your own postures, that's an equally good reason to sit far in the back — where you won't be a bother to the rest.[7]

---

[6] Fiedrowicz, *The Traditional Mass*, 228.
[7] Fr. Zuhlsdorf offers similar advice in "What are the authentic rubrics, postures for lay people at the Traditional Latin Mass. Are we doing it wrong?," *Fr. Z's Blog*, February 15, 2020. An entirely separate question is whether or not pews belong in Catholic churches. Were they a good invention? Do they have serious drawbacks? See my article "Are Pews in Churches a Problem?"

❧ 24 ❧
The Liturgy as a Temple

TOWARD THE END OF HIS LIFE ON EARTH, Our Lord Jesus Christ was walking one day through the temple in Jerusalem—a vast structure of noble design, made by human hands, fashioned by Israelites who dared to dream that this was "God's house" the way that Herod's palace was Herod's house. The fact that the first temple built under Solomon had been razed to the ground by the Babylonian army does not seem to have convinced the children of the covenant that their dream was doomed to failure.

> And as He was going out of the temple, one of His disciples said to Him: "Master, behold what manner of stones and what buildings are here!" And Jesus answering, said to him: "Seest thou all these great buildings? There shall not be left a stone upon a stone, that shall not be thrown down." (Mk 13:1–2)

The temple was only ever meant to be a temporary sign of God's indwelling in Israel—a union destined to be fulfilled in the Word made flesh, the temple *not* made by human hands, where God and man are one, indissolubly and forever. The body of Christ is the tabernacle of the Most High, the place where His glory dwelleth. Hence, in the plan of Divine Providence, the Romans in A. D. 70 destroyed the temple made by human hands, clearing the way for the worldwide temple of the Mystical Body of Christ.

This is not to say that the Christian religion is disembodied, as a certain spiritualistic strain in Christianity, with a strong tendency towards iconoclasm, has been tempted to believe, especially in the eighth, sixteenth, and twentieth centuries. On the contrary, we have *a new and better temple*, the Body of Christ, which—or rather Who—is really, truly, substantially present in the Most Blessed Sacrament of the Altar, housed in every tabernacle of the world.

Each Catholic church is a place in which "the whole fullness of deity dwells bodily" (Col 2:9), making even the humblest chapel greater, worthier, and more glorious than the first temple of Solomon or the second temple of Zerubbabel, expanded by Herod. What Our Lord says about the lilies of the field could be applied to Catholic churches: "I say to you, that not even Solomon in all his glory was arrayed as one of these" (Mt 6:29)—for "behold, a greater than Solomon is here" (Mt 12:42).

It is fitting, then—indeed, more than fitting, *required* by the moral virtue of religion—that our churches be designed and decorated in such a way that they point unambiguously to and boldly proclaim the temple that is Jesus Christ Himself, inseparable from the temple of His Mystical Body, the Catholic Church.[1] In this way, a church imitates and continues the mission of the forerunner who cried out: "Behold the Lamb of God! Behold Him who taketh away the sins of the world" (Jn 1:29).

The sacred liturgy, too, should point to Christ and proclaim Him. As the *opus Dei* or work of God, as an action primarily *from* God and *for* Him, it should share in His own attributes as He has revealed them to us in the history of salvation, and present them to us for our internalization. It should appear to be what He Himself is: ancient of days, stable, indestructible, permanent, strong, holy, transcendent, mysterious, at times bewildering. Above all, it must not seem to be "made by human hands"—that is, a merely human, temporal, this-worldly, secular project—for we would rightly hold it in contempt, and it would have to suffer the same fate as the Solomonic and Herodian temples. Rather, we could place on the lips of the liturgy, as a living reality fashioned by a divine hand in the womb of the Church, the words of the psalmist:

> Thou didst form my inward parts, thou didst knit me together in my mother's womb.... My frame was not hidden from thee, when I was being made in secret, intricately wrought in the depths of the earth. Thy eyes beheld my unformed substance; in thy book were written, every one of them, the days that were formed for me, when as yet there was none of them. (Ps 139:13, 15–16 RSV)

How different, shockingly so, is the *Novus Ordo* (*Seclorum*, one is tempted to add), where the liturgy is, and displays itself as, the work of human hands, revamped according to modern ideas, subject to human manipulation, in a cacophony of vulgar tongues, forming ever new cultural compounds like an unstable element!

> And some saying of the temple that it was adorned with goodly stones and gifts, He said: "These things which you see, the days will come in which there shall not be left a stone upon a stone that shall not be thrown down." (Lk 21:5–6)

In reading these haunting words, how can we not be reminded of the reformed liturgical rites, which were built up by committees of men, experts with flowing phylacteries of scholarship, who were

---

[1] See my article "Unambiguous Theocentricity: Church Architecture and the Traditional Mass," *OnePeterFive*, June 6, 2018.

adorning (as they saw it) the liturgy with "goodly stones and gifts" specially conceived for Modern Man? These "great buildings," all of them, will be thrown down, for they are not the temple formed over the ages by the Holy Ghost in the womb of Holy Mother Church, where the traditional liturgical rites in all their wonderful extravagance were knit together, intricately wrought, fashioned in secret.

"A house divided against itself cannot stand" (Mt 12:25). The new liturgy is a house divided against itself: it is no longer the Roman rite organically developed over many centuries, but a new fabrication made up of bits and pieces of antiquity and modernity. It is like the vision interpreted by the Prophet Daniel:

> Thou, O king, sawest, and behold there was as it were a great statue: this statue, which was great and high, tall of stature, stood before thee, and the look thereof was terrible. The head of this statue was of fine gold, but the breast and the arms [were] of silver, and the belly and the thighs of brass: and the legs of iron, the feet part of iron and part of clay. (Dan 2:31–33)

Even so is the new liturgy, an imposing work of human hands that is fatally flawed by its lack of unity, integrity, consistency, and cohesion. It is not the one Roman rite of the ages, but a voluntaristic product of hundreds of "experts" working in tandem on little committees, murdering to dissect. The only "unity" their product enjoys is the positivistic approval of Paul VI, which is incapable of fusing the statue into one substance and breathing into it the breath of life.

A compilation known as *The Lives of the Desert Fathers* tells us about a certain John the Hermit:

> His only food was the Communion which the priest brought him on Sundays. His rule of life permitted nothing else. Now one day Satan assumed the form of the priest and went to him earlier than usual, pretending that he wanted to give him Communion. The blessed John, realizing who it was, said to him: "O father of all subtlety and all mischief, enemy of all righteousness, will you not cease to deceive the souls of Christians, but you dare to attack the Mysteries themselves?"[2]

This, on a massive scale, is what the father of all subtlety and all mischief, enemy of all righteousness, has dared to do in our times: he has attacked, at their root and in all their branches, the Mysteries of our salvation. He has done so by inducing men to corrupt the liturgical rites of all the sacraments and sacramentals, and the Divine Office, and then to cling to these as if they were better than the visible image of

---

[2] *The Lives of the Desert Fathers*, trans. Norman Russell (Cistercian Publications, 1981), 93.

the invisible God we had received from our forefathers. He has sown doubts, errors, and confusion in dogma and morals, finding many willing accomplices among those who proudly boast of the superiority of modern times, of modern ways of thinking and acting.

We know what happened to the great statue of Nebuchadnezzar's dream:

> Thus thou sawest, till a stone was cut out of a mountain without hands: and it struck the statue upon the feet thereof that were of iron and of clay, and broke them in pieces. Then was the iron, the clay, the brass, the silver, and the gold broken to pieces together, and became like the chaff of a summer's threshing floor, and they were carried away by the wind: and there was no place found for them: but the stone that struck the statue became a great mountain, and filled the whole earth. (Dan 2:34–35)

Like all symbolic visions, this one admits of multiple fulfillments and applications. Daniel interpreted it in regard to a succession of kingdoms, culminating in a kingdom that shall never be destroyed. Can it say something further to us today?

The stone that strikes the great fabrication of human ingenuity is "cut out of a mountain without hands." The giant and terrifying monolith towering over us, a product of feverish squadrons of laborers, is shattered by a little stone that owes its existence to a supernatural sculptor. This stone grows to become a great mountain that fills the whole Earth.

Does this not sound like the Catholic traditionalist movement? It began small, but it is growing, and its growth, being of the Holy Ghost, cannot be thwarted. It loves and defends and promotes not the "banal on-the-spot fabrication" of committees, but the accumulated and inherited treasury of the ages, the worthy vessel of the Incarnate Word, the singing and silent witness of the glory of God. This movement will become a great mountain that fills the whole Earth, as the experiment in monumental statuary falls to pieces, decade after decade.

To adapt an ancient liturgical text from the Easter Vigil, we could cry out: "O happy fault, that preserved for us so great a liturgy!" The radicalized Liturgical Movement in the middle of the twentieth century was hell-bent on tinkering with the Roman liturgy, slowly denaturing and disintegrating it, especially from 1948 onward. Should we not, as counterintuitive as it sounds, be grateful that the proponents of change went as far as they did? Their hubris made them eventually turn away from the historic Roman rite and create a new rite to replace it; but this meant the abandoned Roman rite was left more or less intact, and returning to it is far simpler than if it had continued to be endlessly tinkered with. The outrageous magnitude of the liturgical revolution was permitted by Divine Providence in order to make it possible to return to the preceding tradition *in full*, as faithful clergy and laity over time come to see the corruption and the reasons for repudiating *all* of it—including the antiquarian simplifications and disfigurations introduced during the 1950s under Pius XII, who provided the opening that Paul VI needed. Around the world, traditionalists are awakening to the full magnitude of the harm that was wrought. Ever more clearly, they see the only way forward: total adherence to the Roman rite in its Tridentine form, prior to the arrogant meddling of myopic experts.

The Holy Sacrifice of the Mass in its potent purity, and the traditional liturgy in general, exorcises the spirit of modernism out of the Church. Nothing is more urgently needed than this exorcism—and it is already happening, wherever tradition has established a beachhead on the enemy's territory.

Epilogue

THE SACRAMENTAL SACRIFICE ACCOMplished by the double consecration is always pleasing to God *in itself*. To the extent, however, that the new rite fails to respect the gifts of tradition that Our Lord Himself inspired in His Church and fails, moreover, to give Him, here and now, the honor and reverence due to Him in our external worship, to just that extent is it displeasing to the same Lord of history and of holiness, and should not continue in existence. The innovations and antiquarianisms that dominate the modern rite of Paul VI cannot but be harmful to the Church's identity, coherence, and mission. There is no future for a liturgy that has severed its ties to the past, its bond to the Faith of every generation, unfolding across the ages. The ersatz *lex orandi* is defective in its texts, rubrics, and ceremonies; it fails to embody adequately and communicate clearly the full *lex credendi* of the Catholic Church.[1] This is an objective wound in the Body of Christ and cannot be papered over with charitable intentions or surreptitious improvements.

While I sympathize with a priest who wishes to do his utmost to offer the Novus Ordo as best he can, with the right intention and spirit, it is hard to find objective historical or theological grounds for supporting that approach as a formal policy or principled project, which is what I take the phrase "reform of the reform" or even "doing the Novus Ordo well" to mean: a way of reconnecting the Novus Ordo to the organically developed liturgical tradition of the West embodied in the Vetus Ordo—a tradition from which it departed *in toto* by the simple fact that everything was submitted to the scrutiny of the experts and filtered through their ideological system (what a friend calls "the Great Unfreeze"). By dint of this process, which is forever baked into its existence, whatever remains is thoroughly modern, even the elements that come from the past.[2] If the liturgy is not treated as a gift of tradition that we humbly receive, it becomes a product we make, a thing we validate and give rights to—which we could just as easily toss aside. It seems to me that this is part of the reason why some clergy, such as Fr. Bryan Houghton and Fr. Roger-Thomas Calmel, said from the first moment that they could not, in good conscience, offer the Novus

---

[1] As has been demonstrated by now too many times to count. Scholars whose names quickly come to mind: Dobszay, Pristas, Fiedrowicz, Barthe, DiPippo, Foley, Hazell.
[2] For the full argument, see my aforementioned series "The Reign of Novelty and the Sins of the Times," and "Clarifications on the Reign of Novelty: A Letter Exchange with a Friendly Critic," *Tradition and Sanity* Substack, September 9, 2024.

Ordo. They were spiritually sensitive, and their judgment was correct, against the backdrop of their intimate experience of the traditional rite.

Do I think that a priest sins by saying the modern rite? No, *if* in his mind and heart he considers it to be a worthy and acceptable rite for offering the always-worthy sacrifice of the Cross. I used to consider it to be such, as one may find in many articles of mine from years past; but my shift in thought and the reasons for it have been articulated no less clearly.[3]

What I have written above may sound like an exaggeration, a failure to make various distinctions. I assure you: as a Thomist, I am capable of making distinctions till the cows come home. However, distinctions are not magic; they cannot overcome certain kinds of fundamental difficulties. I don't agree with the opinion that the Church may never err in matters of universal discipline; if her rulers unmoor themselves from traditional principles and practices, they are bound to enforce on the people something that will occasion harm and damage, even if it is, strictly speaking, free of heresy. Deducing an infallible soundness of universal discipline from the dogma of papal infallibility requires a number of assumptions and a lot of whistling in the dark; a negation of it does not threaten indefectibility.[4] One assumption in particular deserves to be rejected, namely, that liturgy is merely a matter of changeable discipline over which popes have complete disposal. To the extent that any pope has spoken or acted as if he has absolute power over cumulative tradition, he is undermining the nature of his own office.[5]

I believe a great deal of messiness is compatible with the human governance and divine support of the Church, provided that access to the means of salvation (especially sacramental grace) remains available to those who seek it out and that the tradition of the Church continues to endure somewhere, anywhere, without deformation. There is no question that the tradition does endure, not just here or there, but in many places, in many minds and hearts. Even if the barque of Peter

---

[3] See Kwasniewski, *Bound by Truth* and "The Reign of Novelty."

[4] The argument about the so-called "secondary objects of infallibility" can be grossly exaggerated. This is why we have people going around saying canonizations *must be* infallible, even though this is a theological opinion that has never been definitively accepted. It's a begging of the question: they assume canonizations have a strict and necessary relationship to faith and morals, and so are infallible, instead of analyzing whether the premise is correct (see Kwasniewski, ed., *Are Canonizations Infallible?*). Similarly, with the liturgy, there are aspects that pertain to infallibility—I think validity and lack of explicit heresy are the only ones—but the rest can be argued to be subject to defectiveness, even a harmful defectiveness. That is one of the reasons I reject the invoking of *Auctorem Fidei* to justify the new liturgy: for the reform endorses the very errors of the Synod of Pistoia that *Auctorem Fidei* condemned.

[5] I argue this point at length in my book *Bound by Truth*, but also in my essay "The Pope's Boundedness to Tradition as a Legislative Limit," in Kwasniewski, ed., *From Benedict's Peace to Francis's War*, 222–47.

has been overtaken by pirates, ransacked, and crippled, it will not sink to the bottom and perish. The ship will need a complete change in captaincy and crew before there is any real hope of the liturgy being restored to its immemorial and venerable form, in accord with the sovereign law of Divine Providence. Lest anyone object that such a change is unrealistic, that the old rite will never be restored, it is well to remember that this kind of defeatism is not what drives salvation history, which is filled with twists and turns not even the most imaginative human author could concoct. Thankfully, a Divine Captain is at the helm, which should fill us with undying hope.

It can hardly be surprising that there will be enormous differences of opinion on how to interpret the strange liturgical situation into which churchmen of the twentieth century have maneuvered the Bride of Christ on earth. I have no desire to attack the good intentions of a priest who seeks to improve his local parish's liturgical life. Especially since *Traditionis Custodes*, tradition-loving priests have been put in an almost impossible situation: what is most precious and inspiring to them, the celebration of the old rite, has been rudely withdrawn; they have little guidance and even less support when it comes to the restoration of the sacred. So they make shift; they do what they can, according to their own lights, to replicate this or that aspect of liturgical tradition, as far as it can be accommodated or tolerated. Often they do so for the sake of their own sanity, for their peace of soul. All this is undoubtedly true. Nevertheless, I have argued that taking this path of an attempted *sanatio* and *elevatio* of the modern rite of Paul VI is inherently problematic, counterproductive, and even spiritually dangerous, and that it must not be seen as "the way forward" or even as "a good path," simply speaking. It is an approach riven with violent internal contradictions, one that will only perpetuate the deepest flaws in the new rite and in the mentality that forced it upon us.

What, then, is a devout, tradition-loving priest to do? I have given a lot of attention to this question in my books *True Obedience* and *Bound by Truth*, but the short answer is: a priest of Jesus Christ, to be most fully conformed to the Eternal High Priest from whose wounded and glorified humanity the sacred liturgy of the Church streams forth across all centuries of the Church, should commit himself in a principled way to the *exclusive* celebration of the traditional rites of the Church, finding a way to do so even when it means struggle, displacement, or ostracization. He should not imagine that he can turn the Novus Ordo into the Roman rite, that is, into a legitimate and authentic rite of the Catholic Church, for this is altogether impossible. There is no incremental way to get from the one to the other. Instead, the priest must take up a traditional Catholic rite—it could be the Roman rite, the Dominican use, the Sarum use, etc., depending on circumstances—and commit himself to providing it for the faithful. As Martin Mosebach succinctly puts it:

> The liturgy IS the Church—every Mass celebrated in the traditional spirit is immeasurably more important than every word of every pope. It is the red thread that must be drawn through the glory and misery of Church history; where it continues, phases of arbitrary papal rule will become footnotes of history.[6]

The faithful, for their part, must stand fast and truly be what they are called: *faithful* to all that the Catholic religion is and does.

What might this look like in practice? I cannot outline every possible scenario, but we could envision the following. A diocesan priest goes to his bishop and says, with all simplicity: "I no longer celebrate the Novus Ordo; I just can't do it anymore in good conscience. I celebrate only the traditional Roman rite. I understand if you have no place for me, but I hope that you will find pastoral work that I can do, as I am eager to continue serving." An understanding or at least a flexible bishop may react by assigning this priest to hospital or prison work, letting him go to a Carmelite convent as a chaplain, or sending him to a remote country parish attended by only a small number of people. A less friendly (not to say heartless) bishop might simply "cancel" him on the spot, saying: "If that's your settled view, then I have no work for you to do, and you are discharged from all responsibilities, with your salary cut in half." Such a priest might then take steps to incardinate into another friendlier diocese; petition to join the Priestly Fraternity of St. Peter or other institute or community, if they will have him; or clandestinely minister to underground communities of traditional faithful. Thanks to Pope Francis, Cardinal Roche, Archbishop Viola, and the middle managers who implement their vicious policies, such underground communities exist in well-established networks and are prepared to be very generous in financial and personal support for clergy who keep tradition alive in our midst.

Let's not forget, too, that with the ever-growing number of deaths and retirements among the clergy, soon any bishop who wants to staff a decent number of parishes will be compelled to use every priest he can find; and so, if *more* priests were *more* resolute and absolute in their commitment to tradition, more bishops would be forced to accommodate them. A bishop who still believes the Catholic faith and cares for the spiritual good of his flock—I realize this may be a minority, even a rather small minority at this point—will not fail

---

[6] Mosebach, *Heresy of Formlessness*, 188.

to assign the TLM-exclusive members of his presbyterate to parishes, chapels, oratories, and the like. There is strength in numbers and, paradoxically, in fewness of numbers; there is strength equally in an uncompromising black-and-white stance, where one does not leave the door open by a crack ("I prefer the TLM but I'm willing to do the Novus Ordo") but closes it firmly: "I celebrate exclusively the TLM."

In short, a priest should make the *right* decision and let Divine Providence decide what further use to make of him, rather than feeling he should continually repeat decisions that, in his heart of hearts, he knows to be compromises or capitulations concerning what is most intimate and important, what is most priestly and most divine. These are so many detours to a dead end. What is needed now is simplicity, clarity, consistency, courage, and zeal. Such qualities will mark out the priests who have lent themselves wholeheartedly to the Lord's work of purifying and restoring His Church, which has fallen into ruins. May His Providence grant that there be more and more such priests as time goes on.

In the state where I grew up, New Jersey, there are three exclusively TLM chapels I have often visited as an adult. All three began as independent chapels in the evil days of the immediate post-council, when I was just an infant. The priest in charge of each had simply said, "I am not going to stop offering the traditional Mass and sacraments for my flock. It would be wrong to do so." Of course, all the usual penalties were thrown at them, but they persevered. In time, the priests died and the people were left with a conundrum. The stories are complicated but we can simplify by saying that, in each case, the chapel was regularized with the diocese in which it stood: the Our Lady of Fatima chapel in Pequannock was entrusted to the FSSP (and it was there that my wife, a convert, made her first confession and her first Holy Communion); the Mater Ecclesiae chapel in the town of Berlin was erected as a diocesan parish, one of the few TLM-only parishes in the country run by a diocesan priest (and it was there that my wife and I were married in 1998, in a Tridentine High Mass on the feast of St. John); the St. Anthony of Padua Oratory in West Orange was entrusted to the care of the Institute of Christ the King (and it was there that a priest, a friend of mine, offered a Requiem Mass for my mother's soul shortly after she died). All three of these places, for obvious reasons, have a special place in my heart and in my wife's heart. All three chapels began in acts of overt "disobedience" to papal and episcopal tyranny; all three are flourishing today, "in full communion with the local bishop," as the saying goes. The Lord does indeed write straight with crooked lines. None of them would exist but for the stalwart priests who established them and the unyielding faithful who built them up in their love for the unchanging Catholic faith and for the venerable Roman rite that perfectly expresses it.

Without heroic individuals among the clergy and the laity who stood up for what they knew to be right, in spite of any and every command, prohibition, threat, or penalty, *there would not be a traditional movement today.* Today's tradition-loving faithful are often ignorant of the inspiring and harrowing stories from the years after the Council, and therefore often do not understand the determination and wisdom necessary to resist ecclesiastical self-destruction whenever it flares up, like a benign tumor that turns malignant again. I highly recommend becoming familiar with this history, for it is not only inspiring but *instructive.* Without such loyal resistance, our Mass and much else in our Roman tradition would long ago have been torn from us forever, thrust down the memory hole and utterly forgotten. That is what the architects of reform intended, as I recalled in Part I, and it looked for a time as if they might succeed. The Fraternity of St. Peter and the Institute of the Good Shepherd, to take two major examples, simply would not exist without Archbishop Lefebvre and the Society of St. Pius X. *Summorum Pontificum* was, in part, the fruit of Joseph Ratzinger's reflections on the sad state of affairs in which faithful Catholics who love the faith and love the liturgy were treated worse than sorted and recycled garbage.

Underground chapels and independent chapels will be the temporary placeholders, the well-planted seeds, of future parishes run by the so-called "Ecclesia Dei communities" or by diocesan priests, once a future pope restores something like the policy of *Summorum Pontificum* (or an even better policy). Of this we may be confident. Just as in the 1970s it was necessary for some priests to work outside the canons and norms when the Church structures were dominated by modernists dismantling the Faith, so too in our era it will be necessary for some priests to work outside the canons and norms precisely with a view to preserving and handing on the Faith in its fullness, protecting the flock from preying wolves. In God's good time, the Church structures as Christ willed them will be replenished by the influx and participation of those who, in the time of crisis, refused to collude with the forces of dissolution and desacralization. It is more important to keep the great liturgical tradition alive than to fall into line with irrational ecclesial diktats or to preserve a self-destructive "communion" with hierarchs who spurn tradition and the common good.

We are again at a crossroads, just as Archbishop Lefebvre was in the early 1970s;[7] and again, the same boldness and conviction will

---

[7] Here I would like to make a brief remark, entirely positive, about the vital contribution that the Society of St. Pius X has made to the fight for tradition. While I am

be needed. Obviously, I advocate working with the Church's pastors—to the extent that they are willing to be worked with, reasonably and charitably—and thus I believe that, wherever bishops still care about their flocks, the best way forward is to bring into a diocese the Ecclesia Dei institutes, as long as they have not been forced by the Vatican to undergo "*aggiornamento.*" At this moment in time, both the Vatican and most bishops are ready to hurl traditional Catholics under the bus, and run over them backwards and forwards. Faced with such persecution, the true lover of the fullness of Catholic tradition does not simply surrender and abandon the fort to its enemies. He resists, in a calm and principled manner. In such grim circumstances, independent and underground chapels will arise of necessity—*and they should*. I see disobedience, irregularity, and independence as last resorts; but I also do not condemn them, as long as the individuals involved understand clearly that their stance is and must be temporary, that is, it will last only until better episcopal counsels prevail and regularization becomes possible with the diocese, under the local bishop.

I therefore condemn and have no truck with sedevacantism in any of its varieties. I wish to be as clear as possible: it is one thing to work outside legal structures in a case of necessity, and quite another to reject the visible structures of the Church and its rulers. The independent priests *I* am speaking of here and encouraging to carry out their pastoral work—it is better, perhaps, to call them priests who have been forced into an independent situation against their will—are still praying for the pope and the local bishop in the Canon of the Mass. They have been forced out of the institutional structures, but their intention is always to remain within them and united to the one and only Church established by Jesus Christ. A sign that this is their true belief is that they are always ready to be canonically regularized by those who will not persecute them for being Catholics.

I would even say—and I am aware of independent and underground priests who are already in the habit of doing this—that once a year the priest de facto in charge of a community should send a courtesy letter to the local bishop, telling him that the community is praying for him and for the pope every day in the Mass and that he is prepared to meet with the bishop to discuss an amicable arrangement whereby the chapel may be incorporated into the diocese as a parish, an oratory,

---

not prepared to say that it alone is responsible for the traditionalist movement—this would be an unhistorical oversimplification—nevertheless Lefebvre was the galvanizing and organizing figure who gave it structure and worldwide prominence, and his Society today continues to bring authentic divine worship and orthodox preaching, catechesis, and schooling to many Catholics. For this we must be grateful.

a shrine, or what have you. Naturally, nine out of ten times this letter will either be ignored or receive a reply to the effect of, "We don't recognize you, we don't want you, go away and stop bothering us." Still, it's the thought that counts, isn't it? "The Lord seeth not as man seeth; for man looketh on the outward appearance, but the Lord looketh on the heart" (1 Sam 16:7).

Hardly a day goes by when one does not hear the objection: "Obedience is the surest way to sanctity, as is demonstrated by the Saints time and again. We have no other choice than to trust Holy Mother Church. A person cannot separate himself from the pope and the magisterium without risking danger in his personal life, or even risking his salvation." I would reply: Fair enough; this is true as long as it really *is* Holy Mother Church at work, and not renegade churchmen; as long as the pope is teaching and practicing the Faith; as long as the Magisterium is in fact coherent with perennial doctrine and sound discipline. A failure to make distinctions like these is a failure to exercise both the faculty of reason and the gift of faith.[8] Let's not forget that the "obedience above all things" mentality has been a major instrument in the dissolution of Catholic tradition and the sex-abuse crisis.

I am someone who tries to see things realistically and sympathetically from all points of view, without committing myself so definitively to one course of action that I rule out every other defensible opinion or prudential avenue. I view the diocesan TLMs, the SSPX, the non-sede independents, and the Ecclesia Dei communities as being like the Army, the Navy, the Air Force, and the Marines. *All* are needed to win through to victory. The rupture with Catholic tradition after Vatican II is a metaphysical wound in the Church that must be healed if the Church is ever to flourish again. Its loss is not merely something to be regretted as unfortunate, like a church felled by earthquake, a manuscript lost by negligence, or a diocese rattled by bankruptcy. The loss of traditional Catholicism is a profound and grievous loss for the spiritual lives of *all* the faithful, with the gravest consequences for the living out of the Faith in the modern world and for the transmission of this inestimable gift to future generations. Therefore, I regard the retention of the TLM as a life-and-death matter, as something immeasurably more important than obedience to those who would crush it or who would treat the faithful attached to it as untouchables and outcasts.

Just as a homeowner may use lethal force against an intruder breaking in, though he may not do so in any ordinary situation, so I believe

---

[8] See my article "Hyperpapalism and Luther: Strange Bedfellows," *Tradition and Sanity* Substack, November 27, 2023.

that there are times when bold steps need to be taken against those who are violating our fundamental rights and duties as Catholics. Everyone who loves the Church's traditional rites must agree with this perspective to one degree or another — why else would we bother having *any* attachment to an old rite that Pope Paul VI made very clear should be discontinued? The traditionalist movement exists because it disagrees, and disagrees strongly, with the prudential judgments of several popes in a row.[9]

Legal positivism is no way to live a coherent Catholic life, since it would mean putting on and taking off our beliefs and practices like cheap clothing, depending on which drill sergeant happens to be in charge. No sane person had ever thought or acted that way prior to Vatican II, but now it seems to be taken as a virtue. Not only is it no virtue, it is the vice of inconstancy — a form of psychological promiscuity, contempt for truth, negation of life-experience, an unseriousness about spiritual things and a superficiality of life that is worse than outright defiance (cf. Rev 3:15–16), an insult to one's ancestors, and a refusal of one's patrimony. In a word: inhuman and unchristian, and thus, offensive to God.

Above all, let us not underestimate the sinfulness of what this pope, his curia, and his toadies in the hierarchy are doing as they seek to suppress the most venerable rite of Christendom and, in so doing, injure the faithful legitimately attached to it. The pope is the *servus servorum Dei*, the servant of the servants of God: his role is to preserve and protect the tradition he has received and to feed the flock in abundant pastures. Instead, this pope and his henchmen have uttered the cry *Non serviam*: I will not serve the orthodox Faith, I will not serve sound Catholic morality, I will not serve Catholic tradition, I will not wash the feet of the disciples of Christ. Therefore, the bishops who follow the lead of Francis and his court make this *Non serviam* their own; and the priests who follow these bishops do the same. As obedience cascades down through the chain of command, so too does disobedience. Of this hated and hateful disobedience, we wish to be absolutely free and uncontaminated, as, with all the saints and angels, we yield our willing obedience to Christ, to His truth, to His divine worship handed down across the millennia.

The stakes are high, and that is why it is not a time for niceties, compromises, or shoulder shrugs, but a time for integrity, honor, and fortitude. Ours is a dire situation, but faith, zeal, and perseverance will pay off in the long run, as it did for our forefathers in the traditional

---

9 All these points in the present Epilogue are developed at much greater length in the second book of the trilogy of which I spoke in the Preface — namely, *Bound by Truth*.

movement. To me, a poignant sign of the care of Divine Providence is the return of growing numbers of Catholics to the use of just those liturgical books that were placed on the butcher's block over half a century ago, Catholics who are now praying the very prayers that were canceled out and pasted over. The Benedictines have a motto: *Succisa virescit*, "hewn down, it flourishes anew"—itself a variation on one of the oldest sayings of all: *sanguis martyrum semen christianorum*, "the blood of martyrs is the seed of Christians." There may well be a special fruitfulness in the blood of witness that, over the centuries, so many priests and faithful have shed, literally or metaphorically, as their Catholic worship was attacked by iconoclasm, be it of the imperial Byzantine, Protestant, or Modernist variety.

The Catholic churches that manage to stay open in the coming decades—as opposed to the vast number of buildings that will either be shut down as the mainstream Church collapses into its predicted demographic sinkhole or be burned down by progressivist radicals—these open churches will sooner or later get the Mass of the Ages back. The movement to recover and restore Catholic worship cannot be eradicated. That has been tried, and the attempt failed. Tradition can be cut down by the blades of persecution or wither for lack of support, but deep in the soil its roots abide, full of vigor. Watered by blood and coaxed by the light of grace, new growth will come taller and stronger. *Succisa virescit*.

APPENDIX I

Are We Justified in Calling Paul VI's Rite the "Novus Ordo"?

THOSE WHO SPEND TIME IN LITURGICAL DISCUSsions are guaranteed to encounter at some point the following objection: "You shouldn't be speaking of the 'Novus Ordo' or the 'Novus Ordo Mass.' This isn't what it's called. That's a *traditionalist* label—a way of attacking the reformed missal of Pope St. Paul VI," etc.

This matter deserves a closer look.

While "Novus Ordo [Missæ]" is not a typical way in which the Vatican itself, post-1969, has preferred to denominate the Order of Mass created by the Consilium and promulgated by Paul VI on April 3, 1969, it is nevertheless a phrase found in a couple of official documents and does not seem to have ruffled feathers until later on.

The first thing to establish is that Paul VI constantly attached the word "new" to his ongoing liturgical reforms of the 1960s. For example, in his general audience of March 7, 1965, he spoke of a "new order [of worship]," a "new scheme of things," "new liturgical books," "new form," "new liturgy," "new habit," and "liturgical innovation"—and all this, about changes far less drastic than those he would promulgate four years later. *A fortiori*, the application of *novus* to the missal of 1969 is entirely justified on the basis of its own promulgator's habits of speech.

Let us not forget that many things people today would assume must have entered with the Novus Ordo in 1969 were already around *prior* to it, as the traditional liturgy was progressively dismantled in the 1950s and 1960s: the priest praying *versus populum* instead of *ad orientem*, a deviation endorsed in Pius XII's revamped Palm Sunday and Easter Vigil services;[1] having the people say the Lord's Prayer at the liturgy together with the priest, something *never* done in the Roman tradition prior to Pius XII's Good Friday service; praying the Mass in the vernacular, which came in here and there experimentally; dropping the prayers at the foot of the altar and the Last Gospel, an amputation executed in 1965; bringing in new *ad experimentum* lectionaries; the admission of multiple Eucharistic Prayers; the discarding of some liturgical vestments; and so forth.

---

[1] At the one, the priest is instructed to bless the palms facing the people, as opposed to blessing them at the altar; at the other, a basin of paschal water is blessed facing the people, the priest having his back to the altar. See also my article "Seeking the Origins of 'Versus Populum' in the United States."

Coming nearer to our topic: in the general audience of November 19, 1969, which attempted to explain why a new missal was to be imposed, Paul VI—this time with much greater justice—referred to "a new rite of Mass" (four times), "a new spirit," "new directions," "new rules," "innovation." In the general audience one week later, he mentioned "the liturgical innovation of the *new rite of the Mass*" and mentioned the "new rite" seven times; he used words like "new," "newness," "renewal," "innovation," "novelty," a total of eighteen times. I comment in detail on these two general audiences in chapter 4 of my book, *The Once and Future Roman Rite*. As if to drive home the point, the words "*Novus Ordo Missæ*" were stamped on the front cover of the original edition.

Interestingly, the phrase "*Novus Ordo Missæ*" was used, if I am counting correctly, eighteen times in the famous *Short Critical Study of the New Order of Mass* of September 25, 1969, submitted to Paul VI with the signatures of Cardinal Alfredo Ottaviani, one of the highest ranking Vatican prelates (in spite of the hatred directed at him by the anti-Roman faction at the Council) and long-time head of the Holy Office, and Cardinal Antonio Bacci, one of the greatest Latinists of modern times.[2] This tract employs the expression as if it is obvious, familiar, and unobjectionable, and to my knowledge no one at the time disputed the appropriateness of it, even though much else in the critical study was the subject of hot debate.

As far as I am aware, the first time the expression "*Novus Ordo Missæ*" shows up in a papal magisterial document is in an address delivered by Paul VI at a consistory for the appointment of twenty cardinals on May 24, 1976.[3] In this address he uses the expression *novus Ordo [Missæ]*: *usus novi Ordinis Missæ* and *novus Ordo promulgatus est* ("the use of the new Order of Mass"; "the new Order has been promulgated").[4]

In April of 2010, the Office for the Liturgical Celebrations of the Supreme Pontiff placed a short document on the Vatican website entitled "The Priest in the Concluding Rites of the Mass." Although the text is redolent of Benedict XVI and the reign of his MC Guido

---

[2] Alfredo Ottaviani, Antonio Bacci, and a Group of Roman Theologians, *The Ottaviani Intervention: Short Critical Study of the New Order of Mass*, trans. Anthony Cekada (Philothea Press, 2010). For more on its history, see Clemens V. Oldendorf, "Lessons from the Sixties: Selective Synodality and Princely Protests," *NLM*, October 24, 2019.
[3] The text, in Italian, may be found at www.vatican.va/content/paul-vi/la/speeches/1976/documents/hf_p-vi_spe_19760524_concistoro.html.
[4] Nowadays the phrase "Novus Ordo" has been extended to mean virtually the same thing as "the reformed liturgical rites." Thus, one will hear people speak of "Novus Ordo baptism," "Novus Ordo breviary," and the like. Although we readily understand what is meant, it would be more accurate to say the "new rite of baptism," the "new liturgy of the hours," and so forth, since "Novus Ordo" is just an abbreviated form of "Novus Ordo *Missæ*": it is specifically about the order followed in the offering of Mass. However, one may justifiably refer to the "Novus Ordo lectionary" and "Novus Ordo calendar" because of their close association with the Mass.

Marini, and although it refers plentifully to "ordinary" and "extraordinary" forms, it remained on the Vatican website long into the reign of Francis; it was finally removed not long ago.[5] This document refers to the "Novus Ordo" (*tout court*) and the "Vetus" [Ordo], albeit using scare quotes for the latter term.

All of the foregoing was known to me prior to discovering an article at *Pray Tell* by Max Johnson dated January 14, 2010: "From Where Comes 'Novus Ordo'?" (Would that *Pray Tell* had opted for the more eloquent title "Whence Cometh 'Novus Ordo'?," but the spirit of *Comme le Prévoit* has long prevailed in those quarters.) As one would expect, the article complains that the phrase has become weaponized by traditionalists into a "title" for the Mass instead of being a simple passing description, like saying "new hymnal" or "shiny new book," that has no substantive (theological) meaning. This view would seem to be difficult to sustain in light of Paul VI's veritable paean to innovation in the 1969 audiences mentioned above and the Vatican's use of the term as late as 2010. The changes made to the Mass are not merely incidental or superficial, like a new typeface or a new binding for a missal, but cut into the bone and marrow of the rite.

The conclusion I reach is, understandably, quite different from *Pray Tell*'s. I think it is fair to call the Consilium's fabrication "*novus*," which means both novel and strange. Whatever it is, it is most definitely *not* the Roman rite, as I demonstrate on multiple grounds in *The Once and Future Roman Rite*. The relentless traditionalist critique has indeed made of "Novus Ordo [Missæ]" a pejorative term — and that is no worse than it deserves.

---

5 An archived version of the document is available at https://web.archive.org/web/20230326025515/https://www.vatican.va/news_services/liturgy/details/ns_lit_doc_20100422_sac-riti-conclusione_en.html.

APPENDIX 2
Discovering the Latin Mass Brings Lots of Questions

Author's note: the following was a real correspondence that took place mostly in the year 2022. Its themes closely track those of this entire book. My correspondent describes in deeply insightful ways her discovery and conversion to traditional worship. I believe readers will benefit from this personal, existential witness.

DEAR DR. KWASNIEWSKI,

My family and I are attending the Latin Mass more and more often these days, and finding it exerts, to our surprise, a strong pull. I say to our surprise, because for such a long time we were die-hard devotees of the reverent Novus Ordo that has long been available to us and where all our friends are. But the confidence that once came easily is now wavering.

I'm writing to you to ask about a possible doctrinal basis for what I'm experiencing in the TLM in contrast to the new rite. I've been attending the TLM nearly every morning for the past week. It feels throughout the Mass as though a steady and continual stream of grace or assimilation to Christ is pouring forth. I don't experience this in the Novus Ordo, which for a long time has felt dry and almost burdensome to me, though I attended the Novus Ordo daily and had always sought out the most reverent expressions thereof. After the TLM, I feel as though I'm in a heightened state of contemplation which remains until I get up to leave. Again, this rarely happened with the Novus Ordo, and when it did, it didn't occur in the same expansive and effortless way. Every few years, God seems to surprise me in a manner that renovates my entire outlook. This feels like such an occasion. I'm full of wonder and in search of a doctrinal basis for what I'm experiencing.

Might it have to do with the TLM being a more objective rite, a fuller expression of Christ's form, as you discuss in *Reclaiming Our Roman Catholic Birthright*? I'm much intrigued by your discussions of the TLM's objectivity as it pertains to Christ's form communicated in and through the Mass. I would love recommendations for written analysis of how the heightened objectivity of the TLM might relate to Aquinas's understanding of form and our conformity to Christ that occurs through grace and the sacraments.

I should say that I'm not at this point following the specific prayers of the TLM in a missal, though I know generally the order of what is occurring.

With gratitude,
Amator Veritatis

Dear *Amator Veritatis*,

Your experience is exactly mine and that of so many others: the grace of contemplation is given more easily in this rite. I think there are a lot of reasons. The "sonic iconostasis" is one of them. The role of the Latin sacral language cannot be overstated. More subtly, the "sacerdotalism" of the old rite—its concentration in and on the person of the priest offering Mass—is not only superlatively beneficial to the priest, but paradoxically augmentative for the laity's experience. In a more obvious way, the spaciousness and silence of the rite allow "time to absorb the mysteries."[1]

The position of the priest *ad orientem* is incalculably helpful in orienting the Mass to God, and therefore the souls of all who participate in it. Either stance, *ad orientem* or *versus populum*, transmits a manifold "message"—and that message is transmitted independently of subjective intentions.

Finally, since you mentioned objectivity, I have written in a couple of places about the contrast between a "Benedictine" approach and a "Jesuit" one,[2] and suggest that we can understand a lot about our situation through that contrast.

Yours in Christ,
Dr. Kwasniewski

Dear Dr. Kwasniewski,

I was thinking on the way home from Mass this morning that thanks to immersing myself in the TLM for the last several weeks (by attending it almost daily and reflecting on it afterwards), I now have a new grasp of Aquinas's sensibility—the understated dignity, expansiveness, and grandeur of his writings. I had long thought I needed to attend and appreciate the Mass that is closest to the one he himself would have celebrated. Thanks be to God I finally did. What I didn't realize was how much more wonderful—wonder-full—it would be! As I said, God seems to surprise me every few years with something that drastically but joyfully revises my perspective. Perhaps this is his way of keeping me humble.

---

[1] See chapter 10 above.
[2] See "Different Visions, Contrary Paths" in Kwasniewski, *Noble Beauty*, 115–33; "Objective Form and Subjective Experience: Life Teen under Scrutiny," in Kwasniewski, *Good Music*, 227–33.

Above all, I continue to be awestruck by the overwhelming sense of God's presence in the TLM. I'm still reeling from the contrast but in a good way. I finally understand all of the references to the Mass as a cosmic reality. I finally understand why preconciliar authors attained to such profundity and to such reverence for the Mass. I keep waiting for all of this to wear off as novelty recedes, but it isn't. Deep down, I don't expect it to. The experience is too profound to be delusional.

Most of our friends are "reform of the reform" people, as we ourselves were up until recently. We've not yet disclosed to them our attraction to the TLM and are discerning how to go about this, even as we try to retain enough memory of our former mentality to be able to communicate the new perspective more intelligibly.

With gratitude,
Amator Veritatis

Dear *Amator Veritatis*,

I quite agree—Aquinas (and the medievals in general) make much more sense when one lives in the realm of prayer they inhabited.

One thing I have realized over the past three decades is that Catholic tradition had developed organically for millennia to a point where everything "clicked," where it all made sense: the doctrine, the discipline, the liturgy, everything mutually reinforced and reflected everything else. That's what we'd expect, isn't it, from an institution led by the Holy Spirit, and with so much time for refinement? I'm convinced, too, that a major reason why the revolutionaries could gain control in the mid-20th century is that most Catholics were taking too much for granted and running on the fumes of a great tradition, and so were unprepared for the challenge of modernity or its distillation, modernism.

It's rather difficult to break through to "reform of the reform" [ROTR] types, because they are (a) already in possession of a lot of truth and so can't imagine they are missing something major, (b) they have a sort of subtle defensiveness, because they *know*—at some level—that the liturgy was massively changed and that the changes have been destabilizing, but they figure if the pope wants the new thing, it must be good; (c) they feel judged if someone says "I used to think the way you do (or go to the church you still go to), but I've found something richer and deeper..."

I think the *Mass of the Ages* films, especially episode 2, can be very powerful aids in this process, if people are willing to watch them. I am particularly eager to hear your thoughts on it, as I consider it one of the best exposés ever produced on a difficult subject—difficult in both senses: challenging to present accurately, and a bitter pill to swallow... unless and until one sees it as a "red pill" that frees us from comfortable, harmful illusions.

Yours in Christ,
Dr. Kwasniewski

Dear Dr. Kwasniewski,

I must first apologize for stating the obvious in my prior email about Aquinas being analytical. I've had so many new insights in the wake of this "conversion" to the TLM that I've not yet sorted them all out. I think the point I was groping towards was this: Aquinas was an analytical type and yet never called for, or never would have been drawn to, a rationalistic Mass along the lines of the Novus Ordo. He was too immersed in the lofty mysteries of theology to think that a liturgy should be "clear and distinct" and instantly accessible to an "audience"; he of all men would have appreciated the silences, the language of symbols, the melismatic chants, the objective rituality.

By the way, "ROTR" is a very funny acronym. It looks like "rotor" and suggests the robotic quality of the rationalistic rite along with the forced conglomerations of argument that often imbue the ROTR outlook. Humor is a welcome tonic in these days of cultural insanity. (It's funny, too, that Pope Francis speaks of an "automatism" in the TLM without apparently recognizing the rationalistic seedbed of the Novus Ordo.) I agree with and find helpful your analysis of why ROTR types might have a hard time breaking through to a deeper appreciation of the TLM. It seems that some of the ROTR folks who do break through have started to *wear out* with the Novus Ordo — it's as if they just can't pretend anymore that this actually *is* the "source and summit" of our religion. If it is, the religion seems kind of pathetic. This was happening to me, as I've already related, though I didn't understand exactly what was happening or why until I broke through with the TLM.

It seems to me that ROTR rationalism leads to an overreliance on moral teachings as fuel for prayer and holiness. The Novus Ordo, even in its most reverent forms, lacks the fullness of what the Mass ought to be, so ROTR people turn to moral theology in a quest to recover the coherence lacking in the Novus Ordo. But this is problematic on a number of levels and has bad side effects. Of course, one ought to affirm and adhere to orthodox moral teachings, but they shouldn't be used as substitutes for the integrity that ought to subsist in the Mass. The liturgical and cultural life should sustain and inspire the moral life. Morals are only interesting, let alone livable, when there's something else behind and beneath them.

I'm still trying to get my mind around the fact that there's a valid rite which mediates grace (and isn't devoid of Christ's Eucharistic presence and sacrifice, as was the Protestant liturgy in which I grew up) and yet does not mediate the grace of contemplation as effectively as the TLM. I'm also trying to understand why God allowed us to remain in the Novus Ordo for decades. Ultimately, I'm grateful for the ease and depth of prayer in the TLM, and I'm grateful we're being led in this direction. But I'm working to fathom the implications of it. Perhaps God uses all the efforts one made to attend reverent Novus Ordo Masses through the years—the habit or exertion entailed in that, in swimming against the current to pray as well as one can amid the rationalism and other deficiencies of the Novus Ordo—to fuel one's prayer in the TLM. As one eventually wears out with the Novus Ordo, God then uses whatever depth of prayer one attained through it, despite that rite's objective deficiencies, within the new TLM context, as analogously God might do when an ardently practicing Protestant converts to Catholicism. At the same time, using the holiness reached through the grace mediated in the deficient Novus Ordo would be an instance of God, through the grace of the Cross, bringing forth good in spite of privation. The privation itself finds no justification except in so far as it can be the occasion of a greater good by the grace of the Cross.

I'm not owed a perfect understanding, and God may want me not to understand it fully, for the sake of humility. With a seismic shift like this, I feel obliged to understand the implications as best I can. It is always painful to realize how much better off one would have been had one seen the light sooner, but the endurance of this pain gives one something else to offer up in union with Christ's sacrifice, drawing closer to Him thereby.

With gratitude,
Amator Veritatis

Dear *Amator Veritatis*,

You have suffered the neglect of anyone who writes a long and intelligent letter, precisely because it deserves a real response and not a quickly dashed-off "reply"!

I get what you're saying about Aquinas. I went through the same process of discovery. It had seemed to me for a long time that Aquinas was a proto-rationalist; indeed, that is the main reproach leveled against him by the Eastern Orthodox. But then I spent more time on his poetry, his sermons, and his actual life (as narrated to us by those who knew him), and I began to realize that his style of writing and arguing is an aesthetic (rhetorical) choice, much as the choice of oil or watercolor or charcoal is for an artist. He wanted to present the *logoi* as clearly as possible, to minimize the danger of equivocation, fallacy, and recourse to the imagination or the emotions. Yet what we see is only the tip of the iceberg of Thomas's spiritual depths, as we catch a glimpse of them in his biography and non-academic writings.

Your comment about an overreliance on moral theology to fill the gap of a religion without much liturgical substance is very perceptive. I think this is part of the reason people got so excited about John Paul II. In his moral theology, in his theological anthropology, he offered something of real intellectual substance, which looked wonderful next to the postconciliar pablum. But it was always rather rarefied and highbrow. The liturgy is high theology translated into symbol, gesture, chant, and art, and everyone can relate to it, indeed relatively easily, although without ever exhausting the meaning.

That we have a valid rite that does not mediate the grace of contemplation is part of the "mystery of iniquity" of our times. Every age of the Church has its own version of this mystery. Ours is the bungled liturgical reform, which ended up undermining everything it claimed to be achieving. It seems to me that the Church's indefectibility requires that there always be a rite that mediates *sanctifying* grace, i.e., the grace apart from which we cannot be saved; but it would not require that a rite mediate other graces, gifts, fruits, perfections, attainments.

You wonder about why the Lord left you for so long in a postage-stamp yard, so to speak, when just outside there was a vast and beautiful forest to wander in! Your conclusion is the same as the one I came to in my own life: through this inadequate diet, God was teaching me how to hunger and thirst for Him, and when I finally got to the pure source (liturgically speaking), I was more than ready for it—I was panting for it. It frightens me to think of souls that do not find this oasis, this garden... I think some of them muddle along well enough, but others lose interest or drift away. There is a deeply *tragic* aspect to the past sixty years: the Council that was called to make the faith come alive among modern men has nearly suffocated it. And although churchmen apologize nowadays for everything under the sun, including plenty they should not apologize for, they never apologize for having caused or tolerated or ignored this tragedy.

When you speak of God's using even a privation as an occasion of good, you state a profound truth. Just as we would not defend Scott Hahn's Protestantism (nor would he) and yet we thank God for what it prepared him to become as a Catholic and how it has fitted him to be a great ambassador for the Bible among Catholics, so too we can thank God for what He has given us on the way to the fullness of liturgical

Tradition, because, no doubt, we—I mean, you and I—would likely not have been able to reach this final point without passing through the earlier stages. Other people will have other paths, like those blessed offspring nowadays who grow up exclusively with the TLM, or the people one meets who convert directly from Protestantism to traditional Catholicism; but without a doubt, speaking for myself, I would never have been able to be a "TLM apologist" without having first had a long and intimate familiarity with the Novus Ordo—indeed, with several *kinds* of Novus Ordos (since it is more like a genus than a species).

Thus, when you write "it is always painful to realize how much better off one would have been had one seen the light sooner," are you not simply stating salvation history in a nutshell? The story of Israel is the story of humanity is the story of each man: we could always have been "better off" from this or that point of view, and yet God manages to bring good out of evil and greater goods out of lesser goods. This is precisely what enables us to recognize His hand, His largesse, when it intervenes, which in turn magnifies our gratitude and our humility. It's enough to make one dizzy with His ingenuity and infatuated with His affection. He truly is a "God of surprises"—just not in the way that our poor misguided pope thinks!

Yours in Christ,
Dr. Kwasniewski

Dear Dr. Kwasniewski,

I finally have time to reply to your generous response. I enjoyed *Mass of the Ages*, Episode 2. It is very well done—surely one of the best video treatments of this subject to date, if not the best. While respectful of the ecclesial authorities involved and any aspirational intentions, the video is unabashedly truthful as to the reality and the damage done. The restraint and respect shown by the commentators make the critique all the more poignant and powerful. I thought Alcuin Reid summed up the reformers and reform superbly when he said they were "culturally naive."

This is the sixties in a nutshell. There seems to have been this sense that humanity could wipe the slate clean and recalibrate everything according to simplistic premises. It does indeed remind one very much of the Protestant Reformation. "We're tired of complexity. Let's get rid of this gobbledygook and start over!" And just as mainline Protestant denominations swelled like red giants headed for collapse, Catholic revolutionaries decided to adopt their failing schema! It's very sad. The mainliners were able to put up a pretty good front still in the sixties, especially in the USA, so I can see how a group of shallow-minded

Catholics might be deceived into thinking they needed to imitate the model or else face extinction. This is also the pattern of today's Catholic progressivists with whom I became well acquainted during my years in college. They were eager to embrace already collapsed ideologies "or else we'll be made fun of and won't fit in socially or survive!"

It reminds me also of the lesser but still egregious cultural naivete of Cavadini, Healy, and Weinandy in their *Church Life Journal* series. Why don't these writers on liturgy spend a month or maybe several months attending the Mass that they think needed reforming, if only to be better informed about the nature of the reform? How can one assess the progress made by a new technology without understanding how the old technology worked? It only makes logical sense. But that's where the "we all need to be united in worship and trust the popes" argument comes in. That *does* make a degree of sense according to the principle *lex orandi, lex credendi*—but not if the TLM is vastly better and the reform a deracination of the original. In this case, one needs to see that we should all be united in worship through a return to the TLM and then assess the liturgical reform by its superior light.

What is especially salutary about your writing, I find, is that you have confidence that the traditional rite will one day be the central and standard rite. This is critical. Just as progressivists falsely imagine a story of inevitable progress, one can also succumb nowadays to a vision of accelerating and inexorable decline, especially in times as degraded as these. We must rather put our confidence in Christ and His sacraments and then let the historical drama unfurl. As Christ said to Peter, what concern is it to you if John lives and you die? These are lesser matters. The one thing needful is to keep our eyes on the Lord perceived through the sacramental forms in which he chooses to appear to us.

I had a good meeting with Fr. *N*. a couple of weeks ago. He emphasized that God is outside of time and can therefore in an instant restore to us the graces we might have been given had we been attending the TLM our whole lives instead of spending decades in the Novus Ordo or worse. This gets back to the salvation history theme you summarized. God brings forth good from every evil. We need not and should not justify the evil or try to make it fit into a logical progression towards the good. Rather, we call it what it is and fight against it, while also asking God to bring forth good from it by the power of the Cross. Each of us can recognize the good that God has brought forth from evils that have marked our lives and the broader course of history, but we don't think the evils were good in themselves. The latter approach tries to defang evil by naturalizing it, whereas the former puts faith in the grace and power of the Cross.

I agree too that obsessive recourse to the life and theology of John Paul II is another instance of people seeking substitutional forms of coherence which ought to have been available in the liturgy properly celebrated. This overreliance on two orthodox popes and their theological works makes conservatives like Weigel vulnerable to errors and to intra-Church leftist critique. At the same time Weigel looks similar to progressivists in the sense that there's an appearance of trying to create from whole cloth—via John Paul II and Benedict—a new Catholic culture from the ruins of the reform, infamously attributing the ruins to poor "implementation" of the reform rather than acknowledging the depth of problems *in* the reform.

In 2006, Joseph Bottum published an essay in *First Things* that confronted the destruction of Catholic culture in the USA.[3] I remember reading and meditating on this essay at the time it was published, when I was fresh from years of chaos in a theology department and had experienced a number of Catholic parishes in different states, and was beginning to realize how inadequate our own RCIA formation had been. I remember being struck by the essay and wondering, "How did this happen?" I recall hypothesizing at the time something like: "These are huge cultural movements; the immigrant communities that kept this cultural element of the Church going likely dispersed when they started making money, gaining wider acceptance, and moving to the suburbs; these changes were bound to happen because of Weigel's thesis about institutional maintenance, because the Church can't be based on cultural identities forged defensively; and at least we still have the Real Presence, the re-presentation of Christ's sacrifice, and a core of sound doctrine, which is what matters anyway even if some rebel against it..." But now I see that changing the Mass was at the causal epicenter of these other negative changes, to say nothing of wider cultural changes it detonated in America, Europe, and elsewhere.

It's a bitter pill to swallow but made less so when one experiences the beauty and richness of the TLM and feels a flood of graces pouring forth from it as I have in recent months. One realizes at once, fully and wrenchingly, the tragedy of the liturgical reform and the needless cultural destruction that followed upon it—but one sees this, mercifully, in the refreshing, calm, relieving, and peaceful light of Christ's presence in the TLM. Yes, one shouldn't have a closed Catholicism that expels anyone who isn't part of one's cultural group (à la Weigel's and the progressivist's portrayal of the Church's tendencies or problems pre-Vatican II), but neither should one have a Catholicism that is non-cultural, ahistorical, formed-purely-along-doctrinal-lines (however sane

---

[3] Joseph Bottum, "When the Swallows Come Back to Capistrano: Catholic Culture in America," *First Things*, October 2006.

and sound the doctrine), and harmfully-stripped-down-sacramentally (however valid Christ's work therein). This is, as Alcuin Reid put it, culturally naive. And this isn't the Catholicism of St. Thomas Aquinas, however pure and clear was his understanding of doctrine. It's the Protestant error all over again.

Gratefully yours,
Amator Veritatis

Dear *Amator Veritatis*,

I'm glad you enjoyed *Mass of the Ages* Episode 2, and I certainly agree with your analysis of the 1960s "counterculture," which, ironically, was really an intensification of the evils already present in Western liberalism.

As for poor Cavadini, Healy, and Weinandy, they are so convinced of the superiority of "everything Vatican II" that they cannot imagine a world in which an older way of worshiping turns out to have been right all along. It's a form of the modernist prejudice that all things new are better. And for such people, even entertaining the scenario of attending a TLM for a while to check it out would feel like disobedience and pride. In this way they deprive themselves of such a great good. It's interesting how fallen human beings don't realize when a principle they would normally agree with applies back to them: for surely, CHW would say "Of course one cannot write well about a subject with which one is not well acquainted," but then they go and do it in spades.

As for having confidence that the superior rite will win out again, I'll admit that I'm hoping for a miracle on the scale of Noah's flood or Pentecost, since right now the "new paradigm" seems to be baked in, hard-wired, fused like metal, injected into the bone marrow. But we do know that huge systems can collapse with astonishing speed: the history of empires shows this, with the rise and fall of rulers and their armies. Indeed, the triumph of Christianity itself could never have been humanly predicted, and yet it happened, in the teeth of persecution of all kinds.

It sounds like Fr. *N.* was very helpful in his way of discussing how God brings good out of evils. A seminarian once tried to persuade me that it would be more humble to accept liturgical defects or ugliness or even abuses in a self-denying spirit like that of St. John of the Cross, who sought out sufferings rather than consolations, than to pursue the restoration of tradition when the hierarchy, who are our fathers in Christ, do not support it, or positively forbid it. My response to him develops an account of how patience and toleration differ essentially from acceptance or approval.[4]

---

[4] Peter Kwasniewski, "Finding Christ in Present Sufferings Does Not Mean Embracing Abuse, Error, or Deformation," *OnePeterFive*, February 8, 2023.

I loved what you had to say about Weigel and the weakness of the neocon position. They do not see that "it's the Mass that matters," or, as Lefebvre once memorably said: "The Mass is the Church and the Church is the Mass." Obviously that is a hyperbolic expression; he is not asserting a simple equivalency. What he perceives is that the Mass mystically sums up and presents the Church to us, it is the clearing house, the axis or nexus, the core, the primary symbol, the point of departure and point of arrival. Because it is what it is, change to it necessarily cascades into change everywhere.

I've often wondered if God permitted this terrible calamity of the 1960s/70s to reanimate and reenergize the Catholic love for the Mass and the Holy Eucharist. Not immediately, but rather in the way the Jews became more devout due to the Babylonian captivity, and paved the way for the coming of Christ and the first disciples. It seems an extraordinarily dangerous "gamble" on His part, but it wouldn't be the first time God has acted with breathtaking boldness. For example, where the TLM has revived in our time, it is celebrated with great beauty and care, with fervent participation, moreso (it seems) than was the case in some places before the Council. God seems to be forming for Himself a remnant. Not that we should too quickly assume we are that righteous remnant, but rather, we should humbly give thanks that we, for no merits of our own, were chosen to carry on the tradition of the Faith at a time when it is being literally bartered away by our bishops, who shutter their churches as dioceses fail.

Cordially in Christ,
Dr. Kwasniewski

Dear Dr. Kwasniewski,

It is good to acknowledge the full reality of the calamity and the ensuing decline in order to develop a proper strategy of response. "Managed decline" is a good term for it. Bishops today often act as though it's inevitable, as though secularism has a more compelling and merciful narrative to which the Church must adapt, damaging its own integrity. I know this defeatism and its lamentable results all too well. Secularism and its false mercy merely enable people to damage themselves through disordered actions. Thanks be to God that we have the Mass and Blessed Sacrament, the foundation of all order, as you said. No wonder Satan wants them suppressed. You wrote somewhere that faithful adherents of the Latin Mass will be the ones still standing when all else is reduced to rubble. The glory will be God's, for He is, even now, bringing about a renaissance through those who are being hunted down and villainized from all sides, by both ecclesial and secular authorities. It is an astonishing story that will inspire future generations.

Our Lord seems to have been laying the groundwork in our family for quite some time. Providentially, my children and I had read together Ronald Knox's *The Mass in Slow Motion* a couple of years ago. My instinct then was that to understand the present Mass as fully as possible, one ought to understand how it used to be. Also, I wanted them to have a concrete sense of the Mass that the great saints had celebrated down through the ages, the Mass that had undergirded most of the history of the Church, because we were studying the saints and the history of the Church and of Europe, and I thought we would be leaving something out if we neglected the Mass that was in place for most of the saints and this history.

Perhaps I imagined the relationship between TLM and Novus Ordo as being similar to the relation between an original classic work and an abridged version. I remember saying something like "to fully understand and appreciate the Mass we celebrate, we must make an effort to understand how the original one was structured." It seemed like common sense to me. In our home studies we've always emphasized the superiority of original works of literature to abridged ones, so at some level I must have been aware that an abridged version of the Mass was bound to be inferior! But I felt at the time that it might be somehow *subversive* to pay too much attention to the original, especially when the Novus Ordo, with Christ's sacrifice re-presented and his Real Presence therein, was so far superior to the Protestant liturgies I grew up with. I didn't know what to make of this feeling. And the typical arguments and narratives about "how necessary and good the reform was" kept a hold on my thinking.

As I have gotten to know the TLM better and better, one thing for which I'm very thankful is that the TLM makes a person less dependent on or desperate for charismatic priests and homilists — which is what one obsesses over in the Novus Ordo realm, where you practically have to develop a rolodex of the priests who say Mass "well" and/or preach the Gospel faithfully. Of course, one always hopes for excellence in any priest, but I feel relieved that the Mass is less *about* the individual priest in the TLM. In our experience it is pretty much the same from priest to priest. This is the way it ought to be.

Gratefully,
Amator Veritatis

Dear *Amator Veritatis*,

So true that the priest in the TLM makes less of a difference — and that is a such a relief for him and for everyone!

Your story is quite interesting to me. It's like Francis Thompson talking about "the Hound of Heaven": Our Lord was pursuing you and trying to reveal more to you, and happily, you were docile!

I love your comparison of new and old rites to abridged and unabridged literature. It's true that one can keep the "essence" of a story while dropping out lots of details or digressions, but then one loses so much richness, atmosphere, the world the author subcreated. Martin Mosebach puts it this way: who would ever say that any element in a painting by Raphael was superfluous, even if there are bits and pieces that could be omitted without destroying the subject? Even the empty spaces, the weeds on the ground, the wisp of cloud in the sky, has a role to play, like the face, hands, and body of the main saints depicted. That is the way any great work of art is, and the traditional Mass is abundantly that way. You see this especially in a well-executed Pontifical Mass.

You mention once feeling subversive just to be thinking about the old Mass. But the most challenging moment for any Catholic, I personally believe, is when he comes to the realization that evil operators have been working behind the scenes and even at the highest hierarchical levels to transform the "faith once delivered to the saints" into a modernist or quasi-modernist, quasi-protestant "catholicism lite" for Modern Man. *They* are the true subversives. This is challenging because the depth of iniquity, the cynicism, the deception, and the consequences for the loss of souls are staggering. It is, has been, the biggest shock of my life, and I feel like it's taken me decades to process it and come to a place of interior peace, where I can see the evil for what it is, put my trust in God, and adhere to the truth no matter how unpopular it may be.

Yours in Christ,
Dr. Kwasniewski

Dear Dr. Kwasniewski,

You describe well the challenging moment in which one has the negative realization about corruption in the Church. I've had three such lightbulb moments: first, when I realized that Protestantism was a deviation and Catholicism vastly superior; second, when I realized post-conversion in graduate school that the Catholic Church was deeply divided and had people in it who were trying to modify or eliminate essential doctrines; and most recently, in my awakening to the superiority of the TLM and the catastrophic impact of the liturgical reform. This latter has been a startling surprise because I had thought lightbulb #2 was the final such realization I needed to have. Little had I known all of these years that #2 had in large part been caused by #3.

Has anyone to your knowledge written a book or article on ways the TLM harmonizes with principles of good design? I've ordered Dr. Shaw's new book on the petitioning by artists and intellectuals on behalf of the TLM. I'm looking forward to reading it — it's telling that artists and intellectuals, even non-Catholics, perceived what Novus Ordo architects did not.

I have noticed the use of design principles in your and others' writing, which is partly what gave rise to this question. It would be interesting to look at the TLM through the lens of recent theorists on what constitutes good design and/or "branding." I was watching an interview today with Paul Rand, who designed iconic logos for IBM, UPS, ABC, and others. He related the following story. About 20 years after he designed the ABC logo in the 1960s, he heard, in the '80s, that some ABC executives had the impulse to update Rand's logo for the times. They devoted many dollars and much angst to exploring the possibility. Finally, they decided to conduct a survey, from the results of which they concluded that the original logo had accumulated such massive recognition and associative value, due to decades of use, that it would be far too costly to dispense with it. Would that Paul VI and his reformers had been as wise and humble as the ABC executives!

Gratefully,
Amator Veritatis

Dear *Amator Veritatis*,

That book, *The Latin Mass and the Intellectuals*, is fantastic! You will *love* it. I ranked it one of my favorite books of 2023.

I don't know of an *ex professo* treatment under the heading of design principles, although innumerable commentators talk about symmetry, order, parallelisms, symbology, the "architecture" of the Mass, etc. The comparison between Classic Coke and New Coke is so obvious that it's given rise to a plethora of articles, posts, and memes. Eric Sammons's fine article on the subject is verging on ten years old (a classic, in internet terms!).[5]

You could be describing my own journey, except that #1 for me was from mainstream lukewarm Catholicism to the charismatic movement; then #2 from there to "conservative" Catholicism; then #3 to tradition. Just as Our Lord healed a blind man on one occasion in steps, it seems that most of us need to be led from station to station — as if, to paraphrase T. S. Eliot, we cannot bear too much reality, and have to be expanded and toughened up for it.

---

[5] Eric Sammons, "New Coke: If Today's Catholics Were In Charge," *OnePeterFive*, December 9, 2015.

I wish you and your entire family many blessings as you put your roots down in the traditional Faith—a mighty tree whose roots plunge into the depths of the ages and whose massy trunk supports far-flung branches heavy with fruit, proffering shade to weary pilgrims. Thanks be to God that, in spite of our unworthiness, we have been led to a home on earth that reflects the beauty and echoes the song of the heavenly Jerusalem. *Gloria in excelsis Deo!*

Yours in Christ,
Dr. Kwasniewski

WORKS CITED

ECCLESIASTICAL AND LEGAL DOCUMENTS

Benedict XVI. "For the Record: Full translation of Benedict XVI letter of support to Müller after dismissal by Francis." Translated by Francesca Romana. *Rorate Caeli*, January 2, 2018.

———. Homily at the Inaugural Mass for the Beginning of the Petrine Ministry. April 24, 2005.

———. Letter to Bishops Accompanying the Apostolic Letter *Summorum Pontificum*. July 7, 2007.

———. Post-Synodal Apostolic Exhortation *Sacramentum Caritatis*. February 22, 2007.

———. Vigil on the Occasion of the International Meeting of Priests: Dialogue of the Holy Father Benedict XVI with Priests, St. Peter's Square. June 10, 2010.

Congregation for the Doctrine of the Faith. Decree *Cum Sanctissima*. February 22, 2020.

———. Decree *Quo Magis*. February 22, 2020.

Fortescue, Adrian, J. B. O'Connell, and Alcuin Reid. *The Ceremonies of Holy Week & the Vigil of Pentecost Described According to the Missale Romanum editio XXIX post typicam 1953*. Éditions Pax inter Spinas, 2022.

Francis. Apostolic Letter *Desiderio Desideravi*. June 29, 2022.

———. "Comments during meeting with youths in Singapore." September 13, 2024.

———. "Document on Human Fraternity for World Peace and Living Together." Co-signed by Pope Francis and Grand Imam Ahmad el-Tayeb in Abu Dhabi. February 4, 2019.

———. Letter to the Bishops of the Whole World Accompanying the Apostolic Letter *Traditionis Custodes*. July 16, 2021.

Gregory the Great. *Epistola* 76. PL 77:1215–16. www.fordham.edu/Halsall/source/greg1-mellitus.txt.

International Commission on English in the Liturgy. *Documents on the Liturgy 1963–1979: Conciliar, Papal, and Curial Texts*. Translated by Thomas C. O'Brien. The Liturgical Press, 1982.

International Theological Commission. "*Sensus Fidei* in the Life of the Church." 2014.

John XXIII. Apostolic Constitution *Veterum Sapientia*. February 22, 1962.

John Paul II. Apostolic Exhortation *Catechesi Tradendæ*. October 16, 1979.

———. Encyclical Letter *Ecclesia de Eucharistia*. April 17, 2003.

Paul VI. Apostolic Exhortation *Evangelii Nuntiandi*. December 8, 1975.

———. "Paul VI on liturgical reform, Part 6." *Pray Tell*, September 6, 2018.

Pius XII. Encyclical Letter *Mediator Dei*. November 20, 1947.

Wuest, Joseph. *Matters Liturgical (the* Collectio Rerum Liturgicarum*)*. Translated by Thomas W. Mullaney. Frederick Pustet, 1956.

WORKS BY THE AUTHOR

"The Acorn and the Oak Tree: In Defense of Liturgical Growth and Maturation." *Tradition and Sanity* Substack, January 23, 2025.

"Adorning the Soul with Allegorical Gems." *OnePeterFive*, July 19, 2023.

"Adventures in the *Lex Orandi*: Comparing Traditional and Modern Orations for St. Augustine of Canterbury." *Rorate Caeli*, May 28, 2020.

"Adventures in the *Lex Orandi* #2: Old and New Versions of St. Ephrem the Syrian." *Rorate Caeli*, June 18, 2020.

"Adventures in the *Lex Orandi* #3: Comparing the Old and New Orations for Our Lady of Sorrows." *Rorate Caeli*, September 15, 2021.

Are Canonizations Infallible?: Revisiting a Disputed Question. Edited by Peter Kwasniewski. Arouca Press, 2021.

"Are Pews in Churches a Problem—and, If So, How Much of a Problem?" *New Liturgical Movement*, July 27, 2020.

"The Beautiful Death: Why We Favor Cut Flowers in the Sanctuary." *New Liturgical Movement*, May 1, 2023.

"Benedictine Monks on Incense: Sourcing It and Making It." *New Liturgical Movement*, February 10, 2020.

"Between Christ the King and We Have No King But Caesar." *OnePeterFive*, October 25, 2020.

Bound by Truth: Authority, Obedience, Tradition, and the Common Good. Angelico Press, 2023.

"The Centenary of the Last Integral *Editio Typica* of the *Missale Romanum*." *New Liturgical Movement*, July 25, 2020.

"Clarifications on the Reign of Novelty: A Letter Exchange with a Friendly Critic." *Tradition and Sanity* Substack, September 9, 2024.

"A Collect Worthy of Royalty." (On St. Hedwig.) *Rorate Caeli*, October 16, 2020.

"Comparison of Old and New Prayers for Blessing of Ashes." *OnePeterFive*, February 26, 2020.

"A Comparison of the Old and New Blessing of Candles on Candlemas." *New Liturgical Movement*, February 1, 2021.

"The Council Fathers in Support of Latin: Correcting a Narrative Bias." *New Liturgical Movement*, September 13, 2017.

"Crocodile Tears and Hand-Wringing: No GPS Coordinates for the Unicorn." *Tradition and Sanity* Substack, August 26, 2024.

"Defending So-Called Doublets by Understanding Parallelism." *New Liturgical Movement*, September 30, 2024.

"Deliver Thy Church, O Lord, from a flawed liturgy." (On St. Felix of Valois.) *Rorate Caeli*, November 20, 2018).

"Deliver us, we beseech Thee, O Lord, from all evils past, present, and to come." *Tradition and Sanity* Substack, October 10, 2024.

"Divine Drunkenness, Mystical Madness." *Tradition and Sanity* Substack, May 25, 2023.

"Don't stop celebrating: After Christmas Day, Christmas continues." *LifeSiteNews*, December 24, 2019.

"An Expansive Counter-Reformation *Lex Orandi* Retains Its Relevance." (On St. Anthony Mary Zaccaria.) *New Liturgical Movement*, July 5, 2021.

"False Antiquarianism and Liturgical Reform." *New Liturgical Movement*, September 2, 2024.

"Fidelity to Liturgical Law and the Rights of the Faithful." *OnePeterFive*, July 3, 2017.

"Finding Christ in Present Sufferings Does Not Mean Embracing Abuse, Error, or Deformation." *OnePeterFive*, February 8, 2023.

"'The Fingers that Hold God': The Priestly Benefits of 'Liturgical Digits': Historical, Theological, and Liturgical Conclusions." *New Liturgical Movement*, March 8, 2018.

"'For I Will Not Give You a Kiss as Did Judas': On Sacred and Profane Kissing." *New Liturgical Movement*, April 6, 2020.

"The Four Qualities of Liturgy: Validity, Licitness, Fittingness, and Authenticity." *New Liturgical Movement*, November 9, 2020.

"Freemasonry and Catholicism: Implacable Enemies." *The Remnant* online, July 22, 2020.

From Benedict's Peace to Francis's War: Catholics Respond to the Motu Proprio Traditionis Custodes *on the Latin Mass*. Angelico Press, 2021.

Good Music, Sacred Music, and Silence: Three Gifts of God for Liturgy and for Life. TAN Books, 2023.

"'The heathens have defiled Thy holy temple… Revenge the blood of Thy saints!': On the Thymotic Realism of the Traditional Latin Mass." (On SS. Nazarius, Celsus, Victor I, and Innocent I.) *Rorate Caeli*, July 28, 2020.

The Holy Bread of Eternal Life: Restoring Eucharistic Reverence in an Age of Impiety. Sophia Institute Press, 2020.

"The Homily Is Not Part of the Liturgy." *The Remnant* online, January 15, 2021.

"Homogeneity vs. Hierarchy: On the Treatment of Verbal Moments." *New Liturgical Movement*, October 16, 2017.

"How Can We Elevate the Quality of the 'Prayer of the Faithful'?" *New Liturgical Movement*, May 11, 2015.

"Hyperpapalism and Luther: Strange Bedfellows." *Tradition and Sanity* Substack, November 27, 2023.

Illusions of Reform: Responses to Cavadini, Healy, and Weinandy in Defense of the Traditional Mass and the Faithful Who Attend It. Edited by Peter Kwasniewski. Os Justi Press, 2023.

"In Praise of Irregularity." *New Liturgical Movement*, April 4, 2016.

Is African Catholicism a "Vatican II Success Story"? Questioning the Conventional Narrative. Edited by Peter Kwasniewski. Os Justi Press, 2025.

"Is Modern Man 'Incapable of the Liturgical Act'?" *New Liturgical Movement*, October 12, 2020.

John Henry Newman on Worship, Reverence, and Ritual: A Selection of Texts. Edited by Peter Kwasniewski. Os Justi Press, 2019.

"Large Catholic families are promoted by the traditional liturgical calendar." (On St. Felicitas and her seven sons, as well as Rufina and Secunda.) *LifeSiteNews*, July 6, 2021.

"The Lie That Was Told to Over 2,000 Council Fathers at Vatican II." *New Liturgical Movement*, May 27, 2024.

"The Lifting of the Chasuble at the Elevations: Touching the Hem of Christ's Garment." *OnePeterFive*, November 9, 2022.

"'The Liturgy Has Been Dismantled': Portland Archbishop Robert Dwyer's Assessment in 1971." *New Liturgical Movement*, September 16, 2024.

"The Mass Should Not Be a Torture Device." *New Liturgical Movement*, February 7, 2022.

"May His Kingdom Come: Catholic Social Teaching, Part VII—The Kingship of Christ, Source and Summit of the Social Order." *Catholic Family News*, October 25, 2020.

Ministers of Christ: Recovering the Roles of Clergy and Laity in an Age of Confusion. Crisis Publications, 2021.

"'Moments of Liturgical Action': Recovering the Sacramentality of Biblical Lections." *New Liturgical Movement*, January 24, 2022.

"The Mounting Threat of Coercive Concelebration." *New Liturgical Movement*, July 22, 2019.

"New historical evidence emerges in support of Bugnini's association with Freemasonry—Names are named." *Rorate Caeli*, May 6, 2020.

"New Interview with Fr. Charles Murr on Mother Pascalina, Bugnini, Paul VI, and Other Major Figures." *Rorate Caeli*, October 10, 2020.

Noble Beauty, Transcendent Holiness: Why the Modern Age Needs the Mass of Ages. Angelico Press, 2017.

"No Eucharistic Revival without Restoration." *Tradition and Sanity* Substack, April 20, 2023.

"The Normativity of *Ad Orientem* Worship According to the Ordinary Form's Rubrics." *New Liturgical Movement*, November 23, 2015.

"Not Just More Scripture, But Different Scripture—Comparing the Old and New Lectionaries." Foreword to Matthew P. Hazell, *Index Lectionum: A Comparative Table of Readings for the Ordinary and Extraordinary Forms of the Roman Rite*. Lectionary Study Press, 2016.

"The Omission of 'Difficult' Psalms and the Spreading-Thin of the Psalter." *Rorate Caeli*, November 15, 2016.

The Once and Future Roman Rite: Returning to the Traditional Latin Liturgy after Seventy Years of Exile. TAN Books, 2022.

"Ordained, Assistants, and Faithful: On Hierarchical Participation in Three Spheres." *OnePeterFive*, February 23, 2022.

"Paul VI: A Pope of Contradictions." *New Liturgical Movement*, December 10, 2013.

"Polluting the Internet with Falsehoods." *OnePeterFive*, October 10, 2023.

"Prophets of Truth in a Decadent Age." *New Liturgical Movement*, May 18, 2015.

Reclaiming Our Roman Catholic Birthright: The Genius and Timeliness of the Traditional Latin Mass. Angelico Press, 2020.

"The Reign of Novelty and the Sins of the Times: Why the Novus Ordo Is Solely Modern in Content." *Tradition and Sanity* Substack, August 5, 8, 12, and 15, 2024.

Resurgent in the Midst of Crisis: Sacred Liturgy, the Traditional Latin Mass, and Renewal in the Church. Angelico Press, 2014.
The Road from Hyperpapalism to Catholicism. Volume 1: *Theological Reflections on the Rock of the Church*. Arouca Press, 2022.
"Rooms broken into, dossiers stolen, death threats, armed guards, assassinations… Fr. Charles Murr on Vatican intrigues surrounding Cardinals Baggio, Benelli, Villot, and Gagnon." *Rorate Caeli*, December 18, 2020.
"Roundup on the CDF Decrees on New Saints and Prefaces for the TLM." *New Liturgical Movement*, July 13, 2020
"'The Rupturist Rubric': The Attempt to Cut Off the Liturgy from Tradition." *New Liturgical Movement*, July 14, 2022.
"A Saint—and a Mass—for Our Times: St. Camillus de Lellis." *Rorate Caeli*, July 17, 2020.
"The Sanctoral Killing Fields: On the Removal of Saints from the General Roman Calendar." *New Liturgical Movement*, November 16, 2020.
"Seeking the Origins of 'Versus Populum' in the United States." *Tradition and Sanity* Substack, October 19, 2023.
"Should the Feast of Christ the King Be Celebrated in October or November?" *Rorate Caeli*, October 22, 2014.
"St. Catherine of Alexandria—broken on the Consilium's wheel." *Rorate Caeli*, November 24, 2017.
"St. Thomas on the 'Asperges' (Sprinkling Rite)." *Views from the Choir Loft*, August 7, 2014.
"The Stigmata of Saint Francis, Appearing and Disappearing in the Liturgy." *New Liturgical Movement*, September 17, 2018.
"Sun, Moon, and Stars: Tradition for the Saints." *OnePeterFive*, February 3, 2021.
"A Tale of Two Lectionaries: Quality versus Quantity." *New Liturgical Movement*, January 16, 2017.
"Things That Remit Venial Sins—The Traditional Liturgy Is Full of Them." *New Liturgical Movement*, February 8, 2016.
"Translation of Ratzinger's Preface to the French Edition of Klaus Gamber." *New Liturgical Movement*, February 8, 2023.
True Obedience in the Church: A Guide to Discernment in Challenging Times. Sophia Institute Press, 2021.
Turned Around: Replying to Common Objections Against the Traditional Latin Mass. TAN Books, 2024.
"Two Attitudes toward Ordinary Form Rubrics: Kantian Duty and Aristotelian Epikeia." *New Liturgical Movement*, January 8, 2018.
"Two Collects Most Appropriate for Our Times." (On St. John of Matha and St. Scholastica.) *Rorate Caeli*, February 10, 2018.
Ultramontanism and Tradition: The Role of Papal Authority in the Catholic Faith. Edited by Peter Kwasniewski. Os Justi Press, 2024.
"Unambiguous Theocentricity: Church Architecture and the Traditional Mass." *OnePeterFive*, June 6, 2018.
"Vatican II as Cause of Cultural Revolution: Questioning the Victim Narrative." *Tradition and Sanity* Substack, February 19, 2024.

"Vatican II: *Requiescat in Pace*." In *Sixty Years After: Catholic Writers Assess the Legacy of Vatican II*, edited by Peter Kwasniewski, 93–122. Angelico Press, 2022.

"'Vera fraternitas': June, the month of brothers." (On SS. Primus and Felician, Mark and Marcellian, Gervase and Protase, and John and Paul.) *LifeSiteNews*, June 8, 2021.

"Was the chief architect behind the New Mass a Freemason? New evidence emerges." *LifeSiteNews*, October 12, 2020.

"We, Too, Are the Sacrifice We Offer." *OnePeterFive*, June 17, 2020.

"What modern Catholics can learn from Eastern Christians and Protestants about reverent Communion." *LifeSiteNews*, May 18, 2021.

"What the Ordinary Form Could Be: The Vienna Oratory." *Views from the Choir Loft*, June 5, 2014.

"What They Requested, What They Expected, and What Happened: Council Fathers on the Latin Roman Canon." *New Liturgical Movement*, August 8, 2022.

"Who Was Captain of the Ship in the Liturgical Reform? The 50th Anniversary of an Embarrassing Letter." *New Liturgical Movement*, June 24, 2019.

"Why Are Laity So Involved in the Liturgical Debate? And Why Is the Continued Struggle Necessary?" *New Liturgical Movement*, July 10, 2023.

"Why Restricting the TLM Harms Every Parish Mass." *Crisis Magazine*, August 13, 2021

"Why the Epistle Should Be Read Eastwards and the Gospel Northwards." *Tradition and Sanity* Substack, December 16 and 19, 2024.

"Why the 'Word of God' for Catholics is not only the Bible, but more importantly, Jesus Himself." *LifeSiteNews*, August 29, 2019.

WORKS BY OTHER AUTHORS

Adams, John. "Letter to the Officers of the First Brigade of the Third Division of the Militia of Massachusetts." October 11, 1798. In *The Works of John Adams, Second President of the United States*, ed. Charles Francis Adams, 9:229. Little, Brown, and Co., 1854.

Ahmad, Joseph. "Droning at Mass." *New Liturgical Movement*, January 3, 2020.

———. "Singing Upon the Book: Further Methods of Chant Harmonization." *New Liturgical Movement*, October 7 and 8, 2020.

"All-or-Nothing vs. 'Progressive Solemnity': A Response." *New Liturgical Movement*, December 10, 2014.

Amorose, Mark. *City under Siege: Sonnets and Other Verse*. Angelico Press, 2017.

"Archbishop Roche: Vatican is Preparing New Document on Liturgical Formation." *Gaudium Press*, English edition, May 16, 2022, www.gaudiumpress.ca/archbishop-roche-vatican-is-preparing-new-document-on-liturgical-formation/.

Arendt, Hannah. *Eichmann in Jerusalem: A Report on the Banality of Evil*. Penguin Classics, 2006.

Aristotle. *Sense and Sensibilia*. Translated by J. I. Beare. In *The Complete Works of Aristotle*, edited by Jonathan Barnes. Princeton University Press, 1984.

Augustine. *The City of God*. Translated by Marcus Dods. In *Nicene and Post-Nicene Fathers, First Series*, vol. 2, ed. Philip Schaff. Christian Literature Publishing Co., 1887. Revised and edited for New Advent by Kevin Knight, www.newadvent.org/fathers/120117.htm.

Baldovin, John F. "Vatican II's liturgy constitution turns 60—preparing the constitution." *The Pilot*, November 3, 2023.

Baresel, James. "The Liturgists and the Fascists." *Rorate Caeli*, August 3, 2023.

Barthe, Claude. *A Forest of Symbols: The Traditional Mass and Its Meaning*. Translated by David J. Critchley. Angelico Press, 2023.

Benofy, Susan. "Footnotes for a Hermeneutic of Continuity: *Sacrosanctum Concilium*'s Vanishing Citations." *Adoremus Bulletin*, vol. 21, no. 1 (Spring 2015): 8–34, https://web.archive.org/web/20160817074120/http://adoremus.org/AdoremusSpring2015.pdf.

Benson, Robert Hugh. *Confessions of a Convert*. The Cenacle Press, 2022.

Berg, John. "An Interview with Father Berg, FSSP." *The Latin Mass*, vol. 22, no. 1 (Winter/Spring 2013): 6–13, www.latinmassmagazine.com/pdfs/Berg-interview-LM-2013-1-WinSpr.pdf.

Blake, Ray. "Mystery of the Trinity." *Fr Ray Blake's Blog*, June 15, 2014, https://web.archive.org/web/20240523184152/http://marymagdalen.blogspot.com/2014/06/mystery-of-trinity.html.

Blanchard, Shaun. *The Synod of Pistoia and Vatican II: Jansenism and the Struggle for Catholic Reform*. Oxford University Press, 2020.

Bottum, Joseph. "When the Swallows Come Back to Capistrano: Catholic Culture in America." *First Things*, October 2006.

Boughton, Lynne C. "An Imagined Past: Initiation, Liturgical Secrecy, and 'Mass of the Catechumens.'" *Antiphon*, vol. 25, no. 2 (2021): 161–210.

Bouyer, Louis. *The Memoirs of Louis Bouyer: From Youth and Conversion to Vatican II, the Liturgical Reform, and After*. Translated by John Pepino. Angelico Press, 2015.

Bradshaw, Paul. "Gregory Dix and the Offertory Procession." *Theology*, vol. 120, no. 1 (2017): 27–33.

Brill, Patrick John. *The Great Sacred Music Reform of Pope St. Pius X: The Genesis, Interpretation, and Implementation of the Motu Proprio Tra le Sollecitudini*. Os Justi Press, 2025.

Brockhaus, Hannah. "Vatican archbishop: Traditional Latin Mass 'experiment' not successful in reconciling SSPX." *Catholic News Agency*, November 16, 2021.

Brusoe, Reyers, ed. *The Latin Mass and the Youth: Young Catholics Speak About the Mass of Ages*. Cruachan Hill Press, 2024.

Buck, Roger. *Cor Jesu Sacratissimum: From Secularism and the New Age to Christendom Renewed*. Angelico Press, 2016.

———. *The Gentle Traditionalist Returns: A Catholic Knight's Tale from Ireland*. Angelico Press, 2019.

Buckley, William F., Jr. *Nearer, My God: An Autobiography of Faith*. Doubleday, 1997.

Bugnini, Annibale. *The Reform of the Liturgy 1948–1975*. Translated by Matthew J. O'Connell. The Liturgical Press, 1990.

———. "Rinnovamento nell'ordine." *Notitiæ* 61 (February 1971): 52.
Bullivant, Stephen. *Mass Exodus: Catholic Disaffiliation in Britain and America since Vatican II*. Second edition. Oxford University Press, 2019.
Campbell, Phillip [Boniface]. "The Novus Ordo and Conversion." *Unam Sanctam Catholicam*, September 20, 2020.
———. "The Obedience of St. Padre Pio." *Unam Sanctam Catholicam*, July 29, 2023.
———. "The Problem of the 'Reverent Novus Ordo.'" *Unam Sanctam Catholicam*, September 10, 2020.
———. "Reform of the Reform: Liturgical Russian Roulette." *Unam Sanctam Catholicam*, December 5, 2022.
———. "Two Deaths and Two Masses: The Healing Power of the Requiem." *Unam Sanctam Catholicam*, September 13, 2024.
———. "The Unsalvageable Novus Ordo." *Unam Sanctam Catholicam*, December 25, 2019.
Cekada, Anthony. *Work of Human Hands: A Theological Critique of the Mass of Paul VI*. Philothea Press, 2010.
Charlier, Michael. "'He is damaging the entire series of his predecessors... and thus himself and the papacy': The insoluble contradiction between Francis and Paul VI." *Rorate Caeli*, January 21, 2022.
Chautard, Jean-Baptiste. *The Soul of the Apostolate*. Translated by A Monk of Our Lady of Gethsemani. TAN Books, 2008.
Chesterton, G. K. "The Queer Feet." In *The Complete Father Brown*. Penguin, 1981.
Chiron, Yves. *Annibale Bugnini: Reformer of the Liturgy*. Translated by John Pepino. Angelico Press, 2018.
———. *Between Rome and Rebellion: A History of Catholic Traditionalism with Special Attention to France*. Translated by John Pepino. Angelico Press, 2024.
———, with François-Georges Dreyfus and Jean Guitton. "Entretien sur Paul VI." Éditions Nivoit, 2011.
———. *Paul VI: The Divided Pope*. Translated by James Walther. Angelico Press, 2022.
Chupungco, Anscar J. "Costituzione conciliare sulla sacra liturgia. 150 anniversario." *Notitiæ* 149 (December 1978): 580.
———. *The Prayers of the New Missal*. Liturgical Press, 2013.
Cipolla, Richard. "The Devirilization of the Liturgy in the Novus Ordo Mass." *Rorate Caeli*, June 26, 2013.
———. "The End of the 'Reform of the Reform': Father Kocik's 'Tract 90.'" *Rorate Caeli*, February 12, 2014.
———. "Epiphany and the Unordinariness of Liturgical Time." *Rorate Caeli*, January 10, 2014.
———. "A Primer for a Tradition-Minded Celebration of the OF Mass." *New Liturgical Movement*, September 14, 2017.
Ciszek, Walter J., with Daniel Flaherty. *He Leadeth Me*. Ignatius Press, 1995.
Clayton, David. "Using Drones as Harmony—A Simple Way to Add to the Spiritual Effect of Sacred Music." *The Way of Beauty* blog, December 27, 2017.

"The Crimes and Heresies of Pope Francis, Their Causes and Effects, and the Action to Be Taken." *Rorate Caeli*, May 2, 2024.

Daoudal, Yves. "Enough is Enough." *Rorate Caeli*, February 1, 2022.

Darroch, Leo. *Una Voce: The History of the Fœderatio Universalis Una Voce*. Gracewing, 2017.

Dashiell, David, ed. *Ever Ancient, Ever New: Why Younger Generations Are Embracing Traditional Catholicism*. TAN Books, 2022.

Davies, Michael. *Cranmer's Godly Order: The Destruction of Catholicism through Liturgical Change*. Revised edition. Roman Catholic Books, 1995.

———. *Pope Paul's New Mass*. Angelus Press, 2009.

Day-Milne, Peter. "Remember the Ember Days? (Part I)." *Adoremus*, November 22, 2021.

De Corte, Marcel. "Sur les variations du clergé catholique." *Itinéraires* 210 (February 1977): 92–104.

de Mattei, Roberto. *The Paths of Evil: Conspiracies, Plots, and Secret Societies*. Translated by Nicholas Reitzug. Sophia Institute Press, 2023.

———. "Resistance and Fidelity to the Church in Times of Crisis." In *Love for the Papacy and Filial Resistance to the Pope in the History of the Church*, 105–30. Angelico Press, 2019.

———. *The Second Vatican Council: An Unwritten Story*. Translated by Patrick T. Brannan et al. Loreto Publications, 2012.

———. "True and False Conspiracies in History. In memory of Father Augustin Barruel (1741–1820)." *Rorate Caeli*, January 13, 2021.

de Nantes, Abbé Georges. "Letter to My Friends," no. 178, August 6, 1964.

Devillers, Arnaud. "Ember Days of Lent." *The Missive*, March 13, 2019.

DiPippo, Gregory. "Did the Roman Rite Anciently Have Three Readings?" *New Liturgical Movement*, November 17, 2013.

———. "An Important Liturgical Reform of the Eighth Century." *New Liturgical Movement*, March 31, 2011.

———. "Is the Ambrosian Lectionary an Older Form of the Traditional Roman Lectionary?" *New Liturgical Movement*, November 20, 2013.

———. "Is the Ambrosian Liturgy a Source for the Modern Lectionary?" *New Liturgical Movement*, November 22, 2013.

———. "Is the Medieval Liturgy a Source for the Modern Lectionary?" *New Liturgical Movement*, December 2, 2013.

———. "Liturgical Notes on the Presentation of the Virgin Mary." *New Liturgical Movement*, November 21, 2021.

———. "Muphry's Law Comes After Mass of the Ages (Part 1)." *New Liturgical Movement*, July 23, 2022.

———. "New Prefaces and Feasts for the EF Missal." *New Liturgical Movement*, March 25, 2020.

———. "The New Rite Prefaces for Advent." *New Liturgical Movement*, December 24, 2015.

———. "A Note on External Solemnities in the EF." *New Liturgical Movement*, April 27, 2016.

———. "The Octave of Pentecost: A Proposal for Mutual Enrichment." *New Liturgical Movement*, June 16, 2011.
———. "Paul VI's Dislike of the Liturgical Reform." *New Liturgical Movement*, April 19, 2018
———. "A Reform-of-the-Reform Paladin Throws in the Towel." *New Liturgical Movement*, January 29, 2022.
———. "The Revolution Is Over." *New Liturgical Movement*, August 1, 2021.
———. "*Sacrosanctum Concilium* and the New Lectionary." *New Liturgical Movement*, December 11, 2013.
———. "The Theology of the Offertory—Part 6: Prolepsis in the Offertory." *New Liturgical Movement*, June 26, 2014.
———. "The Theology of the Offertory—Series to Resume." *New Liturgical Movement*, February 27, 2015.
———. "Torah and Haftarah in the Roman Liturgy." *New Liturgical Movement*, September 20–October 21, 2023. "Part 1: Torah and Haftarah in the Roman Liturgy"; "Part 2: The Ember Saturday of September"; "Part 3.1: The Ember Saturday of Lent"; "Part 3.2: The Ember Saturday of Pentecost, and Good Friday"; "Part 4: An Inheritance Repudiated"; "Part 5.1: The Easter Vigil"; "Part 5.2: The Easter Vigil, Concluded."
———. "A Tradition Both 'Venerable' and 'Defective.'" *New Liturgical Movement*, February 3, 2015.
———. "What Is an Ideology?" *New Liturgical Movement*, May 7, 2022.
Dugan, Conor. "A Deeper Context: Overlooked book provides insight into Vatican II debates." *Catholic World Report*, September 2, 2020.
Durand, William. *Rationale IV: On the Mass and Each Action Pertaining to It*. Translated by Timothy M. Thibodeau. Brepols, 2013.
———. *Rationale Divinorum Officiorum*. Translated by Janet Gentles. Paschal Light, 2019–2021.
Edwards, Kate. "Not the Octave of the Epiphany!" *Saints Will Arise*, January 7, 2014, https://saintsshallarise.blogspot.com/2014/01/not-octave-of-epiphany.html.
Escrivá, Josemaría. *The Way*. Scepter Publications, 1992.
Esolen, Anthony. "Tradition and Treachery." *Crisis Magazine*, December 27, 2024.
Farret d'Astiès, Cyril. "Les laïcs et la defense de la messe traditionnelle: Entretien avec Cyril Farret d'Astiès à propos de son ouvrage les cinquante ans du missel de Paul VI." *Paix Liturgique* Letter 776, December 18, 2020, www.paixliturgique.com/aff_lettre.asp?LET_N_ID=3064.
———. "The Mass of Paul VI 'Well Celebrated'—a Myth!" *Rorate Caeli*, November 17, 2021.
Fassino, Nico. "The Epistles & Gospels in English: A history of vernacular scripture from the pulpit, 971–1964." *Hand Missal History*. https://handmissalhistory.com/Feature-Epistles/, 2023.
Ferrara, Christopher, with Thomas E. Woods, Jr. *The Great Façade: The Regime of Novelty in the Catholic Church from Vatican II to the Francis Revolution*. Angelico Press, 2015.

———. "*Sacrosanctum Concilium*: A Lawyer Examines the Loopholes." Text available online at https://salbert.tripod.com/SClel.htm.

Fiedrowicz, Michael. *The Traditional Mass: History, Form, and Theology of the Classical Roman Rite*. Translated by Rose Pfeifer. Angelico Press, 2020.

Flanders, Timothy. "Why do the Freemasons Love Pope Francis?" *OnePeterFive*, April 7, 2017.

Foley, Michael P. "The Glow of the Ember Days." *Rorate Caeli*, September 23, 2015.

———. "The Origins and Meaning of Ordinary Time." *Antiphon*, vol. 23, no. 1 (2019): 43–77.

———. "The *Per Evangelica Dicta*." *New Liturgical Movement*, October 18, 2024.

———. "A Reflection on the Fate of the Feast of Christ the King." *New Liturgical Movement*, October 21, 2020.

———. "The Reform of the Calendar and the Reduction of Liturgical Recapitulation." In Reid, *Liturgy in the Twenty-First Century*, 321–41.

———. "The Whence and Whither of the Kiss of Peace in the Roman Rite." *Antiphon* 14 (2010): 45–94.

Folsom, Cassian. "*Summorum Pontificum* and Liturgical Law." A talk given at the London Oratory, December 13, 2013. www.scribd.com/document/202923510/Summorum-Pontificum-and-Liturgical-Law.

"Freemasons Celebrate Vatican II. . . . " *Catholic Truth*. June 23, 2014. https://web.archive.org/web/20221129143607/https://catholictruthscotland.com/2014/06/23/freemasons-celebrate-vatican-ii/

Friel, David. "Progressive Solemnity." *Views from the Choir Loft*, December 21, 2014.

Gagliarducci, Andrea. "The increasing influence of the liturgical school Sant'Anselmo in the Vatican." *Catholic News Agency*, July 22, 2021.

Gamber, Klaus. *La Réforme Liturgique en Question*. Éditions Saint-Madeleine, 1992. [English: *The Reform of the Roman Liturgy: Its Problems and Background*. Translated by Klaus D. Grimm. Una Voce Press/The Foundation for Catholic Reform, 1993.]

Gasquet, F. A., and E. Bishop. *Edward VI and the Book of Common Prayer*. John Hodges, 1891.

Gayford, Martin, and Philippe de Montebello. *Rendez-vous with Art*. Thames & Hudson, 2014.

Gélineau, Joseph. *Demain la liturgie: Essai sur l'évolution des assemblées chrétiennes*. Cerf, 1976. [Translation: *The Liturgy: Today and Tomorrow*. Translated by Dinah Livingstone. Paulist Press, 1978.]

Giampietro, Nicola. *The Development of the Liturgical Reform as Seen by Cardinal Ferdinando Antonelli from 1948 to 1970*. Roman Catholic Books, 2010.

Gilder, George. "The Materialist Superstition." *The Imaginative Conservative*, September 8, 2012.

Gnocchi, Alessandro, and Mario Palmaro. *The Last Mass of Padre Pio: The Secret Soul of the Stigmatic Saint*. Translated by Marianna Gattozzi. Angelus Press, 2019.

Graham, Daniel. *Lex Orandi: A Comparison of the Traditional and Novus Ordo Rites of the Seven Sacraments*. Loreto Publications, 2017.

Grillo, Andrea. "Il papa bambino e il primo compleanno di *Traditionis custodes*." *Munera: Rivista Europea di Cultura*, July 15, 2022.

Guardini, Romano. *The Spirit of the Liturgy*. Translated by Ada Lane. Crossroad, n.d.

Guéranger, Prosper. *The Liturgical Year*. Volume 1: Advent. Translated by Laurence Shepherd. The Newman Press, 1948.

———. *The Traditional Latin Mass Explained*. Angelico Press, 2017. [Originally entitled *Explanation of the Prayers and Ceremonies of Holy Mass: Taken from Notes Made at the Conferences of Dom Prosper Guéranger, Abbot of Solesmes*.]

Guillou, Edouard. *Le livre de la messe: Mysterium fidei — Le texte de la messe de saint Pie V*. Foreword by Msgr. Marcel Lefebvre. Éditions Fideliter, 1992.

Guitton, Jean, and Giovanni Battista Montini. *The Pope Speaks: Dialogues of Paul VI with Jean Guitton*. Meredith Press, 1968.

Gullickson, Thomas. "Liturgy Summer Course 2019: Moving Forward — My Plea for Full Liturgical Restoration." *ad montem myrrhae*, August 2, 2019, https://admontemmyrrhae.blogspot.com/2019/08/the-best-vehicle-for-church-renewal-and.html.

———. "Velocity: Haste as Liturgical Abuse." *ad montem myrrhae*, January 12, 2020, https://admontemmyrrhae.blogspot.com/2020/01/velocity-haste-as-liturgical-abuse.html.

Gushurst-Moore, André. *Glory in All Things: Saint Benedict and Catholic Education Today*. Angelico Press, 2020.

Hannon, Urban. *Thomistic Mystagogy: St. Thomas Aquinas's Commentaries on the Mass*. Os Justi Press, 2024.

Harrison, Brian. "The Liturgy and 'Supersessionism,'" *CatholicCulture.org*, item 9168.

Hazell, Matthew. "'All the Elements of the Roman Rite'? Mythbusting, Part II." *New Liturgical Movement*, October 1, 2021.

———. "Demanding the Impossible: *Traditionis custodes* and Vernacular Readings." *Rorate Caeli*, July 20, 2021.

———. "The Eastertide Collects in the Post-Vatican II Missal: A Problematic Reform." *Rorate Caeli*, May 17, 2021.

———. "Ember Days in the Post-Vatican II Liturgical Reforms: An Accidental Elimination?" *Rorate Caeli*, March 10, 2022.

———. "'Expert Consensus' in the Post-Vatican II Liturgical Reforms: More Half-Truths and Dated Scholarship." *New Liturgical Movement*, August 24, 2024

———. "The Prayers for the Feast of St. Lawrence in the Post-Vatican II Liturgical Reforms." *Rorate Caeli*, August 10, 2021.

———. "The Scattering of the Propers: A Case Study in the Mass Formularies of the Ordinary Form." *New Liturgical Movement*, July 15, 2020.

Heid, Stefan. *Altar and Church: Principles of Liturgy from Early Christianity*. The Catholic University of America Press, 2024.

Hickson, Maike. "New biography describes great influence of Fr. Joseph Ratzinger in Vatican II." *Rorate Caeli*, December 11, 2020

Hoffman, Michael. "Putting the Nail in the (Pope's) Coffin." *Crisis Magazine*, December 6, 2024.

Holmes, Jeremy. *Cur Deus Verba: Why the Word Became Words*. Ignatius Press, 2021.

Honorius Augustodunensis. *Jewel of the Soul*. Translated by Zachary Thomas and Gerhard Eger. Harvard University Press, 2023.

Houghton, Bryan. *Unwanted Priest: The Autobiography of a Latin Mass Exile*. Edited by Gerard Deighan. Angelico Press, 2022.

Howard, Thomas. *The Night Is Far Spent: A Treasury of Thomas Howard*. Edited by Vivian W. Dudro. Ignatius Press, 2007.

Hull, Geoffrey. *The Banished Heart: Origins of Heteropraxis in the Catholic Church*. T&T Clark, 2010.

Hunwicke, John. "Liturgy and Vatican II: what did they think they were voting for?" *Fr Hunwicke's Mutual Enrichment*, March 23, 2019.

———. "Some priest called Ruff... and: Did Archbishop Marcel Lefebvre make a big mistake? (1)." *Fr Hunwicke's Mutual Enrichment*, March 3, 2017.

Huonder, Vitus. "An Interview with His Excellency Bishop Vitus Huonder." Society of St. Pius X, District of the USA, October 1, 2021, https://sspx.org/en/news/interview-his-excellency-bishop-vitus-huonder-26764.

Husslein, Joseph. *The Reign of Christ, the Immortal King of Ages*. Arouca Press, 2024.

Innocent III. *The Mysteries of the Mass* and *The Four Kinds of Marriage*. Translated by David Foley. Angelus Press, 2023.

Johnson, Samuel. "On the 'Epitaph to James Craggs.'" In *The Works of Samuel Johnson*, vol. 6: "Life of Pope." J. Nichols and Son, 1810.

Joncas, Michael. "An Issue for Future Liturgical Translation (I): Correcting Already-Approved Mistranslations." *Pray Tell*, October 16, 2017.

Journet, Charles. *The Theology of the Church*. Translated by Victor Szczurek. Ignatius Press, 2004.

Kabel, Sharon. "Catholic fact check: Jean Guitton, Pope Paul VI, and the liturgical reforms." July 7, 2023. https://sharonkabel.com/post/guitton/.

Kappes, Christiaan W. "Consilium and Vatican 2: Everything You Wanted to Know About Its Make-Up, Function, etc. (Replete with Graphs)." https://www.academia.edu/8837932.

Kidd, B. J., ed. *Documents Illustrative of the Continental Reformation*. Clarendon Press, 1911.

Kirby, Mark. "Home from the Liturgical Thirty Years War." *Vultus Christi*, February 23, 2014, https://archive.ph/Lw8RV.

———. "Let nothing be preferred to the Work of God." *Vultus Christi*, February 20, 2014, https://archive.ph/lTOsz.

———. "Sung Theology: The Liturgical Chant of the Church." In *Beyond the Prosaic: Renewing the Liturgical Movement*, ed. Stratford Caldecott, 127–48. T&T Clark, 1998.

Kocik, Thomas. "Reforming the Irreformable?" *New Liturgical Movement*, February 9, 2014.

———. "Reforming the Irreformable? A Postscript." *New Liturgical Movement*, March 1, 2014.

———. "A Reform of the Reform?" In Reid, *T&T Clark Companion to Liturgy*, 317–38.

———. *The Reform of the Reform? A Liturgical Debate: Reform or Return*. Ignatius Press, 2003.

———. "The Reform of the Reform." In Reid, *Liturgy in the Twenty-First Century*, 19–50.

Kreuter, Joseph. "A 1933 Sermon on the Missal: 'Having perfectly worshiped God in this life, the faithful will be prepared to take part in the heavenly praises.'" First published in the journal *Orate Fratres* of October 7, 1933; reprinted at *Rorate Caeli*, June 28, 2019.

Kunitz-Dick, Alisa. "AUDI, ISRAËL: Jewish Feasts in the Propers of the Traditional Roman Rite." *Rorate Caeli*, August 31, 2021.

Lamb, Christopher. "Stubborn opposition to Vatican II 'not Catholic' says cardinal." *The Tablet*, August 28, 2022.

Lameri, Angelo. *La «Pontificia Commissio de sacra liturgia praeparatoria Concilii Vaticani II». Documenti, Testi, Verbi*. CLV, 2013.

Lamont, John. "The Catholic Church and the Rule of Law." In Kwasniewski, *Ultramontanism and Tradition*, 78–106.

———. "Dominican Theologian Attacks Catholic Tradition: Defending Kwasniewski against Donneaud's Positivist Reductionism." Published at *Rorate Caeli* in four installments in September 2023; a PDF of the whole is available at https://bit.ly/4gSSqTz.

Lang, Uwe Michael. *Turning Towards the Lord: Orientation in Liturgical Prayer*. Ignatius Press, 2009.

Larson, David. "Live Like the Amish?" *Crisis Magazine*, September 8, 2021.

Lazu Kmita, Robert. "Sacred Gestures and Symbols: Why Communion in the Hand is Unacceptable." *The Remnant* online, September 20, 2024.

Lebrun, Pierre. *The Mass: A Literal, Historical, and Dogmatic Explanation of Its Prayers and Ceremonies*. Translated by Harry B. Oesman. Ubi Caritas Press, 2024.

Lefebvre, Marcel. "The Infiltration of Modernism in the Church" (1982). Originally published in *Angelus* magazine, vol. 15, no. 3; text online at www.sspxasia.com/Documents/Archbishop-Lefebvre/The-Infiltration-of-Modernism-in-the-Church.htm.

Lemna, Keith. *The Apocalypse of Wisdom: Louis Bouyer's Theological Recovery of the Cosmos*. Angelico Press, 2019.

Leonard of Port Maurice. *The Hidden Treasure: Holy Mass*. TAN Books, 2012.

Lewis, C. S. *A Preface to Paradise Lost*. Oxford University Press, 1942.

Lewis, Mike. "Liturgical Renewal and Traditionalist Trolls." *Where Peter Is*, December 11, 2021.

Lewis, Mike (@mfjlewis). "They have plenty of arguments for why even the stupidest parts are absolutely necessary." X, December 11, 2021, https://x.com/mfjlewis/status/1469847612484472837.

Liedl, Jonathan. "The City of Big Shoulders—and Liturgical Confusion: Chicago Faithful Flummoxed by Inconsistent Liturgy Policy." *National Catholic Register*, June 27, 2022.

———. "Personal Experience, Not Moral Absolutes, to Steer Synod Study Group's Discernment on Sexuality Questions." *National Catholic Register*, October 3, 2024.

The Lives of the Desert Fathers. Translated by Norman Russell. Cistercian Publications, 1981.

Luther, Martin. *Formula missæ et communionis pro ecclesia Wittembergensis* (1523). In *Works of Martin Luther*, vol. 6. Muhlenberg Press, 1932.

Mabry, Zac (@ZacMabry). "There are two pizzas in front of you: A and B. You could have Pizza A, but you choose Pizza B. Then you put all your effort into making Pizza B more like Pizza A." X, August 24, 2019, https://x.com/ZacMabry/status/1165337938210766848.

Maggioni, Corrado. "Fifty years of the Missal promulgated by Paul VI: A reform for the renewal of the Church." *Pray Tell*, April 17, 2019.

Mahrt, William. "Unintended Consequences." *Sacred Music*, vol. 142, no. 2 (Summer 2015): 3–7.

Mares, Courtney. "Vatican doctrine office reaffirms that Catholics cannot be Freemasons." *Catholic News Agency*, November 15, 2023.

Maritain, Jacques. *Liturgy and Contemplation*. Translated by Joseph W. Evans. P. J. Kenedy & Sons, 1960.

Martindale, C. C. *The Words of the Missal*. Os Justi Press, 2023.

McInerny, D. Q. "Reflections on the Loss of Latin, Part I." *Latin Mass Magazine*, vol. 28, no. 4 (Christmas 2019): 33–34.

McNaspy, Clement. *Our Changing Liturgy*. Hawthorn Books, 1966.

McShea, Bronwen. "Bishops Unbound." *First Things*, January 2019. www.firstthings.com/article/2019/01/bishops-unbound.

[Mechtilde of Hackeborn.] *The Love of the Sacred Heart, Illustrated by St. Mechtilde*. Burns, Oates, and Washbourne, 1922.

Mectilde of the Blessed Sacrament. *The True Spirit of the Perpetual Adorers of the Most Holy Sacrament of the Altar*. Angelico Press: forthcoming.

Meloni, Julia. *The St. Gallen Mafia Exposed*. TAN Books, 2021.

Meyer, Garrett. "'Other Things Being... Equal'? A Critique of *Sacrosanctum Concilium* 116." *New Liturgical Movement*, October 14, 2024.

Miller, Peter. "Bible by the Pound: Would the Holy Spirit Agree that More Bible is Better at Mass?" In Kwasniewski, *Illusions of Reform*, 180–97.

Mitsui, Daniel. "Altar Cards for the Requiem Mass." *Liturgical Arts Journal*, April 15, 2021.

———. "New Illuminated Altar Cards." *Liturgical Arts Journal*, November 24, 2017;

Montagna, Diane. "*Traditionis Custodes*: More Facts Emerge (What the Bishops of the World Actually Told Francis)." *The Remnant*, October 28, 2021.

———. "*Traditionis Custodes*: Separating Fact from Fiction." *The Remnant*, October 7, 2021.

———. "*Traditionis Custodes*: A Weapon of Mass Destruction." *The Remnant*, November 29, 2021.

Morello, Sebastian. *Mysticism, Magic, and Monasteries: Recovering the Sacred Mystery at the Heart of Reality*. Os Justi Press, 2024.

Morgan, Jason. "Triumph of the Will: The Novus Ordo, RIP." *The Remnant* online, August 3, 2021.

Mosebach, Martin. "The Church's reform disaster: No one wants to see the causes of the abuse scandal. Yet they can be clearly identified." *Rorate Caeli*, July 24, 2024.

———. *The Heresy of Formlessness: The Roman Liturgy and Its Enemy*. Translated by Graham Harrison. Angelico Press, 2018.

Moynihan, Robert. "Letter #8: The Long Hand." *Inside the Vatican*, April 23, 2020.

Murr, Charles Theodore. *The Godmother: Madre Pascalina, A Feminine Tour de Force*. Independently published, 2017.

———. *Murder in the 33rd Degree: The Gagnon Investigation into Vatican Freemasonry*. Independently published, 2022.

Murray, Gerald. "Papal Abuse of Liturgical Law." *The Catholic Thing*, March 22, 2022.

Newman, John Henry. *Apologia Pro Vita Sua*. Edited by David J. DeLaura. W. W. Norton & Co., 1968.

———. *The Arians of the Fourth Century*. University of Notre Dame Press/Gracewing, 2001.

———. *An Essay on the Development of Christian Doctrine*. Longmans, Green, and Co., 1909.

Nichols, Aidan. *Looking at the Liturgy: A Critical View of Its Contemporary Form*. Ignatius Press, 1996.

The Nine Ways of Prayer of St. Dominic. www.fisheaters.com/stdominic9ways.html.

Normandin, Yves. *Pastor Out in the Cold: The Story of Fr. Normandin's Fight for the Latin Mass in Canada*. Angelus Press, 2021.

O'Connell, Gerard. "Pope Francis: There will be no 'reform of the reform' of the liturgy." *America*, December 6, 2016.

Oesterreicher, John M. "*Pro Perfidis Judaeis*." *Theological Studies* 8 (1947): 80–96.

Oldendorf, Clemens V. "Lessons from the Sixties: Selective Synodality and Princely Protests." *New Liturgical Movement*, October 24, 2019.

"The Old Liturgy and the New Despisers of the Council." *Rorate Caeli*, July 5, 2022.

Olier, Jean-Jacques. *The Mystical Meaning of the Ceremonies of the Mass*. Translated by David J. Critchley. Angelico Press, 2024.

O'Loughlin, Michael J. "Mass for LGBTQ Catholics met with protesters in St. Louis." *Outreach*, April 26, 2024, https://outreach.faith/2024/04/mass-for-lgbtq-catholics-met-with-protesters-in-st-louis/.

O'Malley, Timothy P. *Bored Again Catholic: How the Mass Could Save Your Life*. Our Sunday Visitor, 2017.
Ottaviani, Alfredo, Antonio Bacci, and a Group of Roman Theologians. *The Ottaviani Intervention: Short Critical Study of the New Order of Mass*. Translated by Anthony Cekada. Philothea Press, 2010.
The Our Lady of Mount Carmel Hymnal. Os Justi Press, 2023.
Parsons, John. "A Reform of the Reform?" in Thomas M. Kocik, *The Reform of the Reform? A Liturgical Debate: Reform or Return*, 211–56. Ignatius Press, 2003.
Pasqualucci, Paolo. *The Parallel Council: The Anomalous Beginning of the Second Vatican Council*. Gondolin Press, 2018.
Peachey, Roy. *50 Books for Life: A Concise Guide to Catholic Literature*. Angelico Press, 2019.
Pecknold, Chad. "Why do so few US Catholics believe in the Real Presence? Look at the liturgy." *Catholic Herald*, August 9, 2019.
Pentin, Edward. "After Outcry, Vatican Eases Restrictions on Individual Masses in St. Peter's Basilica." *National Catholic Register*, June 22, 2021.
Pepino, John. "Cassandra's Curse: Louis Bouyer, the Liturgical Movement, and the Post-Conciliar Reform of the Mass." *Antiphon* 18.3 (2014): 254–300
Perricone, John A. "Chicago: Where Eucharistic Revival Goes to Die." *Crisis Magazine*, January 2, 2025.
"Pillar Investigates: USCCB gen sec Burrill resigns after sexual misconduct allegations." *The Pillar*, July 20, 2021.
Pope, Charles. "A Look at the 'Actual Mass' of Vatican II: the 1965 Missal." *Community in Mission*, January 28, 2015.
"Pope Francis simplifies papal funeral rites." *Aleteia*, November 21, 2024.
Pristas, Lauren. *The Collects of the Roman Missals: A Comparative Study of the Sundays in Proper Seasons Before and After the Second Vatican Council*. Bloomsbury T&T Clark, 2013.
———. "Theological Principles That Guided the Redaction of the Roman Missal (1970)." *The Thomist* 67 (2003): 157–95.
Pullella, Philip. "Pope kisses feet of South Sudan leaders, urging them to keep the peace." *Reuters*, April 12, 2019.
Quoëx, Franck. *Liturgical Theology in Thomas Aquinas: Sacrifice and Salvation History*. Translated and edited by Zachary Thomas. Catholic University of America Press, 2023.
Ratzinger, Joseph. *Theology of the Liturgy*. Edited by Michael J. Miller. *Collected Works*, vol. 11. Ignatius Press, 2014.
———. *Milestones: Memoirs 1927–1977*. Translated by Erasmo Leiva-Merikakis. Ignatius Press, 1998.
———. *Salt of the Earth: Christianity and the Catholic Church at the End of the Millenium*. Translated by Adrian Walker. Ignatius Press, 1997.
Reid, Alcuin. "Active Participation and Pastoral Adaptation." In *Liturgy, Participation and Sacred Music*, 35–50. CIEL UK, 2006.
———. "*Beyond Pius V* by Andrea Grillo — Review by Dom Alcuin Reid." *New Liturgical Movement*, January 21, 2014.

———, ed. *A Bitter Trial: Evelyn Waugh and John Carmel Cardinal Heenan on the Liturgical Changes.* Expanded edition. Ignatius Press, 2011.

———. "The 'Consilium ad Exsequendam' at 50 — An Interview with Dom Alcuin Reid." *New Liturgical Movement*, February 7 and February 12, 2014.

———. "Does *Traditionis Custodes* Pass Liturgical History 101?" In Kwasniewski, *From Benedict's Peace to Francis's War*, 252–59.

———. "The Liturgy, Fifty Years after *Sacrosanctum Concilium.*" *Catholic World Report*, December 4, 2013.

———, ed. *Liturgy in the Twenty-First Century: Contemporary Issues and Perspectives.* Bloomsbury T&T Clark, 2016.

———, ed. *Sacred Liturgy: The Source and Summit of the Life and Mission of the Church.* Ignatius Press, 2014.

———. "*Sacrosanctum concilium* and the Reform of the *Ordo Missae.*" *Antiphon* 10.3 (2006): 277–95.

———, ed. *T&T Clark Companion to Liturgy.* Bloomsbury T&T Clark, 2016.

Rheinschmitt, Monika. "Further thoughts on 'inculturation': Why ignore the liturgy that sustained the evangelization of the entire globe?" *Rorate Caeli*, July 5, 2022.

Ripperger, Chad. "The Spirituality of the Ancient Liturgy, Part 2." *Latin Mass Magazine*, vol. 10, no. 4 (Fall 2001): 28–31. www.latinmassmagazine.com/articles/articles_2001_FA_Ripperger.html.

Rivoire, Réginald-Marie. *Does "Traditionis Custodes" Pass the Juridical Rationality Test?* Translated by William Barker. Os Justi Press, 2022.

Roche, Arthur. "Ecclesial Communion and the Motu Proprio *Traditionis Custodes.*" Dicastero per i Vescovi, *Il Ministero Episcopale in Una Chiesa Sinodale*, 137–53. Libreria Editrice Vaticana, 2024.

Romero, Jesse. *What Attracts Men to the Sacred Liturgy — and Why.* Sophia Institute Press, 2024.

Ross Williamson, Hugh. *The Great Betrayal: Thoughts on the Destruction of the Mass.* Arouca Press, 2021.

———. *The Great Prayer: Concerning the Canon of the Mass.* Gracewing, 2009.

Salvucci, Claudio. "Forming Scholars of Native American Liturgical 'Uses.'" *Liturgical Arts Journal*, February 27, 2018.

Salza, John, and Robert Siscoe. *True or False Pope? Refuting Sedevacantism and Other Modern Errors.* STAS Editions, 2015.

Sammons, Eric. "New Coke: If Today's Catholics Were In Charge." *OnePeterFive*, December 9, 2015.

———. "The Politicization of *Ad Orientem.*" *Crisis Magazine*, February 7, 2022.

Sarah, Robert, with Nicolas Diat. *The Power of Silence: Against the Dictatorship of Noise.* Translated by Michael J. Miller. Ignatius Press, 2017.

Savage, Christian Gregory. "Music and the Writings of the Helfta Mystics." Thesis for the Master of Music, Florida State University, 2012.

Schluenderfritz, Malcolm. "Prayer Cards, Painting Class, and Liturgy Wars." *Where Peter Is*, December 9, 2021.

Schneider, Athanasius, with Diane Montagna. *Christus Vincit: Christ's Triumph over the Darkness of the Age*. Angelico Press, 2019.

Schrems, Wolfram. "The Council's Constitution on the Liturgy: Reform or revolution?" *Rorate Caeli*, May 3, 2018.

Schuler, Richard. *Sacred Music and Liturgy After Vatican II*. Edited by Virginia A. Schubert. Arouca Press, 2024.

Scrosati, Luisella. "The clique of Saint Anselm conducts the war against ancient Mass." *Rorate Caeli*, February 27, 2023.

Scruton, Roger. "Rousseau and the Origins of Liberalism." *The New Criterion*, October 1998, https://newcriterion.com/article/rousseau-the-origins-of-liberalism/.

"The Sensible Bond: Why I left the SSPX milieu." *Learning My Catholic Faith*, September 28, 2013, https://web.archive.org/web/20231124125101/https://learningmycatholicfaith.blogspot.com/2013/09/the-sensible-bond-why-i-left-sspx-milieu.html.

Shaffern, Robert W. "The Mass According to Vatican II." *The Catholic Thing*, July 10, 2022.

Shaw, Joseph, ed. *The Case for Liturgical Restoration*. Angelico Press, 2019.

———. "The Death of the Reform of the Reform?" Series in five parts. Part 1, February 23, 2014. Part 2, "The Liturgical Movement," February 24, 2014. Part 3, "Falling Between Two Stools," February 25, 2014. Part 4, "Novus Ordo in Latin?," February 26, 2014. Part 5, "1965?," February 27, 2014.

———. "*Evangelii gaudium* 3: open and closed worship." *LMS Chairman*, January 1, 2014.

———, ed. *The Latin Mass and the Intellectuals: Petitions to Save the Ancient Mass from 1966 to 2007*. Arouca Press, 2023.

———. *The Liturgy, the Family, and the Crisis of Modernity: Essays of a Traditional Catholic*. Os Justi, 2023.

———. "The Mass of 1965: back to the future? Why it is not an option." *Rorate Caeli*, February 27, 2014.

———. "Must I Go to Mass on Monday?" *Catholic Answers*, November 19, 2024.

———. "The Old Mass and the Workers." *LMS Chairman*, July 3, 2013.

———. *Sacred and Great: A Brief Introduction to the Traditional Latin Mass*. Os Justi Press, 2023.

———. "Survey reveals why Catholics leave Church, including because of watered down teaching." *LifeSiteNews*, July 19, 2019.

———. "Transferred Holy Days, 2: The Dates." *LMS Chairman*, January 10, 2014.

———. "Vatican II on Liturgical Preservation." *LMS Chairman*, January 17, 2017.

———. "What Sort of Mass Did 'Vatican II' Want?" *LMS Chairman*, May 24, 2016.

———. "Why Catholics started leaving the Church in droves after Vatican II." *LifeSiteNews*, July 18, 2019.

Shivone, Andrew. "The Glorious Form of the Liturgy." *Humanum Review*, Language: Issue Two, https://humanumreview.com/articles/the-glorious-form-of-the-liturgy.

Sire, H. J. A. *Phoenix from the Ashes: The Making, Unmaking, and Restoration of Catholic Tradition*. Angelico Press, 2015.

Solari, Grégory. "Traditionalism creates a distance between the heritage of past generations and the contemporary ecclesial community." *La Croix International*, October 4, 2024.

Somerville Knapman, Hugh. "The Lament of a Liturgical Loner." *Dominus Mihi Adjutor*, February 18, 2014.

———. "Pursuing a Point." *One Foot in the Cloister*, April 13, 2019.

———. "Saving the New Mass?" *Dominus Mihi Adjutor*, July 15, 2019.

Sonnen, John Paul. "The Custom of Festive Hangings in Rome: The Chiesa Nuova." *LAJ*, January 1, 2025.

———. "Requiem Mass Altar Cards." *Liturgical Arts Journal*, December 9, 2020.

Steckler, Gerard G. *The Triumph of Romanticism*. Os Justi Press, 2023.

Stickler, Alfons. "Recollections of a Vatican II Peritus." *New Liturgical Movement*, June 29, 2022.

Stridon, Jerome. "The *Cœtus [Internationalis Patrum]*: Trad Godfathers at Vatican II." *OnePeterFive*, December 12, 2022.

Thomas Aquinas. *Commentary on the Letters of Saint Paul to the Galatians and Ephesians*. Translated by Fr. Fabian R. Larcher, op, and Matthew Lamb. Emmaus Academic, 2018.

———. *Commentary on Psalms*. Translated by Albert Marie Surmanski and Maria Veritas Marks. Emmaus Academic, 2021.

———. *The Summa Theologiae of St. Thomas Aquinas*. Second and Revised Edition, 1920. Literally translated by Fathers of the English Dominican Province. Online Edition by Kevin Knight, 2017.

Tolkien, J. R. R. *The Letters of J. R. R. Tolkien*. Revised and expanded edition. Edited by Humphrey Carpenter and Christopher Tolkien. HarperCollins, 2023.

Tribe, Shawn. "The Development of the Shape of the Eastern Phelonion (Chasuble) and Its Parallels to the Same in the Latin West." *Liturgical Arts Journal*, November 18, 2024.

———. "Hand Illuminated Altar Cards by Pelican Printery House." *Liturgical Arts Journal*, June 9, 2021.

———. "The Historical, Theological, Liturgical and Artistic Case for Altar Frontals." *Liturgical Arts Journal*, November 16, 2017.

———. "Inculturation: Japanese and Chinese Madonnas." *Liturgical Arts Journal*, May 15, 2018.

———. "Keeping Feasts with Greater Festivity." *Liturgical Arts Journal*, July 5, 2019.

———. "Liturgical Arts Quarterly 1935: 'Christian Art in the Far East,'" *New Liturgical Movement*, April 20, 2010.

———. "The Missal Cushion." *Liturgical Arts Journal*, February 4, 2020.

———. "The Oriental Chasuble of Dom Pierre-Célestin Lou Tseng-Tsiang, OSB." *Liturgical Arts Journal*, October 4, 2017.

Turner, Paul. *In These or Similar Words: Praying and Crafting the Language of the Liturgy*. World Library Publications, 2014.

Ureta, José. "A Brief Study of Certain Theological Deviations in *Desiderio Desideravi*." https://onepeterfive.com/wp-content/uploads/2022/08/Ureta-Complete.pdf.

von Hildebrand, Dietrich. *The Devastated Vineyard*. Franciscan Herald Press, 1973.

———. *Liturgy and Personality*. The Hildebrand Project, 2016.

Ward, Maisie. *The Wilfrid Wards and the Transition*, vol. 2: *Insurrection versus Resurrection*. Sheed & Ward, 1937.

Welborn, Amy. "Up...off your knees!" *Catholic World Report*, December 13, 2024.

"Why Doesn't Pope Francis Kneel Before the Blessed Sacrament?" *Torch of the Faith News*, June 2, 2016, www.torchofthefaith.com/news.php?extend.1332.

Winters, Michael Sean. "As Francis reinforces limits on Latin Mass, it's past time to embrace Vatican II." *National Catholic Reporter*, February 27, 2023.

Wooden, Cindy. "Archbishop says most bishops see importance of 'Traditionis Custodes.'" *National Catholic Reporter*, January 21, 2022.

Zuhlsdorf, John. "Can't get 'Liturgy of the Hours' in Latin." *Fr. Z's Blog*, September 6, 2017.

———. "A diocese smells the coffee: starts planning for decline of the Novus Ordo and growth of the TLM." *Fr. Z's Blog*, January 20, 2020.

———. "Excessive pious gestures during Mass." *Fr. Z's Blog*, January 12, 2019

———. "A Pentecost Monday lesson: 'And Paul VI wept.'" *Fr. Z's Blog*, May 21, 2018.

———. "What are the authentic rubrics, postures for lay people at the Traditional Latin Mass. Are we doing it wrong?" *Fr. Z's Blog*, February 15, 2020.

INDEX OF PROPER NAMES

Abbazia di San Benedetto in Monte, 228, 342, 358
Abel, 45, 115n21
Abraham, 45, 198, 258, 268, 301, 328
Abu Dhabi, 58, 63n33, 114
Adam, 45
Adams, John, 40
Adoremus, 37n25
Africa, 96–97, 103n39, 111n9, 230, 274n8, 316, 348
Age of Aquarius, 123
Ahmad, Joseph, 347n13
Amalarius of Metz, 265
Amazon, 71, 103, 211
Ambrose of Milan, St., 214n9, 239, 320, 343n3
Amerio, Romano, 4n3
Amish, 119
Amorose, Mark, 53
Anthony of Egypt, St., 213
Antiphonale Monasticum, 236n18
Antonelli, Ferdinando, 17, 95n23
Archer, Anthony, 37n26
Arendt, Hannah, 52
Aristotle, 23, 35n18, 129, 202, 237n19, 283n20, 344, 349
Asia, 96, 117, 230
Assisi, interreligious meeting of, 58
Athanasius of Alexandria, St., 30n8
Auctorem Fidei (Pius VI), 7, 374n4
Augustine of Canterbury, St., 88n10, 136
Augustine of Hippo, St., 23, 26, 65, 141, 166n14, 188, 221, 225, 250n2, 257, 291, 304, 367
Austria, 65, 175, 273n6, 308, 348

Babylon, 8, 368, 396
Bacci, Antonio, 384
Bach, J.S., 338
Bacon, Francis, 4, 20, 22–23
Baldovin, John F., 7
Baresel, James, 363n2
Barron, Robert, 327
Barruel, Augustin, 56n17
Barthe, Claude, 218n21, 258n17, 260–61, 263–69, 373n1
Basil of Caesarea, St., 314

Basilica of St. Peter, 111, 317
Baudelaire, Charles, 263
Benedict of Nursia, St., 49, 117n2, 186n18, 320–21
Benedictines, 29, 33, 49, 98, 153n17, 154, 183, 199, 229, 236n18, 238, 252, 342, 348n16, 382, 387
Benedict XIV, 56
Benedict XV, xiv, 86, 236
Benedict XVI, xi, xv, xxi n6, xxiv n11, 11, 27, 35, 46, 62, 70, 74–76, 97, 105n50, 106, 110–12, 118, 124, 134, 143, 159, 191, 193, 203, 225, 231, 283–84, 285n24, 301, 329, 364, 384, 394
Benofy, Susan, 37n25
Benson, Robert Hugh, xix
Berg, John, 237
Bergoglio, Jorge Mario, 76, 99n30, 115; *see also* Francis
Berlin, 108
Bernard of Clairvaux, St., 264
Beyond the Prosaic (Caldecott), 32, 343n2
Bishop, Edmund, 92
Blake, Ray, 189, 278n14
Blanchard, Shaun, 7n11
Blignières, Louis-Marie de, 12
Book of Blessings, 217
Book of Common Prayer, The, 92
Bottum, Joseph, 394
Boughton, Lynne C., 224n33, 225n34
Bouyer, Louis, 18, 27, 49, 57, 63, 106, 223, 243, 271
Bradshaw, Paul, 216n17, 310
Brandsma, Titus, 120n25
Brill, Patrick John, 348n15
Brompton Oratory, *see* London Oratory
Brusoe, Reyers, 257n15
Buck, Roger, xxii, 101
Buckley, William F., Jr., 63
Bugnini, Annibale, x, 6–10, 13–17, 22–23, 26, 27n1, 47–58, 61, 64, 68–69, 76n9, 87, 94, 98–101, 104, 120n25, 129, 144, 152, 168n15, 179n4, 196, 209, 213, 232, 234–35, 271, 275, 340
Bullivant, Stephen, 94n22, 210n3
Burchard, Johann, 259
Burrill, Jeffrey, 55
Byrnes, James, 154–55

Cabasilas, Nicholas, 258
Cabrol, Fernand, 224, 225n34
Calmel, Roger-Thomas, 31n9, 134n12, 373
Calvet, Gérard, 14n31, 134n12
Calvinism, 14, 95–96, 299
Camillus de Lellis, St., 240n3
Campbell, Phillip, 36, 308n5, 329n3
Canada, 139, 366
Cassingena-Trévedy, François, 262
Catechesi Tradendæ (John Paul II), 327
Catherine of Alexandria, St., 240n3
Cavadini, John, 24n58, 393, 395
Cecilia, St., 241
Cekada, Anthony, xiii, 113n17, 145, 314, 384n2
Celsus, St., 240n3
Charlemagne, 43
Charlier, Michael, 87n4
Chartres Cathedral, 5, 229, 270–71, 274–75
Chautard, Jean-Baptiste, 354–55
Chesterton, G.K., 47
Chiron, Yves, 4n3, 13–14, 15n32, 22n54, 47–55, 95n25, 232, 275
Chupungco, Anscar J., 99–100, 314n13
Cicognani, Amleto Giovanni, 234
Cipolla, Richard, 28–29, 34, 38, 234n10, 283
Ciszek, Walter J., 324
City of God (Augustine), 166n14, 304
Civil War (English), 130
Clayton, David, 347n13
Clear Creek, 358
Clement XII, 56
Coetus Internationalis Patrum, 234n8
Comme le Prévoit (Consilium), 385
Comte, Auguste, 20
Con Grande Fiducia (Benedict XVI), 112, 134, 193, 196, 238
Congar, Yves, 83
Congregation/Dicastery for Divine Worship and the Discipline of the Sacraments, 85, 90, 104, 172, 230, 278
Congregation/Dicastery for the Doctrine of the Faith, 56, 105, 330n6, 336, 329
Consilium ad exsequendam Constitutionem de Sacra Liturgia (Consilium), x, 7–9, 17–18, 23, 25, 27, 36, 38, 54, 57, 69, 87, 95, 98, 105, 118, 129, 144, 168n15, 179n4, 206, 216, 240n3, 245, 263, 278, 285n24, 383, 385
Coppen, Luke, 98n28
Crane, Paul, 14n31
Cranmer, Thomas, 92–93, 96, 144n27, 151, 205, 261
Crashaw, Richard, 129–30
Crouan, Denis, xii n1
Cum Sanctissima (CDF), 329, 336
Cupich, Blase J., 142n23, 159, 229
Cyril of Alexandria, St., 173
Cyril of Jerusalem, St., 96n26

Damasus, St., 54
Daniel, 370–71
Dante Alighieri, 257, 298
Daoudal, Yves, 199n3
Darboy, Georges, 85
Darroch, Leo, 143
Dashiell, David, 257n15
David, 45, 54, 62, 221
Davies, Michael, xiii, 4n3, 31n9, 69, 92, 93n20, 95n24, 118, 144n27, 168n15, 232, 261, 311
Day-Milne, Peter, 19–20
de Bus, César, 120n25
De Corte, Marcel, 309–10
de Foucauld, Charles, 120n25
de Lubac, Henri, 300
de Mattei, Roberto, 4n3, 23, 31n8, 56
de Montebello, Philippe, 242
de Nantes, Georges, 83
Dei Verbum (Vatican II), 71
Delalande, Dominique, 342–43
Depression, Great, 216
Descartes, René, 4, 20, 22–23, 50, 129, 242, 320
Desiderio Desideravi (Francis), 35n19, 93n20, 116
Deutsche Messe (Schubert), 273n6
Devillers, Arnaud, 20
Dicastery for Institutes of Consecrated Life and Societies of Apostolic Life, 230
Dionysius the Areopagite, St., 175, 302
DiPippo, Gregory, xii n1, xxv, 58n24, 92n18, 95n23, 106, 116n22, 190n26, 213n9, 214n11, 218n20, 223n31, 233n5, 239n2, 267n39, 329n1, 330, 335n13, 373n1

Divina Commedia (Dante), 5
Dix, Gregory, 216n17, 310
Dobszay, László, 373n1
Documents on the Liturgy 1963–1979, 50n5, 147
Dominic de Guzmán, St., 263
Dominicans, 5n6, 39, 376; of the Holy Spirit, 226–29
Donneaud, Henry, 227n37
Douglas, Mary, 37n26
Dreyfus, François-Georges, 14n31
Dugan, Conor, 15
Dumas, Antoine, 199
Durandus, William, 255, 264, 269
Dwyer, Robert J., 19

Ecclesia de Eucharistia (John Paul II), 110, 166n14
Ecclesia Dei, Pontifical Commission, 238n21, 270, 329–30, 378–80
Edward VI, 92nn18–19
Edwards, Kate, 29
Egidio da Viterbo, 130
Eichmann, Adolf, 52n8
Eliot, T.S., 399
Elizabeth of the Trinity, St., 329
Elliott, Peter J., 136
El-Tayeb, Ahmad, 63n33
England, 27, 92, 129, 153n17, 234, 366
Ephemerides Liturgicæ, 23n55
Ephrem the Syrian, St., 88n10
Escrivá, Josemaría, St., 191
Esolen, Anthony, 142n23, 326n32
Europe, 7, 55, 57, 96–97, 101–2, 162, 170, 196, 202, 274n8, 347, 362, 394, 397; Eastern, 96
Evangelii Nuntiandi (Paul VI), 146

Farret d'Astiès, Cyril, 11–12, 77n11, 105n52
Fassino, Nico, 270n1
Fatima, 55n14, 377
Felicitas and her seven sons, Sts., 240n3
Felix and Nabor, Sts., 239, 243
Felix of Valois, St., 239, 240n3
Fernández, Victor, 56n19
Ferrara, Christopher, 14, 69, 197n2
Fessio, Joseph, 3
Fiedrowicz, Michael, 88–89, 104, 139, 173n19, 255, 259–62, 315n14, 367, 373n1

First Vatican Council, *see* Vatican I
Flanders, Timothy, 56n20
Flavigny, 229
Foch, Ferdinand, 85
Foley, Michael P., 19, 27n1, 29n3, 218–19, 223n29, 272n4, 373n1
Folsom, Cassian, 29–30
Fontgombault, 93, 227
Ford, Henry, 22
Fortescue, Adrian, xiv n7, 256, 310
France, 4n3, 55, 106, 133, 273
Franciscans, 259
Francis de Sales, St., 354
Francis of Assisi, St., 228n40, 240n3,
Francis Xavier, St., 201
Francis, pope, x, xxi n7, xxiv n11, 34n15, 35n19, 54, 56, 62n31, 63, 66n38, 71, 78, 87n4, 90n14, 105, 110–17, 120, 138, 147, 159n3, 211, 376, 381, 385, 389
Fraternity of St. Vincent Ferrer, 227
Freud, Sigmund, 50
Friel, David, 341
FSSP, *see* Priestly Fraternity of St. Peter

Gagliarducci, Andrea, 98n29
Gagnon, Édouard, 51, 55
Gamaliel, 141
Gamber, Klaus, xiii, 31n9, 32n12
Gasquet, Francis Aidan, 92
Gaudium et Spes (Vatican II), 88, 236
Gayford, Martin, 242
Gelasius I, St., 19
Gélineau, Joseph, xiii n5, 8–9, 99
General Instruction of the Roman Missal, 70, 363, 365
Gennadius of Massilia, 311
German Synodal Way, 106
Germany, 273, 366
Gervase and Protase, Sts., 240n3
Giampietro, Nicola, 17n38
Gihr, Nicholas, 59
Gilder, George, 256
Glagolitic Mass, 151
Gnocchi, Alessandro, 329
Goethe, Johann Wolfgang von, 59
Graduale Romanum, 136
Graham, Daniel, 70n4, 92n17
Gregory III, 218n20
Gregory XIII, 239n2
Gregory XV, 239n2

Gregory XVI, 56
Gregory of Tours, St., 312
Gregory the Great, St., 8, 54, 64n36, 136, 199n3, 221, 255, 258n17, 314, 336
Grillo, Andrea, 97–99, 190n26
Guardini, Romano, 266
Guéranger, Prosper, 6, 59, 242–43, 259
Guillou, Edouard, 154
Guitton, Jean, 14–15, 95, 299
Gullickson, Thomas, 126, 231, 235n15, 354n2
Gushurst-Moore, André, 186
Gy, Pierre-Marie, 37n25

Hahn, Scott, 391
Hamlet, 47, 340
Handel, G.F., 338
Hannibal, 6n10
Hannon, Urban, 269
Harrison, Brian, 51, 305n12
Haun, Will, 159–60
Hazell, Matthew, xiii, xxv, 18–20, 88nn6–7, 89n11, 104, 113n15, 145, 214, 233n6, 294n4, 310n8, 373n1
Healy, Mary, 24n58, 393, 395
Hedwig, St., 240n3
Heenan, John, 24, 234
Heid, Stefan, 158n1, 317
Helfta, 153nn17–18
Heraclitus, 69, 73, 314
Herod, 368–69
Hickson, Maike, 13n29
Hobbes, Thomas, 68
Hoffman, Michael, 112n12
Holmes, Jeremy, xxv, 44n37, 155n24, 325–26
Homer, 298
Honorius Augustodunensis, 269
Houghton, Bryan, 85, 91, 133, 373
Howard, Thomas, 158n2, 311nn9–10
Howell, Clifford, 115
Hull, Geoffrey, 7n11, 232
Humanæ Vitæ (Paul VI), 65
Hunwicke, John, 24, 37n22, 129n8, 305n12
Huonder, Vitus, 197
Husslein, Joseph, xxii n9

In Sinu Jesu, 199–200
India, 67, 202

Innocent I, St., 240n3
Innocent III, 269
Institute of Christ the King Sovereign Priest, 124, 227, 238, 240, 357, 377
Institute of the Good Shepherd, 227, 238, 378
International Commission on English in the Liturgy (ICEL), 50n5, 314n13
International Theological Commission, 107
International Theological Institute, xviii n2, 175, 308
Ireland, 101n36, 360, 366
Iroquois, 151
Isaac, 268

James, St., 314
Jedin, Hubert, 10, 93
Jefferson, Thomas, 79
Jerusalem, 52n8, 96n26, 184, 188, 260, 268, 368, 400
Joachim and Anne, Sts., 239n2
Jogues, Isaac, St., 155
John, St., 46, 164, 167, 180, 186–87, 196, 218, 265, 339, 377
John and Paul, Sts., 240n3
John Chrysostom, St., 8, 314
John Gualbert, St., 239
John of Matha, St., 240n3
John of the Cross, St., 395
John Paul II, xv, xxiv n11, 34n15, 70, 110, 118, 166n14, 198, 234, 327, 391, 394
John the Baptist, St., 246
John the Hermit, 370
John Vianney, St., 200
John XXIII, 86, 212, 274, 301, 334
Johnson, Max, 385
Johnson, Samuel, 298, 313
Jonah, 258
Joncas, Michael, 314n13
Jones, Anthony, xxv
Joseph, St., 200, 244–46, 266n38, 332–33
Jounel, Pierre, 27n1, 29n3
Journet, Charles, 312n11
Judas, 162n9
Jungmann, Josef A., 149

Kabel, Sharon, 14n31, 299n10
Kant, Immanuel, 4, 20, 129, 283n20
Kappes, Christiaan W., 17n37

Index of Proper Names 427

Kathrein, George, 134n12
Kierkegaard, Søren, 180
Kirby, Mark, 32–33, 39, 75–76, 343n2
Knox, Ronald, 397
Kocik, Thomas M., xi–xvi, xxv, 7n11, 31–32, 34, 38
Kreuter, Joseph, 154, 360n9
Kunitz-Dick, Alisa, 233n5

Lamb, Christopher, 91
Lameri, Angelo, 179n4
Lamont, John, 5n6, 21, 227n37
Lang, Uwe Michael, 158n1, 317n17
Larson, David, 119n23
Lateran IV, 25n60
Lateran V, 130
Latin America, *see* South America
Laud, William, 129–30
Law of Separation (1905), 55
Lawrence, St., 113n15, 329n2
Lazu Kmita, Robert, 219–20
Le Barroux, 14n31, 358
Le Corbusier, 61
Lebrun, Pierre, 269
Lefebvre, Marcel, 24, 48–49, 69, 154n20, 222, 232, 234–35, 238n21, 275, 378, 396
Legionaries of Christ, 118
Lehnert, Pascalina, 51n7
Lemna, Keith, 63
Leo the Great, St., 19, 221
Leo XII, 56
Leo XIII, 40, 56, 116, 186n17, 276
Leonard of Port Maurice, St., 355
Lewis, C.S., viii, 58, 103, 256, 281–82
Lewis, Mike, 103–4
Liber Usualis, 343
Libertas Præstantissimum (Leo XIII), 116
Linus, St., 329n2
Lives of the Desert Fathers, The, 199, 370
London Oratory, 11n23, 30n5
Longenecker, Dwight, 11
Loreto, Santa Casa di, 130
Lou, Tseng-Tsiang (Pierre-Célestin), 103n40
Louis de Montfort, St., 65
Lucifer, *see* Satan
Lumen Gentium (Vatican II), 71
Luther, Martin, 92–93, 96, 162, 298–99, 380n8

Mabry, Zac, 125n2
Maccabees, 153
Madiran, Jean, 31n9
Maggioni, Corrado, 235n13
Mahony, Roger, 65
Mahrt, William, 163–64
Mantovani, Maria Domenica, 120n25
Marini, Guido, 384–85
Marini, Piero, x
Maritain, Jacques, 15, 366
Mark and Marcellian, Sts., 240n3
Martha of Bethany, St., 206
Martindale, C.C., 306n2
Marx, Karl, 85, 266n38
Mary Magdalene, St., 75, 206
Mary, Blessed Virgin, 42, 88n10, 130, 164, 167, 181–83, 200, 202, 239n2, 243–47, 252, 267–68, 270, 322, 332–33, 340, 343–44, 348, 377
Mass in a Connemara Cabin (O'Kelly), 360
Mass of the Ages (films), 95n23, 388, 392, 395
Maximilian Kolbe, St., 55n14
Mayan Use, 71
McCarthy, Matthew, 313n12
McInerny, D.Q., 15–16
McNaspy, Clement, 100
McShea, Bronwen, 21
Mechtild of Hackeborn, St., 153, 182–83, 297
Mectilde de Bar, Mother, 183
Mediator Dei (Pius XII), 6n10, 37, 182, 188, 257n14, 316–17, 340, 361
Melchisedek, 45, 220
Mellitus of Canterbury, St., 136
Meloni, Julia, 105n50
Mencken, H.L., xxiv
Meßner, Reinhard, 93
Mexico, 55
Meyer, Garrett, 78n12
Michael the Archangel, St., 19, 55n14
Miller, Peter, 214n10, 230n44, 293n2
Milton, John, 181
Missa Papæ Marcelli (Palestrina), 221
Mister Rogers, 67
Mitsui, Daniel, 346n8
Montagna, Diane, 90, 96n26, 105
Montini, Giovanni Battista, 10, 104, 340; *see also* Paul VI

Morello, Sebastian, 115, 156, 320n22
Morgan, Jason, 115n20
Moriarty, Professor, 52
Mosebach, Martin, 64, 112–13, 142–43, 145–47, 194, 241, 272, 285–86, 296, 319–20, 376, 398
Moynihan, Robert, 56n19
Mozart, W.A., 337, 344
Müller, Gerhard Ludwig, 62
Murr, Charles, 51
Murray, Gerald, 111n8

Nazarius, St., 240n3
Nebuchadnezzar, 371
Netherlands, 96
Newman, John Henry, St., xix, 5, 10, 30n8, 34, 44, 73–74, 128–30, 147, 226, 315–16, 320
Nichols, Aidan, xiii, 15, 149
Nicodemus, 206
Nietzsche, Friedrich, 217
Nine Ways of Prayer of St. Dominic, The, 262
Noah, 395
Norcia, *see* Abbazia di San Benedetto in Monte
Normandin, Yves, 134n12, 139
Notitiæ, x, 99n32, 100n33, 189n23, 283–84
Notre-Dame de Paris, 85
Novum Organum (Bacon), 23

O'Connell, Gerard, 159n3
O'Connell, J.B., xiv n7
O'Kelly, Aloysius, 360
O'Malley, Timothy P., 257n15
Oesterreicher, John M., 305
Offertoriale Triplex, 344
Oldendorf, Clemens V., 384n2
Olier, Jean-Jacques, 258n17, 269
Opus Dei, 147
Ordines Romani, 221, 260
Orth, Stefan, 93
Orwell, George, 10n18
Ottaviani, Alfredo, 384
Oxford Oratory, 11n23
Oxford Movement, 34, 129

Pacelli, Eugenio, 32, 236; *see also* Pius XII
Pacem in Terris (John XXIII), 88

Pachamama, 12
Padre Pio, see Pio of Pietrelcina
Palazzolo, Luigi Maria, 120n25
Palestrina, Giovanni Pierluigi da, 221
Palmaro, Mario, 329n3
Paris Commune, 85
Parmenides, 314
Parsch, Pius, 59
Parsons, John, 7n11, 10n20, 31n9
Pascalina, Madre, *see* Lehnert
Pasqualucci, Paolo, 13n29
Patrick, St., 336
Paul, St., 67, 107n55, 144, 213, 245–46, 251, 258, 311, 313n12, 332, 339
Paul VI, xi–xiii, xvii–xx, xxiv, 7, 9–12, 14–15, 17–18, 22, 25, 30n6, 31, 34, 36, 39, 48n3, 49, 51–52, 54–55, 57–59, 61, 66, 69, 74n8, 81–82, 86–87, 89, 95, 102, 110, 112, 115, 120, 123, 125, 127–30, 137–39, 143, 145–47, 149, 151, 154n19, 162, 172, 178, 179n4, 18n8, 205, 210, 212, 214, 222, 234–35, 239, 244, 262, 271, 283–84, 286, 288n1, 299, 301, 325, 330, 339, 363, 370, 372–73, 375, 381, 383–85, 399
Paulinus of Nola, St., 311
Peachey, Roy, 129n7
Pecknold, Chad, 172–73
Pentin, Edward, 111n10
Pepino, John, xxv, 271n2
Perricone, John, 142n23
Peter, St., 54, 111, 196, 245–46, 332, 374, 393
Pillai, Devasahayam, 120n25
Pio of Pietrelcina, St., 65, 83n19, 285, 329
Pistoia, *see* Synod of Pistoia
Pius V, St., 3, 5n7, 25, 60, 86, 103–4, 125, 171, 190n26, 239, 283, 286,
Pius VI, 7, 102, 272
Pius VII, 56
Pius VIII, 56
Pius IX, Bd., 56
Pius X, St., xi, 12, 55, 63, 211, 220, 231–32, 236n16 236n18, 237, 331, 348n15, 361
Pius XI, xxii n9, 63, 222, 237
Pius XII, xiv, 6n10, 37, 63, 117, 182, 188, 225, 231–32, 235–38, 247, 257, 301, 316–17, 331, 340, 361, 372, 383
Planned Parenthood, 55
Plato, 10, 23, 129, 325n31

Index of Proper Names

Poland, 110, 366
Pontifical Commission Ecclesia Dei, *see* Ecclesia Dei
Pontificale Romanum, 171n16
Pontius Pilate, 328
Pope, Charles, 232n3
Populorum Progressio (Paul VI), 88
Pray, Tell, 102
Priestly Fraternity of St. Peter, 124, 139, 200–201, 227, 237–38, 274, 357, 376–78
Primus and Felician, Sts., 240n3
Pristas, Lauren, xiii, 18, 30n7, 36n20, 89, 113n16, 139, 199n3, 214, 314, 373n1
Prosper of Aquitaine, 6n10

Quas Primas (Pius XI), xxii n9, 222
Quo Magis (CDF), 329
Quo Primum (Pius V), 3n2, 286
Quoëx, Franck, 269

Rahner, Karl, 210n3
Rand, Paul, 399
Raphael, 241, 398
Rationale Divinorum Officiorum (Durandus), 255, 269
Ratzinger, Joseph, 3, 5n7, 11, 13n29, 19, 32n12, 37n23, 37n25, 51, 56, 62, 71, 80, 93, 97, 103, 110, 123, 158–59, 161n8, 165n13, 171, 179, 209, 211, 378; *see also* Benedict XVI
Redemptionis Sacramentum (CDWDS), 110
Reform of the Liturgy 1948–1975, The (Bugnini), x, 8n14, 23n55, 64, 99nn30–31, 152n15, 168n15, 179n4
Reformation Sunday, 222
Reid, Alcuin, xiv–xv, xxv, 17n37, 52, 69n1, 190, 212, 392, 395
Responsa ad Dubia (CDWDS), 90, 120
Rheinschmitt, Monika, 34
Ricci, Scipione de', 7
Ripperger, Chad, 188
Rivier, Anne-Marie, 120n25
Rivoire, Réginald-Marie, 6n7, 293n3
Roche, Arthur, 85–107, 120, 159n3, 172, 376
Romanus the Melodist, St., 314
Romanus, St., 329n2
Romero, Jesse, 257n15

Rose, André, 30n7
Rousseau, Jean-Jacques, 44n37, 325n31
Rowland, Tracey, 114
Royal, Robert, 15, 23
Rubatto, Maria Francesca di Gesù, 120n25
Ruff, Anthony, 24n57
Rufina and Secunda, Sts., 240n3
Rule (Benedict), 177n2, 320
Russia, 85, 106, 274
Russolillo, Giustino, 120n25

Sacramentum Caritatis (Benedict XVI), 11n21
Sacred Congregation of Rites, 275, 278
Sacrosanctum Concilium (Vatican II), x–xii, xiv–xv, xix–xx, xxiv, 3–26, 37, 69, 76, 78n12, 89, 91, 95n23, 97, 209, 212–13, 214n9, 231–37, 248, 292
Salvucci, Claudio, 103n40
Salza, John, 54n12
Sammons, Eric, 104n45, 399
Samuel, 262
Sant'Anselmo, Pontifical Athenaeum, 89, 98–99, 116
Santocanale, Maria di Gesù, 120n25
Sarah, Robert, 159, 179–80, 193, 270, 275, 296
Satan, 55n14, 58, 82, 117, 280, 370, 396
Savage, Christian Gregory, 153n18
Saxons, 136, 324n28
Schießler, Rainer Maria, 108
Schineller, Peter, 64
Schluenderfritz, Malcolm, 102–3
Schneider, Athanasius, 96
Scholastica, St., 240n3
Schrems, Wolfram, 5n7, 233n6
Schubert, Franz, 273n6, 275
Schuler, Richard, 11n23
Schuster, Ildefonso, 59
Scrosati, Luisella, 98n29
Scrovegni Chapel, 5
Scruton, Roger, 44n37, 325n31
Second Vatican Council, *see* Vatican II
Sedulius Scottus, 64n36
Sergius I, St., pope, 64n36, 218
Shaffern, Robert W., 69n1
Shakespeare, 59, 266, 298
Shaw, Joseph, 12n26, 27–28, 37n26, 38, 69n1, 86n3, 104, 126, 147–51, 184n14,

189–90, 210n3, 227, 231, 232n3, 234n7, 235n14, 274n8, 299n11, 305n12, 399
Shivone, Andrew, 72
Short Critical Study of the New Order of Mass ("Ottaviani Intervention"), 384
Silverstream Priory, 358
Simeon, 268
Singapore, 58, 63n33, 117
Sire, H.J.A., 4, 23, 48, 61, 165n13, 232, 316
Siscoe, Robert, 54n12
Sistine Chapel, 234
Sixtus V, 239n2
Society of St. Pius X, 104n47, 187n19, 197n1, 238n21, 275, 378, 380
Solari, Grégory, xxi n7
Solesmes, 259n19, 337, 347
Solomon, 60, 62–63, 368–69
Somerville Knapman, Hugh, 33, 38, 100, 231–32
Sonnen, John Paul, 346n8, 347n12
Soul of the Apostolate, The (Chautard), 354
South America, 55, 103n39
Spaemann, Robert, 155
Spellman, Francis, 333
Spinoza, Baruch, 20
St. Gallen Mafia, 105n50
Staffa, Dino, 51
Steckler, Gerard G., 21n50
Stein, Edith, *see* Teresa Benedicta
Stephen, St., 301
Stickler, Alfons, 52, 58, 69n1
Stravinskas, Peter, 213–26, 248
Stridon, Jerome, 234n8
Summa theologiæ (Aquinas), 5, 184n15, 255n11, 261n25, 279–80, 302–4
Summorum Pontificum (Benedict XVI), xi, xiv–xv, xxiv n11, 12, 30n5, 54, 90, 111n6, 121, 134, 143, 191, 193, 196, 231, 238, 271, 288, 295, 353, 378
Synod of Pistoia, 7, 25, 102, 272, 374n4

Teresa Benedicta of the Cross, St., 329
Thérèse of Lisieux, St., 236n16
Thomas Aquinas College, 65, 308
Thomas Aquinas, St., 23, 26, 45, 46n42, 64n36, 65, 112, 141, 176n1, 183–84, 250, 255, 261, 269, 279–82, 302–5, 336, 386–91, 395

Thompson, Francis, 398
Tolkien, J.R.R., 324
Tra le Sollecitudini (Pius X), 220, 348n15
Tract 90 (Newman), 34
Traditionis Custodes (Francis), xxiv n11, 6n7, 54, 57n22, 66n38, 69n1, 76n10, 81, 85n1, 87, 90n14, 97–98, 105–6, 108, 111–16, 119–21, 134–35, 145, 159n3, 172, 203, 286, 293, 294n4, 295, 375
Trent, Council of, xxiv, 14, 81, 92n18, 93, 103, 139n19, 144, 162, 164, 171, 232, 236, 276, 339
Tribe, Shawn, 103n40, 121–22, 335n14, 346nn8–10, 349n17
Turner, Paul, 321n26

Una Voce, 143n26
United Kingdom, 366
United Nations, 5
United States Conference of Catholic Bishops (USCCB), 55
United States of America, xii n2, xv, 39–40, 82, 94n22, 119, 127–28, 173, 274n8, 294–95, 334n12, 346, 362, 366, 392, 394
Universæ Ecclesiæ (Ecclesia Dei), 270–71, 277
Ureta, José, 93n20

Vandeur, Eugène, 59
Vatican I, 37n23
Vatican II, xi–xv, xx–xxiii, xxiv n11, 3–26, 31–33, 35n19, 37nn23–25, 38, 43, 48–50, 54, 56, 69–71, 78, 80, 87, 89–96, 99–105, 108, 114–19, 121, 142–43, 159, 169, 172, 174, 189n23, 191, 196, 197n2, 210–15, 218, 223, 231–37, 245, 273n6, 288, 366, 380–81, 384, 391, 394–96
Vehementer Nos (Pius X), 55
Vendée, 118
Verdier, Jean, 85
Veronica, St., 8
Veterum Sapientia (John XXIII), 274
Victor I, St., 240n3
Vienna Oratory, 3n1, 11n23
Viganò, Carlo Maria, 55
Viglione, Massimo, 115
Vincent of Lérins, St., xvi
Viola, Vittorio Francesco, 99n30, 376

Virgil, 298
Virginia, 118, 228–29
von Hildebrand, Dietrich, 4n3, 31n9, 58, 62, 83, 151n10, 320n21

Waldstein, Wolfgang, 5n7
Ward, Maisie, 299
Ward, Wilfrid, 299n11
Waugh, Evelyn, 24n58
Weakland, Rembert, 142
Weigel, George, 394, 396
Weinandy, Thomas, 24n58, 393, 395
Welborn, Amy, 142n23, 189n23
Where Peter Is, 102, 103n43
White, Hilary, 245
Williamson, Hugh Ross, 261–62
Wiltgen, Ralph, 4n3

Winters, Michael Sean, 105
Woodstock, 123
Works Progress Administration, 216
World War I, 21
World War II, 5, 21, 52n8, 61, 140, 238, 266n38, 282, 324
Wuest, Joseph, 333n8, 334n10, 346n11
Wyoming Catholic College, xviii n2, 65–66, 190

Zaccaria, Anthony Mary, St., 240n3
Zaire Use, 71, 97
Zerubbabel, 368
Zuhlsdorf, John, 58n24, 111n11, 134, 365n4, 367n7
Zundel, Maurice, 59

www.ingramcontent.com/pod-product-compliance
Lightning Source LLC
Chambersburg PA
CBHW021138160426
43194CB00007B/619